THE BOOK OF TAḤKEMONI

THE LITTMAN LIBRARY OF
JEWISH CIVILIZATION

Dedicated to the memory of
LOUIS THOMAS SIDNEY LITTMAN
who founded the Littman Library for the love of God
and as an act of charity in memory of his father
JOSEPH AARON LITTMAN
יהא זכרם ברוך

'Get wisdom, get understanding:
Forsake her not and she shall preserve thee'
PROV. 4:5

The Littman Library of Jewish Civilization is a registered UK Charity
Registered Charity no. 1000784

THE BOOK OF TAḤKEMONI

Jewish Tales from Medieval Spain

JUDAH ALḤARIZI

TRANSLATED, EXPLICATED, AND ANNOTATED BY

DAVID SIMHA SEGAL

London · Portland, Oregon
The Littman Library of Jewish Civilization
2001

The Littman Library of Jewish Civilization
74 Addison Road
London W14 8DJ, UK

Published in the United States and Canada by
The Littman Library of Jewish Civilization
c/o ISBS, 5824 N.E. Hassalo Street
Portland, Oregon 97213-3644

A catalogue record for this book is available from the British Library

Library of Congress Cataloging-in-Publication Data applied for
ISBN 1-874774-03-X

Publishing co-ordinator: Janet Moth
Production manager: John Saunders
Design by Pete Russell, Faringdon, Oxon.
Copy-editing: Leofranc Holford-Strevens
Proof reading: Lindsey Taylor-Guthartz
Indexes: Bonnie Blackburn
Typeset in Caslon by Footnote Graphics Warminster, Wilts.
Printed in Great Britain on acid-free paper by
MPG Books, Cornwall

To the memory of
my mother and teacher

ETHEL SEGAL

Give her of the fruit of her hands
PROVERBS 31: 31

נר זכרון
לנשמת אמי מורתי

אסתר בת אברהם ולינה שול

תנו לה מפרי ידיה
משלי לא: לא

Contents

THE BOOK OF TAḤKEMONI
JUDAH ALḤARIZI

ANALYSES

Abbreviations and Conventions Used in the Text

BDB F. Brown, S. R. Driver, and C. A. Briggs, *A Hebrew and English Lexicon of the Old Testament with an Appendix Containing the Biblical Aramaic, based on the Lexicon of William Gesenius, as translated by Edward Robinson* (Oxford, 1959, reprinted with corrections)

BT Babylonian Talmud

EI *Encyclopaedia of Islam*, new edn. (Leiden, 1960–)

EJ *Encyclopaedia Judaica*, 16 vols. (Jerusalem, 1971)

JT Jerusalem Talmud

SSG *Sidur r. sa'adiyah gaon: Kitāb jamī*ᶜ *aṣ-ṣalawāt wat-tasābīḥ* [*The Prayerbook of Sa'adiah Gaon: The Book of All the Prayers and Petitions*], ed. I. Davidson, S. Assaf, and B. I. Joel, 3rd edn. (Jerusalem, 1970)

ST *Sefer Taḥkemoni*, ed. Y. Toporovsky, *Rabi yehudah alḥarizi: Taḥkemoni* (Tel Aviv, 1952). References are to page and line number: *ST* 13. 4–23 = page 13, lines 4–23

Tractates of the Babylonian Talmud

BB	*Baba batra*	*Meg.*	*Megillah*
BK	*Baba kamma*	*Men.*	*Menaḥot*
BM	*Baba metsia*	*Pes.*	*Pesaḥim*
Ber.	*Berakhot*	*RH*	*Rosh hashanah*
Eruv.	*Eruvin*	*Sanh.*	*Sanhedrin*
Ḥag.	*Ḥagigah*	*Shab.*	*Shabbat*
Kid.	*Kiddushin*	*Suk.*	*Sukkah*

/ In translation: a play on words in the original

[ ] In notes: a biblical allusion introduced by the translator

Translator's Preface

JUDAH ALḤARIZI (1165–1225) appeared on the scene of Hebrew *belles-lettres* following the golden age of Hebrew poetry in Muslim Spain (*c.*1000–1140), a point he emphasizes in his own historical literary surveys (Gates 3 and 18).[1] Andalusian Jewish patrons, following Muslim example, fostered a court-centred culture whose poets wrote in strict quantitative metre, and within set conventions, and that in a restricted number of genres: panegyric, complaint, lament, reflective verse, and poetry of wine, eros, and nature, to cite the major groupings of secular poetry.[2] This Jewish creativity was eradicated when Andalusia was overrun by the fundamentalist Almohad invaders from North Africa, who imposed on non-Muslims the choice of conversion or death; Hebrew culture moved north to Christian Spain, where, oddly enough, it took on, in delayed reaction as it were, a further Arabic influence, that of *maqāma*—rhymed prose narrative, with some metric verse thrown in, depicting the adventures, or encounters, of a narrator and a wandering, often roguish, poet.[3]

More I shall not say at this point, directing the interested reader to Alḥarizi's Introduction and Gate 1, which lay out the genesis of the work;

[1] A recent study by Sadan, 'Rabbi Judah Alḥarizi as a Cultural Crossroads' (Heb.), cites an eyewitness account by a contemporary of Alḥarizi, who records the precise date of our author's death at the age of 60 in Aleppo, namely 3 Dec. 1225, pointing to 1165 as the year of his birth (apparently in Toledo). For a brief discussion of Alḥarizi and *Sefer Taḥkemoni*, see *EJ* ii. 627–9. For brief overviews in Hebrew, see Schirmann, *Hebrew Poetry in Spain and in Provence*, ii. 97–103, 688–9; id., 'Judah Alḥarizi, Poet and Storyteller'. The most recent comprehensive discussion of the author and his works will be found in Schirmann–Fleischer (hereafter S–F), *History*, ii. 145–221; the biographical information at ii. 146–68 is based in some measure on *Sefer Taḥkemoni* itself.

[2] See Gates 3 and 18. For histories of Hebrew poetry in Spain, including the outpouring of liturgical verse, see Gates 3 and 18 with their analyses. Earlier Hebrew sources that used rhyme include the Bible (infrequently) and early synagogue poetry, or *piyut*. The use of rhyme in these genres is discussed concisely and illustrated in 'Prosody, Hebrew', *EJ* xvi. 1202–10 and 1218–20. Other early Hebrew sources include polemic, such as the reply of Sa'adiah Gaon (882–942) to the freethinker Hiwi the Balkhite (on which see Rosenthal, 'Hiwi al Balkhi'); personal and official correspondence; and moral-didactic treatises. The last three categories are discussed briefly in Alloni, 'An Anthology' (Heb.).

[3] The two major predecessors of Alḥarizi, al-Hamadhani and al-Ḥariri, are discussed in the Analysis of the Introduction. Earlier and more general meanings of the term *maqāma* include addresses on various subjects (possibly delivered while standing), especially sermons; assemblages where persons—especially literati—gathered to hear addresses or tales; and compilations of matter typically delivered at such gatherings. The Hebrew term *maḥberet*, used

to the literary histories of Gates 3 and 18; and, of course, to my analyses of these and all gates in Part II, and to the Afterword, where I summarize my findings. Surprise, contrast, and veiling are integral components of this work: to lay its contents out in advance would constitute a serious disservice to the reader. In my prefatory remarks I have chosen rather to focus on my method of translating Alḥarizi's singular medium of rhymed prose.[4]

With zest and very little modesty, our author lays out in his introduction to *Sefer Taḥkemoni* the cornucopia of themes and genres that will characterize the work—chicanery, romance, proverbs, moral exhortation, history, prayer, debauchery, travel, panegyric, and more—all this touted as a storehouse of instruction for the pious, and for worldlings an amalgam of delights that will ultimately lead them to 'the good of the Lord'.[5] Herein, says he, 'each seeker will find his heart's desire and will attain of his longing sufficient for his need of that which he lacks'.[6] So reads the word-for-word translation —which is not the goal of this work; all the less in view of the existence of a literal translation by V. E. Reichert.[7]

In this book I have sought to reconstitute in English the variety, verve, and power of the original with its wide canvas. The need for this approach is self-evident in those 'gates' (chapters) that are showpieces of rhetorical skill—competitions or challenges to the protagonist, such as penning a letter readable forwards and backwards, with conflicting messages (Gate 8); praise of a Maecenas, in rhymed prose and metric verse, with every word using, then shunning, a specified letter of the alphabet (Gate 11); creating double-homonym poems (Gate 33); matching, in content and style—and even in precise poetic metre—a rival's utterance (Gates 16 and 32); and more. But the task of parallel rendition, rather than literal translation, demands more than reconstituting all these verbal acrobatics.

Alḥarizi, more than any other practitioner of his medium, has exquisitely exploited the potential of rhymed prose for all manner of themes, tones, and genres. He chills his reader as he limns the butchery of rival armies (Gate 7) and innocent fawns (Gate 25); skewers religious hypocrites (Gate

as the translation of *maqāma* and as an appellation for like creations, has been termed as particularly apt, containing the two meanings of assemblage and literary composition. See Goitein, 'The *Maqāma* and the *Maḥberet*', and Klar, 'Four Titles of Compilations', 246–52.

4 Even here my discussion is brief: further detailed discussions, more readily appreciable after further reading, are to be found in Analyses 5, 8, 9, 11, 16, 24, 32, 33, and 34; scattered remarks are also found in the analyses of several other gates. Summary remarks on the medium of rhymed prose are to be found in *EJ* xiii. 1218–20.

5 *ST* 13. 4–23.

6 *ST* 13. 10–12; tr. Reichert, i. 37.

7 Reichert has rendered a valuable service to Hebrew-speaking readers in providing an aid to the understanding of every word of the original.

10), poetasters (Gate 18), the *nouveaux riches* (Gate 34), and tightwads of all colours (throughout the work); creates contrasting claims in serious, as well as frivolous debates—Karaite versus Rabbanite (Gate 17), pen versus sword (Gate 43), and more.

Our author's rhyming prose, a step down from the high style of poetry in set metres, affords something akin to the freer rhythms of Skelton and Ogden Nash (if without the comic neologisms[8] and exceedingly long rhyming phrases of the latter). In this loose structure the poet varies his emphases with the number of rhyming units (e.g. *aa*, *bb*, *cccc*, *dd*, *eeeeee*, *fff*, and so on), and with the number and length of words in these units. A further, and crucial, element is the interweaving of scriptural citation, frequently wrenched out of context for dramatic effect, serious or humorous, and often situated at the end of a clause, sentence, or discussion for added emphasis. All this, of course, is further enriched by the standard building-blocks of belletristic writing—figurative language and considered repetitions of motifs and key words.

This dense blend yields a rare product that demands re-creation. At the outset, the English reader might sense a certain artificiality of effect—but the same can be said of the modern reader of the Hebrew text.[9] Rhyme, rhythm, and citation are not cream on the cake, but lie at the heart of Alḥarizi's accomplishment; the translator who strips these away offers a composition that is pale, and unjustifiably so.

Let us consider an example—a sampling from the condemnation of wine in Gate 27. In the literal translation of Reichert this reads:

> He who goes astray through it will pawn his wealth and will squander all his money. He will lose the handicraft that he possesses. For through it he will cease from all his work.[10]

My rendering:

> The bibbler ravages his health and dribbles away his wealth: stript of goodly occupation, the mock of his neighbours, he rests—seven days a week!—from all his labours.[11]

Characteristic of my method is the 'liberty' of the added 'mock of his neighbours', introduced for the explicit purpose of forging that sense of

[8] The rare instances of neologisms in this version—one example being 'Their modesty is unbodicedty, their industry sindustry' in Gate 19—are a liberty of the translator's.

[9] It is true that Hebrew allows for a far greater number of units in a rhyming sequence, necessitating the rendering of four or five rhyming units by three, or three—sometimes four—by two; but this concession by no means mars the overall effect.

[10] *ST* 243. 25–7; tr. Reichert, ii. 140–1.

[11] Gen. 2: 3.

comic climax present in the original due to the wedding of rhyme and witty biblical citation. My addition, at the same time, is wholly consonant with the overall tone and content of the preceding section.

Indeed, in my translator's practice I follow the preferred style of Alḥarizi himself in his rendering of al-Ḥariri's *Maqāmāt* into *Maḥberot Iti'el*.[12] As more than one critic has noticed, the Hebrew author variously expands, deletes, or changes the Arabic (especially by Judaizing Islamic references),[13] nothing loath to insert a plethora of citations wholly absent from the original. Now it is quite true that one underlying motivation on Alḥarizi's part was to Judaize the text, this as part of a larger artistic, nationalistic programme of combating Arabic culture;[14] the outcome, however, was that his readership received a text whose allusions it could readily recognize. In this spirit, I have freely introduced English references not present in the original. The following example comes from the diatribe in Gate 2 against worldly pleasures. My rendering is followed by the English source I have exploited, a poem by Hart Crane, then Reichert's literal translation of the Hebrew original.

Read on this frame, once aflame with passion's breath, the livid hieroglyphic of Death.... Far, far beneath the feet of grasshoppers and mice, the bones' abandoned dice take the slow roll of lice.

---

[12] First published by Chenery, *Machberoth Ithiel*, on the basis of the one surviving, and incomplete, manuscript, this work was re-edited and vocalized by Perets and published as *Maḥberot iti'el betirgum rabi yehudah alḥarizi*. On the history of this work and its relation to *Sefer Taḥkemoni*, see the Introduction, Gate 1, and the respective Analyses.

[13] Lavi, 'Comparative Study', looks quite closely at parallel texts from these two works, paying minute attention to the implicit logic of Alḥarizi in advancing parallel/appropriate Hebrew words and phrases for the Arabic. See also id., 'The Rationale of al-Harizi'. Two major earlier studies of Alḥarizi's translation method are Schirmann, *Die hebräische Übersetzung*, and Percikowitsch, *Al-Harizi als Übersetzer der Makamen Al-Hariris*. Both men emphasize the replacement of Koranic and other Islamic sources with Jewish, particularly biblical, references; and both note, if without close scrutiny, three major avenues chosen by Alḥarizi in his renderings: close and literal translation (in a minority of instances); broad reworking (also a minority of cases), as in rendering untranslatable gates (for example, a text where every other word in the Arabic is pointed); and, for the most part, freer rendering. Schirmann asserts (S–F, *History*, ii. 180 and n. 143) that Alḥarizi in his freer renderings seems to follow the counsel of Moses ibn Ezra in his *Kitāb al-muḥādara wa'l-mudhākara*: 'Now if you seek to render a matter from Arabic into Hebrew, first comprehend its intent and spirit. Do not convert what it says word for word, for languages are not identical' (ed. Halkin, 177). See also, generally, 'The Translation of the *Maqāmāt* of al-Ḥariri', in S–F, *History*, ii. 177–84. In a future article, I intend to offer a closer examination of gate 9 of Alḥarizi's *Maḥberot Iti'el*; more specifically, the Hebrew author's rendering, and modification, of the themes, progressions, and ironies of gate 9 of al-Ḥariri's *Maqāmāt*.

[14] On this point see Analyses 15 and 35.

Often beneath the wave, wide from this ledge
The dice of drowned men's bones he saw bequeath
An embassy . . .
And wrecks passed without sound of bells,
The calyx of death's bounty giving back
A scattered chapter, livid hieroglyph,
The portent wound in corridors of shells . . .[15]

And see what death has left of their voluptuous forms and corpulent and luxuriant bodies. . . . From the preserved shapes and lasting likenesses there only remain signs engraved upon the bones.[16]

Similarly I have not hesitated to draw, with varying effects, from Mother Goose rhymes: in a diatribe of this same preacher castigating worldly pursuits: 'Pleasure's cupboard is bone bare' (Gate 2, citing 'Old Mother Hubbard'); or in the excoriation of a cantor who drives away his congregants with his insufferable expansions of the liturgy, 'Lo, the shepherd had lost his sheep—some deep in Dream's haystacks, fast asleep' (Gate 24, citing 'Little Bo Peep').

Blake's introductory poem in *Songs of Innocence* together with Poe's 'The Raven' afforded me phrases for Alḥarizi's explanation of his own method:

fearing that my readers might find my matter dreary and grow bleary-eyed or weak and weary . . . I wrote my lines with cheery pen that all might joy in reading them.

There are many such liberties that the reader will encounter, drawn from such diverse sources as Shakespeare, Yeats, Frost, and English poets and authors of other eras; as well as twentieth-century popular song.

Inasmuch as the felicitous blending of rhyme, rhythm, and biblical citation in the Hebrew are fused smooth-seamedly in Alḥarizi's work, I have not committed myself to slavish reproduction of each and every one of these elements—which would in any event be an impossible task—except that in those few places where the original dispenses with rhyme, I do likewise, since the emphatic effect was clearly intentional. For the recreation of the essential effect of the original, as I perceive it, I lay greater stress on this or that facet in the search for a parallel English articulation, at times condensing, expanding, and (more rarely) slightly rearranging Alḥarizi's text.[17]

15 Hart Crane, 'At Melville's Tomb', *Complete Poems*, 34.

16 *ST* 33. 25–6, 34. 5–6; tr. Reichert, i. 63.

17 One example of such rearrangement is to be found in Gate 2. My translation says of the preacher that he could 'with his chastisement dig the graves of Lust'—referring to Num. 11: 34–5 and 33: 16–17. This allusion appears a few lines later in the Hebrew text, which says, 'I longed to subdue, through his chastisements, my whoring desire (ever) turning to its delights and camping in the graves of lust' (*ST* 31. 9–10).

To illustrate citation-replacement, here is a word-for-word rendering from the beginning of Gate 24, lamenting the tight-fistedness of a local Jewry:

but all of them—their money pouches are tight-drawn in their palms with no breaching or breaking out; no, not a grain falling to earth.[18]

The sources cited refer to healthy cattle, none dropping stillborn calves (Ps. 144: 14); and God's loving care of Israel, such that not a single one will be overlooked or abandoned (Amos 9: 9). My version reads:

Stripling, greybeard, husband, wife—each tends his purse like the Tree of Life,[19] whispering, *Thine are greatness, might and majesty, splendour and eternity;*[20] *Death, only Death, shall come betwixt me and thee.*[21]

In so rendering the citizenry's tight-fistedness I have opted for sources slightly more recognizable to a twentieth-century English-speaking readership—the Garden of Eden, a scriptural quotation used in the Sabbath-morning Torah service, and Ruth's loyalty unto death to Naomi. Similarly, my citations, like Alḥarizi's, are wrenched out of context: verses that praise God are used to depict people who worship money; like Alḥarizi's, they foreshadow a lampooned precentor's horrendous misuse of biblical citations from the morning service.[22]

At times I retain the same citation, but moved slightly from its place; at others, I retain the same biblical episode or utterance while citing different words from the same verse, or rendering the source more transparent, or both. To illustrate this last point: in Gate 50's Hebrew opening we find, literally,

Now when I drew near with astonished heart *to behold this sight* I found a group of savants . . . hewing from their hearts' mines jewels and from the fount of their intelligence drawing up living waters . . .

Here Alḥarizi evokes the episode of Moses and the burning bush:

An angel of the Lord appeared to him from out of the bush and he beheld and lo the bush was burning with fire, yet the bush was not consumed. Moses said, 'Let me turn aside *and see this sight* . . .' (Exod. 3: 3)

[18] *ST* 223. 12–14.

[19] [Gen. 2: 9; 3: 22.] Any scriptural citation that is mine, rather than Alḥarizi's, is indicated by square brackets. In translating biblical phrases, I have, as in each case seemed appropriate, sometimes based myself on published translations and sometimes made my own.

[20] [1 Chr. 29: 11.]

[21] [Ruth 1: 17.]

[22] See Gate 9 and Analysis for further replacements of biblical citations and a consideration of the logic thereof; and Analysis 34 for the discussion on translation methodology.

I translate:

I mused, What have we here? and, drawing near, found—happy sight!—a noble company whose speech flamed bright; yes, brighter than the bush that summoned Moses. From the hotbeds of their intellects sprang scarlet roses . . .

I wish to emphasize that the translation method adopted here is no impediment to literary analysis—and specifically not to structural-aesthetic literary analysis, the major focus of this work. On the contrary: it is precisely my attention to, and mirroring of, repeated motifs and words, parallel and contrasting situations, characters, and citations, and, above all, tone and register, that facilitate analysis even as they render the work all the truer to the original, while also more comprehensible and enjoyable to the English-speaking reader.[23]

Finally, I call attention to an archaic usage harking back to English literature at least as late as the prose and poetry of Blake, and still well rooted in German—the occasional capitalization of common nouns for personification. Thus the reader will usually encounter such abstract nouns as Time, Fate, Song, and other words capitalized, albeit with deliberate inconsistency, especially when representing autonomous entities.[24]

A word on my analyses is in order. The work before the reader is very broad in scope, both in terms of genres used and of topics covered. The main purpose of this study is the aesthetic and structural analysis of *Sefer Taḥkemoni*, though I occasionally identify hitherto unrecognized sources and explore the historical background. Hence I have not provided exhaustive references to persons, places, periods, movements, and topics; frequently, only the most recent, best, overview on a topic is presented—with a note that further bibliographical information is to be provided there. Similarly, I have often referred the reader to discussions in the *Encyclopaedia Judaica*, and to bibliographies there—whether as sufficient background reading, or in addition to specialized articles, as in my analysis of Gate 17.

It is my pleasure to acknowledge the input and assistance of the many people who have helped me in this long enterprise.

I begin with deep gratitude to the editors of the Littman Library,

[23] On the few occasions where necessary, I provide literal renderings of key passages together with transliteration. See e.g. discussion of the egregious errors of the boorish cantor in Analysis 24, the addendum to Analysis 32, and Analyses 34 and 49.

[24] The translation follows the gender of personifications in the Hebrew: thus World, for *tevel*, is feminine, Time or Fate, for *zeman*, masculine.

Connie Webber and Janet Moth, whose careful guidance has been a staff and stay.

To Leofranc Holford-Strevens, who examined and polished my efforts with painstaking care, my heartfelt thanks—above all for his trilingual rendering of Alḥarizi's trilingual poem in Gate 11.

Several colleagues have shared their expertise with me on my journey. Professor Gerald Blidstein of Ben-Gurion University graciously afforded me his knowledge of rabbinic sources on numerous occasions; Professor Daniel Lasker offered sound guidance on all that pertains to Karaism; and Professor Howard Kreisel provided critical comments on Alḥarizi and Jewish thought on prophecy in the Middle Ages. My discussion of several gates, especially Gate 24's satire on a pompous precentor, profited from the rich input of Professor David Golinkin of the Schechter Institute of Jewish Studies in Jerusalem. Professor Reuven Hammer directed me to several relevant surveys on reward and punishment for my discussion of Gate 25; and Professor Edward Greenstein of the Jewish Theological Seminary of America called my attention to two sources on the suffering of Job for my analysis of that gate. Dr Peretz Rodman, my former student, pointed out a pun based deftly on the Italian prayer rite in Gate 24. Professor Lenn Goodman of Vanderbilt University shed light on several fine points of philosophy in Alḥarizi's introduction; and like service was rendered for the body–soul debate of Gate 13 by Professor Alfred Ivry of New York University.

For the resolution of fine points of Hebrew grammar I am obliged to Professors Moshe Bar Asher, chairman of the Hebrew Language Academy of Israel, and Haim Cohen of Ben-Gurion University. Colleagues who have generously shared their knowledge of Arabic language and culture with me include Professors Yitzhak Sadan and Rina Drory of Tel Aviv University, Alberto Arazi and Pesah Shinar of the Hebrew University, and Yael Blau of Ben-Gurion University.

My thanks go to the efficient staff of the Ben-Gurion University library, and especially to three hard-worked reference librarians, Pinhas Ziv, Gisella Davidsohn, and Tsviya Polani, and to inter-library loan specialists Herta Yankovich and Sabina Sapirstein. I am grateful, too, to the library and administration of Gratz College, where I spent many fruitful hours during a two-year stay in Philadelphia.

I owe a large debt to students too numerous to mention—at Ben-Gurion University, Brandeis University, and Gratz College: the very preparation of lectures on *Sefer Taḥkemoni*, coupled with the frequently challenging questions and comments they offered, deepened my understanding of this extraordinarily fecund text. Three especially dedicated and insightful students I cite by name: Gila Malamud, Haya Sheli, and Ali Ramadin—the last also my research assistant many years back.

I am beholden to the input and encouragement of early readers and listeners: Dr Naomi Graetz, Dr Judith A. Segal, and my daughters Gilia Segal and Dvora ben Shimol.

My wife Marilyn's acumen and astute eye have been put to the test time and again, as she has variously edited translations and analyses, researched footnotes, brought order to burgeoning files and folders, and cheered me on. This work could not have been brought to completion without her wisdom and dedication.

From my earliest years, love of the written word was tendered me by my late mother, Ethel Segal, through lullabies, recitations of poems and stories, and many shared hours in the kingdom of letters. To her I dedicate this work.

D.S.S.

THE BOOK OF
TAḤKEMONI

JUDAH ALḤARIZI

Hear the vision of Poesy's prophet,
the prince whom Fate's sword has near slain,
Who breathed—and the shadow of Poesy's dial
turned back[1] like a twirled weathervane,
Whose words cleave the Heavens with lightning,
reviving dead bones[2] with their rain;
Who, while others are thrown by Song's stallion,
commands Song with a tug of the rein.
In rhymed prose and strict verse he has written
adventures profound—and profane:
Full fifty, with tropes of rare colour
a-bubble with Wisdom's champagne.
But he sinks to the depths of despondence
whom Heaven had summoned to reign:
He who hung from Song's neck like a pendant
is now shackled in Wandering's chain;
He who lived in a Garden of Eden[3]
Fate has marked for a wandering Cain.[4]
He abandoned his land and his dwelling
to run trembling to Zion's domain.
He is Judah, wise Solomon's offspring,
whose birthplace and country is Spain.

[1] 2 Kgs. 20: 9–11. [2] [Ezek. 37: 1–11]. [3] Ezek. 28: 13. [4] [Gen. 4: 12–14].

INTRODUCTION

In His Name who Teaches Man Wisdom

THAT MAN WHO IS WISE, who is deeply clever, takes Wisdom for his guide and shield, his compass and his lever: Wisdom, who prospers his every endeavour, converses with him ever, and leaves him never. Wisdom it is who impels us to God's praise and tells us, Tell God's ways: He who, without eye, tongue, hand, formed Heaven, sea, and land; who, in the beginning, hung the high sphere above the void and set it spinning. He spoke—the sea upreared; he called—the heavens appeared and Chariot Beings thronged to lift His Chair, that being their holy service in the Upper Air.

Praise God, the Ever Near but unknown dweller of Heaven's highest sphere; Ever Apart, yet habiting the human heart; All-Present, yet beholden of no eye; hid, but to His seekers nigh. Extol Him, ye devout, Him, who, like a curtain, stretched the heavens out. See, in the mind's eye, His gloried throne, where He sits austere and lone. See blazing angels, seraphim in holy flame, cry loud His Holy Name, there where all souls sit silent at the cosmos' hid foundation, whose outer boundary is the rational soul's last station. Should she seek final vision in that awesome place, ask to gaze upon her Maker's face, the gates would close and a voice would cry, Come not nigh—this you cannot understand; you shall not pass through my land.

Now the souls of the righteous aspire to wing home to that

In His name who teaches man wisdom Ps. 94: 10.
hung the high sphere above the void Job 26: 7.
Chariot Beings thronged to lift His Chair Ezek. 1: 4 ff.
Him, who, like a curtain, stretched the heavens out [Ps. 104: 2].
See blazing angels, seraphim in holy flame, cry loud His Holy Name Isa. 6: 2–3.
you shall not pass through my land Num. 20: 18.

glory, but they tire in the flesh's mire. Therefore, to gain the outer hall, they strip off their bodies all, to be given, from the treasuries of the King, royal garments worn of the King to put on when summoned to the King's side: those who come nigh the Lord shall be sanctified. Thereupon, pearl-white and bright as nacre, they laud and magnify their Maker, who, from primal rock in the pit of obscurity, formed the soul in all purity, yea, hewed her, drew her forth from the first light to be His daily delight. And when her time came He saw her and declared her, searched her out and prepared her.

Then the angel of the Lord found her, faithful and pure, by the fountain of Wisdom/Shur on the way of Shur; and the angel said unto her: Leave your essence, whence I mined you; forget your people, put your father's home behind you and sit a lowly servant at the body's board; yea, bow low to him for he is your lord.

So she went and sat against him a good way off and anon, as though donning a robe, she put the body on. Then she breathed Heaven's heat into that earthly form and the child's flesh grew warm. Yes, by the soul's fire man rose from nothingness, as Holy Writ proclaims: The Lord descended thereon in flames. For her house is upon the town wall and she dwells upon that wall, standing sentry atop the body, seeing all; and lighting the body like the sun the skies, she eats of his loaf, drinks from his cup, and in his bosom lies.

Then, from her light's shade, sprang the animal soul and the

from the treasuries of the King Esther 3: 9, 4: 7.
royal garments worn of the King Esther 6: 8.
when summoned to the King's side Esther 4: 11.
those who come nigh the Lord shall be sanctified Exod. 19: 22.
hewed her Isa. 51: 1.
to be His daily delight Prov. 8: 30.
He saw her and declared her, searched her out and prepared her Job 28: 27.
Then the angel of the Lord . . . of Shur Gen. 16: 7.
Leave your essence, whence I mined you; forget your people, put your father's home behind you Ps. 45: 11.
bow low to him for he is your lord Ps. 45: 12.
So she went and sat against him a good way off Gen. 21: 16.
she breathed Heaven's heat into that earthly form and the child's flesh grew warm 2 Kgs. 4: 34.
The Lord descended thereon in flames Exod. 19: 18.
For her house is upon the town wall and she dwells upon that wall Josh. 2: 15.
she eats of his loaf, drinks from his cup, and in his bosom lies 2 Sam. 12: 3.

vegetative soul, to form a tripartite whole, the two latter joined in common goal—to serve the upper soul and revere her. Then the handmaids and their children came near her, nothing proud, and low bowed.

*N*ext the Intellect comes apace to dwell above the soul, then return to Ramah/the Heights, his dwelling-place. He strides like a groom to the bridal tent intent to unite with his beloved soul, his undefiled, for he loves her as when he reared her like his child. And if on holy manna she has fed, her will he dower and wed, yes, seize her, lie with her upon love's bed, her whom he so prizes—this while Desire sleeps, knowing not when she lies down and when she rises. The Intellect shall woo her from Lust, raise her from the dust, from the Pit's consummation, to highest station. This is the law unto every generation: if she be chaste when she departs the body's waste she shall wing eagle-swift to that high domain which blameless souls alone attain; but if, self-willed, she caroused and swilled, sold her body to Sin and his broad fields tilled—let her dwell in Sheol, let her touch no hallowed thing nor enter into the sanctuary until the days of her purification be fulfilled. Then shall she be given recompense meet for her from the palace of the King because she did not perform the commandment of the King. She shall come no more before the King unless she be desired of the King; only when the wrath of the King is appeased shall the maiden come unto the King.

*T*herefore God sent the Intellect to be her guide and lover,

Then the handmaids and their children came near her, nothing proud, and low bowed Gen. 33: 6.

then return to Ramah/the Heights, his dwelling-place 1 Sam. 7: 17.

He strides like a groom to the bridal tent Ps. 19: 6.

as when he reared her like his child Esther 2: 20.

seize her, lie with her Deut. 22: 28.

knowing not when she lies down and when she rises Gen. 19: 33–5.

raises her from the dust [Ps. 113: 7].

This is the law unto every generation [Num. 15: 15, and elsewhere].

let her touch no hallowed thing . . . until the days of her purification be fulfilled Lev. 12: 4.

Then shall she be given recompense meet for her from the palace of the King Esther 2: 9.

she did not perform the commandment of the King Esther 1: 15.

She shall come no more before the King unless she be desired of the King Esther 2: 14.

the wrath of the King is appeased Esther 2: 1.

shall the maiden come unto the King Esther 2: 13.

spread his wings above her, hover over her, restore her sight, lead her aright, and slake her thirst with his crystal water. Then God opened the eyes of His errant daughter and she saw a well to make her well. So she took her cup, went down and filled her pitcher, and came up.

*T*hen may the Intellect save us and our sons and daughters with the Source of Life, the Fountain of Gardens, the Well of Living Waters. May he open the eye of the mind that we put Sin behind and find upper light. Oh, might we strive to feed our souls at Knowledge's tree and grow and thrive, ever for our good, to keep ourselves alive.

*I*t is then our holy obligation to laud the Author and Reviser of Creation for all His love and grace: Lord, we seek Your face, You who escape Your loving world's embrace, for Your world contains You not: You are the world's space! Before You brought the mountains forth, before You scorched the south and froze the north, Your kingly chair hovered in empty air. Before You told Creation's story You hewed the highest Intellect from the rock of Your glory, summoned Your darling before You lit the sun, crowned him mankind's king before aught was begun—him, Your dear son whom You loved, Your only son. Through him the void gave birth, as it is written, *By Wisdom the Lord founded the earth*; as well the heavens, sea, and dry land, giving earth into man's hand, but reserving Heaven for the secret throne where You hid when the business was in hand. All rational souls race after Your secret, but stumble and fall: *you may see its outermost part, but you may not see all.* They who stare heavenward, straining to understand, go astray in the land; in their drought and dearth they

spread his wings above her Deut. 32: 11.
Then God opened the eyes of His errant daughter and she saw a well Gen. 21: 19.
So she took her cup, went down and filled her pitcher, and came up Gen. 24: 16.
the Source of Life Ps. 36: 10.
the Fountain of Gardens, the Well of Living Waters S. of S. 4: 15.
ever for our good, to keep ourselves alive Deut. 6: 24.
Lord, we seek Your face [Ps. 27: 8].
Before You brought the mountains forth Ps. 90: 2.
Your kingly chair hovered in empty air Lit. 'You sat in the seat of God (Ezek. 28: 2) and stood in no place.'
Your dear son whom You loved, Your only son Gen. 22: 2.
By Wisdom the Lord founded the earth Prov. 3: 19.
You hid when the business was in hand 1 Sam. 20: 19.
but stumble and fall [Ps. 27: 2].
you may see its outermost part, but you may not see all Num. 23: 13.
go astray in the land Exod. 14: 3.

set their mouths against the heavens and their tongues walk the earth. Oh, we stare after Your mystery but cannot see, for You are mightier far than we. Yet those from whom You are hidden are bidden to look within their hearts and there uncover You, for Your petitioners shall find You, Your seekers discover You.

And now, Father and Maker, fulfil our desire, answer us, draw us ever higher where our lips and thoughts aspire. Uphold us as we speak, lead us to Wisdom's peak; lower Your ladder and guide us up those shining rungs, guarding our way that we sin not with our tongues. Light our path, fright us not with Your wrath. Protect us from the arrogant, we who revere You: shine Your countenance upon us, draw us near You; number us among the souls who truly love and fear You.

THE WORD OF JUDAH son of Solomon son of Alḥarizi of blessed memory: The Lord has gifted me with a skilled tongue and lifted me above my kin that I might place within the Intellect's palm the gold of my thought, subtly wrought, long sought-after and too precious to be bought, that he might make thereof bands for princes' necks and dear companions' hands. Shine, then, my muse, while the downcast and the righteous light lamps from your holy cruse: bring joy and gladness, feasting and good days to the Jews!

Then I lifted my voice and sang:

My speech is refined,
with cunning designed,
green, garland-entwined,
well bred and well versed.

they set their mouths against the heavens and their tongues walk the earth Ps. 73: 9.
You are mightier far than we Gen. 26: 16.
lower Your ladder and guide us up those shining rungs [Gen. 28: 12].
guarding our way that we sin not with our tongues Ps. 39: 2.
shine Your countenance upon us Ps. 4: 7.
of blessed memory This phrase indicates the addition of a later editor, although one cannot rule out a very tongue-in-cheek witticism of the author.
The Lord has gifted me with a skilled tongue Isa. 50: 4.
joy and gladness, feasting and good days to the Jews Esther 8: 17.

Rich sentence, ripe clause
I pour without pause,
penning Poesy's laws,
the last and the first.
I lift my folk up,
raise Poesy's cup,
bid Jewry come sup:
come, drink, ye who thirst.
Then rise, Hebrew hopes,
on the wings of my tropes:
behold, my tongue's ropes
bind up Judah's dispersed.

I slept but my heart woke, indeed near broke in passion's squall. Then did my Intellect call, to rouse me from vanity, restore me to sanity, saying: Son of man, how can you sleep? Open your eyes, leap to your feet, sweep folly aside, gird Thought's mail, lift the tongue's flail, fail not the Lord, but wield your sword for the Holy Tongue, currency of prophecy. Ah, see how she falters! Pray for her, speed with your sacrifice to Song's pure altars. With zeal and truth renew her youth, redeem her from the tooth of the marauding beast, save her from the lion's feast.

I answered, Alas, Lord, my spirit's drouth: my right arm fails, my tongue cleaves to the roof of my mouth; and who am I to save our scattered flock from the lions' claws, lead the Hebrews from bondage back to God's holy laws?

*T*hen he answered: I will be with you, do not resist; sound your voice on high, smite ignorance with Wisdom's fist. All the people you dwell among shall see the work of the Lord, for I will do marvels in their midst.

the last and the first [Isa. 44: 6, 48: 12].
raise Poesy's cup [Ps. 116: 13].
come, drink, ye who thirst [Isa. 55: 1].
bind up Judah's dispersed Isa. 11: 12.
I slept but my heart woke S. of S. 5: 2.
Son of man e.g. Ezek. 2: 1 and elsewhere.
how can you sleep? Jonah 1: 6.
my tongue cleaves to the roof of my mouth Ps. 137: 6.
And who am I to save our scattered flock from the lions' claws, lead the Hebrews from bondage Exod. 3: 11.
I will be with you Exod. 3: 12.
sound your voice on high [Isa. 58: 4].
All the people you dwell among shall see the work of the Lord, for I will do marvels in their midst Exod. 34: 10.

Then the Intellect seized a coal, touched my lips, and spoke my name; and my soul took flame. My word is yours, he called, my voice, your declaration; I ordain you poet of your nation. I give you Folly's arbour to pull down and uproot, Song's arbour to raise and plant with precious fruit.

So roused by the Divine Mind, I put fear behind, struck fires that soared to heaven to sight the blind, that all earth might know our Holy Tongue beyond compare. Prisoners of hope, I cried, Israel has a son and heir who can, with loving care, with words and song and parables rare, front Hebrew, the abandoned bride, and loud declare, You are fair, my love, you are fair! I clear the way that our Holy Tongue might lead her chariots down victory's thoroughfare to her rivals' despair; fright her foes like a ravening bear and all our wastes repair, stripping Esau and Ishmael bare. See her conquer, take heroes in her snare: yea, we have seen sons of the giant there.

Now in ancient times Hebrew was a golden plough, but in our day villains flay her with brazen brow: righteousness lodged in her, but murderers now. She is banished from her children, none mourn her loss, her silver turns dross. Heartsick, she cries in pain, lifting her refrain to deaf ears again and yet again. What sin is mine? she cries in vain. Lo, when you ringed Sinai to hear God's word, me it was you heard. Think on Jerusalem, where the Presence did resort: I was the Queen in God's holy court, standing you and Heaven between, that you might know what God's injunctions mean. And now your children race to kiss a stranger's face. They shun my delights, saying, Come, let us sell her to the Ishmaelites! She is unfit! Thereat they

seized a coal, touched my lips Isa. 6: 7.
I ordain you poet of your nation Jer. 1: 5.
I give you Folly's arbour to pull down and uproot, Song's arbour to raise and plant with precious fruit Jer. 1: 10.
to sight the blind Isa. 42: 7.
Prisoners of hope [Zech. 9: 12].
Israel has a son and heir [Jer. 49: 1].
You are fair, my love, you are fair [S. of S. 1: 15].
I clear the way [Isa. 57: 14].
and all our wastes repair [Isa. 61: 4].
Esau and Ishmael Christendom and Araby.
we have seen sons of the giant there [Num. 13: 33].
righteousness lodged in her, but murderers now Isa. 1: 21.
her silver turns dross Isa. 1: 22.
you ringed Sinai Exod. 19: 12.
standing you and Heaven between Deut. 5: 5.
Come, let us sell her to the Ishmaelites Gen. 37: 27.

seized me and flung me into a pit, they all but doomed me, moaning—the hypocrites!—that an evil beast had consumed me! They set Hagar the maidservant in my place and rushed to her embrace, kissing her hand and pressing her teat—for stolen waters are sweet. Me they have abandoned, the Rose of Sharon, saying, Hagar is fecund and Sarah barren.

While Hagar bears glorious
children, shall Sarah
conceive not?
Jealousy sears me, but
as for my people—
they grieve not.

Therefore I girt my loins and fixed my eyes on Scripture's golden coins wherewith to redeem our ancient dream, save my mistress from her barren state and once more make her teem; I vowed to gain Splendour's crest, bring her to her heritage and rest, swore that I would draw water from her holy spring that our folk might drink their fill and sing.

So I set out upon my way and came to the fountain this day that I might no longer be accurst, that I might draw up Wisdom's wine and slake my thirst; and I said, O Lord God, I pray Thee: recall my faithfulness and this day repay me. Help me fulfil my vow: bring before me, even now, Wisdom's daughters as I stand here at the lip of flowing waters. That maiden, pitcher-laden, whom I shall ask, as she leaves the city gate, fair one, wait! My spirit falters, slips: let me drink of the phrases dripping from your lips; that maiden who answers, Drink at your will and of my flame your spirit fill—she it is whom you have appointed for me, your own anointed.

Now scarcely had I finished this thought when she whom my

they seized me and flung me into a pit Gen. 37: 24.
an evil beast had consumed me Gen. 37: 20, 34.
They set Hagar the maidservant in my place [Gen. 16: 3].
for stolen waters are sweet Prov. 9: 17.
the Rose of Sharon [S. of S. 2: 1].
Sarah barren Gen. 11: 30.
bring her to her heritage and rest Num. 10: 33.
came to the fountain this day Gen. 24: 42.
whom you have appointed for me Gen. 24: 13–14.

soul sought appeared, sun-bright with Wisdom's light, and neared me with her pitcher; and never was maiden beauty-richer. Before I could speak, her lips were on mine and I tasted wondrous wine. Drink deep my thoughts, she whispered—ah, her touch was silk!—seek 'neath my tongue my honey and my milk.

*T*hen I asked her, Fairest on earth, who gave you birth?

I am an orphan, she replied, though my Father flourishes; yet my hope perishes, for my mother's sons, my brothers, have reviled me—I, who wore a royal crown; they have defiled me. I am your Mistress, the Holy Tongue: if I find favour in your sight, I will be your heart's delight—only be zealous for God's name: sanctify me, who am put to shame. Be you my redeemer from every slanderer, renegade, blasphemer.

*T*hen, thanking God on bended knee that she had set her love on me, I rose to deck her neck with jewellery, her ears and wrists with my rare filigree. I did her shoulders drape with silken cape—even so I clothed her—and then in awe and righteousness betrothed her without ring or coin or witness. Straightway I lay with the prophetess and from this union sprang one who godly sang. God's spirit began to move him, never was warrior bolder; sovereignty lay upon his shoulder. A mighty liege, he marched on Wisdom's towers and laid siege, drawing from a mighty store of tools of war: for battering-rams—bold maxims, saws, and epigrams; for armature—thoughts deep and pure; for pike and sabre—reflection's labour; for blade—soft utterance, marvellously made, transmuting to fence, or wall, or shade; for haft, the rhymer's skills and the jokester's craft

she whom my soul sought [S. of S. 3: 1].

and neared me with her pitcher Gen. 24: 15.

seek 'neath my tongue my honey and my milk [S. of S. 4: 11].

my mother's sons, my brothers, have reviled me S. of S. 1: 6.

only be zealous for God's name Ezek. 39: 25.

I rose to deck her neck with jewellery, her ears and wrists with my rare filigree Gen. 24: 47.

in awe and righteousness betrothed her Hos. 2: 21.

without ring or coin or witness i.e. I consummated the relationship at once. See BT *Kid. 1a*.

I lay with the prophetess Isa. 8: 3.

and from this union sprang one who godly sang i.e. Hever the Kenite, or *Sefer Taḥkemoni* itself.

God's spirit began to move him Judg. 13: 25.

sovereignty lay upon his shoulder Isa. 9: 5.

(here none dare say, Wherefore hast thou laughed?); for spear, diction dazzling clear; for catapult, scriptural verses deep and occult. And with these awesome blades and shields and slings sprung of Eden's springs, these heroic themes that turn day night—he put thousands, tens of thousands, into frenzied flight.

Now I will tell you what moved me to compose this book: A certain Arab sage, the pride of his age, master of incision, who turned rivals to a mockery and derision, whose mouth was an open vision, one known as al-Ḥariri, who left all rivals panting and weary, composed a stunning work in Arabic, rhymed prose wed with metric stich—even if he dealt in contraband: for, lo, his vessel is with Hebrew sailors manned! Demand of its every trope, How came you here to stand? and the latter will reply, I was stolen away out of the Hebrews' land.

Now when I saw this book my tongue turned leather, the heavens of my joy rolled together, for all peoples, old or young, take heed to their ways that they sin not with their tongue. But our Holy Tongue, Beauty's very mother, is turned Cain's brother. Vulgarity supplants clarity; homeliness, comeliness; tarnish, varnish. We are unsound, unwound, a dry root in dry ground. Alas our language: our folk have slandered and defaced her, all but erased her, saying, Hebrew is lean and lacking, so much faded sacking; but they are too obtuse to realize that they are blind to her use, too dense to know that theirs is the offence—like a man with a great sty in his eye who, unable to see the sky, holds sunlight night. Even so, most of our folk malign our Holy Tongue, a wonder and a sign—and baldly fear not; the burning bush beckons—but they near not; ears have they—but they hear not.

Wherefore hast thou laughed? [Gen. 18: 13].

he put thousands, tens of thousands, into frenzied flight Deut. 32: 30.

his vessel is with Hebrew sailors manned Lit. 'despite the fact that his themes are hewn from the holy tongue and all his precious parables are taken from our books and thence transmitted'.

I was stolen away out of the Hebrews' land Gen. 40: 15.

the heavens of my joy rolled together Isa. 34: 4.

that they sin not with their tongue Ps. 39: 2.

is turned Cain's brother i.e. Abel/Ḥevel—*ḥevel* also meaning 'vanity' or 'nothingness'.

a dry root in dry ground [Isa. 53: 2].

a wonder and a sign [Deut. 28: 46].

the burning bush beckons—but they near not Exod. 3: 1–5.

The manna fell long since—but they found it not; David's harp lies by—and they sound it not.

Alas for closed eyes:
manna covered the ground;
They went out to gather
and nothing found.

Hence I wrote this book to raise Hebrew's holy tower, to show our holy folk her suppleness and power, for they are now struck blind, they cannot find the gateway leading to her lush green shades, her gushing fountains, and her lark-filled glades. Here let them revel with rich lads and maids, maids bright as stars, swaying in dance or strumming songs on gay guitars, sisters to the dove who, with their lays of lust, fan fires of love, turn many a head, turn hearts a deeper red; yes, lay Love's bed. Now all this I have done with words sprung from my heart, for mine is virgin art, mine myrrh-steeped figures that have known no other's touch, little or much: nay, no stranger has seen them, much less shown them: no man has known them.

Now I have included in this work matter of all manner: anthems for Love's banner, riddles and saws, lore and laws, reflection, censure, the wayfarer's adventure, tales of times past or of death's blast, the grace of every season, the way of reason or treachery and treason, godly wrath and the penitent's path, the beloved's face and hot embrace, wooing and bedding and holy wedding—and divorce as well.

Yes, I tell of teetotallers and drinkers, of warriors and thinkers, spin tales of journeys, of kings and poets' tourneys, prayers and supplication, praise and protestation, the rebuke of the wise and good fortune's demise, the role of Love's gazelles and the cool of desert wells, stint's harsh breeze and beggars' pleas, wind and water, sword and slaughter, harts' hunt and heart's want, travellers' treks and slippery decks and vessels' wrecks, slandering, pandering, and Youth's meandering, Nazirites' vows and drunken carouse, paramours, ills and

ears have they—but they hear not Ps. 115: [6].
The manna fell long since—but they found it not Exod. 16: 27.
manna covered the ground; they went out to gather and nothing found Exod. 16: 14, 27.
they are now struck blind, they cannot find the gateway [Gen. 19: 11].
no man has known them Gen. 24: 16.

cures, blockheads and boors, guile's school and the gulled fool, gibe and jeer and snub and sneer, song enchanted, wine discanted, witty invention, brazen contention—all this, that this book might be Song's manse and garden, wherein every seeker might sate his quest, every petitioner gain his behest: herein shall the weary rest. Then enter, all, my dazzling manor, each in his camp, each man beneath his banner. He who stands in awe of the Lord shall find prayer and preachment and fear of the Lord; and he who sets not his heart on the word of the Lord shall here find this world's dalliance—and thence stream to the good of the Lord. And every dimwit or dolt, greybeard or colt, can seat himself at Wisdom's session, learn judgement and equity, knowledge and discretion. Let the wise of heart, the man of discerning, hear and increase learning; and as for the seeker of worldly knowledge—here is his tutor, here his college; and every poet who would sharpen his wits, who has sought pure waters in muddy cisterns and broken pits—hither let him turn his feet: God shall show him a tree to cast into the waters and make them sweet.

He who longs to burst the gates of Wisdom's hold, he who hungers for Song's jacinths and fine gold, and thirsts for saws and maxims new and old—let him here enter and prosper tenfold, daily grow richer, drinking from an unending pitcher; yes, let him gorge on Wit's meat and Learning's ale, for the barrel of meal shall not waste neither shall the cruse of oil fail. Fie, fie on hunger's threat: the board is set with pheasant and quail, every manner of meat. Let all who are hungry enter and eat.

wherein every seeker might sate his quest, every petitioner gain his behest In openly advocating, and then providing, maximum variety in his works, Alḥarizi echoes Arab philosophy and practice in the literature of *adab*—enlightenment and entertainment—with its frequent digressions and shifts from one subject to another. On the term *adab* see the analysis of Gate 36.

herein shall the weary rest [Job 3: 17].

each in his camp, each man beneath his banner Num. [1: 52].

and thence stream to the good of the Lord Jer. 31: 11.

judgement and equity, knowledge and discretion Prov. 1: 4.

Let the wise of heart, the man of discerning, hear and increase learning Prov. 1: 5.

who has sought pure waters in muddy cisterns and broken pits Jer. 2: 13.

God shall show him a tree to cast into the waters and make them sweet Exod. 15: 25.

neither shall the cruse of oil fail 1 Kgs. 17: 14.

Let all who are hungry enter and eat Passover Haggadah.

And well shall this feast serve our people from west to east, for too often is their Hebrew mangled, their phrases tangled, their clauses jarred and jangled. Let the limp, the halt, the twisted, the unsightly read this work and speak rightly. Let their eyes be opened, let them know the plight that they are in, let them flee their sin, weave new garments and cover their skin. Yes, here let them renew their hope, enlarge their scope with gleaming thought and shining trope.

And in this that I have written, all the lot, I took nothing from the Arabs, not a jot; unless, perchance, I forgot—or it came into my hand and I knew it not. No: all, all my matter is free and fresh, bone of my bone and flesh of my flesh. Now many asleep in the earth of folly shall awake and free their throats for Song's and Heaven's sake.

Now as for al-Ḥariri's work, some rash souls set out to alter him to Hebrew but sore did falter, for they wore profane robes yet dared approach Song's altar. For all their fits and starts they captured rightly but one in fifty parts. Hungry readers, who have Song long cherished, shall leave these poets' tables undernourished—poets (so-called) who trembled at the thunder of al-Ḥariri's tongue: the hail fell upon them and they perished. Storming his palace, they had as well stormed Fate: they massed their troops, but came too late; lo, as night fell their prey slipped out the gate.

—Lieutenant, where have they fled to?

—No one knows.

No one. Until I arose and plucked the Arab's rose. I did his gold retrieve; I took his tapestry and made fresh weave. With consummate taste I wove a holy girdle for Song's waist and left the poetasters howling in the waste.

I turned my eyes to Intellect's heights, I prayed and willed:

---

weave new garments and cover their skin Gen. 3: 7.

it came into my hand and I knew it not Gen. 28: 16. The statement is very tongue-in-cheek. See the Analysis.

bone of my bone and flesh of my flesh [Gen. 2: 23].

many asleep in the earth of folly shall awake Dan. 12: 2.

for they wore profane robes yet dared approach Song's altar Exod. 39: 1, 41; Ezek. 22: 26.

the hail fell upon them and they perished Exod. 9: 19.

lo, as night fell their prey slipped out the gate Josh. 2: 5.

Until I arose Judg. 5: 7.

down gushed Wit's rain; my spirit thrilled, I spoke to Song's rock; its water spilled, and all my furrows filled. For Spain's patrons, awed at this Arab's display, bade me render it in Hebrew for my fellows straightway—and could I say them nay?

But after I had translated the treasure of this all-but-prophet to my readers' pleasure and profit, I left the west, dared mountain peaks and the wave's curled crest, and eastward came—where I was struck with shame. Forgive me, Lord, I cried, for I am much to blame! Alas my name and my fathers' name, that I diverted the Bible's crystal brook to fructify a foreign book. I mistook my purpose. Look: I tended strangers' vineyards and my own forsook.

In consequence I have my harp fresh strung to sing new song in our holy Hebrew tongue—new warp, new woof, new sword, and bright new stones: here I invigorate dry bones. For this battle of honour I have mustered the language of visions—our fathers' speech, in fifty divisions.

Now here is my scheme: I set this work in the mouth of Heman the Ezrahite and Hever the Kenite of Zaananim—but know that they, their histories, all this delectation, are but a fabrication, the child of my imagination.

And now, dear readers, all you who taste my art: if you find aught sour or tart, bid harsh judgement stand apart—let Judah's sin be not writ upon your heart. Bid impatience halt: love covers every fault. Consider: whose the hand with iron grip will never slip? Not mine such anatomy! Look, what king has not stumbled, what head of what academy? If giants mar their tomes, what of gnomes? If, midst tall cedars, lightning fall, what the lot of the hyssops on the wall?

Then may He who teaches man wisdom purge our lips with

I spoke to Song's rock; its water spilled Num. 20: 8.

I tended strangers' vineyards and my own forsook S. of S. 1: 6.

I invigorate dry bones Isa. 58: 11; Ezek. 37: 4 ff.

Heman the Ezrahite and Hever the Kenite of Zaananim Ps. 88: 1; Judg. 4: 11. On the significance and uses of these biblical names, see the Afterword.

let Judah's sin be not writ upon your heart Jer. 17: 1.

love covers every fault Prov. 10: 12.

If, midst tall cedars, lightning fall, what the lot of the hyssops on the wall BT *Mo'ed Katan* 25*b*.

Then may He who teaches man wisdom Ps. 94: 10. Here, repeating the very words that opened the Introduction, Alḥarizi rounds out his exposition.

holy fire, command our hearts that we rightly aspire, answer us from Heaven and grant us our desire.

SAID THE AUTHOR:

Now when I stood back from my canvas and its blazing palette, tasted my words so pleasing to the palate, from the Euphrates to the Nile I sought a patron's smile, a champion of Generosity's camp to lend my work his stamp. Long I looked that I might seize and bind him: I sought him, but I did not find him. I searched until appalled: no one answered when I called. Yet scarce had I passed them by when I found him whom my soul loves and God approves, for He has set him Prince above his generation, a lion whom we roar in acclamation, Probity's girdle and Kindness' glove, Wisdom's tiara and the sceptre of love, a rising sun, a Joseph for awe, a David guarding godly law, a leaping stag, discernment's crag, an eagle soaring proud and lone, a Solomon seated on Wisdom's throne. He strums on sapience' lute—rhetors and sages fall mute; before his lineage all nobles are ashamed, and when he gives, all givers are defamed. Gabriel bright, our pride, our knight, the breath of our nostrils, our light and very sight—his hands are as capacious as his hall, where rich and poor are welcome all. He is the great prince of blazing merit, Israel's wall and turret, the great Maecenas, that shining soul, Rabbi Samuel son of Alberkol, the Lord preserve him! Egypt and Damascus vie to serve him; Zova, Assyria, Babylon admit that they in no way deserve him.

Now when I saw this champion, none bolder, saw that his people's governance fell upon his shoulder, I made his love my staff and crook and set his diamond name upon my book, then gave it him for his livery—for necklace, sceptre, and crown that all the world might see; and I cried before him, *Avrekh*/Bow-the-knee!

Well knew I that on seeing my progeny, my rightful seed, he

---

sought him, but I did not find him S. of S. 3: 2, 5: 6.

Yet scarce had I passed them by when I found him whom my soul loves S. of S. 3: 4.

the breath of our nostrils Lam. 4: 20.

people's governance fell upon his shoulder Isa. 9: 5.

my staff and crook [Ps. 23: 4].

***Avrekh*/Bow-the-knee** Gen. 41: 43, as interpreted by the medieval commentators ibn Jannah, Bekhor Shor, and Abraham ibn Ezra.

would lift me to Heaven, gift me, meet my every need, be my father and my brother, that I might never need turn to any other. Lo, even as we respect him and to high station gratefully elect him, we pray God guard and protect him, yea, bless his memory to the farthest generation: high Heaven be his station. Let his name, moon-bright, be tomorrow's, as today's, delight.

Now this tome, this rare medallion, this unmatched stone is meant to grace Lord Samuel's neck alone. For he it is who is the intimate of Wisdom and of Truth, serving them faithfully since his youth. Herein shall his hand be strengthened and his rule lengthened, for when I set before my readers his virtue's store, they will believe me and love him all the more. And when his days be flown and when his children, grown, rise to take his throne, this work shall serve as a tutorial and memorial, setting sight within the blind man's reach and teaching the mute speech, that they might bless my lord's days and hymn his praise and ever laud his godly ways.

And his two brothers, the esteemed Prince Rabbi Yosef and the fair Prince Rabbi Ezra, God stand them by, are manna from on high, bold riders after Him who rides the sky, pillars of Right and the Torah's guarding eye, cherubs with wings outspread, rule's channel and princedom's bed, joy's beam and modesty's stay, pride's night and kindness' day, who have gathered all virtue and cast all wrongs away, so that their names are a joy to behold—more to be desired are they than gold. God ever light their lamp and bright their camp.

And here I end. May God ever bend my will to His until He end my life; but let Him send me life—for His are the paths that lend me life.

manna from on high [Exod. 16: 15–35].
Him who rides the sky Deut. 33: 26.
cherubs with wings outspread Exod. 25: 20.
more to be desired are they than gold [Ps. 19: 11].
His are the paths that lend me life Prov. 4: 23.

GATE ONE

Whence this Work Sprung and by Whom it was Sung

THUS SPOKE HEMAN THE EZRAHITE: The author of this work gifted me with his tongue's gems and his thought's diadems, saying:

*I*n Kiriath-jearim, Judah's city of groves and Wisdom's treasure troves, I probed high truths with Hebrew youths whose emerald words were darting birds, whose generous hands were streams. Their eyes' fierce beams illumed the skies, as their praise flashed diamond rays that bade dawn be gone. Angels they, who left earth behind to gain Heaven by the ladder of the mind. By their light, light was undone: they shamed the moon and sun; their intellect's least spark lit darkest dark. Above them sailed the cloud of their humility, before them the Ark of Irreproachability; praise rested where their cloud of glory took repose and lifted when that thick cloud rose. Their thoughts were a wonder on the earth: nor pangs nor midwives and lo, they had given birth. Youths pure and glowing, Wisdom's river overflowing, each pitched Torah's camp within his breast. At their command the Intellect journeyed or took rest; ere they would cry, he would reply. Poetry's lords and guards of Wisdom's

---

Kiriath-jearim, Judah's city of groves 'City of groves' is the literal translation of the Hebrew *kiryat ye'arim*, located in the territory of the tribe of Judah (Josh. 15: 60 and elsewhere).

Angels they, who left earth behind to gain Heaven by the ladder of the mind Gen. 28: 12.

Above them sailed the cloud of their humility, before them—the Ark of Irreproachability Num. 9: 15–23.

praise rested where their cloud of glory took repose and lifted when that thick cloud rose Num. 9: 19–22.

nor pangs nor midwives and lo, they had given birth Exod. 1: 19.

journeyed or took rest Num. 9: 17.

ere they would cry, he would reply Isa. 65: 24.

fords, their tongues were drawn swords issuing, to all men's wonder, lightning and thunder. Fierce did their words advance, rank upon rank of targe and lance to turn *instanter* to a lover's glance, a courtly dance, or hid romance; and steeped as they were ever in heady thoughts, that deep were they ever in ruddy draughts.

Now among us was a Hebrew youth towering and regal, Wisdom's eagle streaking and soaring, Faith's very torrent leaping and roaring. When he loomed, giants shivered; when he boomed, heroes quivered. His was splendour and wondrous grace: Beauty camped upon his face. Wisdom took refuge beneath his wings: lions feared him, much more so kings. Consummate rhetor, none more versed, in every endeavour he was ever first, whether staking Wit's claim or slaking his thirst. Convivial in the tavern, Wisdom's storehouse and wine's cavern, he plucked the lute that the Tree of Joy bore fruit and Grief's bowers withered to the root. When he sang, the ocean shook to its very bed; ah, he could wake the dead. And when he entered the tourney of sacred lore, Time wore the mail of fear: Wisdom's knights threw down their shields when he drew near. He spoke: the world rejoiced; yea, the waves of Praise reared up, full-voiced.

A voice from Heaven declaims, proclaims:
Who is the man who seeks after life?
Let him speed to the lands of high learning's lord,
there to discover the path of life.
With his tongue's high art he restores the dry heart,
this youth whose fresh streams give us waters of life.
At his towering wall his rivals fall,
but seekers, uncov'ring him, bask in life.
To sun in his rays is to sing his praise
who showers us all with the fountain of life.

Now among us was a Hebrew youth Gen. 41: 12.
took refuge beneath his wings Ps. 91: 4.
reared up, full-voiced Ps. 93: 3.
A voice from Heaven declaims, proclaims [Isa. 40: 3].
Who is the man who seeks after life? Ps. 34: 13.
the path of life Ps. 16: 11.
waters of life Num. 19: 17.
bask in life Prov. 4: 23, 8: 25.
the fountain of life [Ps. 36: 10].

He is Wisdom's increase, whose lush lips release
black arrows of death and the balm of life.
Set, then, your eyes on the flaming sword
that guards the bright path to the Tree of Life.

Then he cried, Attend, all ye who Wisdom's walls defend. Wherever truth be rung in all that men have said or sung, have you seen, heard, read, or tasted sweeter words than those of the master of rhymed prose, the Ishmaelite, that font of delight, right riddler, teller of tales who never fails, al-Ḥariri? Have you paid him note, heard that honeyed throat, seen the rare *maqāmāt* that he wrote? Behold how poetasters pant and run but cannot touch the fringes of his coat! His lines are Eden's furrows laid anew, dripping with Heaven's dew.

Now if his work were writ in any but the Arabs' tongue it were an instrument ill strung, a mixed multitude, halting, crude, an affliction and malediction; for Arabic is a sail unfurled to bear us wide-eyed to a magic world. It is a faerie melody, a holy fire, an endless sea.

SAID THE AUTHOR OF THIS TOME:

My heart near broke. Alas, I admitted, I must bear Truth's yoke: Arabic rules the ages, former and latter. Beside her all tongues are tin chimes and patter, idle chatter—except the Holy Tongue, wherein God spoke at Sinai to His chosen folk, for Heaven forbid that the Creator of speech should teach His law through want and flaw. All know and own that Hebrew, of old, held stores untold and treasures manifold; but once we bent beneath the exile's yoke, we stooped to speak the tongues our captors spoke. This, our own defection, engendered the perception of Hebrew's imperfection. On the first day of our captivity, no later, did we turn traitor to Hebrew Sarah's seed, seeking the Egyptian Hagar's son to meet our need. Hence are we bereft and our tongue cleft: our speech, once whole, is all but swallowed by Sheol—see what little the hail has left.

But with this tiny residue heed what we yet shall do: write

the flaming sword that guards the bright path to the Tree of Life Gen. 3: 24.

mixed multitude Exod. 12: 38.

It is a faerie melody, a holy fire, an endless sea Lit. 'It is sweet and beloved of its hearers, hewn from fire (Ps. 29: 7), and wider than the sea (Job 11: 9).'

the Egyptian Hagar's son Gen. 21: 9 (Ishmael, ancestor of the Arabs).

see what little the hail has left Exod. 10: 12.

poems and tomes in a swirl of ruby utterance and pearl, indite lines of jacinth and of chrysolite, write scrolls of opal, pen carnelian lines, work wonders and signs, fashion trope after trope of spinel, jade, and heliotrope—verse golden and diverse, blazing announcements, amazing pronouncements; with verve and expedition we shall grace our rich tradition with many a composition flashing wit and erudition, spin song in golden chains and chatelaines. Bright as Aaron's breastplate, our new art shall cleave the heart; songs beyond worth shall be fruitful and multiply upon the earth. And let this be a sign that ours is a godly legacy, the tongue of Prophecy: though narrow, it shall be broad; it shall suffice us all to censure, argue, teach, and laud.

*T*he man replied, If that be true, tell me why no Jew can do what many an Ishmaelite can do? Why has no Jew arisen to ransom Hebrew from dishonour's prison?

I replied, The answer you demand is close at hand. Should we unsheathe our pens and charge that mighty summit, we would go up and win the land, for we could surely overcome it. But for whom shall the author write, for whom indite, when ears are plugged for spite and fists clenched tight, when Time has wrenched mankind from Right's path, when God, in His wrath, has flung humanity into Passion's den, blinding all: the men at the gate are smitten with blindness, great and small. None can see, none can hear, none comes near. Up, get you gone, scour the world's Jewries from Egypt to Italy, Spain to Babylon, and find nowhere men of uncommon sense who dispense rich recompense for Wisdom's jewels.

*Y*ou know Art's rules. Write not for jeering fools, but for the plenty of open-handed cognoscenti! All pleasant wisdom comes to fruition upon the fulfilment of the following conditions: on her finding a Maecenas or a sage or a grandee unto whom she shall be sold into slavery; then, happy maid, her light will never fade! If these three things be not done, do this, according to God's Constitution: free her

---

Aaron's breastplate [Exod. 28: 4–28].
be fruitful and multiply upon the earth [Gen. 1: 28].
charge that mighty summit, we would go up and win the land, for we could surely overcome it Num. 13: 30.
the men at the gate are smitten with blindness, great and small Gen. 19: 11.

without restitution. But now holy stones tumble on the streets, men pass them by; poems and rhymed prose are offered for slaves and handmaids, but none buy. Maecenases ply a bastard art, bubbling praise from the lips but not a whisper from the heart. And everywhere I camp, I cry, Is there no man of learning nigh? But I hear no word: not a cough, not a ghost of a reply. Wonder not why: I stand in a sty!

How can the wise soul rise and shine, how speak her words divine, how consign her precious wine—even her simplest pearled line—to goats, to kine, to swine? How shall we sing? In our people's eyes, wisdom is but a stone in a sling!

The man replied, Sooth, you speak truth! In this shrunken age what moneyed gnat or mite can set things right? Now hear: turn your back on your kinsmen and their lack; make short shrift of their worthless gift. But let not evil so shadow good, that to weed thorn and thistle you would uproot a lush wood. For if you can compose a work of metric verse and rhyming prose insightful, delightful, well groomed, perfumed; a work that will sweetly preach and neatly teach, complaining of folly's yoke, explaining with saw and quote and joke—and, withal, entertaining the learned as well as simple folk; a work lush with winging tropes and singing hopes, erudite and recondite with gems and apophthegms, with ringing stories and winging allegories—you will open the mouths of Jewry's scattered congregations and bare Hebrew's gold unto the nations. Go now: in every chapter you indite I will be with your tongue, teaching you what to write!

And now, if you seek a noble patron for your book, on whom the world would joy to look, I have found even such a one—behold Jesse's son, Majesty's best resort: kings bent with tribute crowd his court. He is wed to Sovereignty in bonds no man can sever, for God has sworn that he shall reign forever. On the day he was born a voice came from Heaven in thunder and in flame: My people, a son is born to David's house—Josiah shall be his name. Rule shall be his alone!

If these three things be not done . . . free her without restitution Exod. 21: 11.

holy stones tumble on the streets Lam. 4: 1.

offered for slaves and handmaids, but none buy Deut. 28: 68.

I will be with your tongue, teaching you what to write Exod. 4: 12, 15.

behold Jesse's son 1 Sam. 16: 18.

a son is born to David's house—Josiah shall be his name 1 Kgs. 13: 2. The grandee is most likely an exilarch who lived in Syria, possibly Mosul. See the close of the Analysis.

Then He breathed His spirit into the corpses of Praise and bone drew nigh to bone. Splendour was given him for bride; wise in all his paths, God stands him beside; the key of the house of David is on his shoulder and he dwells inside.

Splendour was made in his image; then Rule
was presented as helpmeet to him alone;
He breathed his gold breath on the corpses of Praise:
lo, flesh wed to flesh, and bone to bone.

Two witnesses attest to his renown: Solomon his seal and David his crown. With them for chariots and cars, he rules the stars. Before him angels peal, Lo, the age's prince—kneel, kneel, O Israelites: thus shall be done to the man in whom the king delights! He is Praise's walls and ground, his virtue knows no bound, his speech no flaw; his heart is an endless ocean of God's law. His mouth is Wisdom's gushing fountain; his mighty arm, Salvation's mountain. By God appointed, he is with Praise's oil anointed.

On his mind's broad plain kingly notions camp; his face is the Temple's eternal lamp. He boasts his forebears' wit, their regal thought and grace, and his sons shall rise to take his place. His eyes hold the burning bush's flame: God lifts his bannered name and sets it on the highest peaks of Fame. He speaks—all men defer; strides to his throne—no man dare stir. Cease! Earth, render tribute to the great counsellor, the prince of peace who shall habit David's throne without surcease.

Our prince and our rod, the gift of our God
on the pallet of virtue, God's masterpiece;

then He breathed his spirit into the corpses of Praise and bone drew nigh to bone Ezek. 37: 7.
the key of the house of David is on his shoulder Isa. 22: 22.
was made in his image Gen. 1: 27.
was presented as helpmeet to him alone Gen. 2: 20.
He breathed his gold breath on the corpses of Praise: lo, flesh wed to flesh, and bone to bone Ezek. 37: 7.
Before him angels peal: Lo, the age's prince—kneel, kneel Gen. 41: 43.
thus shall be done to the man in whom the king delights Esther 6: 9, 11.
the Temple's eternal lamp [Exod. 27: 20].
the burning bush's flame [Exod. 3: 2].
the prince of peace who shall habit David's throne without surcease Isa. 9: 6.

Josiah, bright spark who illumes Exile's dark,
our banner and ark, our sorrow's release.
In his day may High Heaven call, Israel: Forgiven!
behold a son given you, Prince of Peace

—as it is written, *A child is born unto us, a son is given unto us; and the government shall be upon his shoulder. His name shall be called Wonderful, Counsellor, Almighty God, Eternal Father, Prince of Peace.*

Before Perez' scion, redeemer of Zion,
Josiah, fierce lion—our foes have all fled.
Our wonder and sign sprung from David's bright line,
our bread and our wine, and our enemies' dread.
Kings bow him before—Might's column, Right's floor:
then fear we no more with the Lord at our head

—as it is written, *He who makes a breach passes before them; they enlarge it to a gate and leave thereby. Their king marches before them and the Lord at their head.*

He has sown a rich field whose high wheat, whose lush yield
are our buckler and shield: Josiah, our own!
Lift, Israel, your voice in high praise of God's choice:
loud, loud we rejoice as our enemies groan;
Who dare now refute God's word absolute:
Of thy body's sweet fruit will I set on thy throne

—as it is written, *The Lord swore unto David in truth, He will not turn back therefrom: of the fruit of thy body I will set on thy throne.*

You blest of the Lord, reconfirmed, reassured—
let your throats afford praises: sing loud the Lord, sing!
And praise you his name who has stripped us of shame,
who has crowned us with fame—God's signet and ring;
The weak and downtrod are redeemed by his rod:
they thrill, seeking God and bold David their king

A child is born . . . Prince of Peace Isa. 9: 5.
redeemer of Zion [Isa. 59: 20].
He who makes . . . the Lord at their head Mic. 2: 13.
The Lord swore unto David in truth . . . set on thy throne Ps. 132: 11.

—as it is written, *Afterward shall the children of Israel return, and seek the Lord their God, and David their King; and shall thrill over the Lord and His bounty in the days to come.*

What tongue can so brim with sea-praise as to hymn
this wide ocean? Who swim him? What brave polyglot?
Then drink we this wine, our Witness and Sign,
bright Joseph, that vine who faileth us not.
Our garden of gold with blossoms untold,
whose fathers, of old, came forth from Ephrat

—as it is written, *And you, O Bethlehem of Ephrat, least among the thousands of Judah, out of you shall come forth one unto Me who is to be ruler in Israel—whose origins are from of old, from ancient days.*

He is our master of bright renown, our God-fearing crown of piety, agate and coronal of our society, seed of kings and our prince and lord, our outstretched arm, our bared and gleaming sword, our pillar of fire, dispelling darkness for us, the Ark of the Covenant journeying before us, our holy throne, our song and our refrain, who turns the hills and twisted ways to a level plain, our rabbi, teacher, lord, and king, Wisdom's signet-ring: Josiah, the high prince, prince of Israel's exile, son of our great, eminent, holy rabbi, lord, teacher, and ruler—Jesse, great prince and prince of all the exiles of Israel, be his holy memory a blessing; son of Solomon; son of Josiah; son of Nehemiah; son of Hodiah, seed of Zerubbabel; son of Shealtiel; son of king Jechoniah; son of Josiah; son of Hezekiah; son of Jotham; son of Uzziah; son of Asa; son of Avijah; son of Solomon; son of David, the man set on high, the anointed of the God of Jacob, sweet singer of Israel, and Salvation's cup.

Afterward shall the children of Israel return . . . in the days to come Hos. 3: 5.

Joseph, that vine Gen. 49: 22.

And you, O Bethlehem . . . from ancient days Mic. 5: 1.

outstretched arm Exod. 6: 6 and elsewhere.

our bared and gleaming sword Num. 23: 20 and elsewhere.

our pillar of fire, dispelling darkness for us Exod. 13: 21.

the Ark of the Covenant journeying before us Num. 10: 33.

who turns the hills and twisted ways to a level plain Isa. 40: 4.

David, the man set on high, the anointed of the God of Jacob, sweet singer of Israel 2 Sam. 23: 1.

Salvation's cup [Ps. 116: 13].

Now a prince so heaven-sent, one who boasts such descent, so wise and fair a lord, will surely give you your due reward. Then let his praise be rung upon your silver tongue; not lightly shall he esteem your work and rightly shall he redeem your work; for, faced with such worth, he would pay any quittance on earth. Then praise your prince, rise, task him: he will not flinch, whatever price you ask him.

Proffer the best of the first of your fruits,
your mind's brightest clusters, on bended knee
To the king of all givers—all praise is his,
for all of earth's rivers run down to the sea.
He is prince above princes who lay down their necks
to the tread of his heel, swearing fealty.
Them ridden by envy his breath consumes,
till seekers ask, wond'ring, Where might they be?
The sons of the exile exult in his name,
uplifting his praise like the waves of the sea,
For he is their banner, their strength and their song,
he is their potion and remedy.
Splendour has raised him a castle on high
wherefrom he looks out on a world in fee.
Song's daughters have wove him a garment of silk
with rubies and emeralds and gold filigree
Till a voice loud as thunder resounds through the camp:
Enough has been given. Let be, let be!

SAID THE TELLER OF THE TALE:

His words rang true, his counsel was prudent. So, acting the zealous student, I dedicated this work to that mighty and munificent suzerain, knowing that my labours would not be in vain, confident that my invention, once sold, would gain redemption. Yes, on my readerless and flagging songs I breathed his praises sweet; the spirit

Proffer the best of the first of your fruits [Deut. 26: 2].
all of earth's rivers run down to the sea Eccles. 1: 7.
seekers ask, wond'ring, Where might they be? Job 20: 7.
uplifting his praise like the waves of the sea [Ps. 93: 3–4].
their strength and their song [Exod. 15: 2].
Till a voice loud as thunder resounds through the camp: Enough has been given. Let be, let be! Exod. 36: 6–7.

entered them, they stood upon their feet. But inasmuch as all praise that I can muster pales before his lustre, I resort to condensed report; for when the torrents of his virtues roar, I can do no more than stand humbly on the shore. Therefore I but hint at his good, this much can my pen afford. How else shall this man be reconciled unto his lord?

SAID THE AUTHOR:

He spoke—I heard; and on my mind's scale weighed his every word. Finding them well founded, rooted in truth, and in probity grounded, I did as demanded, composed this tome as shown me in Heaven, prophesied as commanded. Loud did Wisdom's spirit entreat until I approached the Tree of Intellect and of its fruit did eat. I waved rhetoric's staff above my dreams, raising Knowledge's Tabernacle by Righteousness' streams: the beams—high preachment, the sockets—savants' schemes; then I brought together sockets and beams and the Temple was one.

My lines are beams to light men's dreams,
Hermon's rich streams in a world gone dry.
My rivals gnash their teeth, they lash
the air, they smash their brows, cry Ay!
They had as soon outflown the moon
as tilt with me: how dare they vie
With one whose song can admit no wrong,
whose sandal thong they cannot tie,
One whose least note shames each their throat,
whose figures smite them hip and thigh!
With ease I best the Pleiades,
they sink to their knees, they shake, they cry.
My light so burns—the Jordan turns
its back and flees, the mountains fly.

the spirit entered them, they stood upon their feet Ezek. 37: 10.

How else shall this man be reconciled unto his lord? 1 Sam. 29: 4. In utilizing this quote in a radically new context, Alḥarizi here imitates Solomon ibn Gabirol in *The Kingly Crown*, at the close of §32.

prophesied as commanded Ezek. 37: 10.

and of its fruit did eat Gen. 3: 6.

Hermon's rich streams [Ps. 133: 3].

smite them hip and thigh [Judg. 15: 8].

the Jordan turns its back and flees, the mountains fly [Ps. 114: 3–7].

The angels throng to hear my song,
I call and seraphim reply.
I raze the walls of folly's halls:
I lift my voice, I prophesy.

However, fearing that my readers might find my matter dreary and grow bleary-eyed or weak and weary until leery of further assay, I wrote my lines with cheery pen that all might joy in reading them; look—a little child is leading them.

Now when the man saw that I had accepted his counsel he kissed me between my eyes, saying, Blest be you to the Dweller of the Skies, for you have rescued Hebrew's golden reputation and gilded your name unto the utmost generation. And praised be God Most High who has this day brought a redeemer nigh. Loud, loud his name be sung who comes in the name of the Lord to wed the Hebrew tongue.

Then I said to him, Sir, I shall not sleep nor stand until I fulfil your command. But before I sing, tell me your name and your torrent's spring.

He answered, I am Hever the Kenite, singer supreme, sprung from Elon Zaananim. Often shall I meet you, indeed in every chapter greet you: be your petition large or small, I shall answer you before you call.

Now when I had heard these words of Hever I joyed to have found a friend so godly clever, and knew our hearts were bound in love for ever. But swift he turned to depart and my soul leapt from my heart; and my ears strained after his parting lay as he walked away:

Sage counsels are keener than lances:
use them and conquer tenfold;
More to be desired are they than gold,
yea, than much fine gold.

Blest be you to the Dweller of the Skies 1 Sam. 15: 13; [Isa. 33: 5].
unto the utmost generation Ps. 48: 14.
praised be God Most High who has this day brought a redeemer nigh Ruth 4: 14.
Loud, loud his name be sung who comes in the name of the Lord [Ps. 118: 26]. The last words open the traditional wedding ceremony.
from Elon Zaananim Josh. 19: 33.
I shall answer you before you call Isa. 65: 24.
More to be desired are they than gold, yea, than much fine gold [Ps. 19: 10].

GATE TWO

Brimstone and Wrath against the Worldly Path

THUS SPOKE HEMAN THE EZRAHITE: I heard tell of an august sage who could wondrous preach, who could command the waves of figured speech to pound perversion to the ground and so save the sinner from the yawning grave. He could tread Folly to the dust, run Evil through with his tongue's keen thrust, and with his chastisement dig the graves of Lust. He spoke: lo, hearers' ears would smart; tears gushed when he struck the flintstone of the heart.

Now when I heard the noise of the people loudly sounding this astounding rhetor, I longed to be his debtor, imbibe his passionate outpouring that he might quell my innards' roaring and turn my eyes back from their whoring. I yearned to have him snap Depravity's iron band and put Virtue's sword into my hand, that I might make fresh stand: perhaps I might smite my desire and drive it from the land.

Turning my back, then, on profligacy, I sped to the sea, gave rest and ease the slip to board swift ship; and no sooner did I tread on foreign sod, than I sped to the camp of this holy man of God. Once come to the house of prayer I joined the congregation, raising my voice in fervid thanks and supplication, when suddenly from the pulpit's height, the voice of the preacher broke in loud indite, turning sin's bloody red snow-white:

the graves of Lust [Num. 11: 34–5, 33: 16–17].
he struck the flintstone of the heart Ps. 78: 20.
the noise of the people loudly sounding Num. 32: 17.
my eyes back from their whoring [Num. 15: 39].
perhaps I might smite my desire and drive it from the land Num. 22: 6.
turning sin's bloody red snow-white [Isa. 1: 18].

Dreamers and schemers—for your souls' sake, wake! Think! Put aside your drink, you, even you who cede your share of Heaven for a pot of stew. Is this the journey's end, you stocks and stones? Listen, Time intones: come down from your heights, come down to the valley of bones and fall to your fathers' dust—for die you must.

See, understand: you are strangers in a strange land, a land of avarice and sin, a land consuming all who dwell therein, a land—oh, there is no denying!—of thievery and lying, of grief undying, a land where Time's leprous hand renders the cup of confusion and error, of heartache and terror; where Truth and Hope dangle from the hangman's rope. Well is it called the World, where the soul is whirled through lust and ill-got gain to endless pain.

Lo, the harlot World: broad-hipped, wet-lipped, gowned and jewelled, she will lure you, assure you of eternal love, and stroke you with her silken glove. But her gown is treachery; her jewels and gloves lechery; her lips traduction, seduction to destruction. The end of her revels, of her nether desires, are earth's nether fires. See how she toys with the sons of men: she weds them, divorces them, beds them again; and again and again, on to infinity—the blood of the guiltless slain is the blood of her virginity. She slits the prince's throat, flings warriors to the moat—this lusting, snorting goat. Levelling kings, corrupting sages, her promise is ecstasy, but death her wages.

Now you panting lovers of your whoreson money, will you sell your birthright for this bowl of honey? Your winking wine is scorpion's brine; your breezy good holds hellebore, death camass, and monkshood. Know that the fruits of worldly gain are pain; the end of miser-y, misery; of gilt, guilt; of striving for fame, the riving flame. Merchant rich and regal, your money is an eagle: net him today, tomorrow he wings away. Do you think yourselves safe your castle

who cede your share of Heaven for a pot of stew [Gen. 25: 34].

the valley of bones [Ezek. 37: 1].

strangers in a strange land [Exod. 2: 22].

a land consuming all who dwell therein Num. 13: 32.

the blood of the guiltless slain is the blood of her virginity Deut. 22: 15–17.

this lusting, snorting goat Jer. 2: 23 [and 24].

will you sell your birthright for this bowl of honey? [Gen. 25: 28–34].

hellebore, death camass, and monkshood Poisonous plants or roots.

walls within? You habit an inn whence, at dawn, the guests are hurried on, gold and good gone.

My children, be not sloth: God is wroth. Beware! Prepare! Take care! Rally your hearts to war on your inner parts. Groan, aspire, disown desire! Brothers, know, know whence you come, whither you go.

*O*h, man, inanity sprung from Vanity; chip, blot, fetid spot, a leaping fish in a sea of lust and wish: on your milky bones proud Death will gnaw and with your children glut his maw.

*T*hough you charge and conquer till your fame be sung, till your names be hung on Time's broad wall like shields of the heroes on David's tower—of what avail your fame and power, your gains fair-won, ill-got? Your blood, flesh, veins will all unknot till, joys forgot, you rot in an earthen plot. Judgement comes—with pain, as of a woman first giving birth. Look past the joys of earth to that day when none are spared, when all hid histories are bared, when souls reel glassy-eyed, when Sin sits them astride, when Death holds the narrows and none can turn aside. Grieve, leave Sin, and win reprieve. Death is upon you, the final cancer: cry, cry out to God that He might answer!

*G*o now to where your fathers lie, brush the dust from off each putrid eye, look well—then tell who is pious, who a knave, who the freeman, who the slave. Evince the difference between thief and prince. Sift through this muck, the stinking remnants of Death's feast, and tell the mightiest from the least. Inhale the reek of the rancid cheek, see the ghost of the cracked flesh squirm under the soft cover of the worm. Follow the grey-white track of maggots winding through the skull and chest and back. See how they drip like wine about the memory of the lip; see the hot grip of larvae about thigh and hip. Regard: the seat of ardour is turned into the grubworm's larder. Find dung where swelled the lusty lung; and the eye find dry, as well

know whence you come, whither you go Mishnah *Avot* 3: 1.

fetid spot Mishnah *Avot* 3: 1.

hung on Time's broad wall like shields of the heroes on David's tower [S. of S. 4: 4].

with pain, as of a woman first giving birth Jer. 6: 24.

Death holds the narrows and none can turn aside Num. 22: 26.

the brain, the heart, and each moist part. About the body's rolling shape observe the worm's slow rape, while in the ribs' lax cage the beetles rage.

Lo, tendons are cut and sinews severed, the body's upright walls are cantilevered. Read on this frame, once aflame with passion's breath, the livid hieroglyphic of Death. Where once sat the liver, maggot rivers while; and to the banks of the residue of that black bile come larvae, file on file.

Far, far beneath the feet of grasshoppers and mice, the bones' abandoned dice take the slow roll of lice. The arteries are ravaged highways, the veins—savaged byways. Of high, proud thoughts what now remains? Grubs rule the brains. Lo, see the brave design of worm on worm, twining about the spine, a column of columbine; but no, that once-taut cord has been slashed by the ant's black sword.

Woe to the eyes that see this restitution! Woe to the ears that hear this whispering dissolution! Woe to the nostrils stung by this pollution! Men: turn, then, do not falter: with tears for incense and prayer for psalter, offer your innards up on Penitence' earthen altar.

Let fasting and nakedness be your security, let weeping stand you for surety until you win to purity. Put Sin by and tremble; raise your eyes to Heaven, cry to God Most High, do not dissemble. Turn about, cast Sin's host out, and strike till her legions reel in rout!

Beware: be not like them who come into the temple bowed, hands clasped in prayer, all meek and cowed, or alternate, who beat their breasts and cry aloud while their flesh is Virtue's shroud, and within their bosom Sin roars long and loud. Flesh draped in white, but heart in scarlet, each plays the saint, yet lives the harlot. Wrapped in phylacteries and prayer shawl, they sway, eyes closed, about the study hall, but are wolves and vultures all. Bright their weeds but slight their deeds; beaming virtue without, but within—teeming sin.

By Heaven, be not so, but scour your hearts of evil beyond trace. With rule and Justice, riot Sin replace, else never shall you look upon the Lord God's face nor bring your humpback souls into His Holy

offer your innards up on Penitence' earthen altar [Exod. 29: 17–18].

raise your eyes to Heaven Isa. 51: 6.

never shall you look upon the Lord God's face Exod. 34: 23–4.

Place. O mortal men, come, be you dwellers of high halls or mouldy cellars: as others left for you, prepare to leave for others; prepare to join your fathers and mothers, your sisters and your rotted brothers. Make haste to the waste, you cannot long abide: seek Naḥal-Kerit/ Excision's river and there hide: the Last Judge calls, who cannot be denied. You blind men—see! You deaf—give ear! Oft has Time called and you refused to hear. Oft have you laughed at Time's raised spear and turned, without fright, to the Garden of Fleshly Delight to bask and loll and sun. Oh, what is this thing that you have done? Lust swells like yeast at your frenzied feast. You have rooted in offal to raise foul shoots and hollow fruits. You have swilled down forgetfulness until drunken, gorged on lies until your souls are warped and shrunken. Wake, wake from your dreaming before Death drives you from your chambers, naked and screaming!

You differ nothing from them who, in their pride, raised walls high and wide and crammed their goods inside: upon their backs the grubworms ride—oh, soft contortion—Death's high priests who shall not be denied their portion; earth's last, true gentry, the richly landed: when they depart, they shall not go empty-handed.

Where be the proud folk that sported sword and cloak, broad chapeau, opal, and peridot, twining gown and shining crown, women with silk chemise whispering round ivory knees? Where be the wearers of moonstone, sard, and chrysolite, and all eyes' delight? In death the cloak is sheared, the sword broke, silk turns ash, and opal—smoke; the crown is shattered, sard and moonstone scattered, chrysolite's lustre fades, and so all the eye's charades. Velvet loot is trod underfoot. Time's mongering hand trades measured chamber for unordered land; for lofty manse, the centipedes' soft dance; for blood-red hose, blood-bed's repose. Men quit their palace for the

nor bring your humpback souls into His Holy Place Lev. 21: 18–24.

seek Naḥal-Kerit/ Excision's river and there hide 1 Kgs. 17: 3.

You blind men—see! You deaf—give ear! Isa. 42: 18.

what is this thing that you have done? [Judg. 8: 1].

high priests who shall not be denied their portion [Exod. 29: 26].

when they depart, they shall not go empty-handed Exod. 3: 21.

opal and peridot rare gems.

trades measured chamber for unordered land Job 10: 22.

pit—proud barons gone into the barrens, bartering high house and land for a wild of sand. Crumbled the castles, fallen the forts, as the people go forth from Ḥatserot/Courts.

The bravest of warriors must yield their breath and pitch in the Valley of the Shadow of Death. The well-thewed lovers, bright, robust, must trust their lusting flesh to dust; yea, chill and shaking, they must lie down to the sleep that knows no waking. Alas this night of endless sorrow! Alas the day that knows no morrow—the tourney done, naught won, and hope nor flight nor comfort none. Men of discernment, shall sin and silver be your souls' sole spawn? Ready for the journey ere Time bid you be gone; feast your hearts and then pass on.

An end! May Heaven drench us with Salvation's showers; God answer all your prayers—and ours.

Then he lifted his voice and sang:

Sleepwalkers, stumblers in Folly's morass—
up, you are misplaced!
Up, sons of men, circling Lust's mount,
how long will you walk the waste?
Wanderers, wayfarers, look to the worm,
homes build beyond the dust.
Tomorrow—the sorrow of Heaven's scales
and the cost of mead and must.
Deaf ears have you turned to many a call,
but Death's call will not be denied.
Then scour your hearts, seize Penitence' staff:
to Sinai—and there abide!

SAID THE TELLER OF THE TALE:

Now when I had heard this winged creation, this stinging adjuration, I sloughed off Lust's mud to wash my thought of Sin's blood, buried Pravity's filth in Penitence' tilth. Then, when the crowd

the people go forth from Ḥatserot/Courts Num. 12: 16.
the Valley of the Shadow of Death Ps. 23: 4.
feast your hearts and then pass on Gen. 18: 5.
circling Lust's mount, how long Deut. 2: 3.
to Sinai [Exod. 34: 2].

had lifted, I approached this gifted preacher, hungry for the face and further wisdom of my new-found teacher. My eyes met his. Joy without end: it was Hever the Kenite, our mentor and friend! I clung to his side, plucking Poesy's fruits and gathering Wisdom's healing roots. Then, rich and full-hearted, I blessed him and departed.

GATE THREE

The Mystery and History of the Hebrew Song of Spain

THUS SPOKE HEMAN THE EZRAHITE: When Youth's harp was firmly strung, when grey hairs hung not from my forehead's height, I leapt with antelopes on myrrh-drenched slopes to snare delight, swifter than mountain partridges in flight. Sporting, with friends, Dawn's golden rings, I lashed my wings to eagles' wings, decked my temples with Love's garlandings, drank must and spikenard at Love's very springs—all this while Time stooped to kiss my hand and Days scurried to and fro at my command, eager, expedient, in all things obedient. Before I spoke they gave assent, heads bent; wherever my spirit wafted them, they went.

But Wandering winked and fluted and my tent stakes were uprooted. Stripped of silken rest I covered my shivering chest with Parting's crude vest and was in a moment gone, nor made stop till I was come to Babylon.

Now one day, after bobbing through the market like a ship gone astray, I gained entry to a mansion of one of the gentry, a palace azure and sunny, a land flowing with milk and honey. Around that courtyard sprang golden towers myriad as flowers, housing frescoed chambers rich with streams, lakes, deer, and shaded bowers. What cheer! And to joy the ear—lutes plucked by Beauty's fairest daughters, by warbling crystal waters. And the banquet—a dream, a fable: table upon groaning table whose wealth I would describe if I were able. And round about—rugs plush and spacious, lush and capacious.

myrrh-drenched slopes [S. of S. 4: 6].
swifter than mountain partridges in flight 1 Sam. 26: 20.
wherever my spirit wafted them, they went Ezek. 1: 12, 20.
a land flowing with milk and honey Exod. 3: 8 and elsewhere.

And the golden porticos! The ivory porches! The wine in the jugs—flaming torches! Each cup was a hungry mould trembling to hold the grape's molten gold. Yes, the goblets, burning bright, were cast of pure light and then gilt with the sapphires of Love's delight. Oh, cups of Ophir of golden cheer! Thereat I declared:

Wet tongues of fire from crystal mouths
the eyes confound:
See lightning dart amidst the hail,
yet hear no sound.
Ponder a rush of molten gold
in ivory bound.
Expound: how can the Dew of Light
with flame abound?
Ah, raise we, down we the mysteried joy
so fair-renowned!

The memory of that feast sets my lips a-quiver: mounds of quail, of carp, of pheasant, and roseate liver; and the wine—a thick, red river. Round about flowed young and eager serving men—say, rather, pleaders—lissom as willows and fragrant as cedars; yes, beaming retainers bearing crystal and ivory containers which house that brook that will no sadness brook. And look: the cook!—sword dripping sliver after sliver of lamb-cum-onion, braised beef, hot scallion, and steaming liver. Ah, high did each heart leap to see that cook's arms gather in the sheep, a sight much cherished: here Hunger would be flayed until he perished!

Now I spied among this assemblage an aged guest, his eyes a falcon's searching for a nest, his arms snake-coiled, a predator who would not be foiled. What his swooping fingers found they slipped tightly round; then loud his teeth ground—better, pounded, for each tooth was a mallet. And what a hippopotamal palate: his lower jaw

Ophir Ps. 45: 10 and elsewhere.
Wet tongues of fire from crystal mouths the eyes confound This poem is built on the conventional literary paradox of the impossible conjoining of opposites—wine/fire and goblet/ice.
lightning dart amidst the hail Exod. 9: 24.
the Dew of Light Isa. 26: 19.
arms gather in the sheep Isa. 40: 11.

stretched endless as the Oral Law, even as he flung his tongue the hills of food among. Oh, all the king's tailors with all the king's leather could not tie those clickclacking jaws together!

The bread popped to his lip while his kindly grip steadied the goblet that it ne'er might slip. Before him thick slabs of meat trembled like sinners at the Judgement Seat; for an instant they stood his gaping jaws beneath, then fell to the verdict of his grinding teeth. Lips a-slaver and fingers truculent, his was every dish most succulent. Shoulder, shank, breast near or remote leaped down his throat. Incarnate lust, he swooped to his fatty prey like a wintry gust, to grind all to dust.

His hands raised the wine bowl, font of his desire, higher and higher while his eyes shot fire. The trays of sweetmeats were enemy troops, his eyes scoured them; he shot out his arms, he overpowered them, then avidly devoured them. The carp trembled before him like a sobbing harp; the very bread before him fled; the roast sheep did fearful leap; the sturgeon shunned his embrace like a trembling virgin; the meat, scarce within his teeth, cried out before our eyes, *The Lord hath given me over into hands wherefrom I cannot rise!*

Lo, he seemed the host's creditor, disaster's author and editor, ever lean and mean, as though he had a lien upon the plate, such that, when it came upon the scene meat-laden, he wiped it clean above and beneath with tongue and teeth, sucking all up with a tidal roar and coming back for more.

He honoured the cup like his father and mother, smothered it with kisses like a long-lost brother. Slavering, slurping, belching, burping, he careened like a mad sloop through salads, vegetables, and soup. On, on he raced: before him the land lay like Eden; after him, a waste. But for our good breeding, in our choler we would have seized him by the collar, hauled him to his feet, and flung him to the street.

We said one to another in shocked hiss, have you ever known the likes of this? For lips—hinged clips or iron grips; a lion's maw for a jaw and a moat for a throat!

Now the greybeard, cocking an ear, seemed to hear, but

The Lord hath given me over into hands wherefrom I cannot rise Lam. 1: 14.

before him the land lay like Eden; after him, a waste Joel 2: 3.

occupied with duck-grease and with goose, calmly suffered our abuse. Then, fuelled more by his engorgement than ours, we struck up a conversation on the power of those bright bells that through Spain's halls loud rung—bards of the Hebrew tongue. At this the old glutton, poking the remnants of a piece of mutton, began to eye us with the look a caliph reserves for a thrice-convicted crook, or a creditor who holds his mangy debtor's promissory letters. Looking down as on a darkling plain he turned to a guest at his left hand and said, with mountainous disdain, Sir, pray, say: these straggling, bleating sheep—what do they seek? Of what do they speak?

I answered, They rehearse the masters of rhymed prose and metric verse, the golden poets of Spain. Now all maintain that no poems seize the soul more passionate than those of Solomon ibn Gabirol; none more depth evince than those of Samuel the Prince; for smoothness and sweetness, none can vie with those penned by ben Ḥisdai; none are better moulded, none, than those of Takana's son; none more mixed an offering, beryl and bone, than the songs of ben Khalfon; none harder to understand than those penned by Yitsḥak ben Giat's hand; and for song well crafted—none more than those of Yosef ibn Avitor; and for an old-time feast, none better than the songs of Moses the priest.

*T*he songs of Barukh's son stand apart, being kissed of the heart; no songs are as illumined by charm's beam as those of Rabbi Adonim; none so inscribed upon the heart as those sprung of Rabbi ben Giat's art; none as refined and rare as Moses ben Ezra's, poet extraordinaire; none as meet for the soul's throat than those Rabbi Yosef ben Sheshet wrote; none linked so well or fawned upon as the poems of ben Tiban; none as bright and hot as the songs ben Bakoda begot; none like the songs of ben Re'uven, stolen from heaven's domain; none as solid, none, as the songs of Abraham, Ḥarizi's son; none of greater variegation than those of Yosef ben Sahal's creation; none as lofty and as shining as those of Rabbi Abraham ben Ezra's designing; none like the songs from ben al-Mu'alim's hold, beaten gold; none like the songs of ben Barzel's charm—bracelets upon the arm; none like ben

They rehearse the masters of rhymed prose and metric verse, the golden poets of Spain For histories of the Hebrew poetry of Spain, see p. 441, 'Further Reading'.

Tsadik's poetic retinue, faithful/*tsadikim* and true; none like the songs that Judah the Levite sings, honey-sweet and rising on eagles' wings.

Having heard my words he fell into a still surmise, then fixed me with his beady eyes and said, Now have you not all reviled me, styled me a glutton, with your black spleen defiled me? Yes, you had near pounced on me and trounced me, all but bounced me from wall to wall and flung me from the hall. Now, were it not that humility unclenches my fist, that I band my wrist with restraint, I would leave you weak and plantive faint, up to your ears in ignorance's muck, plying your luck. Yes, I should stand aside and watch you weep and moan, yes, reap as you have sown. Thank fortune that I choose not to do so! Whoso would repent his sin and my forgiveness win, his head shall I bind with Wisdom's cords: let vengeance be the Lord's.

SAID THE TELLER OF THE TALE:

Hearing this declaration, the assemblage was seized with trepidation—but then great expectation: they knew that his thunderous speech tokened Wisdom's rain, knew that the lightning words that lit their plain augured standing fields of grain. Here was an end of drouth. Shamefaced, each man put his hand across his mouth.

The speaker commenced, You whom Wisdom would sustain, open wide your mouth to my early rain. Attend, look, as I open each locked book. Now these names you dandle, these secrets you would crudely handle, and thrust towards Wisdom's candle—I know each poet's sword and shield, am come this instant from their battlefield. In me they dwell, sensorial and incorporeal; I am their scroll, I am their living memorial. And now attend my narrative, that your souls might live.

Rapt, the congregation opened their ears to the wizened seer's oration.

He declared, Know that the best song, dearer than pearls and the gold of Ophir, poured forth in Spain and thence fell to the world like mountain waters to the plain. For the poets of Spain wield

reap as you have sown [Ps. 126: 5].
let vengeance be the Lord's [Deut. 32: 35].
each man put his hand across his mouth Mic. 7: 16.
open wide your mouth to my early rain Job 29: 23.
that your souls might live Isa. 55: 3.
the gold of Ophir Job 28: 16.

puissant pens, springing like lions from their dens; all others' lines are women's, theirs only—men's. Now it is true that at the start some untried songsters plied the poet's art. Like reeds sprung by the river's banks they do not stand in Poesy's first ranks. Such be Menaḥem ben Saruk, Dunash ben Labrat, Shmuel, and Abun, and many others whose songs faded, being sung too soon, rawly, and out of tune.

But then came the mighty prince, Rabbi Samuel the Levite of blessed memory, whose themes sprang new and princely from Song's armoury; yet so deep and difficult was his creation that most of his lines require explication. One of his contemporaries was Isaac ben Khalfon, some of whose lines were well sown and well grown; others, Time did disown. There was Yosef ben Ḥisdai, father of 'The Singular Song', commencing, 'Can the deer-like youth, proud and strong'—a poem singular to its mother; seek not its like, our language knows no other. And the poems of ben Takana betoken Wisdom's chain unbroken. And as for the poems of Rabbi Solomon the Short—all shrink before their report. No Hebrew singer has reached his station. His peers were efflation and afflation; but of Solomon we read, *the smallest shall become a mighty nation*.

Through Poesy's high gate he alone burst: yea, Poesy bore him on Wisdom's knees, and sweet Wisdom that infant nursed, after threading his wrist with silk and crying, This one came forth first! All poets preceding merit scorn and laughter; and none rose to be his like thereafter. To him all later poets' fame belongs: lo, King Solomon and his Song of Songs. Would that our poets, luminous and astute, could probe his depth and brilliance to the root, for his lines are flown high as his renown; who can ascend to Heaven to bring them down? In penning poems for the house of prayer he was beyond compare, especially his crowning gem, made for Atonement Day, 'The Kingly Diadem'.

the smallest shall become a mighty nation Isa. 60: 22.

bore him on Wisdom's knees Gen. 50: 23.

after threading his wrist with silk and crying, This one came forth first Gen. 38: 28.

King Solomon and his Song of Songs S. of S. 1: 1.

who can ascend to Heaven to bring them down Deut. 30: 12.

'The Kingly Diadem' This poem is still recited on the High Holidays in the Sephardi tradition.

*O*h, the gleam of the poetry of Rabbi Adonim, wisdom's hoard: he is Learning's Tabernacle, built socket by board. The poetry of Rabbi Yitsḥak towers like a rock; lo, his prayer for Yom Kippur is the song of a prophet, blinding pure. As for Rabbi Yosef ben Sheshet—his verse is with Wisdom's velvet shot; happy his and his readers' lot. The poems of ben Barukh are blessed—a great ox fitly dressed for the deserving guest. And the poetry of Judah ben Giat is by Wisdom upon Piety begot; lo, his brothers' praise is Judah's lot. Rabbi Moses ben Ezra's amazing rays light his readers' eyes—all praise! And his pearls for the season of awe summon his people to God's law. He, too, wrote a sequence of poems for Yom Kippur silver-sure. Rabbi Moses ben Sheshet set Poesy his target and well shot. Rabbi Levi and Rabbi Jacob, sons of Taban, with their fecund tropes bid want be gone; and Rabbi David ben Bakoda—skill is his prelude, praise his coda. And the poems of Yitsḥak ben Re'uven—who can their hidden good explain? Wondrously he did all God's commands rehearse in gushing verse; read this poem, hear it, and stand before God's holy spirit.

*N*ow, the work of Abraham son of Ḥarizi/He-who-rhymes is Wisdom's vine that ever upward climbs. He runs, he speeds, his lines are comely circlets for the cheek, and for the neck, bright beads. Rabbi Yosef ben Sahal shall ever please, for Poesy is born on Yosef's knees. His relative, Solomon ben Zakbel, is a spring that shall never fail, author of that charming delectation, 'Asher ben Yehudah's Declaration'. And the poems that Abraham son of Ezra wrote are a help in woe/*ezra betsarot*. He is wisdom's endless spout, a copious rain in time of drought. His liturgical works are fresh and green, of wondrous sheen: the like no eye has seen. He, too, wrote an opus for Yom Kippur with Faith's tried bonds and Wisdom's rare allure.

*H*is son Yitsḥak drank deep, as well, from Song's pure well, but when he came to Eastern domains loosed faith's firm reins. He pierced his father's flesh with cruel barb, for he stripped off his garments and

---

his brothers' praise is Judah's lot Gen. 49: 8.

Abraham son of Ḥarizi/He-who-rhymes Schirman, *New Poems*, 284 and n. 17. The relation of Judah Alḥarizi to this poet, who precedes him by two generations, is unknown.

comely circlets for the cheek, and for the neck, bright beads S. of S. 1: 10.

is born on Yosef's knees Gen. 50: 23.

'Asher ben Yehudah's Declaration' A love burlesque in rhymed prose.

ezra betsarot Ps. 46: 2.

put on different garb. Rabbi Judah ben Abbas, too, turned his steps towards the East and brought to Song's feast lines succulent and fat, if others less than that; and still others dry and flat. He bore as well a son who had no peer, to speak with charity, in venality and vulgarity.

The poetry of al-Mu'alim's son, Shlomoh, flows light as moonbeams and with brighter glow. Rabbi Yosef ben Barzel/iron penned smooth, spiced song iron-strong. Of most distinguished, royal mien was the great prince Rabbi Yitsḥak ben Krispin, author of *Sefer Hamusar*/'The Moral Tome', in which bright demesne shine some of the wisest lines our eyes have seen. Now as for Rabbi Yosef ben Tsadik—his mighty lines most thunderous speak, cleaving Wisdom's sea and shaking Sapience' peak and turning giants weak: when the daughters of Song are brought low, behold the towering horns of the righteous/*tsadik*.

Now as for the poems of Judah the Levite, our heritage and garland of pure light—they be Song's strong right hand, awesome in might. This Judah is Adino the Eznite, javelin-bright, setting titans to flight. Song's law and lamp, Song's seal and stamp, he dwells in Shevet Taḥkemoni/Wisdom's camp. In Wisdom's gale his songs set sail; before his galleon the sons of Korah quail; yea, Asaph and Jeduthun near fail. He stormed Song's ramparts like the sea, stripped all her chambers of gold and finery, then left and barred the door and threw away the key. They who would unbind his sovereign seals do not reach unto his heels; they cannot win to the dust of his chariot-wheels.

His songs for the synagogue leave angels agog. His encomia know no compeers, his coal-bright love-songs burn through the years, and his eulogies rear biers of crystal tears. Study his letters written without metre and find none godly sweeter, for his notes and bars are

stripped off his garments and put on different garb Lev. 6: 4, here denoting conversion to Islam.
behold the towering horns of the righteous/*tsadik* Ps. 75: 11.
awesome in might [Exod. 15: 6].
Adino the Eznite 2 Sam. 23: 8.
he dwells in Shevet Taḥkemoni/Wisdom's camp Ibid. On the meanings of *Sefer Taḥkemoni* and, relatedly, the names of author and protagonists, see the Afterword.
the sons of Korah Pss. 87: 1, 88: 1, and elsewhere; *EJ* x. 1190–3.
Asaph and Jeduthun 1 Chr. 25: 1.

very angel cars that soar beyond the stars. He entered Song's Tent of Meeting by the Lord's high grace and there beheld his Maker face to face. He strums his lyres—David wakes; he raises Song's rod—the sea of folly quakes; he roars, leaps like a lion from Jordan's brakes: victory is his in all he undertakes.

Then he lifted his voice and sang:

Song has set Judah her paramour—
she kisses his lips, she laves his hands
Whose wine and whose honey rejoice the East,
whose light the farthest West commands.
In the tourney of Song, his praise is a blade
will succour his friends; foes fear his wrath.
Many the rival would win to his gold:
none past or present has found the path.
Alone, he leapt to the chamber of Song,
departed, and barred fast the door behind—
That portal long locked by the hand of God
but burst by the ram of Halevi's mind.
See Poesy's garden shine of his dew,
her flowers unfold in his sun's great blaze;
Men's hearts are too shrunken to hold this rich cup,
their songs too puny to limn his praise.
Yet sing we the pen and the hand and the lips
that never have failed:
When his brothers contended in song's riving wars,
bold Judah prevailed.

SAID THE TELLER OF THE TALE:

Now when this illuminate was through, our mouths filled with

Study his letters . . . that soar beyond the stars Literary correspondence in non-metric rhymed prose was highly esteemed in Arab society and was adopted thence in Jewish circles.

He entered . . . face to face [Exod. 33: 9–11; Num. 7: 89].

He strums his lyres—David wakes [1 Sam. 16: 16].

he raises Song's rod—the sea of folly quakes [Exod. 14: 16].

leaps like a lion from Jordan's brakes [Jer. 49: 19, 50: 44].

victory is his in all he undertakes Ps. 1: 3.

bold Judah prevailed 1 Chr. 5: 2.

ash, and our hearts with rue, as Conscience called, *Go to! Go to!* For well we knew: all his pronouncements were true.

Then the people asked him for his birthplace and the name he bore. And he declared:

Come from the fields of Zaananim
I shine o'er the Pleiades.
The Ox, the Bear behold me and flee,
the Archer falls to his knees.
If tropes be held flowers, I be their rose;
if water, my tongue is the sea's.

SAID THE TELLER OF THE TALE:

Now when I heard that crashing thunder, that crystal speech, that flashing thought—small wonder that I knew him for the king of our generation, Hever the Kenite, our friend and our salvation. Swift made we to seize him in sweet Friendship's grip, raise high Love's beaker, inhale and sip, and kiss the lips of Fellowship; but he, hot as lust, still smarting from our snide distrust, cast our hopes—like our pride—to the dust, and left in disgust. Tongues near cleaving to the mouth from this new and bitter drouth, we cried: Ours the guilt—oh, our brother and Wisdom's firstborn son! What have we done? What ever have we done?

The Ox, the Bear behold me and flee, the Archer falls to his knees Ox, Bear, and Archer are constellations. For a similar declaration, see the boast of the stargazer in Gate 22.

Tongues near cleaving to the mouth Ps. 137: 6.

Ours the guilt—oh, our brother Gen. 42: 21.

What have we done? What ever have we done? [Exod. 14: 5].

GATE FOUR

A Descant on the Flea and the Ant

THUS SPOKE HEMAN THE EZRAHITE: When I was young and thriving, I saw two Hebrews a-striving, men of letters and seasoned rhetors, Wisdom's own guides, to whose thunderous invection crowds streamed from all sides. One combatant was old, his strength dissipated; the second was a youth, his sight undimmed, his vigour unabated. Their eyes flashed like Sinai's laws, their mouths yawned wide as lions' jaws, their words swooped eagle-like with outstretched claws.

The one contended, I am the Lord's, who gifted me with Poesy's shields and swords. Heaven, cried the other, is my domain: I reign! —whereat they clashed in fiercest sport, until, at last resort, they brought their case to court.

Your honour, they thundered, pray put us under oath: set your hand upon us both! Let the truth out!

Gentlemen! No need to shout! What is this all about? Plead each his cause that justice be sped, that the sin of the evildoer come down upon his head.

The elder began: My lord, I cry *Violence!* in the face of my rival, who threatens Decency's survival. Tongue cleaving to his palate, he yet dares sing—this fledgling who would wing to Heaven and be poets' king.

Pooh, the youth cried, your neck is fat with pride! Stand aside!

---

saw two Hebrews a-striving Exod. 2: 13.
his sight undimmed, his vigour unabated Deut. 34: 7.
I am the Lord's Isa. 44: 5.
I reign 1 Kgs. 1: 5.
set your hand upon us both Job 9: 33.
that the sin of the evildoer come down upon his head [Ps. 7: 17].
My lord, I cry *Violence!* Hab. 1: 2.
Tongue cleaving to his palate [Ps. 137: 6].
your neck is fat with pride Ps. 73: 6.

What can you mean? Show us your strength—we shall judge if it be fat or lean. Commence! Do you live in strongholds or in tents? Stand ready for rebuke and scorning! Dare be tested, bare your jewels and your adorning. We shall see if your light break forth as the morning!

Ha, cried the greybeard, you overreach! I am the spring of counsel and fountain of figured speech. I have climbed Wisdom's ladder to the farthest rung; my tongue lifts beggars to heaven, hurls princes to a heap of dung. Now you: though you rode the whirlwind, outroared the thunderblast, were the clouds your chariots, could you cast down hail and lightning till the heavens stood aghast; yes, could you fright the spheres with the thrum of your arrows, the flash of your spears—before my fire you would melt away. Back, I say! Recant, until you crown the downtrod Ant with fame and praise will shine to the end of days.

La, laughed the other, drum your pots and kettles! Will you fright the cedar of Lebanon with brambles and nettles! You jest! This you call a test? Still, I shall fulfil your request.

He began: She is a stranger to the human race, yet her black face is comely as she sits in an open place. Formed of dust, she is light, yet robust, labour her lust—the more fortunate she, for toil she must. Spurred by maternal urges, she emerges from the pit; yes, out she surges, never late, to wake the dawn in the city gate. Black-robed, devout, she scurries about on her endless route, now within, now without. Supine, sequestered through winter weather, when summer comes she knows no tether, putting sleep behind her: seek her in her month and you shall find her. Industry's very spouse, her feet stay not in her house. Seeking food for her household, she sallies through streets and alleys, up hills, cross plains, down valleys: she paces races

if it be fat or lean Num. 13: 20.
Do you live in strongholds or in tents? Num. 13: 19.
if your light break forth as the morning Isa. 58: 8.
climbed Wisdom's ladder [Gen. 28: 12].
heap of dung [Ps. 113: 7].
your arrows, the flash of your spears Hab. 3: 11.
the cedar of Lebanon Ps. 29: 5.
brambles and nettles Isa. 34: 13.
her black face is comely S. of S. 1: 5.
she sits in an open place Gen. 38: 14.
to wake the dawn Ps. 57: 9.
now within, now without Prov. 7: 12.
seek her in her month and you shall find her Jer. 2: 24.
her feet stay not in her house Prov. 7: 11.

hurries scurries darts and starts and dashes, hustles bustles strains her muscles lunges plunges flashes. She knows no rest. She is obsessed. Possessed.

All usefulness and thoughtfulness, she eats not the bread of idleness. Slight and slender, she stoops, she slaves, dragging heavy burdens through the heat's thick waves to build vast storage caves in the dust, beneath earth's crust, the which she fills with tiers of bulging ears of corn. Morn after morn she stands by the crossroads, peers and turns; in the evening she departs, on the morrow she returns. When earth shivers in Winter's icy gown she lies in prison, wondrously gone down. But when summer comes, zealous for her brood, she makes ready to purchase food, and specially at the prime of harvest time.

She girds her loins with strength, opens her door, and sets her face towards the threshing floor where, with shy demeanour, she turns gleaner: walking among the reapers, she retrieves what falls from their sheaves. Wherever she turns she may freely approach: she gleans among the sheaves and no man offers her reproach. She finds such favour in the workers' sight that they, benign, drop her handfuls by design. They never rebuke her; rather, they willingly let her glean and gather, this their text: Let her alone, her soul is vexed; she knows no greed—her house is empty, she has no seed.

So daily, like a bondsmaid, she stoops and strains to cull the harvest's remains, the scattered and forgotten grains. Zeal her lodestone and Wisdom her star, she brings her food from afar, laying corn and wheat away for a rainy day. The slightest grain she chances to spy she guards as the apple of her eye. The late-ripening millet and wheat

she paces . . . Possessed Lit. 'she labours, but wearies not; she runs, but disdains that not; she harvests, resting not'.

she eats not the bread of idleness [Prov. 31: 27].

she stands by the crossroads Prov. 8: 2.

in the evening she departs, on the morrow she returns Esther 2: 14.

wondrously gone down Lam. 1: 9.

She girds her loins with strength Prov. 31: 17.

she retrieves what falls from their sheaves Ruth 2: 7, 15.

she gleans among the sheaves and no man offers her reproach Ruth 2: 16.

they, benign, drop her handfuls by design Ibid.

Let her alone, her soul is vexed 2 Kgs. 4: 27.

she has no seed Lev. 22: 13.

to cull the harvest's remains, the scattered and forgotten grains Lev. 19: 9, 23: 22.

she brings her food from afar Prov. 31: 14.

she guards as the apple of her eye Deut. 32: 10.

The late-ripening millet and wheat Exod. 9: 32.

she brings under earth to guard from cold and heat and the crush of human feet. And when she sees Earth tremble in the hold of the awesome Cold, when none come and none go, locked fast in their walls like the dwellers of Jericho, then she opens her treasure chambers up and lets her household sup, yes, savour the fruits of her labour. Her smiling children eat as much as they are able, for she has richly provisioned her table. Her clothing is strength and honour; God's bounty rests upon her. Lo, by her acts she shows how God is great: let her own works praise her in the gate.

Happy the wise man who takes her for teacher and will not turn from her; woe to the sluggard who will not learn from her: his to kiss Sadness' lips and suck Want's shrivelled breast, to stand confessed an empty vine, a hollow clapboard chest.

Then he sang:

A woman of valour, of daughters blest,
who never knows pallor and scarce knows rest,
Girded with strength, with virtue groomed,
black as myrrh, though not perfumed—
Look! You can see her at dawn's early light
hurrying, scurrying, shortening the night,
Bringing the grain in (learn from her, shirkers!),
bending, contending with all of the workers.
She swoops like a swallow, roves like a gamin,
gathering barley and corn against famine.
Each precious grain she devoutly entombs
in the belly of Earth in her treasure rooms.
Dashing and flashing, swift as a runnel,
never a thief, though found in a tunnel,

none come and none go, locked fast in their walls like the dwellers of Jericho Josh. 6: 1.
she has richly provisioned her table Prov. 31: 15.
Her clothing is strength and honour [Prov. 31: 5].
let her own works praise her in the gate Prov. 31: 31.
learn from her Prov. 6: 6.
Then he sang The ensuing poem basically recapitulates what has been said in rhymed prose, a frequent tactic in this work.
A woman of valour [Prov. 31: 10].
Girded with strength Prov. 31: 17.
never a thief, though found in a tunnel Exod. 22: 1.

Hid in the cold, she leaps forth in the heat,
preceding all men to each highway and street.
As Winter approaches she labours prodigiously
hoarding her bread and her matzah religiously.
Harvest time ends. She descends to Earth's cellars
pent up, yea locked in, like old Jericho's dwellers.
Spring comes; she shatters her gates with all speed,
seeking Bethlehem's bounty to answer her need:
Knowing that Exile will pay for her sins
she leaps to her journey ere day begins.
She is Virtue embodied, ne'er guided by preacher.
O sluggard, observe her and make her your teacher!

SAID THE TELLER OF THE TALE:

His song come to an end, he said to his friend, there you have turns of speech can split the heart apart, pluck it from the breast like a doily from a linen-chest. Behold my talents manifold: more to be desired than gold, they would shame the sun though its light shone sevenfold. So, then—go to! Which way went the spirit of the Lord from me to speak to you? What next, pray? Will you liken carnelian to clay? When did God's spirit last light your eyes or Wisdom dip to anoint you from the skies?

I lift my hand to God Most High: if you could raze mountains, bid Dawn be gone, unmotion the raging Ocean; yes, if you could dry up the seas, if all the host of heaven were your soldieries, your slaves—Orion, Betelgeuse, the Pleiades; if all these powers were yours and more than these, your blood would curdle to hear me bellow, your knees would knock, your skin turn yellow, your mighty men should be dismayed, your muse turn scullery maid, your mincing and

matzah The unleavened bread to be eaten during Passover.
locked in, like old Jericho's dwellers Josh. 6: 1.
with all speed, seeking Bethlehem's bounty 1 Sam. 20: 6.
Exile will pay for her sins BT *Ber.* 56*a*.
O sluggard, observe her and make her your teacher [Prov. 6: 6].
more to be desired than gold Ps. 19: 11.
they would shame the sun though its light shone sevenfold Isa. 30: 26.
Which way went the spirit of the Lord from me to speak to you? 1 Kgs. 22: 24.
I lift my hand to God Most High Gen. 14: 22.
your mighty men should be dismayed Obad. 1: 9.

prancing turn to donkey dancing. Eat dust, my friend, eat, eat: you cannot rise above my feet until you can expound, like me, the glorious history and pedigree of the mighty Flea. Let him that would glory, glory in this! Speak, or drop your eyes as passers-by wag heads and hiss.

Ha! laughed his rival, shall auks fright hawks and beagles, eagles? Holla, sir clown: shall I shiver, now you have flung your gauntlet down? Lend your ear, turn here, witness the skills that won me my renown and the Prince of Poets' crown!

Whereat he launched his soliloquy upon the Flea.

Said he: Behold an Ethiop, yet not of the sons of Ham, who weighs less than a gram. Oven-hot and coal-black, shieldless, yet impervious to whack or thwack of hands outspread, the bread of wickedness is his bread: he enters your house with thief-like tread, he waits until your clothes are shed—in your bedchamber, yea, upon your very bed. He sets teeth to your flesh and gleeful frets; and though you deny him his meal all day he neither fumes nor frets: you must deliver it him when the sun sets.

Yes, when souls are snared in the cords of sleep, then, when deep sleep falls on men, he comes to track you, torment you, wrack you, seek occasion against you, attack you. Wake you or sleep, he drains you without surcease, shedding the blood of war in peace. Try to seize him and he flees him. Cry out, I will run after you, lout!—he has fled and got him out. At times he lingers: you lunge, aha!—you have him! No, he slips between your fingers! Like riches, he takes

---

your muse . . . like me Lit. 'the prancing of your mighty ones would weary and the stallions of your utterances stumble to attain to the dust of my chariot and ascend to the heights of my declaration.'

Let him that would glory, glory in this [Jer. 9: 23].

as passers-by wag heads and hiss [Lam. 2: 15].

Lend your ear . . . crown Lit. 'Now lend ear to your question and hear your reply.' Toporovsky's text here inserts three dots, probably indicating a lacuna in the manuscript employed.

the sons of Ham Gen. 10: 6.

Oven-hot Hos. 7: 7.

the bread of wickedness is his bread Prov. 4: 17.

in your bedchamber, yea, upon your very bed Exod. 7: 28.

you must deliver it him when the sun sets Exod. 22: 25.

when deep sleep falls on men Job 4: 13.

seek occasion against you, attack you Gen. 43: 18.

shedding the blood of war in peace 1 Kgs. 2: 5.

I will run after you S. of S. 1: 4.

he has fled and got him out Gen. 39: 12.

wing, flies eagle-like to Heaven only to return and sting. With nubile maid beneath the embroidered quilt he lies, covering hips to thighs to nuzzle, nip, and champ; then skips to her ample breasts, the scamp, calling that place Maḥanaim/Doublecamp.

Let him find a virgin—or even a wedded wife—he will crave her, lay hold on her, lie with her, enslave her; yes, deprave her, until she cries out at his foulness—but there is none to save her. And if she be asked, Why weep you so bitterly? She answers, The black servant is come in unto me. For hours he sports with me, then rests, a bag of myrrh, between my breasts. All night he lies with me in contravention of God's law, eating me raw, taking for his portion shoulder, cheeks, and maw.

I lie down in sorrow, the unwilling feast of this sprinkling priest (the beast!), who, none bolder, seizes the breast of the wave offering, the heave offering of the shoulder. Skirling under and above, he takes the whole rump and the fat thereof. Spearless, yet fearless, all saucy fresh, he skewers my flesh, rolls over me like Noah's flood, and lies not down until he eats of the prey and drinks the body's blood.

Despised and unesteemed, vile and unredeemed, he has achieved what few have dreamed. The arrow cannot force him to flee, the net is an empty mockery. Before him mighty men despair, warriors gnash their teeth and flail the air; he prisons heroes: we have seen the sons of giants there. Lock your home with gates, raise walls thrice

flies eagle-like to heaven Prov. 23: 5.
the embroidered quilt Judg. 5: 30.
covering hips to thighs Exod. 28: 42.
calling that place Maḥanaim/Doublecamp Gen. 32: 3.
lay hold on her, lie with her Deut. 22: 28.
she cries out at his foulness—but there is none to save her Deut. 22: 27.
Why weep you so bitterly? 1 Sam. 1: 8.
The black servant is come in unto me Gen. 39: 17; Jer. 38: 7.
rests, a bag of myrrh, between my breasts S. of S. 1: 13.
taking for his portion shoulder, cheeks, and maw Deut. 18: 3.
I lie down in sorrow Isa. 50: 11.
sprinkling priest JT *Ber.* 7: 4.
seizes the breast of the wave offering, the heave offering of the shoulder Exod. 29: 27.
he takes the whole rump and the fat thereof Lev. 3: 9.
lies not down until he eats of the prey and drinks the body's blood Num. 23: 24.
Despised and unesteemed Isa. 53: 3.
The arrow cannot force him to flee Job 41: 20.
we have seen the sons of giants there Num. 13: 28.

seven, he will burst through, descend on you from Heaven. You can never forsake him: you must nest him in your bosom, on your shoulder take him. And though, all confidence, you wipe his troops out, say, and their bodies splay—his relatives will come to spill your blood that very day: the blood-revenger shall himself the murderer slay.

*I*f the king's gates be barred, he is not perturbed; he slips into the royal cape or bedclothes, he cannot be curbed: that night the king's sleep is disturbed. The tossing monarch, churned to a froth, hot as boiled broth, summons his serving-men to spread the cloth. Shouting maidservants join the rite with candlesticks of pure gold, five on the left side, five on the right. They wait, he hides; they curse, he laughs until he splits his sides. Would he were flushed out: then were he crushed without a doubt.

*P*ity the monarch, pity: each royal garment serves the criminal for a refuge city. Now if the king, fuming, asmoke, could catch him in his cloak, he would not rest until the creature were killed, until his bile were spilled, until his limbs and frame were splayed: then would the king's wrath be allayed.

*A*nd these be but a fraction of his ways, the palest record of his pirate nights and days!

*P*ious, he sings Heaven's bounty (*amen, amen*): then, when the sun sets, he is clean and eats again. Daily he condemns the guiltless in his magistrature, then sucks impartially the blood of rich and poor. King, hero, knave he swallows like the grave: blood touches blood. Lo, he is evil come to bud.

*N*ow after he has supped the longest time, when he sees the day shorten, the sun's heat decline, when thunder crashes, lightning

on your shoulder take him Job 31: 36.
the blood-revenger shall himself the murderer slay Num. 35: 19.
that night the king's sleep is disturbed Esther 6: 1.
to spread the cloth Deut. 22: 17.
candlesticks of pure gold, five on the left side, five on the right 1 Kgs. 7: 49.
serves the criminal for a refuge city Num. 35: 6–32 and elsewhere.
until his bile were spilled Job 16: 13.
then would the king's wrath be allayed Esther 7: 10.
And these be but a fraction of his ways Job 26: 14.
then, when the sun sets he is clean, and eats again Lev. 22: 7. A priest who has become ritually impure may not eat of Sacred donations until washing and waiting for evening.
he swallows like the grave Prov. 1: 12.
blood touches blood Hos. 4: 2.

flashes, rain splashes, and the wind lays on its lashes, he flees like a spurned lover, burrowing beneath earth's cover. All his troops don Exile's gear and disappear. They flee, they flit: they and all that appertain to them go down alive into the pit. Brothers to the mole, they winter in Sheol; they abide in their places in the camp until they are whole. Then, when they see that they, and Time, are mended, see that the rain has ended, the cold suspended, see that the sun has extended its warm invite, they prepare for fresh flight. Soon their mildewed quarters are forsaken; many of them that sleep in the dust of the earth awaken.

Then he lifted his voice and sang:

Dark as pitch, sprung of fire,
the flagon of blood his sole desire,
A cunning thief whose noiseless flight
engenders terrors of the night—
He claims my flesh, this arrogant lord,
and bolsters his claim with his tooth's keen sword.
What use the latched window, what good the barred door?
Unhindered, he plunders my blood's rich store.
He steals to my chamber to fret on my flesh
and leaves in the morning, red-mouthed and fresh.
He shortens my slumber, this foul bat's brother,
lengthens my night, ties one end to the other.
Behold: a black coal sears my flesh by degrees,
a scarce-visible vampire afloat on the breeze.
He the brash beggar, I the forced giver;
he the dry elephant, I the full river.
Yet withal, this vile demon, ripe blood on his lip,
is an inkspot unleashed by the pen's black tip.

don Exile's gear Ezek. 12: 3.

they and all that appertain to them go down alive into the pit Num. 16: 33.

they abide in their places in the camp until they are whole Josh. 5: 8.

many of them that sleep in the dust of the earth awaken Dan. 12: 2.

he the dry elephant, I the full river Lit. 'as though he found in me streams of honey, coming upon me wearied by his heart's thirst'.

With this, the two men had their say and put their figured speech to rest for another day. Now the judge, with ever-widening eye, declared: I lift my hand to God Most High: my eye has never seen the like nor have my two ears heard such mastery of the spoken word. Lo, none approach your station in this generation. None be so adept as to have risen and conquered while others slept. Now hear my charge: let your hearts grow large in love for one another. As God made you brothers in song, be you each the other's loving brother.

Thereat the magistrate inundated the two with his generosity, saying, That for your wit, old man; and that, young fellow, for your precocity! They, aglow from his praise and presents, cheerily left his presence.

Now as they left I followed, to ask the greybeard's name and how he came to warm himself at Wisdom's holy flame.

He answered, saying:

Before you stand lions of Poesy; I
am Hever and this is my son. Behold:
He shores the wrecked tower of Song, while I—
I buttress the timbers of Wisdom's hold.

His song done, I knew them—Hever and son. Amazed at their art, I turned to depart, gifting them both with my awestruck heart.

I lift my hand to God Most High Gen. 14: 22.

GATE FIVE

Twelve Poets Sound the Months' Round

THUS SPOKE HEMAN THE EZRAHITE: I was one of a cordial band clasped tight in Beauty's hand till all were one: nobles with tongues well tuned, whose speech shone red as coals or torches, or the very sun. It was the month of spring, beloved Nisan, Time's robe and ring, when dew tears streak the lily's cheek, when rings of roses play the garden round, and the proud ground sports mantles of fresh flowers and jewelled bowers; when bush and thicket are bright with aspens' light, when Joy springs sudden on the plains serene, scattering green, bright green; when the garden's spices to the breezes spill and flow at the wind's sweet will; when the sun lifts its lamp in the ram's broad camp; when green folk rise from the depths to people wood and strand, when they shake a mighty hand, appoint themselves one head and come up out of the land; when the world sails forth with leafy sails; when the fleeting cloud, bid to bear earth greeting at the thunder's hand, gives lightning/*barak* command, saying, Loose your sword combative: arise, Barak, and take thy captive, tell trembling earth my troops are ranked row on row; and Barak answers her, Go thou with me—then will I go; and thereat she, Thou shalt not go singly, I will surely go with thee; when Thunder roars and Earth gives back the blast, and the rain's troops muster fast as Barak chases after chariot and host, o'ertaking their uttermost; when the garden pulls on robes of bright and varied hue and the lily laughs in life-restoring dew (although she weepeth, weepeth in the

appoint themselves one head and come up out of the land Hos. 2: 2.

arise, Barak, and take thy captive Judg. 5: 12.

Barak answers her, Go thou with me—then will I go Judg. 4: 8.

Thou shalt not go singly, I will surely go with thee Judg. 4: 9.

Barak chases after chariot and host Judg. 4: 15.

night, upon her cheeks her tears); when the garden peers like a latticed maid of gold-wove coats, all cinnamon and myrrh, as myrtles publish her and leafy tongues give green report of her; when Wine disowns the dry of driest bones, lifts up the denizens of Sheol, yea, restores the dead soul—

At that bright time there shone within our midst the tower of wit and rhyme, the lord of rhetoric and prince of sages who leads in his cortège the savants of the ages—Hever the Kenite, whose lines, sun-bright, deck Song's fair neck; pearls rise from seabeds at his beck.

He addressed the assemblage, saying, Young trees of life whose blessed shade shelters Right's throne: you stand arrayed in splendour that makes daylight fade. This day, Time laughs open-eyed; then mount and ride, Song's captains and defenders: appoint twelve singers to chant the year's splendours. Let your first come on in praise of bright Nisan, your last unbar hid treasures of Adar. Come you: sing bright and true.

Then all the company replied, Sir, what shall we speak, what say? Wisdom is yours to sway. Set your servants the way with your gifted tongue, that they might mount Song's ladder rung by rung.

Then Hever the Kenite approached, saying: Nisan, the dawn of Spring, is the months' acknowledged king, for in his reign is Time renewed with sanctitude. Listen: song fills the air as dew buds brightly glisten, while from Winter's bleak prison a new king is arisen. Sound horn, strike cymbal, strum lyre and crewth, for Time, like an eagle, renews his youth. He strips his black sack from his back, doffs his dull robe to don the garb of priestly order, he bathes him in pure water. He who was grown old and hoar is young once more: the garden shouts, night's starry glow routs woe, joy buds and sprouts, the lilies blow; Earth, restored to former health, sports flowered wealth. She who was to Winter wed, dispirited, has put aside that dotard cursed, saying, I shall betake myself to him I wedded first. Yea, though she be

she weepeth, weepeth in the night, upon her cheeks her tears Lam. 1: 2.
what shall we speak, what say? [Gen. 44: 16].
that they might mount Song's ladder rung by rung [Gen. 28: 12].
like an eagle, renews his youth Ps. 103: 5.
doffs his dull robe . . . he bathes him in pure water Lev. 14: 8.
I shall betake myself to him I wedded first Hos. 2: 9.

divorced from the season of cold and rain, her first mate Nisan, who sent her away, may take her back again.

This, too, is the month of miracles and awesome signs and chiefest of holy times, for God's beloved then stepped free, casting her chains into the sea with Egypt's chariots close behind; yes, the sea was cleft by a great east wind, drowning Egypt's throng, and the redeemed sang a new song. Pharaoh plunged from the heights to the depths of the Red Sea's water; he was washed clean without hands, he was scoured and rinsed in water; as it is written, the entrails and the legs shall be washed with water. Then the Israelites strode boldly on the heights: risen from slavery's plain, they came forth from prison to reign.

This, too, is the month when the sun draws near and wine is doubly dear. To the cup's daughter am I sped: though aged, she is young and fair-faced, blushing red; her I wed and bed. All night she lies by my side, a warm and spicy bride. My nostrils revel in that fragrant cup, I raise her up for honeyed sips, I am kissed full upon the lips. I drink her dry, that bitterly doth she cry, Is this my reward? Full I went forth but am brought back empty by my lord.

Then he sang:

Imbibe the roses of Nisan,
nest in gold gardens of the dawn;
Chant with the swallows of swaying boughs,
gambol with Spring on the greening lawn:
Laurel your joy with the cup's bright gold—
the blessings of Eden alight thereon.

Then one of the company, second to Hever the Kenite, declared: Iyar is darling of the year by far—that loved boy who girds

Yea, though she be divorced . . . may take her back again Deut. 24: 4.
with Egypt's chariots . . . a great east wind Exod. 14: 21.
drowning Egypt's throng Exod. 14: 27–8.
and the redeemed sang a new song Prayerbook, morning service, toward the close of the last blessing following the Shema.
Pharaoh plunged from the heights to the depths of the Red Sea's water Exod. 14: 27–8.
the entrails and the legs shall be washed with water Lev. 1: 13.
risen from slavery's plain, they came forth from prison to reign Eccles. 4: 14.
Full I went forth but am brought back empty by my lord Ruth 1: 21.

the weak and is the joy of God and man. And if Nisan be the months' crowned king, fresh and fecund, Iyar is his second: he stands his monarch by, camps by his side, and in the chariot next him doth he ride. Heat shows his goodly power and in that rich shower the garden comes to flower. Frost flees and is soon brought to his knees: by Heat's troops is he hot pursued till utterly subdued. Then the rain's hands bare hidden treasure; they bring up chequered woven-wear cut to Earth's measure—green, red, and blue and many a dazzling hue. Earth, who had worn widow's weeds and wept bitterly in hills and meads for Winter, her fallen sweet, is clasped by the season of heat. He wipes the chill tear from her face; to raise fresh seed, he wraps her in his warm embrace. Comforted and joyed, she doffs her widow's gown, throws her sackcloth down, decks her head with diadems, her ears with gold, and her hands with gems.

Then Wine calls to drinkers, Prepare me a bower in the garden; yea, my palate is myrrh-spiced—drink me straight away. Delay me not, seeing that the Lord has prospered my way.

Then he sang:

Aye, buds of the garden are each a star;
walk by their light through bright Iyar.
See Time's embroidery on petals stitched
in turquoise, myrtle, and cinnabar.
Toast ye the banner of conquering Joy
as Sorrow's gaunt legions show heels afar.

Then the third declared, Of all months, let us boast Sivan and his saving host. Then Earth is girt round with Light's white shield and all once hidden is revealed. Heaven's dew falls in profusion and buds spring up in gay confusion. The turtle sings, the garden wafts spiced odours on the wind's young wings. Fruit-bearing limbs are richly appointed; the lily bush is Aaron's staff anointed. All fruits are Eden-sent, firm and succulent, choice, new, and bright with dew,

the joy of God and man Judg. 9: 13.
in the chariot next him doth he ride Gen. 41: 43.
Delay me not, seeing that the Lord has prospered my way Gen. 24: 56.
The turtle sings [S. of S. 2: 12].
the lily bush is Aaron's staff anointed [Num. 17: 23].

glistening like the oil on the priests' right lobes: yea, the goodly oil that streamed down Aaron's beard, that streaked his robes. Time greets us as he should, in his hand all of his Master's good.

This month marks the designated time of God, when He on Sinai trod to give the devotees of His mysteries His statutes and decrees. But His thundering voice slew every soul, so He brought down the dew of light to make them whole: exuding His healing breath, He saved their souls from death.

Hearts joy, then, in fair Sivan as the bride-like garden puts her gay skirts on. The wind strikes a tune, the fruit trees smile and sway, we are washed with the vine's bouquet. Time kisses us with his plenty as every heart turns sweet and twenty. The cup chants, Wouldst thou a charm to stay, to wash away Woe's harm? Set me as a seal upon thine heart, a seal upon thine arm.

Then he sang:

Filter your woes through the grape's sweet sieve;
suffer no gloom in gold Sivan.
Lift eyes to the cup and straight revive:
Joy springs anew with Sorrow gone.
Let heat and thirst attempt their worst—
cup-clarions hurry Gladness on.

Then the fourth spoke, saying, My theme is Tammuz' sweet, when sorrow tastes Time's defeat. Joy burbles at Tammuz' feet, for grief is then destroyed and happiness is unalloyed. Oh, time endearing! And specially in every wood and clearing men drink deep of leisure, leaving courtyards and dens for the field's wide pleasure.

the oil on the priests' right lobes Exod. 29: 20.

the goodly oil that streamed down Aaron's beard, that streaked his robes [Ps. 133: 2].

in his hand all of his Master's good Gen. 24: 10.

This month marks . . . His statutes and decrees Traditionally, the revelation at Sinai was calculated to have taken place on the festival of Shavuot, called 'the season of the giving of our Torah'.

But His thundering voice . . . saved their souls from death S. of S. 5: 6—'my soul failed when He spoke', and midrashic interpretation thereof. See *Exodus Rabbah* 29: 4. See also *Song of Songs Rabbah* on S. of S. 5: 6 and *Midrash Tanḥuma* Leviticus, 1: 11.

Set me as a seal upon thine heart, a seal upon thine arm S. of S. 8: 6.

Who, say, is unable to house in the garden with furrow for table, downing draught after draught engendering cheerful, vigorous thought? On every branch a joyous bird is heard; the swallow's shower spills from each bower, the sweet cry of the lark from every leaf and bark, and from above—the cooing of the dove.

Yet this is the month that chokes all hearts, for then were the Tablets shattered and the walls of Jerusalem battered and breached; this is a time of mourning for all Jews, who, crowns shorn and honour gone, sit and bewail Tammuz.

Still, ought one not his sorrows down, deep in the brimming cup his hot griefs drown? Let everyone bit by sorrow's snake look to the goblet lenitive: And it shall come to pass that everyone that is bitten, when he seeth it, shall live.

Then he sang:

Seize Time's glad portion, do not refuse
the purple kiss of ripe Tammuz.
Spill out your coin for gushing wine:
wink, toss, gambol, and nothing lose.
Choose to rejoice while you walk the earth:
soon you are dust and can nothing choose.

Then the fifth spoke, saying, The month of Av brings salve to aching hearts and Joy's sweet song. Days lush and long are stolen coffers, rich with the loot of bursting fruit. The figs swell plump and sweet, grapes follow suit, the pomegranate blushes and the apple gushes spice, and in a trice date palms are dark and glowing, succulent and overflowing.

Now if this be the month bitter and tart, burdening the heart, wherein is the ruin of the Lord's House, that is overgrown with thorn and thistle, crows nesting there (even the bird finds her a house); and if this be one thousand, one hundred, and fifty years that we are banished like a bird from its nest, bartered by slavers and denied all

for then . . . battered and breached Jer. 52: 6–7; JT *Ta'anit* 4: 8, 68*c*; BT *Ta'anit* 28*b*.
sit and bewail Tammuz Ezek. 8: 14.
And it shall come to pass that everyone that is bitten, when he seeth it, shall live Num. 21: 8.
even the bird finds her a house Ps. 84: 4.

rest, that we weep in impotent rage, for the years are many and our eyes dim with age, even while our Aged One is He who has brought us this degradation and devastation, driving off His nation, that we no longer worship in His holy fief—ought not one drown this grief long pent, down the grape's liquor until woe be spent? Ah, if your hearts be weary of pain's leaching, hear, O children, a father's teaching: firmly take hold of a burnished chalice cast from Ophir's gold and tenant that cup with Yeoman Wine, who roams the heart and roots grief up. Know, the grape's son is crafty wise; many a charm he can devise to banish anguish; knowing, suave, this wise son gladdens Father Av.

Then he sang:

Set you the cup beside and thrive:
bear Nisan's physic to stricken Av.
Avaunt, soul's gaunt! Away, warped want!
Poultice the heart with cup's warm salve.
Bury Av's griefs in the vineson's sweets:
*a wise son gladdens a father/*av.

Then the sixth spoke, saying, The month of Ellul knows joy's bright rule; then bounty spins from an endless spool; the heart sings with joy profuse as the mountains drip with juice and granaries bulge with grain. God's blessings sweep the plain even to the barrens and the river; the wine press flows and all hearts stream to the good of God the Giver like a mighty river. The gardens run with honey's bright, the overflowing fields are bathed in light, the juice of the vine drips

our Aged One is He who has brought us this degradation and devastation Lit. 'We have an aged father (Gen. 44: 20—Judah, speaking before Joseph, refers to Jacob) and he it is who has exterminated us and destroyed us.'

hear, O children, a father's teaching Prov. 4: 1.

from Ophir's gold Isa. 13: 12 and elsewhere.

this wise son gladdens Father Av The biblical citation, 'a wise son gladdens a father' (Prov. 10: 1, 15: 20), is turned into a pun and a personification. The Hebrew word *av* designates both a month of the year and 'father'.

a wise son gladdens a father/*av* Prov. 10: 1, 15: 20.

the mountains drip with juice Amos 9: 13.

stream to the good of God the Giver Jer. 31: 11.

God's blessings . . . like a mighty river The translation mirrors the atypical repetition (twice) in the Hebrew of the same rhyme word, *nahar*, 'river'.

glistening home, sweeter than honey and the honeycomb. Cool breezes lap earth's shore that do the soul restore, as we win to Joy's field. Earth's four ends yield gentle winds and Summer ends with a call to Time, prophesy unto the wind; and the pourer bids his cup, Give these, woe's victims, what you alone can give: breathe upon these slain that they may live.

Then he sang:

Scoop bubbling joys from the goblet's pool:
lull woes to sleep in fair Ellul.
Bow in the morn to the fruit-filled bough;
kneel to the tree-stock in evening's cool.
Sate on the grape, that revives the dead:
your cheek, turned crimson, shall flaunt its rule.

Then the seventh spoke, saying, Tush—the best of months is Tishrei, when Joy holds sway, bearing all men to Glee's heights away. God made this month the keystone of our year, season without peer. Herein is the year's start: according to this moon's decrees, by ancient art Jews know which days to set apart as holy and which not, from first to last, when to hold feast-days and when fast. Its first day is a day of 'membrance and of awe, a day when Virtue wins recognizance before Heaven's Law, when all men come to God like sheep, some to exult, some weep; some to win grace, and others—lasting sleep.

Through prophets' declaration God informed His holy nation to ready them for this day of visitation, a day for surcease from strife, a day for listing in the Scroll of Life all those who should be writ down for life; but they worthy of death shall be blotted out from the Book of Life. This is a day of God's judgement on all creatures, lordling and

sweeter than honey and the honeycomb Ps. 19: 11.
prophesy unto the wind Ezek. 37: 9.
breathe upon these slain that they may live Ezek. 37: 9.
kneel to the tree-stock Isa. 44: 19.
when all men come to God like sheep A citation from the *Unetaneh tokef*, a prayer of Kalonymus ben Meshullam (11th-c. Germany): 'all who enter the word dost Thou cause to pass before Thee, one by one, as a flock of sheep.'
a day for listing in the Scroll of Life all those who should be writ down for life See 'and inscribe us in the Book of Life' (repetition of the Amidah, Hertz, *Authorised Daily Prayer Book*, 844–5).

underling, a day whereon He commands to bring the Book of Records of the Chronicles that they be read before the King; a day of pain and agony when each man shall be held a rotted tree, his terror mounting: for a fire shall go forth from Ḥeshbon/Accounting. Happy the soul that day who wins God's grace, who shall be pure enough to look upon His face, for he shall blossom like a fruitful vine; ample shall his table be, his cup run over with Salvation's wine.

Drink shall be sweet that day for every soul seized of Dismay. Then, when hours shift and fly off swift, Wine calls, Men, heed life's lesson: days shorten, moments lessen; speed to the grape, no moment wait, for the day is short and the work great.

Then he sang:

Cup's crimson share throughout Tishrei
whose shimmer gladness doth bewray.
Hath trembling seized your guilt-rid heart?
Seize you the goblet for shield and stay.
Get Joy to mistress, cede her to none:
the vine shall all your cost defray.

Then the eighth spoke, saying, Fair is the realm of Marḥeshvan; the flocks of gladness light thereon. Swiftly heat wilts in icy light and takes frantic flight, with Winter's heroes thundering after, vengeance in their icy laughter, for they remember how Nisan did undo them, bringing all his forces down to strew them and subdue them. They will be quit with him, yea, eagerly smite him, for a man's deeds shall requite him. Then the plain is seized by the rain's chill hold as all rush home to escape the cold. Road and turf wince at the snow's reproof; Time heralds his servants to bring his cattle under roof.

Then most dear the fireside to all who draw near, to bask in its

He commands to bring the Book of Records of the Chronicles that they be read before the King Esther 6: 1.
for a fire shall go forth from Ḥeshbon/Accounting Num. 21: 28.
he shall blossom like a fruitful vine Ps. 128: 3.
his cup run over with Salvation's wine Ps. 23: 5; [Ps. 116: 13].
for the day is short and the work great Mishnah, *Avot* 2: 20.
for a man's deeds shall requite him Job 34: 11.
heralds his servants to bring his cattle under roof Exod. 9: 20.

heat and gaze on its charm while roasting their meat and readying sweet, mixed wine. Ah, brother mine, with cup for sister and roast for brother, take pride in the one as you joy in the other. Here be sweets and steaming meats to be deep whiffed: while the one speaks, the other comes on swift. And you revel, and regally, too, standing like a king between the two while the grape's flushed daughter richly kisses you. Yes, if Time weight you with woe, let Wine's love sate you head to toe. Her taste is sweet and sharp, Eden's own scion, sweeter than honey and stronger than a lion.

Then he sang:

Moist well your bones in Marḥeshvan;
drink deep till grief be past and gone.
If wayward days have given you hurt—
Cup's pardon pour their heads upon.
Though Time has warped Joy's yellowbrick road,
the cup repairs it—travel on!

Then the ninth spoke, saying, The months' best kiss is that of Kislev, when waves of Calm the willing heart enslave. See, then, how Heaven spins glistening strands of silver rain to weave pine wreaths and standing fields of grain. Then, left and right the snow wings in, in leisured flight, binding the brows of hills in silky white. Now see before you an angry Ethiop maid, in coals' scarlet 'rayed, fronting Cold unafraid, her blazing weaponry displayed: she warms to battle and pricks him to the heart, dart after dart.

This, too, is the month of miracles abounding, the enemies of God's chosen flock confounding, when the Greeks streamed to the Temple Mount and surrounded God's House; they desecrated the courtyard and the House until the Hasmoneans crushed them and drove them from the House; yea, they cast the unclean ones out, who lay about the House; and sought to light the lamp—but lo, the heathen had defiled all oil within the House. Then the priest called unto

while the one speaks, the other comes on swift Job 1: 16–17.

sweeter than honey and stronger than a lion Judg. 14: 18.

the Greeks streamed . . . the heathen had defiled all oil within the House BT *Shab.* 21*a*. See also Hertz, *Authorised Daily Prayer Book*, 150–3.

the storeroom of the House, Tell me, what hast thou in the House? whereat she replied, Save for a pot of oil thine handmaid hath not anything in the House. Then Joy waxed great; yea, great was the honour of the House: praise was offered up to God, they sang the song of the dedication of the House.

Therefore, at this season it behoves all men of reason to rise at Joy's behest, bless God for the grape and render Noah blessed—him who, discovering wine, endowed mankind with rest. Of this, one reads in Scripture (if one rightly understands): this one will comfort us from our work and the toil of our hands.

Then he sang:

You whom sorrows and hot fears lave,
kiss the lov'd cup throughout Kislev.
Though Time shake shackles before your eyes,
the Cup's bright wink shall Time enslave—
The Cup, redeemer of flesh and blood
who lifts dry bones from out the grave.

Then the tenth spoke, saying, Lo, Tevet, veteran comforter of the disconsolate, tends Grief relief. Then Cold musters his regiments and takes to the field to pitch his tents: bold he grows, ever more bold (who can withstand his cold?), shaking the body from head to toe and bringing down stinging tears in constant flow. The snow raises banners on every hill, his minions spill chill pain upon the plain. Bonfires roar—drawn, flaming swords to battle Cold's hordes with blazing breath, even to the death.

But this is a month unclean, the like no eye has seen: Heaven wept for pity as Babylon pitched against David's city. Yet if, when Tevet's tenth day falls, Israel, fasting, recalls the first breach of

Tell me, what hast thou in the House? whereat she replied, Save for a pot of oil thine handmaid hath not anything in the House 2 Kgs. 4: 2.

Then Joy waxed great; yea, great was the honour of the House BT *Shab.* 21*a*. Hertz, *Authorised Daily Prayer Book*, 150–3.

the song of the dedication of the House Ps. 30: 1.

render Noah blessed—him, who, discovering wine Gen. 9: 20 ff.

this one will comfort us from our work and the toil of our hands Gen. 5: 29.

who lifts dry bones from out the grave [Ezek. 37: 11–13].

who can withstand his cold? Ps. 147: 17.

Jerusalem's walls, and eyes pour water forth like waterfalls—shall not Wine Grief displace, blot it out without trace? Though Grief grow daily and grip man tight, let Wine break that grip by night and blackest Sorrow drown: though it flourish in the morn, in the evening it shall be cut down. Let Wine take the heart's part, for when he gains the ribs alongside the heart he seizes all sorrows, dooming them: a fire went forth from before the Lord, consuming them.

Then he sang:

To the vat of the vintner without debate;
swim in those juices throughout Tevet!
Sink in the cup, that sea of balm;
suck like an infant, she shall thee sate.
Oh, seize the grape's daughter of golden breasts
and honeyed tongue for thy willing mate.

Then the eleventh spoke, saying, Shevat makes short shrift of the heart's duress: he is a fortress in the wilderness for refugees from plundering Distress. This month, sweet offerings in his hands, great good commands: he lights the darkened lands, opening fountains wide till rivulets lace the wooded mountainside and silver rivers glide over ivory pebbles. Then wee, green rebels break through earth's crust, as Joy jack-in-boxes from the dust; Earth bursts forth in leafy showers with moonblest plenty and carpetry of flowers. Dawn's laughing hero wings eager to his goal, sowing sweet rays to heart the faltering soul. Cold's gloom flees the blazing sun as the wide-eyed furrows smile each one. The physic cup makes rounds to staunch Grief's wounds, curing all pained by her, for she hath cast many down; yea, many strong men have been slain by her.

Then he sang:

Shatter malaise throughout Shevat:
with winesword smite the misbegot!

---

though it flourish in the morn, in the evening it shall be cut down Ps. 90: 6.

a fire went forth from before the Lord, consuming them Lev. 9: 24, 10: 2.

moonblest plenty Deut. 33: 14.

Dawn's laughing hero wings eager to his goal [Ps. 19: 6].

many strong men have been slain by her Prov. 7: 26.

Strip off Grief's grey, don Joy's red robes;
gather them gaily, knot well the knot.
Dance in the light before you turn shade,
before the sun seek you and find you not.

Then the twelfth declared, Radiant Adar by far is fairest of the fair: all Joy's troops stand readied there. The breach of sighs is sealed, Cold's proud legions yield and quit the field. With industrious hands the clouds spin silky strands; the sun skips beaming through her heavenly rooms as the garden exudes its sweet perfumes.

This, too, is the month of miracled salvation God wrought for His beleaguered nation. God heard and chose to joy me when Haman the Agagite rose to destroy me; He paid him in coin for all he sinned: he and his seed swung gaily in the wind. Yes, Heaven heard my pleading tongue: me He restored to my post, but him He hung. As Haman and his ten sons came the scaffold nigh, the tree called, Sir, no need to sigh: lo, I lift you high upon clouds' pinions, high, for all the world to see. Mourn not: am I not better than ten sons for thee?

Then let the wise laud Adar with Revel's troupes, trounce Misery with the cup's red troops until none can descry the difference between *Curst be Haman!* and *Blest be Mordecai!* Let each call the grape's daughter, Maid, help me, I pray: pour into all these vessels and bear the full away!

Then he sang:

Laud rose and lily with gay guitar
and drink to their health in dear Adar;
Yes, drink of the wine, which, in the cup,
glisters like gold in an ivory jar.
Here be your months: I have ordered them all
in bright constellation, nor skipped a star.

Haman the Agagite rose to destroy me Esther 9: 24.
he and his seed swung gaily in the wind Esther 9: 25.
me He restored to my post, but him He hung Gen. 41: 13.
Am I not better than ten sons for thee 1 Sam. 1: 8.
trounce Misery with the cup's red troops until none can descry the difference between *Curst be Haman!* and *Blest be Mordecai!* BT *Meg.* 7*b*.
pour into all these vessels and bear the full away 2 Kgs. 4: 4.
I have ordered them all in bright constellation, nor skipped a star Isa. 40: 26.

Now when this *maqāma* was sent to far and sundry parts, bold drinkers wrote it fast upon their hearts, yea, set it on their heads for crowns as well. Damascus' Jewry, fallen beneath its spell, soon had it fast as *Hear, O Israel!* Learning like Scripture its minutest stricture, they observed it to the letter; none kept it better. It was their pride and their delight: daily they did it each indite within their gardens before one might distinguish between blue and white. Yes, they probed these mystic airs before their morning prayers and at night knew no rest until they had it read each man upon his bed; they studied it from tot to hoary head, chanting it with deepest veneration, they and their sons and each succeeding generation.

Learning like Scripture . . . before one might distinguish between blue and white BT *Ber.* 9*b*.

they and their sons and each succeeding generation Ezek. 37: 25.

GATE SIX

Of One Too Swiftly Sped to the Marriage Bed

THUS SPOKE HEMAN THE EZRAHITE: I pitched by Thebez' height to don Joy's many-coloured coat and couch in Eden's delight. Now it chanced on a day when I chose to play with loved and noble friends who love Love's bonds and pleasing songs, that, looking up, I saw a fellow crestfallen and hobbling, weak and wobbling. Approaching, whom did I discover but Hever the Kenite, none other! Hever, I greeted him, where be you bound? Where have you been and what found?

He answered, I come from the far isles of the sea where seething waters near devoured me; and now I mean to make rest a stranger, however great the danger.

How long, I asked, these endless wanderings, as though you pitched on the wind's broad wings? Stay, we will treat you gently; loved friend, live contently. Say the word and I will ease your weary soul, get you a wife to freshen you and make you whole!

By all the prophets' lives, he shouted, not a word of wives, though you bore a command stamped by God's own hand! One horror will suffice: never twice!

I laughed, then said, What grief and care make you swear?

He answered, I was tempted by the Serpent, yes, stabbed by Passion's knife to seek a wife, a soulmate for my weary life, to shine, I thought, upon my spirit, heal it and cheer it. It is not good, thought I, that I should live alone: I must get me a helpmeet, for I am grown old, I know not when I shall die; and when shall I provide for my

Thebez' Judg. 9: 50.
many-coloured coat Gen. 37: 3.
seething waters near devoured me [Ps. 124: 5].
I was tempted by the Serpent Gen. 3: 13.
I must get me a helpmeet Gen. 2: 18.
I am grown old, I know not when I shall die Gen. 27: 2.

home? In this way did my thoughts roam a stormy ocean until, dizzy with the motion and wet with passion's sweat, my heart shouted, *Yea!* then, *Nay!*—steamed, then cooled straightway. Now as I bobbed about in this fashion, the dupe of Passion, aimless and lone, lo, a crone prune-faced, features and limbs and what-not else displaced, came apace, a wispy veil drawn over her face, foulness to perfection, incarnate evil: Fate must have hauled her straight up from the Devil.

In a trice she was down on her knees with a *Please, sir, please!* and with oil-smooth smile and honeyed guile showering piety like a fountain of water, and she Perversity's first-born daughter! Feet such as hers are not confined to home, but roam; her paths lead underground; on every side her victims abound.

Peace, my sweeting, she oozed in greeting, God grant you long life and all that you seek, and guard that rosy cheek. My, my, you are a joy to the eye! Indeed, your own eyes are darts piercing helpless hearts. Beauty has robed you sweetly and paid your debts completely. In truth, the tree of your youth has yielded wondrous fruit. Now what a shame the likes of you should simmer o' nights in passion's flame, no wife to meet your need, no meat, no mead, no field for seed. Why should you search out broken cisterns of foreign daughters, seek sweetness in foul and stolen waters? Let me show you a maid whose cheeks bring on the morning light, whose locks, the night. In this singular princess shall you be Eden-blest, a maid made to serve you best: warm in your bosom shall she rest, fast by your table shall she trill and shine, her mouth a cruse of wine. In the valley of deep shadow, walk by her light: her candle burns the night. All spikenard and must she is, all spice; far distant from rubies her price.

Sir, rise from the dust to a nubile, doe-eyed maiden faint with

when shall I provide for my home Gen. 30: 30.
Feet such as hers are not confined to home Prov. 7: 11.
paid your debts 2 Kgs. 4: 7.
the tree of your youth yields wondrous fruit Lev. 26: 4.
search out broken cisterns Jer. 2: 13.
sweetness in foul and stolen waters Prov. 9: 17.
bring on the morning light, whose locks, the night Evening service, conclusion of *Ahavat olam*: 'Blessed be You, O Lord, who bring on the evening'.
in your bosom shall she rest 1 Kgs. 1: 2.
In the valley of deep shadow [Ps. 23: 4].
her candle burns the night Prov. 31: 18.
far distant from rubies her price Prov. 31: 10.

lust. She is supple, her body warm and moist, well-spiced, glistening like amethyst, pure, holy, blest. Her eyes are two lions, her teeth strung pearls, each breast a trembling fawn. On, sir, on! Feast your eyes on each succulent part and feel your senses fall apart; ah, me: *thou shouldst go mad at the sight of thine eyes that thou shouldst see*. Oh, happy the man who clasps her to his side, who mounts this chariot to ride; oh trebly sweet the lot of him who bows, falls down, and lies between her feet.

Now he who would bed her—let him pay two thousand coins and wed her, a small price to own the morn: if a man offered all his wealth for love, he would be laughed to scorn.

SAID THE TELLER OF THE TALE:

She had not uttered her last word and I was a snared bird. Only let me see this girl, I said; then shall I trip lighthearted to the nuptial bed.

Heaven forbid, she countered, that I should spew lies or in any way devise. No, all that I have told to you you will find doubly true.

Well, I replied, if the maid be half so fetching as you say, I will gladly pay whatever I must pay.

Ah, she smiled, wait till you see her gentleness, this doe that ravens like a lioness; then you will taste of my tongue's truthfulness. I shall be back at dawn to ease your hurt and moan: even tomorrow the Lord will shew who are his own. And so she went her way, bearing my heart in her teeth away.

That night sleep fled; I could not get to bed. I paced about, tethered by Passion's rope, a prisoner of Hope. By morning my chest was ready to burst: I gnashed my teeth, I slapped my thighs, I cursed; but then the sun leapt into the blue, and lo, the old woman came into view. My heart leapt and thumped, and up I jumped.

God cherish you, she called, for ever; be your seat vacant never.

each breast a trembling fawn S. of S. 4: 5.
thou shouldst go mad at the sight of thine eyes that thou shouldst see Deut. 28: 34.
bows, falls down, and lies between her feet Judg. 5: 27.
if a man offered all his wealth for love, he would be laughed to scorn S. of S. 8: 7.
a snared bird [Prov. 6: 5].
even tomorrow the Lord will shew who are his own Num. 16: 5.
That night sleep fled Esther 6: 1.
a prisoner of Hope [Zech. 9: 12].
I gnashed my teeth [Ps. 112: 10].
be your seat vacant 1 Sam. 20: 25, 27.

Young man, your joy is sped, grief and sighing are fled. Wandering wings off like a dove: this is the season of love. Look: the girl's kin and father come this way to hear what you would say and strike a pact with you this day.

Ere long, the city's elders ringed me in jovial throng. When they had gathered all and packed the house from wall to wall, the girl's father rose, coughing aloud, to address the crowd:

Peace be with ye, dear brethren, Fidelity's heirs and loving confrères. Know that this gentleman, a model of propriety, would be compacted to our society; to wit, he would enter our chariot and ride; to wit, take our daughter to bride. His praises have been recited us; his gifts and merits have delighted us; his cheer, his generosity, and noble birth excited us. Now, then, I risk my soul this hour, empowering him to take my daughter and her handsome dower. Only let him pay two thousand shekels as her bridal price and not defer: whene'er she shall demand it, let it be given her.

Then the elders of the gate asked me, Do you accept these terms as stated? and I, ill-fated and thoroughly flustered, rather than weigh the agreement, blustered, C-c-correct! I-I-I accept!

Before I could further think, they rushed in a scribe with pen and ink, who tossed off a certificate of stylish marriage could fill a carriage; and I objected not a whit to all they had contrived for me but declared with Jeremy, bowing to destiny, *I am come with the rolled-up scroll prescribed for me.*

They brought in a scribe to fix her price
by document cum *explications*
Binding me fast with Holy Writ
arresting in its innovations.
They raised the wine, chanting God's name
to bind the nuptials with legal force
While Time stood by with my joy in tow,
whom wed I would not, but would swift divorce.

grief and sighing are fled Isa. 35: 10, 51: 11.
the season of love Ezek. 16: 8.
whene'er she shall demand it, let it be given her [Esther 2: 13].
the elders of the gate Ruth 4: 11.
I am come with the rolled-up scroll prescribed for me Jer. 36 and Ps. 40: 8.

*N*ow when the scribe had dotted all his *i*'s and looped his *q*'s, the wedding compact was read to all the Jews; and I, I brought in witnesses, wrote in the scroll and sealed it: black bells—toll!

*T*he sun set, never faster, and lo—disaster! Earth sunk beneath Blackness' tide: here comes the bride! As they lined the festive road, mouths gaping wide, the people bellowed, *Joy, bridegroom, in your bride!* On stretched the revelry with merry song from early evening until midnight's gong. Then the company departed all, great and small, leaving me alone with my chickadee seated next to me. Thought I, I shall restore youth like an eagle, I shall dip and soar: this is a night of vigil, sure.

I turned eager to my bride, loosed her gown swiftly, flung her veil aside, raised my candle high, fixed her face with my hungry eye, and—*Ay!* A holy blunder! The mouth of Balaam's ass with a voice like thunder! Cheeks like Jeroboam's calves, but sunken, black, and dry—and foul as a sty, as though Satan had smeared them with sulphurous pitch. A bitch, a witch, a dark misshape, an Afric ape! Yet if her face was a black fright, her hair was silver white in memory of her years' long flight. Her lips flew upwards on bent wings; her teeth were fangs, her eyes were scorpion stings. I cried out,

Her teeth are fair as a bear's,
though clogged with hairs.
Her head is pocked; her eyes,
Grief's own surmise.
A palm tree—tall, with bumps,
flesh thick with lumps.
Her lips are black as coals,
her cheeks, dark holes.
Her breasts—why waste my breath:
a walking death!

*S*eeing this fiend, my toes curled and my head whirled; but holding myself back, I took a gentle tack. Fair spouse, I whispered,

the wedding compact was read to all the Jews Neh. 8: 3.
restore youth like an eagle Ps. 103: 5.
this is a night of vigil, sure Exod. 12: 42.
The mouth of Balaam's ass Num. 22: 23.
Jeroboam's calves 1 Kgs. 12: 28.

sweet mouse (prithee, delouse), tell me—what have you in the house? Cloaks and silken strings? Baubles, bangles, and rings? Pearls and shining offerings?

She answered, I have fine stuff: God has dealt graciously with me and I have enough. I left all my things packed at home, in my father's house, in my room.

Darling, I murmured, give me pleasure: describe this treasure.

M-m-m-m, she bleated, I have three socks, two sacks, a ball of flax, three forks, a plate, a grate, a dried date, a napkin, an apron, a bent cane, a pouch of grain, ripped shoes, stained sheets, four bowls, and two pots with holes.

I heard her and clutched my head. My thoughts fled swifter than Adam from the cherub's flaming sword: I found no vision from the Lord. Then, waxing poetic, I cried:

Did you drop from an imp or a ghoul,
you nightmare, you scalded pot!
Satans your sisters all,
but you be the queen of the lot.
Oh, goat of Azazel,
how fled you the waste so swift?
Time, hot for Lilith's flesh,
presented her you as a gift.
Oh, mockery of Adam and Eve,
God formed you of muck, not earth.
Happy your dam to have borne you not
or at least to have died giving birth.
You slobber with lips of an ape,
your mouth is a charnel pit.
Your yellow-black teeth are a bear's
slopping over with torrents of spit.

---

what have you in the house 2 Kgs. 4: 2.
God has dealt graciously with me and I have enough Gen. 33: 11.
the cherub's flaming sword [Gen. 3: 24].
I found no vision from the Lord Lam. 2: 9.
Oh, goat of Azazel, how fled you the waste Lev. 16 (entire).
Lilith's flesh In Jewish legend, Lilith was Adam's first wife; she became a satanic figure. See *EJ* xi. 245–9.
God formed you of muck, not earth [Gen. 2: 7].

Your eyes are twin buckets of smoke,
your face is a pan thick with grease,
You loom like the gallows of Haman—
pray hang there and leave me in peace.
Ah, spare me the sight of your face,
ah, spare me the stench of your breath.
This night I compare to the last of the plagues,
when God missioned his angels of Death;
To the night Pharaoh sank in the sea,
to the day Haman swung like a bell,
To the hour when Sisera fled to Jael,
to the day Eglon, skewered, fell.
Your face is your fortune, black;
your belly's a pot, and your rump.
Your palms are a flea-bitten monkey's,
your fingers, each one, a stump.
Your mouth is a five-metre pit,
your stomach, a festering ditch;
You savage your food like a cur,
you wolf down your meal like a bitch.
God give you the death you deserve,
overturn you like fest'ring Sodóm;
Be your winding-sheets lions' maws:
go, be their bellies your home!

Now when I had done my song I saw that poems could not right my wrong. No, no cure for misery in poetry; in verse, no relief for grief. So, half berserk, I seized three sticks and set to work. In the dark of that cursed house I gagged her with her blouse, and laid on with many a thwack and crack until her heart's blood coursed down her

the gallows of Haman—pray hang there Esther 7: 9–10.
This night I compare to the last of the plagues, when God missioned his angels of Death Ps. 78: 49.
the night Pharaoh sank in the sea Exod. 14: 15–29.
the day Haman swung Esther 7: 9–10.
the hour when Sisera fled to Jael Judg. 4: 17–22.
the day Eglon, skewered, fell Judg. 3: 15–22.
overturn you like fest'ring Sodóm Deut. 29: 22 and elsewhere.

neck and back. I tore her limb from limb, I made her swim in the blood of her virginity. Then taking all her clothes with me I loaded my mule and was gone well before dawn. Leaving behind a ravaged waste, I rode in haste: by day I slept and by night rode fast, crossing deserts and forest till all danger had passed. Then, waxing poetic, I declared,

Praised be He who guarded me,
who showed me His pity on the day of wrath;
Creature lust had fogged my brain
but lo, the Creator illumed my path.
Deep I had plunged to Sheol's dark womb
when He saw me and lifted me up from death.
I shall praise and extol Him, my lamp and my shield,
I shall praise and extol Him with every breath.

SAID THE TELLER OF THE TALE:

Hearing Hever the Kenite's misrepresentations, his mad concoctions, his ludicrous fabrications, I laughed my fill, then bade him goodbye, and off went I; and off went he—dreams, wit, and wondrous falsity.

on the day of wrath [Lam. 1: 12].
Deep had I plunged to Sheol's dark womb when He saw me and lifted me up from death [Ps. 89: 49].
I shall praise and extol Him [Ps. 34: 2].
my lamp [2 Sam. 22: 29].
my shield [2 Sam. 22: 3; Ps. 18: 3].

GATE SEVEN

Of Battle Lords and Dripping Swords

THUS SPOKE HEMAN THE EZRAHITE: I journeyed from crowned Tyre's great halls to Shushan's towering walls with Hever the Kenite, heart's delight, larkspur and riddling raconteur, who graced my ears with tales of what his eyes had seen through his long years.

He said: Before my black hairs had suffered loss I journeyed from Persia to the lands of Meshekh and Tiras with upright men of many parts—warrior princes with lions' hearts, yet the grace of harts. Now once come to the tents of Kedar we found we could no farther win: the desert crawled with thieves like nits on a camel's skin; the wilderness had shut us in. Armed bands filled the desert like thistle and thorn: travel forsworn, the very roads, forlorn, seemed to mourn. Wayfarers left the highways to wind in and out through byways roundabout.

Our elders, seeing the waste, turned chaste as virgins tightly laced. We would not stir, said they, from where we were but would outwait the war, hold till the roar of battle stilled that we might sojourn safely as before. So there we stayed at Time's caprice, awaiting the soft release of peace.

Now on the tenth day we heard far off the blare and bray of two camps readying for fray. Forward each army pressed, prancing-grand, with an outstretched arm and a high and mighty hand. Our ears

crowned Tyre's Isa. 23: 8.
Shushan's Esther 2: 3, 8 and elsewhere—Shushan, the capital of Persia.
Meshekh and Tiras Gen. 10: 2—Arabia.
the tents of Kedar S. of S. 1: 5—Arabia.
wilderness had shut us in Exod. 14: 3.
the very roads, forlorn, seemed to mourn Lam. 1: 4.
Wayfarers left the highways Judg. 5: 6.
Forward . . . with an outstretched arm and a high and mighty hand Exod. 14: 8; Num. 33: 3 [and Deut. 5: 15].

attended with dismay, even as our thoughts fell into disarray: who, say, would win the day? And we, we were caught between two armies primed for battle—they, slavering lions; we, blood-rich cattle.

When the two forces had come to Emek Habakhah/Vale of Tears, they formed in ranks, spears fronting spears, raging, bold, limbs cast in iron mould—some from Savta and Raamah, others from Togarmah; as well Hadad and Temah, Jetur, Naphish, and Kedmah, Mishma and Dumah. On flowed the troops, ever faster, as we prayed against disaster.

Huzzah! With yells and jeers that slashed our ears, with brandished swords and polished spears, surging, dashing, armour flashing, hot blades crashing, wild eyes large and bright, the foemen rushed to death's rite as to love's delight. Yes, not a one dared falter, but rushed to offer up his blood on Battle's altar; with eager breath they stretched their tongues to the honeyed taste of death.

At that, waxing poetic, I sang:

Men who hold death their life,
their spearpoints honed for death,
Rush to embrace their foes
with panting lovers' breath.
They hunger for death's release,
Ruin the banner they bear;
Sweet on their lips is the taste of their blood,
sweeter the kiss of the spear.
Death is a crown to their heads;
their adornment, the slashing sword.
Seeing them, mountains shudder and quake,
Mount Tabor dissolves at their word.
Giants turn grasshoppers, eagles turn doves,
lion hearts melt at their cry.
They crack o'er the field like lightning,
taking broad earth for their sky.

Emek Habakhah/Vale of Tears Ps. 84: 7.
Savta and Raamah Gen. 10: 7.
Togarmah Gen. 10: 3, Ezek. 27: 14.
Hadad and Temah, Jetur, Naphish, and Kedmah Gen. 25: 15.
Mishma and Dumah Gen. 25: 14.
polished spears Jer. 46: 4.
Mount Tabor As in Jer. 46: 18.
Giants turn grasshoppers Num. 13: 33.

A sea of hot spears their hands thrust up,
a star-flecked meteor flood;
And earth, set afire by the flaming sword,
runs red with thick rivers of blood.
Their blades like lightning leap and dance,
the blood-cloud bursts and flows.
Kissed on the lips by their swords' wet mouths,
heads fall in uneven rows,
Transmuting the field to a furrowed park
with many a blood-red rose.

Yet prior to this grisly dance two warriors made advance from their respective camps, lions roaring and taunting, vaunting their power in a shower of rebuke and boast, each claiming to be the bravest swordsman a chieftain could desire. Each, raging, kindled flames of fire, a very pyre. Necks taut, faces red, one cried to the other and said:

I am sprung from Lord Battle's loins
and seek death on the field of my lord:
Life poisons my blood and my breath,
I crave the release of the sword.
My spear, my shield, attest my fame
who am made half of ice, half fire.
I cut terror's waves like a knife—
front my blade who dares call me liar!
When my sword cries, Water! Water!
I sate it with traitors' red.
Gold and possessions I set at naught,
seizing bow and sword instead.
I shun the cedared hall,
let winter work its worst;
I lie with the scorpion, rise with the wolf,
on snakes' blood sate my thirst.
He who would brave me shall quickly learn
that my last thrust is true as my first.

kindled flames of fire Ps. 29: 7.
one cried to the other and said Isa. 6: 3.
I cut terror's waves Ps. 78: 13; Neh. 9: 11.
the cedared hall 2 Sam. 7: 2, 7 and elsewhere.

Then his rival rose up before his foeman had done; while one was yet speaking the other came on:

Twins clawing at one breast
we suckled, Death and I.
I blast the eagle's rock
when I sound my battle-cry.
Until it be caked with blood
my sword disdains its sheath;
It dyes the dreams of my foes—
they shiver in their sleep.
Behold, there, terrors of old,
there angels of darkness sit.
Forged on the anvil of Death,
for disembowelling fit,
It provenders jackal and worm,
spilling bushels of skulls to the pit.

War struck, and when the torchlike arrows flashed home, thick-fleshed, well meshed; when yawping throats bawled Battle's fierce refrain; when flapping banners rushed like wind across the main; when battle-axes crashed on leather shields, dashed heads to the ground, when horses clashed and earth could scarce contain the rain of blood and thunderous pounding of the plain; when swooping sword-beaks sucked neck and head, when heaving chests ran red; when tiers of red-tipped spears flashed starlike in the sky; when dust clouds spilled wide and high, that the sun was eclipsed; when arrow-showers hissed ever higher, a serpentine fire; when hip from thigh was reft, when the everlasting hills were cleft; when Death's flames, sprung of javelin and mace, held heated race to lay the worm's and lion's feast, yes, proffer holy offerings to desert beast; when bows bent back with viper arrows, never spent, and sent them frenzied forth to

while one was yet speaking the other came on Job 1: 16–18.

terrors of old Deut. 2: 10 ('The Emim dwelt there in times past'; the literal meaning of *emim* is 'terrors').

when the everlasting hills were cleft Hab. 3: 6.

sting; when shooting swordstars, shining all too soon, blinded the eye at noon; when liberal Sword and generous Mace endowed the field with the heart's rich red; when Earth drank not rain, but cloven hoof and head; when lungs and groins were sluiced to right and left by mace and sabre; when warriors writhed like women in labour, yes, groaned like mothers on the birthstones, or fell like wheat, to be ground under feet: then the camps faced each other, stunned and wide-eyed, as Death rose them between—Goliath, legs astride—and raucous, voiceless cried.

Heaven darked, the sun blackened and died; the sword's tongue rang its message to the deaf, the cold rebuke of the blade's hot breath. War seized command with his outstretched arm and mighty hand, glaring without eye and roaring his voiceless cry.

Now when the spears, devoid of tongue and lips, had sucked down the blood's last pips; when the blades of vengeance were sheathed, having had their fill of the hearts' spill, unable to down more of guts and gore; when War's palate was cloyed, when one camp joyed to see their foes destroyed; when the dust cloud cleared and the pale sky reappeared, even as the mountains settled into dust, the smoking embers of Battle's lust—then we rose to our feet to journey on, to make our way to our beloved home. Amazed at what our eyes had seen, we turned from frighted to affrighter, from smitten to smiter, that we might dwell in the shadow of their hand. Their envoy bore us from that land of devastation, then led us to our peaceful habitation.

blinded the eye at noon [Deut. 28: 29].
warriors writhed like women in labour Jer. 30: 6.
between—Goliath 1 Sam. 17: 4.
the sun blackened Joel 2: 10, 4: 15.
outstretched arm and mighty hand [Deut. 5: 15].
in the shadow of their hand [Isa. 49: 2].
peaceful habitation Isa. 32: 18.

GATE EIGHT

In Praise of a Letter of Praise Read Two Ways

THUS SPOKE HEMAN THE EZRAHITE: In spring I came to Egypt, Beauty's crown and ring, when earth was fair as dew-blessed Zion, carpeted with aster, jasminth, and cheery dandelion, spilling fruits new and old, green, ruby, gold: Egypt, fair bride who sports the necklace of the Nile, bright candle in the inky world's defile. There I found gracious and keen-witted youths a-brim with truths, sure travellers through complexities, unravellers of perplexities, crossing the Sea of Knowledge on dry land and shattering on every hand Wisdom's boulders. If ornate speech be lamps, they be the holders; if nebulae, they be the sky. From the tower of their intelligence they cast bright gems in trains, with the power of their elegance unleashed abundant rains. For parched nomads their words were a crystal well; their hearts, Prophecy's citadel. Abloom with purity, like Aaron's rod, all were steeped in knowledge of the Most High God.

Now amongst them was a greybeard who gathered scattered herds; with Rhetoric's magic he revived dead words, now weaving bright carpets trimmed with golden wit, now plunging into Wisdom's main to split its waves, emerging from its deep-hid caves with pearls and corals of ornate speech beyond all others' reach. The youths who

dew-blessed Zion [Ps. 133: 3].
fruits new and old S. of S. 7: 14.
crossing the Sea of Knowledge on dry land [Exod. 14: 22, 29].
shattering on every hand Wisdom's boulders 1 Kgs. 19: 11.
their hearts, Prophecy's citadel Lit. 'their hearts were a valley of vision [Isa. 22: 1] for song's prophecy'.
Abloom with purity like Aaron's rod [Num. 17: 16–26].
knowledge of the Most High God Num. 24: 16.
plunging into Wisdom's main to split its waves Exod. 14: 16.

had this sage surrounded, eagerly imbibing what he expounded, asked him to teach them the craft of verbal invention to its utmost extension, to guide them through those highways and byways, those oceans wide and uncharted that weary thought's heroes, even the lion-hearted, they who rush foremost to the fray; for that is the path whereon the eagle fails: on that sea of rhetoric no ship sails.

He told them, I shall pass all my good before you, putting forth conundrums that will outsoar you. Know that the realm of riddles, literate letters, metres, and rhymes boasts numerous terrains and climes can perplex the most well-tried guide. Now the profoundest entertainment, the royal and ultimate attainment is the reversible letter, that bow back-bent with double intent: fair it is when read forward, in no way froward; but turn it round, and lo, around you flow the waters of the raging Nile, pure wrath: a very Jordan turning back upon its path.

Then all the assemblage cried, This virgin soil no feet have walked upon; this path no man has won. Wed us to this way and win rich dower of us this day.

He began, Listen, O children, and I shall teach you the fear of the Lord, seeking at your hand no offering or reward. I shall pour upon you manna of ancient lore, a lissom missive soft-eyed and submissive, cast from Discernment's mould, refined gold, fair as a doe but with a lioness' roar. It is a changeling, sure, the only one of her mother: no heavens have given birth to such another, yea, to such wonder of warbling and thunder. Eyes rush to its silk to caress it; maidens rise up and bless it.

Read it from beginning to end and commend it as wholesome, virgin praise, blameless in all ways. But read it from finish to start and the maid turns tart: rare speech, bare screech, *laudes*, *lewdes*, and benediction, malediction. Bright beams that would earth's iciest peaks

I shall pass all my good before you Exod. 33: 19.
putting forth conundrums Judg. 14: 12.
Jordan turning back upon its path Ps. 114: 3–5.
Listen, O children, and I shall teach you the fear of the Lord Ps. 34: 12.
Seeking at your hand no offering Mal. 1: 10.
I shall pour upon you manna Exod. 16: 11–36; Num. 11: 6–9.
refined gold [Mal. 3: 3].
the only one of her mother S. of S. 6: 9.
maidens rise up and bless it Prov. 31: 28.

unfreeze to set the sundial back ten degrees, leaving readers astounded, nay—dumbfounded. Here is a black but comely maid, laughing and unafraid, modesty's cowl but inwardly foul, tongue tinkling like a bell, but with the bite of hell; two faces to behold, like the shewbread of old. All who taste her in the usual manner will raise Joy's banner, saying, This is the bread of the Lord, yea, this is the table set before the Lord; but reverse the offering wholly and find the loaves unholy. Here good and evil coeval loom, twins striving in one womb: the first comes forth blameless, a dweller of tents, but the second a hunter, a man of violence.

Here, then, find my wreathed gem, my lethal diadem of laud and hissing twined, sprung from the vineyard of my mind, wondrous of scent, myrrh-redolent. No man can pen the like: I have set it in Time's right hand as a cunning pike, therewith to war on ass and boor, jolt clod and dolt. Its theme, the abject object of my disesteem, is a sheepish shepherd of wide renown, a princeling clown I praised till Praise was left behind but who paid me no mind. To black his name, then, unto latter times, I penned these rhymes. Him they found; and when he groped them round he thought himself Heaven-borne, but in truth was scourged with Mockery's thorn: wool-robed at dawn, he was at sunset shorn, as it is written: *Morning's* Well met! *is evening's scorn*. Now hear, lend ear as my words take wing and sing:

Our unparalleled lord	*our life and our blood*
Who unsheathes	*our glory*
Who strips us of	*sadness*
Who bids us sip	*gladness*
Wasting	*trepidation*
Hasting	*salvation*

set the sundial back ten degrees 2 Kgs. 20: 10, 11; Isa. 38: 8.
a black but comely maid S. of S. 1: 5.
two faces to behold, like the shewbread of old Exod. 35: 13, 39: 36.
This is the bread of the Lord Lev. 21: 6, 22.
this is the table set before the Lord Ezek. 41: 22.
twins striving in one womb Gen. 25: 22.
the first comes forth Gen. 25: 25.
blameless, a dweller of tents Gen. 25: 27.
the second a hunter Gen. 25: 27.
a man of violence [Ps. 140: 12].
myrrh-redolent [S. of S. 3: 6].
he groped them round Gen. 27: 22.
Morning's* Well met! *is evening's scorn Prov. 27: 14.
Hasting salvation [Isa. 60: 22].

Shield against calumny
Crown of our community
Known throughout the isles
Famous among the nations
Terrible in praise
A stranger to base ways
He robes him in truth
Spurning mere wealth
Burning for right
Sickened by slander
Quickened by candour
Uprooter of decadence
Suitor of excellence
Foe of vulgarity
Fountain of charity
Storming at arrogance
Kissing veracity
Hissing mendacity
Suing sagacity
Eschewing mordacity
Wooing God's face
Effacing malevolence
Embracing benevolence
Rejecting stupidity
Respecting lucidity
in short
Beauty without taint
The Prince
God guard him
Never be his candle dim
God his glory
Cease each his pain

Known throughout the isles Isa. 42: 12.
Terrible in praise Exod. 15: 11.
Wooing God's face [Pss. 27: 8, 105: 4; and elsewhere].
God guard him [Deut. 32: 10].
be his candle dim Prov. 20: 20.

Increase	*his gain*
Destroy	*his contenders*
Joy	*his defenders*
Bend low	*his foemen*
Defend	*his yeomen*
Down	*all who distress him*
Crown	*all who bless him*
Raze	*his foeman's gate*
Raise high	*his horn*
Cut off	*his moan*
Double	*his revels*
Trouble	*his rivals*
Save	*his companions*
Enslave	*hateful minions*
Bless	*O Lord*
Bless him	*with abounding love*
Never	*perish*

O our lord

Here is lion praise (read: lion preys) for this is ravenous verse—or worse: Lo, I set before you this day the blessing and the curse. Read it straight through and walk a broad-paved, ivoried avenue; but if you choose to turn it round you bring the castle to the ground. Start at the close, go back; take the second, winding track, thusly:

O our lord	*perish*
Never	*with abounding love*
Bless him	*O Lord*
Bless	*all hostile minions*
Enslave	*his companions*
Etc.	*etc.*

Bend low his foemen [Ps. 89: 24].

Crown all who bless him Gen. 27: 29. The Hebrew, citing the same verse, reads, 'curse them who curse him'.

his foeman's gate [Gen. 22: 17].

Raise high his horn 1 Sam. 2: 10.

Lo, I set before you this day the blessing and the curse Deut. 11: 26.

Then he said, Now here is another, and this time metric, rhyme, rife with further crime:

Sire: Oh, thine be joy; no evil stands thee nigh!
Right lyre: thine blinding speech; none this deny!

And now, he offered, this reverse—and thus rehearse:

Deny this none: speech blinding thine, right Liar.
Nigh thee stands evil. No joy be thine, oh sire!

Having ended, he fell quiet a moment and then said, I lift my hand to God Most High, to Him who dwells apart but knows each secret of the human heart: this potent letter can no poet better. Of Jews' and Arabs' pens, know it is best, unmatched in East or West. No hands have twisted chain so fine, no lips turned phrases sweetly tuned at mine. Look you to Arab song renowned: all the high hills beneath the Heavens are drowned. Yes, all men conversant with sweet melody of Jewry and of Araby can savour properly its subtle flavour and—by Song's daughters!—separate waters from waters.

SAID THE TELLER OF THE TALE:

Our hearts melted like wax beneath the savant's light: we were like grasshoppers in our own eyes and so were we in his sight. Numb, overcome, near dumb, we barely lisped, Who be you, Sir? Whence come?

Loud rang his laughter as he sang:

I am Hever, whose princely pen the praise
of princes loud rehearses;
My tripping tongue spills accolades
that garland my foes with curses.
My words restore the eyes of the blind
but the seeing rob of sight

I lift my hand to God Most High Gen. 14: 22.
all the high hills beneath the Heavens are drowned Gen. 7: 19.
separate waters from waters Gen. 1: 6.
Our hearts melted like wax Josh. 2: 11; [Ps. 22: 15].
we were like grasshoppers in our own eyes and so were we in his sight Num. 13: 33.

As I lie with Song's virgin daughters, who laugh
at all others, with legs locked tight.
To him who pursues my heights I say:
Prudence! Do not over-dare.
Why will you pain and nothing gain?
Ascend not the altar's stair.
Why strive to defame your limping name,
your shame to all men bare?

Hearing his song I placed him—Hever the Kenite! Swiftly I embraced him and stayed him close, day after day, thinking to sweetly pass my years away firm at his side; but that, tight-fisted Time denied. The raven wandering raised his cry and I journeyed on with trembling eye: clutching the Kenite's name for drink and food, Judah went into exile in great affliction and great servitude.

As . . . tight Lit. 'All the daughters of song (Eccles. 12: 4) are possessed (sexually) of me, though they are virgins to all others beside me.'

Ascend not the altar's stair Exod. 20: 26.

your shame to all men bare Exod. 20: 26.

Judah went into exile in great affliction and great servitude Lam. 1: 3. 'Judah' points to an overlap of identity between Heman and Alḥarizi, on which see the Afterword.

GATE NINE

Poetic Invention: One and Thirty in Contention

THUS SPOKE HEMAN THE EZRAHITE: When I was young, eagerly would I rise to garner the words and dark sayings of the wise. Now one day I found myself with thirty poets, keen and discerning, heroes of Learning, one of whom declared, Let him who can climb Song's ladder to Heaven's height lead us aright: in ignorance' storm let him seize the helm, bare Rhetoric's holy arm, and show us the riches of his realm.

His fellows answered, This is a hid path; we do not know it. Who could be such a poet?

He replied, He who would win to Song's mansion must master rhyme and scansion, wed poetic convention to athletic invention, traverse vast realms, immerse himself in rules diverse; and, to be crowned king, rear poems resting each on a prophetic verse.

Now off to the side sat a scruffy fellow stooped with age, but a towering sage who could body forth kingdoms with his mind's swift brush and with his diamond tongue make rubies blush. His face was hid by a disguise: I could see no more than his eyes.

He declared, Men of understanding, hearken unto me: shun folly and obliquity. If you would dare this thoroughfare, attempt this

One and Thirty in Contention On citation substitution in this gate, see the Analysis.
dark sayings of the wise Prov. 1: 6.
ladder to Heaven's height [Gen. 28: 12].
bare Rhetoric's holy arm Isa. 52: 10.
show us the riches of his realm Esther 1: 4.
rear poems resting each on a prophetic verse Actually, only most, not all, of the rhyme verses chosen derive from the second section of the Bible, i.e. 'The Prophets' (Joshua to Malachi).
His face was hid by a disguise Lit. 'his face was covered'. On the issue of the disguises of Hever, see the Afterword.
Men of understanding, hearken unto me Job 34: 10.

sea, choose you a champion to come down to me. With words my arms, none can best me. Come, test me.

Thereat one of the company approached him and said, If you would raise Song's wave to a mighty wall, strike lines that close, *The young men shall utterly fall.*

Then he lifted his voice and sang:

Shall I wait for the Lord any longer, my soul?
I am old. ***Fear and serve him; recall:***
They who wait on the Lord shall renew their strength
while the young men shall utterly fall.

Then the second of the company declared: If you would have your fragrance blown, strike lines that close, *Through the might of Your arm they are still as stone.*

Then he lifted his voice and sang:

Rise against Evil, cross swords with Pride,
Storm Falsehood's tower, though you ride alone.
Behold, lips that slander the righteous are sealed:
through the might of your arm they are still as stone.

Then the third declared: If you would show your mind to be coeval with Jeremiah's, strike lines that close, *They proceed from evil to evil.*

So he lifted his voice and sang:

I look to the right—Right's sun is eclipsed;
I look to the left—darkness primeval.
Earth shakes at the tramp of the godless' feet—
they proceed from evil to evil.

choose you a champion to come down to me 1 Sam. 17: 8. Here Alḥarizi evokes the Arabic literary tradition of warrior poets debating before the fray. See Analysis of Gate 7.

raise Song's wave to a mighty wall [Exod. 14: 29]. Lit. 'If it is your desire to kindle the flame of intelligence'.

The young men shall utterly fall Isa. 40: [30].

They who wait on the Lord shall renew their strength Isa. 40: 31.

Shall I wait . . . utterly fall The literal rendering of this poem is: 'Son of man, trust on your Rock on the day of your pain for in Him shall the weary find rest [Gen. 8: 9]. Those who trust in vanity labour in vain, but they who hope in the Lord shall renew their strength.'

Through the might of Your arm they are still as stone Exod. 15: [16].

They proceed from evil to evil [Jer. 9: 2].

Then the fourth declared: If you would have your verse bear the stamp of piety and urbanity, strike lines that close, *Extending the finger and speaking vanity.*

Then he lifted his voice and sang:

Muck sucks at your feet, Death rises fast:
return to your Maker, errant humanity.
Banish the yoke from your midst, put an end
to extending the finger and speaking vanity.

Then the fifth declared: If you would be richly esteemed, strike lines that close, *What is this dream that you have dreamed?*

Then he lifted his voice and sang:

Oh nodding soul—your bed of lust,
this World for which you toiled and schemed
Is but a plot of writhing worms.
What is this dream that you have dreamed?

Then the sixth declared: If you would lead the dance in Poesy's wood, strike lines that close, *He hath shown thee, O man, what is good.*

So he lifted his voice and sang:

God's voice breaks like thunder: yours to obey
nor pretend you have not understood,
Love mercy! Walk humbly with God! Be just!
He hath shown thee, O man, what is good.

Then the seventh declared: If you would raise Song's banner and Wisdom's shield, strike lines that close, *Heal me, O Lord, and I shall be healed.*

Extending the finger and speaking vanity Isa. 58: 9.

What is this dream that you have dreamed Gen. 37: 10.

He hath shown thee, O man, what is good Mic. 6: 8.

God's voice breaks like thunder [Ps. 29: 4].

Love mercy! . . . what is good Mic. 6: 8.

Heal me, O Lord, and I shall be healed [Jer. 17: 14]. The translator-introduced source is recited daily in the thrice-repeated Amidah prayer, where the first person singular has been changed to first person plural. (See Hertz, *Authorised Daily Prayer Book*, 140.)

So he lifted his voice and sang:

My festering soul runs thick with pus,
the flesh of my spirit is pocked and wealed.
I seize on God's name for physic and cry,
Heal me, O Lord, and I shall be healed.

Then the eighth declared: If you would wed the muse's daughter, strike lines that close, *Order the rock to yield its water.*

So he lifted his voice and sang:

My heart, sin-snared, is turned to stone;
then war on my heart, soul, grant no quarter.
Strike with God's word till she weep with remorse:
Order the rock to yield its water.

Then the ninth declared: If you would set your hearers' hearts aglow, strike lines that close, *If Thou go with me, then will I go.*

So he lifted his voice and sang:

Hide not Thy face—my heart is wax,
my soul turns water; I spill, I flow.
Help me, my God, and I shall be helped,
stay me, O Lord, my shaft and bow;
Seize Thou my hand, go where Thou wilt:
If Thou go with me, then will I go.

Then the tenth declared: If you would set your words on Wisdom's shelf, strike lines that close, *The Lord will take Judah unto himself.*

So he lifted his voice and sang:

God's word my lamp, God's law my light,
I turn my back on Pride and Pelf.
Let Mammon seize seekers of silver and gold:
the Lord will take Judah unto himself.

Order the rock to yield its water [Num. 20: 8].
If Thou go with me, then will I go Judg. 4: 8.
Hide not Thy face Ps. 27: 9.
my soul turns water Josh. 7: 5.
The Lord will take Judah unto himself Zech. 2: 16. Here Alḥarizi hints at the amalgamation of the character Hever with himself. See the discussion on this phenomenon in the Afterword.
God's word my lamp [Ps. 119: 105].
God's law my light [Prov. 6: 23].

Then the eleventh declared: If you would send forth Wit's scents till our nostrils be sated, strike lines that close, *His eyes were undimmed, his vigour was unabated.*

So he lifted his voice and sang:

Plant Justice' tree within your heart; and lo—
Right's fruit blooms fair, the air is permeated.
Live so, that when you die men shall declare,
His eyes were undimmed, his vigour was unabated.

Then the twelfth declared: If you would have your store of wisdom shown, strike lines that close, *It is not good for man to be alone.*

So he lifted his voice and sang:

When man lay raw upon Creation's floor,
Chaos and Dark but six days overthrown,
Let Wisdom be man's helpmeet, God decreed;
it is not good for man to be alone.

Then the thirteenth declared: If you would have us revere your words as though Heaven itself revealed them, strike lines that close, *He sent forth His word and He healed them.*

So he lifted his voice and sang:

Sinners, find health in the Torah of God:
He set there His nostrums and sealed them.
Join those who drink Scripture like physic, and lo—
He sent forth His word and He healed them.

Then the fourteenth declared: If you would blaze among the Sons of Light and bright the Age's night, strike lines that close, *My sheaf uprose and also stood upright.*

So he lifted his voice and sang:

In many a battle was my tongue a scourge,
lashing my rivals into frenzied flight;

His eyes were undimmed, his vigour was unabated Deut. 34: 7.
It is not good for man to be alone Gen. 2: 18.
He sent forth His word and He healed them [Ps. 107: 20].
My sheaf uprose and also stood upright Gen. 37: 7.

But at Song's quiet harvest I have ruled as well:
my sheaf uprose and also stood upright.

Then the fifteenth declared: If you would have your song shine sevenfold, strike lines that close, *That they made them gods of gold.*

So he lifted his voice and sang:

Let tight-fisted men fear Judgement's wrath
like sheep cut off from the fold.
This their reward, that they bowed down to Coin,
that they made them gods of gold.

Then the sixteenth declared: If you would have us number you among the great, strike lines that close, *Lovely indeed is my estate.*

So he lifted his voice and sang:

Let lust-rid men storm the gates of the World—
I lust after God, I hold to His gate.
I stand in His Presence in perfect joy:
Lovely indeed is my estate.

Then the seventeenth declared: If you would bind poetic wit to battle's brawn, strike lines that close, *The sword, the sword is drawn!*

So he lifted his voice and sang:

I rest in the West, I rise in the East;
my verse outshines the dawn.
I raise my Pen: Song's waters split
as the troops of my thought rush on.
Let scribblers and quibblers flee my wrath
for the sword, the sword is drawn!

Then the eighteenth declared: If you would spring like a lion from Poesy's brake, strike lines that close, *And the rod which was turned to a snake.*

That they made them gods of gold Exod. 32: 31.
Lovely indeed is my estate Ps. 16: 6.
I stand in His Presence in perfect joy [Ps. 16: 11].
The sword, the sword is drawn [Ezek. 21: 8].
Song's waters split [Exod. 14: 16].
spring like a lion from Poesy's brake [Jer. 4: 7].
And the rod which was turned to a snake Exod. 7: 15.

So he lifted his voice and sang:

I lift up my arm—my foes fall back;
I speak and the mountains quake.
For mine is the pen which devours like a lion
and the rod which was turned to a snake.

Then the nineteenth declared: If you would have Song's chariots wheel at your command, strike lines that close, *Stretch forth your rod, smite the dust of the land.*

So he lifted his voice and sang:

Stretch out your pen o'er the Torah's sea
till its secrets are bared to the sand.
As for rivals—those stones, those clods—why, stretch
forth your rod, smite the dust of the land.

Then the twentieth declared: If you would pay Fame's fee, strike lines that close, *Vengeance belongs to Me.*

So he lifted his voice and sang:

His eyes shoot arrows, vessels of wrath—
the gazelle who attacks me ruthlessly.
Then shine forth, my cheek, till he stumble and fall:
Vengeance belongs to Me.

Then the twenty-first declared: If you would prove yourself Song's turtledove, strike lines that close, *Ascend not the mount nor touch the border thereof.*

So he lifted his voice and sang:

Ruin stands waiting for worldlings who climb
the high ridges of Pride and Self-love.
Take care then, beware then, ascend not the mount,
nor touch the border thereof.

I lift up my arm—my foes fall back [Exod. 17: 11].

Stretch forth your rod, smite the dust of the land [Exod. 8: 12].

Vengeance belongs to Me [Deut. 32: 35].

vessels of wrath Gen. 49: 5.

stumble and fall [Ps. 20: 9].

Ascend not the mount nor touch the border thereof Exod. 19: 12.

Then the twenty-second declared: If you would have your songs loved best in East and West, and lauded from North to South, strike lines that close, *Let him kiss me with the kisses of his mouth.*

So he lifted his voice and sang:

I wait for the love of the fair gazelle
as Earth waits for rain in drouth.
His juices are sweeter than wine; so I say,
let him kiss me with the kisses of his mouth.

Then the twenty-third declared: If you would lay Song's board with Wisdom's meat, strike lines that close, *Then take it to your father to eat.*

So he lifted his voice and sang:

Reverence your teacher and father, and set you
his words as bright lamps to your feet.
Pluck Wisdom's fruit from the mind's ripe tree,
then take it to your father to eat.

Then the twenty-fourth declared: If you would climb Poesy's peaks till you can climb no higher, strike lines that close, *He and they both shall be put to the fire.*

So he lifted his voice and sang:

Havoc and Cruelty rut with Lust,
Perversion reigns in the Land of Desire.
Therefore must man guard his heart and his soul
or he and they both shall be put to the fire.

Then the twenty-fifth declared, If you would wing your muse and fly, strike lines that close, *For whatever he did to draw blame thereby.*

Let him kiss me with the kisses of his mouth
S. of S. [1: 2].
His juices . . . the kisses of his mouth
S. of S. [1: 2].
Then take it to your father to eat
Gen. 27: 10.
his words as bright lamps to your feet
[Ps. 119: 105].
He and they both shall be put to the fire
Lev. 20: 14.
For whatever he did to draw blame thereby
Lev. 5: 26.

So he lifted his voice and sang:

That man who lives dead to the Living God,
who plugs up his ear, who covers his eye,
Shall gain his reward at the final day
for whatever he did to draw blame thereby.

Then the twenty-sixth declared: If you would gild your name with our praise, strike lines that close, *Take me not away in the midst of my days.*

So he lifted his voice and sang:

My heavens of tears cloud over with sighs;
O God, cleave my dark with Repentance' rays.
Lord, shine in my heart, grace Your servant with Life,
take me not away in the midst of my days.

Then the twenty-seventh declared: If you would have us say of your handiwork, Behold, it is very good, strike lines that close, *Here, then, is the fire and here the wood.*

So he lifted his voice and sang:

My sighs rise thick as altar smoke;
would I could act as I know I should!
The flame of remorse consumes my heart:
Here, then, is the fire and here the wood.

Then the twenty-eighth declared: If you would prove your worth, strike lines that close, *Arise, O Lord, and judge the earth.*

So he lifted his voice and sang:

Answer us, God, our strength is gone;
we wail like a woman who crouches in birth.
The heathen rage, the nations roar:
Arise, O Lord, and judge the earth.

Take me not away in the midst of my days Ps. 102: 25.

Behold, it is very good [Gen. 1: 31].

Here, then, is the fire and here the wood [Gen. 22: 7].

Arise, O Lord, and judge the earth Ps. [82: 8].

we wail like a woman who crouches in birth [Isa. 42: 14].

The heathen rage, the nations roar [Ps. 2: 1].

*T*hen the twenty-ninth declared: If you would seize Song's river and hold the fords, strike lines that close, *And the kingdom shall be the Lord's.*

*S*o he lifted his voice and sang:

Lord, speed the day when You free your crushed folk
from the feet of the servant hordes.
Restore our lost glory to Zion,
and the kingdom shall be the Lord's.

*T*hen the thirtieth declared: If you would sit foremost at Song's holy board, strike lines that close, *Make haste, O God, to deliver me; make haste to help me, O Lord.*

*S*o he lifted his voice and sang:

Faint is my heart upon enemy soil:
terror within, and without—the sword.
Make haste, O God, to deliver me;
make haste to help me, O Lord.

SAID THE TELLER OF THE TALE:

*N*ever, ah, never, had I seen like endeavour! Was ever poet so keen, so deep, so clever? I looked more closely and lo—Hever the Kenite, Heaven-sent, wandering dweller of Wisdom's tent! Seeing that face I shed all distress, ah, quivered for very happiness! My heart leapt free to see my sea of friendship and sincerity. Long days we spent in quiet walks and sweet discourse until jealous Time flung us to horse and drove us off, each to his separate course.

---

and the kingdom shall be the Lord's Obad. 1: 21.

Make haste, O God, to deliver me; make haste to help me, O Lord Ps. [70: 1].

Faint is my heart upon enemy soil [Lev. 26: 36].

terror within, and without—the sword [Deut. 32: 25].

dweller of Wisdom's tent Gen. 25: 27.

GATE TEN

Of Rustic Propriety and Winged Piety

THUS SPOKE HEMAN THE EZRAHITE: Soon after I came to the Land of Kasdim from the Valley of Siddim my name shone bright from every height and rang in every street; the very hills turned footstool to my feet. Now one fine morn, resolved to view the foreigner and native-born, I spied a stranger seated off by himself; so down I sat, as travellers often do, to while away the time with a tale or two.

Sir, good cheer! I opened. Who be you and what brings you here?

A prosperous foreigner I am, who sometimes snares a fox, sometimes a ram.

Where you have been, then, and what seen on your wanderings?

Strange and wondrous things. But in all my days, through all my winding ways, never did my eyes light on as strange a sight as I saw before sundown last night.

Pray share, said I, this curious affair.

He began: I was in a pleasant company of true Aristocracy, born nobles, granaries of Generosity, awesome givers, their hands rivers, their liberality a theme to tax the bard, their speech of topaz, sapphire, and sard, their faces bright as dawn's first light, putting the stars to flight, outshining moon and sun, and making day of blackest night. Now yesterday, when dawn broke, we woke early to repair to the country for fragrant air, to revel in fresh flowers and loll in shady bowers. Ordering our servants to ready the teams, we set out, ringed

the Land of Kasdim Mentioned often in Scripture—e.g. Jer. 24: 5 and Ezek. 1: 3; essentially the land of Babylonia. See BDB, 505.

the Valley of Siddim Gen. 14: 3, 8, 10.

footstool to my feet Isa. 66: 1.

before sundown 2 Sam. 3: 35.

with youths, for woods and streams, our horses sleek and spry, eager to outrace the eye.

Then the chief of our company said, Sirs, I suggest we take rest on yonder mountain's ripe green crest, a choice location, stunningly beautiful; and you will find the villagers most dutiful: they are mine, you see, beholden to me and to my generosity.

On we rode, our horses sweating, and approached the village as the sun was setting: as we entered that delightful place, she took to her chamber, veiling her face with crimson lace.

A cluster of farmers rushed out to meet us, bowing low before our coaches to greet us. Their leader helped us down and led our horses to a grassy mound where, without delay, he laid out drink and rich, sweet hay; then he made our steeds lie down in green pastures and led them beside still waters. Beaming, he rejoined us and took us to his home on the range, his sprawling grange, straw strewn about within and without, and, witness to his plenteous flocks and herds, layered lavishly with turds. Wielding a zesty broom, he swept free each room of thistle, thorn, and broom; yes, whirring about like a comet, he cleared the floor of dung and vomit. That done, he removed his wives and daughters, sequestering them in his innermost quarters, and came before us to implore us: M'lords, permit me to set the boards—he flashed a broad smile—with milk, butter, and curds, mountain style.

Sir, we replied, as you prefer.

In a trice the man was off and running and that swift returning with a cup of goat's milk churning, which he congealed instanter, tendering it with the following banter:

M'lords, here's your cup: drink it up. You know, we mountaineers and farmers try our best: we go all out for a guest, we don't squeeze the penny till our hands get gritty, like folks from the city. They're downright mean, table always clean—you know what I mean: they'd grudge you a stringbean. Sure as I live, they'd serve milk in a sieve. But us, why for us it's a sterlin' delight to get hold of a guest

he made our steeds lie down in green pastures and led them beside still waters Ps. 23: 2.

and feed him right. Way we do it can't be beat—servin' up a good, thick chunk o' bloody meat.

Then he cleared his throat and sang:

M'mouth, sir, it waters to bring in guests:
that's as tasty a treat as a jug o' whey
Or burnt-out crumbs come in butter vats,
if you know how to make it the mountain way.
When I hear a guest sing out in the dark
I call to my boys, Unlock the lock!
I'm as tickled to take in a guest for the night
as a wolf lopin' off with the best o' my flock.
I'm as hot on the tail of a guest, I tell you,
as a ploughboy hot on the tail of his ass.
I get pitapat hostin' a guest in my house
like a half-starved pony a-chompin' dry grass.
I'm plumb hungry for guests like a calf for full teats
or a donkey a-waitin' and droolin' for grits.

This said, our host took a lamb of one year, trussed and served it, then hovered near. After we had eaten, he led us to plush beds of down where, weary from the way, we laid us down.

Next morning, when the sun gilt each blade of the country glade, we tossed our covers off, rose and prayed, mounted our horses and eager set our courses for the bright scenery of country greenery, picking our way through arbours' shades and flower-thick, pungent colonnades. Now as mealtime neared, the farmer appeared. He brought us to his home, where we found the food set out, gay country dishes all about. *No trouble, sirs, no trouble; m'pots are all a-bubble.* Howbeit, only green beans filled the pots; alas, all flesh was grass. So there we sat, a sorry scene, ringed round with bowls brimful of every kind of country green.

SAID THE TELLER OF THE TALE:

Now I had earlier observed that the rustic owned a plump and juicy bird, a broad-winged rooster begging to be served, yes, one designed to whet the appetite, particularly since he had kept me up

all flesh was grass Isa. 40: 6.

half the preceding night. So I said to the farmer, Sir, we are beholden to you for your generous attitude and can scarce express our gratitude; but I am somewhat ailing and failing, and nothing would me more refresh than that rooster's flesh. My doctors, you see, have told me what I should and should not eat; fowl is fine, but never meat.

M'lord, you shan't lack: if you'd wanted the skin off my own boy's back I wouldn'ta held it back, he answered, as he and his wife, without any strife, went for the cock with a carving knife. Thereat the rooster, to the servants' guffaws, squawked round the room in flight from Death's claws.

*T*he puffing farmer, seeing no gains for all his pains, called in his young men, who gave chase in throngs with jeers and songs and clanging gongs, until one youth prevailed, seizing their prey by the tail. Thereat the frenzied rooster pecked him and checked him, flew swiftly to the ladder's furthest rung, and fervent sung—yea, sung as he would never be outdone—God's praise on the day that the Lord had delivered him from the hands of his enemies, every one.

*W*inging next to the roof of the house of prayer, for a large and noisy crowd had gathered there, the fugitive opened wide his beak and did impassioned speak: *Blessed art Thou, our Rock, who givest wisdom to the cock*—and at the sound, the people cocked their ears and gathered round.

*D*raw near, crowed Chanticleer, pursuers of justice and men's commendation, who come to tender supplication to the Dweller on high, to cry to the Lord of all lands, to lift your hands to Him who commands Heaven's host, you who bluster most: what avails the reverent word? Your hands run red with blood! Why loud implore, you murderers of the innocent and the poor? How dare you pray, who lie in wait to slay the guiltless each and every day? Refrain! Bring no more oblations vain! Come not to Bethel: with blood your hands

God's praise on the day that the Lord had delivered him from the hands of his enemies, every one Ps. 18: 1.
Blessed art Thou, our Rock, who givest wisdom to the cock First of the *birkhot hashaḥar* or morning benedictions.
pursuers of justice Isa. 51: 1.
you murderers of the innocent and the poor Jer. 2: 34.
lie in wait to slay Prov. 1: 18.
Bring no more oblations vain Isa. 1: 13.
Come not to Bethel Amos 5: 5—lit. 'to the House of God'. On the cultic centre of Bethel, see *EJ* iv. 728–30 and v. 1163 ff.

be full. Shall your mockery atonement win? It is a commemorative offering, commemorating sin!

The people, staring at each other in astonishment, asked the meaning of this sharp admonishment. Then the bird spoke: To you, O men who front the foemen in the gate, I shall my tale relate. Has God's fear vanished, is Justice banished from your midst? Desist! If you betray all who enter your door, who will trust you more? Allies and friends despise, and all your truths turn lies. Is it a light thing to play false to them that love you? Beware: God stands above you! Have I not served you selflessly in truth since first I came within the shadow of your roof, waking you the night through that you might offer God His due? Have I not lavished on you wondrous pullets, fair sons and daughters to titillate your palates? But you, thoughts lewd and crude, would see me skewered: from the day that I knew you, you have been rebellious against the Lord!

By my faith! While I am yet alive with you, you have been rebellious against the Lord—and how much more so after my death! I adjure you: through all my days and years have I not ever kept my word? Witness against me before the Lord! You have seen and known that I own no other occupation but offering Song and Supplication, seeking as recompense bare sustenance, chanting to God my roundelay, my litany night and day. See, see: the Lord doth command His Lovingkindness by day, and by night His Song shall be with me.

And now that I am aged and bleary in your service, weak and weary, my youth long flown and hoar years come, you give, for my good, foul compensation, repaying my love with detestation. Rudely from my sons and daughters you would force me and from my consorts' sweet bosoms divorce me, leaving my chickadees helpless and alone and my widowed wives to moan. Yet had you profited

with blood your hands be full Isa. 1: 15.
atonement win Isa. 22: 14.
It is a commemorative offering, commemorating sin Num. 5: 15.
men who front the foemen in the gate Isa. 28: 6.
from the day that I knew you, you have been rebellious against the Lord Deut. 9: 24.
While I am yet alive . . . after my death Deut. 31: 27.
Witness against me before the Lord 1 Sam. 12: 3.
the Lord . . . with me Ps. 42: 9.

therein I had held my tongue, nor had this accusation sung; but my flesh is flinty—a fact indisputable, hence for sacrifice unsuitable. My juice is dry, my eye is blurred, my strength as brittle as a shard. My bones are turned very stone to the measure of my days and years long gone. My smell is foul, my flesh doth crawl, my taste appal. My meat is rich as mud and vile as pigs' blood. My grinders have ceased, my eyes film with mist; my ribs bear no meat and, beyond that, my innards no fat. My legs totter, I am poured out like water, my bones are out of joint: sirs, what is the point?! Should a sick man eat my rot he would die on the spot, and bear his sin to Hell as well. And should the sound man wolf me down, he would not renew his strength, go he—the glutton!—to any length.

Shall such be my recompense? Shall such be your name when you are carried hence? Surely you can find among my sons, with virtue graced, one amply fit to take my place! By the Law, they are all wholesome, without flaw, deliciously soft and a joy to gnaw; each fat as a goose, ribs moist with juice, and bones with marrow richly blessed would joy a royal guest. And my daughters: aspire no higher—the very heart's desire! Each is a plumpish treat—ah, ah, their nubile meat: flaky-tender, oh what flavour! Let the sick man savour thereof and he will stand again in Health's good favour and never waver. Moreover, look you in Scripture and plainly see: *Let the dam go and take the young to thee.*

Then the bird sang:

Tender me comfort, O trusty friends,
the faithful servant vilely served.
Great anguish mine, paid foul for fair;
yea, almost for supper I had been served.
Friends have forgot my kindness past:
they seek me out, they seek my blood.
For all my love they bear me hate—
me, me, who ever sought their good!

Yet . . . I had held my tongue Esther 7: 4.
my strength as brittle as a shard Ps. 22: 15.
My grinders have ceased Eccles. 12: 3.
I am poured out like water Ps. 22: 15.
renew his strength Isa. 40: 31.
Let the dam go and take the young to thee Deut. 22: 7.
the faithful servant [Num. 12: 7; 1 Sam. 22: 14].

Listen: they whisper! Listen: they plot!
They raise the black banner against my life.
I proffer them daughters and handsome sons—
in answer they proffer the butcher's knife.
Gen'rous, I feed them my children's flesh—
they seek out pretexts the more to eat.
I am old and wizened, gristle and bone,
yet the fools consider me plump and sweet!
Miscreants jeered me in hot pursuit,
in but a moment they had me slain;
But God in His mercy succoured me,
frantic they sought me, but sought in vain.
Had God not writ me down for life
my bones were shattered like dry sticks
And I sent forth from my wives' fair arms,
yea, banished from my tender chicks.

SAID THE TELLER OF THE TALE:

Now when the people had heard his complaint, they knew him for a very saint. Indignant at this repugnant history, they bade the rooster's owner stand and did him reprimand: How could you do it, who put you to it, to lay hands on our wise old teacher, our holy preacher who tells us what God's wantin' us to do and, when the sun starts rayin', calls us out of bed to set us prayin'?

Then the rustic replied, I won't say you nay. From the start, this bird's been crowin' out his heart; like you're sayin', he's always prayin'. But last night a bunch of Jewish guests walked in my door, bigwigs for sure. One of 'em got sick, and his doctors've told him what not to eat—meat. And, all polite, he asked me to prepare this rooster there; and 'pon my soul, I'm not the sort to hand a guest an empty bowl!

Then the elders answered all, All right, that was sweet to offer him such a treat. But another bird can do the trick—so fetch one quick!

Yes, they adjured the farmer by his faith and farm to bring the

Had God not writ me down for life As in the *Avinu malkenu* prayer, 'Our Father, our King, inscribe us in the book of good life' (Birnbaum, *High Holiday Prayer Book*, 271).

cock no harm; whereon the rustic vowed aloud, I wouldn't touch a feather, 'pon my word, or nothin' else neither on that bird.

Now when the rooster had heard them out he raised his voice, yes, loudly shouted in exultation for the miracles and redemption and salvation: loud did he revel, seeing that God had repented of the evil. Clearing his throat, he sang:

God bless these kindly, noble folk,
these honeyed tongues who bear God's yoke.
Their hearts and souls cleave fast above:
they met my need with faith and love.
Except for them the foeman's stone
had ground me to nothing, flesh and bone.

SAID THE TELLER OF THE TALE:

Now when the stranger had finished his declaim, I asked him his name, whereat he said:

I am Hever, choice chanticleer of Song
jewel-studded from ancient story;
From my laughing heart I spin out my
melody sweet and my allegory.

SAID THE TELLER OF THE TALE:

Hearing his song I knew him quite as Hever the Kenite and said to him, Your concoctions are incredible, your honeyed invention all but edible! God's life! You have not heard this tale from any human tongue but from your own heart have it sung!

Chuckling at that, my friend turned, walked on, and was gone.

for the miracles and redemption and salvation Amidah of the daily service, the start of inserted prayer for Ḥanukah (Hertz, *Authorised Daily Prayer Book*, 150–3).

God had repented of the evil Jonah 3: 10.

GATE ELEVEN

Of Verbal Show: Using and Refusing the Letter O

THUS SPOKE HEMAN THE EZRAHITE: My thoughts' progeny seized me, wrist and knee, and lifted me, bore me across the sea to that fair land where Israel flourished proud and free. There I leapt like an antelope across Myrrh Mountain in swift pursuit of riddle, saw, and trope; and turned thereafter to Bethlehem of Judah, full of hope and trust, to slake my wanderlust in that sweet dust and there find many a roe and hind. So it was that I arrived at the gate of a city wondrous pretty and spied men streaming from every direction, frenzied, as from an insurrection. Now when I asked, Why all this flurry, this hurry and scurry? they answered that a man of rare order had just crossed the border, a sign and a wonder, very lightning and thunder. So I said in my heart, Let me join this race and see this wizard face to face. Once come to where he had pitched his tent I spied a savant, wizened and bent, whose speech was kingly ornament.

He declared: Come, master and sage, here gauge the wonder of your age, whose tongue is Learning's ever-turning page, who holds the bird of Scripture in his mouth's gilt cage, whose arbours are dowered with shining rows—metric verse and rich, rhymed prose. Before my tropes' fierce thunderbolts wise men wobble like newborn colts or drop their lower jaws like dolts. Before my speech the stars retreat; the everlasting hills melt in my utterance' heat; Heaven's lightnings cannot reach unto the dust of my feet.

Then the chief of that company declared: Behold, here are high claims aired, Pride's lofty arm and bright sword bared; but is wisdom

I leapt like an antelope across Myrrh Mountain S. of S. 2: 17 [and 4: 6].
Bethlehem of Judah Ruth 1: 1 and elsewhere.
a sign and a wonder [Deut. 28: 46].
the everlasting hills [Ps. 36: 7].
lofty arm and bright sword bared Isa. 52: 10.

thereby snared? Your words are many, but your deeds few: gain honour when your prophecies come true.

The old man said: I stand before you with Song's rod, yea, I stand between you and God. Reach now as far as you can reach for strongest song and deepest-figured speech. Set me against Orion, the Pleiades; come, climb my Pyrenees. Search me as you please, your search shall prove barren; you will find no thorns round my rose of Sharon.

They replied: If you speak true, this do: swell your lungs; climb Poesy's highest rungs to sing us a song in three tongues.

Then he lifted his voice and sang:

My song shall praise His name
Dont de beauté suprême
EST OPIFICIUM.
The word of God is strong:
Louer le Tout-Puissant
FANDI PRINCIPIUM.
All speak His name in awe
Au Créateur Très-Haut
MUNDI DOMINIUM.
With all-resplendent sheen
Sa justice illumine
TENEBRAS NOCTIUM.
Knowledge to man is barred
de celui qui regarde
OMNE MYSTERIUM.
To the parched earth His love
Que jamais rien n'entrave
INMITTIT FLUVIUM.
His kingdom evermore
S'arbritera du sort
REGUM MORTALIUM.

I stand between you and God Deut. 5: 5.
no thorns round my rose of Sharon [S. of S. 2: 1].
climb Poesy's highest rungs [Gen. 28: 12].
Then he lifted his voice and sang Again, I thank Dr Leofranc Holford-Strevens, who has rendered a trilingual poem—shortened, at my request—analogous to the Hebrew–Arabic–Aramaic original. For the literal translation of Dr Holford-Strevens's lines, the reader is directed to the addendum at the close of the Analysis.

He shall exalt the meek
Et l'orgueil tyrannique
PREMET POTENTIUM.
The horn shall sound that day
Mettant fin au sommeil
HUMI MANENTIUM.
His counsel hid no more,
Rendra la vie aux morts
VINDEX VIVENTIUM.
Once more the Lord shall set
Son tabernacle au faîte
ALTORUM MONTIUM.
And my song shall not cease
d'être le sacrifice
DEUM TIMENTIUM.

Then he declared, See and record: here find Song's lord! Whose cunning hand can sever this threefold cord? Ho, trembling listeners, is my strength now proved? For these three shall the earth be moved. Search eastward, westward: here is Wit's font, the pick of tripping rhyme and triple stich, built brick by brick in Aramaic, Hebrew, and—yes—Arabic.

Awed, they said, Song's tongue and eyes who foil the wise—claim love's prize, for it is clear you know no peer for figured song to sweet the ear. Now gain Spain's throne if this you own—praise spun from rhymed prose to match the metric magic you have shown. Give us a letter that will singularly record the lustre of a noble lord with flashing rhyme and dashing trope; and this be its scope and show: let its every word contain the letter *O*.

*O*ho! cried he. Approach, then, and see. Breathe myrrh and frankincense, for I commence:

O people, come forth from south to north! Unloose your throats, pour out notes of generous laudation; offer adulation, proffer

Whose cunning hand can sever this threefold cord Eccles. 4: 12.
For these three shall the earth be moved Prov. 30: 21.
let its every word contain the letter *O* In the Hebrew, the challengers speak of the letter *resh*.

oblation & libation, carol for joy, do not forbear, loose chariots of song down Glory's thoroughfare & summon footmen to follow; sound Poesy's horn through mount & hollow. Loose Rhetoric's downpour, soak meadow & moor, oh, disgorge your showers &, thereupon, grow, Poesy's golden flowers! Bloom, honouring Honour's seignior & Illustriousness' groom!

Countrymen, hoist Song's torch, commanding stoneblind orbs, Behold! Hold out your coronals, took of Wisdom's hold, to your uncontested lord. Of one accord, commend our precious potentate who, godly & lone, occupies Splendour's throne. Blazon Probity's cloak & Morality's yoke, noble of blood, of choicest derivation & spotless lineation, Prose's perfection & Poetry's consummation, our Solomon, author of glowing tomes whose reputation throws contenders into consternation & bottomless frustration; whose strophes command acclamation & whose tropes, intoxication: tropes of topaz, opal, tourmaline, diamond—oh, wondrous beyond designation!

Eulogize our goodly goblet & our overflowing bowl, explicator of our Holy Scroll who roars & lions cower; whose scorching discourse topples mound & tower; our paramount whose valour powders mountains, whose coal-hot exhortation vaporizes fountains, whose horses' hooves shoot firebolts, who storms & conquers & none revolts.

Extol our gracious doctor, our sagacious practitioner, whose generosity bolsters poorling & petitioner. Companions, bow to your Joseph, Wisdom's lode & rock, saviour of our worn flock, who looks for lost journeyers &, those once found, restores broke bones, looses bonded & bound. Loud, loud afford encomia to our benevolent lord, who buoys our downcast people; oh, shout roundelays to one whose wondrous odours & bouquets overrun Zion's wood—odours of rose oil, olibanum, bergamot, & cedarwood. Our second-to-none, our people's worthiest son, to whom Goodness proffers benison, our champion & tower before whom colossi cower.

Adore our religious vower & prodigious endower, our incomparable donor, gold's distributor, not owner, whose door

bow to your Joseph [Gen. 41: 43]. **looses bonded & bound** [Ps. 146: 7].

evermore opens upon our poor, whose unalloyed coin sows Salvation; terror of error & our foes' subjugation, to whom monarch & sovereign offer veneration, governors—approbation. Commemorate our worthy's progenitors, whose instruction & dedication begot goodness, candour, & probity—our lord's vocation.

Lord of creation, hoist to topmost station our rector & regeneration, restorer of Your holy congregation, protector of Your downtrod nation & luminous hope of our liberation. Forbear to show our Moses Your vexation & hot indignation. Compass our monarch's leastmost aspiration. Lord God of Hosts: bestow upon our champion honour & unparagoned renown unto Mortality's utmost generation.

Then he declared: Behold your request; and now I shall sing, to fatten this bequest. And he lifted his voice and sang:

Shout Sovereignty's joy & sovereigns' veneration,
whose noble blood boasts noblest derivation,
Our Cloud of Glory journeying before,
conducting our folk to holy elevation,
Who took for compass Torah &, ironwilled,
approached God's throne—oh, Holy Destination!
Our lord, above whose brow glows Wisdom's crown,
before whom monarchs proffer adoration,
Troth's bow, gold's flow, wrong's foe, Good's hoe, souls' glow,
God's own strong word, our anchor & salvation.
Oh, potent Providence, protect our lord
from dolour & misfortune's devastation.

Now when he had fulfilled their strict requirements every one and had outshone the very sun, he rested from all the labour that he had done. Thereon they declared, Our tongues cleave to our palates, we are astounded, confounded, dumbfounded! But now release a second letter from your puissant bow wherein no word, not

Lord God of Hosts [2 Sam. 5: 10; Isa. 22: 5; and elsewhere].

Our Cloud of Glory journeying before [Num. 9: 17–22].

he rested from all the labour that he had done Gen. 2: 2.

Our tongues cleave to our palates Ps. 137: 6.

one, contains the letter *O*; then shall we laud you to Heaven, none more fervent; let your deeds be seen now by each your eager servant.

Then he spoke, saying: Regard Israel's leader, her mighty & supernal cedar, Justice' planter & Virtue's breeder, fairest tent amidst Israel's tents, like waterside palms dripping rarest scents, an unfailing light, Evil's bane & Darkness' fright & his kinsmen's delight, beaming as the sun in his might. He issues his decree & silver gushes like the sea. He wears Integrity's triple plume, his name is fragrant as spilt perfume. See his eyes, burning & discerning, and his lips, sweet with learning. Ah, what a matchless giver, a blessed tree planted by Largesse' river; better: Largesse is his vessel & daily he embarks, his tack—the patriarchs'. In this tree's mighty branches Israel's wanderers make their nest: there the weary rest. Yes, Jewry dwells safely beneath this spreading vine that slakes their keen thirst with Deliverance' wine.

His race's stay, he bars the heart's gates, turning Grief away. He makes yesterday's slaves dawn's regents; willingly his kinsmen render him allegiance. Exemplary dispenser, ruler & sage, Virtue's standard & Faith's wage, he is Jewry's master, their bulwark against Disaster, their unchallenged chief, their shield & buckler against Grief. His is Right's lance, skewering Mischance. Their greatest & least accept him as father & priest. We laud his dam & applaud his sire: they, kindling in his breast charity's flame & virtue's fire, made learning his chiefest desire, wherewith he purchased fame & a bright & enduring name.

Then happy his children, happy his kin, happy all that win his presence & his seemly face, alive with care & heavenly grace. Happy his dwelling-place, happy they that enter his gates & walls: he sits them in his banquet halls where, manna-like, his endless nurture falls.

let your deeds be seen now by each your eager servant Ps. 90: 16.
her mighty & supernal cedar [Ezek. 17: 22].
palms dripping rarest scents Num. 24: 6–7.
beaming as the sun in his might [Judg. 5: 31].
his name is fragrant as spilt perfume [S. of S. 1: 3].
a blessed tree planted by Largesse' river [Ps. 1: 3].
there the weary rest Job 3: 17.
Jewry dwells safely beneath this spreading vine [1 Kgs. 5: 5].
Deliverance' wine [Isa. 12: 3].
father & priest [Judg. 17: 10; 18: 19].
manna-like, his endless nurture falls [Num. 11: 9; Ps. 78: 24].

Yes, his alms' balm shades needy guests like a leafy palm. The faint & weary kneel at this gushing stream where they eat their fill & drink wine & mead & thick, rich cream. The dead hear his name & revive, & he keeps the living alive. He salves pain: pity camps within his heart as Abram camped in Mamre's plain. Time chants his praise, garlanding his just head with leaves & bays.

May Israel's Redeemer grant him his desert: guard him against all hurt & dress him with Deliverance as with a skirt. All-Merciful, attend: extend him divine blessings passing any uttered & penned: ah, richly reward Israel's pride & Justice' best friend. Give him Thy ladder & help him ascend: raise his standard high, be his tent the sky, send him bright harvest until Time's end.

Then he lifted his voice and sang:

Judea's bright pride & her singular prince—
singular praise his acclaimers sing:
Justice his staff, Mercy his stay,
Sapience his signet & Faith his ring.
His merit is music that thrills Jewry's hearts,
his lineage a lute & he the chief string.
Kingly, delightful his liberal heart;
his kinsmen, delighted, exalt him as king.

SAID THE TELLER OF THE TALE:

The people, spellbound at that their happy ears had found, swept the shining rhetor off the ground, placed him on their shoulders and danced him round. They shouted, ululated, whooped; they wheeled, they swooped, spun, regrouped; then stuffed the poet's pockets till his shoulders drooped. At that his face glowed and his eyes flamed, and turning to leave he exclaimed:

I am Hever the clever: Song's cedars & palms
spring lush & green from my generous breast.
My tropes trip lightly: even as I rest
they dance to the ends of the East & West.

Abram camped in Mamre's plain [Gen. 13: 18, 14: 13].
dress him with Deliverance as with a skirt [Isa. 61: 10].
Give him Thy ladder & help him ascend [Gen. 28: 12].
cedars & palms spring lush & green [Ps. 92: 13].

I fit them for arrows to down my foes,
as a sword to cleave Time's helm & crest.
What penman, what lover, can match my joy
who have, at once, three brides possessed:
Arabic, Hebrew, & tongue of Aram—
three songbirds of Eden who trill from one nest,
They rise to the heights of the Zodiac
my name & my fame to manifest.
Enviers swarm round my head like bees,
they buzz incessant—but find no rest.
They pant & they puff, lame mountaineers;
crestfallen, crushed, they ne'er reach my crest.

swarm round my head like bees [Ps. 118: 11–12].

GATE TWELVE

Of the Ferocity of the Wars of Stint and Generosity

THUS SPOKE HEMAN THE EZRAHITE: I found myself in a large company of men of high degree whose acts proclaimed their pedigree, knights of Largesse confronting the theme of Stint, that bone-strewn wilderness. Their leader was Hever the Kenite of Zaananim, rhetor and arbiter supreme, whom the assembly asked to disclose where Stint was formed and whence arose.

*K*now, he said, that this beast first pitched amidst the sons of the East: from Babylon his kingdom mushroomed forth eastward and westward, and south and north. At the start he was but a greasy pot, a leper, a living rot, one sent beyond the camp; yet he it was whom the Creator chose to stamp with notability, and so commanded Generosity, Take you my robe of glory, my chariot, my horse and set your course—for thus I choose—for the house of Stint, and crown him king of the world's Jews.

*S*o Generosity took horse and robe at his Lord's beck, clothed Stint and looped the golden chain around his neck, set him upon the chariot in regal rite, crying, Thus shall be done unto the man who is the King's delight! With that, proud Stint was to the King's gate sped while Generosity slunk home with covered head.

*T*hen all asked Hever the Kenite to explain the start of Stint's

the sons of the East Gen. 29: 1.
from Babylon his kingdom mushroomed forth Gen. 10: 11.
eastward and westward, and south and north [Gen. 13: 14].
a leper, a living rot, one sent beyond the camp Lev. 13: 45–6.
Take you my robe of glory, my chariot, my horse Esther 6: 10.
crown him king of the world's Jews 1 Kgs. 12: 20.
took horse and robe . . . the King's delight Esther 6: 11.
home with covered head Esther 6: 12.

reign, his elevation to high station, how and when the Jews proclaimed him king of their scattered nation.

Know, he said, that in ancient times, in eastern climes, Stint and Vileness clung to one another like brother to brother, one roof above their head, sharing the selfsame bed. When the time came to set forth, they wandered north to Shinar's fair valley and there did dally. There the Lord gave them second birth and from thence scattered them over the face of the earth.

Now one day Stint spoke unto his companions and to his faithful minions, saying, I dreamed a dream this night: lo, I stood on a mighty height whence rose a fortress sky-high, awesome to the eye, its foundation wider and deeper than Creation. Suddenly I heard behind me a mighty sound: all danced before my eyes like lambs and crumbled to the ground.

His friends answered, Know that the mighty fortress is the Torah of the Lord, which is a mighty fortress; and the vast foundation signifies the leaders and elders of the far-flung Jewish nation; and as regards the tower's collapse to thunderclaps—know that God's folk shall be yours to command: the Kingdom of Israel shall be established in your hand. Nod, smile, or frown and their princes shall all bow them down. Stand tall, then, and crush your foes: what you close none shall open; what you open, none shall close.

After a few days' space Stint came upon a savant in the marketplace bearing the Book of Destiny, which sang his praise: *It shall come to pass in the end of days that the broad wall of Babylon shall be razed and the land of Shinar be upraised. Earth shall spawn a new creation, a hideous malformation from Babylon's land, who shall the East command. Stint shall be his name, child of Stinginess and Shame.*

At this, Stint was dazed, even amazed. Onward the seasons rolled, while he remembered all that had been foretold.

they wandered north to Shinar's fair valley and there did dally Gen. 11: 2.

and from thence scattered them over the face of the earth Gen. 11: 9.

I dreamed a dream Gen. 41: 15.

danced before my eyes like lambs Ps. 114: 4.

the Kingdom of Israel shall be established in your hand 1 Sam. 24: 20.

what you close none shall open; what you open, none shall close i.e. you shall have the absolute authority of a sovereign (Isa. 22: 22).

It shall come to pass in the end of days Isa. 2: 2.

the broad wall of Babylon shall be razed Jer. 51: 58.

Now it came to pass after some days that his dream became known to all the Holy Communities from Babylon's Elam to Egypt's No-Amon, that they did joyous say: Now we shall have a king to lead us on our way and turn our night to day. Oh Gates of Cheer, wide ope! We have a judge to raise our hope!

One day, Stint and his attendants set out to make their rounds through villages and towns. Scarce had they left the city's thoroughfares when four knights of Generosity overtook them unawares.

Behold, they said, he comes—this dreamer, this schemer who prophesies our slavery. Fellows in bravery, let us slay him and fling him to a pit; let us be quit of him, rid earth of his vile schemes and then see what will become of his dreams.

At this their leader said: Hush, let no blood be shed! Rather, loop his neck with hempen bands and likewise deck his hands. Let him be banished; let his lackeys scour the hilltops and find him vanished. Cast him in a cell in a lonesome citadel, the pompous fool; there let him rule, let him drool over scant water and meagre bread till he be dead.

At once they spurred on to surround him. They seized his horses, downed him, drew his blood, and in brass fetters bound him, then locked him in a citadel with only clouds around him. Yes, they flung him in a murky chamber all apart. Listener, smite your heart and grieve: none could come there, none leave that dungeon, lit by two sunbeams squeezed through a stony slit. To guard him in this hold his captors chose five hundred warriors strong and bold, Generosity's picked corps—skilled swordsmen, mighty men of war.

At that, the Jews of Sepharvaim and Babylon loosed a cry of

Now it came to pass after some days Gen. 4: 3.
No-Amon Nah. 3: 8—Thebes (in upper Egypt).
Now we shall have a king to lead us 1 Sam. 8: 19.
Behold, they said, he comes—this dreamer Gen. 37: 19.
and then see what will become of his dreams Gen. 37: 20.
let no blood be shed Gen. 37: 22.
scant water and meagre bread Isa. 30: 20.
in brass fetters bound him 2 Kgs. 25: 7.
none could come there, none leave Josh. 6: 1.
skilled swordsmen, mighty men of war S. of S. 3: 8.
Sepharvaim 2 Kgs. 17: 31 and elsewhere; city usually identified with Sippara, between Baghdad and Babylon (BDB, 709).

shame, which to Assyria came and flowed to Aram Naharaim, a mighty hum, then roared on to Egypt and thence to the Beautiful Land was come: that Stint, their lord, was prisoner ta'en, seized of their foes and given over to cruel pain.

Now the men were sore aggrieved, choked with bile, that their king was sent forth to exile. This, they said, is a sore predicament: we thought our monarch had been Heaven-sent to rule over us, to go us before in peace and war that we, God's people, lose not our way like sheep gone astray. And now robbers from among our people have set cruel snares, that our sweet Sun has set: the breath of our nostrils, God's anointed, is caught in their net—him whom we had held a very tree of life, our light and Salvation's, him of whom we had said, In his shade shall we live among the nations. Brothers, lift hands and plea: Lord, look down from Heaven and see!

Now after many days in prison pent, Stint, desolate and spent, recalled how he had left at home a dove that did him deeply love and daily voiced that love, note after dulcet note. These thoughts constrained his throat. Embittered, he sank upon his iron bed and lo—a man stood by his head and said: *Even for those of you who live among the sheepfolds there are wings of a dove sheathed in silver, its pinions in fine gold. When the Almighty scattered the kings, it seemed like a snowstorm in Salmon.*

Then, waking with moan and sigh and streaming eye, whom did the dazed monarch spy but his own true dove, cooing on the sill, hopping about and thrusting with her bill, bitter, heartsore, and unreconciled as a mother who has lost her only child.

At this strange waking, the king, his heart near breaking,

Aram Naharaim Gen. 24: 10 and elsewhere; Mesopotamia (BDB, 74).
the Beautiful Land Dan. 11: 16, 41; the land of Israel.
their king was sent forth to exile Jer. 49: 3.
to rule over us, to go us before in peace and war 1 Sam. 8: 19–20.
like sheep gone astray Num. 27: 16.
have set cruel snares [Jer. 18: 22].
the breath of our nostrils, God's anointed, is caught in their net Lam. 4: 20.
a very tree of life Gen. 2: 9, Prov. 3: 18.
our light and Salvation's [Ps. 27: 1].
him of whom we had said, In his shade shall we live among the nations Lam. 4: 20.
Lord, look down from Heaven and see Lam. 3: 50.
a man stood by his head Gen. 28: 13.
Even . . . Salmon Ps. 68: 14–15.

scooped up his soul's delight and, holding her tight, lifted his voice and sobbed:

O distant dove: by God above
I am now remembered! Oh, sweet my love,
Dost thirst? Have no fears: drink deep of my tears
or I thine as we bleed from the thrust of Fate's spears.
God safeguard thee whose loyalty
shames turncoat friends—oh, perfidy!
I rot out of sight in an endless night,
while none, ah none, bring my cause to light.

My dear, who told you I was here that you wing to my side with comfort and cheer? Be you recompensed of the Lord and for this work gain full reward. Oh, fair lily of Faith's green season, you have not joined the ranks of Treachery and Treason. And now, dear bird, who dost so deeply love me, spread Compassion's wings above me: stir up my people with your sweet chirrup, resort to my capital and bear report of how I am made Time's butt and sport.

That said, with many a purposed wink and blink he moistened a sliver of coal for teary ink. Then, finding a scrap of parchment in his cage, he shaped a tiny page whereon he penned two lines, then a third, and then a fourth; binding it to the dove's wings, he sent her forth as the sun died in the west. Eschewing rest the bird was gone, to speed to the palace in Babylon where she hovered before one, and now another, courtier's face, trilling her lord's distress and disgrace. Exhausted, and flayed by fear's knout, she lighted, then hopped frantically about until the servants saw the scroll attached to her wing with a mangy string.

At once they took the missive out, read it, and raised a thunderous shout. Mightily vexed, they sent it from one city to the next; but not before they took the dove, embraced her, kissed her, and placed her on a satin cushion and did her deck with gold and silver

distant dove Literal translation of the second and fourth words of the Hebrew phrase prefixed to Ps. 56, *al yonat elem reḥokim*, probably identifying the melody to which it was to be sung.

Be you recompensed of the Lord and for this work gain full reward Ruth 2: 12.

dove's wings, he sent her forth Gen. 8: 12.

links about her neck; and therein did the dream unfold: *wings of a dove sheathed in silver, its pinions in fine gold.*

And this is the content of the missive sent by Stint from his prison cell to those who wished him well:

Greetings from on high to them that stand me by, though they be few. O comrades tried and true, who do me cherish: I am sold to be destroyed, to be slain, to perish. My eyes darken, shallow my breath: there is but one step between me and death. It is beyond my ken: the faithful fail from among the children of men. Shall I, your king, lie lice-rid and spurned? Where be the hearts that once for battle burned? Warriors turn cravens, chiefs—churls, guardsmen—girls. Have you forgotten all that I have won for you, dismissed all that I have done for you, you who have eaten of my bread and drunken of my cup? Recall, I have swaddled you like my own children and brought you up.

Ah, see how Time has paid me: I am forgot by them who should have succoured me and stayed me, I have nurtured and brought up children and they have betrayed me. O my people, recall your king, I pray: uphold your covenant with me this day. My cup of bitters swells up to the brim, I sink in Misery's waters and cannot swim; keep faith—my vigour fades, my eyes grow dim. Fate skewers me and turns me on his spit: ah, friends, what profit you that I go down unto the Pit? Take arms, stand by me, be my stay and staff; and know that the Lord will fight on your behalf.

Now when this missive reached Jewry's scattered congregations they played their harps no more but wept full sore, raising a mighty roar from Zion's heights to Africa's northernmost shore. They laid

wings of a dove sheathed in silver, its pinions in fine gold Ps. 68: 14.

I am sold to be destroyed, to be slain, to perish Esther 7: 4.

there is but one step between me and death 1 Sam. 20: 3.

the faithful fail from among the children of men Ps. 12: 2.

who have eaten of my bread and drunken of my cup 2 Sam. 12: 3.

I have swaddled you like my own children and brought you up Lam. 2: 22.

I have nurtured and brought up children and they have betrayed me Isa. 1: 2.

uphold your covenant with me this day Jer. 33: 20.

my vigour fades, my eyes grow dim Deut. 34: 7.

what profit you that I go down unto the Pit Ps. 30: 10.

the Lord will fight on your behalf Exod. 14: 14.

they played their harps no more Ezek. 26: 13.

away their robes, hearts weak and failing, put off their broidered garments, dizzy and ailing: in every province where the king's word came there was great mourning for the Jews, much weeping and much wailing. The ram's horn loosed its blast as many lay in sackcloth and in ashes and in fast. Then, stirred by God's hand, the people's leaders gathered in the Glorious Land, in Emek Habakhah/the Valley of Tears, whence they sent a letter telling their compeers of their anguish and their fears: how their sins had recompensed them, how God's arm was raised against them.

And these were the lines upon that parchment traced:

Peace to our holy congregations! Brothers, make haste! Is it time for you to dwell in your wainscoted houses while the house of our king lies waste? Shall you sound harp and drum, and leap and bound, kill kine and pass the goblet round while our king lies bound? Know you that our God has bid us end our monarch's pains, snap the oppressor's whips and chains. Who among you of his people (God be with him!) will echo our alarm, will revenge our king with a mighty hand and an outstretched arm? Rise, rise! Choose Jews of valour with swords on thighs; choose lions, soaring eagles, hissing adders—then storm the heavens with your own shot shafts for ladders. Surge forward like rivers, gushing and true, bows ready, hands steady, firm of heart and thew: come to Emek Habakhah and let us found the kingship anew!

Like lightning did this missive strike the hearts of old and young alike. Inspired of God, Jews rallied to the banner, full fifty thousand men, and in this manner: they streamed from Egypt and Jordan, proud and tall, from the Beautiful Land, Damascus, and Hamath in answer to their monarch's call, from Haran to Aram Naharaim to

They laid away their robes Ezek. 26: 16.

in every province . . . much wailing Esther 4: 3.

in sackcloth and in ashes and in fast Joel 1: 13–14.

Emek Habakhah/the Valley of Tears Ps. 84: 7.

Is it time for you to dwell in your wainscoted houses while the house of our king lies waste Hag. 1: 4.

our king lies bound S. of S. 7: 6.

Who among you of his people (God be with him!) Ezra 1: 3.

with a mighty hand and an outstretched arm Deut. 4: 34.

come to Emek Habakhah and let us found the kingship anew 1 Sam. 11: 14.

Beautiful Land . . . Ashur On the locales and communities designated by Alḥarizi see the Analysis, esp. n. 5.

Ashur—a pounding waterfall thundering from Arbel to Adinah, yea, to proud Babylon's wall.

*B*rows knit and with a high hand, they surged to Hermon's pleasant land, vast as the sea's waves or the shore's sand. Long blasts upon the ram's horn were blown as the faithful fell like snow—in fulfilment of the ancient dream—on Mount Hermon: *When the Almighty scattered the kings, it seemed like a snowstorm in Salmon.*

*N*ow when this report reached the defenders of the fort, they felt like felons in a court of last resort. Hearing the trampling feet and horn and rattling sword and sabre, they shook like women in labour.

*T*hey sent out messengers to their fellow patrons, crying, Brothers, awake, awake! The lintels of the door are smit and the posts shake! Oh, for sweet Heaven's sake, Right's minions: how long will you be slack, how long halt between two opinions? Ruin stalks Lord Generosity's dominions! Mount and ride, fly to our side, else shall we rise, flee by night, and leave the city open wide.

*T*heir comrades answered, Stir not: tomorrow you shall have help before the sun be hot.

*N*ow on the third day in the morning Terror came a-borning: there was thunder and lightning from the swords' crash and the spears' flash, shrouding the mountain with a thick cloud as the voice of the trumpet waxed exceeding loud. The troops of Generosity drew up, a paltry force, ringing the castle, man and horse, to front the sons of Judah and Ephraim, their awesome foe, thick as the driven snow. Indeed, the camp of the patrons and generous men were like two little flocks of kids in a pen, while their opponents, ready for the slaughter, filled the land like a body of mighty water. Horns blew, and blood-

with a high hand Deut. 33: 3.
vast as the sea's waves or the shore's sand Gen. 22: 17.
they shook like women in labour Isa. 13: 8.
The lintels of the door are smit and the posts shake Amos 9: 1.
how long will you be slack Josh. 18: 3.
how long halt between two opinions 1 Kgs. 18: 21.
and leave the city open wide Josh. 8: 17.
tomorrow you shall have help before the sun be hot 1 Sam. 11: 9.
Now on the third day in the morning Exod. 19: 16.
there was thunder and lightning . . . waxed exceeding loud Exod. 19: 16.
like two little flocks of kids in a pen 1 Kgs. 20: 27.
filled the land like a body of mighty water [Isa. 11: 9].

red standards pricked the sky; the troops of Judah and of Ephraim drew nigh, numerous as the sands of the sea and the stars of the sky.

Suddenly their princes shouted, Brothers, cease! The Torah says: When you approach a city to attack it, first cry peace. Now every man who fronts us is our brother, flesh of our flesh, our spirit and none other. Let us sue for peace, let not one bone be broken!—to which the warriors cried, Well spoken!

So Judah and Ephraim sent messengers to the fort's defenders suing for surrender, saying, Our brothers, flesh and kin: stay your hands from sin. Open wide your gates that we might enter in and win our king's release, then go our way in peace. Pray let us be of one accord: ask what you will, only afford us the freedom of our lord; but rebel, and you shall be devoured of the sword, yea, we shall smite you hip and thigh. Then turn you from your evil ways: why, why, O house of Israel, should you die?

Now when their brothers received this message they held it rubbish, broken crockery: they laughed, they jibed, they made of it a mockery, so that their kinsmen turned into a raging band, pouring out to battle with a high hand; and first to take the field were the princes of Adinah, bright with sword and shield. Singing, they declared:

Who dares to stand and front us,
dares bark in the face of our throng.
We are sons of Abel, the light of the world,
Time's pride and Praise's song.
What matter to us if the sun be hid?
Our swords shall serve for suns.
What matter to us if we die on the field?
We bequeath our bright name to our sons.
Rest we eschew; we shall live on in pain
till we rescue our master from Slavery's chain.

numerous as the sands of the sea and the stars of the sky Gen. 22: 17.
When you approach a city to attack it, first cry peace Deut. 20: 10.
flesh of our flesh Gen. 2: 23.
Open wide your gates that we might enter in Ps. 24: 7, 9.
but rebel, and you shall be devoured of the sword Isa. 1: 20.
smite you hip and thigh Judg. 15: 8.
turn you from your evil ways: why, why, O house of Israel, should you die? Ezek. 33: 11.
with a high hand Exod. 14: 8.

Then the magnates of Ashur approached and said:

Before our swords' flash, the light of the sun
is grey slate in a coal-black hole.
If battle be form, we be that form's form;
if body, then we be its soul.
Beware our spears' lightning—it burns, it burns,
consuming the light of day.
We seek our lord's vengeance and never shall rest
till we bear him from prison away.
Never we rest, sirs, never we falter:
our lives we bear, forfeit, to Faithfulness' altar.

Then the aristocrats of Arbel came forward and declared:

Before our swords' lightning the sun and the moon
are as dark as black, worm-eaten shrouds.
Our weapons rain blood till the earth turns to mud,
our giving inspires the clouds.
Rest we forswear till we die, sword in hand,
redeeming our leader. We chorus:
Time, heed—God's anointed delays; rise you up,
make a God who will walk on before us.

Then the merchants of Haran declared:

With the crash of our swords and the flash of our spears
we leave enemies' mothers barren;
Our blades, roving free in the flesh of the foe,
are redder than roses of Sharon.
Revenge for the king! is our cry; we press on,
resting never; no, never; nay, never!
If we die for our monarch, the happier we,
resplendent in glory forever.

if body, then we be its soul This superlative refers to the Platonic dualistic concept of form versus matter, body versus soul—form/soul being foremost in value.

make a God who will walk on before us Exod. 32: 1.

roses of Sharon S. of S. 2: 1.

Then the sons of Aram Naharaim declared:

Front us, O Heavens, for never we shrink,
we sons of Aram Naharaim.
Rest shall we never until we renew
righteous rule for the sons of Ephraim.
Shouting, we leap into carnage and slaughter
till earth runs with blood and with guts as with water.

Then the heroes of Calneh declared:

We be heroes of Calneh, the pride of the age,
we crouch, we snarl, we leap.
We ravage the bowmen of foemen like lions
set loose in a pen full of sheep.
We rush to greet death with our arms open wide:
ere he calls us, we answer the call,
Eschewing all rest till the lord of our lives
is released from black Anarchy's thrall.
Though his crown be removed, though he lie in the dust,
he shall rise, he shall shine—yes, command;
Though his sheep be removed to the earth's farthest ends
they shall pass 'neath their shepherd's fair hand.

Then the heroes of Pisgah declared:

We Pisgites are noblemen, warriors, hot flames—
yea, moulded of flames from on high.
Let the ocean confront us, we care not a whit:
with a roar we shall render it dry.
All rest we eschew till we succour our lord,
restore him from darkness to light.
We shall shatter the foe, for one man of us, one,
can set thousands, ten-thousands, to flight.

ere he calls us, we answer the call Isa. 65: 24.
they shall pass 'neath their shepherd's fair hand Jer. 33: 13.
one, can set thousands, ten-thousands, to flight Deut. 32: 30.

Then the men of Hamath declared:

The wrath of the men of Hamath forges flames:
we are Battle's own fathers and scions.
We savage our foes with the teeth of the wolf,
we ravage our foemen like lions.
We shall swallow our enemy up like the flood
till we haul up our king from the mire.
In battle's mad swirl we have hearts will not flinch
being hewn out of shot flames of fire.

Then the men of Damascus declared:

God's chosen are we, cunning merchants of death:
we approach, and the enemy fears.
Whenever we fight, Heaven's stars shine the brighter
rekindled by sparks from our spears.
From the day that our lord was enchained we wear
sackcloth and ashes—we shun all dissembling.
Sleep we forswear; we shall harry his foes, yea,
serve them a cup full with trembling.
We shall skewer his foes till the nations proclaim:
Behold ye this nation and praise ye its name.

Then the hosts of the Beautiful Land declared:

God's messengers we in the Beautiful Land,
deer-swift, we are masters of earth.
Should the stars from their courses attack us—why, poof:
we would fling them back, each to his berth.
From the day that the foe caught and prisoned our lord
our hearts are perplexed and downcast.
We say to our souls: Hide yourselves—as it were—
for a moment, till anger be past.

hewn out of shot flames of fire Ps. 29: 7.
we wear sackcloth and ashes [Esther 4: 1].
serve them a cup full with trembling Zech. 12: 2.
Should the stars from their courses attack us Judg. 5: 20.
Hide yourselves—as it were—for a moment, till anger be past Isa. 26: 20.

Then the picked troops of Fustat declared:

Behold: Heaven's Lord comes to Egypt once more,
He rides swiftly, He mounteth the cloud—
To give aid, as of old, in the day of fierce fray,
to bold Judah and Ephraim proud.
Lions of battle, we leap and we roar
as the foe flies like chaff o'er the plains.
Our hearts will not rest nor our lips know a smile
while our monarch lies weeping in chains.
In battle's hot flame we press on, give no quarter
till all of our foemen are splattered like water.

Then the mighty men of No-Amon declared:

The waves of our soldiery sweep o'er the field
bold as lions and swifter than harts.
The points of our spears are the lightning-bolt's flash,
they skewer our enemies' hearts.
We weary of life, we hunger for death,
lamenting the loss of our lord.
We never shall rest till the foe turns and flees
in hot terror before our bright sword.
Though the light of the day be as white as the moon,
the dust that we raise turns it black;
When the hosts of our soldiery spill o'er the field
the sea flees and the Jordan turns back.

THEN THE TELLER OF THE TALE DECLARED:

At that, bows arched and swords were drawn. Words set like dead suns as the warriors pressed on into battle's black dawn. The sun set at noon and dust covered the moon. The sword planted corpses in the groaning earth; heroes cried out like women giving birth. Blood

He rides swiftly, he mounteth the cloud Isa. 19: 1.
We weary of life Gen. 27: 46.
the sea flees and the Jordan turns back Ps. 114: 3–5.
The sun set at noon Amos 8: 9.
cried out like women giving birth Isa. 42: 14.

flowed like the Nile, as many plunged shouting to Death's defile. Swords intermittent sent up spark after spark while earth sank in a flood of dark: yea, the mountain burned with fire to the midst of the heavens, with darkness and clouds and thick dark.

Now it came to pass at midday, that the troops of Generosity gave way and the sons of Judah and Ephraim took sway. Shouting *Hurray! Hurray! Hurray!* they broke the lines of Generosity like flaxen cords; they chased their foe through hill and dale with waving swords; they battered them, scattered them, shattered them, then took the fords until the survivors, trembling slaves, buried themselves in the holes of rocks and in earthen caves.

Then every holy congregation surged forward as one man, a mighty aggregation, to burst the fortress gates with booming voice: *Rejoice! Rejoice!* At the sound of their thunder the ground beneath them nearly clove asunder. Stint, drawn and pale from long confinement and travail, they led forth from his chamber of stone to set upon a golden throne.

Then was the monarch ringed by the leaders of each congregation: to his right, Adinah's princes, high of station; to his left, Ashur's venerables, a numerous legation; before him Calneh's faithful, sounding acclamation; behind him Pisgah's warriors, breathless with adoration; and opposite, Damascus' doctors, richest of an exiled nation. Their king passed before them as their wet eyes gleamed; they praised the Lord their God that thus He had deemed to shower them with good: their monarch was redeemed. They bowed down all, great and small, and their ruler's eyes beamed, for he remembered the dream that he had dreamed. With hearts overjoyed, with gladness unalloyed, all his subjects, known and obscure, rich and poor, young and mature, proud and demure, let their voices loud ring, Long live

the mountain burned with fire to the midst of the heavens, with darkness and clouds and thick dark Deut. 4: 11.

they broke the lines of Generosity like flaxen cords [Judg. 15: 14].

they battered them, scattered them, shattered them, then took the fords Judg. 12: 4–5.

buried themselves in the holes of rocks and in earthen caves Isa. 2: 19.

the ground beneath them nearly clove asunder Num. 16: 31.

he remembered the dream that he had dreamed Gen. 42: 9.

the king! They made that day a day of feasting and of gladness, then kept it year by year to raise up cheer and banish sadness.

*F*rom that day forth, my friends, Stint's rule has spilled to the Diaspora's ends. So widespread is his never-ending feast that throughout the lands of the East Generosity is stripped of station and protection, even lost to recollection. Stint holds the Diaspora in fee from Adinah to the Beautiful Land, from the Great Desert unto Lebanon and the Last Sea, leaving Generosity but crumbs and lees or two or three berries in the tops of the boughs of the uttermost trees.

SAID THE TELLER OF THE TALE:

*F*or this our hearts are faint and our eyes grow dim, for this our spirits melt, the cup of bitters overruns the brim—for the mountain of Generosity that is desolate, its sweet prince gone; foxes walk thereon. Oh, Lord, let our petition not be spurned: turn us unto Thee and we shall be turned. Raise high the horn of Generosity, so long enslaved; in his day Judah shall be saved.

They made that day a day of feasting and of gladness, then kept it year by year Esther 9: 17–18.

the Last Sea The Mediterranean, as in Deut. 34: 2.

two or three berries in the tops of the boughs of the uttermost trees Isa. 17: 6.

For this our hearts are faint and our eyes grow dim Lam. 5: 17.

for the mountain of Generosity that is desolate, its sweet prince gone; foxes walk thereon Lam. 5: 18.

turn us unto Thee and we shall be turned Lam. 5: 21.

Raise high the horn Ezek. 29: 21.

in his day Judah shall be saved Jer. 23: 6.

GATE THIRTEEN

Wherein Shall a Man be Whole? A Debate of Body, Mind, and Soul

THUS SPOKE HEMAN THE EZRAHITE: Long pent in Sin's coil, all fraught and spent, I longed to repent, longed to scour my heart and make new start, depart in haste from Deception's waste, and taste the manna of the soul's hosanna. Now it chanced on a day that I made my way to Hever the Kenite, who thus to me did say: No longer can I roam; I must go home. Before I am taken from you, ask what you will.

Dear friend, I answered, one request fulfil. Lend me a portion of your power and glory: teach me an allegory deep and bright that will lead me from darkness into light. Show me the recompense waiting body and soul: shall it be split between the two, or given one or both whole?

Well asked, said he, for in this, there is no other redeemer but me. I shall reach into the store of our fathers' lore and unscroll the truths of body and soul.

Said I, God grant you full reward; lead on to where your gems are stored.

He said, Know that on Judgement Day, when the ledgers shall be opened and assessed, and men find themselves cursed or blessed, when deeds shall prove potent seeds flowering to salvation or damnation, when heavenly scribes tell each man's tale, when sins and good deeds dance in God's scale, then shall sinners shake and shudder, then shall poor helmsmen quake and curse the rudder. Then shall

taste the manna [Num. 11: 7–8].

Before I am taken from you, ask what you will 2 Kgs 2: 9.

there is no other redeemer but me Ruth 4: 4.

God grant you full reward Ruth 2: 12.

body and soul perforce resort to Heaven's high court, stand before God and give report.

Then the Soul shall speak, addressing the Body: O destroying flesh that through marsh and mire hast trod—art thou not ashamed before thy God? Thou turnest Resolve's mansions to rubble; thou it is that art the cause of all this trouble. Daily hast thou fanned my desires, yea, stoked my fires with thy vice, filled me with ill advice, sweet lies of wine and breasts and thighs. Oh, thy roving eyes ever meant to rob me of my breath and sell me in perpetuity to Death.

Then the Body answered, saying, Soul impure, that ever did me sway and lure—ho, my daughter, thou hast destroyed me sure! What, am I to blame? What power have I for sin or shame?

Said the Soul, I sat in that high ring closest the King, made my singing nest in God's own breast; yet I abandoned Heaven's board, departed the sons of the Lord to be thy guide and truest friend, to better thy end; but thou through lust didst deprave me and enslave me, leddest me to drink and dine on meat and wine, leave the sweet breezes of God's laws for Belial's storms to revel in lissom forms, to glut on cherries ripe and fresh, with white garments cover thy flesh—and never those linens soil—and anoint thy flesh with oil. But what are oils and finery to me? Is it my place to seek fair forms' embrace, fill a belly and tremble at a face? This is thy exercise and gaiety, pertaining naught to me.

The Body replied, Not so! I lay a cast-forth stone, mute and lone, till thou didst swoop down from the skies and open my eyes, set me on my feet, teach me to feel, to speak, to eat. Of such delights what had I known until thou didst claim me as thy own?

At these words, the Soul paled her, turned faint, her courage failed her. Now when Intelligence saw the Soul step back in confusion at Passion's attack, saw that the foul Body in Reason's guise was

---

art thou not ashamed before thy God? Ezra 9: 6.
thou it is that art the cause of all this trouble Jonah 1: 7.
sell me in perpetuity Exod. 21: 1–6.
ho, my daughter, thou hast destroyed me sure Judg. 11: 35.
the sons of the Lord Gen. 6: 2, 4; Job 1: 6, 2: 1.
to better thy end Deut. 8: 16.
white garments cover thy flesh Eccles. 9: 8.
anoint thy flesh with oil [Ps. 23: 5].

crushing Truth with his lies, he roused himself and cried, Pure Soul, taken from God's glory and in fleshly gaol forsaken—awaken! Guard early and late against the lion that croucheth at the gate, who would, at his whim, rend thee limb from limb. Scrape off the Body's mire, purge thy uncleanness in Repentance' fire. Rest not until thou fulfil thy desire and God's intent—to live in Glory where first thou didst pitch thy tent.

Then he spoke, saying:

My Soul, if thou be naked of good,
raiment seek above:
Robe in the bright of Creation's light,
wing skyward like the dove.
What wilt thou say on Judgement Day,
what answer shall be thine?
Wash well thy heart in the Stream of Right,
scour it till it shine.
Disperse, for thy health, thy worthless wealth,
barter today for tomorrow;
Look to thy years gone up as mist
and hang down thy head in sorrow.
Provide. Make journey to Mitkah/Sweet;
Marah/Bitters depart.
Send down grief's bolts, rain tears, in clouds
of penitence wrap thy heart.
Sleeper—behold: thy companions rise
at midnight to weep and to praise.
Lust's waves rear high, thy vessel lists—
up, the vessel raise!
Bricks hast thou baked aplenty and thick
to build thyself cities of leisure.

against the lion that croucheth at the gate Num. 24: 9; [Gen. 4: 7].
where first thou didst pitch thy tent Gen. 13: 3.
Wash well thy heart Jer. 4: 14.
Make journey to Mitkah/Sweet; Marah/Bitters depart Num. 33: 8–9, 28–9.
thy companions rise at midnight to weep and to praise The reference is to the awakening during the early hours of the morning for penitential prayers. See *EJ* xiv. 1133–4; and Fleischer, *Hebrew Liturgical Poetry* (Heb.), 39, 402–3.
Bricks hast thou baked aplenty and thick to build thyself cities of leisure Exod. 1: 11–14.

Thy lust's stores mount; thou shalt render account
at Judgement for each day's measure.
Behold thou a crucible of gold
burning bright in the Lord's right hand.
If thou prove pure—why, thy good is sure;
if not, how shalt thou stand?
Storm-tossed, near-lost, when shalt thou heave
to the port of God's Truth and Good Sense?
How long wilt thou ride at Rebellion's side
and take refuge in Pride's black tents?
Whistling at Virtue, thy rightful lord,
thou liest with the sons of Lust
And on that frail reed, the traitor Time,
darest to set thy trust!
Delay not, cast off thy shackles all,
seek thy Master, anchor weigh;
Sail to the camp of our Holy God
and there with me ever stay.

Then the Soul said to the Intellect: How can one break the bands forged by cruel and iron hands? What charm, what potion shall draw me up from this raging ocean? Lust hisses, strikes, and never spares me; the Body ever snares me. The one is a whip, the other a bar: woe is me for I have dwelled in Meshekh, have pitched in the tents of Kedar.

Then she lifted her voice and sang:

From highest Heavens my crystal stream
to the darkest Pit down spilt.
Yes, exiled from Heaven I entered the flesh
and there my castle built.

thou shalt render account at Judgement for each day's measure Exod. 5: 6–19.

on that frail reed, the traitor Time, darest to set thy trust 2 Kgs. 18: 21; Isa. 36: 6.

and there with me ever stay At this point (*ST*, 142. 13) the translator has taken the liberty of moving a bloc of seven stichs of the Hebrew, which seem inexplicably out of place here, to the end of the gate, where they comprise the final thanksgiving of the soul. Standing here they destroy the drama and logic of the entire debate.

woe is me for I have dwelled in Meshekh, have pitched in the tents of Kedar Ps. 120: 5.

Loved, entwined in my Father's arms,
laughing, virginal, young,
I found me betrothed on a day to the flesh
and into his rude arms flung.
He seizes me foully, day and night,
despite my tears and pleas;
Offspring I bear him daily—
tens of thousands upon his knees.
Oh, Thou, my first love, by day and by night
I weep on my fate and my need,
I sicken in longing, the while my heart moans,
moans like a hollow reed.
Earth cannot bear the keen love of my Love,
but I bear it, yea, ask even more.
Why hath He held me a faithless wife
who never have played the whore?
Why hath He tendered me bitter drink,
who never have gone astray?
Could the drops of my eyes match my sorrow's flood
I had washed the world away.
I shake at the sight of souls soaring to God
whilst here I must remain!
My tears ever rise to my staring eyes,
then furrow my cheeks like rain.
Recalling my years on the Mountains of Spice
I sway and I seize my head.
Flee! I must flee from the flesh and step free,
for locked in the flesh I am dead!
Wayfarers: blessings convey to my Love,
Him whom my soul holdeth fast.
Say: since I dined at His nectared board
I tremble in weeping and fast.

laughing Prov. 8: 30–1.
Offspring I bear him daily . . . upon his knees Gen. 20: 53.
have played the whore Ezek. 16: 30; Hos. 2: 7, 9: 1; and elsewhere.
tendered me bitter drink Num. 5: 18–27.
the Mountains of Spice S. of S. 8: 14.

Since the day He denied me His goblet of love
I drink to the lees cups of gall.
No taste will I have but His tongue's: wine, milk,
mead, honey—I spurn them all.
My eyes, once bright, are with Wandering's shafts
harsh smitten, yea, stricken blind;
Others have found the straight path to God,
my own I cannot find.
I quiver, a near-extinguished flame
who shone bright in God's innermost room;
At the thought of Last Judgement my spirit swoons:
oh, the certainty of doom!
Lo, as a servant lifts eyes to his lord
I lift up mine eyes to God's throne
And pray I may walk unafraid once more
in the halls where I brightly shone.

Then Desire said to the Soul: Wretched Soul, arise—thou whose cup runneth over with the wine of sighs. Time shall Youth's regency banish; in the wink of an eye thy splendour shall vanish, thy flesh o'ergrown with wormwood in a house of stone; in an instant thy ruin shall root and bear bitter fruit. Do not alloy thy happiness with tears nor all thy good destroy; in this world, cleave to Joy! Know what awaits the close of life's hard tourney—no joy, no peace, no rest, no further journey. Decide thee: live with Merriment beside thee—for in death all shall be denied thee. In the Pit thou shalt not make good thy loss, nor refine thy dross. Now leave off Intellect with his prating and his upturned eyes; he shall never make good his pack of lies.

Then he lifted his voice and sang:

Rebuff the Intellect's folly, Soul;
chirrup and frolic, cavort and shout.
Take of sweet Time thy portion whole
before thou reclinest with dust about.

I drink to the lees cups of gall Lam. 3: 15.
harsh smitten, yea, stricken blind Gen. 19: 11.
Lo, as a servant lifts eyes to his lord . . . to God's throne Ps. 123: 2 [and 121: 1].
cup runneth over Ps. 23: 6.

Then wilt thou dance? Then raise the cup?
Sing in thy blood, now! Sing in thy breath!
Pamper thy tongue with sweet kisses and wine
before thou slide down the wide tongue of Death.
Then leave the dull preachers their rant and their cant,
moan thou for pleasure: rejoice, be glad;
Only in flesh, the sweating flesh,
the fretting flesh, can joy be had.
The tall gates of Grief thou openest wide
but joy and contentment thou lockest away.
Assassins raise swords to end other men's lives;
weaponless, thou thy poor self dost slay.
The World is a garden, the World is a vault
with diamonds abounding—why wouldst thou flee it?
The Intellect lures thee to Lie's thick cage;
open thy eyes and see it!
Flesh ripe and fresh, silk flowing like milk—
Soul, these be thine, all these!
God in His mercy these portions allots—
do thou thy portion seize.
Refrain thy voice from weeping, dear heart,
refrain from tears thine eye.
Rise from the pit of wretchedness
to beam forth in Pleasure's sky.
Thou art, in the Body, a morning star;
in the pit, a maggot art.
Know: thou shalt not be summoned to joy
once to dust thou dost depart.

Then the Intellect said to the Soul, O holy Soul, ringed by Desire's chain: thy self restrain! Be not tempted by the Body's lies: his coin naught buys. Know that a mortal king, an earthly lord, rests not till he tenders due reward to them who serve him with pen, plough, or sword. Now if a ruler of flesh and blood, sprung from worm and

do thou thy portion seize Eccles. 5: 18.

Refrain thy voice from weeping, dear heart, refrain from tears thine eye Jer. 31: 15.

mud, can open wide his purse, how much more so the Master of the Universe! On this depend: thy God, who hither did thee send, knoweth foe from friend: He shall raise thee to Eternal Life; there is hope for thy latter end.

Said the Soul: May I find favour in thine eyes! Thy wise comfort and counsel hath strengthened me in every wise and hath rescued me from the Evil Inclination's lies. Trust I shall in the merciful Ancient of Days to restore me to the fields of light and praise. I know, I hold that one must ever believe God's mercies manifold. As God lives, I know He pities and forgives.

Then the Soul lifted her voice and sang:

My Rock, Thou hast tested and tried me,
who would bury her sins in the sand.
I fly—but Lust rides me ever nigh,
Satan at my right hand.
Thee I forgot; me Thou hast not—
in Thy field of Love I dwell;
And now I recall, sweet Master,
Thou habitest me as well.
Lord of the world, reach down, touch my brow,
declare to my soul: ***Awake!***
Pity and Grace are afforded thee, not
for thy sake, but Mine own Name's sake.
Eden lies open before thee
with streams of Salvation—draw near;
Troubled, thou called and I answered, for I
am thy Lord, who responds, I am here.

Then he lifted his voice and sang:

I was born in Elon in fair Zaananim,
I am Hever the Kenite by name.

there is hope for thy latter end Jer. 31: 16.
May I find favour in thine eyes Ruth 2: 13.
Satan at my right hand Zech. 3: 1.
not for thy sake, but Mine own Name's sake Ezek. 20: 9, 14, 22.
I am thy Lord, who responds, I am here Isa. 52: 6.

I shoot darts of rebuke into somnolent hearts,
sear the sleeper with words forged of flame.
Penitence' gates I reveal and fling wide
to the righteous and faithful nation;
I save the frail flesh from the cauldron's fire,
the soul from the Pit's conflagration.
The evil desire, the body in lust
are but straw or a smoking brand;
Then happy the man who for Father takes God
and is led by that Father's firm hand.
He shall root from his heart transgression and sin,
plant contrition and right in their place.
Then shall he bask in Eternal Light
and look on his Maker's face.

gates I reveal and fling wide to the righteous and faithful nation Isa. 26: 2.
a smoking brand Isa. 7: 4.
bask in Eternal Light Job 33: 30.
look on his Maker's face Deut. 5: 4.

GATE FOURTEEN

Of a Prayer Beyond Price
Hewn from the Mountain of Spice

THUS SPOKE HEMAN THE EZRAHITE: Come through rough seas and Toil's straits to Gaza's gates, I found myself blessed, for there I came upon a man possessed of awesome wealth, knowledge culled like eggs from a nest.

He sat in a rich courtyard, if you please, students clustered round his knees, one of whom begged him, Pray you, my lord, cast us a gem you can so readily afford—a supplication to be shield and sword, cleave Heaven's gates, and win to the throne of the Lord.

As you ask, said he; come, drink of Wisdom's flask.

Thereat he swung Thought's pick and bared Wit's hidden lode; he spoke to the rock of his tongue and Wisdom's waters flowed.

Pursuers of Righteousness, come near me, hear me; attend my prayer, fair beyond compare. Recited with conviction, it will cast off affliction through godly benediction.

O King of every land and nation, Lord of Eternity, Master of all creation, Mansion of souls, the Cosmos' First and Last Foundation—I have come to bow before Thee, Thou who art singularly One, One before Time was begun and One when Time shall be done; true

Hewn from the Mountain of Spice [S. of S. 4: 6].

culled like eggs from a nest Isa. 10: 14.

spoke to the rock of his tongue and Wisdom's waters flowed Num. 20: 8. Here the speaker is characterized at once as prophet and miraculous source of poesy.

Pursuers of righteousness Isa. 51: 1.

Lord of Eternity Start of *Shokhen ad* prayer in the Sabbath liturgy.

Thou who art singularly One See ibn Gabirol's 'The Kingly Crown' in *Selected Religious Poems*, ed. I. Davidson (Philadelphia, 1924), cited below as KCD, §2, pp. 83–4, ll. 28–38.

One before Time was begun See KCD, §3, 84, ll. 42–3.

Good, supernal and eternal; unending Delight and inner Light seen only in Thought's sight; Saving Splendour, Good's fountain and defender, whose oneness knows no history, Pure Being and Ultimate Mystery, Primal Cause, Source of the Cosmos' laws, Spring of Probity, Honour, and Right, and Fountain of Justice' Might.

*A*ll creatures spring forth from Him; all that is, wings forth from Him. Immeasurably distant, yet responding in an instant, He exists for Himself alone: none share His life or His throne. His life, might, and wisdom are given at no other's hand; He it is who leads us in the paths of Righteousness through Probity's green land. Angels seek His essence and stumble; yet He abides with the lowly and the humble. Master of kindness and dispensation, He pours forth good—but through no obligation. Kindness and luminosity, He forgives sinners through the might of His generosity. Champion, who by power of His might, in the midst of His rage wipes transgression from His sight, turning sin's scarlet white.

*C*reator, not created; Originator, not originated. Ruler, with none to command Him; Mind beyond mind, with none to fully understand Him. Effector of all, with none at His right hand; Decreer, with none to second His command; Judge who sets bounds and borders, bound by no other's orders. Necessity does not curtail Him; never do His judgements nor His counsels fail Him.

*U*nto You I call, Upper Light, in the hid chambers of Your lofty

true Good, supernal and eternal See KCD, §1, p. 83, ll. 19–20.
seen only in Thought's sight KCD, §2, p. 84, l. 34.
knows no history KCD, §3, p. 84, l. 42; §4, p. 85, l. 46.
Pure Being and Ultimate Mystery KCD, §3, p. 84, l. 44.
Primal Cause KCD, §9, p. 88, ll. 96–106.
All creatures spring forth from Him; all that is, wings forth from Him KCD, §1, p. 83, ll. 22–3.
He exists for Himself alone: none share His life KCD, §3, p. 84, l. 41.
His life, might, and wisdom are given at no other's hand KCD, §4, p. 85, l. 46; §9, p. 87, l. 90.
He it is who leads us in the paths of Righteousness [Ps. 23: 3].
yet He abides with the lowly and the humble Isa. 57: 15.
He forgives sinners through the might of His generosity KCD, §6, p. 85, ll. 60–1.
turning sin's scarlet white [Isa. 1: 18].
Ruler, with none to command Him Sa'adiah Gaon, *Bakashah* 1, *SSG* 48, l. 2.
Mind beyond mind [KCD, §9, p. 87, ll. 90–1].
Upper Light KCD, §7, p. 86, l. 64.

site, Thought's quest, the lusting Soul's sought rest: O mysteried God, I ask Your grace; I ask Your aid, O near, yet distant Face, who, before space was formed, inhabited Your endless space.

*L*ord of Infinity, endless Divinity, I call upon You, even with impunity: by Your enduring might, by Your hid unity—lave me, save me from the pit of Desire, smother Perversion's fire, lift me from Lust's pyre, clothe me with right thought, You whose purity my soul has ever sought. You whose counsel knows no defect—give me good teaching, let me stand erect, bring me to the company of the elect, robe me with the silk of pure intellect.

*S*anctify me with holy thought that You have wholly wrought. Fountain of Knowledge, water me to the root that I might bear sweet, not bitter, fruit; that I might live truth-centred, that I leave not this world as I entered, a raw seed naked of high and holy deed.

O God, who bade me drink of Mercy's grape before I had matter or shape, yes, who thought of me kindly before my flesh knew form, who blessed my soul before my blood grew warm, who leaned from Heaven and fated me to be created, who called on the spheres and they spun, that my life might be begun; yes, He called on Heaven above and earth beneath, to wed the high-born soul with sinews, veins, blood, teeth; who, before He made me, fed blood's nurturing repast to my ancestors in ages past—which beneficence reached to my father and my mother. He, none other, bade Emptiness shatter, the Void scatter, and Nothingness yield matter; yes, He drew me forth from non-existence' hole and lent me His spirit that I might be whole.

*G*entle in His kindness I lay curled, deep in my mother's womb, until He drew me out into the world, breathed the breath of life into my chest, and fed me the bounty of my mother's breast. Then He graced me in my parents' eyes: they shouldered my pains, bowed low that I might rise. I grew, and generously He fed me, clothed me, guided me, bred me; yes, by Virtue's still waters led me. He lit Right's

in the hid chambers of Your lofty site KCD, §1, p. 82, l. 14.

who, before space was formed, inhabited Your endless space KCD, §3, p. 84, ll. 42–3.

give me good teaching [Prov. 4: 2].

I leave not this world as I entered, a raw seed naked of high and holy deed Job 1: 21; KCD, §36, p. 114, ll. 498–9.

bade Emptiness shatter, the Void scatter, and Nothingness yield matter KCD, §9, p. 88, ll. 101–2.

by Virtue's still waters led me [Ps. 23: 2].

torch and lighted my way, He showed me His Torah and brighted my day. My pulse His drum, He showed me, in the mind's eye, the light of the World to Come.

How often did I, laughing, trip Sin's path—but He withheld His wrath. He could have, should have removed me, but only lovingly reproved me.

Often I averted Him, never He averted me; oft I deserted Him, never He deserted me. O my sweet God who lovingly begot me, oft I forgot You but never You forgot me.

Ever deeper His good rooted and His kindness grew, as if it were all my due; and no matter what ill or dangers might befall, He saved me from them all. Then how can a slave as foul as I, a pig in a sty, repay with praise but one of His untold kindnesses, thousands upon thousands, oh, tens of thousands?

May it be Your merciful will, Abode of Will and Road of Truth, shield and stay from my youth, my Maker and Former, to make my latter end fairer than my former. Stay not Your hand from Your servant, raze not that good which You erected, uproot not that plant which You have lovingly protected. As You have begun, ever deal with me kindly—until I have cleansed Your lustrous garment I have fouled so blindly. Light my eyes that I might see You beckoning, save my soul from Your grievous reckoning; for I know that You would much prefer to cure the proud and cunning of their errors than lash them with Retribution's terrors.

O God, whose mercies ever warmed me; You who of Your own volition formed me, poured me like rich wine, shaped me, chest and spine, made soul and body mine, who stretched out my heart like a tent and therein went; who in Chaos' wilderness cleared me a way,

Gentle . . . brighted my day See KCD, §35, pp. 110–11, ll. 441–7.

no matter what ill or dangers might befall, He saved me from them all KCD, §35, p. 111–12, ll. 450–6.

Then how can a slave . . . tens of thousands See the middle of the *Nishmat* prayer (Sabbath morning liturgy) (Hertz, *Authorised Daily Prayer Book*, 418).

to make my latter end fairer than my former Job 42: 12.

Light my eyes [Ps. 13: 4].

who stretched out my heart like a tent Isa. 40: 22.

in Chaos' wilderness cleared me a way Isa. 40: 3.

who bore me on Mercy's hands into my natal day, who taught me as I lisped and crawled, who answered me even before I called—though I were to laud You on my knees for centuries, I could not pay You back for all these kindnesses, no, not for one of these.

What have I not owed You, I, who did my best to gall and goad You? I clutched Sin's hem, I neared You not; I turned a brazen face, I feared You not; I walked apart, in the hardness of my heart, smug in Your mercies, knowing You forgiving to all men living. Had You taken strict measure of my limp and meagre deeds, You had ploughed me under like a field of weeds.

But You would show how unlike flesh and blood You are.

When a servant thwarts his king, the monarch stifles affection and gives that man his due; but not so You. You deal lovingly with sinners, all toleration—that they, at their latter end, might lack justification. You know that Your restraint while the sinner draws breath secures him in his death; then, when his journey is through, he must return to You and render reckoning for all he chose to do; yes, he must strip off his harlot's raiment and render payment.

May it be Your will, O Source of Will, Voice small and still who unto Moses and Elijah spake—that I do all for Your Great Name's sake, that I turn to You in utter resignation, make Your service my vocation, Your will the object of my meditation, my chiefest joy, my jubilation. Healer, rock of my salvation, be my delight, let me serve You with all my heart, with all my soul, with all my might. Set not my portion with those who fall on this world's bosom and linger,

---

who answered me even before I called Isa. 65: 24.

though I were to laud You . . . one of these See the first *bakashah* of Sa'adiah Gaon, *SSG*, p. 60, ll. 8–18: 'And even if we attempted all the days of our lives and deprived all sleep from our eyes, and stood like cedars . . . we would not attain to one portion of your thousands, of your tens of thousands of praises.'

I clutched Sin's hem [1 Sam. 15: 27].

I turned a brazen face Prov. 21: 29.

I walked apart, in the hardness of my heart Deut. 29: 18.

But You would show how unlike flesh and blood You are Our author chooses not to rhyme here, for emphasis.

he must strip off his harlot's raiment [KCD §37, p. 117, l. 548].

May it be Your will KCD, §39, p. 120, l. 596. This is a frequent form of address in rabbinic prayer.

Voice small and still [1 Kgs. 19: 12].

my chiefest joy [Ps. 137: 6].

rock of my salvation [Ps. 95: 1].

serve You with all my heart, with all my soul, with all my might [Deut. 6: 5].

with men who wink the eye, who point the finger, mockers and scoffers, champions of disdain, who look upon Your Law as so much chain.

O Source of Life and Fount of favouring Will, may it be Your will to tend me, defend me from their misperception, from the sinners' rank conception. Turn my heart to fear You, fear Your Day of Retribution, recall ever Your grim restitution, turn me wise, let the sun of Your awe rise to burn like frontlets between my eyes. Oh hear my prayer when I cry out to You! Blessed art Thou, O Lord, who hearest prayer. May the words of my mouth and the meditations of my heart be acceptable before Thee, O Lord, my Rock and my Redeemer.

*T*hen he said to them: Ascend now prayer's second peak, majestic and unique, shining with praise, Wonder's winding maze, resplendent as the sun's first rays.

*H*e began, saying: Where, my God, is Good's song that once I sung? My flesh is wrinkled, but my lust grows young. I have sown offal and reaped dung; therefore I cover my lips, I hold my tongue.

*F*or these I shudder and my chest heaves: I have drunk Lust's cup to the lees, I am turned a dry oak with rotted leaves, a field with few and blasted sheaves, a rudderless ship on swollen seas. My life is plundered, my deeds the thieves: for these things I weep, and my soul grieves.

*L*ust's troops pursued me, but I discerned them not; hot harlotries wooed me and I spurned them not; I cast off God's teachings, I learned them not; Sin fouled my garments and I burned them not.

I renounced regret; now Sin, wet with Desire's sweat, winds me

men who wink the eye, who point the finger [Prov. 6: 13].

frontlets between my eyes Deut. 6: 8.

Oh hear my prayer when I cry out to you Ps. 28: 2.

Blessed art Thou, O Lord, who hearest prayer Daily service—the last of the middle blessings of the Amidah, based on Ps. 65: 3 (Hertz, *Authorised Daily Prayer Book*, 147).

May the words of my mouth . . . and my Redeemer Ps. 19: 15—a line that ends the silent meditation at the conclusion of the Amidah (Hertz, *Authorised Daily Prayer Book*, 157).

I cover my lips Lev. 13: 45.

For these things I weep [Lam. 1: 16].

round, binds me in his tight-wove net. Reason's face is pocked and scarred, my white soul charred, I am hoist on Desire's petard.

Once the doves of innocence knew me; now Sin's horned beasts pursue me, eager to pay me what is due me. They catch me at the ford and swift subdue me.

Sin grips me; the hand of Abandon strips me; my blood turns water as Time loudly sips me.

Alas, my good deeds—where are you, former shepherds? My flock of days is ravaged by Lust's leopards. Alas the flowers that I have plucked, alas the lips that I have sucked, alas hips wide and fecund: never, never I reckoned that pride and power could vanish in a second. Drunkenness plugged each my ear that I might not hear, *Glory short lingers*; and now Joy's spine cracks at the snap of Fate's fingers.

What life remains for these dry, these wasted bones that show no flow but streams of moans, fountains of weeping, seas of groans? Woe's rivulets careen, hot streams of grief convene, they drown all life until the highest branches of Joy's trees cannot be seen. I hear no lutes but Sorrow's strum; now Woe sounds his pounding drum; now Misery strings his bow, his arrows thrum.

Awake and sing, you sleepers in Sin's dust, rise from the bed of Lust, turn back the kiss of mead and must; yes, you whose scarlet lips suck Sin's pleasures to the pips, renounce the vine, denounce the harlot wine who will laughing leave you naked and lone with naught but moan in a field to stubble mown. Lift and polish Virtue's glass, see your foul forehead turned to brass, your eyeballs sunken in Lust's obsession—you, slaves of Possession, drunken with avarice and oppression, and stinking with transgression.

O my soul, frothing and churning, cast Lust's snake down, lift the staff of Returning, spurn Sin's flame for ever burning. Think! Care! Sink not to Despair! O sickly pale, be whole, be hale: weep, wail, rant, rail. In Sin's flooding dark, be Penitence your barque—board,

They catch me at the ford [Judg. 12: 5–6].
these dry, these wasted bones [Ezek. 37: 2–3].
the highest branches of Joy's trees cannot be seen [Gen. 7: 18–20].
Awake and sing, you sleepers in Sin's dust [Isa. 26: 19].
your foul forehead turned to brass [Isa. 48: 4].
cast Lust's snake . . . staff [Exod. 4: 3–4].

sail! You cannot scale the mountain of Desire; oh, foolish adventurers, climb you ever so high, the peak looms ever higher. Be steadfast firm; else, sprung from low germ, your term is a moment, your hope the worm.

*Y*ou, sweating through life under Lust's hot breath; shall wake to strife: the warrior Death shall seize you, man of might (say, rather, mite), do what you might, and drag you up Retribution's flinty slope, naked of hope, bound in Transgression's threefold rope. Then, when horned sins caress you, hot fires dress you, when thorned whips and briars oppress you—then shall you confess you, then, when all your jeering wrongs possess you?

O Lord, what is man that You know him? What the sons of men that You give them thought? Unwise, untaught, they shall pasture by Death's waters in the Land of Naught, heartsick, footsore on the shore where lions of Retribution roar.

O my God: ere my soul sets sail, dazed and pale, before you drop my shrivelled deeds upon Your scale, before I fully fail, unhealed, unblest—touch my burning breast: Lord God, I would rest. Lift this wretch from the slough of his schemes; strengthen my casements, right my beams—I would see visions, dream new dreams. In the desert of Lust my years fade, with no wisdom for water, no goodness for shade—this as my sins, silk-clad, parade, smacking their lips, sucking the thick grapes of lust to the pips.

*M*ost princely, Perversion hosts me; takes Vice's winking cup in hand and toasts me; then strips me, thrusts me on Sin's spit and in fierce fire roasts me. He takes my youth's glass, leisurely grips me; grins, tips me, languorously sips me.

*D*otard Resolve mutters and mumbles; Resolution, halting, stumbles while, in my groin, Desire rumbles. Sin and Lust join hands, their nomad bands invade my lands, they strike at my belly, they pierce my flanks, Lust's arrows stream heartward, they overflow my banks. Passion fires my gate, I gasp, I choke; my innards flame, my eyes

sprung from low germ . . . your hope the worm [Mishnah *Avot* 3: 1, 4: 4].
threefold rope [Eccles. 4: 12].
O Lord, what is man that You know him? What the sons of men that You give them thought? Ps. 144: 3.
they shall pasture by Death's waters in the Land of Naught [Ps. 23: 2–4].

smoke; Time puts forth his hand and robs me of my cloak. My grain turns chaff, my wheat, stubble; the castle of my youth turns rubble; my dream of endless gain, a bubble.

My sins rain thicker than my falling hair, my fat turns lean and my plenty, spare; at my gates Old Age's clarions blare, while in my heart who couches and makes his lair, but the jackal of Despair.

Wake, wake, my storm-tossed soul, before the goal be lost. Gauge, gauge the cost of the banquet of Avarice, who would ever deceive you. Lo, Vice's volleys cleave you; Virtue's weeping angels leave you; see—the jawing worm, the pit, the smoke, the fire, receive you!

Therefore err no more, defer no more, stir no more the pot of Desire's brew. Renew your youth with truth, give God His due. Death thunders, Judgement's lightning flashes: robe your flesh in sackcloth and your soul in ashes before the body's mansion crashes. Youth's flower fades, the hour grows late; Fate rushes from Death's crest, he will not wait; Doom pounds upon your rusting gate. Cast gaudery aside, be your bawdry denied. How long shall Right's sword rest, how long shall you cower? Seek the aid of your fathers, cry God for power, surround Faith's blessed tower. Yes, yes, salvation is in reach: besiege Faith's city with right deed and speech; with the ram of repentance Forgiveness' tall walls breach.

Leave Lust's pennants flapping in the waste; haste, haste away this day from the glistening world, wet-lipped and fresh, who ever gorges on her children's flesh. See how she laughs as your hot blood rages! Reject her hire, spurn her wages, turn ever higher to the Rock of Ages, the Root of Roots and Author of your creation; rise to your rightful station, set your pillars on His firm foundation, be God your Shepherd, the Lord your light and your salvation.

Amen, amen. God light your path with healing grace that you prove worthy to look upon His face. So may it be His will.

robs me of my cloak [S. of S. 5: 7].
the Rock of Ages Isa. 26: 4.
God your Shepherd [Ps. 23: 1].
the Lord your light and your salvation [Ps. 27: 1].
So may it be His will Traditional closure of many prayers.

SAID THE TELLER OF THE TALE:

The chill of Repentance shook my frame. Trembling, I turned to a student to ask this preacher's name, whereat the rhetor himself strode to my side and replied:

Hever I be, bright destroyer of cares,
who rears Wisdom's altars, stones, and stairs;
Singing for simpletons riddles and airs,
I gladden the pious with paeans and with prayers.

GATE FIFTEEN

A Prayer Sent where Grace Reposes: A Prayer to Godly Moses

THUS SPOKE HEMAN THE EZRAHITE: When I was young and bold and richer than can be told, yes, afloat in silver and gold, I met a merchant company bound 'cross the sea. I gave them my hand and joined their band; but scarce had we left land when God's fist churned the ocean to a vast commotion: the seabreakers leapt and roared, the ship sank and soared; and we, we flung our riches overboard to escape a salt grave and swift they sank beneath the wave. Then our vessel, moaning like a woman in travail and swaying drunkenly with ripped sail, stumbled to land, where I fell vomiting and pale, a Jonah spat from the whale. Homeward I staggered, all misery, where friends and loved ones came to comfort me. As I sat before them, wide-eyed and distraught, Hever the Kenite, lips taut, came to my side, red-eyed at what Time had wrought.

*H*ad I wealth, he said, I would not show you a closed palm but would salve you with gold's balm. However, I must comfort you in different fashion, by sharing with you what God has granted me in His compassion. Let me teach you a prayer to Moses, man of God, which shall bear you through woe's waves dryshod, that your salvation might shine afar, even brighter than the morning star. Accept this as a godly boon and recite it evening, morn, and noon with clean hands

---

A Prayer to Godly Moses Ps. 90: 1. On the abundance of this gate's references to Moses in rabbinic sources, see the Analysis and n. 2 there.

we flung our riches overboard to escape a salt grave Jonah 1: 5.

moaning like a woman in travail [Isa. 42: 14].

Jonah spat from the whale Jonah 2: 11.

a prayer to Moses, man of God Ps. 90: 1.

which shall bear you through woe's waves dryshod [Exod. 14: 29].

recite it evening, morn, and noon Ps. 55: 18.

and a pure heart, secure that God shall do His part, showering you with heavenly largesse to wipe away the memory of distress.

Speak on, dear friend, I said with conviction: let this be my comfort in my affliction.

Here then, said Hever, is my disquisition, the composition that you must be taught: know, naught like it has been wrought.

He began: O winged hosts, come apace; dwellers above, bear countless greetings of heaven's grace to the Lord's portion on high who stands Him beside, the messenger true and tried, rich in pity and poor in pride, lustrous and lone, Prophecy's foundation-stone. Free of taint, he is praised by proud and low alike, by sinner and saint. The burning bush thrums his praise, the Red Sea, Jordan, and Arnon their voices raise; by Egypt are his *laudes* sung, his wonders are rung on the sea's loud tongue, his name whispered by the Nile's bent reeds, Sinai shines memorial to his deeds. Praises pale and tongues fail to limn the virtues of his golden heart, holy and apart.

Ere God had formed him in the womb he was a prophet to the nations come. The Lord called Heaven and Earth and these gave wondrous birth to Virtue's best bloom, sprung from choicest loins and holiest womb, to the master who wrenched us from darkness' maw through Torah's light and law, who loosed us from sin's degradation to serve the Author of Creation.

Earth cleared a mighty swathe for him and then set him foremost among the sons of men. His ear was tuned to the Almighty's word; his tongue taught Torah and all men were stirred. He bore tidings to the meek, healing to the sick and weak. He instructed the perplexed, lit the path of the ignorant and vexed, for until then earth lay in darkness, spawning seed of vice and folly in word and deed. Then Moses rose and spoke and man's dawn broke. Him the nations

clean hands and a pure heart [Ps. 24: 4].
let this be my comfort in my affliction Ps. 119: 50.
messenger true Prov. 25: 13.
The burning bush Exod. 3: 2–4.
the Red Sea Exod. 14: 26–9.
Jordan Josh. 3: 7 ff.
Arnon Num. 21: 13–36.
Ere God had formed him in the womb he was a prophet to the nations to come Jer. 1: 5.
He instructed the perplexed Here Alḥarizi indirectly praises Moses Maimonides, author of *The Guide of the Perplexed*, which Alḥarizi himself translated.

all believed; but we, above all men, perceived the splendour of his prophecy, his witness of Divinity.

God spoke—and Moses, meditating, rose to Sinai's crest, then upward pressed, onward through trial and test, free of fear, rising on clouds of glory to the angels' sphere. On, on he urged as round him bands of winged glories surged and a voice cried him before, Open wide High Heaven's door and loud rejoice: behold, the choicest of the choice. Rise, sing: greet him who is honoured of the King!

He entered and before him rose the dwellers of the High Realms Seven, saying, O blessed teacher, welcome to the hosts of Heaven! Then the seraphim, in blazing streams of white, bore him headlong into the inner sanctum of God's might, and throneward he stepped as earth quaked with fright. In Humility's glow he entered that holy place and spoke with his Creator face to face. He probed deep mysteries with eyes that saw no wrong; no, foulness and evil never he looked upon. He took God's comeliest portion with hands sin-free, mighty in integrity. He spoke with God, lip to pure lip, and then descended, grasping in his hand a gift undreamt of by mortal man: the Tables of the Covenant, bounty of the Divine Mind to light man's way and sight the very blind.

This lord of all mortals with high-held rod inscribed upon our hearts the fear of God. He sets our hands in our Creator's hand; he is the highway to the Promised Land. Through him we are privileged in the World Supernal to see the face of the Eternal. He brings us to the Tree of Life and feeds us of its delectations; under his shadow we live among the nations. That his pure flesh has perished no man can deny; but he lives, shining in Thought's eye, our dear master, blessed of the mouth of the Most High. Peace be to the dust made holy by

Moses, meditating, rose . . . the angels' sphere See BT *Yoma* 4*a*.

Open wide High Heaven's door Isa. 26: 2.

him who is honoured of the King Esther 6: 9–11.

spoke with his Creator face to face Exod. 33: 11; Deut. 34: 10.

with eyes that saw no wrong [Hab. 1: 13].

the Tables of the Covenant Exod. 32: 15.

the Tree of Life Gen. 2: 9, 3: 22.

under his shadow we live among the nations Lam. 4: 20.

he lives, shining in Thought's eye Lit., 'He who lives, though his pure body is dead; revealed to the eye of thought, though his soul is hid'. See BT *Sotah* 13*b*, where Moses is described as not having died, but as living and standing before God as he did at Sinai.

his every bone! Peace to his soul's dwelling-place beneath God's holy throne—from his servant and his handmaid's son, reverer of his teachings every one.

*M*oses, man of God, to you I cry with aching heart and bloodshot eye, ribs racked with pain, again and again, my tears streaming free as the waters of Galilee. O towering fortress of mercy and salvation, of pity and consolation: our deeds, blasted and mean, stand us and God between. Weak and afraid, we are stripped of Heaven's shade. I come before you low and beaten, my soul wormwood-eaten. Let your righteous acts of old be my advocates; lead me forth from Misery's gates. I seize the hem of your mercies and confess me; I shall not let you go until you bless me. Oh speak me good, take my debtor's part: angels learned of you that art. Earth's pillar, Fountain of Right, let my soul be dear in your sight. Hear my plea and set my prisoned spirit free, for the sake of the Lord thy God, the Holy One of Israel who hath glorified thee.

*T*hen he raised his voice in song:

Peace, peace unto you, first prince of God,
abiding in Heaven, ringed round with cloud:
The swiftest tongue falters to hymn your praise,
the heart is dizzied, the mind is cowed.
When the brook of Salvation turned weary and dried,
you appeared, bringing water to barren ground;
From under God's shadow, your hearth and home,
send down your bright merit and ring us round.
May we, with you, God's rescue see—
the return of Zion's captivity.

SAID THE TELLER OF THE TALE:

*W*ith that, his prayer was told and I seized upon it like gold; I learned it by heart and won relief, yes, therein found a cure for grief;

his servant and his handmaid's son Ps. 116: 16.
I seize the hem 1 Sam. 15: 27.
I shall not let you go until you bless me Gen. 32: 27.
let my soul be dear in your sight 2 Kgs. 1: 13–14.
for the sake of the Lord thy God, the Holy One of Israel who hath glorified thee Isa. 55: 5, 60: 9.
the return of Zion's captivity Ps. 126: 1.

for the Creator so loved those lines I well rehearsed that He made my latter end fairer than my first. Pitying, he sought my door and filled me with His plenty's store: His mercy endureth for ever; be His name praised for evermore.

He made my latter end fairer than my first Job 42: 12.

His mercy endureth for ever Ps. 106: 1 and elsewhere.

be His name praised for evermore [Ps. 113: 2].

GATE SIXTEEN

Airs of Song's Seven Heirs

THUS SPOKE HEMAN THE EZRAHITE: While Love's svelte leaves on Stillness' stems were green and sessile; ere Fellowship's flowers were ripped from Rest's fair trestle; ere Serenity's nest dispossessed Hope's best and Roaming's egrets came to nestle; ere the pods of Peace were pounded by Separation's pestle and Hope's daughters were poured from vessel to vessel; ere Severance' Angel seized my thigh and thundered, *Wrestle!*—I lay light on lush leas, plucking Joy's lilies under Indolence' trees; but an ill dispensation gripped me and savaged me, a chill visitation whipped me and ravaged me: Fate shrilled his whistle, that I sped from my bed, shed silkenware and in its stead bound my loins with sackcloth and with thorns my head and, wed to Wandering, fled.

*Y*es, I traded Rest's torque for Roving's shackle, and in the wilderness of ostrich, owl, and jackal, where satyrs gambol and liliths cackle I slacked my tongue with moaning, blacked my lungs with groaning, and raised the Tent of Weeping for my Tabernacle.

*T*hought's daughters drank deep from Depression's waters, then limped despondent to their quarters. Yea, the rock of the ribs was struck and streams rushed forth—scathe gusheth from the north: anger, wrath, rage, and a pack of evil angels fourth.

were poured from vessel to vessel Jer. 48: 11.
Angel seized my thigh and thundered, *Wrestle!* [Gen. 32: 25–6].
plucking Joy's lilies S. of S. 6: 2.
bound my loins with sackcloth [Gen. 37: 34].
torque An ornament for neck or arm.
ostrich, owl, and jackal, where satyrs gambol [Isa. 13: 21–2].
raised the Tent of Weeping for my Tabernacle [Exod. 40: 17–38].
the rock of the ribs was struck and streams rushed forth [Ps. 78: 20].
scathe Severe injury, harm, loss.
from the north [Jer. 1: 14].
anger, wrath, rage, and a pack of evil angels [Ps. 78: 49].

Many of Bale's couriers rose to waylay me, many his minions to flay me and splay me, spoil me of Hope's gold and with Cark's coppers pay me.

Grief's ocean is lashed by Despair's White Whale: Woe's wild winds wail; waves of travail the Straits of Concord flail and, megrim-crested, Calm's cliffs assail. Lo, Love's mountain is laid low and chilling vapours overflow Camaraderie's plateau; oh, the sweet child Joy is no more, and I, whither shall I go? Ravaged the realm of Amity: calamity upon calamity!

The chariots of Distress pressed across my spirit's wilderness, firing arrow after arrow without cess. The Daughters of Days, in unholy collusion, robbed water from my eyes in wild confusion.

Then at last Weeping's welkin cleared, Joy's radiance reappeared and daytide's billows neared: Gloom's galleons, exile-geared, veered to Woe's westward and disappeared.

Thus, when Time stilled his thunder, filled lips with laughter, and hearts with wonder, tore Sadness' cloak asunder, beat his sword to a coulter and ploughed Sorrow under, I chanced, on a day, to join a gallant troop of bard and maker, tropes' sard and nacre, whose surging speech struck Wisdom's beach breaker upon breaker.

Ah, their poesy's sweet scent, heav'n-sent and dew-besprent! Here Lebanon's cedars were found together; and loud from their branches did Song's orioles sound together. At these masters' hands, song's silken strands were instant wound together.

Brave herdsmen they, who sought and found Song's scattered hordes; brave swordsmen they, who fought and downed Song's bogus lords. Brave borers they, who with Percipience' picks Wit's shining lodes uncovered; explorers they, who with divining stichs Song's gold abodes discovered; outpourers they, whose diamantine clouds above the Tent

Bale Woe or pain.
Cark Care, anxiety.
megrim Depression of spirits.
vapours Desolation of spirit.
the sweet child Joy is no more, and I, whither shall I go [Gen. 37: 39].
calamity upon calamity [Jer. 4: 20].
welkin Sky.
exile-geared Jer. 46: 19; Ezra 12: 3.
filled lips with laughter [Ps. 126: 2].
beat his sword to a coulter and ploughed [Isa. 2: 4].
maker Poet.
sard and nacre Reddish-brown chalcedony and mother-of-pearl.
Lebanon's cedars [Ps. 104: 16 and elsewhere].

of Wisdom's meeting hovered. Their eyes spoke swords broke Dark's thraw shields; their lips spilled ploughs, tilled Wit's broad fields.

Now their company comprised Ken's glowing river and bow and quiver, Song's lumer and lawgiver, giants compliant to his will, a-tremble at his lips' least trill; the prince whose tongue weaves Song's silk sleeves, and mystery sleaves; liege lord who, casque and greaves, Cacophony grieves; the pancratiast of iron grasp, whose strong-thewed words clasp Song's angel fast with Keenness' hook and hasp—the prince: Art's height, hearts' light, Benevolence' site, Truth's defender till time's end, our lord and friend, Hever the Kenite, of might unreckoned, him whom Poesy beckoned, then crowned Song's suzerain to no man second; singular singer whose bounding tropes, swift antelopes, mount Wisdom's slopes; whose hue and cry tarn torrefy, mere dry, and salt sea arefy; whose tongue's taut gust and fiery thrust blow Folly's heights to dust.

He sets Thought's stones in Rhetoric's slings; aims, flings, and brings down kings. He is Wit's lamp and lustre: round this bright panion Might's heroes muster and Song's companions cluster to suck his former and his latter rains, to trek his mind's meadows, pluck his psyche's plains, cull the last, least remains of his harvest's cast-off grains, yes, lie in wait for the weakest of his fold. Inebriate of his mandrake and his marigold, their souls take wing; yea, angel-souled and makers made tenfold, they soar toward the splendour of Heaven's high hold, the better to behold their sun and deck their necks with his beat gold.

---

the Tent of Wisdom's Meeting hovered [Exod. 40: 34–8].
thraw Twisted.
Ken Cognizance.
lumer Light.
sleaves Disentangles.
casque and greaves (With) helmet and armour that protects the leg from the knee to the ankles (translator's licence—as with all terms depicting medieval European weaponry).
pancratiast Participant in an ancient (Greek) athletic contest that combined boxing and wrestling.
clasp Song's angel fast [Gen. 32: 26–7].
tarn torrefy . . . arefy Dry out a small mountain lake, pond, and the ocean.
He sets Thought's stones in Rhetoric's slings; aims, flings, and brings down kings [1 Sam. 17: 49–50].
panion Fellow, companion.
his former and his latter rains [Deut. 11: 14; Jer. 5: 24].
cull the last, least remains of his harvest's cast-off grains Lev. 19: 9, 23: 22.
lie in wait for the weakest of his fold Deut. 25: 18.
makers Poets.

These Samsons of Song, with lions to their heels, captains of airy chariots with many-eyed wheels, leave earth's aiguilles to urge ever higher, mad with desire to reach their high priest's altar and scoop coals from his white fire.

They sanctify themselves, rise on Song's gold pinions to Heaven's dominions, join angel minions—seraphs, hearts aflame, and fiery loins and lips the same; in wild declaim they burst the gates of fame, whir, whirl, yea, twirl in angel dance, then down the beakers of prophetic trance. Their ringing declaration draws form for Thought's matter from the wells of Salvation for a thirsting Hebrew nation.

Seven the choicest of these voices numbered, who in Song's service neither slept nor slumbered, but waking, dreamed: from back Song's brattice, from out Song's lattice their bright eyes beamed. Each, with Thought's brand and mace, claimed pride of place in Song's hot race, each called to his brother, Come, let us contend one with another! Thus they gathered before their master and mentor, Poesy's pure precentor, Hever the Kenite, bidding him say who sang most rarely, bidding him rise up early to the vineyards of their song and judge them fairly.

Then the first approached and said:

Let all men see, let all men hear
the cry that quashes lions with fear.
Earth's olden mountains shake at my tread
who am scourge of dolts and Folly's bier.
My thought weaves hail with thunderbolts,
leaves fields of foemen blast and sere,
My lightning retrudes hot Battle's steeds,
footman unmans, snaps sword and spear;

chariots with many-eyed wheels [Ezek. 1: 1–22].
aiguilles Needle-shaped peaks.
scoop coals Isa. 30: 14.
gold pinions Ps. 68: 14.
from the wells of Salvation [Isa. 12: 3].
neither slept nor slumbered [Ps. 121: 4].
from back Song's brattice From behind Song's parapet.
from . . . beamed S. of S. 2: 9.
Come, let us contend one with another 2 Kgs. 14: 8.
precentor Cantor.
rise up early to the vineyards [S. of S. 7: 13].
judge them fairly [Pss. 96: 13, 98: 9 and elsewhere].
weaves hail with thunderbolts Exod. 9: 24.
retrudes Repels.

Yet my tropes and lines are sockets and beams
Song's tent of meeting proudly rear.
Strive, rivals, but never attain my mind,
the Cosmos' last, vast outer sphere.
I raise my staff o'er the Sea of Song:
its waters split, its waves uprear,
Pursuers rush in; I lift my pen:
the waters enfold them, they disappear.

Then the second spoke, saying:

Fast by my tent Song's daughters vie
to enter, then serve in, my serail,
To don my bracelets of chrysolite,
my chains of lapis lazuli.
Mine the bright sword of Wisdom's realm
that smites pretenders hip and thigh,
Poets manqués—bald, limping fools,
dullards who dare to versify.
What wonder Song's realm lies desolate—
Wit's wells are barren, her fields are dry!
I raise Song's staff, strike Wisdom's rock,
and Learning's furrows fructify.
I lay Song's beams, her sockets set,
her altar raise, alone draw nigh
And with my fragrant sacrifice
the sins of thousands rectify.

sockets and beams Exod. 26: 11.

tent of meeting proudly rear [Exod. 40: 2, 18].

the Cosmos' last, vast outer sphere Medieval Aristotelian philosophy—and, in general, Neoplatonism—envisaged the cosmos as a series of concentric spheres, the last being the active intellect, which controlled the terrestrial world. See J. Guttmann, *Philosophies of Judaism* (London, 1964), 146 f., and 'spheres' in index.

I raise my staff o'er the Sea of Song: its waters split, its waves uprear [Exod. 14: 16–29, 15: 8].

Pursuers rush in; I lift my pen: the waters enfold them, they disappear [Exod. 14: 27–8, 15: 10].

serail Seraglio, a harem.

smites pretenders hip and thigh [Judg. 15: 8].

I raise Song's staff, strike Wisdom's rock [Num. 20: 11].

her sockets set [Exod. 26: 11].

Then the third spoke, saying:

Upon the flint of my Desire
my tropes' swift sword strikes fire.
The forts of Folly, Jerichos all,
crumble before my lyre.
Upon the ladder of my mind
my nimble thoughts climb ever higher
To turn with cherubs in holy dance,
with seraphs perne in holy gyre
Of searing tunes, of arcane runes,
which, e'er reborn, ne'er halt nor tire.
Wisdom, that Sheba, comes to test me,
kneels at my feet and calls me Sire,
Rich sets my board with meat and wine,
affords me all that I require
That Song's high towers I raise anew,
yea, raise the realm of Song entire.

Then the fourth spoke, saying:

The crags of Thought are my domain,
mind's mountains my mortmain;
What madbrain risk ascend my ramps,
whose legions mount my terreplein?
What rival's spears lift up their heads
to strike my cuirass and my poleyn?
None dare lift verses from my hands,
who can Orion's light restrain.

The forts of Folly, Jerichos all, crumble before my lyre [Josh. 6: 12–20].

Upon the ladder of my mind my nimble thoughts climb ever higher Gen. 28: 11–13.

Sheba, comes to test me, kneels at my feet and calls me Sire 1 Kgs. 10: 1–13.

Rich sets my board with meat and wine [Prov. 9: 2].

mortmain Inalienable possession.

terreplein Upper surface of a rampart beyond the parapet.

cuirass A piece of armour reaching down to the waist, comprising a breastplate and backplate.

poleyn A piece of defensive armour covering the knee.

My singing sword, Wit's light and lord,
is the pride of Jubal and Tubal-Cain:
By its swift blade are men unmade;
Song's thousands, tens of thousands, slain.
But though I bury Folly's hordes,
my wine and meat the wise sustain:
Green my thought bursts through Wisdom's soil
to plenish the earth with standing grain.

Then the fifth spoke, saying:

Through me are Earth and Heaven reborn:
my lyre awakes the morn.
Song's flocks drink deep of my thought's pure streams
fresh sprung from my mind's wide bourne.
My fancy's seed endows the mead
of Poesy with bursting corn,
While arid fields of rivals yield
dry stichs that savants laugh to scorn.
The Muses' midwives kneel at my feet
to leave all others' songs stillborn.
My notes are pearls to sages' throats,
my gems kings' diadems adorn.
At each my word, Wit's daughters joy—
that, while the sons of Darkness mourn.
I loose bound tropes from Folly's ropes
as loud I trumpet Freedom's horn.

Then the sixth spoke, saying:

Time's sons hear my song, stop, quiver, and quake;
Orion and Pleiades shiver and shake

My singing sword, Wit's light and lord, is the pride of Jubal and Tubal-Cain [Gen. 4: 21–2].

thousands, tens of thousands, slain [1 Sam. 18: 7].

my wine and meat the wise sustain [Prov. 9: 2].

to plenish the earth with standing grain Isa. 27: 6.

my lyre awakes the morn [Pss. 57: 9, 108: 3].

I trumpet Freedom's horn Lev. 25: 9–20.

At my leonine verse that savages fools
as it crouches, then leaps from out Valour's brake.
Keen prophet am I, restoring the axehead
of Song deep sunk in Sapience' lake.
You, hung'ring for wisdom, enter and eat;
at my fountain's issue your soul-thirst slake;
Yes, joy in my wine and my balm, loved friends—
to foes, a stinging, venomed snake.
My lute and my lyre awake the dawn;
my strings the springs of Discernment wake.
The waves of my song rise vast and long
and on Wisdom's beaches thunderous break.
For the sake of my brothers I ne'er shall be still,
and for Heaven's and for the future's sake.

Then the seventh spoke, saying:

Though Heaven and all its hosts stand massed
they must flee my clarion blast.
I raise the temple of Holy Song,
but have Folly's altars—all!—down cast.
I am he who ushered his muse into Song's
dominions; she shuddered—heart, eyes aghast:
Little foxes had ravaged the standing corn,
the wheat was blighted, the vineyards blast.
Furious she raised her sceptred hand
that the winter of woe in an instant passed:
The fields shone gold with harvest untold;
she set the table for Joy's repast.

brake Thicket.

Keen prophet am I, restoring the axehead of Song deep sunk in Sapience' lake [2 Kgs. 6: 1–7].

You, hung'ring for wisdom, enter and eat [Passover Haggadah: 'Let all who are hungry enter and eat'].

My lute and my lyre awake the dawn [Pss. 57: 9, 108: 3].

For the sake of my brothers [Ps. 122: 8].

I ne'er shall be still [Isa. 62: 1].

I raise the temple of Holy Song, but have Folly's altars—all!—down cast [2 Kgs. 23: 8, 12, 15].

Little foxes had ravaged the standing corn, the wheat was blighted, the vineyards blast [S. of S. 2: 15].

the winter of woe in an instant passed [S. of S. 2: 11].

Search through the Heavens, and ages past:
my meteor rhyme find unsurpassed.
Regale at the board of Song's proud lord:
I am the first; yea, I am the last.

Now when every bard had his braw might bared and Song's broad halls repaired, Hever the Kenite declared: This tourney will bear no sequel; each man is champion, each his fellow's equal. All have conquered, none failed: each would illume deep darkness were his face unveiled.

Wit is slaved of the first, and shall never gain release; the second dons Poesy's gold pelisse; the third is to scribblers as lark to geese; the fourth—sard and onyx are his field's increase; the fifth's verse is Song's masterpiece; the sixth wins sovereignty without surcease; the seventh is given Song's covenant of peace.

SAID THE TELLER OF THE TALE:

What could my heart do but adore them? I stood dumbstruck before them. What chains of song! What wondrous intellects had wrought them! Or was Hever's the laurel? He it was who had taught them. Yet all had raised staves to Song's waves and deep cleft them: grateful and reverent, I left them.

I am the first; yea, I am the last [Isa. 44: 6, 48: 12].
each would illume deep darkness were his face unveiled Exod. 34: 33–5.
Wit is . . . release [Exod. 21: 2–6].
sovereignty without surcease [Isa. 9: 6].
is given Song's covenant of peace Num. 25: 12.
raised staves to Song's waves and deep cleft them [Exod. 14: 16, 26, 27].

GATE SEVENTEEN

Rabbanite versus Karaite

THUS SPOKE HEMAN THE EZRAHITE: When young, I left home to roam the world for maxim, song, and gnome sweeter than honey and the honeycomb, and happily discovered a group of youths above whose heads the Cloud of Wisdom hovered. Drawing near to drink of their pure well, I found the Philomel of intellect, whom that band elect queried on the strange and sickly sect of the Samaritans.

Sect! Say moral insects, the Kenite replied, for they are everywhere denied, by Christians, Muslims, Jews. Whose be they, whose, this malformation–miscreation, this monstrosity, this budless branch and rootless tree? Unfit, yea, counterfeit, these slaves dare sit upon a lordly throne usurping Holy Writ. Fired by their prophet, Sanballat the Horonite, and their prince Tobiah, slave and Ammonite, they are thieves, no less: they openly transgress, flaunting their godlessness; they call our Torah their own, yet all its truths disown. Adamant, perverse, they traduce and traverse, clutch our scrolls, claim our Law, and do the reverse. Blind and halt, stupid to a fault, they are a drunken lot, and shrunken, too: less than a thousand—a twisted crew, evil and few.

They continued, What have you to say of the schismatics, the Karaites, who close their eyes to our sages' lights?

sweeter than honey and the honeycomb [Ps. 19: 11].
above whose heads the Cloud of Wisdom hovered [Exod. 40: 34–7].
the Samaritans On this group, see the Analysis.
Sanballat the Horonite, and their prince Tobiah, slave and Ammonite Neh. 2: 10, 19.
Blind and halt [2 Sam. 5: 6–8].
evil and few Gen. 47: 9.
the Karaites, who close their eyes to our sages' lights The nature and history of this movement, treated subjectively by Alḥarizi, is discussed in the Analysis.

He answered, They are nearer, essentially kin; yet their faith is adulterine. Accepting Sinai's revelation, they spurn rabbinic explication, and hence are not numbered in our congregation. They stumble after their desire like sheep gone astray; they have turned aside quickly from the way.

How, asked the youths, can they be so thick as to confound the dead and the quick? Know they not that the Torah is an impregnable fort whose chambers hold blooms and gems of every sort; that rabbinic discourse unlocks those barred rooms, those gems and rare perfumes; that, without this key, all is mystery?

He answered, They understand, but plug their ears to Reason's reprimand. Their forebears would not leave our heritage intact, but attacked our sacred Pact. Now their sons, faith sick and maimed, stand naked but unashamed.

They pressed further: But what, precisely, have they claimed? What articles of faith have they proclaimed?

They are, he answered, querulential, their arguments inconsequential.

Still, they countered, their errors must be ample: pluck their larder for one example.

He replied, Know that in days of old the Torah's guardians formed two camps: those who respected our sages—and those who rejected our sages. The former reverenced Ashi and Ravina, Akiba and Tarfon; the latter, God and Moses alone. They took the Torah, wondrous fair, of silken wear, and stripped her bare. They are like a farmer who cherishes his field, then discards the yield.

Then said the faithful Rabbanites to the schismatic Karaites: Is it not odd that you, who know evil from good, should shun the

like sheep gone astray [Isa. 53: 6].

they have turned aside quickly from the way Exod. 32: 8; Deut. 9: 12; Judg. 2: 17.

stand naked but unashamed [Gen. 2: 25].

Ashi and Ravina The initial editor of the Talmud (335–427/8 CE) and his pupil or colleague, who, with Ashi, closed the talmudic period. See *EJ* iii. 709–10; xiii. 1584–5.

Akiba and Tarfon Rabbi Akiba was a major systematizer and explicator of Jewish law (*EJ* ii. 488–92); Tarfon, his frequent adversary (*EJ* xv. 810–11). Neither of these two men is cited in the Hebrew text.

who know evil from good 2 Sam. 19: 36.

greenwood for dead wood? How can one accept what the Torah commands without explication of those demands? Without the Mishnah's lucid text, the Written Law would leave us utterly perplexed; without the Gemara, we had stumbled from Mitkah to Meribah. Without talmudic interpretation, the Torah were a tower without foundation; were it not for the Pharisees, we were sailless sloops upon stormy seas. Were it not for rabbinic intervention, how could one shun error and dissension, flee arbitrary invention, know which commandment is weighty or light; in short, grasp the Text's intention?

The Schismatics replied, Of this we read, Behold this dreamer! What, has Israel no Redeemer that we should pursue your fantastical sages? God forbid that we should turn our backs upon the Rock of Ages and His Inheritance! Hence! We shall keep faith with the Law, the which we rightly understand, given at Moses' hand, adding nothing thereto nor diminishing therefrom: keep your bizarre compendium. You hawk usurpation, you distort the Torah with reckless explanation. Your fancy never spent, spurning the Text's intent, you leave God's Tree of Life blast and bent, in disregard of what our Maker meant.

The Faithful countered, Awful, awful! You dare claim the mantle of the lawful! Is this your offering, is this your sweet savour? How long shall you stand between two thresholds and waver? Cut cord: choose Baal or the Lord. Let each camp present one champion, one, and let these two battle till the argument be won, that truth shine brighter than the noonday sun.

Done! cried the assemblage. To the debate! Whereat each camp sent forth an advocate.

from Mitkah to Meribah i.e. 'from sweets to quarrel'. Alḥarizi interprets allegorically two placenames in the Israelites' journey to Canaan, echoing scriptural practice. See Exod. 17: 1–7; and Num. 20: 1–13, 24.

the Pharisees See *EJ* xiii. 363–6.

Behold this dreamer [Gen. 37: 19].

has Israel no Redeemer 2 Kgs. 1: 3, 16.

the Rock of Ages [Isa. 26: 4].

adding nothing thereto nor diminishing therefrom Deut. 4: 2.

God's Tree of Life [Prov. 3: 18].

is this your sweet savour? [Num. 29: 8 and elsewhere].

How long shall you stand between two thresholds 1 Kgs. 18: 21.

choose Baal or the Lord Ibid.

shine brighter than the noonday sun [Isa. 58: 10].

The Believer declared:

They who lay claim to Moses' Law
but rabbinic dicta jeer
Are like subjects who swear to obey the king
then scoff at the king's vizier.

The Schismatic declared:

I hold to the Torah of Moses alone,
I keep faith with our prophet and seer;
Let your sages interpret, emend, and recast
and revise—I turn a deaf ear.
I lean on the Law of the Lord, that uplifts
the believer, that grants him good cheer.
I lean 'gainst the tree trunk, not branches or leaves,
God beside me—and never fear.

The Believer declared:

Show me that lore that is self-contained
in the annals of humankind!
Think: if doctors' recondite tomes
had remained both unsealed and unmined
How many had languished on Suffering's couch,
to torment, then dust, consigned!
Even so are God's dictates: the veiled and complex,
the specific and general are twined;
Except for the Rabbis' sagacity
their secrets were never divined.
The literal reader, with blinders for guide,
leaves wisdom and reason behind.
All praise to the Sages! Except for their light
we had stumbled on, wilfully blind.

The Schismatic declared:

What need for a guide over mapped terrain
or a highway well signed? What need
For your tortuous, thumb-dipping logic?
Your field is run over with weed.

God beside me—and never fear [Ps. 118: 6].

The Believer declared:

Rise up, my son, come, show me your strength
in the knowledge and fear of the Lord:
Choose you a verse and tender me
all of the meaning that verse can afford.
Tell me its dictum, its laws, implications,
its logic; come, show me its sword—
This with no reference to Mishnah or Talmud
or law codes; then claim your reward:
I will take up your banner and fight at your side,
I will kneel and proclaim you my lord.

The Schismatic declared:

So long as I live I shall cleave to God's word
and give it my sons as their right;
Shall I worship false idols, your sages, so called,
who turn sunset to dawn, and dark, light?
I shall not. I walk in my ancestors' paths,
who habited Zion's height:
They took their delight in the Law of the Lord
therein delving both morning and night.
No sage, no gaon, *could entice them to turn*
from God's Word to the left or the right.

Mishnah The compendium of Jewish law governing all areas of behaviour, personal and public, civil and criminal, cultic and non-cultic, finally edited by Judah the Prince *c.*200 CE. See 'Mishnah' in *EJ* xii. 93–109, and bibliography there.

Talmud Rabbinic explication and expansion of the mishnaic code, in the form of a running commentary. This same corpus is more often called Gemara, the term Talmud referring to the two works combined. See 'Talmud' in *EJ* xv. 755–68; and 'Gemara' in *EJ* vii. 368–9.

law codes Lit. 'halakhah': Jewish law in its entirety, especially in its historical development through the Mishnah and Gemara, later explicators, the responsa of leading rabbinic authorities through the ages, and such well-known law codes as Maimonides' *Mishneh torah*, called *Yad haḥazakah* after his death; Jacob ben Asher's *Tur*; and Joseph Caro's *Shulḥan arukh*. See 'Halakhah' in *EJ* vii. 1156–66.

They took their delight in the Law of the Lord therein delving both morning and night [Ps. 1: 2].

gaon The *geonim* were the heads of the chief talmudic academies of Babylonia. From the 9th to the 13th cc. they won and maintained religious authority over diasporic Jewry. See *EJ* vii. 315 ff.

from God's Word to the left or the right [Deut. 2: 27].

The Believer declared:

Your fathers and ours kept faith with God's law
through the Levites and Priests—kohanim;
And through Prophets as well, who brought down the
Lord's word in a mighty and thundering stream.
Now these are all gone: risen in their stead
are God's gift to his folk—geonim.

The Schismatic declared:

I could have considered your rabbis' remarks
had they not washed God's teaching away,
But the rabbis come forward with fanciful strictures
no right-thinking man could obey.
The Lord gave straightforward command: you may kindle
no fire on the Sabbath day;
But, kindling dissension, they bid us light candles,
and so God's effulgence betray.

The Believer declared:

He who is blessed with a sensible mind
will rightly perceive and obey:
Life and law are no black-and-white corpus,
but a field of perplexing grey.
Should I foul the bright Sabbath by sitting in darkness?
Heavy my sin would weigh!
More: when are candles kindled?
On the sixth, not the seventh, day.
And if someone should note that the altar fire burned
on the Sabbath—why, what would you say?
Then open, once more, the eyes of your heart;
let our Sages' bright reason take sway.

the Levites and Priests—*kohanim* The first recognized authorities of Jewish law were the *kohanim*, 'priests', or *kohanim-levi'im*, 'levitical priests' (Deut. 17: 9, 18, 18: 3, 19: 17, 24: 8).

you may kindle no fire on the Sabbath day Exod. 35: 3.

the altar fire burned on the Sabbath As in Num. 28: 9–10.

The Schismatic declared:

Words grow weary; all streams feed the sea;
enough, then, of false surmise.
God's Dictate is perfect, restoring the soul,
and pure, enlightening the eyes;
It buds on the trees of the geonim,
it shines in the rabbis' skies.
And he who contests, who rejects this truth
does nothing but fantasize.
Yet how can I stir from my fathers' paths,
men righteous, steadfast, and wise,
To label them evil, who ever sought good,
to hold their instruction lies?

The Believer declared:

If your fathers digressed from the Pathway of Right
must you, then, walk retrograde?
No! Pluck up the stones, lay the highway down;
play not the renegade.
Turn heart and reins to the Law of the Lord,
to the truths that never fade.
Regard God's command as the festive booth
with wisdom and love inlaid—
Now, except for the Rabbis, how could you know
if that booth were properly made,
How know the right length, the right width, or the proper
proportion of sunlight to shade?
Could you know if it rightly can share a wall,
stand as well in a grove as a glade?

Words grow weary Eccles. 1: 8.
all streams feed the sea [Eccles. 1: 7].
God's Dictate is perfect, restoring the soul, and pure, enlightening the eyes Ps. 19: [8], 9.
Pluck up the stones, lay the highway down Isa. 62: 10.
heart and reins e.g. Ps. 26: 2.
with wisdom and love inlaid [S. of S. 3: 10]. For discussion of Rabbanite–Karaite debate on the laws of the sukkah and the Sabbath, see the Analysis.

Further: we read, Let none leave his tent
on the Sabbath. Does one, then, invade
The domain of the public by crossing one's door?
Who shall teach you, who come to your aid?
Now all this is explained by the Sages;
their answers are sweetly arrayed
In debates of our wondrous Sanhedrins
with prooftexts well picked and well laid.
Then turn to the prosperous Pathway of Life;
save your soul from descent to the Shade.

SAID THE TELLER OF THE TALE:

Finally, after folly had been proudly touted and loudly shouted, it was soundly routed: the Karaites bowed to the Rabbis' endeavour, vowed the *geonim*'s words were a Tree of Life and that he who tastes their fruits shall live for ever. They fled their false doctrines and sped, out of breath, to save their souls from death. Yes, they rushed to God's Laws, nevermore to contravene them, saying of their fathers and mothers, *I have not seen them*. They ate of the fruit of the Tree of Knowledge and their eyes opened wide; they cast from their necks the mantle of pride, to let Truth mount and ride. Enmity was put aside: their elders made peace; Israel was unified.

Let none leave his tent on the Sabbath [Exod. 16: 29].

Sanhedrins Lit. 'the lesser and greater Sanhedrin'. Alḥarizi here echoes tannaitic sources that view the Sanhedrin as chiefly a legislative body dealing with religious matters. See *EJ* xiv. 836–9; Tosefta (*Ḥag.* 2: 9, *Sanh.* 9: 1); JT *Sanh.* 1: 7, 19*c*; and BT *Sanh.* 88*b*.

save your soul from descent to the Shade Job 33: 24.

a Tree of Life and that he who tastes their fruits shall live for ever Gen. 3: 22.

to save their souls from death Ps. 33: 19.

saying of their fathers and mothers, *I have not seen them* Deut. 33: 9.

They ate of the fruit of the Tree of Knowledge and their eyes opened wide Gen. 3: 6–7.

cast from their necks the mantle of pride [Ps. 73: 6].

GATE EIGHTEEN

The Rise and Reign of Monarchs of Song in Hebrew Spain

THUS SPOKE HEMAN THE EZRAHITE: I left Hadrakh, in my youth, for that holy site where shone the Presence' light—beauty's height, the world's delight, where Kingship's crown shone bright; and did for fellows choose God's chosen Jews. A few days passed and I found savants unsurpassed in song, Song's rudder, sail, and mast, and Rhetoric's ripe repast, hot in deliberation on Song's generation, asking whose hands laid its first foundation, who bared its spring to a thirsting Hebrew nation.

Some said: Surely our fathers have told us of old that Poesy shone forth from the Arabs' lands; that its gold bands decked their hands since first they ruled the desert sands. But none here can tell when Poesy came to dwell within our walls. Who led our fathers through Song's gates, who fed them in her banquet halls? Whose mighty palm took those charmed waters' measure? Who brought us forth with untold treasure? Whose finger made Song's heavens firm? Who brought the babe of Poesy to term?

Now after they had floundered about, they sought a route to lead them out of puzzlement and doubt. Vainly they urged their craft to shore, but the more they rowed, the louder did the waters roar. Then the greybeard spoke.

Say, is it shamelessness or aimlessness leads you to Wit's recess? Confess: you are come to a wasteland with no egress; you are shut in by

Hadrakh Zech. 9: 1; a district near Damascus and Hamath (BDB, 293).
the world's delight [Ps. 48: 3].
our fathers have told us of old Ps. 78: 3.
Whose mighty palm took those charmed waters' measure? Isa. 40: 12.
heavens firm Isa. 40: 12.
urged their craft to shore Jonah 1: 13.

the wilderness. You would probe deep oceans or mountains high—where none can reach but I.

SAID THE TELLER OF THE TALE:

The debaters, worn and fraught, their efforts come to naught, rushed to the fire of the savant's thought, hot for his showers to quench their draught.

Know, said he, that golden Poesy was the Arabs' legacy. Masters of scansion, they healed her every hiation and raised her mansion, led strong-thewed stallions into her stable, with wine and choice meat set her table, raised high her towers, straight laid her floors, hewed her crystal windows and silver doors. They raised gold ladders to Song's firmament and made, and ever make, the first ascent. And though every land and clime rears singers swift to climb the golden rungs of rhythm and of rhyme—all they compose, compared with Arab song, is prose. For the clearest chime Time's bells have rung, the boldest songs that ever lips have sung, have spilled from the Arabs' tongue. The Arabs are dawn's blinding, puissant sun: before them are the nations all undone.

Yet our fathers, émigrés in Exile's winding maze, reached Arab lands and bathed in their sun's strong rays, yes, learned their speech, thought, song, became their protégés, even as Scripture states: *They mingled with the nations and learned their ways*; for in Jerusalem, metre was unknown to them. Job, Proverbs, and Psalms were our Poesy's sole store—these three and no more. This triad's balanced waves, long or short, marked Hebrew Poesy's sole port—we knew none meeter; but we lacked true verse, writ in rhyme and metre.

Yet inasmuch as some of Judah's exiles crossed the main, as it is written: *And the exile of Jerusalem that is in Spain*; and inasmuch as

you are shut in by the wilderness Exod. 14: 3.

rushed to the fire of the savant's thought, hot for his showers to quench their draught Mixed metaphors are common in *ST* and in medieval Hebrew poetry generally. See Pagis, *Secular Poetry*, 91–2.

with wine and choice meat set her table Prov. 9: 2.

They raised gold ladders to Song's firmament and made, and ever make, the first ascent [Gen. 28: 12].

all they compose, compared with Arab song, is prose Lit. 'all their poems compared with the Ishmaelites' are of no help and all their words are emptiness, of no use'.

They mingled with the nations and learned their ways Ps. 106: 35.

And the exile of Jerusalem that is in Spain Obad. 1: 20.

Spain's boundary marks Wisdom's feast, being situated, in the West, parallel with Babylon in the East (such the plan of the Creator, who set them on earth's equator)—Wisdom spilled forth to these two equidistant points from Heaven's generous hand: they be the pillars of the overarching sphere, awesome and grand; thereon does the house stand. Yes, these two lands shine in Heaven's love; as it is written: *It shall have the two shoulderpieces thereof joined at the two edges thereof.* Babylon unfurled Wisdom's banners over all the world; while in Spain arose masters of all learning, specially poetry and rhymed prose. Therefore is their pure speech unsoiled, its fine flavour enduring, its bouquet unspoiled. Yes, Song camps in Spain's fair land, and at the Spanish bards' command her hosts set forth or stand.

Then he waxed poetic and sang:

When Poesy's sages were bound in chain,
Song's silver spring burst forth from Spain.
When visions of God were denied in the East
Song's prophets arose on the Western plain.

Now it came to pass in the year four thousand seven hundred past the world's creation, there rested on Spain's sons the spirit of counsel and might; Heavenly lumination blessed the Hebrew nation: in the seventh century, dawn broke and first our singers spoke. Then fires of figured speech lit up our skies, then from our cities did our pillars of smoke cloud rise; but withal, our infant speech was spare and scrimping, our infant metre bare and limping—this until the eighth century, when they woke the lyre and made sweet melody, set Poesy's feet firm on the ground and with gold filigrees her sweet wrists bound.

Spain's boundary . . . thereon does the house stand Judg. 16: 26, 29.
It shall have the two shoulderpieces thereof joined at the two edges thereof Exod. 39: 4.
its fine flavour enduring, its bouquet unspoiled Jer. 48: 11.
Song camps in Spain's fair land, and at the Spanish bards' command her hosts set forth or stand Num. 9: 18–23.
visions of God were denied Lam. 2: 9.
Now it came to pass in the year four thousand seven hundred past the world's creation i.e. 940 CE.
the spirit of counsel and might Isa. 11: 2.
from our cities did our pillars of smoke cloud rise Judg. 20: 40.
they woke the lyre [Pss. 57: 9, 108: 3].

*A*t that time there shone in Spain our lordly sun, Greatness' firmament, the prince, Heaven-sent, who held Dominion's rod, Rabbi Isaac ben Ḥisdai the Spaniard, may he rest in the shadow of Almighty God, whose viscounty showered petitioners with endless bounty. Wisdom's pearled waters rushed through his halls, then stood upright as walls; and God opened wide the eyes of every soul, that well each saw that honeyed well, and straightway bent to pour those waters to her jug till it could hold no more. For that prince saved Folly's victims with his sweet noblesse, hauled in exiled Jewry with the nets of his largesse; yes, he won the hearts of Abraham's seed, crying, He who is God's—here speed: I shall meet your every need!

*T*hen swift did each resplendent scholar come, from East and West, from Araby and Christendom. He spread them the table of his loving care and set his Cloud of Glory hovering there, then raised his pillar of fire, blinding bright, to give his people light. There the age's winged spirits soared to set fair Wisdom's board. Inspired by their prince, they plumbed Wisdom's inner parts and fired Hebrew hearts, raised Learning's awesome see, whence Wisdom filled the earth as the waters cover the sea—oh, gloried breakers: first singers came, then music-makers. Lo, he freed mute tongues, this bold defender; and poets poured him praise starlike in splendour. Then did eyes open on Song's gold demesne: the heavens parted, and godly sights were seen; waking poet vied with dreamer, for here was Poesy's intimate and redeemer. But then faded that lustration: the enchanted castle sank to its foundation; the prince had died and all his brethren and all that generation.

*T*hen the ninth century broke and Isaac ben Khalfon spoke:

may he rest in the shadow of Almighty God Ps. 91: 1.
waters rushed through his halls, then stood upright as walls Exod. 14: 29, 15: 8.
God opened wide the eyes of every soul, that well each saw that honeyed well Gen. 21: 19.
He who is God's—here speed Exod. 32: 26.
I shall meet your every need Judg. 19: 20.
He spread them the table Ps. 23: 5.
set his Cloud of Glory hovering there, then raised his pillar of fire Exod. 13: 21.
Wisdom filled the earth as the waters cover the sea [Isa. 11: 9].
first singers came, then music-makers Ps. 68: 26.
the heavens parted, and godly sights were seen Ezek. 1: 1.
intimate and redeemer Ruth 2: 1, 3: 2, 9, 12.
the prince had died and all his brethren and all that generation Exod. 1: 6.

eastward and westward his bright lines burst; in Poesy's lists he rode forth first. His the blest beginnings of poetic might: he opened doors shut tight. Then came the Jews down to the gates to taste his palm's sweet dates. Yet his choicest trees were too few, his orchards often unblest with dew; many his fields grew blasted corn, even thorn—this while his compeers, who sought to be Song's heirs, grunted from their lairs like sleeping bears.

Yet his era bore the glory and might of the great prince Rabbi Samuel the Levite, blest be his memory, who burst forth from Song's armoury to fight the wars of poetry, unbaring many a deep and cunning mystery.

Toward the end of his reign rose Poesy's bright soul, her singular and splendid oriole, Song's altar and incense bowl, Solomon ibn Gabirol. So strong and sweet his least conceit, none other then or since could win unto the dust of his feet. And what wonders more had this man written had he not been smitten down at the height of his strength: twenty-nine years his short life's length. Bleak sum: unto thirty he was not come.

And in the ninth century these poets died, yet left bright coin in trains: they were gathered to their fathers, but their praise remains.

Then came Song's April morn, men waving like lilies in a field of thorn. This was the wondrous age of Poesy, its singers risen to prophecy. Foremost among them was the Levite, Rabbi Judah Halevi of fair renown, learning's diadem and Torah's crown. And as for the others, peace be upon them, if even not a one of them attained the heights of Rabbi Solomon—his sweetness and his strength, no, not a one—yet their words were a sign and a wonder, and their verses, thunder. Awesome each their poem and hymn, as though wrested from the cherubim, or of diviners captured; we read of them in Scripture: *Them the spirit enraptured*. Oh, could they prophesy again, all would draw near them: awesome their speech, the leaders of the nations gathered to hear them.

Then came the Jews down to the gates Judg. 5: 11.
the dust of his feet Nah. 1: 3.
unto thirty he was not come 1 Chr. 11: 25.
they were gathered to their fathers Judg. 2: 10.
like lilies in a field of thorn S. of S. 2: 2.
Them the spirit enraptured Num. 11: 26.
the leaders of the nations gathered Ps. 47: 10.

Then he waxed poetic and sang:

Princes be these, who donned the poets' robes
then beamed forth godly light from our lore and law.
Men of discernment trembled before their lines,
Time bent his knee, yea, bowed his head in awe.
With Wisdom's planks they raised their towering songs,
sockets and nails each furnished from his heart.
Choicest of men among the chosen folk,
their chosen verses stand all songs apart.
These men were visioned by their Maker's grace,
prophets that Song enlivened, face to face.

Alas, the aftermath of that great age was wrath and derision: Song's well ran dry, our bards found no godly vision. Years passed as many sought Song's lost daughter, but hewed broken cisterns and drew up bitter water. For with kingly Solomon gone to his reward, and Abraham his prince, and Judah, wielder of Song's sword, and Moses his prophet—lo, the angel of the Lord retired and prophetic Song expired; the splendour and the glory banished, that bright fountain vanished. None rose again to wield like godly pen. We here today are beggars in ravaged fields, gleaners among shrunken yields, trailing their footsteps ever but gaining on them never—a ragged horde brandishing Folly's sword. They ate the choicest wheat by half, leaving us chaff.

Now I have seen the communities of the East, there where God's glory bade the world's soul feast; and the communities of Rifat, Germany, and France, bold in wisdom's dance; those of Persia, Meshekh, Tiras, and Greece/Yavan—lying between Dishon and Alvan. What wisdom, what virtue have they not inherited? What blinding praise not merited? But for all their fame, the fields of rhyme

sockets and nails Exod. 36: 20–38.
prophets that Song enlivened, face to face [Deut. 34: 10].
found no godly vision Lam. 2: 9.
they hewed broken cisterns Jer. 2: 13.
drew up bitter water Exod. 15: 23.
Solomon gone . . . Moses his prophet i.e. Solomon ibn Gabirol, Abraham ibn Ezra, Judah Halevi, and Moses ibn Ezra.
the angel of the Lord retired Judg. 13: 21.
Rifat Gen. 10: 3.
Dishon Gen. 36: 25 and elsewhere.
Alvan Gen. 36: 23.

and metre they cannot claim, never having entered the same. Amorous for song, long they wooed her, hot pursued her, thought they had subdued her, but alas—they misconstrued her: she has barred them her doors, she will never step forth; she will come them no nearer than the South the North. Their weary souls circle that kingdom's rim, but cannot to that kingdom win: You may see it with your eyes, but you may not enter in. Yet ask them of their prowess and hear them rail: *No poet's barque like ours, no swifter sail!*—who, as they speak, fail. For the poet of high ambitions must satisfy seven conditions if he would walk Song's peaceful paths and pleasant ways to the heights of praise. But he who regards these dicta not shall find his work forgot: his lines shall melt when the sun waxes hot.

The first condition: the poet must rid his verse of dross, strip away foreign gloss, lest he resemble Greek Jews who blur Song's prism, muddying their poems with many a foreignism, making verse a shambles, weaving garnet with granite and jewel with brambles, such that their poems *sont ganz* perplexed, one line or *Wort* being *étranger* to the next.

The second condition: the poet must keep the poem's metre to the millimetre, lest he resemble some moderns whose feet, too short or too long, cannot bear proper song.

The third condition: a poet's themes should have depth and scope and be fitly dressed in figured speech and trope, lest he resemble Shinar's bards, beggars beyond hope, who rant and stumble, clutch and grope, struggling to draw deep waters from the brain without bucket or rope.

The fourth condition: the poet's meaning must be transparent to the discerning reader, at once apparent—lest he resemble the poets of France whose scrambled lines are an obfuscation groaning for explication.

You may see it with your eyes, but you may not enter in Deut. 34: 4.
peaceful paths and pleasant ways Prov. 3: 17.
melt when the sun waxes hot Exod. 16: 21.
such that their poems *sont ganz* perplexed, one line or *Wort* being *étranger* to the next i.e. 'are entirely perplexed, one line or word being stranger to the next'. The translator takes liberties here: the Hebrew does not employ foreign words.
Shinar's Babylon's.

The fifth condition: the poet must strictly hew to the rules of grammar, lest he stumble and stammer like Damascus' bards, and especially the prince of their discard blackguards, Isaac son of Barukh/Blest, the physician, whose every curst poem is a fetid emission. His pen is rigid, his matter frigid, his schemes barren and his themes bores, his men women and his heroes whores, his words foul and inconsonant, to the vowel and consonant. He depends upon fools to applaud his scribbling, on mules to laud his quibbling, who know not whether he mints chrome or crime, spews rhyme or slime.

The sixth condition: upon finishing his work, the poet must not be quick to bare it before he repair it: let him strike limp tropes, criss-cross and make good each loss, fire his dross, burnish and gloss—lest he resemble poetasters who know not words' worth: before their thoughts conceive, they give birth.

The seventh condition: the poet must sift his lines, take six from ten, then unsheathe his pen and strike again—take even four from seven to purge his leaven, thus freeing his songbird to wing to Heaven.

Now he who ploughs Song's fields with these seven tillers has set up Wisdom's seven pillars: through these virtues Spain's poets were known far and wide, took Poesy to bride while others gnashed their teeth and stood frustrate aside. Yes, Song was Spain's betrothed and sanctified, to all other swains denied.

And now attend: there be three groups of men—fools, savants, and wielders of the poet's pen. Then, poet, toss some tinselled, minnow themes into Song's pools to please the fools; but with strong word and theme poeticize to please the wise; last, pass your thought through the myrrh of trope and figures' nard to please the bard. For know that Poesy's troops divide into these three groups. The poem that accords with the first group's rules will bore the wise but please the fools; and poems where strong matter lies will repulse the fools but draw the wise; and that poem where rich tropes and fancy be sisters and brothers will please the poets but not the others—albeit the poem that binds these three virtues fast is unsurpassed, as in Judah the

before their thoughts conceive, they give birth Isa. 66: 7.

set up Wisdom's seven pillars Prov. 9: 1.

Levite's multiplicity: smoothness and simplicity, deep thought's authenticity, and music's felicity—a blest triplicity.

As for the poems of young Rabbi Solomon: the wise pursue them, but simple folk eschew them; and Rabbi Moses ibn Ezra's poetic troops please poets far more than the other two groups, for the waves of his figured speech fall wondrous clean on his thought's pure beach.

Now I have seen in the West's domain two lands flanking Spain: the first, Provence, whose poems are profound but spill not sweet or meet as Spain's upon Song's holy ground; and to the other side the Ishmaelite domains under the King of the Moravides, may his rule be erased and his name effaced.

There, before the forced conversion, lived the world's greatest sages, the crowns of the ages; but their knowledge of Song was incomplete: their works were neither strong nor sweet; their fields showed blasted wheat, except for one man's, whose song waved fully grown—Rabbi Yosef bar Yehudah bar Shime'on. His heart-sprung song shines clean and strong. His limpid lines the heart beguile; all others' are vomitous-vile. He crafted a *maqāma* all delectation, a wondrous figuration, commencing *Toviyah ben Zidkiyah's Declaration*. All snarling tongues fall still before his vision and his skill—that you might know the Lord makes sharp distinction between his and others' poems, doomed to extinction. His manse alone I found sweetly built in the West's broad zone. Yes, pity the traveller's bones who stumbles upon those others' stichs and stones. A pox on blind craftsmen with warped woofs and warps; not a one of their houses is lacking a corpse.

I saw, in France, sages who could all hearts entrance, minds wider in wisdom than the rolling sea, who be the root and branch of Knowledge's tree. But their poetic compositions are misrequisitions, gaunt apparations, sickly, bleeding, not worth the reading, pinched

There, before the forced conversion See *EJ* xv. 225.

Rabbi Yosef bar Yehudah bar Shime'on . . . *Toviyah ben Zidkiyah's Declaration* See Analysis, n. 1.

All snarling tongues fall still Exod. 11: 7.

the Lord makes sharp distinction Exod. 11: 7.

not a one of their houses is lacking a corpse Exod. 12: 30.

and pale, sin-laden like the goat of Azazel. Their metres are mangled, their rhymes jangled, their lines a spoliation straining for innovation; none can read them without explication. (Some of these bards do furnish explication—the same requiring further explication!)

*Y*ou will find like errors without surcease in our communities of Greece, bright Learning's site whose folk delight in right; but oh, their dull songs, their clanging, banging gongs! Thence repair and find no garden fair to scent the air, but bushes scraggly bare. Thankfully, at times God raises there a palm with fragrant dates—such be the fruits of Michael son of Caleb from the city of Thebez, some of whose poems are the ear's delight; for he went to Spain in his youth and learned to write. Like praise is due Rabbi Moses son of Avtalion, among his fellows lone.

*T*ravelling to the East I found virtuous communities praise-crowned and rightly renowned. But, oh, the sad offerings of their clumsy bards: shards, not sards. Their poets leap agile as pregnant sheep—whose offspring were better throttled, being streaked, speckled, and mottled.

*A*nd in the city of No-Amon I saw the learned—God help us!—Elazar whose song bizarre plummets earthward (*thud!*) like a falling star—although one finds, at times, a glint of intelligence among his rhymes.

*A*h, pity Egypt's poems, how their writers undress them of Glory's bright robes, then task them and distress them: yea, I have seen the oppression wherewith the Egyptians oppress them—excepting Rabbi Abraham of Demira's sweet trills, some wafting over Wisdom's clear rills (the rest having fled to the hills).

*I*n Damascus, too, I saw—sure fact!—masters of kindness, charity, tact, and every godly act; but their songs, less than lucid, are overbearing and mucid. Were they flung to the swines' trough, the latter would shout, *Enough!* Now the cream of their miscognition is Yitsḥak son of Barukh the physician, whose febrile lines call for no

sin-laden like the goat of Azazel Lev. 16: 1–15.
streaked, speckled, and mottled Gen. 31: 10, 12.
Elazar The name means 'God has helped'.
I have seen the oppression wherewith the Egyptians oppress them Exod. 3: 9.
the rest having fled to the hills Gen. 14: 10.
overbearing and mucid Zeph. 3: 1.

diagnostician, being in an advanced state of decomposition—though donkey and cur still sniff them like packets of myrrh.

Now some Damascenes purloin Solomon's and Judah's lines, then twine them with their own blasted vines—oh, sorry tilth! Yes, they strip the former of their mantled wealth and robe them in filth. They cast angel songs, none sweeter, in misshaped metre, prison their attar in fetid matter, then through their banquet rooms parade them as though they themselves had made them.

Moreover, Damascus' bards sport the prince of obsceneness, an Egyptian unrivalled for dullness and leanness, whose bovine lines, in their uncleanness, know no like in all the land of Egypt for meanness. This scribbler, proudly wafting his turds, discredits Gabirol's 'feeble words'; claims his vessels are onyx, and Abraham's, potsherds; that Moses (ibn Ezra) would shepherd his herds; that Judah would judge him Song's dawning light and find Poesy's giants grasshoppers in his sight. In one poem he bawls, in fevered unreason, *My song is like the Spaniard's, each word spoke in due season!*

Ah, would our brave Spaniard Solomon repair again unto his kingly chair, he would bare the buttocks of his would-be heir, clip his tail and smash his pate, show the reprobate the gate, boot him straight into a monkey cage, and leave him there to rant and rage!

I saw as well in Damascus a Hebrew smiting an Egyptian Jew, the smiter being the aforementioned Barukh's son, Yitsḥak, a physician who made Song a laughing-stock, that Song fell on his face and cried, God makes of me a mock: he who hears of this will laugh/*yitsḥak*: Listen how ploughboys and ruffians laugh, hear the jeers and hoots of raff and chaff. This very Yitsḥak reviled the Egyptian's poems, saying:

Rule's splendour and shields—turn to me,
turn your backs on the scribblings of slaves.

packets of myrrh S. of S. 1: 13.
robe them in filth Zech. 3: 4.
bovine lines, in their uncleanness, know no like in all the land of Egypt for meanness Gen. 41: 19.
find Poesy's giants grasshoppers in his sight Num. 13: 33.
each word spoke in due season Prov. 15: 23.
I saw as well in Damascus a Hebrew smiting an Egyptian Jew Exod. 2: 11.
God makes of me a mock: he who hears of this will laugh/*yitsḥak* Gen. 21: 6.

Dig a grave for their lines, drop them in;
if the lines do not fit, dig more graves.

Now I cannot see—is my vision blurry?—how a buried man can yet another bury! You, inter, if you please—who are Song's demise? It is you who are referred to in the saying of the wise: *First heal your own, then another's eyes*. You babbler-none-worse: while you rant and curse, the Egyptians are burying your own dead verse.

And now a word about Zova's Jews: I hold them faith's crystal cruse, recorded all in Virtue's *Who's Whos*; but their song, no paradigm, sinks like a snared bird in a pit of slime.

There, long past, lived a poet named Yosef bar Zemaḥ/plant, whose soul was a jewel but whose song a rank plant, whose root was blast and whose fruit was cant. There, of old, did one Shelah abide who took the Muse to bride but did no more than lie a virgin by her side, that she bitterly cried, yes, cried all her life, seeing that Shelah was grown and that she was not given him to wife.

After him came the cantor dulcet-voiced and able, Yaḥya son of Elkazir who set God's votive table. By nature sweet, in virtues complete, his songs, alas, showed all his fellow poets' wrongs. And there be other poets of his ilk who know not sackcloth from silk: mewling sheep, they penned songs that float like darkness on the face of the deep. Some be young, some old, some cantors, some judges—but all their poems are dolts and drudges.

Now there be among them those who revel in the poems of ben Abbas declaring, *Hélas! No poet has risen in his stead*. Let each such dullard whack his head to restore his wit and admit, with no misgiving, that they have confounded the dead with the living.

I saw also in the city of Calneh—that is, Alraka—a man of first rank rushing to Song's plush, verdant bank. Well, let him browse—with cows, the drooling plodder: he knows no more of wisdom than

First heal your own, then another's eyes BT *BB* 15*b*.
the Egyptians are burying your own dead verse Num. 33: 4.
like a snared bird Ps. 124: 7.
in a pit of slime Gen. 14: 10.
seeing that Shelah was grown and that she was not given him to wife Gen. 38: 14.
darkness on the face of the deep [Gen. 1: 2].
Alraka Like many cities called by biblical names, the identity of this site is unclear: see 'Calneh', *EJ* v. 65.

straw and fodder. Yes, fit, for all his twaddle, for bit and saddle, him the rabble follow and his foul flasks swallow, grateful to their generous donor; well—like ox, like owner. His name is Berakhot/Blessing, son of Yeshuah/Salvation—and is a blest abomination. Of him I wrote:

Wide fling the windows when this scribbler
trespasses the room:
He passes wind, calls it a song,
then wafts it like perfume.
His father fathered a host of sins,
his mother was Evil's womb.
Dead both, they leave the world their son—
a pox, a scab, a rheum.
Beware! He is passing lines again!
No—worse! Arggh—fetch the broom!

Among Arbel's prophets I found a prince of crimes who purloined the homonym rhymes of Moses ben Ezra's masterwork *Anaq*. The name of this rooster was ben Sekhvi /Son of the Cock. He stretched each purloined rhyme into a song tortuous long, which should be flung to a pile of dung, unswept, unhonoured, and unsung. Rise, Moses, and strike this fool's head of rock: who else can give wisdom to this cock?

Now of the Eastern poets of old I cite Rabbi Zekhariah and the academy head Shmariah, heroes of the Talmud and God-fearing men who, had they not lifted the poet's pen, had been in no wise blamed: but they chose to walk naked, both of them—and were not ashamed! Yes, they took Song's mantle and held it between them; then, bare-butted, walked backward—alas every eye that has seen them!

Moses ben Ezra's masterwork *Anaq* See Analysis, n. 1.

Rise, Moses, and strike this fool's head of rock: who else can give wisdom to this cock Prayerbook, preliminary morning service (*birkhot hashaḥar*): 'Blessed art Thou . . . who hast given the cock intelligence to distinguish between day and night' (Hertz, *Authorised Daily Prayer Book*, 19 n.).

but they chose to walk naked, both of them—and were not ashamed Gen. 2: 25.

they took Song's mantle and held it between them; then, bare-butted, walked backward Gen. 9: 23.

Now looking at the poets of Babylon, that land which genius shone upon, I see that the more they be Torah's masters the more have they sown Song's disasters. Their bloated lines bleat or bray, We are sheep gone astray, we have tumbled down folly's scarps: by the rivers of Babylon we sat down and wept; yea, upon their willows hung our harps.

Now the pick of their poets was the academy head Yitsḥak bar Yisrael, few of whose poems were whole and hale; most, pinched and pale, showed weal and wale. He penned a book of *maqāmāt* cold and remote, filled with songs and letters were best unwrote, that tax the eye and tight the throat. There folly rested, nested, and sickly themes egested, all maggot-infested. Silence had suited Yitsḥak better: he penned neither song nor letter, but worms and fetor.

Following upon him was Yitsḥak ben Alawani, with gold in store but as poet, poor; for a thousand gold coins he bought an academy, but was supplanted as its head; he betrothed a maiden but another man lay in his stead. His song is bare, crude earthenware; and if one ask, Where is that poetry loved of fools and sots? God speaks, Here 'tis, hiding among the pots.

All current poets of Adinah chew Folly's cud; they bob, asleep, on Folly's flood; some few pluck our sages' gardens for a random bud then tramp it in their mud. Lo, the skirts of their bards are fouled with blood.

Now Rabbi Moses son of Sheshet came from Spain to teach the Adinites the ways of Song, but could not right their wrong, could not penetrate their minds' thick shield: we have healed Babylon but she is not healed.

Then he lifted his voice and sang:

In truth, the sons of the East stand removed
from Time's savants like peaks from the plain.

We are sheep gone astray Isa. 53: 6.
by the rivers of Babylon we sat down and wept; yea, upon their willows hung our harps Ps. 137: 1–2.
maggot-infested Exod. 16: 20.
he betrothed a maiden but another man lay in his stead Deut. 28: 30.
hiding among the pots. 1 Sam. 10: 22.
Adinah Babylon.
the skirts of their bards are fouled with blood Isa. 9: 4.
we have healed Babylon but she is not healed Jer. 51: 9.

When the sages of France and of Greece set their hearts
on the Torah and claimed its domain,
All knowledge and wisdom they won for themselves—
but abandoned Song's kingdom to Spain.

SAID THE TELLER OF THE TALE:

Now when I had heard his wondrous exposition, his sweet and winning composition, I asked him his name and whence he came; he answered, saying:

Hever the Kenite the name that I bear;
from Elon Zaananim am I sprung.
In Wit's wars I use laudes for arrow and lance
while I raise, for a pitchfork, my tongue.

GATE NINETEEN

Of a Dispute of Poets Seven: Which Virtue is Dearest in the Eyes of Heaven

THUS SPOKE HEMAN THE EZRAHITE: I was in Petor, city of Balaam son of Beor, walking the blue Euphrates' side on grassy carpets plush and wide, whiling away the hours in pungent flowers and shady bowers. There I spied a handsome band—seven youths, fairest of the land, poets striving to prove which of all virtues should be most approved, of God and man most loved.

Said one, To virtues be we dutiful: all are beautiful, all hallmarks of gentility; yet first among them stands Humility, Beauty's own vault: burying every fault, it blots out shame, rids souls of blame—yes, yields a man friends, and fair and goodly name.

Humility—fairest of virtues she,
Wisdom's most blessed dove:
Sin she removes from all men's sight
and hatred turns to love.

His companion said to him, You shepherd wind, leave Truth behind. What worth restraint from boast compared to Industry, captain of the host? Thereby find favour in God's sight and in man's eyes; take wealth and honour for your prize in earth and Paradise. Gain good, yes, flowing gold beyond what treasure-troves can hold.

Then, waxing poetic, he sang:

Industry, unrivalled good—
happy the man she aids.

Petor, city of Balaam son of Beor Num. 22: 5.
of God and man most loved Prov. 3: 4.
shepherd wind Hos. 12: 2.
find favour in God's sight and in man's eyes Prov. 3: 4.

Serve her: she is virtues' queen—
all others be her maids.

Said the third companion, Rant! Cant! All virtues quake in pallor before Valour, who tenders foes their right amends and succours friends. The hero's sword shall never fail: he shall shout, yes, roar, against his enemies prevail. He shall know great sway: before him men shall cry, *Clear ye, clear ye the way!*

Then, waxing poetic, he sang:

Valour, the pride of virtues all:
blest be the man uncommon brave.
Many the foes he shall subdue,
many send early to their grave.

Said the fourth: Slaver! Palaver! Fie on your industry, your valour, your humility: futility! Faith, Faith sets men whole, ennobles the soul, and gives a man honour as naught else can: so shall he find favour and good understanding in the sight of God and man.

Then, waxing poetic, he sang:

God held that Faith be largest writ
on Virtue's scroll;
If Prophecy were body held—
Faith were its soul.

Said the fifth, Pooh! Phoo! On Virtue's height shines Wisdom's light, whose devotees are blest. Wisdom gives life to them of her possessed. But for Wisdom, men were goods and chattel, slavering cattle.

Then, waxing poetic, he sang:

Wisdom: no virtue half so fair—
man's golden crown
Bringing the weakling power and rule
and right renown.

he shall shout, yes, roar, against his enemies prevail Isa. 42: 13.

Clear ye, clear ye the way Isa. 62: 10.

so shall he find favour and good understanding in the sight of God and man Prov. 3: 4.

If Prophecy were body held—Faith were its soul Lit. 'If prophecy were matter, then faith would be its form'.

Wisdom gives life to them of her possessed Eccles. 7: 12.

Said the sixth, Prattle! Rattle! Right's principality is ruled by Morality. He by this highest virtue moved finds his words and acts approved, and all his sins removed. Him the world prizes: tower-like his golden reputation rises. Burnished by men's veneration, his goodly name shines generation after generation.

Then, waxing poetic, he sang:

Naught like uplifting Morality,
in Virtue's sky the sun.
That man, immoral, with good and fame,
good and fame hath none.

Said the seventh, Bibble! Dribble! In the Kingdom of Virtue one man stands apart: he who is possessed of a Good Heart. Blest thereby, he stands high in every eye. Accolades twine him; even his foes cannot malign him. All mortal tongues his praises tell; the very angels speak him well.

Then, waxing poetic, he sang:

Goodheartedness—that garden yielding
fruits of goodly flavour;
The Good Heart is loved of God above;
yes, finds in His eyes great favour.

Now when the old man had heard them all, he said: Stuff! Fluff! Puff! And richly worthy of rebuff! Sooth, you darkly seek the truth! One virtue holds the rest in fee: before her all others bend the knee, yes, stumble and fall—for she excels them all. She robes men in Piety's weeds, for she is the store of righteous, kindly deeds. Through her is sin atoned and hatred disowned. Through her one gains his uttermost desire, though it were in Heaven or higher. Through her one soars to nobles' ranks winged with men's heartfelt thanks. Through her, spared sweat and toil, one wins a name fragrant as goodly oil.

Yes: that man of Generosity devoid shall see his goodly name

finds in His eyes great favour Prov. 3: 4.
stumble and fall [Ps. 20: 9].
she excels them all Prov. 31: 29.
a name fragrant as goodly oil Ps. 133: 2; S. of S. 1: 3.

destroyed, his righteous prayers held ribald songs, his right deeds, wrongs. He shall be held a shivering mouse, be shunned like a louse; by friends maligned, to ignominy consigned, he shall become a stranger in his very house.

But the generous man is honourable by definition: shriven of sin without fasting and contrition, his crimes know instantaneous remission. His largesse is a magic glove to stroke men's hearts and win undying love. His foes shall laud him, enviers and enemies applaud him. Any who dunned him shall breathe his name with awe; any who shunned him, hold him Light and Law.

Through Generosity is the dolt wise and the wretch disarming; the gaunt, full, the proud, charming. Indeed, I have seen rakes and jakes through Generosity transmute their every monstrosity. Lead turns golden in their vault: Love covereth every fault.

Likewise I have seen men deserving all laudation, Wit's consummation, who rear their lives on faith's foundation; but lacking Generosity, they are held void of true religiosity. Their modesty is unbodicedty, their industry sindustry, their lucidity stupidity, their pluses minus, and their sobriety vinous. At Generosity's feet all goodly virtues fall and of her it is written, *Many daughters have done virtuously but thou excellest them all.*

Then, waxing poetic, he sang:

Excelling all other virtues she—
Generosity, with great good swollen;
If other virtues be held fair
know them of Generosity stolen.

SAID THE TELLER OF THE TALE:

Delighted by this alluring outpouring, this dipping and soaring, I sought to learn if the speaker's elegance attested like intelligence, so I said, By Him who lends your lips the power to indite

Any who dunned him shall breathe his name with awe; any who shunned him, hold him Light and Law Lit. 'Those who curse him shall bless him, for through his generosity he conquers their hearts and attracts their love.'

Love covereth every fault Prov. 10: 12.

Many daughters have done virtuously but thou excellest them all Prov. 31: 29.

Excelling all other virtues she Prov. 31: 29.

and gifts you with the spirit of Counsel and of Might, inform me of your spring and of your pasturing. Whereat he said,

Hever, bright hearth of Poesy I:
my tongue shoots fire far and near.
I dower the heart with Wisdom's stones,
sapphire and onyx, opaque and clear.
Fast friends I vest with cloaks of praise
but foemen mantle with robes of fear.

Hearing this art and power, this poetic shower, I knew the speaker as our friend and mentor and guide supreme, Hever the Kenite of Zaananim. For the moment he was me lent I stood him by to smell his goodly scent, inhale his sweet locution's condiment. Then I bade him goodbye and we turned to our tents respective, he and I.

the spirit of Counsel and of Might Isa. 11: 2.

GATE TWENTY

Of Seven Maidens and their Mendacity

THUS SPOKE HEMAN THE EZRAHITE: In youth, when I was garlanded with light, I was pricked by Delight to mount and ride down vale, up mountainside through murky fens and lions' dens. So I loaded Wandering's mule with all I might require—five bushels of Desire; then, bidding Judah's Bethlehem/Bread's Store goodbye, I primed my wings to fly before life's liquor in its cup ran dry, before my bloom were blown, my seed unsown, before bright noon gave way to a silver moon.

*W*ell on my way, I entered a field in the cool of the day and saw seven maidens pass before me on the green, stars pristine: the rippling grass gave back their sheen. Seeing me, they advanced in stately dance, each covered with Beauty's mail—robe, hood, and veil; yet their ivory aura breached my eyes and took my heart as prize. Oh bannered armies, awesome all, with breasts that stood upright as a wall; fragrant they were, elegant and tall, proud as cedars from Lebanon's hills, sprung from Beauty's forests and fed from Eden's rills. Each shining maid was redolent with cinnamon and myrrh and many an unknown scent: Oh magic field of Beauty's richest yield!

*O*ne of the seven, from her shoulder and upward tallest of that band of Heaven, stepped forward with eyes that spoke soft love like the turtle dove, and lashes dark and long that were a siren's song, with breasts designed to rob the heart of rest, with hips that set a-quiver

lions' dens S. of S. 4: 8.
Judah's Bethlehem/Bread's Store Ruth 1: 1.
in the cool of the day Gen. 3: 8.
bannered armies, awesome all S. of S. 6: 4, 10.
that stood upright as a wall Exod. 14: 29, 15: 8.
cedars from Lebanon's hills [Isa. 14: 8].
redolent with cinnamon and myrrh [Prov. 7: 17].
from her shoulder and upward tallest 1 Sam. 9: 2.

loins and lips, and polished thighs to melt the liver and daze the eyes, with white hands radiant as ivory bands, with glowing cheek would turn the strongest warrior weak, with teeth circled by bright scarlet thread—gems guarded by sharp roses' red. Within that garden lie nectar-washed pearls on a soft, pink bed, whereof angels would be fed; who drinks from that spring thirsts never more nor hungers more for bread.

She addressed me: Peace, tiger's whelp and lion's young from the brakes of wisdom sprung.

To which I answered, And may you never cease to walk with the angels of peace. But I adjure ye, O daughters of Jerusalem of haughty gait, with cheeks that Beauty doth bediadem with my blood's red, with eyes blue-tinted not of kohl, but my heart's grief instead, with lids that pierce me as with spears, with cheeks whose glowing coals fire my fears, with teeth whose pearls are but my frozen tears, with fingers that are milky dreams, with lips—sweet tongs!—concealing living streams, with faces' shine against which dawn is night, a glow that drives the sundial backward with its light: restore me my heart and stolen soul; oh, make me whole! Tell me, I must know: whence come ye and whither will ye go?

Then I sang:

Why should a maiden, a gentle doe,
so wound a man when she never knew him?
Pity a lover racked with pain—
Desire's sword hath clean run through him.
Ah, mercy, maiden: show him grace
lest it be said, A woman slew him.

One smiled and opened her moist lips wide while lightning flashed from her eyes to every side. *Bow low before her beauty!* Beauty

with teeth circled by bright scarlet thread S. of S. 4: 3.
thirsts never more nor hungers more for bread Amos 8: 11.
tiger's whelp and lion's young Deut. 33: 22; Judg. 14: 5.
I adjure ye, O daughters of Jerusalem S. of S. 2: 7, 3: 5, 5: 8, 8: 4.
living streams [S. of S. 4: 15].
that drives the sundial backward Isa. 38: 8.
lest it be said, A woman slew him Judg. 9: 54.

cried; and yet that beauty no eye had assailed: hid from all living eyes she was, her face was veiled.

*H*eaven forfend! she cried, We have not harmed you or darkly charmed you. Yet you have come into a dangerous strait. Now, you, son of man, your business state: what brings you beating on Desire's locked gate? Have you no fear? How come you, unsummoned, to your monarch's inner court? What seek you here? How is it that you feared no injury from the eye's dart and from the eyebrow's sword, aimed at your rash heart, feared not to have your liver splayed apart or have your heart ripped out even, sending you on a wingless flight to Heaven? Why feared you not the viper of the eye, the flaming cheek with tress'd snakes curling nigh, the thrusting pomegranates high, the rolling robes and all the mysteries that under lie?

*L*ioness-doe, I answered, slowly, slow! Wound me not unduly nor draw your bow so coolly to slay me cruelly. Know me: since birth I lolled by Comfort's banks and knew my worth, knew myself destined to shine over all the earth. From boyhood I have lived a life of ease, born high on noble shoulders, dandled on royal knees; for my sires bore high rank and name, courageous warriors, intimates of fame. Before them lion hearts blanched like lime: more than a match they proved for pallid Time.

A rare soul couches in this frame, stranger to idle boast and shame, one that dwells beyond Orion and the Bear and shines resplendent there, a soul forged from purity alone, that sits on a high, proud throne. How many lionesses have I stalked, how many sleek deer taken, snared by my love and therein deeply shaken, aflame with love of me—be not mistaken! And all my life I have undertaken the discovery of Wisdom's sweet venue; my heart has striven with God and angels too. I seek and probe, knowledge shall not be denied me: truly there is no redeemer beside me.

*M*y word, she answered, but you are elegant and charming,

Bow low before her beauty! **Beauty cried** Gen. 41: 43.

her face was veiled Exod. 34: 33–5.

Now, you, son of man Ezek. 2: 1 and elsewhere.

beating on Desire's locked gate Judg. 19: 22.

How come you, unsummoned, to your monarch's inner court? Esther 4: 11.

has striven with God and angels Hos. 12: 1.

there is no redeemer beside me Ruth 4: 4.

amorous and disarming! Well, then—it pleases us to act at your behest and grant you your request. Know that this fair, this jewel rare of glowing cheek and spilling raven hair, this glowing creature with her every mysteried feature is Beauty's consummation, singular of station, the mistress of every land and nation. Queen-conqueror decked with ring and booty, she is come out to show the nations and the princes her beauty. This day she has robed herself in Beauty's suit: flowing with milk and honey she, and this is her fruit.

Then she sang:

Behold one fairer than the moon;
her hair and cheek are night and fire.
All other maids have Beauty claimed
while she hath Beauty owned entire.
The luminaries, envious, flame;
they draw their blades, they threaten, Yield!
The heaven's stars are javelins,
the surly moon a blazoned shield.
A dotard long undone by age
at sight of her cheek would be restored:
O lips of springtime, honey-bright;
O kisses, dewdrops of the Lord!
Beauty, long a-wandering,
discovered her meadow and pitched his tent;
The blind, at midnight, stream to her light,
the mute sing, tranced and eloquent.
Let the wisest sage probe her mysteried face—
his thought would drop wide-eyed to the ground.
Honour and Majesty clasp her hands,
Splendour and Radiance ring her round.
Plumb the world's treasures—find not her worth,
not in ocean's blue nor beneath earth's green;
Nor ever say, Have you seen her like?
Know: you have no likeness seen.

she is come out to show the nations and the princes her beauty Esther 1: 11.
flowing with milk and honey she, and this is her fruit Num. 13: 27.
Honour and Majesty Ps. 96: 6.
you have no likeness seen Deut. 4: 15.

Her poem done, she asked, Now tell me of your habitation and of your station.

I answered, Maid, peruse the finest of the Jews, their boldest and their best, he who, shunning ease, flew wingless eastward from the farthest west. Quitting Spain, he crossed the main to Greece and did not cease but urged through raging waves, through deserts, swamps, and bat-filled caves until he came to No-Amon in Egypt, thence went on to Mount Hermon; yes, Memphis put behind with fair Canaan in mind, left the Nile forever for the Jordan River, abandoned Alexandria's rare halls for Jerusalem's bare walls. To Hazor I did aspire and thence passed on to Tyre, from Dibon travelled to Heshbon, from Arnon to Lebanon, from Dan to Dedan, from Ramathaim to the land of Merathaim, from Keilah to Havilah, from Ashur to Geshur, and from Arbel to Babel; and amidst all these lands and sights never have I encountered such delights. And now, if I have found favour in your sight this day, remove your veil, I pray, that my soul not fail: restore my strength and make me hale. Bestow upon me that which you alone can give: truly this place is strait—let my soul live!

The maiden heard me to the last, then burst out laughing like a trumpet-blast, and seized me fast. Lo, she said, I rise to the task and do as you ask. Therewith she stepped back a pace, whisked the veil from off her face and—aagh! A gross mistake!—revealed a beard as thick and tangled as a writhing snake. A man! Who plunged his eager hand beneath his gown, pulled out a sword and swung it round—which seeing, I flashed cold, then hot, then crumpled on the spot.

Seeing me so, strength fled, half-dead, he began to guffaw and snort as though to give the matter wide report. His maidens followed after, rolling on the ground with laughter.

from Dibon travelled to Heshbon . . . from Ashur to Geshur Heshbon is the capital of the Amorite kingdom (Num. 21: 26–30); Arnon is a stream in Moab (as in Num. 21: 13); Dan is the northernmost point in Israel; Ramathaim is in the hill country of the tribe of Ephraim (1 Sam. 1: 1); Merathaim refers to Babylonia (Jer. 50: 21); Keilah is a town in Judah (1 Sam. 23: 1); Ashur denotes Assyria; Geshur (2 Sam. 3: 3, 13: 37) is an uncertain area east of the upper Jordan; and Dibon and Havilah could refer to various biblical sites in Canaan/Israel or outside it.

And now, if I have found favour in your sight Gen. 18: 3, 30: 27; Exod. 33: 13; and elsewhere.

remove your veil Exod. 34: 33–4.

truly this place is strait—let my soul live Gen. 19: 20.

Mercy, he said, but you surprise me: don't you recognize me? At that I forced my eyelids apart—oh, sorry sight: it was Hever the Kenite, arch-actor, ham, master of villainy and sham.

Damn you to Hell, I shouted, damn you! Can't act like a human being yet, can you!?

Hush, hush, you are still alive, said Hever; try to pull yourself together. Whereat, with more than little strain, I came to myself again.

Who, I demanded, who is this strange retinue that netted me with love, and vexed me too?

These, he answered, are the hosts of my love, whom I desire all others above and never from their beauty shall remove. I was out walking with them, savouring the heady pleasure of talking with them—each being matchless for beauty and speech—when who hove into view but you! No sooner did my beauties apprehend that you were my dearest friend, than they told me as I loved you, yes begged and cajoled me, that I must arrest you and test you, twit you and outwit you.

That said, he bade adieu and passed from view; and his maidens fair vanished into air, gone with a godly wind, leaving me lone and stunned behind. Homeward I turned, bitter at rogues and liars, and cursing Hever the Kenite and his Desires.

vanished into air, gone with a godly wind 2 Kgs. 2: 16.

GATE TWENTY-ONE

Of a Sumptuous Feast and a Bumpkin Fleeced

THUS SPOKE HEMAN THE EZRAHITE: In the sprout I set out to cull fruit of the tongues of the wise; and who should greet my eyes, roaming Rehovot's streets and thoroughfares, but chief of my comperes, Hever the Kenite, smiling gloriously and laughing uproariously.

Myself excusing, I asked, What's so amusing?

Ha, said he, I have a story for the taking will leave your ribcage aching.

You do? Well, then, fall to!

He began: I woke this morning with my insides grumbling and rumbling for a take of thick steak, but with hardly a prospect for the same, having not a penny to my name; so I set out for the city, trusting in God's pity. But after poking here and there, street, square, and everywhere, I found no fare and was the worse for wear; so I headed home strained and drained—sorry pass—when lo, I spied a country Arab on an ass, headed my way. Happy day! Joy and laughter! Here was the man I was after!

Hurrying towards him I exclaimed, Twice welcome my lord and my lord's seed, Hassan ibn Sa'id. Where have you been and where are you going? Praised be God All-Knowing: for know that many a year I have yearned after you and every which way turned after you.

Bless you, my lord, but I am not Hassan ibn Sa'id: I am Hussein ibn as-Sid.

roaming Rehovot's streets and thoroughfares S. of S. 3: 2.
poking here and there, street, square S. of S. 3: 2.
on an ass Zech. 9: 9.
Here was the man I was after S. of S. 3: 4.

Hussein ibn as-Sid The Hebrew text gives the Arab's true name as *Avida hagive'oni* and Hever's misnomer, *Avidan ben gide'oni* (both Hebrew!). In the Arabic source (see Analysis) the two names are *'Abū Zayd* and *'Abū 'Ubayd.*

Well, I rejoined, what's in a name? Aren't they all the same? Come, tell me of your health, my brother, and what you've been about, and of your father and mother. Are they yet in their prime or do they wane with time?

At this the rustic bent his head. Ah me, they have fled this world through the sins of their grief-struck son: they have gone to their reward, each one.

Oh, I cried, I cannot bear it!—and seized my robe to tear it.

Leave off, he shouted, by your parents' breath: grief saves no man from Death!

I countered, Were I to take the proper mourner's part I should rend not my robe but my heart; weep blood, not tears, for a brother generous and kind, time out of mind, a comrade ever true to me, a very tower against adversity. But Sagacity bids us abide God's decree. Dear friend, accept my sympathy and come home to break bread with me; or better, let's head down this street to the market, for a sizzling piece of meat.

Now when the word *meat* fell upon his ear he was a snared deer.

Momentarily, amidst the market's crush and jam we found, dripping on a spit, a gorgeous lamb. The fire's tongue set its innards steaming and our tongues dreaming: with its hot powers it raised up meaty flowers displaying morsels thick and choice, tender and moist, snow-white within, ruby-red outside, ruby and diamond riches side by side, the fatty cover gleaming white, a rare delight, an awesome, holy sight designed to split the heart apart.

Now when we drew alongside the butcher I said, Slice me that lamb, sir, succulent and fresh, for Hassan, our brother and our flesh. Tender us tidbits, ruby-ivory strips that will ravish our eyes and teeth and lips.

Obedient to my command the man took knife in hand and showed the butcher's art, slicing us honeysweet meat coal-red as a jealous heart. Ah, did we glut! Ah, did we cram! Ah, blessed, juicy lamb!

Flesh downed, and bread, I turned round to the restaurateur and said, Kind sir, bring on now, fresh as virgin flesh, two plates of

our brother and our flesh Gen. 37: 27. **took knife in hand** Gen. 22: 10.

your choicest dates sweet enough to soothe the fates, dates that melt between the fingers, that kiss tongue and teeth and leave a taste that lingers long after the silky jelly has slid down to the belly.

Obedient to our wish, our host tendered us the dish proudly, the which we sucked down loudly. Finally, after all the food had come to its proper place and we had offered grace, I said to the rustic, I think our steaming stomachs need a drink. Let me go, pray, to the gate, while you wait here, and send for an icy jugful from Mount Senir.

The rustic, all respect, did not object; so I hurried off and slipped behind the wall, waiting to see what would befall.

The moments dragged; the farmer, with furrowed brow and a cough, readied to make off. But in one stride the butcher was at his side. Seizing him by the sleeve he cried, Ho, ho! Very funny! And where is my money?

The rustic blustered, Please! Don't squeeze! I didn't order your meat: it was my friend's treat!

At that the butcher struck the man's back a hearty thwack. Whoreson! Who asked you to come? And where do I know you from? Three dinars, you, before I belt your butt till you empty your stuffed gut!

The rustic sobbed, Damn that robber, blubbering for my father. I told him my name is Hussein ibn as-Sid and he kept calling me Hassan ibn Sa'id—the fake, the snake!

On wept the peasant, cursing his fill, but he could not leave until he had paid the bill. Then bitterly he sang:

That cheat, that liar, he tore me apart:
Oh, I could carve his rotten heart.
I never saw the dog before,
the rotten thief, the son of a whore!
He cried for my father like a hungry calf—
but just to stuff himself and laugh!

SAID THE TELLER OF THE TALE:

Now when I had heard Hever the Kenite out I knew him for

Mount Senir S. of S. 4: 8.
waiting to see what would befall Exod. 2: 4.
Whoreson Judg. 11: 1.
the son of a whore [Judg. 11: 1].

King of Rogues beyond a doubt. I cried, For Heaven's sake, you are a matchless raconteur and rake! You bait your hook with your oily tongue, snaring old and young, nothing loath to gull the traveller and city-dweller both.

Laughing, he sang:

All men are robbers, all men lie,
so I betray each passerby.
I net me lions in my sleep
and tigers rend like mewling sheep.
I make of the savant an earthen crock,
the grey-haired sage a laughing-stock.

At that he turned aside, leaving me wide-eyed at his cunning and his bold displays, his wit and twisted ways.

You bait your hook with your oily tongue, snaring old and young Lit. 'with your tongue you snare heroes and in your maliciousness cast (cunning) spells *ḥover ḥavarim*' (Deut. 18: 11)—a pun on the name of Ḥever.

city-dweller In the Hebrew, *ezraḥ*, 'native' (Lev. 23: 42): plausibly, Heman the Ezrahite, in a veiled pun, here alludes to himself, too, being a victim of the Kenite—in this instance, by being drawn into hearing an immoral tale.

GATE TWENTY-TWO

Of Fate's Rack and the Zodiac

THUS SPOKE HEMAN THE EZRAHITE: When dawn/*zaraḥ* shone bright and I rode fresh and light, when the stars veered right and left at my command, when, on every hand, I grazed on ripe red flowers in leafy bowers, lolled in shady nooks by gurgling brooks, took my ease in every myrrh-steeped breeze and did whatever I might please, even on such a day I made my way through field and plain and came, at last, upon a fellow weary and downcast, near disconsolate, at the city gate whom, at closer sight, I recognized as Hever the Kenite.

Ḥaveri/my friend, what befell you?

Patience; I will tell you.

Yesterday I was with Hebrew friends. At the city's outskirts we saw a large mêlée, a swirling tide, men pushing in from every side. Curious, my Hebrew friends and I hurried toward this stir, this dusty blur, to find that an Arab savant had arrived at the city gate, an intimate, we were told, of stars and Fate, one who unrobed the future before it came, revealing mysteries that bore no name.

My companions ventured, Well, now, let us look into this prophet's schemes and see what shall become of his dreams.

Advancing into the crowd we saw the sage, an imposing figure advanced in age, a broad instrument in his hands and thereon a net of crisscrossed copper bands wherewith he gauged the circuits of the sun, when and where her race had begun, wherein she spun, where her course would run and when be done, declaring the while to observers

grazed on ripe red flowers S. of S. 2: 16.
and see what shall become of his dreams Gen. 37: 20.
a broad instrument in his hands An astrolabe.

of the scene, Ask me what all upper portents mean—these I can explain, yes, read you Heaven's hieroglyphic plain; but ask earth's mysteries and nothing gain. I have not spoken in secret, I said not, Seek ye me in vain. With me commune to learn the secret laws of sun and moon, the Heaven's highroads, the five planets' thoroughfares and byroads: all, all, are *my* roads. I know all the planets' zodiacal stations, their towns and castles and habitations, their ascensions and declinations, twelve princes according to their nations, who, though they in Heaven reign, habit my brain, bound fast in my thought's thick chain.

Saturn's ills I know, know Jupiter and all the good his to bestow, and warrior Mars of the blood-red glow. I hold the sun in his might, Venus with her delight, Mercury, wise and bright, and the moon of silvered light. I know where the Zodiac wends, where one house begins and the other ends.

*I*f Fortune be a throne, I be its legs; if a tent, its pegs. I snap my fingers, the Ram turns lamb; I yoke the Bull and bid him pull; Pollux and Castor call me master; I am the lancer who skewers Cancer; I lift my brows—Leo meows; Virgo, sweet maid, is by me unmade; my mind's fierce flail flips the Scale; my feet sound Scorpio's retreat; I shoot—the Archer makes swift departure; I cut the throat of the bleating Goat; by my frown I Aquarius drown; I carve the Fish on a serving-dish.

Swiftly, sprightly, quickly, lightly, I probe the stars' secrets and judge them rightly. I bring them under the yoke of my law and mend their every flaw. Men bend their ears to me to hear my prophecy: I tell each man where Fate will call him and what shall befall him from his first-drawn breath until his death. I say if his life shall be honey-sweet or he shall taste defeat; shall he root or roam, die at sea, in desert, or at home. I read his planet's flight, its risings and settings, its plain and hidden light, all the acts of its power and its might. His least duress

I have not spoken in secret, I said not, Seek ye me in vain Isa. 45: 19.

twelve princes according to their nations Gen. 25: 16.

the sun in his might [Judg. 5: 31].

judge them rightly Ps. 9: 9 and elsewhere.

all the acts of its power and its might Esther 10: 2.

to his mightiest success are incised, through my art, on the tables of my heart.

Then, waxing poetic, he sang:

Mine is the heart with a thousand eyes
unciph'ring Time's scrawled mysteries.
Tomorrow bows to kiss my hand;
Yesterday falls upon its knees.
Ask: Seer, shall I falter, stoop, or rise?
Ask: shall I stride, or limping go?
Shall so-and-so prosper? Such-and-such beg,
bear sons or daughters? I know, I know!
Say, son of man, shall you win hoar hairs?
Shall your life be the flight of the bumblebee?
Shall your feet root you out of your native soil?
Shall your fingers stroke silver as winds the sea?
To each I unveil what the heart hath hid,
and who can contend with the heart's hid power?
I disclose to each seeker what lies him in store,
season by season, hour by hour.
Ask what you will, step forward and see—
lo, Time has engendered none other like me.

SAID THE TELLER OF THE TALE:

Hearing these wonders, the assemblage, thoroughly cowed, bowed low, then rushed like waves shoreward to learn how Time would bear them forward. They pleaded one by one: What will become of me or my son? Or my wife? Shall I have long life? Health? Wealth?

When he had done answering—or, shall I say, guessing?—each man rewarded him according to his blessing.

Now I, ill-fated and star-led, turned to my friends and said, Shall we believe him or deny him? Let us try him, explore his strange hold, and cull his dross from his gold.

Yes, they answered, let us confirm him or undo him by putting one question to him: when shall Salvation come to the sons of our

Say, son of man [Ezek. 2: 1 and elsewhere]. **according to his blessing** Deut. 12: 15.

scattered nation? Let us ask, of one accord, When shall the Fallen One be restored?

So we came before him and declared, Bare your swift sword: tell us our question and win your reward.

He answered, Set you each man his hand upon the sand and I will split Holiness' domain from that of the profane.

We did as he asked. Then he drew on the sand myriad dots and signs and crisscrossed many lines. Once done these intricate designs he made many a calculation, lifting his astrolabe before his face and fixing the sun in its station; then, with lines for borders and partition, he fixed the ascending planet in its exact position until each star nearly fell from its berth to bow before him to the earth. Long he sat in strange surmise, then raised his eyes to stare.

I swear, he said, by Him who fashioned earth and air, moon and sun, the planets every one, who set the Zodiac turning and the whirling constellations burning, yes, who put each star in place: you be not of us nor do you the Nazarene embrace; no—you are of the accursed Jewish race.

Jews we be, said we.

Thereat the old man raised a cry: I lift my hand to God Most High, who probes men's hearts with His all-seeing eye, who teaches His servant to understand the secrets of stars and sand, who divides the holy from the profane; you ask me to explain deep mysteries and fathom thick-veiled future histories.

You ask, Shall a lost sheep walk through lions' dens and rise from the feast of a seventy-toothed beast? What power, you ask, can raise a fallen tower, seize the helm of a sinking ship and wrest its voyagers from the Maelstrom's grip? You ask if a scattered folk,

the Fallen One i.e. Israel: Amos 5: 2.

Bare your swift sword [Judg. 9: 54; 1 Sam. 31: 4; 1 Chr. 10: 4].

split Holiness' domain from that of the profane Ezek. 42: 20.

to bow before him to the earth [Gen. 37: 10].

you are of the accursed Jewish race Lit. 'but of a nation of despised and lowly folk; and perhaps you are Jews'? See Analysis.

I lift my hand to God Most High Gen. 14: 22.

who probes men's hearts [Jer. 17: 10].

who divides the holy from the profane From the *havdalah* service, marking the end of the Sabbath, based on Ezek. 42: 20.

Shall a lost sheep walk through lions' dens and rise from the feast of a seventy-toothed beast? Lit. 'and of scattered sheep—shall she escape the lions' teeth, while she walks about amidst the beasts?', the reference being to the nations of the world.

laughed to scorn, can be ingathered in a world reborn? You seek the dead's rejuvenation and the nations' devastation; by God and His revelation, you ask Earth's ruination! Sons of death, you would see our kingdom destroyed; you would hurl us to the void!

SAID THE TELLER OF THE TALE:

After the old man had roundly disowned us, the entire congregation would have stoned us. They spat on us, hooted us, booted us, dragged us hands and feet through street after street until, battered and blood-spattered, we were flung at the gate of the city's magistrate.

Spilling us in the dirt, our captors shouted, These dogs seek the king's hurt!

Now this righteous gentile, before whom we had been brought, could, at a glance, discern a man's most secret thought. At once, he took us to a private place and bade us tell him what had taken place—the which we did. Thereat he said, Peace be with you, do not fear: no harm shall come you here. He called loud to a servant, Put these sons of perversity under lock and key! And so we passed the night in prison. But shortly after the sun had risen and the crowd had long gone, he bade us travel on.

God in His clemency had sent an angel to set us free. And now that we have escaped that mob's wide jaws and raking claws, I say, Blessed be the Lord in Heaven above and on earth beneath, who gave us not as prey unto their teeth.

Sons of death 1 Sam. 26: 16.
the entire congregation would have stoned us Num. 14: 10.
Peace be with you, do not fear Gen. 43: 23.
sons of perversity 1 Sam. 20: 30.
shortly after the sun had risen Gen. 19: 15.
God in His clemency had sent an angel to set us free Num. 20: 16.
Blessed be the Lord . . . who gave us not as prey unto their teeth Ps. 124: 6.

GATE TWENTY-THREE

Of Hever the Kenite's Wretched Hour and Sudden Rise to Wealth and Power

THUS SPOKE HEMAN THE EZRAHITE: The tempter Wandering clasped my arm and hugged me close as if to ward off harm. He set me high on Separation's wings that I might fly from one land to the next. So, greatly vexed, I traversed deserts, hills, plains—endless domains. Oh, Wandering buffeted me about till I was utterly worn out.

One day when I had dragged from Syria to Tiberias, I encountered someone in a plight yet more serious—Hever the Kenite, ragged and shabby, blood-streaked, pustulent, and scabby. I rushed to his side and did him importune to tell me of his wretched fortune.

He informed me he had come from Shittim to Tel Hittim, where thieves had seized and overpowered him; they kicked him, clubbed him, all but devoured him. They scored his flesh from his head to his feet, threshed him like wheat. Yet, stripped naked, and dripping red, he somehow fled, even as Death's sword turned above his head.

Now when I had heard his tale, my insides quivered: I sobbed, I wept, I shivered. I seized his hand and home I led him; I spoke him soft, I robed him, richly fed him, hoping to rid his heart of pain and lead his soul to Gladness once again. We downed spiced wine, cups beyond number, until wine had me deep in slumber. When I awoke at dawn and sought my loved friend, I found him gone: I called him, but he answered none.

Shittim Josh. 3: 1 and elsewhere.
sword turned Gen. 3: 24.
home I led him S. of S. 3: 4.
spiced wine S. of S. 8: 2.
sought my loved friend, I found him gone: I called him, but he answered none S. of S. 5: 6.

Anger suffused me like a red tide. I smacked my hands, I chafed my lips, I all but cried: to think I had him naught denied! Sore did I regret it and swore *instanter* never to forget it.

Now the next day, as I walked down a busy street, whom should my eyes meet but Hever the Kenite, dressed like a count and seated on a royal mount and two servants before him—wondrous strange! I was staggered by the change. He had left me battered and shorn, tattered and torn. Lo, Weeping abides the night, but Joy comes by morn!

No sooner did I see him than I turned to flee him, but he leapt from his carriage, overtook me, faced me, fell upon my neck, kissed me, and passionately embraced me.

See here, said he, I know: I have made poor show. My offences are myriad. Period.

How dare you so offend your tried and trusted friend? I cried. How long will you so use me and abuse me?

God knows, he answered, you are graven on my heart till death do us part. But necessity, you see, forced me to leave you and deceive you.

Explain me, then, all this—this metamorphosis! Last night you were a starved and sorry sight; now you ride in silk and ring, decked out like a king.

Said he to me, His praise be sung, who dethrones the king and lifts the needy from the dung. Today He gifts the pauper with a crown; tomorrow, brings princes down. But let me tell you how I came to wealth and power in this blessed hour.

Heart's delight, after slipping from your house last night, I wound round the city, praying God His pity to evince; and lo, I came upon the courtyard of a prince.

There I declared:

Who shall succour a noble son
hurled to the depths by Fortune's wrath?
He trod Orion yesterday,
yea, stars of Heaven laid his path.

Weeping abides the night, but Joy comes by morn Ps. 30: 6.
fell upon my neck, kissed me, and passionately embraced me Gen. 33: 4.
you ride in silk and ring, decked out like a king Esther 6: 6–11 [and Gen. 41: 42–3].
lifts the needy from the dung [Ps. 113: 7].

But now his meteored praise is dark:
Fate lifted up the hand of stealth,
Brigands attacked him on his way
and stripped him of his weal and wealth.
He swathes himself in darkest mist;
lacking all cover, he robes in black.
He would make his home in clayey grave,
yes, sink into the earthen crack.
Oh, had a scribe the sky for scroll,
he could not set down this grief in rhyme.
Is there any a giver will pity me now?
I shall brighten his name to the end of Time.

All this the prince heard, and knew me master of the spoken word. He had me ushered in and said, I heard your keening and grasped its keen, hid meaning: surely such elegance attests great intelligence. Now if you will heed my behest and grant me my request, I will whip you Fortune soundly till he dare not near you and give command that Sorrow fear you.

Ask what you will: I shall your every wish fulfil.

Know, said he, that one of the realm's chancellors, chiefest of the king's counsellors, lost a daughter yesterday and fathered a son today. Now, since dawn I have laboured without cease to compose a suitable poetic piece; but though I strove to hove out of Folly's squall, succeeded not at all. I meant to write a double salutation proffering comfort and congratulation, tears, yet cheer, dirge, yet celebration. But my spring was barren of prophecy: the Lord has concealed, has not revealed this thing to me. Such is the task to which you must prove equal. Speak well; my Purse will speak the sequel.

He swathes himself in darkest mist Job 38: 9.

Oh, had a scribe the sky for scroll, he could not set down This is an adaptation from the third and fourth verses of 'Akdamut', a prayer in Aramaic written by Rabbi Me'ir ben Isaac of France (11th c.): 'He (God) has endless power, not to be described. Were the skies parchment, were all reeds quills, were the seas and all waters made of ink, were all the world's inhabitants made scribes . . .' (Birnbaum, *Daily Prayer Book*, 647–8 ff.)

to the end of Time Ps. 48: 14.

Now if you will heed my behest and grant me my request Esther 5: 8.

strove to hove out of Folly's squall Jonah 1: 13.

the Lord has concealed, has not revealed this thing to me 2 Kgs. 4: 27.

I answered him, No farther fear: joy's very source, right's best resource, is here. Behold Wit's eyes and Song's own throat. Bring ink and quill—the which he did, and I sat down and wrote:

Thine yet shall honour be and comfort fair,
only thy Maker's judgement meekly bear.
God covers thee with sackcloth and with silk,
but all thy overbearing foes strips bare.
The fir tree comes for thorn; thy daughter gone,
thy son shall fame and sway effulgent bear.

*F*ollowing this metric display I went on to say, After tears have stormed High Heaven like a raging sea, God has repented of His evil decree. Tear-clouds close at His command, gone are the rains throughout the land; the waters dry from out the eye; the breached wall is repaired, restored the beam; moonlight gives way to the sun's bright beam. We who swayed vacantly as in a trance, we who were crushed by Chance, run through by Fortune's lance—God fixed in His healing glance; raised us up from Grief's grey circumstance; turned our tears to smiles, our stumbling turned to dance. We of the palsied hand and ravaged eye found a kind sun ruling the noonday sky. Instantly healed, for mourning we were given light a-borning; for sadness, gladness; for mishap, hap; for Woe's rune, Joy's tune; for Grief's throng, song. We stripped off our sacks and put silk on our backs. Though the upper branches of the elm be shorn, a new and mighty oak is born; though last night the moon set, the sun shines yet.

*F*ather, God grants you His relief: your daughter can know no further grief, while your son, in his prime, shall set you lord of Time. Behold: instead of brass, gold; bright be your name: for whispering coal, take blazing flame. God gives you for the myrtle, oak; for a princess' gown, the ruler's cloak; for veil, mail; for soft perfume, the triple plume; for lily's pale, the rose's red; for prayer shawl's fringe, phylacteries of the head; vine's bounty for the fruit tree's yield and for

The fir tree comes for thorn Isa. 55: 13.
God has repented of His evil decree Jonah 3: 10.
gone are the rains throughout the land Gen. 8: 2.
Behold: instead of brass, gold Isa. 60: 17.
prayer shawl's fringe Deut. 22: 12.
phylacteries of the head Exod. 13: 16; Deut. 6: 8, 11: 18.

lacy kerchief, shield; the lover for the love, hawk for dove; for lioness, leader of the pride; for footman, knight astride; for sheath, sword, and for target, arrow; the falcon for the sparrow; the hauberk for the shawl, bright dawn for evenfall, for the women's house, the study hall. Yet shall you be kings' sire; you shall God desire and ring you round with glory as with fire.

Now when the prince had heard my letter and knew me prince of Song, none better, he stripped my filthy sack from off my back and clothed me with ring and jewel and lordly rule; he gave me silken cloaks for my every rag, set me on horse beneath his flag and gave me these two men at my desire; and there you have my tale entire.

SAID THE TELLER OF THE TALE:

When he was through, I said, Praise God, who showers kindnesses on His every servant's head! Whereon he bade me fond farewell and was swiftly gone.

---

the women's house Esther 2: 3 and elsewhere.
you shall God desire 2 Sam. 24: 23.
he stripped my filthy sack from off my back Zech. 3: 4.
set me on horse Esther 6: 10–11.
beneath his flag S. of S. 2: 4.
Praise God, who showers kindnesses Ruth 2: 20.

GATE TWENTY-FOUR

Of a Jolly Cantor and Jolly Instanter

THUS SPOKE HEMAN THE EZRAHITE: These be the words of Hever the Kenite:

Sit down for a spell for I've a wondrous tale to tell of a trip from Geshur to Ashur in a dry spell, when I swept through the streets for gain but found no rain. It is a vast city, Beauty's own repast, brimming with people, in wealth unsurpassed—there the awesome Emim dwelt in times past—a land flowing with milk and honey.

But no money; for the people dwelling there are a strong nation—I speak of our kinsmen, heroes of self-occupation. Champions of stint, hearts and hands of flint, their bold, piercing eyes show Gold's fierce glint. Attentive to duty, they never wince: be their supplicant pauper or prince, they do what they must do—give nothing, from a thread to the latchet of a shoe. Stripling, greybeard, husband, wife—each tends his purse like the Tree of Life, whispering, *Thine are greatness, might, and majesty, splendour, and eternity; Death, only Death, shall come betwixt me and thee.*

I arrived there, weary and sweating, at the eve of the Sabbath, as the sun was near setting. Having no money nor any friend to sup with, I resolved to see what I could come up with; so I took myself to the house of prayer, which proved exceeding fair, and joined the throng

when I swept through the streets for gain but found no rain Lit. 'when the hands of her generous men were as dry as flintstone'.

a vast city Jonah 3: 3.

there the awesome Emim dwelt in times past Deut. 2: 10.

a land flowing with milk and honey Num. 13: 28.

the people dwelling there are a srong nation Num. 13: 28.

from a thread to the latchet of a shoe Gen. 14: 23.

Tree of Life [Gen. 2: 9, 3: 22].

Thine are greatness, might, and majesty, splendour, and eternity [1 Chr. 29: 11].

Death, only Death, shall come betwixt me and thee [Ruth 1: 17].

assembled there. To my side sat two bejowled sextons, towers of pride, each with a belly wondrous wide, a Gargantuan backside, and a beard as flowing as high tide.

I drew them into conversation: Tell me, pray, of your congregation and its ministration.

*W*e have buoyant sages, they beamed, Wisdom's own barques; we have pearls, we have exilarchs; and, thanks be to God on High, a darling cantor, modest and shy, who can sweetly preachify, who fills the heart and even more the eye, a spotless lamb, a cheery, fatted ram. For holy company seek no better choice. And what a voice! Stranger, attend and rejoice! And with what ease he captains us upon Tradition's seas, unravelling the Torah's mysteries, and the Prophets' and Writings', if you please! To boot, he is Poesy's very flute—a master of liturgic verse, to wit, *piyut*.

*H*earing this generous acclaim, I burst forth, *Praise the Name!* and, heartstrings thrumming, reverently waited the cantor's coming, which was forthcoming: lo, as a comet lights the skies he burst into view, phylacteries between his eyes, and they topped by a turban of wondrous size, a cloud of linen some two hundred cubits round. His beard was a thicket on his belly's ample ground, a running spigot—if scarcely revealed, for it lay concealed beneath his prayer shawl, elegantly fringed, the which he trod on as we cringed. Seeing this awesome apparition we hurried forward, trembling in contrition and bowing in submission, awaiting his rendition of our awesome tradition.

*H*e opened his mouth as we tendered rapt attention; and lo: our ears imbibed one hundred crystal-clear mistakes—and others not worthy of mention. But I breathed not a word; why do him the disservice? This was the Sabbath; perhaps he was tired, or nervous, or distraught by the demands of the longer service.

*T*he next day, when dawn broke, I swiftly woke, donned Piety's cloak, and sought God's house once more with my holy folk. Lo, the

we have exilarchs The *resh galuta*, or exilarch, held a descendant of the Davidic house, was the lay leader of the Babylonian Jewish community. See *EJ* vi. 1023–34.

a cheery, fatted ram Deut. 32: 14.

liturgic verse, to wit, *piyut* A poetic composition designed to ornament an obligatory prayer, or the totality of such compositions. See Analysis.

phylacteries between his eyes See Analysis.

cantor entered and took his honoured seat, and in tones dulcet sweet began the daily blessings, as is meet. According to the practice of our nation, he begged God's lumination, thundering, *Make the words of Thy Torah pheasant in our mouth*, rather than *pleasant in our mouth*; and *May the Lord flavour you and grant you peas*, instead of *May the Lord favour you and grant you peace*.

In the next section of the service, his zeal mounting, he made errors beyond counting. For *It is our duty to bless and hallow Thy name* he said *It is our duty to blast and hollow Thy name*; for *Exalt the Lord our God*, he said *Assault the Lord our God*; for *Praise the Lord, O my soul*, he said *Prize the Lard, O my soul*; for *Thine, O Lord, is the greatness and the power*, he said *Thine, O Lord, is the gratings and the flour*; for *Thou rulest over all*, he said *Thou droolest over all*; and on he went until I grieved that I had ever seen that place; *a-a-rgh*, the disgrace! I pressed my palms against my burning face.

Now when the cantor had finished this prefatory atrocity, he launched into higher religiosity. Cloaking his head, he waxed ever bolder, shaking each meaty shoulder, lifting his left foot, then his right, hunkering for sheer delight until—welladay!—he put his vaulted treasures on display. He showed us his own, his original *piyutim*—a foul dream, a madman's scheme, a limping, misyoked team, a parade no ear could halt of the blind and the halt; rank crime without metre or rhyme, splume and splatter without form or matter.

For hours he bawled forth *piyutim* to his dimwit flock, called forth mucky streams from his mind's dull rock, drowned his listeners with his poppycock, this while a few of the livestock continued to snore; but most had slipped out the door. Lo, the shepherd had lost his sheep, some deep in Dream's haystacks, fast asleep; but most had gone astray, leaving behind four gaping jaws to bray and pray, a donkey choir for a poet manqué. So the fat buffoon drew out his serenade till

began the daily blessings, as is meet See Analysis.

he put his vaulted treasures on display 2 Kgs. 20: 13.

the blind and the halt 2 Sam. 5: 6–8.

called forth mucky streams from his mind's dull rock [Num. 20: 8–11].

leaving behind four gaping jaws to bray and pray, a donkey choir for a poet manqué On choirs in synagogues, from early times, see Fleischer, *Hebrew Liturgical Poetry*, 280–1.

noon (*puff-puff, squeak-squeak*), until no one had voice with which to speak.

Now when he had done his *piyutim*, when he had curdled his cream, finished his *la-dee-dees* and *tra-la-la*, and returned to the completion of the cantor's repetition of the Amidah, the service's essential prayer—the synagogue was bare; no one was there: the people were at home, lost in Lethe's lair.

Now one man of that community was of pious extraction, a man of godly action; hearing of this affair, he was driven to distraction. Can it please the Lord, he cried, to compose such trivia for worship of the Lord, and send the congregation packing with the Amidah lacking? This is rank sin, vice—for no longer can we offer incense and sweet sacrifice; the Amidah alone must suffice. Instead of rams and cows, the utterance of our lips must pay our vows; as it is said, Instead of bulls we will render the offering of our lips. Dare we be so lax, let duty melt like wax as to suffer a yak serenading yaks?

Taking deep offence, another man rose to the cantor's defence. Sneering, he taunted: Your logic slips; falsehood drips from your lips. The essence of adoration is laudation; song, sir, before supplication! In Temple times, song held sway: the Levites sang new song to God each day—and these were dear in God's eyes; yes, dearer than the fat of lambs, than breasts with meaty thighs. Now, in exile, poems and *kerovot* are the essence of our liturgy, Faith's pulse and vital energy. Moreover, consider our far-flung congregations: scattered throughout the nations we show God our esteem through *kerovot* and *piyutim*, through *seliḥot*—the penitential prayers—and laudatory airs. Would you have us stray from this set way? Say nay!

---

returned to the completion of the cantor's repetition of the Amidah The central component of all three daily services—preceded, in the morning and evening service, by the Shema ('Hear O Israel') and its attendant blessings—the Amidah is generally referred to in rabbinic Hebrew as *tefilah*, '[the] prayer'.

Instead of bulls we will render the offering of our lips Hos. 14: 3.

sang new song to God Ps. 96: 1 and elsewhere.

dearer than the fat of lambs Ps. 37: 20.

breasts with meaty thighs [Lev. 10: 15 and elsewhere].

kerovot Poetic embellishments to the first three benedictions of the Amidah on Sabbaths and holidays—possibly the most ancient form of *piyut*. See Idelsohn, *Jewish Liturgy*, 40–1, and 357 nn. 24–8; and *EJ* xiii. 598–9.

seliḥot Prayers of supplication (Idelsohn, *Jewish Liturgy*, 43–5; *EJ* xiv. 1133–4).

There is truth, said the other, in what you say: in an earlier day, when the Temple stood, thanksgiving and the psalms of David our king were the heart of our tongues' offering; but when did this pure song resound? When the Presence walked Zion's holy ground, when the writers of psalms boasted clean palms, when each singer was a saint without taint, when the Levites sang David's songs and no others, and all listeners were Wisdom's brothers. Now, however, we have neither Temple nor altar fires, no praise, no fresh song, no holy choirs; no harpists, saints, neither Levite nor priest, no man to set the board for Right's fair feast.

Harpists today are a harping fright, flatting for spite. No poets have we, but poetasters, wastrels, and wasters. Our bovine congregations shame us, and every cantor is an ignoramus. Instead of singing David's holy Psalms they hoot like harlots, without qualms. Each oaf, each clod dares blur his speech with the words of the living God, transmuting shewbread to offerings of the dead. While the cantor goes on squawling, belching, and bawling in wild pretence, none know if he makes sense, if he praises or laments; no, none can say if he prays—or brays.

Now how can this please God, that a simple man who knows not his right hand from his left, bereft of reason, should suffer such theft? One Sabbath hour a week he comes to God's house: shall he enter in vain and leave in obfuscation? He cannot pray: the cantor has not fulfilled his obligation.

Hereat his collocutor opened his mouth wide and replied: Shall your limping argumentation wrench us from the practice of every self-respecting congregation? Look to the prayer halls of the west, to Spain; and look again to Greece, where our wise brethren never cease to offer *kerovot* and songs that give their souls release. Surely, there, congregations are not lacking in fools a-mooing and a-quacking. For

clean palms [Ps. 24: 3].
shewbread [Exod. 35: 13 and elsewhere].
offerings of the dead [Ps. 106: 28].
who knows not his right hand from his left Jonah 4: 11.
shall he enter in vain and leave in obfuscation? Eccles. 6: 4.
the cantor has not fulfilled his obligation Lit. 'he does not know how to pray and the cantor has not exempted him from his obligation'. See Analysis n. 3.

the sake of a bestial fold would you turn us from the ways of old? Why, in obduration, do you seek a new creation?

Enough, said his collocutor, enough pretension! In all the lands you mention there is no like Abyss, no congregation thick as this, no, none controlling folly with so unchallenged a monopoly—from Memphis to Samarkand, from Seville to Thermopylae. See here: in every congregation you will find some ghost of thought a-glimmer—a glint, a glow, a shimmer, some comprehension of the Hebrew word, some eardrums stirred, such that when the cantor sounds the convocation to offer adoration, they at least have an inkling of what he is saying and can begin praying.

But here, no such luck: sooner milk a duck! Here none are ready, none able, for this is a stable! Here ox and ass give wisdom the *coup de grâce*; here the cantor is a knock-kneed horse who cannot walk his course. He neither sees nor comprehends, he knows not where the service starts or ends; and the mob about him know even less: they cannot tell if he curse or bless.

If he should err, he need not fear it—for none would hear it. If he butcher the text, who knows? And if he blaspheme—why, so it goes! Unchecked, he pastures cattle with his grunts and groans, and speaks to the trees and the stones. To whom, I say, does this cantor pray with twitching hand, with lurching gait, with squeaks and squalls—the synagogue walls? As Scripture attests: *To whom shall he teach knowledge—to them just weaned, just taken from the breast?* If any community had a congregation like this, they would clap their hands and hiss, groan, scream. So I say again: You are forbidden songs and *piyutim*. Lo, any man who offers *piyutim* to this congregation—his adoration is abhorration; his paean, pain; his glorification, whorification. Best that the congregation should stay their homes within: need they heap sin upon sin? Here the blind

from Memphis to Samarkand, from Seville to Thermopylae The Hebrew does not specify communities.

He neither sees nor comprehends [Isa. 44: 18; Ps. 82: 5].

speaks to the trees 1 Kgs. 5: 13.

To whom shall he teach knowledge—to them just weaned, just taken from the breast? Isa. 28: 9.

they would clap their hands and hiss [Lam. 2: 15].

groan and low: they come in mist and in darkness go. Hence say that poems and *kerovot*, if unbidden, are permissible everywhere, but here forbidden. Here be goats, not men: this is a pen.

Now when his opponent had heard this scholar out, he saw that he had been put to rout, saw that his fellow's arguments were solid and his own, rank and squalid; so, stung, he covered his mouth and left his bell unrung; he put a halter on his tongue.

Now in the city of Arbel, passing fair, there lived a Jew called Binyamin Heḥaver, Wit's pit and Intellect's despair. Hearing this locutor's argument he made reply and gained just punishment—an end to his life's none-too-silent session; he died in his trangression. His every assay was as graceful as a knock-kneed giraffe: all who heard him could but laugh; yes, laugh at him or come with staff at him. Had he only held back, he had not been bared a babbler and a quack; but he chose to show his forehead brass, so God opened the mouth of the ass. His arguments were gross, grotesque, each one a right-angled arabesque, a bald burlesque, an idiot romp, a house built on a swamp. He claimed that the biblical account of God's revelation to Moses alluded to one particular place—the penitential prayers, wherein we read, *And God passed before his face*. And for a further offering from his brain's shredded wheat: the Amidah was not the service's meat, but merely perfume or roses—not having been enjoined in the Five Books of Moses. And as for the rabbinic interpretation, *Thou shalt serve the Lord thy God*—serve meaning the reciting of the Amidah—this he held a bogus explication, a fabrication.

they come in mist and in darkness go Eccles. 6: 4.

Heḥaver The sage.

all who heard him could but laugh Gen. 21: 6.

his forehead brass [Isa. 48: 4].

God opened the mouth of the ass Num. 22: 28.

And God passed before his face Exod. 34: 6. 'The verses Exod. 32: 11–14 and 34: 1–10 are traditionally recited during public fasts. Among these is the verse "And God passed before his face, etc." (Exod. 34: 6) recited by the congregation at the end of each penitential prayer.' Schirmann, *Hebrew Poetry*, ii. 168, explanation at bottom of page.

Thou shalt serve the Lord thy God Exod. 23: 25.

serve meaning the reciting of the Amidah BT *BK* 92*b* and *BM* 107*b*: 'This [service of God] refers to the Shema and the Amidah.'

this he held a bogus explication, a fabrication See Analysis.

But anyone who maintains that penitential prayers have pentateuchal backing, while Torah authority for the Amidah is lacking, does more than bray and plod: his sin cannot be atoned, for he blasphemes the great, the mighty, the awesome God.

He who declares, The kerovah *must be said,*
but say the Amidah at your will—
Is tongue-tied, tilted, twisted;
drivelling, dribbling, ill.
His eyes are shut, his neck is stiff,
his slanting forehead brass—
The flaming fool, the goat, the ox,
the foaming, snorting ass!
Away he would gallop with Truth, the thief,
but Folly has carted him off
To slosh in the slime of ignorance' pen
and muck in deception's trough.
Could this ass lock his jaws, keep his braying tongue chained,
he might yet his honour save;
But holding each moment the year of release
he keeps freeing his mangy slave.
His criminal argument brands his brass brow
with the fiery mark of Cain:
He would light up the East with his sunshine wit
but instead drowns the world with black rain.
Sooner sing to a plugged and uncircumcised ear
than offer kerovot *to an ass;*
Sooner water a thornbush in bright hope of grapes,
sooner hunt for a dolphin in grass.
The cantor who offers seliḥot *to this folk*
will find no forgiveness for sin:

forehead brass [Isa. 48: 4].
the year of release he keeps freeing his mangy slave [Deut. 15: 1–18].
with the fiery mark of Cain [Gen. 4: 15].
uncircumcised ear Jer. 6: 10.
Sooner water a thornbush in bright hope of grapes, sooner hunt for a dolphin in grass Lit. 'and like one who says to a tree, "Wake, get up!" and like one who knocks on a locked door, and one who leaves a well-laid road to walk about a pit and comes close to falling [therein]'.

He has ravaged our highways with ditches and pits—
the ox and the ass fall therein.
Let death be his bounty, the dribbler who claims
that piyut *makes us holy and whole,*
That we may—la-dee-da—do without Amidah:
Let him sink to the depths of Sheol.
God save us from heresy, schisms, and fools,
and preserve and protect our lucidity.
Oh, grant that we ever cleave fast to Thy Will,
and not the fouled skirts of Stupidity.

pits—the ox and the ass fall therein [Exod. 21: 33].

GATE TWENTY-FIVE

Of a Hid Place and a Champion of the Chase

THUS SPOKE HEMAN THE EZRAHITE: Journeying from Ashkelon to the Valley of Ayalon we camped upon a pleasant green, and spoke, each man, of places he had been or seen; whereupon an old man chanced by, whose flashing eye hinted a vision none else could descry.

Let me tell you, he ventured, what my eyes have seen here, for I have not been here in many a year. Long since, I passed this place and, lifting my eyes, saw a champion of the chase who could the desert lion outface; who, with a roar, could mountain peaks displace. He sat upon a steed of awesome speed, whose hooves, all granophyre, struck fire; who of a kind, when given rein, sunders the plain, whose thunder and whose straining flanks shake foemen's ranks; who rears upright in blinding light, turning day night; whose gallop speaks Conquest's yoke and skullcase broke; who takes stars for eyes, for feet, the wind, and the lightning for wings—the while his hot heart sings to the fray; yea, in the fire of his heart his flesh near melts away.

See now, like a crest on a helm, the winged champion of Death's realm; yes, look to the hero's wrist, to his clawed mace; see the falcon, wings gold-tipped, all eager for the race, claws honed for slaughter: before his swoop the heart turns water. With ice-clear eyes he cleaves the skies, spies prey, and down, down to the carcass flies. His spreading wings bind deer in chains of fear. He rends, he tears, naught spares, his blood is steeped in theirs. Eagles bear witness to the hot blood's spatter; yea, all who have wings tell of the matter.

Valley of Ayalon Josh. 10: 12.
lifting my eyes, saw Zech. 2: 5 and elsewhere.
the heart turns water [Josh. 7: 5].
down to the carcass flies Gen. 15: 11.
all who have wings tell of the matter Eccles. 10: 20.

*N*ow round the hero swirl many a fierce and lean-faced hound: they streak, they bound; flame-faced, they ready them to seize their prey though he be Heaven-bound: yea, though he leap to the stars, they will cast him to the ground.

I lift my eyes—and behold, the hero a-horse on his raging course, falcon to hand; and to shoulder, the source of swift death—his quiver. Shiver, now, rocks, at his stallion's attack: fall back, lest flint hooves grind you to powder. Hunter and horn roar louder, louder: leaping on mountains, he halloos, he yells, flushing conies and hares, and wide-eyed gazelles, and the trembling hart.

*N*ow a trail wound deep to the mountain's heart, to a large, rocky glen and, therein, a covert den where none intruded. Here, safe and secluded, lay a camp of deer, tranquil all, large and small, old and young, the fawn nudged gently by the mother's joying tongue, the grazing roe, the watchful buck, the suckling fawn, and mother giving suck. Blest be the babes, now seeking rest upon their mothers' breasts, now sweetly sleeping; then waking, leaping, mother dancing at their sides, now faster, now slower, neck craning higher, now lower, not knowing that her sun will soon set in their tears, that their doomsday nears. Even as she runs from them, faces them, even as she kisses, embraces them, Death's arrow thrums: he comes! The hero comes!

*A*wesome and brave, he storms the green cave like a searing dawn. On he storms, on, his long bow drawn, his lean hounds foaming as if in pain, his falcon straining at the chain. He breasts the threshold of the lair, his bellow cleaves the air. Despair! Terror-struck at the roar and horse-hooves' clatter, the young deer scatter, but the hero rides against them; loosing hounds and hawk, he has fenced them. Teeth, claws are poised to rend them; the javelin shakes: who, who shall defend them? Now the young, harried deer, quaking and quivering, shaking and shivering, think on the mercies of them that bore them: they weep, they implore them, but find, racing before them, the

flame-faced Isa. 13: 8.
though he leap to the stars, they will cast him to the ground [Obad. 1: 4].
I lift my eyes—and behold Zech. 2: 5 and elsewhere.
flint hooves Isa. 5: 28.
grind you to powder Exod. 32: 20.
horn roar louder, louder [Exod. 19: 19].
leaping on mountains S. of S. 2: 8.
their doomsday nears Deut. 32: 35.

warrior in his might; while the fright-struck mothers, put to flight, plunge to earth's bowels or the mountain's height. At the thought of their children, weary and faint, they swoon and faint; and oh, my heart's grief for the younglings, sobbing and weak, scattered on the mountain's peak.

Now the hero's bellow, bursting as from lions' jaws, rakes the deer like lions' claws. No pause, no pause! On he pushes his raging charger; down swoops the falcon, ever larger. He seeks the deer, he finds them; sweeping behind them he turns them, winds them; in Terror's net he tightly binds them.

Now weary unto death, their sun set, flanks throbbing, wet with blood and sweat, the deer are hard beset on every side by the flash of the warrior's steel, by wheeling falcon and the hounds' hot zeal. Hound at neck and hound at heel, barking, nipping, lunging, gripping, rending, ripping thighs, throats, paps, their legs collapse, as many are taken in Death's traps. Growls and barking drown their silent moans as their flesh is ripped from their twitching bones. Yes, the maddened pack pulls their bowels apart, drinks down the blood of fawn and hart, and all for no sin on their part.

Praise God! At whose command the Void gave birth, whose justice rules the earth—though it be veiled from man. Who can grasp our Maker's plan, that makes one creature another's prey, for the killer's life sweeps blameless lives away? He fashions fangs to dismay the weak, yes, slay the weak; casts kid and dam to riving claw and beak, gives the young and feeble unto the command of the murderer's hand. Who shall illume God's laws, that fling the suckling to the lion's jaws? Yes, one creature feeds another; but, in the end, each is the other's brother: all wend earthward, all descend, all feed slug and maggot in the end.

Then he lifted his voice and sang:

All creatures are food; Death's hungry eye,
Death's falcon eye, has scanned them.
The weakest feed the strong. Such are
God's laws. None can withstand them.

scattered on the mountain's peak 1 Kgs. 22: 17.
weary unto death Jer. 4: 31.
many are taken in Death's traps Lam. 4: 20.
for no sin on their part Job 16: 17.

The killers wreak their worst designs
even as they have planned them.
Yet though they snare and feed, the hunter
Death shall snare and brand them.
Eater and eaten shall perish both,
the selfsame Death command them.
All praise to God, whose ways are hid:
no one can understand them.

SAID THE TELLER OF THE TALE:

Astounded by what his tale had taught, dumbfounded by his parable's onslaught, I knew the speaker for Hever the Kenite, and he read my thought. Feet strong and fleeting, he rushed upon me in warm greeting. I rejoiced with him my soul loved best until we were wrested from Friendship's breast and sent to wander, birds scattered from their nest.

him my soul loved best [S. of S. 3: 4]. **birds scattered from their nest** [Isa. 16: 2].

GATE TWENTY-SIX

Travels: Kudos and Cavils

THUS SPOKE HEMAN THE EZRAHITE: Heavy with goods, I sailed to Bozrah cross the surging floods where, roaming about, I chanced upon a diamond-tongued young group, Wisdom's very barque and sloop. Drawing near, I lent an ear and heard—bless every word!—the hum, the thrum of Learning's rain, saw Wit spill like wine across a fruited plain, inhaled myrrh, spikenard, and more—when suddenly a greybeard stood us before, declaring, You who would be wise: wealth despise! Lift eyes to Him dwells beyond the skies, for this world shall rot, forgot. Let the clear knell of Charity's gold bell dispel your fears and turn you from the fires of Hell.

Behold me, Time's slave, tossed like a cork on Wandering's bitter wave, then flung to the lip of the grave. Through travel I have turned up Wormwood's cup until Hope's ship is sunken, and my frame warped and shrunken. What is worse than travel, that does man's thoughts and wealth unravel? Therefore have the bards indited, *Motion is commotion, traversal, reversal, to-and-fro, rue-and-woe.*

He who puts home and 'heritance behind shall, time out of mind, naught find but fear and dread. He shall not lift his head before the Sun smite him, the Wind bite him, Heat blight him, Dark fright him, and Snow white him. Travelling by the sun's or the moon's light,

Bozrah In the Bible, a city of Edom (Gen. 36: 33; Isa. 34: 6; and elsewhere). Inasmuch as Edom became synonymous with Rome and then Christendom, Alḥarizi probably indicates a place in the Byzantine empire. See *EJ* iv. 1284–5, vi. 369–70, 378–80; also vi. 857–9 ('Esau in the Aggadah').

Therefore have the bards indited Num. 21: 27. The author adopts biblical parlance, in a claim lending added weight to the speaker's exhortation; but the assertion is bogus: the sayings are his own.

Motion is commotion, traversal, reversal, to-and-fro, rue-and-woe Lit. 'Peregrination is confusion; travel a curse; and separation, fear'.

he roasts by day or chills by night. Clambering up rocks and hills, splashing through icy rills, tripping—yes, tripping!—on the roots and stones of mountains, slipping in fountains, plunging, lunging, fumbling, tumbling, racked with fever and with aches, he quakes and shakes, stumbling through lions' brakes, through pits of writhing snakes, collapses, and wakes to rains that churn the roads to mud, in which bitter flood his eyes run red with blood. In soggy squalls he moans, lurches, falls from his mount into the muck, cursing his luck. His clothes are a stench, an abhorrence, as the rain beats down in torrents, a wild roundelay that all but bears his horse away. Hail cuts his flesh like a carver at a feast; the Wind is a mad priest pushing him altarwards for slaughter: his innards and intestines are washed with water.

And if this were not enough, what of the Road's dangers, the armed, masked strangers? Woe worth the night or morn when brigands find him, for he shall be borne to earth, flesh bruised and torn, stripped naked as the day that he was born. And if he travel unmounted his woes are uncounted. Sticks and stones shall break his bones: he limps, he falls, he faints, he crawls, clothes muddy, knees skinned and bloody. And if he is snared by the snow—double woe! A prisoning garment clings to chest and back; white without, his heart is black.

And let us suppose seafaring is his choice: what can he do when the Breakers raise their voice—refuse the feast of Terror at the Wind's hands served? Shall he not be utterly unnerved? When the Ocean spits forth its invective, he shall see the world in a new perspective. Then shall he curse his day or weep and pray, seeing the vessel lurch and pitch, careen to a crest, then plummet to a salty ditch. Ah, sad fool (none sadder), his guts climb his mouth as angels Jacob's ladder.

eyes run red with blood The identification of tears with blood in medieval Hebrew litrerature is noted in Moses ibn Ezra, *Secular Poems*, ed. Brody, ii. 168, commenting on ss. 3–4 of poem 87 and s. 35 of poem 131.

his innards and intestines are washed with water Lev. 1: 13.

Woe . . . he was born Here the text recalls the brutal robbery of Hever at the outset of Gate 23.

the Breakers raise their voice Ps. 93: 3.

climb his mouth like angels Jacob's ladder [Gen. 28: 12].

Finally he tosses his merchant's hoard overboard to save his life. And if he escapes the sea's strife to see another morn, he holds himself reborn. Yes, though the waters with his goods be flecked, though his life be wrecked, the fool is overjoyed that he is not utterly destroyed. And if, after all this bitter stress, this moil and toil, this wretchedness, his travel and travail end in no gain, what profit his from all this pain? All was in vain! With such griefs shall the traveller be distressed, like a bird wandering from its nest. Finally, maddened from Fate's blows, he rakes his scalp and cheeks until blood flows.

Then he lifted his voice and sang:

He who has chosen the wanderer's life
wins Want without cessation.
He anoints his head with the oil of Grief,
paints his eyes with the blue of vexation.
He pours out his tears in a land not sown,
the kingdom of Desolation.
Then, when he thinks he has gained Rest's cove,
Fate makes grim salutation:
On, on his legs strive, as though they had sworn
eternal peregrination.
He is turned a smooth stone set in Wandering's sling,
whirled round in unending frustration.
Inhabiting torment, he cries, God, send
me a herald proclaiming salvation!

Now when he had so sweetly sung, one of the listeners ventured: Sir, yours is an angel's tongue. But now that your metric verse and unmetred rhyme have damned Journey's evils till the end of time, laud, if you can, the blessing of horse and caravan; show what good grows in Wandering's wood.

He replied, If travel be injurious, its woes furious, its blessings spurious, is it not curious: in life's harsh tourney, the laurel is won only

he tosses his merchant's hoard overboard to save his life Jonah 1: 5. This episode recalls the seafaring Heman's brush with death in Gate 15.

like a bird wandering from its nest Isa. 16: 2.

He anoints his head with the oil [Ps. 23: 5].

in a land not sown Jer. 2: 2.

a smooth stone set in Wandering's sling 1 Sam. 17: 40–9.

a herald proclaiming salvation Isa. 52: 7.

through journey. Yes, through Wandering's ragwort heal your hurt and every ill avert.

He who girds his loins shall gild his name and gain bright coins. Stir your thighs, else never rise! Be bold! What matter the road's heat or the field's cold if you double your gold? Welcome travel's sorrow: beg today, but rule tomorrow.

What worth the stay-at-home, the lier-in-his-berth? His be shame and dearth until he leave his earth; his no end of agitation till he quit his habitation. Therefore have the bards indited, *Rise and hunt, or win not what you want. Trust Wanderlust; stir dust; drive and thrive or roost and rust. Gamble—ramble: peregrination wins salvation; sail farther, climb higher, and claim your desire; the great trekker greatens his exchequer.*

He who stands fast, stands last; but he who roves wins troves. The globe-girdler's art girdles the heart with joy and bliss, sets Fame's kiss on the wanderer's lips, grips his right hand and returns him to his land with bulging pouch, seats him on Fortune's couch and Honour's seat, supplicants kneeling at his feet.

Then he lifted his voice and sang:

The coward who chooses the stay-at-home life
must drink of the cup of vexation.
The sluggard, a tent-peg thrust deep in the earth,
is a study in want and frustration.
His torment is endless: woe follows woe,
loss follows deprivation.
But the man who is wise travels eastward and west,
till he topple Ill Luck's domination.
The adventurer, spurning the gifts of repose,
wins Wandering's high consummation:
The splendour of mountain, of ocean, and plain;
gold—and illumination.
Winning home he is hailed by expectant throngs
as a herald proclaiming salvation.

Therefore have the bards indited Num. 21: 27.

a herald proclaiming salvation Isa. 52: 7.

Now when he had finished this display and swept his hearers' hearts away, they let their hands fly free: they flooded him with gifts like the sea, then asked the poet who he might be; whereat he replied:

Hever my name, whose rivals, lame
and halting, slink from me, cowed.
I have raised the meek with pearl-like praise;
in a phrase, have princes bowed.
Yea, princes and proud I slay and shroud,
but the lowly uphoist to the cloud.

lame and halting [2 Sam. 5: 6–8].

GATE TWENTY-SEVEN

Of the Cup's Joys and Other Alloys

THUS SPOKE HEMAN THE EZRAHITE: Thinking, in youth, to firm my moral fibre, I cut me off from tippler and imbiber, and seized on Abstinence to be my guide and circumscriber.

Let others glut on sensuous sights: I fled the vine and all vinereal delights. Renouncement to my Nazirite breast I clasped until a solid year had passed. Now when I had fulfilled this holy undertaking—twelve months, as sworn—and strained my patience far beyond the point of breaking, I longed for the solace of the cup that ever buoyed my youthful spirits up. How long, I cried, shall I myself deny—until my years slip by, my life one drawn-out sigh? Let me turn back, moaned I, Joy's wings are clipt enow: then was it better with me than now.

Swiftly did I my monkish garb dismantle, tied on Bacchus' mantle and hurried straight, loud pounded at the tosspots' gate, swift entered that festive place and stood in Joy's bright presence face to face.

Looking about I spied a jolly, youthful band, the goblet's bright planet in the orbit of each hand. Each tippler cried the cup's good loud, filling Laud's cup as well his skill allowed.

Said one, Earth is a maid of flowing hips and wine the liquor

and seized on Abstinence to be my guide and circumscriber Lit. 'and yearned to walk in the ways of the Nazirites', referring to Num. 6: 1–4.

then was it better with me than now Hos. 2: 9.

Swiftly did I my monkish garb dismantle Lit. 'I hastened to strip off the garb of being a Nazirite.'

tied on Bacchus' mantle Lit. 'put on the garments of drunkenness'. There is no reference to Greek mythology in the Hebrew.

of her lips; the flowers, her face; the springs, her eyes; the grass, her thighs.

Said another, Wine is life's joyer and Grief's destroyer.

Said another, But for the vintner's glass our hearts were a clouded glass; Joy, invisible, would pass like wind in the grass.

Said another, Though Grief be leprous, Dr Wine is most obstrep'rous: he breathes his wondrous breath, heals all, and saves our souls from death.

Said another, Wine doth fear affright, sets ills aright, and is both God's and man's delight.

Now next that company, off on a stand, stood a greybeard whose bright eye gave the cup command: constantly it flowed into his hand. Having let the young jugglers go through their paces he at last laughed in their faces.

You call this praise of Wine, the unmatched scion of the vine? A pity on sickly phrases trotted out and driven about! Why not cite Wine's bite and balm? Why slight his sting and calm, his honeyed sweet, his measure meet, his early and latter rains, his springtime showers, his foaming powers, his bright and plume, his mad perfume, his glowing coals, his moist, his hush and roist, his harsh and tender, his glory and his splendour? All this you fail to cite but bumble on as if for spite!

At that the assemblage replied, If you can praise Wine merrily and thoroughly, take our purse for cup in ample share and drink you deeply there.

Thereat he began: Know that Wine is the physician of the sickly soul, brings her remission, has her quickly whole. He is the eye's bright and heart's delight, is godly blest, bestowing Gilead's balmy rest. Wine is of glad possessed: joy lies voluptuous on his glistening chest. With fire his forehead burns; between his eyes the two-edged sword bright turns, the which he wields with high hand, driving the hosts of Gloom from out the land.

and is both God's and man's delight Judg. 9: 13.
his early and latter rains Deut. 11: 14 and elsewhere.
Gilead's balmy rest Jer. 8: 22.
the two-edged sword bright turns Gen. 3: 24.

His crucible purges impure Grief's alloy, his holy dew wakes slumbering Joy. His goblets, whiter than the snow, shine with the grape's red glow. He softs the hardened heart: joy his theatre and art, he assigns the oppressed the prince's part. All burning fire, his sweet is the heart's desire. His is the shade of Paradise, his the reviving dew for pain-closed eyes. He bears from Beauty's mountain wondrous riches: in the heart's field he pitches, calls out his troops that they might Discontent surround and flow upon the foe till he be drowned. Yea, over Woe's coal his gushing waters roll; his fiery commands extinguish Pain's smoking brands. He is our Lord of the swift and golden sword: laughing, he leaps and savages Grief's rumbling horde. Sweet, fragrant, self-reliant, before him are all hearts compliant. Warriors he fronts defiant; puny he, yet downs the giant. Inspiring, inspired, kiss'd and by all desired, his shining light sets dark behind and sights the very blind.

Then he waxed poetic and sang:

By all be heard: my blood is stirred
by the potent juice of the vine's fair daughter.
Bright her cheek glows as her sweet breath flows
with spicèd liquor, healing water.
First ivory-clad, then sudden freed,
hers beauty bare devoid of taint:
See her high blush as though amorous eyes
with flaming red her cheek bepaint.
She lives anew when her blood is spilt
from earthen vessel to crystal vial:
The cup's ivory canyon turns red, bright red,
as down she rushes its defile.
Though years asleep in prisoning jar,
at the drinker's kiss she springs awake;
She is the sun of Beauty's Heav'n:
bright cups, about her, orbit make.

his holy dew wakes slumbering Joy Isa. 26: 19.
the reviving dew Isa. 26: 19.
smoking brands Isa. 7: 4.
sets dark behind Isa. 58: 10.
sights the very blind Ps. 146: 8.

Now when he had finished his peroration, his audience voiced their approbation: Well sung, O tripping tongue! And now if you can limn Wine's fault as smooth you did its purity exalt, be known as singer without peer, our leader and our seer.

Then he answered, saying: Ho, heroes to down the draught, take thought: you are naught! Are you boasters so of sense devoid to see not that you walk upon the void? Know you not the daughter of the vine's renown? Many a man she has cast down. Take but a sip of her and know the fiery grip of her. Head turning, brain churning, you will wake to find your wits quite fled and a tent-peg in your head.

Wine is the very seed of Evil, brew of the devil, sure road to crime, to turpitude, to slime.

Over the winecup witching Evil cackles among a pack of sadists, rogues, and jackals gathered to work their filthy schemes, guzzling malt and corn in streams. Elbow to elbow, pimp and tart, men and women stand not apart: out come the instruments, virtue snoring, the pipes their brazen tunes outpouring, till in the night's dark pitch—shameless coupling of cur and bitch. Oh, adversity! Perversity!

Behold your wine that strips off all contrition and inhibition, that soddens the brain, drives the sober man insane until, making light of God's weightiest laws, he trots panting to Hell on wobbly paws. Wine joins beneath one roof the knight and knave, master and slave, head and tail, rust and nail, sweet and stale, rheum with perfume, gilt tongue with dung. The bibbler ravages his health and dribbles away his wealth: stript of goodly occupation, the mock of his neighbours, he rests—seven days a week!—from all his labours.

Then he waxed poetic and sang:

The knowing eye sees through the veil,
straight to the face of the vine's foul daughter.
Ambrosial her liquors to sotted tongues
but spurned by the wise as muddied water.
Seized and possess'd, she runs red with blood,
forever tainted, infectious—worse;

Ho, heroes to down the draught Isa. 5: 22.
Many a man she has cast down Prov. 7: 26.
a tent-peg in your head Judg. 4: 21.
he rests—seven days a week!—from all his labours Gen. 2: 3.

He who dares hold her a glowing saint
will find her repugnant, a lee-rid curse.
Conceived and born in vile and muck
she spends her life in muck and vile:
Discernment's eyes shrink back from her face—
never shall she his Pure defile.

SAID THE TELLER OF THE TALE:

*T*he people, hanging on his every word, marvelled at that they had heard. Cups were emptied with assiduity as many swore off wine in perpetuity.

I adjured him, By Him who gifts you with poetic flame, tell me your name! To which he answered, Elon Zaananim proclaims my fame; the wise man knows the same.

*T*hat spoke, I seized him by the cloak. Surely, I cried, you are our lord and light, Hever the Kenite!

I am, said he, your faithful and true friend; on that depend.

*T*hen all too briefly I stood him beside, for he would not bide: leaving, he left a fire within my breast and my soul wondrously oppressed.

GATE TWENTY-EIGHT

Praise and Pity for David's City

THUS SPOKE HEMAN THE EZRAHITE: Let me recall how time tossed me like a ball until I left Memphis for the Western Wall, thinking, Draw no more water, hew no more wood: I shall bring you up from Egypt's wretchedness, that you may see Jerusalem's good. Then I set my feet for the mountain of the Lord, the city chosen of the Lord, once home of a noble race who sat all men above, who looked upon the King's bright face. Once come unto that holy ground I turned myself round to count turrets and towers, then knelt amid showers of the scorpion's hiss to kiss the dust and loose my moans upon my Beloved's stones, crying, Zion, goodly are your tents: I shall not stir hence. Soul, fly, for I have seen her face; I shall not leave this place. Then, waxing poetic, I sang:

Thirsting from Spain for Zion's pure light
I rise from the depths to Heaven's height.
This is the day the Lord has made:
O Faithful City, my chief delight!
So many the pious who yearned for this sight;
what merit has guided this sinner here?
Near dead in the West, my soul revives:
my pulse is a fountain, my vision clear.

Draw no more water, hew no more wood [Josh. 9: 21–7].
I shall bring you up from Egypt's wretchedness Exod. 3: 17.
see Jerusalem's good Ps. 128: 5.
I set my feet for the mountain of the Lord [as in Ps. 24: 3].
the city chosen of the Lord 1 Kgs. 14: 20.
I turned myself round to count turrets and towers Ps. 48: 14.
goodly are your tents Num. 24: 5.
This is the day the Lord has made [Ps. 118: 24].
O Faithful City [Isa. 1: 21, 26].
my chief delight [Ps. 137: 6].

Babylon, Athens, Tyre, Rome—
what joy can you offer my flowing eyes?
The clouds flock like doves about my bright feet:
O Salem, towering Paradise!
Here shone the Presence in sight of all men;
here Wonder's pupils opened wide.
Sucklings and children drank both at God's light,
before they sought vision they prophesied.
She is fair, though stripped of glory and good;
though unjewelled and uncloaked, I say she is fair.
But my heart turns ashen, my tears pour forth,
I strike palm to palm, I pull at my hair.
Where is God's Presence, that vanished sun,
where is the splendour of yesteryear?
O haste, Beloved, to the Mountain of Myrrh,
haste, my Beloved, even as the deer.
The daughter of Zion is cast from her halls:
brazen, she fronted her Maker's will.
Haughty, she spurned the bright Love of her youth,
sought stolen waters and drank her fill.
Then the Lord, filled with jealousy, filled up her cup
with the waters of bitterness, forcing her drink.
She became, in the midst of her people, a curse;
her belly did swell and her thigh did shrink.
She prayed Exile's waters would wash off her sin
but God holds her sinful, though long she roam.

Sucklings and children drank both at God's light, before they sought vision they prophesied BT *BB* 12*a*: 'Since the day of the Temple's destruction prophecy was taken from the prophets and given to sages . . . Rabbi Yohanan declared, "It was taken from the prophets and given to fools and children."'

She is fair . . . she is fair [S. of S. 1: 15, 4: 1].

I strike palm to palm [Ezek. 21: 22].

O haste, Beloved, to the Mountain of Myrrh [S. of S. 4: 6].

haste, my Beloved, even as the deer [S. of S. 2: 17, 8: 14].

stolen waters Prov. 9: 17.

filled . . . did shrink Num. 5: 14–27.

Exile's waters would wash off her sin BT *Ber.* 56*a*.

One thousand, one hundred and forty-eight years—
her Sabbaths unpaid, she is barred yet from home.
Sorrowing, dreaming, her sad eyes are ringed
with black circles of longing: long has she cried—
Cried at the sight of the stranger ascending
God's Mountain while she, Zion's child, is denied.
But the mercies of God are unending; again
He shall shower salvation and rescue like rain.
His beloved, though old, shall renew her sweet youth:
she shall lie in the arms of her Lover again.

Now when my song and prayer were ended I rose from off my bended knees to walk about the city, afire with grief and pity. Lifting my eyes I saw the Temple's inner court, there where the heathen came to rip out the candelabrum and light a pagan flame. On I walked, feverish and weak, tears sluicing each cheek like streams cascading from a mountain peak. At length I met a citizen, who said, You have a foreign look, young friend: do you come from the Exile's end?

Yes, I answered, and would question you if I may.

Surely, he answered, say what you would say.

When did Jews return here?

When the city fell under Arab sway.

But why had the Christians driven us away?

They claim we shamelessly killed their God, who did then disown us: if we sacrifice the abomination of the Egyptians before their eyes, will they not stone us?

By what grace, I continued, did you re-enter His sacred place?

The Lord, zealous for His Name's sake, had pity on His

One thousand, one hundred and forty-eight years This calculation yields the date of 1218, ostensibly the date of Alḥarizi's visit to Jerusalem. R. Brann observes that 'the maqāma must have been written before 1229 when Jerusalem was occupied by Emperor Frederic II' (R. Brann, 'Power in the Portrayal', 26 n. 68).

her Sabbaths unpaid, she is barred yet from home Lev. 26: 34.

God's Mountain Ps. 24: 3.

the mercies of God are unending [Lam. 3: 22].

shall renew her sweet youth [Ps. 103: 5].

if we sacrifice the abomination of the Egyptians before their eyes, will they not stone us Exod. 8: 22.

The Lord, zealous for His Name's sake Ezek. 39: 25.

namesake, saying, It is not right that Esau seize Mount Zion's tents and Jacob be driven thence, lest the envious nations scoff, saying God has driven His firstborn off, setting the divorcee's child His firstborn above, preferring the son of His beloved wife over hers whom He does not love.

So, 4,950 years since the first day's light God roused the Ishmaelite ruler to fight, granting him the spirit of counsel and of might, so that he marched up from Egypt with his minions liege and against Jerusalem laid siege. God gave it him to have and hold, and he told the city's dwellers young and old, Speak unto Jerusalem's heart: let all the sons of Ephraim who dwell apart, yea, all Egypt's and Assyria's remnants speed like the hart! From every corner, come; build you your home!

So here we be, by blessed calm approved—unless we be suddenly removed; for we fear the evil that here befalls, the rapine and the violence within these walls, the churning contention and burning dissension defying comprehension. For the cruel leaders of this community are masters of impunity, each the next man's stumbling-block and pain; then how shall we remain? They seek their fellows' hurt, each one: the son, his father; the father, his firstborn son. Yet father and son together do not falter to gather kindling for the pagan altar. Within each chest curls a poison snake: nothing is done for Heaven's sake. With shouts and bitterness the streets are rife: each eye is a lance, each tongue, a knife; I call this city Even Hamaḥlokot/the Stone of Strife. And leaders aside, there are yet others who pit brothers against brothers. They are rogues and liars: one spreads his net, one draws a mighty bow, a third conspires, a fourth prepares contention's altars for new fires.

Then let us pray until God Almighty heeds, and rids us of these noxious weeds. Let Him fill our lungs with Salvation's breath; let Him rid us of this death.

preferring the son of His beloved wife over hers whom He does not love Deut. 21: 16.
the spirit of counsel and of might Isa. 11: 2.
Speak unto Jerusalem's heart Isa. 40: 2.
all Egypt's and Assyria's remnants Isa. 27: 13.
speed like the hart! From every corner, come S. of S. 2: 17, 8: 1.
father and son . . . altar Jer. 7: 18.
let Him rid us of this death Exod. 10: 17.

Then he declaimed:

Shall we tempt God with
stubborn reprehension?
All wounds have cures, but who
can cure contention?
All sins the Lord forgives—
except dissension.

SAID THE TELLER OF THE TALE:
When he had no more to declaim I asked him his name.

Ho, he said, laughing at my woe; do you not apprehend Hever the Kenite, your closest friend?

Then gladness took us by the hand, bound us with his golden band, and fanned Love's fires all the days I dwelt within his land.

GATE TWENTY-NINE

Beggars' Arts versus Frozen Hearts

THUS SPOKE HEMAN THE EZRAHITE: When Profit's alarums sounded, I bounded from my bed, seized goodly merchandise and all but fled to Nineveh, Wealth's hold and hoard—Nineveh, a mighty city before the Lord. When I arrived, December rose and roared, all but crushing me in his icy hold: who can stand before his cold? The snow padded forward on mammoth paws as the wind unsheathed its ivory claws.

*T*hrough the biting air I advanced to the house of prayer and there found a crowd of middling size gathered round a man in shabby guise, who with rolling eyes moaned and cried while a youngster shivered by his side. His upper lip shone with crystal tears, his cheeks were blue, and bluer still his ears. The wind wrenched his hair and hit him like a hammer until his thoughts were a jumble and his speech a stammer.

*T*he congregation's prayers having been said, the wretch lifted his hands above his head, praised God, faced the crowd, and cried aloud:

*O*h goodly sirs, you blessed with sealskins and with furs: I call upon you, swathed in velvet and felt and ermine pelt, you who jeer at winter with his icy pinions, who scoff at the snow and his minions, whose cloaks are shield and buckler bold against the cold, and downed hats a sure device against the rain and ice, you who wealth and health command, lain by with men and maids at every hand, you who think pomp is yours alone, and rich beside you none—fear Time's wheel and wild zeal! We who splurged and gorged beyond our farthest needs, who decked ourselves out in silken weeds, who pranced about

Nineveh, a mighty city before the Lord Jonah 3: 3.

who can stand before his cold? Ps. 147: 17.

on jet-black, well-fed steeds, who were borne shoulder-high, who did our vanity nothing deny and deep in ripe and fragrant flesh did lie—Time spied us and had a change of heart: he brought out Wrath's weapons and cast his dart. Our ease flew off like the breeze; we who sipped deep at the vine of days, drank lees; our veloured tags turned rags; dumbstruck, we foundered in the muck, changing our satin wear for wormy cover and despair; none plunged faster to disaster.

*O*h, while you yet have power, heed this story, before Time leave you gaunt and hoary and you step naked from your glory. See our distress, walking the wilderness in ashes and in sacks. Turn not your backs! Appallingly sunken, our orphan eyes beseech you: we reach out for your mercies—let us reach you. Is there among you one of princely birth will prove that Virtue and Pity yet walk the earth, one whose mercies can be stirred, whose heart will melt at this that he has seen and heard, one whom fear can grip, imagining like reeling cup pressed to his lip, and he forced to sip?

*H*e choked and made long pause, as though his tongue clove to his jaws, then looked for comfort with ever-narrowing eye—but none such did espy. Seeing that his seed had fallen on rocky hills, that he had nothing gained for all his skills, he sat down on the ground a-shiver and a-quiver, hissing to his lad, Do what you can: no comfort here of any man!

*A*t that the boy sprang up, staggered, swayed, unsheathed his tongue's broad blade and unleashed a keen tirade.

S-sir, he began, I c-can but shake and s-stutter when ch-charity no word doth utter but m-m-m-melts away like butter; our hopes are c-c-cast into the gutter!

*C*ruel folk, he cried, that which you have heard this day could deep sea-chambers s-s-swift unlock, extinguish fire, bring water from a rock, could halt the sp-sp-sp-sp-spitting serpent in his track and flip him rigid on his back. How, how can you turn away from all our pain

well-fed steeds Jer. 5: 8.
brought out Wrath's weapons Jer. 50: 25.
drank lees Ps. 75: 9.
Appallingly sunken Lam. 1: 9.
reeling cup Isa. 51: 17, 22.
his tongue clove to his jaws Ps. 137: 6.
S-sir . . . into the gutter The youth's stuttering is a liberty taken by the translator.
water from a rock Num. 20: 8–11.

and wrack? God save us from the palsied soul and hardened heart, and from plugged ears, and palms that will not pull apart; yea, save us from these granite hearts, these b-boulders, from these cold eyes and shoulders, from these arid hands b-b-barren as desert sands. Oh, unrepentant and b-b-brazen-faced: may this your land lie desolate and waste! This day you have heard Ruin's roar in measure never heard before; yet you stare unblinking, turn away you do, as though this preachment taught you nothing new, as though this charge fell on anyone b-but you.

Now think you all on Him who kindled your souls' fire: repent, shatter your evil d-d-desire! Let each man chastise his sp-sp-spirit, till it turn mild; let heart and shut hand be reconciled: this fate tomorrow could befall each man his child. Yes, picture your sons, plunged to like poverty, stretching their hands to hearts as hard as yours for charity, compelled to sob and b-b-beg like me.

SAID THE TELLER OF THE TALE:

Now when the son had done, their stony hearts were shattered every one. The dazed crowd, lashed and cowed, both suppliants most generously endowed, each as his means allowed. Thereat the father, clutching his bulging purse, burst forth in verse:

God bless these giving, noble folk
for all their mercies mild.
At first their hearts were adamant,
their spirits rank and wild;
But the Rock converted their stony hearts
to pity my age and my child.

Now when he had ended his song to the smiling throng, I looked closely and—lo, it was Hever the Kenite in the flesh, and that sapling fresh, his son, flesh of his flesh, up to their ears in fraud as ever, man and boy, now with the Pity-me-and-my-wretched-child ploy. But I lacked the stomach to reveal their theft; so, turning neither right nor left, I straightway left.

brazen-faced Lit. 'of bronze forehead': Isa. 48: 4.

this charge fell on anyone b-but you Mal. 2: 1.

let heart and shut hand Deut. 15: 7.

their stony hearts [Ezek. 11: 19, 36: 26].

each as his means allowed Deut. 16: 17.

At first their hearts were adamant Zech. 7: 12.

GATE THIRTY

Of a Quack and his Bogus Pack

THUS SPOKE HEMAN THE EZRAHITE: One day I trekked from the River Arnon to Fortunesville/Baal-Gad in Lebanon. While wandering the streets to cull gilt Speech's sweets, I saw a great commotion, a mighty motion towards the city gate, where straining bodies grouped about a greybeard voluble and stooped, who proffered piles of bottles and vials filled with unguents, creams, and oils for blisters, sores, and boils—countless concoctions for countless infections, stretching in all directions. He trooped out instruments without pause: needles and lances, knives and saws, and the three-pronged fork, all sharp as a two-edged sword, as well a gleaming cutting-board; yes, nothing forgetting for deft and copious bloodletting. Then, facing his attendants he cried far and wide:

Hear me, O peoples, attend, O ye nations: I have fled from Time's lists, escaped vast conflagrations and the seething waters' devastations. I am emerged from gravest danger, have heard marvels and seen wonders, none stranger. I hail from Babylon, where I sought earth's master sages, granaries of the Wisdom of the ages. I have studied medicine under brilliant physicians, poured water on the hands of peerless diagnosticians, drunk their words down passionately, not circumspectly; and not from books, but from their lips directly. I have swum deeply in their inner sea: the pillars of their wisdom stand revealed to me.

And so it is that I, with His help who formed Earth and

Fortunesville/Baal-Gad in Lebanon Josh. 11: 17, 12: 7, 13: 5.
the three-pronged fork 1 Sam. 2: 13.
two-edged sword Prov. 5: 4.
facing his attendants he cried Gen. 45: 1.
Hear me, O peoples Mic. 1: 2.
attend, O ye nations Isa. 49: 1.
the seething waters' devastations Ps. 124: 5.
poured water on the hands of 2 Kgs. 3: 11.
the pillars of their wisdom [Prov. 9: 1].

Sky, can bind up your pain and give you ease again, stanch your every wound and set your strings well tuned. All who ache or ail, be hale! Mine the unguent and salve for every loathsome lesion you might have. Let the snake-bit man take what I give: and it shall be that everyone bitten shall look on me and live. You who hunger for health, come dine: mine is a powder ground exquisite fine to open eyes shut tight, giving the blind full sight. I have a potion sets the barren teeming and the frigid steaming. For each raw wound recalcitrant to medication I am come from the city with Salvation. With God's help I shall put your deafness behind, heal the blind, set the lame skipping like lambs, and butting about like rams. Each and every hurt that casts man down to dirt, yes, your very least distress I shall send loping off to the wilderness.

*G*ood folk, I bring you calm. Mine is the balm for the streaming eye; yea, I shall dry its tear and halt its weal; I can command the twisted leg and broken hand to heal. Yea, they who twist in pain and fright in pitch-black night, sweet sleep in flight, my physic frees. Please let me be specific: my vials can loose the paralytic and the paraplegitic. The tubercular, waste, and gaunt; the palsied frame that is Pain's haunt; the organs that ills tease and taunt—I restore. More: I cure measles and mumps, rid breasts or rumps of bumps and lumps.

*Y*ou who suffer from arthritis, conjunctivitis, laryngitis, appendicitis, or varicose veins—I have the answer to your pains. I can break grippe's grip, halt coronary thrombosis, hirsuteness, halitosis, corectoral palpitation, crepuscular degeneration, or mickle constipation. I root loose teeth, heal swollen lips, tight loose-strung hips. The epileptic thrashing round upon the ground with gurgling sound I raise and render sound. I hold out relief for nerves weak and peaked, for the soul-sick or for victim of flea or tick.

who formed Earth and Sky [Ps. 115: 15 and elsewhere].

and it shall be that everyone bitten shall look on me and live Num. 21: 8.

I am come from the city with Salvation 2 Sam. 18: 3.

I shall put your deafness behind, heal the blind Isa. 35: 5–6.

set the lame skipping like lambs Ps. 114: 6.

I shall send loping off to the wilderness [Lev. 16: 21].

in pitch-black night Prov. 7: 9.

Ho! I extend my royal healer's rod and raise the wretch cast down by God. Where is a woman with unnatural flow? I shall clear her decks below! Who suffers from fetid emission? Through me he shall gain remission no matter how deeply he has sinned, upwind or downwind.

Now, all who are afflicted with any above, or yet unmentioned, sickness—egad! Regain your fitness! Be cured at my hand, as Heaven is my witness! Any among you who have heard me out but harbour further doubt, come forward, try me; test my Truth; and only then deny me!

The mob, ravished by his lush address, fell on him like manna in the wilderness. By the hundreds, by the thousands, they surged forward all, great and small, rich and poor alike, servant and lord, a pocked and pustulent horde: the lame and the halt, the hunchback, the bald pate, the faint, the failing, the whining, the wailing, brandishing fetid specimens varied in colour in vessels diverse from one another: some reddish, some blackish, some greenish, most brackish—a motley hubbub up from the farms, dotards and babes-in-arms, a swain groaning his pain, a dame moaning her name, all pouring forth their grief; and he, clucking sympathy, hurrying his relief in bottles and jars, and garnering their dinars, his humour none the worse for having filled his purse through his sham and baldfaced scam.

SAID THE TELLER OF THE TALE:

I could not approach this charlatan until the well-fleeced crowd had gone. Then striding to his side I cried, By God, sir, answer me aright: are you not Hever the Kenite?

Here I be, sir, he chortled, your true and trusted friend, faithful to the end.

My heart leapt, as one who finds great booty; but I had my duty. Tell me, I said, should such as you despoil your crown, playing the clown in town after town? Whom shall we thank to see you turned rank mountebank?

I extend my royal healer's rod [Esther 5: 2].
as Heaven is my witness Job 16: 19.
fell on him like manna in the wilderness [Exod. 16: 15–33].
in vessels diverse from one another Esther 1: 7.
as one who finds great booty [Ps. 119: 162].
despoil your crown [Ps. 89: 40].

At that he curled his lip as if to curse, but said instead in measured verse:

Because you are my honest friend
your every word I take as manna;
But I must wander far and wide
till I be blest with coin's Hosanna.
Flint-hearted Time rears wavelike up
and strikes me cruel, early and late:
Lodge no complaint at my door, good friend;
lodge your complaint against harsh Fate.

So nonplussed by his wit and his chicanery was I that I could not reply; and, before my thoughts had cleared, Truth's doctor had disappeared.

GATE THIRTY-ONE

Of a Mocking Knight and a Wormwood Cup of Fright

THUS SPOKE HEMAN THE EZRAHITE: I left my native place, unbidden, to scour the world and leave no secret hidden. With Wandering for staff and guide, I roamed far and wide in search of wonders; I would not be denied. Now one day I made my way from Syria to Antioch with friends who sported Friendship's very crown: Hever the Kenite, of high renown, who held our hearts with many a bright story and delightful allegory.

Said he, By your leave, I would tell you a tale you could never conceive.

We answered, Out with your gem and let it glisten: set forth your riddle and we will listen.

Once, said he, I was journeying from Dibon to Heshbon with a star-bright company, men strong-armed and steady, skilled swordsmen, battle-ready. Now one day as we rode across a plain, down from the hills fell a horseman like sudden rain. Downward he plunged, looming larger and larger, masked, on a mighty charger. As for us, we dashed forward with fiery glance, waving sword and lance, to meet his rash advance. In an instant our weapons had rendered him sliced meat when he threw himself to earth to kiss our feet.

Hear me, he cried, my lords, and only after use your swords.

Speak out! What secret enterprise are you about?

At that he ripped the veil from off his eyes and, to our vast surprise, displayed a woman bright enough to put the sun in shade, leave the moon afraid and dawn dismayed! Her tongue was Eden, manna beneath and—ah!—the whiteness of her teeth. Her hair,

Wormwood Cup Lam. 3: 15.
set forth your riddle and we will listen Judg. 14: 13.
he ripped the veil from off his eyes Exod. 34: 34.

shining and jet black, spilled like a flock of Gilead's goats down her fair back. Long did our eyes upon her eyebrows linger, two lines writ by God's finger, cherubim cunningly made: ah, what a maid!

Lady, we said, bare your mystery: give us your history.

She began: Hear my cry; be this fate not yours, all you passers-by. The hand of God has touched me, therefore I moan! Behold and see if there be any sorrow like unto my own. I was a maiden fragrant in royal chambers, protected from all dangers, hid from the light by day and night, unseen by youthful wooers, much less evildoers! But one dark night an avaricious and malicious lord, Deceit's own brother, broke through the wall and stole me from my house, from the chamber of my mother, brought me to this desert, disgraced me, debased me, and placed me in a dark cave, a caged sparrow; he set me as a target for his arrow. For a full year I lived in that vile lair, wasting away in fetid air until one day, distraught and weak, I slapped my cheek, seized my temples, shook my head to and fro, crying: Better to die than live so! Better leap into the hand of Death than rot here till my last breath. The kindness of the Lord has not ended: O soul, be commended to the Lord and flee at any cost; and if I be lost, let me be lost!

Now it came to pass at midnight as he lay in his usual stupor, mumbling away, flat on his back, I tiptoed to his side, heart pounding, lips trembling and open wide, and bared his sword—his last, most naked bride. For an instant I stepped back, then thrust the weapon through his heart and out his back. Up, up he reared: I seized him by the beard, flung him to the floor, wrenched the sword from his breast—and slit his throat (the God of Heaven be blest)! Then I leapt to his horse and set my course, riding, questing over desert rocks and

like a flock of Gilead's goats [S. of S. 4: 1, 6: 5].
writ by God's finger Exod. 36: 8.
cherubim cunningly made Exod. 26: 1.
be this fate not yours, all you passers-by Lam. 1: 12.
The hand of God has touched me Job 19: 21.
Behold and see if there be any sorrow like unto my own Lam. 1: 12.
the chamber of my mother S. of S. 3: 4.
a caged sparrow [Prov. 6: 5].
he set me as a target for his arrow Lam. 3: 12.
Better to die than live so Jonah 4: 3.
The kindness of the Lord has not ended Lam. 3: 22.
and if I be lost, let me be lost Esther 4: 16.
Now it came to pass at midnight as he lay Ruth 3: 8.

sands until I fell into your hands. Now I have said my fill: do with me what you will.

Stirred by what we had heard, we cried, Cursed be that monster, but blest be the slaughtering knife; and blessed be God who rooted out his life. Have no fear: no harm will befall you here. Come, know Kindness at our hand.

Sirs, she answered. I am yours to command and gladly will your least desire fulfil.

As we travelled onward, the maid, no longer afraid, suggested that we go beyond the next plateau to a spring comfortable beyond imagining. To stop there, she offered, would be the better part of sense, as our destination was a long way thence and the heat intense.

Tired, we took her suggestion. Crossing the plateau in question we arrived, in the heat of the day, at a gushing waterway. Our flagging spirits soared: soon we would be restored.

I suggest, said our guide, a midday rest; then, refreshed in body and mind, with sun and hot wind behind, you can proceed. We agreed; so, circling the fount, we proceeded to dismount. She, too, dismounted; took off her bangles, jewels, and flowing vestures; tied all the horses, readied our places and laid us down in green pastures.

Sweet maid, we said, you wed beauty with sincerity and duty with dexterity. She answered, While you may prize my sincerity, you have not apprised my dexterity; for I have skills unseen beyond these plains and hills: let me show you a few.

Up she sprang, then, seized her bow, notched an arrow and let it go—cloud-high, it seemed—with a laugh; then loosed at once a second, splitting the first in half! We were amazed. Dazed.

She continued, Now let me lay another feat before you; you shan't forget it, I assure you.

Leaping to her steed, she galloped at full speed, reached into her quiver, pulled back her bow—and shot one of our comrades in the heart!

do with me what you will Gen. 19: 8; Judg. 19: 24.
no harm will befall you here Ps. 91: 10.
laid us down in green pastures Ps. 23: 2.
let me show you a few The translation imitates the Hebrew's emphasis of not having a rhyme at this point.
reached . . . heart See preceding note.

As he fell I cried, My God! What have you done! At which she hooted, Shut your mouth, whore's son! Found my twin breasts inviting, didn't you; my doe eyes, round thighs, broad hips, soft lips, exciting, didn't you? Imagined you would lie upon me to play hip-and-thigh, have your day, give your hands free play, roam my body like a forest lair, seize me, squeeze me, kiss me, stroke my hair, and touch me everywhere? Well, by God, you are misled! I've something else for you instead! Now listen, you cravens: tie each other up before I feed you to the ravens!

SAID THE TELLER OF THE TALE:

Grief! Horror beyond belief! Our trust fell with us to the dust, desire turned to a black, rank fire, ruddy charms to bloody arms: here was, as he began—a man! We were undone: we could neither fight nor run. With our horses tied, our weapons stacked and set aside, ourselves reclining and he on horse—we had no recourse. No: before that bow, with arrow notched and waiting, there was no debating or hesitating. So we bound each other, one by one. When we were done, with only myself untied, he leaped from his mount and strode to my side, seized my wrist and thwacked me with his fist. Bastard, he hissed, miss being stroked and kissed? Miss your bedtime treat? Take your shoes off your feet!

Yes, yes, I stammered, but these shoes—I began to cough—I—I can't . . . I can't get them off!

Too tight, eh, you son of a bitch, you? C'mere—I'll unhitch you!

He bent over—the last curtsy of his life, for hid in my shoe was a razor-sharp knife. Before he could start I thrust home to his heart; he fell on his face and torrents bled as I wrenched out my weapon and lopped off his head. Then I turned to my friends, struck the bands off their hands; and swiftly we buried our friend in the desert sands. Thereafter we turned to leave with clouded eye, yet giving thanks to God Most High, through whose salvation Death had passed us by.

Then I declared:

Except that God had drawn us up
we had sunk beneath Death's wave;

twin breasts S. of S. 4: 5, 7: 4. **Take your shoes off your feet** Exod. 3: 5.

Except that God had lifted us up
we were swallowed by the grave.
Prisoned we were in the chambers of Death
but God our bonds did sever.
Let Israel say: Thank the Lord, He is good,
for His mercy endureth for ever.

we were swallowed by the grave [Prov. 1: 12]. **Let Israel say: Thank the Lord, He is good, for His mercy endureth for ever** Ps. 118: 2.

GATE THIRTY-TWO

Needlepoint: Point-Counterpoint

THUS SPOKE HEMAN THE EZRAHITE: Sporting youth's rose, I chose for intimates blest minds who rose up early to pluck Sapience' fruit, then Wisdom's lute, setting ready rhetors mute. Now as we wed tropes' gold with riddles' green, weaving mantles of silk sheen and velvet mien, we were met by a greybeard rich in Song's provision and poetic vision. None the perplexity, claimed he, he could not right, nor grey heart light nor gnarled riddle bright.

I be the lord of Song's dutiful daughters; mine the rod to cleave Song's raging waters.

*T*hereat from our midst rose a hero sharp-eyed and young, whose tongue rang song had ne'er been sung, pearl-ringed and sapphire-sprung.

*S*ir, he challenged, prove you speak true: give us our due. Let us race Song's meadow through—but ever with one rhyme between us two. Echo to my pleasure a line laid down to Song's exacting measure: grace my stich's well-laid foundation with your simile's consummation. Bring forth your pearled treasure from Song's deep corals; then, only, parade your laurels.

*S*aid his rival, I am ready, sword drawn, hand steady.

*T*hen the youth advanced and spoke of the pen, saying:

> Comely is the scribe's loved Quill, whose gold-gilt skill
> can heal or kill;

*A*nd the old man answered:

> that golden sceptre, whose dictates spill like fire or
> honey at its wielder's will, whose every whim it must fulfil.

---

the rod to cleave Song's raging waters Exod. 14: 15–21.

golden sceptre Esther 4: 11, 5: 2, 8: 4.

Whereat the youth sang:

Across the scroll's sky the Quill flies:
at the head of black comets find him;

And the old man answered:

Resembling a snae who darts through the dust,
leaving smoothed earth behind him.

Then the youth spoke of the letter, saying:

In beauty's grove the Letter spends her days, a myrrh-steeped maid of modest ways, whose wit can castles raise or kingdoms raze;

And the old man answered:

a comely, black maiden whose moon-soft gaze can transmute to the sun's harsh rays, whose mute tongue might displays and sings God's praise.

Whereat the youth sang:

The Letter, reared in perfect faith,
in sapience effloresces:

And the old man answered:

A fetching maid of ivory cheek
with flowing, jet-black tresses.

Then the youth spoke of the sword, saying:

Behold the silver Blade, haft pearl-inlaid, naked but unafraid, now sheathed and now displayed. Her lightning hand cannot be stayed, nor her mortal cost defrayed.

And the old man answered:

She is Death's red queen, arrayed in crimson livery made by men unmade.

comely, black maiden S. of S. 1: 5.
whose mute tongue might displays and sings God's praise Ps. 19: 1–3.

Whereat the youth sang:

The warrior's Broadsword, flashing,
lights blind eyes,

And the old man answered:

Licking the field like Lightning's
tongue the skies.

Then the youth spoke of the warrior's mail, saying:

Fine-wrought, wondrous feats fierce Mail has wrought, rendered impervious through its maker's thought.

And the old man answered:

Well ought we praise the craftsman's mind, who caught, in metal rings, foes' blades and heroes taught: Advance with camel-speed; fear naught.

Whereat the youth sang:

Keen swords find dullest mail
exceeding wise,

And the old man answered:

Whose links are camels' thews,
whose nails, ants' eyes.

Then the youth spoke of the horse, saying:

Mind the Horse, mind, whose bright hooves bind the mountains' peaks, blind foemen's eyes, and leave the wind behind.

And the old man answered:

Unconquered, unconfined, he leaps on mountains like the hind, soars eagle-like, joys eye and mind.

he leaps on mountains like the hind [S. of S. 2: 8–9].

Whereat the youth sang:

He soars like lightning; fire, his eyes,
his breath, shot steam:

And the old man answered:

A stag on the peaks, an eagle in air,
a fish in a stream.

Then the youth spoke of the torch, saying:

The torch is a red-horned ox can gore through Darkness' stable, wall and door, yet silver Night's ebony shore.

And the old man answered:

He is a red-winged dove can soar Dark's waters o'er; or a widow given rich store of precious oil, and yet—the more given, weeps all the more.

Whereat the youth sang:

The wizard Torch
transmutes the gloom;

And the old man answered:

Ophir's gold branch
with lightning bloom.

Then the youth spoke of the myrrh packet, saying:

Myrrh packets cloister balms that heal; but genteel scents their hidden hearts reveal;

And the old man answered:

like a smitten youth who would conceal his heart's red zeal, but those bright eyes flash what his hot reins feel.

ox can gore [Exod. 21: 28–36].
dove can soar Dark's waters o'er [Gen. 8: 8–12].
a widow given rich store of precious oil 2 Kgs. 4: 1–7.
Ophir's gold 1 Chr. 29: 4 and elsewhere.

Whereat the youth sang:

Through cloistering packets
Myrrh's sweet odours call,

And the old man answered:

A gossip—tongue cut off,
whose eyes tell all.

Then the youth sang of the Vineson, saying:

Blest not of the Nazirite, the Vineson, Joy's fine son, is yet blest with might: he puts sinner Grief to flight, to the heart's delight, as he shepherds Joy's pilgrims to the goblet's holy site.

And the old man answered:

Blest sprite—though blest not of the Rechabite—he is sun's bright, moon's light, myrrh's bite, Joy's rite, and the sufferer's right.

Whereat the youth sang:

The server's hands shed blood-red wine,
whose fire grief chills.

And the old man answered:

Our hearts revive, our dry bones draw breath
as the red blood spills.

Then the youth spoke of the falcon, saying:

Behold the falcon, lightning-swift, whom gold-tipped feathers lift: learning and relearning the preyer's text, his storm-wings churning, he rides the high winds, turning, ever turning;

Rechabite Neither Rechabites nor Nazirites are mentioned in the Hebrew text; both abstained from wine.

dry bones draw breath [Ezek. 37: 1–14].

Behold the falcon . . . turning, ever turning The Hebrew text here shows the unusual feature of two rhyme clusters, rather than one, in the rhymed prose section.

And the old man answered:

an all-seeing judge, stern and discerning, mercy spurning,
plummeting, rending, then heavenward returning.

Thereat the youth sang:

In that razored beak and arrowed claws
Death sings.

And the old man answered:

Death burns in those pearly eyes
and thunder wings.

Then the youth spoke of the wolf, saying:

The keen-fanged wolf works evil without pause: he
authors the hunt's harsh laws, letter and clause;

And the old man answered:

stalks, summer and winter, on silent paws, slaughter his
cause; and rests not till his prey rests in his jaws.

Thereat the youth sang:

His eyes flash lightning, his fangs drip blood
white snow absorbs;

And the old man answered:

Night's grey, grim thief, the flaming torch
between his orbs.

Then the youth spoke of the lightning, saying:

Lightning's gold whip outstrips the eye, flips, strips
night's mantle off, leaps, ripples, dips.

And the old man answered:

High-spirited, Lightning skips; binds heav'ns horizons as
he heaven rips; writes, with pearled pens of flaming tips,
lines spilt from Night's thick lips.

rests not till his prey rests in his jaws Num. 23: 24.

The flaming torch . . . orbs Gen. 15: 17.

Whereat the youth sang:

The joyous hero Lightning
races, leaps.

And the old man answered:

No, no: Night's watchman he,
who blinks, then sleeps.

Then the youth spoke of the stream, saying:

Behold the stream with ivory inlaid glow, a blade to lay the foeman low, yet pure as purest flowers that blow;

And the old man answered:

rain's bright rondeau, a lisping cymbalo, a dewed tableau, mail's silver-linked flow, sword's lightning show.

Whereat the youth sang:

Shining, slow, the waters flow—
bracelets of silver, slender and frail,

And the old man answered:

While the hand of the wind, a craftsman's hand,
hammers those bracelets to linkéd mail.

Then the youth spoke of the pomegranate, saying:

The Pomegranate—joy complete, where blushing charm and spurting passion meet: suck, eager lips, teat after wondrous teat.

And the old man answered:

Greet, in this gold ark, pearl-replete, the ruby's sweet—a text wondrous pointed by Nature's Masorete; eat, friends and lovers, eat.

joyous hero Lightning races Ps. 19: 6.
pointed by Nature's Masorete On the Masoretes, vocalizers of the biblical text, see *EJ* xvi. 1401–82.
eat, friends and lovers, eat [S. of S. 5: 1].

Whereat the youth sang:

The hidden seeds of the pomegran't
are blushing girls.

And the old man answered:

A gold ark, rather; open at will
and lift red pearls.

Then the youth spoke of the nut, saying:

Of the Nut I speak, whose sweet mystique ripe gourmands seek.

And the old man answered:

Gentle and meek, yet in no wise weak, he will no vengeance wreak when struck, but turns the other cheek.

Whereat the youth sang:

The Nut is sweet, but withholds his meat
till broke in half,

And the old man answered:

Resembling a fool who will nothing learn
till taught of the staff.

Then the youth spoke of the harp, saying:

The Harp's mute lips give rise to thunder cries; yet, at the harp's soft sighs grief softly dies.

And the old man answered:

Her all men prize, on whose ripe breast Contentment lies and whose lullabies flow gentle as sunset down twilight skies; yet she hurls Song's polished stone 'twixt Grief's fierce eyes.

turns the other cheek Isa. 50: 6.
a fool who will nothing learn till taught of the staff Prov. 26: 3.
hurls Song's polished stone 'twixt Grief's fierce eyes [1 Sam. 17: 49].

Whereat the youth sang:

Behold, at the maiden's heart, the Harp,
whose strains our hearts beguile;

And the old man answered:

A babe who weeps on his mother's breast,
who croons and laughs the while.

Then the youth spoke of the water-channel, saying:

Circuitous the course she steers even to the garden's flowered frontiers; dizzy in circling dance, cheek streaked with tears, she trips—but perseveres.

And the old man answered:

Swirling her skirts, the dancing maiden nears: her laughter cheers our ears, as she endears herself with moans and cold, clear tears.

Whereat the youth sang:

Wedded to water, she water bears
as she skips the garden o'er.

And the old man answered:

Hers is, at times, the viol's thrum;
at times, the lion's roar.

Then the youth spoke of the citron, saying:

Who holds the fragrant citron fast has cast out Grief and set out Joy's repast.

And the old man answered:

Its colours fast, scent unsurpassed, it tenders beauty ever present, never past.

Whereat the youth sang:

Behold the bright fruit of this goodly tree
gold-girt beneath, above,

And the old man answered:

Flushed like the face of the lover
reflecting the face of his love.

Then the youth spoke of the candle, saying:

The Candle's knight errantry and bright blazonry free us of night's slavery.

And the old man answered:

No. Riven by jealousy, driven by knavery, she in her piracy rips night's bright tapestry, lifts the sky's jewellery.

Whereat the youth sang:

The Candle lifts the captive, form,
from Darkness' hold;

And the old man answered:

In holder set, it seems a tongue
of molten gold.

Then the youth spoke of sunlight, saying:

Praise we the Sun, Day's bright envoy whose beams our spirits buoy—who, Heaven-camped, bids Earth her gifts enjoy;

And the old man answered:

rather, a warrior queen who bids Day's troops: Deploy, Night's armies to destroy, that all who mourned Day's overthrow sing out for joy.

Whereat the youth sang:

The Sun bursts Heaven's silver vault;
gold showers the earth without sound.

all who mourned Day's overthrow sing out for joy Isa. 66: 10.

And the old man answered:

Lo, a cedar springs up in the heavens
with branches bent low to the ground.

Then the youth spoke of the moon, saying:

Heaven's harpist, the Moon, strums her silvered tune,
whose pearly notes the garden's limbs festoon.

And the old man answered:

Night's lutist lilts—sweet boon!—her silent rune: the
stars, in silent gaze, commune.

Whereat the youth sang:

Bent o'er the stream, the Moon binds her hair
with silver cord;

And the old man answered:

Then, frighted, sees in the water's waste
a turning sword.

SAID THE TELLER OF THE TALE:

Now when they had done their sweet, meet vying, their bright and sprightly versifying, the youth said to the old man, I swear by all the wit that I call mine, and by Him who set you a wonder and a sign, your every phrase is gold, your each stich diamantine.

Said the old man: Nor have I ever seen so fine a branching vine spilling so rich a wine. Your eyes' keen levantine and tropes' thick columbine twine listeners' hearts and make them thine.

Thereat the company, grateful for the sage's gift, gave him a bulging purse he scarce could lift; and the youth declared:

I adjure you by Him whose wisdom is unbounded, by whose high grace our hearts have been confounded, by Him who calls you to fame: state your name.

a turning sword [Gen. 3: 24].
a wonder and a sign [Deut. 28: 46].
levantine A heavy, twilled silk fabric.

He answered, saying:

A wonder am I in the eyes of the wise,
a garland on Wisdom's curls;
Know me as Hever, or stringer; to wit,
I am he who strings Song's scattered pearls.

Ah, well I knew that mind's clear bell! Pell-mell I rushed to kiss and snare Song's philomel, quell all my cares at Wisdom's well. But few were the days I drank his tongue's rich mel: cold Parting rang his knell. Farewell, loved friend, farewell.

Know me as Hever, or stringer Lit. 'Truly they call me Hever because I join all scattered delights'. On the significance of the name Hever, and especially its relation to permutations of the Hebrew root *ḥbr*, meaning to link, join, or associate with; and on Alḥarizi's use of the name at the close of chapters of *Taḥkemoni*, see the Afterword.

mel Honey.

GATE THIRTY-THREE

Homily, Hymn, and Homonym

THUS SPOKE HEMAN THE EZRAHITE: When I flourished in the arbours of Youth, basking in Strength's green booth, I hungered after Truth, hungered to take Wisdom's measure; so I set out after Rhetoric's buried treasure, that I might spend my days in richness, my years in pleasure.

In this pursuit I came in full career to Mount Seir and there discovered bards whose tongues bright beryl uncovered; over Song's tent their bright clouds hovered. In their groves lush fruits swelled thick and choice; deep did I rejoice as I drew near to see each countenance and hear each voice.

Then one of them said to his companions: Is there a mouth here breathing sage and thyme, is there among you a tongue can chime the rare, fair song of homonym rhyme?

What, asked some, is this song sublime?

Homonyms, said he, are an equivocation, words writ or mouthed alike but with divers signification. They be twin roses on two vines, closing each of two succeeding lines.

Having heard this explanation, each singer stepped forward with his own configuration, each by his standard, each according to his station.

Now off to the side stood a greybeard tut-tutting like a clock, dour as a rock, a shepherd set to guide a bleating flock. Seeing his fellows' piteous assay, how they could not find their way, but stumbled

spend my days in richness, my years in pleasure Job 36: 11.

over Song's tent their bright clouds hovered [Exod. 40: 35–7].

to see each countenance and hear each voice [S. of S. 2: 14].

each by his standard, each according to his station [Num. 1: 52, 2: 2].

like blind men at the height of the day, he cried, Friends, would you mount and ride unqualified? The way is steep, your steeds untried; this well is dangerous-deep and wide. Now if you would pluck the homonym from Songtree's highest limb, cease and draw near; O house of Jacob, hear!

Then he declared: Praise God! His acclamation raise, Him praised by dawn's mute rays, who bids backsliders, Turn, and others guide in turn; who calls, Wing'd soul with Passion's fires alight, descend from your false Heaven, alight. Sinner, seek no greater feat than wading Jordan's shallows with Repentance' feet, shouting *Forgive, Lord!* true and loud; then find true Heaven allowed.

Will you sail Life's sea on Lust's rotted board? Find Virtue's vessel, climb aboard, hoist Penitence' sail on Resolution's boom to front Temptation's swell and boom. Skim over Lust's waves in full career, with honesty your full career. Unsheathe Right's sword and stiff your back, that pirate Sin might see and straight fall back.

Conceive aright and this notion bear: Pleasure's cupboard is bone bare. Wake, ere your breath be blown, your once-ripe spirit blast and blown. You, in sin bound: burst fetters, flee Temptation's bound. Shall you, goat-eyed, unceasing browse on painted lips and thick, black brows? Know Sin's honied scent to be Hell-sent. Open God's Holy Writ and read: Lean not on Lust, that hollow reed. Shall he lead you fearless to Heaven's pike past Michael's sword and Gabriel's pike?

He who desires Life's best must Lust's arms best. Let Intellect and Soul confer and all their powers on Right Resolve confer, through whose might Desire's surging river shall be dammed; else, be damned! Stumble no more on Sin's decline, and when he bids you to his board, decline; gorge on his meats and sugary desserts and Heaven shall mete you harsh deserts.

Oh, call your revels to a halt before Time leads you, trembling and halt, you and all your hot blood's host, to be the Worm's most

stumbled like blind men at the height of the day [Deut. 28: 29].
O house of Jacob, hear [Isa. 46: 3].
Him praised by dawn's mute rays [Ps. 19: 1–6].
wading Jordan's shallows with Repentance' feet [Josh. 3: 13–4: 24].
Forgive, Lord [Dan. 9: 19].
Lean not on Lust, that hollow reed [Isa. 36: 6].

generous host. Ask Sin no leave but instanter leave the company of mocker, scoffer, liar. Seize Virtue's psaltery and Right's lyre; then strum with passion, raging and livid: accuse your soul till she turn bloodless livid.

Cast evil out, admit your Maker to your heart, race to His service swifter than the hart. Come, end your grief, and your soul commend to Him all souls commend. Step down from silk and satin, linen and down. Hold our forefathers' merits fast, seek God in sackcloth, ashes, and in fast. With Right your standard and Mercy your flag, climb upward, never flag until you hear God's angels sing, Done well! Come, O Beloved, drink of Salvation's well.

Now when he had finished the pressing of Song's grape, when he had draped himself in Splendour's cape, when he had bound Sin fast and left him no escape, we stood minds reeling and mouths agape.

Yet more remained of this sweet extravaganza: Friends, he declared, I shall gift you with homonym stanza, the double-rhymed quatrain at start and close, Wit's reign and Rhetoric's gold vein.

Then he lifted his voice and sang:

A *All ways lead to God when you heed the bright*
thunder of Sinai and give your assent.
Always approach the Lord's Hill with clean hands
and pure heart—and so win the ascent.

B *Beset your name with the best of gems—*
Good Deeds; Better; Best.
Beset by Temptation, your ramparts will hold;
you shall the Attacker best.

C *Confer with your heart and live like a man,*
not like a dog or a cow;

Seize Virtue's psaltery and Right's lyre [2 Sam. 6: 5; 1 Chr. 13: 8; and elsewhere].
race to His service swifter than the hart [Mishnah, *Avot* 5: 20].
seek God in sackcloth, ashes, and in fast [Esther 4: 3].
Come, O Beloved [S. of S. 7: 12].
drink of Salvation's well [Isa. 12: 3].
heed the bright thunder of Sinai and give your assent [Exod. 20: 18, 24: 7].
approach the Lord's Hill with clean hands and pure heart—and so win the ascent [Ps. 24: 3–4].
Confer with your heart [Ps. 4: 5].

Confer on your spirit the staff of Resolve
and Appetite's grumblings cow.

D *Defer not: succour the sick and the poor,*
hold pity and justice dear.
Defer to the Lord: do His will with a will
lion-strong and as swift as the deer.

E *Even and morn He lights my path*
whose good no tongue can full express.
Even as He has served my good
so be my service full, express.

F *Fly, soul, Sin's sea,*
Lust's fleet.
Fly swift to heaven—
swift-fleet.

G *Grown old my flesh, not so my acumen—*
low-bent my frame; halting, my spirit's gait.
Groan, O my soul, as your slow steps lead up
the tortured path of age to Judgement's gate.

H *Hollow, mountain, sea, and sun*
proclaim God's glory: mortals, hear!
Hollow your hearts, that Song ingest,
mirror that splendour—instanter, here.

I *Inspire, poet, the Prophets' fire*
and errant men indict.
Inspire your fellows to holy deed:
reflect, seize pen, indite.

J *Just man: would you whip your steed*
till he turn a jade?
Just so abuse not your soul,
your priceless jade.

K *Keen-sighted Death with outspread wings*
swoops to your castle's keep.

---

succour the sick and the poor [2 Sam. 27: 28; and elsewhere].

do His will with a will lion-strong and as swift as the deer [Mishnah, *Avot* 5: 20].

proclaim God's glory [Ps. 19: 1].

Keen, prince, your wealth, your flesh, your soul:
nothing can you keep.

L *Let the heart's chambers to Truth and Right;*
lead in these tenants by Kindness' light.
Let Meanness leave; then let the Dove
of Mercy upon your lintel light.

M *Mine counsel and strength, bold Wisdom declares;*
mortal, show your mettle:
Mine me to my darkest depths
and find no finer metal.

N *Naysay the pleader Lust,*
that whining nag.
Neigh, say, and whinny on,
you ass, you nag!

O *Ought I repent, my spirit asks,*
and all my folly own?
Ought have you gained, my heart replies;
confess—and pardon own.

P *Part right from wrong and truth from lie;*
take ever the orphan's part.
Part you from evil and cleave to good—
the whole and not the part.

Q *Quack-quack! Meat! Sack! cries the mindless mass,*
slavering for wine and quail.
Quacksalvers! Fools! When will you wake?
Fear judgement! Quake and quail!

R *Render your innards in Penitence' fire;*
your sickly souls repair.
Render to God your lips and deeds
and so to Heaven repair.

S *Sway, heart,* lulav*-like, on the Feast of Booths,*
confession's lyric sound;

Mine counsel and strength, bold Wisdom declares [Prov. 8: 14].
take ever the orphan's part [Ps. 10: 14].
Sway, heart, *lulav*-like, on the Feast of Booths The reference (the translator's) is to the palm frond, waved ritually in six directions in the synagogue during the Feast of Sukkot.

Sway then your heart, your reins, your flesh—
your present and future sound.

T *Turn the heart's iron to water, Lord,*
the turtle Will to tern;
Turn us again unto thee, O Lord—
we shall return in turn.

U *Undue reward I give my God—*
more than my tongue can utter;
Undo your wrong, O rebel soul,
before your ruin be utter.

V *Vail a thick curtain upon your deeds;*
be treacherous, gross, and vain.
Veil each your lie from man and God.
Veil all. And all in vain.

W *World, I have drunk of your wine too deep,*
too oft your silks and satins worn:
Whirled high and low by the winds of Lust
my flesh is wasted, my spirit worn.

X *Exercise daily: push sinning off,*
bend to repentance. Be strict, exact.
Exercise mercy and self-restraint,
and right reward of Heaven exact.

Y *Yield, O my soul, to Him who formed you*
deep in the womb, a quivering yolk.
Yield him the best of your fertile field—
Good's field, ploughed deep 'neath the Torah's yoke.

Z *Zero-hour! Alas, my soul and heart,*
don Prayer's white mantle and Penitence' zone.
Zero achieved, breath failing—God,
bring me in mercy to Heaven's white zone.

SAID THE TELLER OF THE TALE:
Now when the speaker had finished this display and sweetly

Turn us again unto thee, O Lord—we shall return in turn [Lam. 5: 21].

Him who formed you deep in the womb [Isa. 44: 2; Jer. 1: 5; and elsewhere].

zone Girdle.

swept his listeners' hearts away, the grateful people shouted their acclaim and begged him to reveal his name. To which he replied:

I am Hever, ever the silver bell
whereon Poesy's tunes are rung.
Though Wisdom's flocks have strayed round the world,
find them upon my tongue.

GATE THIRTY-FOUR

Of a Host Bombastic and a Feast Fantastic

THUS SPOKE HEMAN THE EZRAHITE: Having journeyed from Maḥanaim to Mount Ephraim, I followed my feet, street after street, until I came upon a fellow standing by his gate weary and distraught, morose and overwrought. Approaching him I asked, Why, sir, your moan? And why stand you alone?

Damn lust, cried he, that sees its owner made a mockery!

Sir, said I, your tale unfold: let your history be told.

Said he, This day a merchant led me home, a guest to his feast. We were but a moment walking and, lo, he was off and talking of his fine wealth and life, and wife.

Know sir, said he, that my ancestors were the nonpareil of the aristocracy, prodigious in their generosity. God graced my father with Means and Name and Mark and Fame. I was born beneath an auspicious sky, a delight to the eye. Now when I had grown and had made Wisdom's path my own, opening my very teachers' eyes and frustrating the wise, my father gave into my hand a daughter of the *noblesse* of the land. Fair she is of form and face (more I would say in another place), shining like a lamp in her labours—the joy of her husband and her neighbours. By heaven, sir, could you but see her beauties as she rushes *sans* restraint to her duties hour by hour, from turret to tower and tower to room, with mop or broom or down on

Maḥanaim In Scripture, a city in the territory of Gad on the eastern bank of the Jordan: Josh. 21: 36 and elsewhere.
Mount Ephraim Josh. 17: 15.
weary and distraught, morose and overwrought 1 Kgs. 20: 43, 21: 4; Deut. 25: 18.
a delight to the eye Gen. 2: 9.
opening my very teachers' eyes Ps. 119: 99.
frustrating the wise Isa. 44: 25.

her lovely belly scouring pots,—the dear!—her fair face flecked with soot and bright eyes blear, you would exclaim, Happy the man of her possessed and happy the people so blessed! And on he babbled until my ears rang.

Now when we arrived at his gate he exclaimed, My good sir, look at this gate and its links, its crest and its chinks, its rings and its poles, its sockets and holes: much Wealth did I spend and great effort expend until I made it fair and prize, the very Vision now before your eyes.

Next we came to the courtyard, where he proclaimed, My good sir, look on this courtyard and its graces, its walls and their delightful faces—Ah, how goodly are its dwelling-places! Mark you the merchants' dwellings round about and look without doubt on the fairest of them all. My good sir, mark this lovely hall and all its windows; look you at each wall, and lift your eyes aloof to rafters and roof, to boards and beams, the very stuff of dreams; and at the chiaroscuros in their perfection, each one a painted, rare confection beaming in every direction like eyes with stibium hued, by Beauty wooed and robed and shoed. My good sir, look at the water pool and, at its brink, the lions who do it rule the while they copiously drool, dripping waters that are the soul's joy quite, yea, God and man's delight.

We then entered the house, where he said, My good sir, look at each lovely chamber royally gilt for slumber, each floor inlaid with ivories without number. There stands my Bed of Bliss—my wife's room, this. Ah, could you but see me alone, outstretched, with my dear bride at my side, her cheeks the light of my eyes, her arms tight round my thighs and her lips like honeyed pies; and she, *sans* restraint, kissing and hugging and panting and tugging and bobbing and sobbing until my very bones be throbbing, your thoughts would be staggered by such glorious Intimacy *and thou shouldst go mad at the sight of thine eyes which thou shouldst see*.

down on her lovely belly scouring pots Ps. 68: 14.
Happy the man Ps. 1: 1.
happy the people so blessed Ps. 144: 15.
the very Vision now before your eyes Num. 8: 4.
Ah, how goodly are its dwelling-places Num. 24: 5.
God and man's delight Judg. 9: 13.
each floor inlaid with ivories Esther 1: 6.
and thou shouldst go mad at the sight of thine eyes which thou shouldst see Deut. 28: 34.

After all of this torment he summoned his servant to bring in the table, which done he said, Look, sir, at this well-formed table, so firm and stable. Note its planks and clasps, its knots and its hasps, its four sleek legs and pegs. I had it made of choicest cedar, King of the Wood, indeed, sir, that it might last forever.

Then to his servant: The water, young man, to wash *les mains!* And when the youth complied, my host began again, My good sir, look at this basin, poured from gold, as it were; yea, the choice gold of Ophir. It is opulent and wide: two men could bathe inside. And mark you, sir, these waters, the dream of a lusting eye, as though from the sigh-filled tears of lovers they had quite congealed, in all their purity revealed as moist gems or filaments of silver drawn out, so—or frozen snow! From the Tigris' waters were they drawn and lolled in ivory vessels till the dawn when they shone forth fresh as morning dew on a rose's cheek, or two.

Then he said to the lad, Heed my command: pour water on your master's hand!

Now when the youth approached he said to me, Good sir, mark this lovely lad's rare figure and pleasant stature: his jet-black hair, his face so fair, and cheek like a red rose rare! Ah, the sweet weave of his face—black eyes, white teeth: what grace! As though his cheek were a plush mound with roses set round and with silk bound, and all this, that no grief might in your heart be found. For him unto Earth's ends have I gone and purchased him in Babylon. His understanding is profound: in him my Soul's desire have I found. What I want he knows; where I go, he goes. He answers ere I call and my needs knows all. Yea, he walks in my way; and as for my bequest of God, I say, *For this lad did I pray.*

Now when my ears were ringing with his prattle he called to his servant, Go fetch the sweets and honeyed treats, yea, all the tasty food well cooked and good, the succulent lambs and wine and yams, for our grief has greatly grown: the Belly's gates are besieged, the weapons of Hunger are drawn.

the choice gold of Ophir Ps. 45: 10 and elsewhere.
pour water on your master's hand 2 Kgs. 3: 11.
jet-black hair S. of S. 5: 11.
He answers ere I call Isa. 65: 24.
For this lad did I pray 1 Sam. 1: 27.
the tasty food Gen. 27: 4.
gates are besieged Isa. 22: 7.

THE TELLER OF THE TALE WENT ON:

I considered: all this song and swelling chorus and no food before us, while there was yet to speak of the bread to eat, as well the harvesting of the wheat, and the oven and the baking, and the fire and wood that went into its making, and the axe used in the undertaking; and doubtless some tales of the meat and abattoir and then a discourse on each condiment and its jar: the nutmeg and capsicum, cubeb and chutney, marjoram, shallot, and mace—and others more commonplace. Not to mention the pots and the pans and the plates and the forks and the knives and the spoons and the bottles and corks—all this to go on for a year and a day, yea, or Eternity, say.

*S*o with a start I sprang up to depart.

*S*aid he, Sir, can I believe you mean to leave?

*S*aid I, I must go home to . . . to attend to a private need; that done, I shall return with speed.

*A*t that he seized and pulled me, faint and numb, until we were unto the privy come.

*W*hat, said he, to think of leaving until you set your eyes on this breathtaking sight, the very Acme of Delight? Look, sir, alone, on Naked Beauty Bare: the water basin firm and fair, the marble floor inlaid with ivories rare. Should a fly walk on this lovely floor, he would stumble and fall; need I say more? Indeed, here one would crave to dine, so fair a place it is and fine!

*S*aid I to him, Sir, with relish eat! I had thought my reckoning complete; but, truth to tell, it had not reached unto the Privy Seat!

*T*hen swift and *sans* restraint I fled him like a hind with him red-faced and shouting close behind, *Mind the meal, sir, mind!*

*A*t that, his servants, hearing the rout, thought some grossness on my part had brought about that shout, so they halloed after, *Mind the meal!* And seeing them swarm about me like flies, my blood rose to my eyes and, taking a stone in hand, I flung it in the middle of one ugly head and left the man half-dead. Then the neighbours all, both great and small, joined eager in pursuit and caught and thrashed me

inlaid with ivories rare Esther 1: 6.
swarm about me like flies Ps. 118: 12.
taking a stone in hand, I flung it in the middle of one ugly head 1 Sam. 17: 49.

fist and boot. By the skin of my teeth I escaped Death's sword; such was the merchant's feast—ah, be reminded of his father's sins, dear Lord!

SAID THE TELLER OF THE TALE:

When I heard his tale I shook for very mirth and fell full-length laughing to the earth. By Heaven, I cried, unless I greatly err, you are Hever the Kenite, my good sir!

And he proclaimed:

I am Hever the Kenite, heart's delight:
Mine be the words that hurry thoughts to flight.
I fashion stories rhymed with riddles sweet
And please the hearer's palate with rich meat.
Fire comes flashing at each my pleasant word:
Out of my granite speech I draw my sword.

Now having heard his poetry I marvelled at his glorious falsity. With his sweet speech he seized me fast and bound me many days in love until, at last, Wandering bore him off on his wing and struck me with the rod of wrath—and I feel yet the sting.

By the skin of my teeth I escaped Job 19: 20.
be reminded of his father's sins, dear Lord Ps. 109: 14.
fell full-length laughing to the earth 1 Sam. 28: 20.
Fire comes flashing Ps. 29: 7.
struck me with the rod of wrath Exod. 21: 20; Lam. 3: 1; and elsewhere.

GATE THIRTY-FIVE

Of the Grave of Ezra the Blest and Poems Celeste

THUS SPOKE HEMAN THE EZRAHITE: Shaken to my soul, I wandered far, even to Shinar, that land of aloed sweets, where, walking one city's streets, I spied by chance—blest glance!—Hever the Kenite; and my heart turned bright. Hever, I cried, be blest of God Most High. What brings you nigh?

*T*he snake, said he, the tempter Wandering, none other, who wrests brother from brother.

I said, Perforce. Yet what brings you here and where lies your course?

I was in Spain, he answered, distraught and distracted, and could not rest until I acted, for daily I heard ringing tales of Ezra, holy to the Lord, such that I could not bind my throbbing thoughts with Sleep's sweet cord. God roused my spirit, then, to set sail, brave wave and raging gale, cross bogs and fens, dare mountains of leopards and lions' dens far from my native clime, to set apart Truth's ring from Falsehood's chime. Judah left his brothers at that time.

*T*hus He who sets His path through mighty seas bore me from Spain's pleasantries to the Gloried Land, where rumours knocked on my heart's door at every hand, each with the same demand: Believe (and could a thousand tongues deceive?) that between the land of Kasdim and Shushan a certain Samra lay (Aḥavah in the Holy Tongue); and, three parasangs away, the wondrous site—since the start of the Second Temple's sway (may God rebuild it in our day!)—of the first grave of Ezra, may his memory light our way.

be blest of God Most High Ruth 2: 4 [and Gen. 14: 19].

The snake, said he, the tempter Gen. 3: 13.

God roused my spirit Hag. 1: 14 and elsewhere.

mountains of leopards and lions' dens S. of S. 4: 8.

Judah left his brothers at that time Gen. 38: 1.

There was the prophet's holy station until, thirteen hundred years beyond the second exile of our nation, the site became a desolation, that his bones uneasy slept: there jackals cackled and satyrs leapt. He lay there lost to sight, a star in cloudy night, a buried chrysolite.

Now, as most reports go, some one hundred and sixty years ago a shepherd came to know, in a dream of the night, that God's own Angel habited that site. Twice came the message, nor could it be ignored, for the vision of the shepherd's blind eye was restored.

The awestruck herdsman left his fold, summoned his people, and told them all he had been told.

Friends, he cried, hear the vision that is mine: this is the grave of Ezra the Divine. Know this as true by this wonder and sign: my two eyes shine!

Again and again he spoke, swore no one had deceived him; and the folk believed him.

Then picks and axes rang until a mighty clang disclosed a tight-sealed iron box, upon whose surface letters raced, tight locks upon the Mystery of that which therein lay. What those words spoke no man could say; no, none could win to the enigma's unfettering until a sage declared that it was Hebrew lettering. Quickly they brought a Jewish reader for the writ's decipherment, who told them at once what the inscription meant: that this was, indeed, the cask of Ezra the priest, graven with his and his forebears' names back to Aaron the high priest.

Back to its place the fear-struck heathen bore the cask away; and there it rests unto this day.

Since then, on many a night that grave is washed with holy light—a godly light, men deem; and thither the nations stream. Moreover, by the holy prophet's side lie seven others, all Righteousness' brothers; and many a night, men tell, their sepulchres shine as well, yes, give birth to tongues of light that walk the earth.

wonder and sign [Deut. 28: 46].
my two eyes shine 1 Sam. 14: 29.
thither the nations stream Isa. 2: 2.
tongues of light that walk the earth Ps. 73: 9.

SAID THE TELLER OF THE TALE:

Now all this talk I held a fabrication, the workings of a strained imagination, mere vapour and mist—until I came and saw, and knew that God was in our midst. Until that moment I had held the veil of Splendour stripped from Ariel, the glory departed from Israel. Therefore I said, if this be no lie, why, let me go and see this thing before I die. So I girt my loins for holy destination, toiled through many a land and nation at Wandering's assignation, until I came to the site of Ezra, holy man of God, and lay me down upon his grave before my God; and soon went out with a large congregation to see that miracled illumination.

But seeing was not yet believing.

I suspected deceiving heathen round about of firing our griefs by lighting high fires in mockery of our beliefs.

Then second thoughts were mine: fire gives off a reddish glow, but this was crystalline.

Furthermore, many men reported with precision the selfsame vision; told of throngs gathered patiently, waiting to see those godly beams rise strong and free to slake their spirits' thirst; and strong those bright beams burst.

Now this account, so widely verified, has been denied emphatically by men who have set faith aside—schismatics/*minim* thick with pride.

They claimed that land had housed a nation which God had singled out for devastation, so that its soil turned sulphur, and pitch its streams; and that the burning sulphur issued forth those beams.
So much, said they, for shepherds' dreams.

A curse, say I, on their vile schemes! Sulphur's flames are blear and soiled, dark-roiled, and pitch-embroiled; but this was haloed

knew that God was in our midst Exod. 17: 7.

Ariel Isa. 29: 1 ff., a poetic designation for Jerusalem.

the glory departed from Israel 1 Sam. 4: 21, 22.

let me go and see this thing before I die Gen. 45: 28.

schismatics/*minim* Possibly an allusion to the Karaites (see Gate 17).

men thick with pride Lit. *paritsim*, 'reprobates' or 'dissolute men' [Ps. 73: 6–7].

its soil turned sulphur, and pitch its streams Isa. 34: 9.

light, pure-bright, dancing to left and right, rising and falling in angel flight, light-swift; and sulphur's hulking flames can scarcely lift.

Yet one more proof descry that no man can deny: I saw that blest light fly eastward from the west across the sky, to light upon the grave of Ezra, may he rest in peace.

Yes, our sight unfailingly records that this work is of no hand but the Lord's.

And so it was that after I had long waited, I came, saw, weighed until my mind was sated. Well then could I discern Truth's tale from claim of fool or schemer. Blest be the Lord who has not left us without a redeemer.

Then I lifted my voice and sang:

Heaven's gates be these? Jerusalem?
An angel camp?
Oh, house of God! My spirit ascends
a blazing ramp—
The beams of our master Ezra's grave
that illume blind eyes
And write God's love of his scattered folk
across the skies.
Oh, light to my night outshining the sun
by seven times seven,
Whose beams sweep earthward like eagle's wings
then breach high Heaven—
Beams scarlet and gold as though Heaven's fields
were sown with two grains!
Ezra, my tears flood your grave
like Noah's rains.

These lines I drew from Sweetness' mines at the grave of Ezekiel the prophet, our master of blessed memory:

Blest be the Lord who has not left us without a redeemer Ruth 4: 14.
Heaven's gates be these? Gen. 28: 17.
An angel camp Gen. 32: 3.
fields were sown with two grains Lev. 19: 19.
like Noah's rains. These lines I drew The lack of transition indicates, perhaps, a lacuna in the manuscript used by Toporovsky.

Grave of Truth's prophet, and prophet—be blest;
and your ramparts, from east and from west.
Your earth is as flesh and Ezekiel its soul,
or a sky where his starred splendours rest.
Daily men seek you, and angels by night,
for the Presence that shines in your rooms.
Your grave is a vial no stopper can seal
for the pow'r of your pungent perfumes.
Kings leap from their chariots to lick your sweet dust
where kid and leopard meet.
Sceptics, and heathens who knew not God's name,
strip the shoes from their trembling feet.
Prophet and priest, Torah's font—God speaks
from your dazzling Urim *and* Tumim*;*
God's mitre is given your forehead; therefrom
Creation's awed secrets beam.
Happy the mother who bore you, and happy
the father who called you his own.
Happy your grave, resplendent on earth;
and your spirit, beneath God's high Throne.
Fused with the angels your glorious soul,
whose splendours can never be told.
Your flesh? Death's worms hold all flesh in thrall,
but never your body hold.
Your soul lives in Heaven, your flesh yet on earth:
your lungs, liver, heart not yet dry—
You, blest with the Chariot Vision of God
where eyed wheels and wild beasts whirl by,

be blest; and your ramparts Ps. 122: 7.

kid and leopard meet Lit. 'Lo the leopard lies down with the kid around you' (Isa. 11: 6).

strip the shoes from their trembling feet Exod. 3: 5; Josh. 5: 15.

God speaks from your dazzling *Urim* and *Tumim* Oracular stones inlaid into the breastplate of the high priest. See Exod. 28: 30, Lev. 8: 8.

God's mitre is given your forehead Exod. 28: 36–8.

Eagle face, lion face, ox face, and man's;
You were brought to the vale of dry bones
That rose at your word (for you spoke, at God's word).
That vision yet holds us, intones
That we, too, shall rise up at Time's weary end,
bones gathered together, and sing;
Yea, the sleepers in dust shall awaken and shout,
revived by the dew of their King.
Beloved of your people, to Earth's farthest ends
your words bring the sightless sight:
Then favour your servant, from Spain's shores come,
to bathe in your glorious light.
Pity my cheeks, rived with rivers of tears,
and my heart, with coal-fire riven.
Grant me a gift of your spirit Divine
like the portion Elisha was given;
Though meagre the gift—sweet prophet, I know—
that I offer your holy name:
My song, sprung from lips anoint with your myrrh
and my innards' incessant flame.
Ezekiel, I pray: Plead God's grace for a man
whom sadness and sin infest;
Who cries from the ends of the earth, O grave
of Truth's prophet, and prophet—be blest!

You, blest with the chariot vision of God where eyed wheels and wild beasts whirl by, Eagle face, lion face, ox face, and man's Ezek. 1.

You were brought to the vale of dry bones Ezek. 37: 1–15.

That we, too, shall rise up at Time's weary end, bones gathered together, and sing [Isa. 26: 19].

Yea, the sleepers in dust shall awaken and shout, revived by the dew of their King Isa. 26: 19.

Grant me a gift of your spirit divine like the portion Elisha was given 2 Kgs. 2: 9 ff. At this point the translation slightly condenses the remainder of the poem.

GATE THIRTY-SIX

Challenge and Reply: Sweet Words Fly

THUS SPOKE HEMAN THE EZRAHITE: When I dwelt in Gladness' tent, when my cheeks were fragrant with youth's sweet scent, my arms firm, my back unbent, joy all my bent, heart resolute to pluck the lute, and Pleasure's trees of bobbing fruit, I journeyed to Sevaim, land of the gipsies, where I came upon a band of tipsies—young blades, their fires a-muster, clustered round the grape's sweet cluster. Amidst them sat Song's firstborn son, Hever the Kenite, in whose right hand the goblet spun and at whose left sat a stag bright as the sun, and he between the two, to each sweet pleasure true.

*L*ong at the cup's ruddy breast he suckled; and when his eyes discovered me he blushed, then chuckled.

*S*tep forward, he beckoned, no need to hide. I complied, stepped to his side, but cried, Hever, how dare you? Dismount Lust's mount: how long shall these things snare you?

*J*olted from his langour, Hever thinned his lips in anger. Stuff! he cried; enough of your pouting! This is Joy's hour and no time for shouting. Remove my sin from before your eyes and turn to a tale will make you wise.

*D*one, I replied, see me turning. Now set me learning.

*O*nce, in my youth, he said, in Kittim's land, the sun turned black, as hosts of Aram made attack, Hittite troops to the right and Philistines at their back. As the city lay besieged, week after week, my eyes spun for hunger and my knees grew weak. With no help to be found and my liver near spilled upon the ground, I took my life in

stag i.e. a fetching youth.
how long shall these things snare you? Exod. 10: 7.
Remove my sin from before your eyes Isa. 1: 16.
Kittim's land Isa. 23: 1.
my liver near spilled upon the ground Lam. 2: 11.

hand—Let fall what may!—and in night's pitch o'erleapt the city wall and made away. Thus I escaped by God's redeeming arm: and Him I praised, who saved my soul from harm.

Now amidst that camp I drank down Slumber's cup and early next morning, when the sun leapt up, I strode to a hill's clear height and cried, Who would delight in Wisdom's light? Draw near, for I am here!

At that, throngs left their tents to circle me, numerous as the sands of the sea.

Men of learning, I proclaimed, incline: eat my bread and drink my wine, find him who, putting rest behind, has mined the varied mind of humankind, whose signet ring proclaims him Hidden Lore's sole king, who has leapt over mountains like a hart uncovering Healing's secret art; who leaves naught to conjecture in the halls of Architecture; who multiplies wonder in the realm of Number while others slumber; who bares, and bears off, buried treasure in the kingdom of Measure; who, on Logic's height, has built a palanquin of delight; who unbars the secrets of the stars; whose penetration unveils the mysteries of scriptural cantillation. I am the vial of the Mishnah's scent, stay of the Talmud's tent; in the fields of the Sabora'im I sport and play, holding sway over *Sifra* and *Sifré*. I am the consummation of exegetic explication. In the counsels of Grammar I sweetly declaim, while others stammer to their shame. In Song's bright chorus, mine is the brightest note, for I am Song's very throat.

Then a blameless youth, his eyes white doves by Learning's pond, rose to respond:

Bold archer, he challenged, let your arrows fly: to each my question, make reply.

---

numerous as the sands of the sea Gen. 22: 17.
eat my bread and drink my wine [Prov. 9: 5].
who has leapt over mountains like a hart [S. of S. 2: 8–9].
a palanquin of delight S. of S. 3: 9.
scriptural cantillation Markings as guides to chant and to syntactical groupings. See *EJ* xvi. 1412–13.
Saboraim Babylonian sages in the generation following the talmudic period, and preceding the geonic, roughly the 6th c. CE.
Sifra A halakhic commentary on the book of Leviticus.
Sifré A halakhic commentary on the books of Numbers and Deuteronomy.
his eyes white doves by Learning's pond [S. of S. 7: 5].

My sword is unsheathed, said I, and my arm steady. Speak—I am ready.

SAID HE: *What spice sweets fellowship all spice above?*
I ANSWERED: *Love.*
SAID HE: *Who owns Wisdom's vault?*
I ANSWERED: *He who owns his fault.*
SAID HE: *Who guards his wit's repute?*
—The mute.
How merit Wisdom's wreath?
—Hold your tongue between your teeth.
What gilds wealth's bright?
—Right.
How conquer in Wisdom's race?
—Set everything in its proper place.
When is prayer heard?
—When griefs grow, tears flow, and the soul bows low is Heaven stirred.
What dims the mind's sight?
—Appetite.
When is death better than life?
—When the noble must dance to the villain's fife.
Define cursed rain.
—Outpourings of a muddied brain.
How is a community slain with impunity?
—For lack of unity.

Who guards his wit's repute?—The mute Lit. 'He said, "What is the virtue hotly desired?" I answered, "Silence"'; similarly, generally, *Mivḥar hapeninim*, gate 32—on which see the analysis in A. M. Habermann's edition (Tel Aviv, 1947), 34–5.

What dims the mind's sight?—Appetite Lit. 'lust for food'; similarly, *Mivḥar hapeninim* 15: 13, 15, 20: '. . . lust is the enemy of intelligence. . . . Intelligence is lost between the evil inclination and lust. . . . Lust is the partner of blindness' (Habermann, 22).

When is death better than life?—When the noble must dance to the villain's fife Lit. 'when despicable men vaunt it over esteemed men'; similarly, *Mivḥar hapeninim* 43: 45, 'Three are more deserving of pity than any other man: a knowledgeable man led by an idiot, a righteous man ruled by an evil man, and a giving man in need of a knave' (Habermann, 47).

By what four evils is man ever tried?
—Folly, Brazenness, Stupidity, and Pride. Each can have the world undone; how much the more so when they act as one!
What carves Might's rod?
—Fear of God.
Who pays for his folly dearly?
—He who serves his king insincerely.
Whose joy knows no abortion?
—He who joys in his portion.
What strips men of longevity?
—Levity.
For whom must Misfortune stand aside?
—He who stands not on his pride.
Who drains Danger's flask?
—One slothful at his task.
What is the best claim to fame?
—An unstained name.
Who can be called a giving man?
—He who gives what he can, though his cloak be a rag and his chair a can.
Who is Folly's sot?
—He whose parents' corpses rot, yet whispers in his heart, Death seeks me not.
How shall the wretch rise?
—By girding Wisdom's sword upon his thighs.

By what four evils . . . they act as one Similarly, *Mivḥar hapeninim* 27: 12: 'Four things bring a man to ruin—pride, stubbornness, laziness, and rashness'; and 43: 27: 'He who withholds himself from four is saved from four: from rashness, stubbornness, pride, and laziness; for the fruit of rashness is regret, and the fruit of stubbornness is brazenness, and the fruit of pride is hatred, and the fruit of laziness is failure' (Habermann, 31–2 and 46).

Whose joy knows no abortion Lit. 'who gets of the world what suffices him.'

He who joys in his portion Mishnah, *Avot* 4: 1; similarly, *Mivḥar hapeninim* 46: 1: 'The wise man said, "There is none so poor as him who is not happy with his lot and whose eye can never be sated."' (Habermann, 55).

When does Silence shriek?
—When the wise should speak.

Who holds Wisdom's springs rank pools?
—Rank fools.

When does high praise falter?
—When mighty givers are given to Death's altar.

What discolours Modesty's blush?
—Pride's black and Lust's flush.

What virtue wins highest reward?
—Fear of the Lord.

Now, when I had met his every thrust, left him nonplussed, and shown my claim just, each man put hand to purse and stilled my pocket's lust.

Then I sang:

Take heed of the fickle clerk of Fate
who sets all men's names on his dreary docket.
Forge, with your mind, Good Fortune's key:
when Good's gate closes, let that unlock it.
Let sluggards lose all of their fathers' wealth;
you, wise and eager, fill each your pocket.

Now when I had heard his every word, I carved his message on my heart, that it ne'er depart. Then I bowed and took my leave, and he put me behind him; I left him and did not find him.

Who holds Wisdom's springs rank pools?—Rank fools Lit. 'He said, "When is the supremacy of the wise revealed?" I said, "In the company of fools".'

What discolours modesty's blush?—Pride's black and Lust's flush Lit. 'He said, "Wherein is modesty fair?" I said, "Through subjugation of pride and lust"'; similarly, generally, *Mivḥar hapeninim* 3 and 15 (Habermann, 13–14 and 21–2).

What virtue wins highest reward? Lit. 'What is the unmatched virtue?'

each man put hand to purse and stilled my pocket's lust Lit. 'Each man endowed me of his goods and conferred upon me his blessings'.

I left him and did not find him S. of S. 5: 6.

GATE THIRTY-SEVEN

In the Clasp of a Deadly Asp

THUS SPOKE HEMAN THE EZRAHITE: I made my way from Tyre to Hazor with a score of brawny men of war. In the midst of a scrub-flecked waste, we came on an oasis laced with chains of colours glorious to behold: magenta, amber, turquoise, green, and gold—flaming blooms and riotous perfumes on all sides; and this with cushioned grass and shaded pools besides. Delighted, we made our quarters in that pleasant land of brooks and waters.

Contented even to sighing, we were soon lying about, man and beast, beneath the trees, as the murmur of the noonday breeze lulled us to a deep and refreshing sleep. How much time passed I cannot tell: but then an ear-splitting yell singed us like a fire from Hell. We sprang from our slumber to see one of our number writhing and moaning, sobbing and groaning. Breath growing shorter, jaws in contortion, he told his misfortune: some creeping thing had hissed at him and struck! Foul luck! What could we do? We knew no charm to vitiate a viper's sting or draw poison from his arm. And what balm could we extract from fountain, rock, or palm? So we stood helplessly amidst the desert sands, red-eyed and wringing our hands. Then from nowhere, it seemed, up sprung a man who spoke with stinging adder's tongue.

Come now, he said, why do you cower and look so at one another? I will heal your brother! Only pay me my fee and gain your goal; every eye shall behold: your friend will leave here whole.

pleasant land of brooks and waters Deut. 8: 7.
who spoke with stinging adder's tongue Prov. 23: 32.
why do you cower and look so at one another? Gen. 42: 1.
I will heal Deut. 32: 39.
every eye shall behold Isa. 52: 8.

What say you? we shouted. Yes, yes, we will gladly pay you! Begin, we implore you; let your righteousness go before you.

Now as we watched in a hush, in a rush the fellow made a ring of tiered stones, the which he overlaid with twigs and brush. These he covered with dirt, until he had made a domed den, whereon he engraved a door of sorts with a stick for pen. Then he sent up a cloud of incense and, as it broke, rose and spoke:

Mountains, attend! List as I contend! Yea, turn your ear to that I say. I now command the desert sand, the sea and dry land, lush valleys, ripe hills, the wastes and gushing rills, lions' dens and monsters' fens; I, even I, Might's lord, by my bared arm and drawn sword, by the storming sky, by the eagle's cry, by mountain and by main, by thunderbolt, by firefount and hurricane—I call upon you: lest all my powers fall upon you, send all your adders forth—your asps and snakes from south to farthest north; divest yourselves of scorpions from east to farthest west. Release the viper with his deadly sting, the flying serpent of fiery wing. All must appear: on the Wind's broad pinions send them here. Gather, despatch them, every size and shape; none dare escape, I show no pity: give them no hiding-place, no refuge city; all must wear my rope, my double bridle, yes, choke beneath my yoke.

Hurry, scurry, helter-skelter, slither hither now! Be known, be shown, converge, merge—now, now, now!

Scorpion, turn in your track; advance, you cockatrice, turn not back; come every adder, green, brown, or black; lizard, drop from your rocky crack; come, salamander, with your scaly haversack; snake, leave your log, dragon, your sea-wrack. Come, come, I would employ you; come—else I will destroy you, snap you asunder with lightning and thunder, cast spells and charms to blast your eyes and blight your legs and arms. Now: swarm, storm, muster, cluster, centre, enter now—lest I blight you with treble devastation: Angels of Evil, Wrath, and

let your righteousness go before you Isa. 58: 6.
Mountains, attend Mic. 6: 2.
turn your ear to that I say Ps. 78: 1.
bared arm Isa. 52: 10.
and drawn sword Num. 22: 23, 31; and elsewhere.
refuge city Num. 35.
double bridle Job 41: 5.

Indignation, a threefold and unbroken cord, an all-consuming sword, by the power of the Almighty Lord.

Then he sang:

You I conjure, crawlers, creepers,
wasteland spirits, desert sleepers,
Adders' spawn and asps' increase,
wingèd seraph, cockatrice,
By thunder, lightning, wind, and rain
and Him who cleft the Sea in twain:
Hither swarm at my command
to work my will; or, at my hand,
Suffer the curses of power primeval—
Wrath, Indignation, and Angels of Evil.

He finished, lowered himself to earth and cocked his ears; and soon the air gave birth to a mighty tumult, an eerie hum, a buzz, a shout strong enough to wake the dead or turn mountains inside out. A massive grey cloud usurped the skies that the sun set at noon; choking, we closed our eyes; and when we opened them, saw a sight would freeze a hawk in flight: a host of grotesqueries descending, eyes multiple and distending, vipers with gnarled and horny covering, limbless creatures humming and hovering, heads sprouting horns, limbs layered with thorns, darting tongues with sagging sheath, conical and recurved teeth, dripping fangs and flashing scales, creatures with two heads, three tails, all hissing, clicking, rattling, whistling, crying—terrifying! Forward they came, squinting, staring, glowering, glaring. How would we survive? On they hopped and crept: they would swallow us alive!

Gripped with terror and dismay we turned to run away; whereat our wizard laughed and shouted, About face! Let no man leave his place.

Angels of Evil, Wrath, and Indignation Ps. 78: 49.
a threefold and unbroken cord Eccles. 4: 12.
Him who cleft the Sea in twain [Ps. 78: 13].
Wrath, Indignation, and Angels of Evil Ps. 78: 49.
mighty tumult Isa. 66: 6.
the sun set at noon Amos 8: 9.
they would swallow us alive Ps. 124: 3.
Let no man leave his place Exod. 16: 29.

Be strong, fear no injury, stand each man at his station: stand and behold the Lord's Salvation.

Quickly he rose; as we watched, grave and grim, he opened the mouth of the den and all the reptiles and the vermin swarmed therein. Then, whispering fiercely, he put into his grasp the soul of every scorpion, adder, and asp. Speaking so softly we could scarce hear, he bade them draw near. Then he opened the door wide and one by one they stepped outside, to depart unconstrained; until only one remained who, the more he tried, the more he could not force himself through the adobe's door. He leapt high and low, slithered to and fro, struggled and strained, yet was chained. Now when we saw his helplessness we knew the source of our friend's distress.

Bring me the patient, called the seer, and see my wondrous Remedy!

We brought and set him by the cage's door. Then our conjurer summoned the viper with a roar that all but shattered the adobe's roof. The serpent, being subtle, grasped the reproof. Out of the entrance he thrust his foul, black head and, as we looked on with dread, placed his lips on the wound and on his own poison fed; which done, our friend arose—and the viper fell down dead!

SAID THE TELLER OF THE TALE:

When we saw his wondrous deeds, we rose to revere him. Blessed be God, we cried, who gives of His Wisdom to them that fear Him! Then, having paid him, every one, for what he had done, we asked his name, his genealogy, and whence he came.

He answered:

In the Kingdom of Speech, I reign supreme
and leap and conquer where bright spears gleam.
I am Hever, ḥaver/*friend to friends*/ḥaverim;
also whisp'rer of charms: ḥover ḥovarim.

Be strong, fear no injury Isa. 35: 4.
stand and behold the Lord's Salvation Exod. 14: 13.
he opened the mouth of the den Josh. 10: 22.
The serpent, being subtle Gen. 3: 1.
who gives of His Wisdom to them that fear Him Traditional blessing on seeing a sage distinguished for his knowledge of Torah.
whisp'rer of charms: *ḥover ḥovarim* Deut. 18: 11.

GATE THIRTY-EIGHT

Of Men and Ship in the Storm's Grip

THUS SPOKE HEMAN THE EZRAHITE: Wandering seized me, bound me, placed me on his back, took wing, until I found me silent and still, with strangers all around me and my soul near expired, heartsick, lone, and far from all I desired. Sore I yearned to breathe free and stand once more upon my native shore, but many a hill and dale, many a vale and many a mile, many a mountain defile, yes, many a river and at last the sea stood between my desire and me; and far from being brave, I feared the pounding wave. Nonetheless I put my life in my hands and, trusting Him who Heaven and Earth commands, boarded a vessel trim and spare, black but fair, even black as an Afric's hair and swift as an arrow to cut the air, a craft with mighty planks and wales, with oars for legs, and for wings sails, a capital ship to rule the ocean gales. And behold: our vessel squatted like a woman giving birth, yet we floated on the wind between Heaven and Earth for a day or two, the waters below gentle as mid-May dew.

But suddenly the heavens trumpeted and the clouds turned bowmen, the sea reared up, a savage foeman, and a gigantic wind stepped these three between—Goliath the Philistine, who seized our vessel with a roar, raised it sky-high, then hurled it toward the ocean floor. Staggering, falling, weeping, bawling, we unleashed groans and shrieks, we pulled our hair, we clawed our cheeks. The wind churned the sea to a boiling pot, while the Ocean shouted, *I have her not!* One moment the waves divested them of all the goods they had ingested; then the ark rested—until once more the billows surged, the vessel

black but fair S. of S. 1: 5.
between—Goliath the Philistine 1 Sam. 17: 43, where the Hebrew reads literally '"the man of the space between"—i.e. between the armies' (*Tanakh—The Holy Scriptures*, ad loc.).
the ark rested Gen. 8: 4.

submerged, and the ship was near digested by the glutton waves. Time's slaves, round, round we widely spun, the revels fresh begun. Lo, oar after oar leapt from the ship to strike for shore. The sails whipped round, slipped down; in the wind's blast, the mast fell to chaff. Against the storm's mad laugh we staggered, sank to our knees, shuddering like men who had downed wine to the lees.

Now with all this, one man on board sat so calmly one might have thought him bored! While sailors screamed, while beams buckled, he sat and chuckled. Long after all began to shriek and squall, to screak and caterwaul, until the ship had turned a drunkards' ball, he sat alone, sans moan and groan, still and silent as a stone.

So I approached him and said, Is your heart lead, good sir, or your thoughts iron, that you will not stir? You sit aloof like a bird on a roof! One might have expected you would be a trifle more affected. Look: we are come to Death's straits, Hell's gates! Now, even now, our feet descend: this is our end! We shout and rock from side to side and you sit wrapped in Pride. Pray, why so gay? When we feed the fish, who will bear your bones away?

The fellow smiled, shook his head and said, He who has the knowledge I possess never need fear distress.

SAID THE TELLER OF THE TALE:

We heard—and every word dismissed at once. A dunce! Insane! Water on the brain! But then, suddenly, the wind lapsed and the waves collapsed. An end to fright! Why—the man was right! We were free from harm, untouched by Death's bared arm. Saved! Unscathed! As before, the oceans rolled gently towards a distant shore; once more the waves took their ease beneath a gentle breeze. Yes, the stranger was neither mad nor proud, but divinely endowed! So the passengers stood round about, attempting to draw the fellow out.

Sir, all this that we have seen—what does it mean? You seem unearthly wise: open our eyes!

Aha, said he: before, I was a loon, of no worth; and now, Heaven's voice on earth! But discounting your stupidity and vice, I shall tell you a secret beyond price. Know that I have a rare device, a scroll will keep its owner safe and whole, yes, save him from the

a bird on a roof [Ps. 102: 8]. **wrapped in Pride** Ps. 73: 6.

descent to Sheol; for it holds the names of all the angels of the water, a safeguard against the sea's mad slaughter. He who keeps it pressed to his side shall know no hurt wherever he abide; or when he journeys, whether he walk or ride. If he be cast into the flames he will not be harmed; or into the depths, he need not be alarmed. Lo, hereby even lions can be charmed!

They said, Sir, we hear you, and no one here dissents. Give us this cunning and win rich recompense. Speak plain—your labours will not be in vain.

He answered, By the life of this secret, loved of God, I swear: before I dare this lore unbar, each man must gift me with a gold dinar. Then will I write him a scroll will ever keep him hale and whole, a scroll precious beyond gold, his to have and hold and thereby unfold, if truth be told, more mastery than Solomon had of old.

SAID THE TELLER OF THE TALE:

So put to the test, most of the travellers granted his request; whereat he pulled forth a pouch, removed ink and quill, and wrote with a will, turning out scrolls neatly and sweetly, adding delicate illustrations to his many oaths and imprecations.

Then he said, My friends, being of this scroll possessed you are richly blest. He who binds it on his arm will never come to harm: heroes will give him wide berth or bow down before him to earth; and if he takes to sea and the tempest falls, the sea will calm, its waters turn to walls.

Now when our feet had once more trod upon dry sod and we had sung a new song unto God, I heard the old man hum a cheery tune, then softly croon:

I am Hever the Kenite, who sucks Wit's breast
with relish—yes indeedy!
Praise God, whose kindnesses ensure
I never need be greedy.

save him from the descent to Sheol Job 33: 24.

If he be cast into the flames he will not be harmed; or into the depths, he need not be alarmed Isa. 43: 2.

binds it on his arm Deut. 6: 8, 11: 18.

its waters turn to walls Exod. 15: 8.

we had sung a new song unto God Prayerbook, morning service, part of the last blessing of the Shema (Hertz, *Authorised Daily Prayer Book*, 128).

Now I sit pretty because I'm so witty:
ah, pity the stupid and needy.

SAID THE TELLER OF THE TALE:

Hearing this declaration, I knew him for our friend, count of Imagination and fount of Falsification. The bawd! All that shipside piety was but a fraud, a bald maraud! Anything to make a living! But I, being over-forgiving, concealed the poem I had heard and said not a word, for had I greeted Hever aloud, I had unmasked him to the crowd; and so I left him, stunned by his rapacity—and his sagacity.

GATE THIRTY-NINE

The Debate of Day and Night: Whose the Greater Might and Delight

THUS SPOKE HEMAN THE EZRAHITE: I was in Rimon Perets with men of many merits—nobles all, standers in the breach, repairers of the wall, Laud's lieges and Sapience' lords, their tongues splitting rocks like two-edged swords. One declared, I will hold forth with dark sayings of old, given by our fathers from Wisdom's hold. They answered, Speak, friend: we attend.

*K*now, he replied, that when the sun, magnificent, set in the ram his mighty tent, lighting earth's darkest crannies to the farthest north, then, in that season when kings march forth, when nights pale and wane and hale days gain in strength and ready for the fray, bright Day put on the cloak of pride and did the Night deride, thundering, I am king over all; the nights be mine in thrall. God set me burning white and bright, captain of the coal-black Night, that lowly Hamite born to kiss my garment's hem—I, sprung glorious from Shem.

*N*ow when Day had had his say, Night cried, Oh, that strutting jay, that knave, that unredeemable slave! Shall he rule me? He, boasting, seamy, roasting? All know that Day was made for toil, for sweat and moil, and therefrom no release until Night come with his blessed peace! In darkest Night the toiler lays aside distress, the poor their wretchedness. Calm comes to the raging breast: therein the weary rest, the miserable slough off their care; servant is free of

Rimon Perets Num. 33: 19–20.
repairers of the wall Ezek. 22: 30.
splitting rocks [Isa. 48: 21].
two-edged swords Ps. 149: 6.
dark sayings Prov. 1: 6.
in that season when kings march forth 2 Sam. 11: 1.
the cloak of pride Ps. 93: 1.
sprung glorious from Shem Gen. 9: 18–27, 10: 21–31.
therein the weary rest Job 3: 17.

master there. Ah, Night of ebony quietude, freeing mankind from servitude!

*Y*ou revile me for my blackness? Oft is the white buffeted and despised and the black coveted and prized. What status the eye's white? Lo, the black pupil is honour-bright: in his path lies light.

I see, groaned Day, that God has made mock of me, that I should see the lowly sprung to Heaven and the lofty fallen so, see every valley exalted and every mountain and hill made low. Shall the Night preen, naked of delight? Barren be that Night! In dark of night men grope and fumble, hopelessly stumble. Only at daybreak do they win content, eyes bright and shining as the firmament. Only in Day's undertakings man succeeds, for then can he see to all his needs, getting or spending, asking or lending; whereas Night is fit but for sprawling and snoring or thieving and whoring.

*T*hen Night jibed, Do you know not? Have you heard not? I am Love's consummation: in me Love's liquors pour to satiation, while you sate lovers with separation. I bring bright lovers close, you push them one from other; I banish Grief, you be Grief's father and mother. In me find Love's hot embrace, face to face; but you wrench lips apart, you sear the heart. Seeing Dawn's light, sad lovers say, Dear heart, away! Here is Joy's foe who would our love lay low.

*T*hen Day retorted, Alas the day that I was born; perish that morn! That I should suffer children's jeers, the mockery of the wet behind the ears! Up creep the waters of the murky deep; lice, fleas, supplant the Pleiades. Know you not? I am the life of the world; my sun breathes life, Creation is unfurled. In her light, plants and flowers come to bloom: the precious fruits brought forth beneath the sun, the precious things brought forth beneath the moon. But you, barren of germinating force, are a doddering, blind horse!

servant is free of master there Job 3: 19.
in his path lies light Job 38: 19.
has made mock of me Gen. 21: 6.
every valley exalted and every mountain and hill made low Isa. 40: 4.
Barren be that Night Job 3: 7.
eyes bright and shining as the firmament Dan. 12: 3.
Do you know not? Have you heard not? Isa. 40: 28.
Alas the day that I was born; perish that morn Job 3: 2.
Know you not? Isa. 40: 28.
the precious fruits brought forth beneath the sun, the precious things brought forth beneath the moon Deut. 33: 14.

Said the Night, Would you laugh me to scorn, boasting your sun, a woman born? Your logic droops: will you drag out a woman to lead the troops? How can the sun withstand the virile moon's command, my awesome lord who lights my path with his silver sword? Sure, when the moon shines the sun cannot stay, but shamefaced to the woman's chambers creeps away. Moreover, your regal sun stands stark in isolation; but Night is legioned of a starry nation who beaming sing, In our multitudes lies the glory of the king! When my moon first shines, your sun declines to a milky blotch, a ghoul, a fading pigeon nesting by Sheol. She slinks off in fear, like craven youths when enemy drums draw near.

Said Day, Rot, you windbag, you steaming pot! Well you know: your moonlight is the sun's reflected glow. Were she to cloud over, your moon would hover like a leprous spot, a blot; and if the moon vaunt it with his tinsel troops night-borne, the Lord will show who are His at morn. At daybreak the moon and his men are fled: like a thief in the night, if the sun be risen upon him, his blood may be shed. And as the thief is shamed when he is found, shame robes the moon when the sun's shafts strike the ground.

SAID THE TELLER OF THE TALE:

Now when they had spoken at length, Night's eyes were opened, that he saw his rival's strength. Showing the white pinion, he ceded Day's dominion:

Your Eminence, rule; be I your second, for yours are all my hosts unreckoned. Let us again to the fields of blessed Friendship and there renew the kingship.

SAID THE TELLER OF THE TALE:

When the speaker had done, my heart was won by his bright show. Seeing me all aglow he sang:

Would you laugh me to scorn, boasting your sun, a woman born? Alḥarizi uses *yare'aḥ* (masculine gender) for moon, rather than *levanah* (feminine); *shemesh*, 'sun', can be construed as masculine or feminine.

In our multitudes lies the glory of the king Prov. 14: 28.

you steaming pot Jer. 1: 13.

the Lord will show who are His at morn Num. 16: 5.

like a thief in the night, if the sun be risen upon him, his blood may be shed Exod. 22: 1–2.

eyes were opened Gen. 3: 7.

Let us again to the fields of blessed Friendship and there renew the kingship 1 Sam. 11: 14.

*A friend/*ḥaver *of all who seek me out,*
I am Wit's scythe; no field can say me nay.
Harvesting Wisdom, through mankind I roam,
turning now here, now there, by night and day.

GATE FORTY

The Battle of Sword and Pen for Mastery of Men

THUS SPOKE HEMAN THE EZRAHITE: In dark, deep night, as I lay tossing on my bed, sleep long fled (ill fate!), I heard a pounding at the gate, fierce as a lover who will not be denied. Who comes in the heart of darkness? I cried. To which a voice replied, One strayed from the main, splayed by rain, flayed by pain.

Now hearing that tongue's thrust and pith, I bade my servant lead the traveller in forthwith. He entered with his staff and pack, rags dripping from his back and—godsend: It was Hever the Kenite, our teacher and friend! I rejoiced as over great treasure, for indeed my pain was changed to pleasure beyond measure. Swift I emptied my larder and my guest attacked with ardour. Now when he could gorge no more, he began to display his wisdom's store; quickly I looked round, and seized scroll and pen to set his baubles down. However, he had hardly spoke when the quill broke, so I took another—which proved the former's brother. Bother! Vexed, I flung it on my unborn text.

Said Hever the Kenite, Dear heart, attend: spurn not God's chosen friend. Would you work harm on Blessedness' right arm, fling to earth as of no worth the very emblem of Nobility? Surely you know of his ability, his broad agility, and quotability! If not, I will tell you—although, of course, I would not compel you.

My ear is pierced at your words' door, said I. Your words' mascara paints my eye.

He began: In olden time the king's chief scribes held fierce debate with the generals of the state. The former declared, We are the

a pounding at the gate Judg. 19: 22.
I rejoiced as over great treasure Ps. 119: 162.
My ear is pierced at your words' door Exod. 21: 6.

knights of Wit and Elegance, the bastions of Intelligence, mortar of the realm's foundation, and mighty banner of the nation. Our hands command the puissant Pen, emperor of men—the Pen who brooks no defiance, who makes wise the simple and topples giants. Puny and unrespected, short, gaunt, and rejected, he is a tower of blinding power who scoffs at wielders of the sword and tramples down the haughty lord.

Then they lifted their voices and sang:

Hymning our monarch, we stand apart,
all through the Pen's bright art.
As sun and stars ne'er quit the sky,
from Wisdom we never part.
Bold warriors kneel at our feet like slaves
or we strike them to the heart.

Then the king's commanders countered, Yield! We are champions of the battlefield each one: our blades shoot fire like the sun, unmanning father and son. We leave green kingdoms dun, hearts quaking and undone. Ours is the Sword, the silent lord that eyeless watches o'er the sward and rains down Death's black horde. When the kingdom's best are called he strides forth first and no other durst, for he is the crown and sceptre of the king, the monarch's seal and signet-ring; safe rests his owner in his hand: his victims are countless as the sand.

Then they sang:

We raise our right hands, in each a sword,
wave offerings to the Lord.
A mountain are we no man can climb,
a river no man can ford.
Our swords spring up like bulging vines
nourished on corpses' red
Or are bolts of lightning skewering the field,
splitting each foeman's head.

---

who makes wise the simple Ps. 19: 8.
rejected Isa. 53: 3.
wave offerings to the Lord Num. 8: 13–15.

Then the Sword and Pen spoke, giving stroke for stroke. Said the Sword, I am the warrior's might and creed, eagle and lion I feed. Let condors track me in the waste; I will dine them to their taste, serving, blood-red and fresh, lean warrior flesh. Now look at this dust, this tinder, how he howls, this pen with his flimsy jowls! What worth this reed, this thorn, this weed? Touch him: he is undone; a wind passes, and he is gone.

Then the Pen answered, saying, I am the prophet who dwells in Wisdom's tent, Jacob upright and excellent: he who clasps me tight grasps true delight. I bare recondite mystery and unknot secrecy, and do the wise regale with hid or open tale. Through me spring the nation's righteous laws, clipping Evil's claws. But for the Pen, story and wisdom and cunning were unknown to men.

Then spoke the Sword, saying, From Earth's bowels I came, blinding in flame. Earth's regents cede me their allegiance, for who can look on my awesome blade and be not afraid? When I spring from my sheath the lion's heart turns wax, heroes quail and turn in their tracks, the giants of the earth drop each as a stillbirth; the brave flee to pit and cave. Now who is this Pen to rise before me, to dare so bore me, this stumbleseer who stuffs his prattle in my ear, this windy staff, this chaff? To brush him is to crush him, pluck his tongue, and fling him to a heap of dung. But I, I rest on the king's broad thigh and stand the proud prince nigh until his foes be fled; to see me is to dread.

Then the Pen answered, saying, Sooth, you speak the truth! When you leave your sheath men suck in their breath, for you are very Death! Cruel, heartless, evil-willed, how much blood have you spilled, how many guiltless killed? From birth you have wreaked havoc cross the earth, strewing corpses east and west, wresting sons from fathers, sucklings from mothers' breasts. Go, boast your brawn that even more men fear it; my glory is my spirit. How can you stand before me, the righteous dweller of tents, you, man of the field and violence, slayer of innocents, ravening on mountain slopes, racing with wild goats, or

a wind passes, and he is gone Ps. 103: 16.
I am the prophet who dwells in Wisdom's tent, Jacob upright and excellent Gen. 25: 27.
the lion's heart turns wax 2 Sam. 17: 10.
the righteous dweller of tents, you, man of the field Gen. 25: 27.

stalking through forest and fen, a lion loosed from den? All who see you flee you, while all men are secure in my kingdom high and pure; all rejoice who hear my still, small voice.

You, you be brother to the thief and Evil's chief, you, Virtue's tomb, drawing the assassin and miscreant from the womb; while I, no evil comes me nigh: foul man or gross shall not come me close. Pious hands alone deserve me; only the upright shall serve me. I am summoned to the king's most secret council to render perfect counsel; honoured and lone, I stand the king beside, while you fret outside.

Then the Sword replied, Fabrications! Abominations! Why do I endure you? Ask of times past, of days that came before you! Read: through me the king lops rebels' heads, digs traitors' guts for flower-beds. The king reigns through my power: I shout, his enemies cower; I leap, and pull down turret and tower. I am my monarch's shield against all foes: my fear precedes him where'er he goes. His rivals I efface, their camps erase without a trace. All tremble at my blade's command: before me who can stand?

Now when the Sword had done his argument, the Pen rose confident and sang:

Though voiceless, I fear not swaggering boys:
my troops their might destroy.
My words bind monarchs' heads with light,
my proverbs, the heart with joy.
I cover the earth with the mantle of Law
and no evil stains that cloak;
Through me God hewed the Tables Two
at Sinai for His folk.
Let the Sword, all leering, loom; I shall fly
my bright banner above his head.
Let him front me in battle, swollen with pride;
he shall lie before me dead.

still, small voice [1 Kgs. 19: 12].
no evil comes me nigh [Ps. 91: 10].
only the upright shall serve me Ps. 101: 6.
Ask of times past, of days that came before you Deut. 4: 32.
before me who can stand? Job 41: 2.
God hewed the Tables Two at Sinai for His folk Exod. 32: 16.

SAID THE TELLER OF THE TALE:

When I had heard this well-honed story, this sharp-edged allegory, I inscribed his words on my heart with iron pen, that never they might part. For many days after I dwelt by his side, soul-satisfied; but Wandering struck, robbing me of rest and weaning me from sweet Friendship's breast.

---

this well-honed story, this sharp-edged allegory Lit. 'his allegory and his figured parables'.

inscribed his words on my heart with iron pen Jer. 17: 1.

GATE FORTY-ONE

Badinage: Man and Woman Rage

THUS SPOKE HEMAN THE EZRAHITE: I joined a caravanserai of merchants making their way from town to town with perfume and amulet, spice and gown. Now one day as we journeyed through the countryside, I spied clusters of rustics sally forth from hill and valley. Pricked by curiosity, I left my company to witness—what shall I say?—a verbal fray, a near mêlée, in a broad plain; a huge mob milled about a fuming twain—an old man dripping disdain and a woman crasser than crass, her face brass.

Praise God! the man cried loud, who placed us over all who fear Him, who set us first of those drawn near Him. We rule all creatures, none dare resist; and what is more, He drew the prophets from our midst. And more—us alone Divine Command bedecks: the blessed burden of His laws complex He denies the weaker sex. Yes, He frees them from the yoke of His holy Law for they are nature's quintessential flaw—sensuality, rank and raw. Maid and dame He bids stay home to hide their shame, whereby we are told that the world and all it holds is man's, being framed for him and named for him. Except for man, woman had never been born and no name borne.

Hey diddle diddle, go whistle and fiddle, jibed she—you piddling fool, you blunt tin sword, forsaker of the Lord, you hollow gourd, you warped board! Tell me then: with no women, how could there be men? You old coot: we're the root and you're the shoot and where's the shoot without the root? Mules! Cross-eyed fools! The truth is as plain as the warped nose on your face. Know your place! If you men had any brains you'd take pains to serve us as we deserve. And what's all this holier-than-thou fuss? As much as we need you, you need us!

her face brass Isa. 48: 4.

—Ugh! Close your bag, hag! Put your hand on your mouth, you fool, you stool, you crusted pan. What! Compare yourself to a man!? Woman, off with the pants! Crawl with the ants! Oh, aren't you glib? Remember: woman was made from man's rib to let her know she is no more than a piece of man—a drop, a drib.

—Noodlehead, sap: how long will you yap? Hold your tongue or take a spade and cover your dung! You creep, you sheep, you garbage heap! Enough of your dribble! Liars, cheats! Go puff your chests out, prance in the streets: we know where the horse eats! When you're hot and bothered aren't you sweet, licking our feet; but when you've had your treat, we're stale meat! You're like slaves out of Egypt, burping, enchanted, every crumb of manna taken for granted. You thumb your noses at God, crying, Who dare enslave us? Then, in lean times, you shriek, Help, Help! God save us!

The man retorted: Oh, we come from you all right, which puts us in a sad plight and a sorry light. But think of us as pearls lifted from mucky mollusc whorls; or think of the sod that gave rise to man, to prophets, and to saints of God. It makes no sense to say—come, no disagreeing!—that dust is superior to a human being.

—You make me laugh. Without us, each of you'd be a sick calf. What airs, what cheek, what gall! When you need us, you crawl. So stick up your noses and keep on ranting; it's us you're after when you're down and panting.

Said he: Craving for a woman is a sadness, a passing madness, a sick man's lust for meat, a curse can only make things worse. Woman is a glutton's cake, a stinging snake. How can a man hold out when his Desire seeks the woman out and temptingly shows her? Then, Heaven help him, he knows her. It's a sure bet: marry a wife and fall to the fowlers' net. Down you go, all a-jitter, to a life hard and bitter. Behold Lust's fruition: raiment, food, and coition; such is her lawful due, naught impedes it. Who needs it! Better the grave's stench than a

Put your hand on your mouth Prov. 30: 32.
woman was made from man's rib Gen. 2: 21–3.
take a spade and cover your dung Deut. 23: 14.
every crumb of manna [Exod. 15: 13–36].
in lean times, you shriek, Help, Help! God save us! Jer. 2: 27.
a stinging snake Prov. 23: 32.
fall to the fowlers' net [Ps. 91: 3].
raiment, food, and coition; such is her lawful due Exod. 21: 10.

wench! Oof! Sit on a roof's edge and live out your life—better there, than with a nagging wife.

—God give me shears and file to shorten your vile liar's tongue! Goat dung! Lunatic! Your tongue could serve for a walking stick! Go on, cloud the skies with your lies. And will you ring a bell for every prophet you can tell? Well: God spoke through us as well. Bray and moo: your reasoning is as bald as you. We were called, too.

The man shouted: Cow, chew your cud! Women prophesy when men are knee-deep in mud; but when men stand tall, women cannot prophesy at all. Only when men glut on sin does female prophecy begin. Deborah rose to wage war when Israel had turned whore; Hulda the prophetess spoke when Israel shucked God's yoke.

Know: if women had all of Heaven's stars for swords, if every woman were hymned by Heaven's hordes, still she would have to stretch out neck and hands for a husband's yoke and cords. Yes, let him seize her and do as his pleasure affords: the woman and her children shall be her lord's.

Then he sang:

Praise God, who gave man Honour,
setting woman in his hand:
Hers to obey her lord's least word,
to leap, to lie, to stand.
On us, the seed of the Living God,
devolves God's high command;
From out our midst the prophets sprang
who oceans turned dry land.
Let woman know her rightful place:
prone—and to be manned.

SAID THE TELLER OF THE TALE:

Now when they had put an end to their dissension and contention, I gave the man further attention and *voilà!*—

Sit on a roof's edge and live out your life—better there, than with a nagging wife Prov. 21: 9.

Deborah rose to wage war when Israel had turned whore Judg. 4: 1–4.

Hulda the prophetess 2 Kgs. 22: 14; 2 Chr. 34: 22.

the woman and her children shall be her lord's Exod. 21: 4.

oceans turned dry land Ps. 66: 6.

comprehension: here was Hever the Kenite, father of Invention, font of Cunning and Pretension. At once I knew his claims to be absurd, knew I had heard the very weasel's word. But I strongly wished to leave, you see, my soul drawn to my company. Who Hever was I did not say, but simply walked away; and who the woman was I know not to this day.

GATE FORTY-TWO

Generosity or Greed—Which the Better Creed or Deed?

THUS SPOKE HEMAN THE EZRAHITE: Once on a day I made my way to a company of free givers whose thoughts were gushing rivers, princes of the assembly, men of renown, each sporting Learning's golden crown, whence jacinth and agate showered down. Now as we rambled through Wisdom's glade under Sapience' sun and Contemplation's shade, whom should we meet but a nobleman, generous and gracious, hands outstretched and heart capacious. Passing by chance, he was drawn to the dance of our wisdom, open and hid; so join us he did, and at once turned leader of our throng in rhymed prose and metric song: the waves of his speech flung to our blessed shore riches whose like we had not known before. Finally, having so liberally gifted us and lifted us to the pinnacle of Thought by what he had taught, he rose, blessed us, and left us. Moved by the honour he had paid us and the gift of victuals he had made us we declared: Behold—Learning's hold, whose pillars rest on sockets of fine gold! What provision! Have you ever seen the like, awake or in vision?

Then one of our number said, Herein we see how Generosity is unequalled for virtuosity: the Virtues kneel before her, great and small: *Many daughters have done virtuously, but thou excellest them all.*

Now one of the group with a tongue sharp as an adder, yet who soared like an angel up Wisdom's ladder, declared: Well sung! You

princes of the assembly, men of renown Num. 16: 2.
jacinth and agate Exod. 28: 19.
the gift of victuals he had made us Jer. 40: 5.
whose pillars rest on sockets of fine gold S. of S. 5: [15].
awake or in vision Num. 24: 4, 16; Ps. 17: 15.
Many daughters have done virtuously, but thou excellest them all Prov. 31: 29.
who soared like an angel up Wisdom's ladder [Gen. 28: 12].

raise Generosity to the ladder of merit's highest rung. But if I choose to loose my tongue I can fling her to a hill of dung.

Are you daft? we laughed. What sleight of hand might turn day night and wrong right?

Thereupon one of our number, a youth, declared: Lo, I come unto you in a pillar of flame to test your claim. I shall crown Generosity queen of morals and deck her brow with golden laurels; you I challenge to dethrone her and disown her.

Agreed, the greybeard countered, lift up your voice; then I will mine, and our hearers shall make their choice.

The youth began: Unto you, men, I call, yes, even all who have been taught from early years the rudiments of thought. Have you known not? Have you heard not? Generosity is Wisdom's queen and the law of Morality's demesne, the princes' tiara from Amghara to Ferrara, from fair Bokhara to bare Sahara.

Be it allowed that she it is who has the nobleman endowed, making his left hand a river and his right a bursting cloud. But for Generosity, Stint's ferocity and tenebrosity would lay men low; Greed would grow noxious in insolence, earth would be filled with violence, corruption would be global; the brave and the noble would be roundly reviled and soundly defiled. Who can be reconciled to see Probity blamed, the pure stripped naked, the strong and healthy maimed, the lofty whipped, the blameless shamed? Let those who have, share, such is God's design; else the vineyard shows but an empty vine.

Generosity, virtues' queen,
in happiness arrays her,
A blessèd river, ever giving,
never aught dismays her.
Her the Lord chose to crown His work
and high to Heav'n did raise her.

a hill of dung [Ps. 113: 7].
Lo, I come unto you in a pillar of flame Exod. [13: 22]; 19: 9.
lift up your voice [Isa. 58: 1].
Unto you, men, I call Prov. 8: 4.
Have you known not? Have you heard not? Isa. 40: 28.
earth would be filled with violence Gen. 6: 11.
an empty vine Hos. 10: 1.

Hers is the arm endowed with might:
no monarch but obeys her.
Before her fair are all virtues bare;
no man can fully praise her.

Then the old man cried, What nonsense have you ventured? Shall your rant go uncensured? What use a lofty trait that hurls its owner to Hunger's gate? Generosity shatters the giver's pride, scatters his coin far and wide, sets Grief astride his drunken heart where he does cackling ride. Through Liberality men's hands are stripped and the coin of plenty clipped. The eminent smashing, the prominent dashing, she robs the prince of his just deserts, makes rags of velvet mantles and silken shirts.

But he who can clench his fist has Fame and Fortune kissed: he lives untroubled, his gold and silver ever doubled. Sure, if the miser turns his pockets out, he must turn sharp about, as life's march triumphant turns a rout. No! Keep your fist tight curled and gain the world; be Fortune round your finger twirled. Let good gush down like rain: as it is said, *Gather little by little—and gain.*

Then he lifted his voice and sang:

He who keeps his fist tight closed
shall in danger find repose.
Shining treasures his in hoards;
they shall ring him, goodly guards.
But the open-handed man
turns his purse an empty can.
Joy the hoarder's in his lair;
in the giver's find Despair.
Sated the miser by Plenty's river;
parched and red-eyed faints the giver.

Then the boy answered, saying, Ye blind, look here; ye deaf, give ear! Shall the fox rule the lion; a mist, Orion? With your gaseous prating, your specious debating, you would turn silk weeds milkweeds, kindness blindness, earl churl, the lofty lowly and noble mean, and the

Shall your rant go uncensured? Job 11: 2. **Gather little by little—and gain** Prov. 13: 11.

generous obscene! What, laud me niggards! Confess: giving does the giver bless; to help your fellow, as you should, is to root your own good. Generosity is a fountain, which, when drunk of, the stronger flows: it swells, it grows; all hale, never shall its waters fail. Were it to stay undrunk, old fool, it would shrink to a brackish pool. So give without temerity and win prosperity; but worship Stint and lose your vaunted mint.

Now if you say me plain that there be villains who have won great gain, that I can explain. Their skill was not the cause, my friend: their gold shall wing off in the end; and if a benefactor's coin has sped and his wealth fled, this was not Generosity's perversity, but God's testing of a good man through adversity.

Then he waxed poetic and sang:

Oh, blessèd Giving that leaves one wiser;
curst are the blessings of the miser.
The miser's good is nothing worth,
forbid to all who walk the earth.
So tight his fist, so pinched his breath,
he starves at gold's ripe feast to death
Like one who stares at streams sublime
but slakes his pounding thirst on slime.
His goods are surety in his hand,
but surety for another man.
Honour and Peace are the giver's prize,
but spurned is the miser in all men's eyes.

The old man rejoined: How fine your logic, how fine! Shall your thoughts answer mine? What would you have me learn? To which of the holy angels would you turn? Look the world over from Egypt to the Indian Sea and find me a spotless prince of Generosity, more than one in a thousand! Nay, but say what you find: prince and churl with fist a-curl and nowhere more than by the Tigris' shore. This, if you will, is proof of Generosity's low station and deprivation: she is trod

never shall its waters fail Isa. 58: 11.
their gold shall wing off in the end Prov. 23: 5.
To which of the holy angels would you turn? Job 5: 1.
the Tigris' shore i.e. in Babylon.

down, reviled in every nation. Were she so worthy she would be eager sought, fought over, wooed by high and low, her tenets universally taught. But since everywhere she is as honoured as a bawd, know that she is a fraud, quintessentially flawed. I would almost say, Generosity is a practice forbid by Holy Writ, that he is an idolater who cleaves fast to it.

The youth rejoined, Do you truly suggest that perversions and monstrosity bring men to Generosity? Say, rather, Nobility, quite beyond the moral pygmy's height. Wait! I can prove that the singular and best is by the high-born and the rich possessed: rare jewels adorn the king's fingers and the queen's breast. Largesse, like Wisdom's feast, is not tendered to fish, fowl, or beast—nor, for that matter, to every man or nation; rather, it is a godly assignation to minds of highest penetration. It is, like Piety, a rarity in any society; find it among spirits pure and holy who give themselves to their Creator wholly. So it is with all goodly virtues such as Faith and Humility, Kindness and Gentility: fools and villains cannot enjoy them, lest they destroy them; they are reserved for the chosen best, who cherish them like a mother the suckling at her breast.

Yes, Generosity is not for clods, for sinners who have bent the knee to foreign gods, but only for the righteous of the earth, who know her worth; not for masters of dissembling arts, but for them who raise God altars in their hearts.

Then he lifted his voice and sang:

Generosity beckons; open your eyes:
she has laid out her secrets before the wise.
Sell all; keep but her; know unending rule.
Yea, purchase her only; prosper, rise.

SAID THE TELLER OF THE TALE:

Now as the argument flashed and the combatants clashed, the people saw the youth revealed as Samson's arm and David's shield, saw that the greybeard would have to yield. Taunting, they jibed the old man, Where is your vaunted skill? You cannot down this boy, do what you will.

who have bent the knee to foreign gods 1 Kgs. 19: 18.

David's shield S. of S. 4: 4.

Said the old man, Folly! I jolly well would pounce on him and trounce him, and with a shrug and a look turn his spear into a pruning fork or hook. But it were unfit to give the victory to Greed and leave kind Generosity to moan and bleed, lest base men hoarsely cry, *Our hand is high*; lest Falsity win the day and wash the memory of Good away.

Well said, sir, cried the company; all here agree. Now tell us who you be.

Then he sang:

Seek, in Elon Zaananim, my domains:
I wander and thrive in those far-off plains.
My name, sirs, is Hever, or Linker; behold:
my song links all virtues in golden chains.

turn his spear into a pruning fork or hook [Isa. 2: 4; Mic. 4: 3].
lest base men hoarsely cry, *Our hand is high* Deut. 32: 27.
Seek, in Elon Zaananim, my domains: I wander and thrive in those fair-off plains. My name, sirs, is Hever Judg. 4: 11.

GATE FORTY-THREE

The Sea Roars its Worth against Proud Earth

THUS SPOKE HEMAN THE EZRAHITE: Having come from Ekron to Shomron I met men of many parts, words swifter than harts and smoother than butter, but war in their hearts. One of their number outshone the rest: Wisdom's fire lit his breast. All the shocks of Wit's harvest bowed down to his shock: his words were a hammer shattering rock.

He declared: Men of understanding, draw near, lend ear to a strange, sweet tale will tax Wisdom's scale.

Sir, they said, proceed; we heed.

Return with me, said he, to yesteryear, when God weighed Heaven in His hand, and gave command that the lower world rise, half ocean and half land—whereat, with a mighty sound, the Ground burst forth, with Water swirling round. At once the Shore was subject to the Water's rasp and roar. Hemmed in on every side by the grasping Tide, the pounding wave, she glowered, an unwilling slave.

Now the Sea, seeing that the Land could not withstand his massive hand, leaned back, puffed and overborne, and laughed Earth to scorn. To whom but the Sea, said he, is given the mastery? The World and they that dwell therein belong to me. Earth, be chary of my indignation, wary of my devastation. Chafe not at my reins, but kneel and don my chains.

At this floodtide of Pride the Land was stupefied. Raging, asmoke, she put on zeal for a cloak, then thundered against the Sea:

words swifter than harts [Mishnah *Avot* 5: 23].

words . . . smoother than butter, but war in their hearts Ps. 55: 22.

All the shocks of Wit's harvest bowed down to his shock [Gen. 37: 7].

his words were a hammer shattering rock Jer. 23: 29.

The World and they that dwell therein belong to me [Ps. 24: 1].

she put on zeal for a cloak Isa. 59: 17.

Now who is he, yea, who is he who so presumes, who foams and fumes, all vanity and puff? Enough! This sloshing fool, this spume, begins to rankle. Why, he cannot reach my ankle! Fiddle-faddle, he is but my saddle: look, I sit astride the drunken Tide and ride!

*I*n me were all humans fashioned; in me the prophets spoke, impassioned; the Torah was given in my realm alone; in me God's Presence shone.

*B*ehold: clouds shroud the Sea and its din that no joyful sound might come therein, whereas God opens wide high Heaven's gate for me, drenching mountain and plain with singing rain to raise the flowers of May and fruits of June—the gifts of the sun and the precious things brought forth by the moon. Yea, sun, moon, and stars light all my paths; bright kings raise high their flags on my low plains and from my fortress' crags.

*W*hence your disdain, dribbling Main? He who abandons me for you abandons breath, you Valley of the Shadow of Death! To lie on your breast is to couple with dread: Death's sword dangles above your head. By day the voyager gasps with fright and his heart takes no rest in the night. What surety can he find until he put your dripping teeth behind? When he flees to me, relief is his; yes, only then does he know what respite is.

*H*earing this, the Deep with a mighty leap rose upright as a heap and let loose a roar that near bore away the Shore.

*Y*ou stone-faced fool, you rebel, you hollow rock, you pebble! You dare compare yourself to me, the Watery Dark, home of the lashing octopus, the gnashing shark, the sounding whale, the roaring gale, before whom seamen pale! Shiver and wail! I sound my reproach and none dare approach: my waves whip men to simpering slaves.

who is he, yea, who is he who so presumes Esther 7: 5.
that no joyful sound might come therein Job 3: 7.
God opens wide high Heaven's gate for me, drenching mountain and plain Deut. 28: 12.
drenching mountain and plain with singing rain Ps. 65: 10–11.
the gifts of the sun and the precious things brought forth by the moon Deut. 33: 14.
Valley of the Shadow of Death [Ps. 23: 4].
his heart takes no rest in the night Eccles. 2: 23.
rose upright as a heap Exod. 15: 8.

Had not my Maker set dry ground my bound, declaring, Halt, O Rolling Salt!—you were my prey. I had borne you away, you chunk of clay, you pile of weeds, you hunk of moss, you ditch, you fosse! Ah, I had purged you of your dross, seized your old vessels, pounding them to chaff with my countless pestles, until—though you were sought for—you would be found no more, being steeped in sleep in the endless Deep.

Recall how Israel's sons and daughters entered my waters, shouting in fear as Pharaoh and his troops drew near; but—praise God!—I heard; my mercies were stirred; yes, when their foes cried, *Look! There they be!* Moses stretched his hand out over the Sea; my waters split, reared upright, did not fall, but formed, on either side of them, a solid wall wherein they quickly crossed, with no lives lost. And when the great Sea Beast flopped after for the feast, I waited at my leisure to repay him, measure for measure: for all his lies and wiles, I pulled him, slavering, down my wet defiles and fed him to the crocodiles.

Now imagine if God's holy folk had been differently inclined and had not put dry land behind: when destruction loomed they would have been doomed, utterly consumed. Then what would you have said? *O hills and valleys, raise them from the dead?*

At that, the Plain taunted the Main: Vapidity! Stupidity! A sorry volley! Fool—return to your folly! Butcher, rucky remnant of the Flood—your hands are full of blood. Deep in your reeking mud rot the bones of dotard, infant, nurse: oh, bitter waters that bring the curse! Gross, wild, defiled, you murderer of woman and child: rapacious to a fault, you are Death's very vault.

Who dares drink the stink of your fetid sink? What soil will your brine ready for men's toil? Dogs shun you, cattle fear you, no foot

set dry ground my bound Jer. 5: 22.
I had purged you of your dross Isa. 1: 25.
Moses stretched his hand out over the Sea; my waters split Exod. 14: 21.
reared upright, did not fall, but formed, on either side of them, a solid wall Exod. 14: 22, 15: 8.
the great Sea Beast Egypt—Ezek. 29: 3.
Fool—return to your folly Prov. 26: 11.
your hands are full of blood [Isa. 1: 15].
oh, bitter waters that bring the curse Num. 5: 24–7.

of an animal dare draw near you. He who would slake his thirst with your emulsions would die of convulsions.

Tormentor, devil's mentor, treachery's inventor, you suck to your bone-strewn floor the innocent, the helpless, and the poor. Ill-renowned, how many ships have you driven aground, how many sucklings drowned? Your drooling lips are Death's straits, your gaping jaws, Death's gates. Oh, twisted and godless city, you have slaughtered without pity.

Woe to the voyager: seeing your walls of water loom, hearing your growls, your hiss, your boom, he is seized with trembling and pain, his tears cascade like rain; his thoughts fly Heavenward and plummet down again. And when wild winds whip your waves to froth, lash your water to broth, the traveller moans and groans, Terror grips him to his bones. He shivers, he writhes, he dies, he lives—and then, again, he dies. And when he finally steps off your pitching boards, free from your screaming hordes, he sinks to his knees and sobs, *Salvation is the Lord's*.

Said the Main to the Plain: Enough of your gall and prating, your mock debating! Can you not hold your peace, keep your filth within? No, no, you must bare your sin. Know yourself—a serpent's fen, a robber's den with denizens malicious, corrupt, and pernicious. He who leaves you for me regains his piety, drinking the wine of high sobriety. He casts his sins away, confessing to his Maker night and day, as it is written: *Let the unrighteous man forsake his thoughts, the wicked man his way*. But let him depart and he recoups his evil heart, becoming what he was at the start. Nothing loath to break his every oath, he turns from penitence to decadence, a born-again adept of sinning, even as at the beginning.

Now after all this din, the elders within both camps made peace 'twixt Sea and Shore: they dwelled together as they had before.

Death's gates Ps. 107: 18.
you have slaughtered without pity Lam. 2: 21.
fly Heavenward and plummet down again Ps. 107: 26.
Salvation is the Lord's [Ps. 3: 9].
Can you not hold your peace Esther 4: 14.
a robber's den Jer. 7: 11.
Let the unrighteous man forsake his thoughts, the wicked man his way Isa. 55: 7.
to break his every oath Num. 30: 9.
even as at the beginning Gen. 41: 20.

SAID THE TELLER OF THE TALE:

Having heard this salty presentation, I looked closely at the speaker and found, to my elation, Rhetoric's towering consummation—beloved prince and preacher, Hever the Kenite, our champion, friend, and teacher; so I raised my voice in song:

Seekers of gold, of Wisdom's hold,
of tales of old will shine forever:
All sages shun for the Age's sun,
the matchless one—speed you to Hever!

GATE FORTY-FOUR

Life's Laws: Proverbs and Saws

THUS SPOKE HEMAN THE EZRAHITE: I journeyed with youths who were Beauty's domicile, from Hamath to the Lower Nile. Once there I found a thoroughfare that led to a mansion ringed with gold, wondrous to behold, wherein I saw a gathering as of hungry supplicants before the king. A greybeard faced them—humility his attire, modesty his desire, piety his veil and virtue his lyre, and God's fear in his eyes like a pillar of fire.

*F*ifty students, wise and sweet, hungry for Wisdom's meat, sat at his feet, kissing his garment's hem.

*K*now, he said to them, that I would test your wit, see if your minds be weak or fit. Now then, to the sport: say each a sweet saw will stop its hearers short.

*T*o it! they answered. We shall do it!

Then the first of the pupils said, Trial genders fame—or shame.

Another said, A slave is free, if content; a freeman—slave, if malcontent.

Another said, Man is hunter and prey: hunter of all that deftly flees him; prey of one who will deftly seize him.

Another said, Slave-buyers want skill: the tongue should buy freemen at will.

Hamath A city in Syria, north of Damascus. See e.g. 2 Sam. 8: 9.

gathering as of hungry supplicants Lit. 'therein [were] many people, and a mixed multitude together with them' (Num. 11: 4, 'And the mixed multitude that was among them fell a-lusting . . . and said, "Who shall give us flesh to eat?"').

piety his veil Exod. 34: 33–5.

a pillar of fire Exod. 13: 21–2.

Wisdom's meat Not in the Hebrew, the phrase further compensates for the allusion to Num. 11: 4 (noted above).

Trial genders fame—or shame Lit. 'A man gains prestige or is denigrated in the hour of trial and test.'

one who will deftly seize him i.e. Death.

Another said, Fate's blight: yesterday's flight, today's despite, tomorrow's night.

Another said, Prudence and piety be your rule: slur not the wise, gull not the fool.

Another said, Eating and drinking muddies thinking.

Another said, Seek your need and naught will entice you; beyond, and naught will suffice you.

Another said, Courtier, keep faith—or court death.

Another said, Be not of them who turn moral in danger, turn to God when wealth turns stranger, and repent when spent.

Another said, Plough the field, harvest the yield: teach the child truth and reap joy of his youth.

Another said, Sin's yoke fouls Virtue's cloak.

Another said, Birth is pain; death, gain.

Another said, Man is a mule on a pitted road, slavering and stumbling beneath Sin's load.

Another said, When God is vexed, misers drink from His pitcher; when pleased, givers grow richer.

Another said, Fawn—and be prisoned of him you seek; show no need—befriend him you seek; be kind—rule him you seek.

Fate's blight: yesterday's flight, today's despite, tomorrow's night Lit. 'Man's days are three: yesterday—whose time is past; today—which is passing and is no more; and tomorrow—veiled, with none to understand it.'

Eating and drinking muddies thinking Lit. 'A man's drinking and eating will blind the eyes of his intellect.' Cf. *Mivḥar hapeninim*, 1: 10, 'Wisdom does not dwell in the place of drinking and levity, but is banished thence' (Habermann, 7).

Seek your need and naught will entice you; beyond, and naught will suffice you Lit. 'If you ask of the world (only) what you require, the little (she gives you) will suffice you; but if you ask for more than you require, all of it will not suffice you.' Cf. *Mivḥar hapeninim*, 10: 6: 'He who desires of the world only to meet his need—his small portion will suffice him' (Habermann, 19).

Sin's yoke fouls Virtue's cloak Lit. 'He who would rise to great virtue/ *la'alot bema'alot gedolot* [also meaning "who would ascend lofty stairs"] will guard himself against [committing] base deeds.'

Birth is pain; death, gain Lit. 'He who enters this world has his fill of bitters, and he who leaves it escapes from woes.'

Another said, Wisdom cries out, Seize me and bind me, before you seek me and not find me.

Another said, Shun the borrower at the gate: loan's end is hate.

Another said, Restraint and moderation are the pillars of Salvation.

Another said, Three seek three again and yet again: the ear, speech; earth, rain; women, men.

Another said, Virtue is ward against Slander's sword.

Another said, See to your tongue or it will see you hung.

Another said, Youth leaps to Lust's rage; thence, to old age.

Another said, Physic makes flesh whole; Penitence, the soul.

Another said, Of all virtues, Silence is fairest—and rarest.

Another said, Youth's dreams turn dust as Youth's chariots rust in the River of Lust.

Another said, He who holds to Virtue's path holds a shield against the Day of Wrath.

Another said, In prattle—distress; in silence—success.

Another said, Man's need for the good is as fire's for wood.

Another said, If the soul be matter, Wisdom is its form; if a tree—its fruit.

Another said, Himself and loved kin the giver sates; the miser hoards for them he hates.

---

you seek me and not find me Jer. 29: 13.

Restraint and moderation are the pillars of Salvation Lit. 'Whoever exercises restraint knocks on the gates of salvation.'

See to your tongue or it will see you hung Lit. 'Guard your mouth and your speech lest you fall victim to your own sword.' Cf. *Mivḥar hapeninim*, 32: 23: 'A man will die through his tongue's failing and not through his foot's; for his tongue's failure will remove his head . . .' (Habermann, 35).

He who holds to Virtue's path holds a shield against the Day of Wrath Lit. 'He who is pure in his deeds—he shall find no complaint against him on the day of judgement.' Cf. *Mivḥar hapeninim* 30: 2: 'He who chooses righteousness for his rule will have a strong shield' (Habermann, 33).

In prattle—distress; in silence—success Cf. *Mivḥar hapeninim* 1: 20: 'Be silent and be saved; attend and learn'; 32: 10: 'Silence serves a man better than untimely speech' (Habermann, 8 and 34).

Man's need for the good is as fire's for wood Lit. 'The soul's need for *musar* (right living or edification or chastisement) is as the earth's need for rain.'

Another said, Though your sin be slight, hold it not light: let his worth, whom you wronged, loom large in your sight.

Another said, Wisdom will enrich you if you be poor; if rich, lead you to Right's door.

Another said, Prepare for Death's laughter, drowning all that precedes yet a whisper of all that comes after.

Another said, Set 'midst the righteous, a Cain will turn Abel; yet shewbread turns mouldy at Evil's table.

Another said, Probity: helm of the just realm.

Another said, Judgement calls. Prepare—with charity and prayer.

Another said, Forget your friend's sin, however great, or get his hate.

Another said, Death's rattle over fools' prattle.

Another said, Store up good deeds, for Time is a knave, enslaving the king and crowning the slave.

Another said, Virtue before station: station demands Virtue—not Virtue station.

Another said, To see the Pit is to flee the Pit.

Another said, Man—a cygnet, earth's joys—his net.

Another said, Much giving breeds want; much speaking—rant.

Another said, Who sets his thought in Passion's bond suffers in this life and beyond.

Another said, He walks in Folly's mist who covets fame with a closed fist.

Prepare for Death's laughter, drowning all that precedes yet a whisper of all that comes after Lit. 'Death is more difficult than all that precedes it, and easier than all that follows.'

shewbread [Exod. 35: 13].

Set 'midst . . . table Lit. 'Even as vices will be corrected in the company of the upright, so will virtues be corrupted in the society of the cruel.'

Death's rattle over fools' prattle Lit. 'Better for a man to be a mute sage than a prattling fool.'

Another said, The wise man is honoured at home and abroad though his father be thief and his mother a bawd.

Another said, Be Time's lord: smite woe with alms; want, with Prayer's sword.

Another said, Flight from the world cures all grief and is the gold for penury's relief.

Another said, An end: repent and be strong; right wrong; still Sin's siren song.

SAID THE TELLER OF THE TALE:

When they had done, the greybeard cried, I do attest: you best the ages' sages, east and west. Be blest!

Thereat I asked a younger pupil his teacher's name and station, city and nation; whereat the old man himself declared:

Had I nothing said, my deeds had spoke,
laurelled long since by Fame.
You who would seek my title out,
who would learn from whence I came—
Elon is my birthplace, in Zaananim,
and Hever the Kenite my name.

Hearing his song, I called out to the learned throng: Behold Wisdom's sweet fruition, the crown of Erudition, the lamp of Wisdom brightly burning, the prince who owns ten portions in the Land of Learning.

Then I pressed his hand, beaming and light-hearted; but, being pressed, I swiftly departed.

The wise man is honoured at home and abroad though his father be thief and his mother a bawd Lit. 'The wise man is honoured though his family be held in contempt, and has many friends though he be in a foreign land.'

An end [Eccles. 12: 13].

repent and be strong; right wrong; still Sin's siren song Lit. 'The choicest of acts is turning away from evildoing, being void of cruelty, and being pure of sin.'

Had I nothing said, my deeds had spoke, laurelled long since by Fame Lit. 'Were I to keep silent my deeds would give witness that splendour called me by his name.'

Elon is my birthplace, in Zaananim, and Hever the Kenite my name Judg. 4: 11.

Behold Wisdom's sweet fruition, the crown of Erudition Lit. 'This is the crown of [instructive] texts and the compendium of all delights.'

who owns ten portions in the Land of Learning Lit. 'who own ten portions in every [field of] wisdom'. In rabbinic literature, a means of affording high praise is to ascribe nine out of ten portions of something (as of beauty or wisdom) to a person or place. See BT *Kid.* 49*a*.

GATE FORTY-FIVE

Hid Learning: Saws of Men of Discerning

THUS SPOKE HEMAN THE EZRAHITE: En route from Alexandria to Tiberias I found my friend Hever—ah, the delight of him: my thought soared, my eyes shone at the sight of him! I seized his arm: Loved friend, come home with me and dine with me. Come to Love's castle, swim in my moat; come, clench the cup and drench your throat.

Said he: I agree.

Home, then, we sped, where he was sumptuously wined and fed. Thirst hushed, hunger crushed, face flushed, he spoke: Friend true and kind, mine it is to reward you from my God-lit mind. Let me gift you with choice proverbs of the ages, culled from the mouths of sages.

Speak, I answered, for your servant listens.

Our fathers apprised us, yes, our forebears advised us that a certain savant, wisest of the wise, took saws and apophthegms for ears and eyes; ever he yearned for them, ever he turned to them, ever he burned for them.

Now one day twenty-six of Wisdom's warriors, singled out by name, gathered before him. He charged them, Let each of you come forward in fine expression to give subtlety to the simple, to the young man knowledge and discretion. Come, silence Sin's baying with wise word and deep, dark saying.

They answered, That which you have said is good.

my eyes shone 1 Sam. 14: 27–9.
to reward you Ruth 2: 12.
Speak, I answered, for your servant listens 1 Sam. 3: 10.
Our fathers apprised us, yes, our forebears advised us Pss. 44: 2, 78: 3.
twenty-six The number cited in the printed Hebrew text is 24; but the number of anecdotes, and tellers of anecdotes, is 26.
singled out by name Num. 1: 17.
to give subtlety to the simple, to the young man knowledge and discretion Prov. 1: 4.
wise word and deep, dark saying Prov. 1: 6.
That which you have said is good Deut. 1: 14.

Then the eldest of them spoke. We are told, said he, that a pious man, coming upon a graveyard, said, Peace, dwellers of muck and mud, sailors of the Last Flood. Tell us what you own or lack: does Judgement's rod lie easy on your back? Do you weep and moan, you who reap as you have sown? Soon, soon we follow; soon lift your cup and swallow. God grant you, and us, His pardon; and usher you, and us, into His blessed Garden.

Another said, A pious man was richly befriended and, by his friends, richly commended. Lifting his eyes Heavenward he declared, Master of the Universe: You know of me what I know not; and I know of myself what these know not. Pray, Lord, reward me at their estimation; but punish me not for their false declaration.

Another said, A certain pious man would pray in adversity, God, let this trial right my path, not fright me with Your wrath.

Another said, A certain pious man, dreaming a-bed, saw a loved, departed friend. Tell us, he asked, what you see and where you be. He answered, Ask not what we see. We see a written account, full with charges, the ledgers open, and a Judge beyond bribing; and we have forgotten Death's anguish for that of judgement, far bitterer than death.

Then he lifted his voice and sang:

Bare to our kin, to our flesh and bone
the pain we bear; bear them our groan.
Writhing, we turn on the coals of wrath,
we tremble before Judgement's throne
Held fast by darkness to left and right
the like no human eye has known.
Would we had seen this the while we lived—
we had repented; now life has flown.
Beloved, take care lest you share our fate,
lest our tears be yours, our moan your moan.

Another said, An Arab woman lost her son. Burying him she

you who reap as you have sown Job 4: 8.

see a written account, full with charges, the ledgers open, and a Judge beyond bribing Cf. Mishnah *Avot* 3: 2: 'the ledger lies open . . . and the judgement is true . . .' (Hertz, *Authorised Daily Prayer Book*, 662).

cried, My son, my son, you were the Lender's loan, the Giver's gift, the Depositor's surety. This day the Lender recalls his loan, the Depositor his surety, the Giver his gift. God grant me, in your stead, good suffering; and recompense me for the good reward that He has taken.

Another said, An Arab woman lost her son but quickly took comfort. Her neighbours asked, How can you be comforted so quickly? She answered, Comfort has two virtues: joy in this world and reward in the next. Much mourning has two vices: loss of suffering's reward and punishment for excessive grief.

Another said, A certain Arab woman would pray in this manner: Master of the Universe, if I offend You, I cannot harm you; and if You forgive me, You will not lack thereby. Pray, then, my God, forgive me that which will not harm You and give me that which You will not lack.

A pious man met an overbearing prince whose every stride spoke pride. Know, he said, that the Creator detests your strutting. The prince replied, If you knew whence I am sprung, you would hold your tongue. He answered, But I know! You spring from a stinking sperm, rot through life's term, and end in the worm.

Another said, A man offended his monarch and was summoned to his justice. He declared, By God! Shall your foes be joyed and your lovers' joy destroyed? Spare me, whose loyalty is unalloyed; spare him your righteousness has oft employed. The king freed him.

Another said, A wise man asked his companion, How much wine do you drink at table? Three cups, he answered. Said the sage, Well done: Nazirite are you none and drunkard none.

You spring from a stinking sperm, rot through life's term, and end in the worm Mishnah *Avot* 3: 1: 'Akavyah son of Mahalel said: "Reflect on three things and you will not come into the grip of sin: know whence you came, whither you are going, and before whom you are destined to give a strict account. Whence you came—from a malodorous drop; whither you are going—to a place of dust, worms, and moths; and before whom you are destined to give a strict account—before the supreme King of Kings, the Holy One, blessed be He." ' See *Mivḥar hapeninim*, 44: 42: 'The king of India gave one of his servants standing before him a manuscript, telling him, "When you see me angry give it to me". On it was written, "Desist, for you are not God but a body going to waste, whose one end will consume the other and will return to worm, maggot, and dust" ' (Habermann, 52).

Another said, A wise man, as he lay dying, begged God forgive his stillborn kindnesses, his self-indulgences, and his lying—the while his friends stood round, praising him and crying. Brothers, he cried, stop braying! Start praying!

Another said, A sage came to comfort a courtier whose son had died. He said, So long as you live, we will not fear Time's rod. Be not mistaken: Death graces us—you were not taken.

Another said, A wise man came to comfort a courtier on his son's death and said to him, God speed you comfort to your need: may you sow new seed.

Another said, A poet eulogized a king whom he had often lauded in life. One of his friends asked, Why has your praise rung truer than your lament? He answered, Praise was my duty; lament, my gift.

Another said, A man was asked to sing the virtues of his beloved. He replied: Manna, her mouth; her soft palms wash away my drouth; and oh, the sweet sail to her tropic south! Hers the lush Garden where my pleasures root; her breasts, my Tree of Life, dripping with fruit; her neck my fingers' lute; her sweet, pursed mouth my magic flute.

Another said, A man was asked to tell his love's beauty. He said, Rare she is, most ripe and fair. Seated, art; rising, a hart; walking, love's dart; speaking, a very fire of the heart.

Another said, A poet composed a poem for a certain courtier. The latter, all liberality, gifted him with honour, coin, and hospitality. Now this courtier had a fair daughter; so the poet penned lines of amorous bent, which he spoke—and she heard, at the entrance to the tent.

He sang:

By Love's raised banner and godly flame
I claim this maiden's love; the same
Who from hid chambers steals my heart
and must me pity or bear the blame.

---

she heard, at the entrance to the tent Gen. 18: 10.
Love's raised banner S. of S. [2: 4].
godly flame [S. of S. 8: 6].
hid chambers Ps. 45: 14.

Moon-fair, sun-bright, I know you hear:
soft rose of Sharon, make good your name.

To this cry she made reply:

Hunt other woods, hold me no game:
your honeyed words your lust proclaim
Attesting to a jaded sire
and to a most blameworthy dame.
Then hold your tongue and leave in peace.
Elsewhere pluck roses. Shame, sir, shame!

Another said, A pious man, walking by the way, saw a vicious evildoer hanging on a tree. The pious man said to his friend, No rein to Evil's way but the gallows' sway.

Another said, An offender was brought before the king, who commanded that he be whipped. Now this man was very tall, and the flayer very short. The flayer said to the flayed, Bend down, that I might whip you. The flayed answered, Damn you, you whoreson, do you invite me to a banquet? God's life, would I were as tall as Og and you short as Gog! The king, laughing, released him.

Another said, A wise man saw his son eyeing a beautiful woman and said to him, My son, my son, why will you love women? Their bellies are pits, puffed gourds their teats; their coin is rust, and all their beauty the Graves of Lust.

Another said to a villager, By your life: when you leave your home, who guards your wife? He answered, Two guards have I set her: I have left her naked, that she go not out with women; and hungry, that she sport not with men.

Another said, A villager was asked, What kind of man would you have to be husband to your daughters? He answered, There are three grooms: gold, pedigree, and the grave. The last is best.

Another said, An old man was asked how fared it with him. He answered, Alas two ills: my belly and my slack desire. My belly: when I

Moon-fair, sun-bright S. of S. 6: 4.
rose of Sharon [S. of S. 2: 1].
Og Deut. 3: 11.
Gog Ezek. 38: 1–23.
the Graves of Lust Num. 11: 34.

hunger, I near expire; but when I eat, I tire. And as for my Desire: when I leap, he sleeps; when I sleep, he leaps.

Another said, One of the poets, whenever he came to the home of a certain courtier, knocked on locked gates. So he said, He whose forehead is brass, whose left hand strokes rumps and whose right the glass, whose mother is crass and whose father an ass, plods through scorn like a cow through high grass.

Another said, A certain Arab was asked about a miser. He said, he is Virtue's shroud: his promise is vapour—a morning cloud; his palms are rainless, his head brainless; his gifts and fests are as dry as his mother's breasts—this drooling cow, this sow, this slough.

Another said, Two warriors traded taunts. The first said to the second, You overreach! I am he who fills the breach! The second replied, Half true: your father filled his breeches with his fear; mine—breaches with his spear.

SAID THE TELLER OF THE TALE:

When I heard Hever the Kenite's thoughts and saws, I housed them in my heart for lamps and laws. For many days I held him in my walls, rejoicing my chambers and my halls; but then he left me, sorely yearning, my insides bare and burning.

forehead is brass Isa. 48: 4. **a morning cloud** Hos. 6: 4.

GATE FORTY-SIX

Of This and That Community Sung with Impunity

THUS SPOKE HEMAN THE EZRAHITE: A caravan of Ishmaelites met me one day as I made my way from Adinah to Elam. There, in the plain, in the tamarisks' shade, we stopped and stayed; and lo, who should greet our sight but Hever the Kenite, come to that very place to light my eyes and bright my face.

Good friend, I called, hallo! Where do you come from and where do you go?

He answered, Gilead was my last station, Persia my destination.

Did you visit all our Jewries on your quest—those of Babylon and Egypt and the West?

Yes, no city towered so high that I should pass it by, nor scan its virtues with my eagle eye.

If you please, then, cite me these by name: sound the fame of every society blessed with good deeds and godly piety; then tell of them who act with somewhat less propriety—or notoriety.

He said, Know that all the communities I saw are righteous to a flaw, fearful of the Lord, with probity and modesty their mail and sword. Um-m-m-m, well, not all of them, truth to tell: some, say, wait Heaven; some, Hell.

Not all pass muster. Consider each group a thick fig-cluster—some nectareous, others nefarious. And now I shall sketch you the worst and the best, that the deeds of the giving and noblest be for ever blest, while evildoers rest in infamy, a stench from east to west.

A caravan of Ishmaelites Gen. 37: 25.
from Adinah to Elam From Baghdad to Persia (BDB 726 and 743).
to light my eyes 1 Sam. 14: 27–9.

Then, turning poetic, he sang:

Come to the Garden of Splendour, heart;
all blooms mark well.
Guard, tend rightly, fruit-bearing trees;
all others fell.

Then he declared, In youth I was told that Spain, noon-bright, the eyes' and soul's delight, was Splendour's seat—its breezes sweet with perfume, its bowers and star-like flowers ever abloom, sprung from fragrant sod—the very joy of man and God: Spain, land of praises beyond tally—the rose of Sharon, the lily of the valley.

Small wonder that Desire's voice rang out, *About, about!* flinging me in wild commotion over hill and dale, over dusty trail, over river, bay, and ocean. Yes, I split the surging main until I touched the golden shores of Spain; and, once there, once I had inhaled that incense-laden air, I found all praises spare to paint her fair. Many a domain I saw in mysteried Spain, first in the lands of Ishmael and then in the Christian pale where dwell the children of Israel.

Thus I came to queenly Navarre, and to Tudela, her brightest star, famed for her towers' high beauty: to laud her dwellers' towering virtues is both joy and duty. There the Lord's tribes came and put the sun and moon to shame, erecting synagogues on every hand throughout the land, therein sounding God's praise through nights and days. Tudela's holy Jewry, Virtue's seed and copious yield, grew

Guard, tend rightly, fruit-bearing trees Gen. 2: 15.

the very joy of man and God Judg. 9: 13.

the rose of Sharon, the lily of the valley S. of S. 2: 1.

Yes, I split the surging main until I touched the golden shores of Spain Though Hever frequently represents the author in this work (see the Afterword in this regard), and of course in this gate with its travel itinerary, here he chooses to represent Hever as not being of Spain. On this point, see the Analysis.

Many a domain I saw in mysteried Spain, first in the lands of Ishmael and then in the Christian pale where dwell the children of Israel By Alḥarizi's time, Andalusia, or Arab-controlled Spain, had shrunken markedly: the greater part of the Iberian Peninsula, excluding the territory comprising present-day Portugal, comprised the four Christian kingdoms of Castile, Leon, Aragon, and Navarre. For histories of Spanish Jewry and, particularly, descriptions of centres of settlement, see Y. Baer, *A History of the Jews in Christian Spain* (Philadelphia, 1966), i and ii; and E. Eshtor, *A History of the Jews of Muslim Spain* (3 vols.; Philadelphia, 1973–84).

There the Lord's tribes came Ps. 122: 4.

numerous as the grass of the field. Their leaders number the late, revered prince Solomon—the great prince Joseph's son and grandson of Shoshan. This Solomon was Right's throne or, better, its foundation-stone. There, now, dwells the keen-witted Abraham ben Shoshan, who has put Grandeur's mantle on. Moses ben Shoshan has built Largesse' forts—hostels where many a passer-by resorts. Other leaders include the virtuous Abraham ibn Alfakhar, known and blessed afar, and Tadros' son, Master Me'ir/Luminator, the Levite, bathed in learning's light, who stands the wise astride with none him beside—albeit he is somewhat stooped beneath his outsize pride!

Discover, in Tudela, Counsel's don—Master Ziza ben Shoshan, Wisdom's best friend and river of charity without end; see, as well, the modest Master Isaac ben Me'ir ibn Megash, with Wisdom's waves awash; and Master Joseph the judge, store of Virtue and holy lore; and his cousin, the doctor and seer, Master Jacob ben Me'ir, light divine, bright ore lifted from Discernment's mine.

From Tudela I journeyed to Kalat Iyob and met Master Joseph Constantino, regal in Faith's robe, a doctor graced with probity and learning, the Lord's lamp sweetly burning. From there I travelled to Laredo to that distinguished Arabist, Master Joseph, as well a keen astronomist. There, too, lives the sharp-witted cantor Joseph Alsiyad, shining vessel of God, if sirened to the shore of Karaitic lore. Thereafter I continued to Barcelona, ringed with princes like a bright corona, including that font of Largesse and Noblesse who knows no peer, Master Makhir. There, too, lived that princely Jew, him whom all men knew as Jewry's deacon: our dear *gaon*, our brightest beacon, our teacher, Rabbi Sheshet, pillar of the earth, who gave Virtue birth. There, too, lives his nephew the courtier, Master Isaac, a potent bard with lines of amethyst and nard; and that prince and light, Master Samuel the Levite, wisdom's source and pulsing force, blessed with five sons, wise and learned every one. There lives the courtier Master She'altiel: sailing under Modesty's taut sail, he is secure in the wildest gale; lo, he is doubly blest, as his children's deeds attest.

grew numerous as the grass of the field Ezek. 16: 7.

Kalat Iyob Calatayud.

if sirened to the shore of Karaitic lore On the Karaitic movement in Spain, see Gate 17 and its Analysis.

*T*here lives the doctor of the silver tongue, Master Judah son of Isaac, wide his praise be rung, prince of the pen and paragon of godly men. There, too, lives the prince the highly renowned, Jacob the Great, of great estate—if somewhat reprobate: he has set a writ of divorce in Generosity's hand and sent her from his gate. He has, however, two sons worthy in their ways, Solomon and Judah, destined for praise. Thence I went to Narbonne, where the house of David boasts a royal son—Rabbi Levi, Rule's mountain height and our eternal light.

*T*hence I came to the city of Balaguer, finding there that prince of great renown, Rabbi Kalonymus, Sovereignty's very crown. The prince, Rabbi Judah, Kalonymus' sister's son, is Israel's champion and charioteer, a captain of the host who knows no fear. There, too, lives the choice prince Isaac, pleasant in his ways, blinding the eyes with Wisdom's rays. There, too, lives the sage Rabbi Judah ben Netanel, who ruled the sea of Hebrew with his golden sail; and his sons five keep that mastery alive. His eldest, the keen Rabbi Samuel, puts to shame wise Lemuel; Ezra, the second son, indites clear as the noonday sun; Isaac, the third, is master of the poetic word; Isaiah, fourth of this house, has taken Geometry to spouse; and the fifth, Netanel, walks in his brothers' path and shall not fail.

*T*hence I came to Marseilles, where the generous prince Rabbi Moses holds sway, keeping adversity at bay. There lives the liberal Rabbi Jacob, appointee of the king, whose goodly, measured deeds all sing.

*T*hence I journeyed eastward on the sea to the realms where God's glory shines eternally; and first to Alexandria, Gilead's very balm, whose sage residents pour saving alms into outstretched palms. Their good citizens number Rabbi Simḥah/Joy the priest, who greets each guest with joyous feast and boasts sons upright and bright, all erudite. There lives the virtuous Obadiah, the king's secretary, a man of action and a prominent Karaitic dignitary. In that city lived, of late, the late Rabbi Hillel, known and honoured in the gate—albeit the gate to his gold chambers shut out the light of day, for he had locked them tight and thrown the key away. There lived, too, the precentor

he has set a writ of divorce in Generosity's hand and sent her from his gate Deut. 24: 1–3.

a captain of the host Deut. 20: 9.

wise Lemuel Prov. 31: 1.

God's glory shines Isa. 60: 1.

Rabbi Zadok: when he sang, the hosts of Heaven awoke; and Wisdom smiled contented when he spoke.

Then I sailed a while by the Nile, journeying through Egypt, of two realms comprised: the first, lofty and prized, is Fustat, kingship's seat, where one may meet a man unparalleled for generosity, and for faith, modesty, and moral virtuosity: he is the giving judge, Rabbi Menaḥem, son of the pious Rabbi Isaac, bless his name. Soul high and spacious, and with hands capacious, he is a pillar of Piety, who with his deeds feeds fame unto satiety.

The second city holds splendour brighter than gold's—Eden's onyx and bdellium, the wise Rabbi Abraham, son of our teacher Rabbi Moses ben Maimon of blessed memory. This splendid youth, learning's agate and emery, though tender of years, has few peers. His father rescued travellers lost by night, that in all their dwellings the Israelites had light. Yes, Maimonides looked and saw Jewry's frantic horde running to and fro to seek the Lord, yea, saw his people's sons and daughters crying out for the Torah's waters, even swooning from hunger and thirst. He saw how Time, accurst, rose up to worst them—and enslaved them; then Moses arose and saved them. He sifted the Talmud through his wondrous brain, lifted the choice grain, and for all languishing in the wastes of Time prepared nutriment sublime—whereat (Hosanna!) the children of Israel fed on manna! No longer had they need to limp or lurch about, search about in vain through the Talmud's vast domain; for he rid his composition of the names of sage or commentator, earlier or later, of fancy, of homily, of aggadic explication, of far-fetched innovation—in short, of obfuscation. He straightened all the Talmud's winding ways, then turned to the Exile and did his voice loud raise: *Enter these gates with thanksgiving, these courts with praise.*

second city Unspecified in the Hebrew.

Rabbi Abraham On Abraham ben Moses ben Maimon, leader of the Egyptian Jewish community, philosopher, and Bible commentator, see *EJ* ii. 150–2.

in all their dwellings the Israelites had light Exod. 10: 23.

Moses arose and saved them Exod. 2: 17.

the children of Israel fed on manna Exod. 16: 14–36.

Enter these gates with thanksgiving, these courts with praise Ps. 100: 4. On Maimonides' codification of Jewish law, see 'Sefer ha-Mitzvot' and 'The Mishneh Torah', *EJ* xi. 766–8, and 'As Halakhist' under Bibliography, *EJ* xi. 781. See also *EJ* v. 761–83, 'The 613 Commandments'; and *EJ* v. 639 and xvi. 330–1.

Now after Moses' death it came to pass that critics wondrous crass, weak minds who held his magnum opus in disdain, whether from Palestine, Babylon, Provence, or Spain, rose up like sheaves blasted with murrain—puffed heroes with blunt dirks and whinyards, little foxes that spoil the vineyards. Now had they fronted him alive, even with sword or axe, they had frozen in their tracks or melted in his sun like wax; or turned from his eagle mind, his lion heart, and fled; or sunk into his sea like lead. But now, any fool who pleases spouts Wisdom's song: the weak say, I am strong.

The weakling, warm in bed with wife,
feels much empowered;
But shows himself, on battle's field,
a naked coward.

Their grandees number the revered high prince Joseph son of the great prince Obadiah: his father was prince over all, raised in Kingship's hall; and now his skilful son, with righteous acts unreckoned, knows no second.

Thence I went to that city God has sanctified, where Heaven opened wide; and walking through Jerusalem's walls and ramps met angel camps—Virtue's lions and Truth's scions, come from Provence to dwell in Zion, at their head the pious master of learning, Rabbi Joseph son of the master Rabbi Barukh/Blest, who sucked Piety's breast, be he blest to his Creator; and the sage his brother, Rabbi Me'ir/Illuminator, with Learning's diadems bedecked, brighting the dark with his intellect.

A notable community are the Ashkelonites, headed by Sa'adiah

like sheaves blasted with murrain Gen. 41: 6, 23.
little foxes that spoil the vineyards S. of S. 2: 15.
sunk into his sea like lead Exod. 15: 10.
the weak say, I am strong Joel 4: 10.
The weakling, warm in bed with wife, feels much empowered; But shows himself, on battle's field, a naked coward See 'Maimonidean Controversy' and 'Maimonides' in *EJ* xi. 746–80, and the substantial bibliography there.
where Heaven opened wide See Gate 28, where Heman the Ezrahite, travelling to Zion, encounters Hever the Kenite, who provides information on the history of the Jewry of Jerusalem.
met angel camps Gen. 32: 2–3.
come from Provence to dwell in Zion On the aliyah of 300 rabbis of Provence see Analysis 28 n. 7.

the Benjaminite, Wisdom's sure and steady light. There, western Jews, too, have a congregation worthy of commendation. Their leader is Elijah of the West, who arrests misery with his largesse, this tower of comfort for his fellows in distress. Yet rumour whispers of deeds untoward, acts foul, abhorred: ah, well: the secret things belong unto the Lord.

Thence I went to Acre, city of dolts and God's wretchedest acre, as ignorant of charity as of their Maker. Next, throughout the Land of Israel I trekked, until I came to Saphad and there found the Lord's elect, who, Jacob-like, strove with God for wisdom and wondrous throve—the righteous Zadok, dean of the academy Geon Yaakov, son of noble and illustrious deans whose charity matched their copious means.

However, mischance clasped him round and flung him down: and the aftermath of sovereignty was wrath—Wandering's path. Yet though he journeyed far and was poured like water from jar to jar, he has not lost his lustre; he still wafts sweet odours like a fresh date-cluster. Though Fate clanks his chains, Zadok still reigns. May God, who has so tried his reins, staunch his wounds and heal his pain and lead him to gladness once again.

Then I sang:

The coin of Learning's realm dark Days debase;
the Torah's banner traitor Days deface.
Yet God shall grace us with His shining face—
restore the Torah to her rightful place.

Thence I went to Damascus and found, lofty of station, a valorous and God-fearing nation, albeit a mixed lot with many a stiff-necked, foul-mouthed, slanderous misbegot; still, the just held sway such that, when tested, they led me to say, Surely God is in this place and I knew it not.

the secret things belong unto the Lord Deut. 29: 28.
Jacob-like, strove with God for wisdom and wondrous throve [Hos. 12: 4–5].
was poured like water from jar to jar Jer. 48: 11.
a mixed lot [Exod. 12: 38].
Surely God is in this place and I knew it not Gen. 28: 16.

The crown of that vast congregation, Virtue's consummation, their pre-eminent leader, their towering cedar distinguished beyond parity, is the great physician Moses bar Zedakah/Charity, a very fort of comfort and support. He has no need of my modest witness: his deeds psalm his fitness. How many men whom wandering and bitterness have enslaved has this man saved! How many starving souls has this man sated, how many from danger extricated! How many men has he shielded from Fortune's whip, how many pulled back from the grave's lip, yes, shaken loose from Death's bony grip! He has, with his accordance and donation, fêted an entire generation.

Then I sang:

Can Metre wed with Rhyme define the gifts
with which this generous Moses is endowed?
God listens when he calls upon His name:
when Moses speaks, God answers him aloud.

There lives the prince Josiah, son of Jesse, the exilarch, Honour's ark, Splendour's mark, and Virtue's banner unfurled: glorious things are said of him throughout the world.

Then I sang:

Honour's image was in his image made;
his helpmeet, Rule, was given him alone.
He breathes his spirit on the corpses of Praise
until they come together, bone to bone.

The rest of the Damascene community are a good and pious lot, but even fine damask can show a spot. One finds, at times, among bloodstones, mudstones; among sweet blooms, foul fumes; among

towering cedar [Ps. 92: 13].

when Moses speaks, God answers him aloud Exod. 19: 19.

the prince Josiah, son of Jesse, the exilarch This is the same Josiah to whom Alḥarizi dedicated *Sefer Taḥkemoni* at the close of Gate 1.

glorious things are said of him throughout the world Ps. 87: 3.

Honour's image was in his image made Gen. 1: 27.

his helpmeet, Rule, was given him alone Gen. 2: 20.

He breathes his spirit on the corpses of praise until they come together, bone to bone Ezek. 37: 7.

pinks, stinks; among violet and gardenia, obscenia. They are sadists and rakes, coiled snakes, jakes, bloated weeds naked of good deeds, bursting with pride but hollow inside. Choosing randomly one rogue in vogue, I mention Barukh/Blessed the physician, scum come from Mount Eval, from a family of Belial who have turned their backs on God and bent their knees to Baal. He is a hack, a quack, spouting his physic's praises to Heaven on the minute; but the pit is empty, there is no water in it. He knows not his left from his right, the addlepated cluck, yet God has lent him luck: he stuffs a failing patient with dog- or donkey-meat and somehow puts him on his feet, then prances open-mouthed before his victims, bringing miracles to pass: lo, words stream from an ass!

His sires were the progenitors of Evil, strong-armed, strong-headed in service of the devil, in cruelty rich and resolute, of goodness destitute, hearts hard as mail, sin-laden like the goat of Azazel. Swifter than deer, they, to lift forbidden skirts and slower than turtles to give God His deserts. Their ranks, scum-swollen, know no lack: each man is an ass who bears a stack of sins upon his stinking back and groans beneath the pack. They number every fulsome bug that creeps upon the earth, yes, every noisome slug.

Such is his father's goodly treasure conveyed in modest measure. But his son Isaac God's patience hard assaults, amassing even more than his father's faults, until he bursts Sin's vaults—for he is high-nosed, foul-mouthed, and tight-fisted; snorting, fuming, and twisted, hoarding his ancestor's virtues like gold and adding thereto a thousandfold. He is an un-Jew, a one-man zoo with the foul of a sow and the brains of a cow, kind as a cat and clean as a rat, true as a fox and quick as an ox, brave as a hare, and sweet as a bear, brazen as a dog, lazy as a hog, witty as a donkey, shitty as a monkey, a baboon's double with a goat's stubble.

Were this contaminant, said Hever, plunged into the ocean for ablution, it were no solution: he would foul the sea with his pollution!

a family of Belial Deut. 13: 14 and elsewhere.
bent their knees to Baal 1 Kgs. 19: 18.
the pit is empty, there is no water in it Gen. 37: 24.
words stream from an ass [Num. 22: 28].
the goat of Azazel Lev. 16: 5 ff.
Swifter than deer Mishnah *Avot* 5: 23.

Were he passed through the refiner's fire, the flames would tremble and expire. The abomination: may his name not survive a quarter-generation! His father called him Ring of Opal, while his proper title is String of Offal. In his father's eyes, none is more prized; in the eyes of the wise, none more despised. And because that ass of a father is so blazing a fool, I have named his son Shekhem, son of Ḥamor/Mule.

Now this scribbler, in all his rashness and brashness, has dared to write poems all scrimpy and seedy, limping and needy, stale and crusty, pale, yet rusty, creaking, leaking, false coin, none worse, verse stolen from his father's purse, barren tilth, full of vomit and filth, poems designed to strip their writer bare or set him up for show at a country fair.

Poems? No—cats' howlings or dogs' growlings. Lo, he barks his lines from sunup until dark and calls them by his name, Novaḥ/Bark—lines highflown, flyblown, wholly unholy, odious, not melodious, peccant, not piquant, mucid, not lucid; like Tamar in roadside disguise, brazenly offering the sacrifice of breast and thighs—and when Judah saw her, she was a harlot in his eyes. Her leprous touch he spurned, crying: *Away with her; let her be burned!* I sent him a wondrous poem, my muse's fairest child, and Shekhem, son of Ḥamor, saw her, took her, and lay with her, that she was defiled. Then I did what I must, no more I could: I robed her in black, and locked her up at home unto the day of her death in living widowhood.

Now if the son was Sin's chariot and horse, Sin's gushing source, the father was Sin's flour and leaven who, rebellious, thrust his horns up to Heaven. And this ram that I saw, having two horns, the foulest creature ever to have been born, a-giggle with joy, none gladder, stormed the angels' ladder and wed into the family of the dean of the academy of Geon Yaakov, Zadok! Was ever a worse

Shekhem, son of Ḥamor/Mule Gen. 34: 2.
full of vomit and filth Isa. 28: 8.
calls them by his name, Novaḥ /Bark Num. 32: 42.
the sacrifice of breast and thighs [Lev. 10: 15].
and when Judah saw her, she was a harlot in his eyes Gen. 38: 15.
Away with her; let her be burned! Gen. 38: 24.
Shekhem, son of Ḥamor, saw her, took her, and lay with her Gen. 34: 2.
locked her up at home unto the day of her death in living widowhood 2 Sam. 20: 3.
thrust his horns up to heaven Dan. 8: 3 ff.
stormed the angels' ladder [Gen. 28: 12].

misyoke? Oh tragic night, when good wed evil, when angel joined devil, and tin linked with mail: one lot for the Lord, the other for Azazel—to wit: an impure, obscure, cocksure boor; intemperate, intoxicate, extortionate; close-pursed, ill-born (none worse), who has his Maker cursed.

*R*ound the world did Stint roam, frustrated till he made his home in this man's heart: who, if he touched the sea, its wet would dry; the rain cloud, and it would fall apart. The wealth that he protects with his strong right arm is wealth hoarded to its keeper's harm. Many an ingenious shackle has he invented for his gold and silver, whom he has mercilessly tormented, squeezing them until they moan in pain, deep in his dungeons where they shall never see the light of day again. Daily his tortured treasure cries, The Lord has delivered me into their hands from whom I cannot rise! Pity me, pity me my friends, for I am ruled by a lord base and mean, mocked by the unclean. Since the day I fell into this curst man's hands I have lain on Death's dark plain: he has hedged me about that I cannot get out, he has thickened my chain.

*I*f he knew that he should profit from his body-lice (he would not), he would gather all the inhabitants of East and West to bring out the lice—but they could not. Were he to hold a banquet beneath his roof, it were but proof of his venal heart and mind. There you would find not roast and wine, but reasty rind, a tasteless joke—burnt offerings, their smoke ascending like furnace smoke. Expect no goose or pheasant under glass, but stringy rump of ox or ass, as though his pot were a pit: an ox or ass passed by and fell into it. His bread—unleavened bread; his wine—black, not red; lamb tender as thistle, his meat all gristle; his table short on meat and long on soup, with peas, beans, broccoli, spinach, cabbage—a gay, green group. For greens and

one lot for the Lord, the other for Azazel Lev. 16: 8.

who has his Maker cursed [1 Kgs. 21: 13; Job 2: 9].

wealth hoarded to its keeper's harm Eccles. 5: 12.

The Lord has delivered me into their hands from whom I cannot rise Lam. 1: 14.

he has hedged me about that I cannot get out, he has thickened my chain Lam. 3: 7.

reasty Rancid.

their smoke ascending like furnace smoke Exod. 19: 18.

a pit: an ox or ass passed by and fell into it Exod. 21: 33.

water none can his feasts surpass: all flesh is grass. Ask for the meat and they will tell you with pious sigh that it is like the soul, hid from the eye.

Generally speaking, his fruits are as inviting as the populace that them inhabits—nits, worms, and maggots; as juiceless his peaches as sick men bled of leeches, his rancid grapes—fit only for apes, his figs—unfit for pigs, each pomegranate red without, white within, and hard as granite; his every date foul as fate, his raisins—the best, exquisitely shrivelled as each his mother's breast; his nuts, fit for study by a botanist—as hard to crack open as his miser father's fist. Instead of ginger, nutmeg, parsley, pepper, chutney, or sage, he offers onion limp with age. Water alone his table does not lack, and greens by the stack; for such was his father's favourite combination, a family delectation. Should a hungry passer-by come nigh he would be told, We have no bread or water or like stuff; but we have all sorts of grasses tender and tough: we have both straw and provender enough.

And when he stuffs his belly like a hog, he spares not a crust for his dog, who, if he could speak, would say: Master, shall you turn traitor, pray? Heaven forfend! Pity your dearest, and your father's dearest, friend! His heart is an inn that Sin loves best: Vice knows no wider camping-ground than in his breast. His forehead is brazenness' bench; none can match his sons and father for their stench. On the Sabbaths and on every holiday his godly way is to flee the congregation, and speed to his garden far from public prayer and supplication, even as Holy Writ prescribes: *God shall set him apart for evil from all Israel's tribes*. He glows like a stump on a burnt-out sward, for he has fled from before the Lord.

Wary lest some charitable issue be raised or some injurious legal pronouncement be made, he dashes home afraid. Herein he is hereditarily nervous, allergic, like his fathers, to God's service. Indeed, his pater and grandpater adjured him early and later to shun the synagogue and never share his wealth with his Creator, all in fulfilment of God's word, *Let no guilt money or sin money be brought*

all flesh is grass Isa. 40: 6.
we have both straw and provender enough Gen. 24: 25.
God shall set him apart for evil from all Israel's tribes Deut. 29: 20.
he has fled from before the Lord Jonah 1: 10.

into the House of the Lord. Scripture says of him, *Bring no harlot's hire nor the cost of a dog into the house of the Lord your God.* Not once a year does he join the congregation, but dwells a lonely nation in leprous degradation: beyond the camp he makes his habitation.

Not for these reasons alone, but for others beside, he puts public prayer aside: for he indulges in sin and filth beyond pardon, in fulfilment of the verse, *They who sanctify and purify themselves in every garden.* I have it on sure testimony that his sires lit pagan fires, slithering out at night by the stars' chill light to offer libations, cakes—sacrifices, even!—to the hosts of Heaven.

For all these reasons he is deserving of universal excommunication: yea, he who slays him on the Day of Atonement need make no reparation nor fear damnation.

Lo, the discoverer of pinch and scrimp—
in quest of avarice, brave Balboa,
Who, should he tread Mount Hermon's lush slopes,
would leave them barer than curst Gilboa.

God, cut him off; blot out his and his father's name; let them burn together and none put out the flame.

Thence I came to Mount Zemara'im and found, among their men of renown, the pious Master Jacob, foe of falsehood, ever spurning evil and choosing good. A choice leader of their community is Master She'erith/Remains, Integrity's saving remnant and remains, father of seven sons all bright with Learning's golden chains. One of the community's most distinguished residents, whose

Let no guilt money or sin money be brought into the House of the Lord 2 Kgs. 12: 17.

Bring no harlot's hire nor the cost of a dog into the house of the Lord your God Deut. 23: 19.

but dwells a lonely nation [Num. 23: 9].

in leprous degradation: beyond the camp he makes his habitation Lev. 13: 46.

They who sanctify and purify themselves in every garden Isa. 66: 17.

to offer libations, cakes—sacrifices, even!—to the hosts of Heaven Jer. 7: 19.

curst Gilboa 2 Sam. 1: 21.

let them burn together and none put out the flame Isa. 1: 31.

Mount Zemara'im 2 Chr. 13: 4—in Scripture, a site in the tribal territory of Ephraim in the land of Israel. The reference here is unclear.

spurning evil and choosing good Isa. 7: 15–16.

sons give evidence of his fine traits, was the refiner, Master Peraḥiah. The grandee, Master Petaḥiah, was lauded for his actions and applauded for his benefactions. Two brothers also live there, anointed priests, honoured guests at all of Virtue's feasts—Master Eliezer/God my Aid and Master Berakhot, God be ever his shade. Their father was a man of true devotion; and his sons, true heirs, Virtue's land of Goshen. Many there, in fact, are joyous practitioners of the godly act.

Thence I journeyed to Hamath, home of Rabbi Uziel, the great prince and king's gold-tongued vizier, in whose day Jewry knew no fear. The king's courtiers scurried about him: no man could lift hand or foot without him. All the king's officers, at his nod, uplifted the people of God throughout the land. Great in spirit, speech, and deed, he was next the king, accepted of the multitude, and spoke peace to all his seed. Praise God, who sent this champion to His nation to raise the fallen to high station, to grant the wanderer rest, the hungry, satiation. May he look upon Jerusalem's salvation, see God shine forth from Zion, beauty's consummation, hear the ram's horn sound our restoration, hear the Messiah's long-awaited proclamation: O scattered children of Israel, rise, prevail, come up from weeping's vale, return with song and sacrifice to Ariel!

Then he sang:

Ho, hungry and weary: feast at the board
of the prince who is chos'n of the Lord,
Who, should he touch the desert crust,
would turn it a blooming sward;
Whose counsel gains more victories
than wielders of the sword.

land of Goshen [Gen. 45: 10 and elsewhere].
Hamath a city north of Damascus (2 Sam. 8: 9, BDB 333).
no man could lift hand or foot without him Gen. 41: 44.
All the king's officers, at his nod, uplifted the people of God Esther 9: 3.
spoke peace to all his seed [Esther 10: 3].
Zion, beauty's consummation Ps. 50: 2.
hear the ram's horn sound our restoration Isa. 27: 13.
come up from weeping's vale [Ps. 84: 7; Lekha Dodi prayer in the service for welcoming the Sabbath].
Ariel Isa. 29: 1.
Ho, hungry and weary: feast [Isa. 55: 1].

Terror of men, his people's shield,
be this his just reward:
To shout with joy in the courtyards
of Jerusalem restored.

The notables of Hamath number the judge, Master Mivḥar/Choice, wisdom's own voice. There lives there, too, Master David the physician, of spotless character and gentle disposition. There lives there, too, Master Isaac, music's master, in truth, and one who has served Moses from his youth—high Wisdom commanding, a man of deepest understanding.

Onward progressing, I came to lordly Aram Zova where the Lord commanded the blessing. Over this diadem of kings Glory shines and sings. Besides a veritable host of notables and pleasant congregations, they boast, these thirty years, a scholar bright as the ephod upon Aaron's chest: the great rabbi of the West, Joseph the Westerner, that imposing sage and luminary of the age. Seekers of King Solomon, no further aspire: here is the burning coal that you desire, the man whose tongue is a consuming fire.

Then he sang:

A roaring lion on Wisdom's field
this holy man of God
Who calls out to Wisdom's sea, Divide!
then strides across dry-shod.
Unique, and father of splendid sons
he is, who has preferred
To teach his children virtue
before they could speak a word.
Come from the west to light the east
he took Splendour's treasure hoard—

in the courtyards of Jerusalem [Ps. 116: 19].
who has served Moses from his youth Num. 11: 28.
Aram Zova (shorter form Zova) Aleppo (Haleb) in northern Syria.
where the Lord commanded the blessing Ps. 133: 3.
the ephod upon Aaron's chest [Exod. 28: 4, 6 ff].
Who calls out to Wisdom's sea, Divide! then strides across dry-shod Exod. 14: 21–9.

This bright Elijah, whom the wise
acknowledge as their lord.
If our age were blest with prophecy
he would lead the prophets' camp;
Had he lived of old in Zion, he
would have been the western lamp.

Pleasant, discerning, a sea of learning, his light is beaten olive oil's, for ever burning. Many a dead mind of upper Syria he restored—wondrous feat: the spirit entered them, they lived, they stood upon their feet. Now one of his students, an ingrate and overreacher, rebelled against his teacher with forehead of brass and heart of wood, returning evil for good, forgetting how Joseph had drawn him out, sought him, whence he had brought him, and how much he had taught him; for he had raised him from a heap of dung to set him among thinkers, seers, and giants, only to merit such defiance.

Now at the head of Zova's generous and noble leaders stand two mighty cedars, the great prince Rabbi Azariahu, whom his folk acclaim, and his brother, Generosity's soul and flame, Rabbi Samuel, God magnify his name. And these heroes, by God appointed, are the seed of God's anointed, Rabbi Nissim, friend and choice of I Am Who I Am and seed of His beloved Abraham, who wields Wisdom's wondrous rod—a soul of splendour who keeps faith with the angels and rules with God. He is Zova's and Damascus' fair renown and the academy head's crown. Within his heart the Holy Presence lies; the fear of God is a flaming torch between his eyes.

God put Master Abraham to rule's test, and found him suited best. And had Father Abraham found this Abraham, he had placed

the western lamp Tosefta, *Sotah* 13: 7.
his light is beaten olive oil's, for ever burning [Exod. 27: 20].
the spirit entered them, they lived, they stood upon their feet Ezek. 37: 10.
forehead of brass [Isa. 48: 4].
returning evil for good [Prov. 17: 13].
he had raised him from a heap of dung Ps. 113: 7.
only to merit such defiance The history referred to here is unknown to me.
I Am Who I Am [Exod. 3: 14].
seed of His beloved Abraham Isa. 41: 8.
keeps faith with the angels and rules with God Hos. 12: 1.
a flaming torch between his eyes Dan. 10: 6.
God put . . . suited best Gen. 22.

him on his breast for a pendant, thanking the Lord for so singular a descendant, who, were he to so decide, could make the sea divide; who, if thrown into the fiery furnace of Ur, would emerge whole and pure—this hero of whom Wisdom boasts, this angel of the Lord of Hosts.

From the patriarchs' days this family is virtue-crowned and wide renowned. Their generous hands are open ocean-wide, showing no ill gain inside. Demeanour's vault and modest to a fault, none in the Beauteous Land can match their high degree, Syria basks in the light of their pedigree, Assyria trembles before their praise, none in Babylon attain to a fraction of their ways. At the great prince Samuel's door the generation begs—for he has gathered up all virtues like abandoned eggs! His mansion home has turned to an inn where citizen or visitor from east or west may feast and rest. Had he wealth to match his boundless piety, he would fill each outstretched hand beyond satiety. He has a son dawn-like, streaming, aptly named Mazhir/Beaming, who has climbed his forebears' ladder to high station, adding to his herited reputation. God grant him years as vast as his approbation.

Now there lives there Dr Elazar/God Aids, who parades his impiety in high and low society, cancelling the laws of Sabbath and of Holiday. Once summoned by the King of Hamath on the Sabbath day, he arose without delay to make his way from the Desert of Zin to Levo Hamat—the fetid spot, the lout, may his name be blotted out! Now, having succinctly set forth this bastard's shame, this dastard's claim to fame, I add how, long years ago, he swelled with pride and sallied forth, a snorting ram pushing south and north; and lo, a lion sprang up from the west, wondrous in size, and bitter smote the ram, broke his two horns and put out his eyes; he was the great doctor, Master Joseph the Westerner, who forced the fool to see his own tumidity, then showed the world his singular stupidity.

could make the sea divide [Exod. 14: 21].
if thrown into the fiery furnace of Ur, would emerge whole and pure BT *Pes.* 118*a*.
he has gathered up all virtues like abandoned eggs Isa. 10: 14.
the fetid spot [Mishnah *Avot* 3: 1].
he swelled with pride . . . broke his two horns Dan. 8: 3–7.

*U*pper Syria, Aram Zova, holds, as well, the choice patrician and just Rule's practition, Master Elazar/God Aids, the king's physician, a courtier and royal scribe of high position who furthers his people's good with strength and expedition. His also is a son of erudition—Intellect come to glorious fruition. His nephews, too, have won them distinguished places: though they be veiled in modesty, God's glory shines forth from their faces.

*T*here be three men in Upper Syria whom their brothers specially revere, being wise, pious, and sincere, precious beyond the gold of Ophir. Rule's emblem they and Virtue's token, a threefold cord that is not quickly broken. Foremost among them is Moses, who has high mountains trod, as it is written, *Moses went up unto God*. He wears Modesty's robe (the which his generation holds too drear): when God calls out, Moses alone draws near. Next is Daniel, greatly beloved and Virtue's token: of him great things are spoken. He walks unscathed through the dens of Passion's beasts; he turns his back on Day's raptures, spurns Time's altars and drunken priests; for Daniel purposed in his heart that he would not defile himself with the portion of the king's meat nor with the wine of his feasts. The third is Joseph, set over Virtue's broad land: Counsel's fenced cities fall to his hand.

Lo, three sons of Eminence
to honour and to prize:
Moses, modest and lowly,
but lofty in Heaven's eyes;
Daniel: praises faint at his gate,
his name outshines the gold;

God's glory shines forth Isa. 60: 1.
the gold of Ophir Job 28: 16.
a threefold cord that is not quickly broken Eccles. 4: 12.
Moses went up unto God Exod. 19: 3.
when God calls out, Moses alone draws near Exod. 24: 1–2.
Daniel, greatly beloved Dan. 10: 11.
of him great things are spoken Ps. 87: 3.
He walks unscathed through the dens of Passion's beasts [Dan. 6: 8–29].
for Daniel . . . of his feasts Dan. 1: 8.
Joseph, set over Virtue's broad land Gen. 42: 6.
fenced cities fall to his hand Dan. 11: 15.
Moses, modest and lowly Num. 12: 3.

Joseph, whose tongue is healing balm,
whose mind is Wisdom's hold.
Imbibing their splendour daily,
their people, of one accord,
Acknowledge these three, all men above,
as angels of the Lord.

By all criteria, two of the greatest leaders of the Jews of Syria are Master Yakhin and Master Yeshuah/Salvation, pillars of rule and royalty's foundation. The noted grandees number as well a father of benignities, Master Hananiah, blessed for his many magnanimities, a man whose forebears' sway spilled forth like the Milky Way. The pride of his people, he has fathered a virtuous son, nor could have been blessed with a finer one. May Master Hananiah live till one hundred and twenty; and as he reaped his fathers' fields, so may his offspring reap his plenty.

Syria's prominent Jews number, too, the sons of the courtier Shmariah, Masters Muvḥar and Obadiah. The father was the crowning glory of his generation; the sons, following in his footsteps, have won like veneration.

There I found Master Joseph, son of the late, pious Master Ḥisdai, God stand him ever nigh. The modest father was a stellar light among the Jews, Wisdom's lamp and Honesty's cruse. Master Joseph, the son, hungry for like reputation, has swallowed each virtue like a delectation, proving himself worthy of his name and station.

Among them lives wise Master Joseph, son of Moses, beaming with godly awe and barer of the mysteries of God's Law. There, too, lives Master Shmariah the sage, son of Rabbi Barukh/Blessed, joy of his age, a man of clean hands, pure heart, a devotee of truth, God-fearing from his youth; and that great prince Master Samuel of bright report, Learning's resort, a scribe in the royal court.

They include a physician heavy on Goodness' scale—Rabbi Hananiah, son of Bezalel, his people's praise: with lowered eyes he

three, all men above, as angels of the Lord [Gen. 18: 1–19: 1].
barer of the mysteries Job 28: 11.
a man of clean hands, pure heart Ps. 24: 4.
God-fearing from his youth 1 Kgs. 18: 12.

walks down Wisdom's ways. Scholars, his door is open wide: enter and see Virtue shining on every side. There, too, lives the famous prince Rabbi Menaḥem ben Zakkai, whose royal father stood monarchs by. The son is the very model of his illustrous sire—if, as a font of giving, somewhat drier. There, too, lives Honour's stream, the pleasant prince, Rabbi Na'im, a leader of his fold, if often led by the love of gold. Virtue's repository, he is coins' lasting depository. Betwixt him and charity is enmity: he squeezes his silver felly, freeing it only for his mouth and belly. Let stranger seek his coin and lo, he hasn't any—not a penny.

There, too, lives Rabbi Judah, the physician, blessed with piety and tact, and master of the righteous act. There lives also the sage Rabbi Yeḥezkel, speeding cross Wisdom's waters at full sail: never shall his vessel fail. There, too, reposes meek Rabbi Abraham son of Moses, true and upright, Honour's torch alight. There, too, lives Rabbi Ḥisdai the judge, whose scroll of honour knows nor stain nor smudge, a man of high spirituality, impeccable morality, a lover of virtue and foe of venality; his life is his art—God's Law in its totality.

There, too, lives the precentor Rabbi Daniel of gifted note and golden throat: his people's hearts are his with one accord as he lifts his voice in the Temple of the Lord. There, too, lives the young scholar Obadiah son of Eli, amiable and calm, his every word pain's balm; robed in modesty even as a boy, his ways are ways of pleasantness, his purity a joy. There, too, lives the prince and Virtue's prince, crowned in all magnificence, Rabbi Se'adel, son of the prince Rabbi Ezra of blessed memory, a vine of noble line. He strides through life on virtuous legs, gathering up goodness like scattered eggs. There, too, lives the eminent sage and doctor Master Pinḥas, few so great, a man most generous with his estate. There, too, is Master Jodiah, cleaving to Righteousness' track and never looking back.

Thence I turned west and found a community richly blessed, the former home of Rabbi Solomon the Westerner, that soul of gold, modesty, and piety manifold, and sons cast all in his mould.

Thence I journeyed to Serug and Rabbi Elazar, Maecenas of

his ways are ways of pleasantness [Prov. 3: 17].

gathering up goodness like scattered eggs Isa. 10: 14.

Babylon known near and far for his sterling clarity, his counsel and charity. He feasts the passer-by as well as he is able; native and traveller grace his sumptuous table. Then I journeyed to Aram Naharaim, home of the godly Master Yefet, afire with duty; and the precentor Master Joseph of lordly beauty. Thence I went to Haran, whence harlots and wastrels had long since gone, with the exception of Pagiel, son of Akhran. There, too, lives Rabbi Zedakah/Charity, God's own delight, if somewhat tight. There the physician Rabbi Matsliaḥ/Succeeds arose: by Wisdom's stream this blessed lily blows; he cries, yea, roars, prevails against his foes.

There, too, lives Obadiah son of Eli, the King's scribe. Sing, Diatribe, the wisdom of this slug, this empty jug, who can shout *Holy!* or *Amen!*—no more; he discerns not behind from before. When I met him, I thought him harmless as a hollow box and so took company with him. Pox! Tradition warns against a boring ox!

Thence I went to Calneh and found a rare congregation, a pious and God-fearing nation, a winged host risen above all temptation—of Charity, their wealth sunk deeper than the sea, wrapt in bronze chains, and kept under double lock and key. Their leader is Rabbi Zemaḥ/Branch, glorious branch of the Lord, endowed with every rare gift—especially thrift. However, his brother, Rabbi Obadiah, had he the power, would greet each supplicant with gold in shower.

Their ranks contain young Isaac son of Moses, a joy and treasure and wise beyond measure. There, too, Rabbis Simḥah/Joy and Halafta dwelled, and happy the eye that them beheld, both men God-fearing, exceeding generous and endearing: when they approach, see God's own cherubs nearing. Their charity shielded Calneh like an iron dome, as it is writ: *And the two angels came unto Sodom.*

went to Haran A city in Turkey, about 100 km. north of al-Raqqa.

Pagiel, son of Akhran Num. 1: 13.

cries, yea, roars, prevails against his foes Isa. 42: 13.

a boring ox Exod. 21: 28–36—the laws pertaining to the *goring* ox. The Hebrew text reads *shor tam*—'an innocent animal, one that did injury for the first time, or before warning had been given . . . B. Kam 1: 4' (Jastrow, 1674–5).

Calneh Isa. 10: 9; Amos 6: 2: al-Raqqa in (Iraq).

glorious branch of the Lord Isa. 4: 2.

And the two angels came unto Sodom Gen. 19: 1.

Thence I took my way to Ashur and there saw Rabbi Nissim, modesty's mount and charity's sea, his gate open wide as the eye can see; stay stranger: Kindness' very soul is he! There I beheld David, our exilarch and lord, and the son of his sister Hodiah, both gifts of the Lord. In this age they beam forth potent rays: none can match their peerless ways; my tongue falls mute to sing their slightest praise.

Therein, too, lives a God-forsaken wretch singularly distressing, Berakhot/Blessings by name, but in no way a blessing. His every feature shouts out the grossness of the creature. You would say, seeing his heinous face, Surely there is no fear of God in this place! Of him the poets say:

Bear's paunch, pig's guts: behold Berakhot,
the acme of uncouth.
Only a fool would take his word:
he cannot speak the truth.
Trust him never, ah, never, with three:
money, maid, or youth.

Arrived in their midst I saw them swathed in mist, snoring in Folly's bosom for all care, no man and no man's voice there, but rather horses' neighing or donkeys' braying. No city, that, but a pit—an ox or an ass passed by and fell into it: for on that day that memory can scarce endure, when Jerusalem's saints were exiled to Damascus and Egypt, and pitched from Havilah to Shur, then came the lost ones to the land of Ashur.

Thence I went to Baghdad, that gloried nation, ever Wisdom's truest station. Today, however, it stands bereft: its elders have departed; only raw youths are left. The wheat is gone, the chaff stays on, Virtue has vanished without a trace, Vileness has seized her place; the lions are all dead and foxes roam the hills instead, fouling the ruins of Giving's hall and tower. I sought but found no vower; no, not

Ashur Mosul, northern Iraq.
no fear of God in this place Gen. 20: 11.
pitched from Havilah to Shur Gen. 25: 18.
then came the lost ones to the land of Ashur Isa. 27: 13.
foxes roam the hills [Lam. 5: 18].

one endower. No man can win grace from them: they hid their faces from me, and I will surely hide my face from them.

Their chief, and in this their chief malefactor and Stint's chief benefactor, is one Joseph son of Shever, whom I saw never. Had God prized this fraud, me had he prized; but his Maker despised him, so me he despised. Nonetheless I found from among their choicest sages Rabbi Isaac, one of the age's finest souls: he walks Right's paths, achieving godly goals. Thence I journeyed to Tavekh, where Jews praise outright the arm of godly might, Rabbi Shmuel, and gladly bear his yoke—the prince who drapes Babylon with Largesse' cloak, whose praise streams Heavenward like altar smoke. His brothers are two funnels of gold whom angel arms enfold. These three are loved and respected, Divinely elected, trebly blessed, nurture and mercy manifest, succour and shade for the weary guest: the very sons of Noaḥ/Rest.

Then he lifted his voice and sang:

Jews least and best of East and West
are here fair praise accorded:
Wise men and bold and fountains of gold;
others who pinched and hoarded.
With iron pen I have limned these men
and have them fair rewarded.
Let future days inspect their ways:
lo, they are here recorded.

and I will surely hide my face from them Deut. 31: 17.
Tavekh Wasit.
streams Heavenward like altar smoke [Josh. 8: 20].
two funnels of gold Zech. 4: 12.
the very sons of Noaḥ/Rest Gen. 9: 19.
With iron pen Jer. 17: 1.
lo, they are here recorded 1 Kgs. 14: 19 and elsewhere.

GATE FORTY-SEVEN

Nation Contends with Nation for Rank and Station

THUS SPOKE HEMAN THE EZRAHITE: When the voice of the turtledove was heard in the land, I arrived in Kaftor from Petor, so faint I scarce could stand; indeed so weak it seemed as though I had not sat a week—and this, when the sun was at its peak, striking at earth with steaming swords, lashing at lions with gold-knotted cords, and driving snakes from their lairs in hordes. As my forehead dripped, I slipped from my horse, hungry for shade and a water course, and spied among tall grasses, all in a heap, a man bound fast in the cords of sleep. I drew near; stood over him; he woke, fearful, and sprang up like a deer.

*C*ome back! I shouted at his fleeing back. I am only a traveller off the beaten track! Come here! Peace be with you; do not fear! At that the man returned and I attempted conversation.

*C*ome, tell me your purpose and your destination, your birthplace, sir, and occupation.

*H*e answered, I am of the Kenites and hail from Elon, and am in place and purpose lone.

*I*nhaling his myrrh, I knew my soul's seigneur: as he had said and even as I had thought, here was Hever the Kenite whom I had long sought, friend of invention in prose or verse; so I begged coin of his mind's rich purse.

*G*ift me, I asked him, with a wise word: can you tell me of that which you have seen and heard?

the voice of the turtledove was heard in the land S. of S. 2: 12.

Kaftor Crete: BDB, 499.

Petor A site in Mesopotamia, home of the prophet Balaam: Num. 22: 5 and Deut. 23: 5; cf. Gate 19.

he woke, fearful Gen. 28: 12–17.

I am of the Kenites and hail from Elon Judg. 4: 11.

I daresay I can, said Hever, and thus began:

We are told that in days of old, the fair lands from the Tigris to the Nile's broad gate struck fierce debate, each staking claim to high estate.

First No-Amon did loud intone, Mine rod and crown, I, prince of God, who reared me as His own. Surely this thing is *known*, even as my name hints: *No*-(Amo)*n*. The great sea-necklace loops about my shoulders, the thundering breakers shatter on my boulders. By me kings reign and princes make decree: I, covenanted lord who hold the world in fee; I, renowned city strong in the sea. Cringe, you who would touch my garment's fringe! Rebel kings beware; yea, front my foaming horses if you dare!

Oh, rebel cities: though you flaunt your strength,
flashing and beaming with pride outgrown;
Though you loose your banners on earth's highest peaks,
in the Seventh Heaven set your throne—
Yet would I dwarf you. Be it known:
no kingdom looms higher than No-Amon.

Then Fustat spoke, saying: Let Jerusalem vaunt her height—I am the eyes' delight. At the thrum of my crossroads Praise strums her lute; in my Eden-sprung waters miracles take root and give fruit. In darkest night, by the Nile's wondered might the Israelites had light. Here marvels have no dearth; here Salvation gave birth; here nations come from the ends of the earth.

Though every far-flung land and isle
ascended Heaven, I should but smile.
Yes, though they soar to High Heaven's floor—
they must raise their eyes to my domicile.

No-Amon Nah. 3: 8—Alexandria.

Surely this thing is *known* Exod. 2: 14.

No*-(Amo)*n Lit. 'God called my name No-Amon because I am as a daughter to him and was as one brought up by him (*amon*)' (Esther 2: 7; Prov. 8: 30).

By me kings reign and princes make decree [Prov. 8: 15].

renowned city strong in the sea [Ezra 26: 17].

Fustat In the Delta of Lower Egypt—today part of Cairo.

the eyes' delight Gen. 3: 6.

Eden-sprung waters On the identification of the two rivers Pishon and Gihon (Gen. 2: 11–13) with the Nile see Cassuto, *A Commentary on the Book of Genesis*, 115–17.

the Israelites had light Exod. 10: 23.

All lands be daughters, vassals, slaves;
their mother—Egypt, Land of the Nile.

Then said Jerusalem: Lo, I shone in my prime on the breastplate of Time. Here was God's camp: upon my every wall and ramp bright angels strode. Here Providence abode, ringing me every side; here children and greybeards prophesied; joy filled my tents—but through my people's sin God's Glory hurried hence: naught was spared, my foundations were bared. Here where David ploughed and sowed, kings' blood flowed. Here, where the prophets spoke, the horns of the altar broke. And now in God's holy court idols resort, images grimace and make sport. Yet I am still held fair, my name raised high in blessing and in prayer.

Then she lifted her voice and sang:

Tongues cleave to palates and knees turn weak
in the city of David, Beauty's site.
Count ye her ramparts, her towers, this camp
of the Living God, of Holy Light.
Oh, pray for the peace of Jerusalem;
may all of your lovers find grace in God's sight.

Then Acre spoke, saying, I am earth's cornerstone, the field where holiness was sown, lily of Sharon, my fragrance blown to the mountains of Carmel, Lebanon, Tabor, and Hermon.

Then she lifted her voice in song:

Acre am I, the pride of the world,
Splendour's unchallenged lord.

the breastplate [Exod. 28: 30].
Here was God's camp Gen. 32: 3.
my foundations were bared Ps. 137: 7.
the horns of the altar broke Amos 3: 14.
And now in God's holy court idols resort, images grimace and make sport For a similar sentiment, see Gate 28.
Tongues cleave to palates Ps. 137: 6.
Beauty's site [Ps. 48: 3].
Count ye her ramparts Lit. 'This is the camp of God: here the Rock opened her gates opposite the gates of Heaven; for she is the light of the world for every eye; she is the life of hearts, a joy to the eyes.'
her towers [Ps. 48: 13].
this camp of the Living God Gen. 32: 3.
pray for the peace of Jerusalem [Ps. 122: 6].
lily of Sharon S. of S. 2: 1.

I border Carmel where Elijah, enraged,
put the prophets of Baal to the sword.
My breezes are charged with Divinity,
my rocks hold the speech of the Lord.

Then Damascus spoke, saying: Mine are the East's dominions—I, who rise on Splendour's pinions. What are Elam and Shinar to my bright star? What feet tremble not on my marble stairs, where Splendour repairs, or in my castles, gardens, and my thoroughfares? The sword of Beauty shines upon my thighs and I bind the sun and stars between my eyes. Behold my ivory palaces with tapestries and cedar panels, behold my gardens with crystal water channels. My pleasures echo far, even beyond Amanah and Parpar. Down my slopes the juice of the vine runs free, thick as the waters covering the sea.

He who boasts of gate and tower,
state and power—
idly boasts.
Stand in awe before my walls,
my lamps and gardens,
pillars and posts.
Small wonder that my halls were picked
to host the light
of the Lord of Hosts.

Then Zova spoke, saying: Here was the reign of Splendour founded, here Rule's trumpet sounded, here was Might's kingdom bounded. Lovers of perfection, no farther seek: when Beauty is summoned, who else dare speak? Descend to my every valley, climb

Carmel where Elijah, enraged, put the prophets of Baal to the sword 1 Kgs. 18.
Elam and Shinar Baghdad.
I bind the sun and stars between my eyes [Exod. 13: 16; Deut. 6: 8, 11: 18].
Amanah and Parpar Rivers near Damascus: 2 Kgs. 5: 12.
Down my slopes the juice of the vine runs free Amos 9: 13.
thick as the waters covering the sea Isa. 11: 9.
Small wonder that my halls were picked to host the light of the Lord of Hosts Lit. 'because my Creator made His glory to dwell in Hadrach, in Damascus his place of rest'—a citing of Zech. 9: 1: 'He will reside in the land of Hadrach and Damascus; for all men's eyes will turn to the Lord.'
Zova Aleppo (Haleb) in northern Syria.

my every peak: find fame resounding, for mine are sages and nobles abounding, savants who can salve the sick, turn dull minds quick—the choicest of men, fierce wielders of the pen.

When Beauty's sheaves stood thick and tall,
Zova's towered above them all.
My throne is raised; earth's nations, bearing
tribute, come—and before me fall.

Then Mosul spoke saying: I am Syria/Ashur and, be you sure, the envied, chosen nation, object of massive veneration. To raise my name is to praise my fame. I capture renown in giant strides; here Glory rides and Providence abides:

Then he lifted his voice and sang:

God lifts me high on Glory's rock,
decks me with jade and ligure.
My sire is Splendour, Beauty my dam,
Renown my paramour.
On Kingship's bow my hands are sure,
sure as my name is Ashur.

Then Baghdad spoke, saying: Behold the kingdom blest, the best of East and West. Other lands, compared with me, are a drop in the sea. I am sister to God's Holy City. When God's hand drove His holy people from their Holy Land sans pity, I gathered, shaded them, I gave them rest, I pressed them to my pitying breast and ever since I prized them: I have not abhorred them or despised them. And my soil has given rise to hosts of the wise, towers of the Talmud who lit Wisdom's skies.

Then he lifted his voice and sang:

Behold Time's crown, fair Babylon,
then travel the earth, fly hither and yon:

sheaves stood thick and tall, Zova's towered above them all Gen. 37: 7.

God lifts me high on Glory's rock Ps. 27: 5.

lands, compared with me, are a drop in the sea Isa. 40: 15.

I have not abhorred them or despised them Lev. 26: 44.

Find crows and buzzards, rooks and daws;
turn back—and gasp at Beauty's swan.
Here dwelled God's sages; here dwelled, as well,
the glory of God—and here lingers on.

SAID THE TELLER OF THE TALE:

Now when he had finished his recital, winning anew the title of prince of Song, I cried, How strong your speech and sweet! How meet! How bright your wine, how spiced your meat! May your wisdom ever find increase; God robe you with His canopy of peace! Thereat he blessed me, turned away, and went his way.

How bright your wine, how spiced your meat [Prov. 9: 5].

God robe you with His canopy of peace *Hashkivenu* prayer of the evening service (Hertz, *Authorised Daily Prayer Book*, 313).

GATE FORTY-EIGHT

The Heart's Grief and Relief

THUS SPOKE HEMAN THE EZRAHITE: Time's true and faithful Dart pricked me to the heart and laid me in sickbed where scarce I slept but ever wept, there where the king's prisoners are kept. For days on end my friends wept rain as I lay gripped with pain no doctor could explain. Then my companions all, great and small, bid me seek Gilead's healing balm for my good and calm. Desperate and spent, to Gilead I went, arriving in that blest land so weak I scarce could stand.

As I dragged through that dazzling city I spied a greybeard self-possessed and richly dressed seated on a pillar high against the sky. Now when I came questioning nigh, I was told that he was a rare physician: he cured the broken-hearted—at no fee!—of their condition. At that very instant a red-eyed fellow came before him; weeping, he began to implore him:

Alas, my lord, your servant is smitten of the sword. I have contended with warring bands, men with death-dealing hands. I was struck by a first and then a second arrow that sought and sucked my very marrow. Now that warrior whose arrows sluiced my heart and split me near apart—he holds my cure, my Physic sure; but the more I roar in pain, he laughs the more. I groan, I plead, I cry; he grants me no balm, he makes no reply. Now I have heard tell that yours are instrument and spell can make men well; that you turn raw flesh fresh and the sick, quick; that yours is poultice and plaster can reverse disaster. Extend then to your servant your healing rod and cure me, for the love of God!

where the king's prisoners are kept Gen. 39: 20.
Gilead's healing balm Jer. 8: 22.
I cry . . . he makes no reply Isa. 46: 7.
Extend then to your servant your healing rod Esther 4: 11, 5: 2, 8: 4.

The doctor answered, Sir: if you come to test me, to riddle me and best me—I have no time to play with you. Away with you! Speak clearly and sincerely; then I shall speedily accede, heed your cry, and meet your need.

The man answered, By Almighty God, before whose Throne I tremble, I shall not veil my meaning or dissemble! I entered hard upon the field of Love, not field of targe and mailed glove. I fought soft-tongued gazelles, not warriors with their yawps and yells. I was struck by swords of the eyes, not blades girt on thighs. Brows' arrows caused my woes, not bows'. Flames sprung from fair lads' hearts in fits and starts have seared my inner parts.

Now one of these youths drew his eyebrow and sent an arrow rushing forth, that the blood of my liver came gushing forth. Then, beneath his ravening eyes' bright banner he treated my heart in the same manner, leaving me, lo, these many days adrift in pain's maze, cheeks hot and red, heart throbbing, as well my head, turning and moaning and burning and groaning abed.

Now that young stag whose eyes have left my heart a tattered rag—my cure is his to command, firm in his hand. He, however, scoffs, leers, laughs at my tears, and frolics in my fears. But I have heard it said of you that in your quiver lies healing for the love-cleft liver.

Then, waxing poetic, he cried:

Succour! I cry with swollen eye;
the foe comes nigh and I lack all shield.
Shall I expire within your sight
great doctor, 'fore whom all ailments yield?
Unless you extend a pitying hand
I shall not live to leave the field.
I pant, I sigh, I bleed, I die—
heal me, my lord, and I shall be healed!

Now when the physician had heard this speech and song he

you come to test me, to riddle me 1 Kgs. 10: 1; 2 Chr. 9: 1.
Away with you Exod. 10: 28.
targe Shield.
beneath his ravening eyes' bright banner [S. of S. 2: 4].
heal me, my lord, and I shall be healed Jer. 17: 14.

laughed loud and long. Fear not, said he, I shall tender you a double prescription that shall rid you of your malediction and sore affliction. I suggest you take the first, by far the best, and gain thereby sure cure and rest. However, if you find it inexpedient, lacking this or that ingredient, down the second solution and stay the grave's dissolution.

*S*o then: we are begun! Prescription number one: take two sprigs of tender Companionship with a half-vial of spiced Fellowship; blend with concentrate of the lips' rose and dilations of the vapours of the nose; mix swiftly—do not rest—and promptly add a touch of eyes' sheen and down of the breast. Add fragrance of lissom limbs swaying in love's breeze, and the sweet pungence of thighs and of the flesh behind the knees. Meld thereto extract of the teeth's pearly white, the hands' softness, and the lips' delight. All these ground fine, mix with the mouth's wine, and sprinkle generously with essence of eyebrow and true-tongue-in-cheek. Take this Physic not for a day or a week or a month, but pursue it indefinite as a daily rite, morning, noon, and night; and, with God's help, all shall be set right.

*I*f, however, the above be beyond your cost and you see that your heart is tempest-tossed and near lost—take a spray of hot Expectation and the rue of Deprivation with the gall of endless Anticipation, plus the bine of Pain and the foliole of Disdain. Beg or borrow the spoon of Sorrow and mix with these herbs the fruit of Separation, bracts of Wrath and Trepidation, the buds of Care and Tribulation, the horns of Agitation, the roots of Discontent, the shoots of Lament, the leaf of Grief, the moss of Loss, the seed of Need, the sprout of Doubt, the bloom of Gloom, and the sage of Rage.

*T*o these add Misery's folia—any variety—and pound with the pestle of Anxiety. Pour thereon one litre of tears laced with the heart's fears and season with a vinaigrette of Sighing and Regret. Pour into an endless pot of Joy Forgot and heat on a high, smoking fire of Constant Desire. Preserve this elixir in a well-washed jug and drink it in Patience' mug—for years at least. Make it your daily feast until, with God's help, your pain has ceased.

morning, noon, and night A reference to the three daily weekday services.

SAID THE TELLER OF THE TALE:

Leaving the doctor, I followed close upon his track, right behind his back. Turning, he saw my look of awe—my shining eyes and hanging lower jaw. Said he:

I am Hever, your friend, your dearest friend;
to the world's far ends I win.
Should you wish to know me, turn to your heart
and find me fast within.

Before his words had echoed, he had left. Bereft, I sought him but found him not. Undone, I called—but answer gave he none.

I followed close upon his track Lit. 'Leaving the doctor's presence, I hurried after him'. On the ambiguity of the Hebrew see Analysis n. 16.

I sought him but found him not. Undone, I called—but answer gave he none S. of S. 5: 6.

GATE FORTY-NINE

In Praise of the Fruits of the Garden Trees

THUS SPOKE HEMAN THE EZRAHITE: When I was a stag afire, ripe with desire, Pleasure my mother and Yearning my sire, I longed to revel in flowery glades and forage in garden shades. So early one morning before dawn broke, before the yawning sun awoke, I set out for pleasure's cove, some shady grove would grace me with the song of Love, when morning's breeze seized my knees, lisping Love's mysteries.

Accept, I heard, my sweet increase, the soft release of peace. My temple beckons—near it, for I would grace you with Love's spirit. Now that my early sun has sweetly caught you, behold me, first fruits in hand—long have I sought you. Taste now the garden riches I have wrought you; take, I pray you, the blessing I have brought you. Enter my green home, pass beneath my gable; come, you who thirst, drink as you are able, dine at my table; I bring you dew of dream and fable. Your foot will not stumble, I shall gently lift you; I shall betroth you and richly gift you.

Joyed at that which I had heard, buoyed by her word, I instructed my heart, Turn now to leaf and fern, test the truth of her report, see if she lead you to Rapture's court.

Then Felicity's springs down-spilled, for what the wind promised she fulfilled: soon I was chambered where sweet leaves chimed and lush vines climbed, where glistening drops of dew kissed knops and blossoms fresh and new, where Time wore a gown of silk green weave, rose at the hem and lilies at the sleeve, as sweet attire as mind could conceive or eye perceive.

first fruits in hand Deut. 26: 2, 10.
take, I pray you, the blessing I have brought you [Gen. 33: 11].
come, you who thirst [Isa. 55: 1].
Your foot will not stumble [Ps. 121: 3].
I shall betroth you Hos. 2: 21.

Then he lifted his voice and sang:

Candles, not buds, bedeck the trees:
the wood turns carnadine.
White snuffer clouds would put them out
but they the brighter shine.

And through the grasses of that Fairyland fanned streams and channels generous as a lover's hand strewing beads of silver, strand upon strand.

Then the poet spoke, singing:

Ivory streams stroke beds of fire
like tears a lover's hand
As singing falls come tumbling down—
beads in a silver strand.

And abutting streams and springs rose columns of ivory, bright as Morn's wings; and sprinkled through this watery confluence lay fragrant aloe tents; and furthering the play of light and shade, many a marble colonnade twined with green bowers, giving to gently rising towers with frescoed rooms whose walls gave back the gardens' blooms; while without ran many a channel flower-dressed, the garden's true *beau geste* to greet each noble guest—vest of violet and lily's crest, gentle shrubs with spicy toppings blest; and apple trees unknown in east or west, with fruits fragrant-pink as a virgin's breast.

Then he lifted his voice and sang:

Speed to the apple orchard's myrrh
and seize your portion sweet.
Here is the fruit of the knowledge of Joy:
eat, friends and lovers, eat.

And then I came upon a stand of pomegranate/*rimon*, each crowned fruit ruddy upon his throne like David in Hebron. Balm for Pain's groan, salve for Woe's moan, these sapphires habit Beauty's

the fruit of the knowledge [Gen. 2: 17].
eat, friends and lovers, eat [S. of S. 5: 1].
upon his throne like David in Hebron [2 Sam. 2: 1–4]. Before being crowned king over all of Israel, David was first crowned king over the tribe of Judah.

torrid zone: within find Beauty richly grown—succulent, lush, the tongue's cologne, flowing scarlet like the waters of Dimon, aglow with the dew of Mount Hermon. Crimson as youth caught in love's embraces, they blush, they flush, near-drown in the blood that rushes to their faces.

Then he lifted his voice and sang:

The winds intone, Behold the rimon
with grace and joy begirt;
Now seize the gold bells, the rimonim,
that fringed the High Priest's skirt.

And alongside them stood a stand of fair nut trees, nutant and lissom in dawn's breeze, green clad above and beneath and a joy to tongue and teeth, each nut fair-formed, a youth to Beauty wed, yet coarse and ill-bred: you may plead for his generosity till your face turn red; never will your fortune be sped until you smite the miser, plant the tent peg deep within his head.

Then I lifted my voice:

Nuts are prosp'rous, but understand:
none be stingier in the land.
Suppliants, finding them stiff-necked and proud,
must strike them with a mighty hand.

Thereby stood a grove of tall palm trees asway in the music of morning's breeze, smooth roes that took their ease in Love's soft reveries.

Then I lifted my voice:

I said in my heart, let me climb the palm
whose taste is bliss and whose smell is balm.
You who seek Heaven's largesse—approach,
and sate your soul with towering calm.

flowing scarlet like the waters of Dimon Isa. 15: 9.

the dew of Mount Hermon Ps. 133: 3.

the gold bells, the *rimonim* . . . skirt Exod. 28: 34, where *rimonim* denotes gold bells.

plant the tent peg deep within his head Judg. 4: 21.

stiff-necked and proud As in Jer. 19: 15 and elsewhere.

I said in my heart, let me climb the palm S. of S. 7: 9.

Opposite them stood thick, twined vines where the sun-drenched daughter of the grape reclines. Happy the tongue can drink her kiss: the garden yields no higher bliss.

Then I lifted my voice:

Well Solomon seized on the grape to body
Love's passioned, gloried lustre:
The smell of your nose is like apples, said he,
your breasts are the vine's rich cluster.

Alongside them glowed moist figs in ripeness' flush. Blood leaps to the nostrils at their perfume's gush, calling for crush of teeth and the tongue's wet brush.

Then he declared, singing:

Figs, are you stol'n from gazelles' moist lips
or from gardens of ripe breasts plucked?
Let figs be the wet-nurse, our mouths the babes:
ah, wondrous the milk we have sucked!

And round about them comely almond trees sporting at Beauty's knees, housing saffron and nard; and, though their backs be hard, yet their hearts are supple: in their hid chambers scent and nurture couple. Then, with staff thick and stout, smash those barred chambers in joyous shout, that those hid beauties come spilling out.

Then I lifted my voice:

Almond: all men desire your kiss
so lush, so fragrance-laden,
You who sequester sweet, pulsing fruit,
rich emblem of the maiden!

Now midst all these lay garden beds with Beauty's wreaths, there where the aster sighs and the lily softly breathes, there where Joy springs ever new, moistening the breeze with kisses of dew.

Then I lifted my voice:

The garden beds are the fairest lines
yet traced in Spring's parenthesis,

The smell of your nose is like apples [S. of S. 7: 9].

your breasts are the the vine's rich cluster [S. of S. 7: 8].

Writ large with petals and tears of dew
the which the breezes gently kiss.
Here thrives the Vine's daughter whose death is my life:
the hour of her grief is the hour of my bliss.

Now in the midst of that flower-drenched lawn sat a high-born maid, Love's very fawn, whose tresses were night but whose cheek was dawn. Moon-pure and fair beyond compare, she held a harp which she gently pressed against her bosom and soft caressed as though it were an infant sucking her breast.

Then I lifted my voice:

Her ivory fingers against the strings
are running water or leaping harts.
She nurses the lyre upon her breast,
she strums, she thrums, and Woe departs;
Then murmurs, trills, raises her brows
and devastates a hundred hearts.
The raging fire of her desire
cleaves flesh as the torch clove Abram's parts.

Before her flowed the Red Sea waters—the blood of the grape's daughters, whose waves the fleets of sorrow rive. Here the faint-hearted plunge and thrive; here Heaven urges the grief-smit, Sip, revive! Bathe here, dead spirits, till you come alive.

So I lifted my voice:

Fire it is, but flameless sweet;
shameless, but blameless, and rich perfumed.
The wine-filled cup is a burning bush
that is ever afire and ever consumed.

Now before that fragrant wood stood choicest youths, the eyes' delight, who, with their light, set sun and moon and stars to flight, and

Love's very fawn Prov. 5: 19.
Moon-pure S. of S. 6: 10.
fire of her desire cleaves flesh as the torch clove Abram's parts Gen 15: 10–17—the sacrificial covenant between God and the patriarch Abraham.
a burning bush that is ever afire and ever consumed Exod. 3: 2.

climbed, with poets' silver tongues, high Wisdom's rungs. They leapt like deer on Discernment's mountain and slaked their thirst at Wisdom's fountain.

Now as I approached this gathering of the wise, they rushed forward to greet me with eager tongues and eyes. Come in peace, they cried, though we do not know you. Whence come you and where go you?

Spain, I answered, is the land of my birth; and I have set my feet toward the fairest land on earth. They replied: High singer, blest be your track. May your body prosper and your soul know no lack.

Then they set me a place among the honoured guests and lo, they were a prophet band who housed the father of songs and gests, Hever the Kenite, who sprang to his feet and faced me, fell on my neck, kissed me, and embraced me, crying to his fellows, You are joyous blest; only now have you come to your inheritance and rest.

One loving month we revelled, hart with hart: I plucked their lips' fruits and fed them to my hungry heart until Time's lash made our spirits smart: he drew his ever-turning sword and drove us far apart.

climbed . . . high Wisdom's rungs [Gen. 28: 12].

They leapt like deer on Discernment's Mountain [S. of S. 2: 17, 8: 14].

the fairest land i.e. the land of Israel: Dan. 11: 16, 41.

they set me a place among the honoured guests 1 Sam. 9: 22.

they were a prophet band 1 Sam. 10: 5, 10.

fell on my neck, kissed me Gen. 33: 4.

only now have you come to your inheritance and rest Deut. 12: 9.

ever-turning sword [Gen. 3: 24].

GATE FIFTY

Varia and Nefaria

THUS SPOKE HEMAN THE EZRAHITE: These are the words of Hever the Kenite, who spoke to me, saying:

One day among the scribes of Jabez, in the land of Thebez, I sucked on Poesy's ripe dates: seeing a mighty crush at the city gates, I mused, What have we here? and, drawing near, found—happy sight!—a noble company whose speech flamed bright; yes, brighter than the bush that summoned Moses. From the hotbeds of their intellects sprang scarlet roses, tropes fresh and true, glistening with saving dew; this as they rose to test each other, brother fronting brother.

Seeing their wit so brightly displayed, seeing them so rightly arrayed for Poesy's list, I gloved my fists, determined to contest them all and best them all, declaring:

Hear me, men of discerning, you with innards burning to own Learning; you with hearts refined, who would put Error far behind. Wisdom's peers, attend, lend me your ears, for I am he whose intellect dries streams and rills, who shakes the everlasting hills, he at whose word Song's rock spills water. Wisdom is my sister, Sapience my daughter; wherefore in Poesy's wars I give no quarter. Now if there be any here would deny me or defy me—let him step forward and try me.

The leader of the assembly answered, How shall your strength be known, your valour shown? Shall we bend submissive before a

Jabez 1 Chr. 2: 55.
Thebez Judg. 9: 50.
the bush that summoned Moses [Exod. 3: 1–3].
Hear me, men of discerning Job 34: 10.
who shakes the everlasting hills [Hab. 3: 6].
at whose word Song's rock spills water Num. 20: 8–11.
Wisdom is my sister [Prov. 7: 4].
How shall your strength be known Judg. 16: 6, 15.

rhymed missive? What do you propose? How shall you your wit disclose—in measured verse or in rhymed prose?

*T*hereat I replied, Both skills has Heaven bountifully assigned me, such that I leave all men behind me; yet seek me and you shall find me.

*W*ell, then, said he, shine forth your beams: sing the songs you have composed on many and sundry themes.

I answered, I shall nothing hide. Stand aside open-eyed, as I mount and singing ride the highway leading back from sin. Lo, I begin:

Lord, be not distant: my vessel sinks,
I cannot reach the shore.
The waters of sin rise fast to my chin,
the winds of judgement roar.
God, quell my fears, dry my tears; let the sin
of Judah be writ no more.

*T*hese lines show our beacon in Exile's fog, the synagogue:

Draw nigh, O hidden God, we cry
with streaming eye and bended knee.
High Lord, revealed and yet concealed,
we toss and moan like a swollen sea.
What frame, what line dare seek confine
Thy majesty and mystery?
Yet these spare walls recall the halls
where Levites offered praise to Thee.
Here turn Thy heart and eyes, for here
our hearts and eyes are turned to Thee.

*T*his I wrote coming from Egypt to Jerusalem:

Salem, shalom! *O city of peace,*
where is the glory of yesteryear?

seek me and you shall find me [Isa. 55: 6].
I mount and singing ride [Isa. 55: 6].
Lord, be not distant Ps. 22: 12.
let the sin of Judah be writ no more Jer. 17: 1.
Here turn Thy heart and eyes 1 Kgs. 9: 3.
This I wrote coming from Egypt to Jerusalem This poem is a variant of Heman's poem in Gate 28.
Salem, *shalom!* O city of peace Ps. 122: 6.

With aching fingers I sift your dust,
my sweetest torment and bitt'rest cheer.
Seeing, in thought, your former might
my eyes flow streams, while my hope is sere.
The Shulamite weeps her Love long gone:
Return, Beloved, and dry my tear.
May He who kissed her from Sinai's peak
proclaim once more, Sweet bride, draw near!

This I wrote after fever had sickened me but God quickened me:

Mercy my Lord:
my flesh and my bones
want healing oil.
Take me not up
in the midst of my days;
pity my toil.
Wealth I ask not.
Give me the soul,
take Thou the spoil.

This I wrote for a godly man, piety's shield and sword, gone to his reward:

You sinned not—
yet, remorseful for sin,
refused to eat.
You planted, and rogues:
they toiled in vain;
your fruits were sweet.
Then rise, blest soul,
redeemed from the Pit:
sit at God's feet.

The Shulamite [S. of S. 7: 1].
dry my tear Isa. 25: 8.
May He who kissed her from Sinai's peak [S. of S. 1: 2, *Song of Songs Rabbah*].
Take me not up in the midst of my days Ps. 102: 25.
Give me the soul, take Thou the spoil Gen. 14: 21.
Then rise, blest soul, redeemed from the Pit Ps. 86: 13.
sit at God's feet [Exod. 24: 9–11].

This I wrote on blest, firm ground, having been near-drowned:

Who, Lord, am I, and what is my life,
that You chose to deliver me?
You planted my feet in Zion's gates,
set soul and body free.
I bring them back from Bashan, saith the Lord,
yea, from the depths of the sea.

Across mountain and wave I sent these lines to Ezekiel's grave:

Oh, to engrave these my words on your grave,
to fly across barrier lands,
Ezekiel, thundering prophet of God,
lauded by angel bands.
Grieving, I vision my palms filled with jewels
brought forth from your wondrous sands,
I picture me breathing your incense and myrrh
till I shout, as my spirit expands,
You have given me joy in Your works, O Lord,
I shall sing of the work of Your hands.

Penitence led me to inscribe these lines for the grave of Ezra the Scribe:

The lame, the blind, the mute, the weak
all stream to this holy shrine
Where the light of Creation leaps to the stars:
Oh, Lord, what wonders Thine!
You, thirsty for healing, drink from this font;
delve, traveller, from this mine

This I wrote on blest, firm ground, having been near-drowned This poem relates to Heman's brush with death in Gate 15.

Who, Lord, am I 1 Sam. 18: 18.

and what is my life [1 Sam. 18: 18].

You planted my feet in Zion's gates [Ps. 122: 2].

I bring them back from Bashan, saith the Lord, yea, from the depths of the sea [Ps. 68: 23].

Across mountain and wave I sent these lines to Ezekiel's grave This poem and the next are variants on the poems of Gate 35.

You have given me joy in Your works, O Lord, I shall sing of the work of Your hands [Ps. 92: 5].

Oh, Lord, what wonders Thine! Ps. 9: 2.

You, thirsty for healing, drink [Isa. 55: 1].

Where the glory of Heaven seeks earth like dew,
opening the eyes of the blind.
Praise Ezra the prophet, ezra betsarot/
Aid in Woe, our wonder and sign.

This I wrote of one who penned a vicious text, warped and circumflexed, assailing Maimonides' *Guide of the Perplexed*:

This fool is but a goat can kick and butt:
let lips that slander righteous men be shut.

I took another shot at the aforesaid sot:

Ensconced in his home, the coward belabours
his wife with his prattle;
But see his bare buttocks in furious flight
on the field of battle.

For our teacher Moses I penned this hymn and from Spain sent it him:

Great prince, by men's praise of your ways
we are raised and renowned.
Through your word and your deed we succeed:
your bright thought girds us round.
For your sake the Lord God fashioned man
from the dust of the ground.

The above I reversed and malfeasors cursed:

Alas for these villains, whose profitless
actions abound.
They are doddering oxen, whose minds
the least thought would confound.
Not for them the Lord God fashioned man
from the dust of the ground.

---

opening the eyes of the blind [Isa. 35: 5].
***ezra betsarot*/Aid in Woe** Ps. 46: 2.
wonder and sign Deut. 38: 46.
let lips that slander righteous men be shut Ps. 31: 19.
For your sake the Lord God fashioned man from the dust of the ground [Gen. 2: 7]. Lit. 'God said, "Let us make man in our image and in our likeness"' (Gen. 1: 26)—echoing *Lev. Rabbah* 36: 4, stating that heaven and earth were created only for Moses' sake.

I wrote this report of a judge who is blessing's best resort, Egypt's Rabbi Menaḥem son of Isaac, Virtue's bay and port, the widow's stay and the poor man's support; happy the plaintiff who stands in his court.

So generous are his flowing palms
that the Nile cries in envy, Outrageous!
Ah, would the niggardly hands of the East
touch yours, that your gift prove contagious:
The iron-tight fists of Zova would gush,
its tight cowards would turn courageous.

*W*hile in Jerusalem I wrote these lines praising the late revered Rabbi Abraham ben Moses ben Maimon, and sent them down to No-Amon:

Count Probity, master of masters,
Abraham's slave—
Abraham, lifted to heaven
on Fame's high wave;
Abraham, taken for ever:
my soul, be brave.

*T*his ditty I made of a girl who dismayed her father and her tutor by lying with an ardent suitor:

This pampered dove,
for all her
education,
Could not decline
the intensive
conjugation.

*T*his I wrote to describe grease on gutter grates, one of Time's foremost reprobates:

Abraham ben Moses ben Maimon Leader of the Egyptian Jewish community and religious philosopher. See *EJ* ii. 150–2.

Abraham's slave Gen. 24: 34, 52, 59.

intensive conjugation A Hebrew (and Arabic) grammatical category, in which the middle consonant of the verbal stem is strengthened, often denoting an intensification of the action.

This miser, his palms wadded tight to all seekers,
his fist Stint's flintstone fist,
Defaces Time's face—this fright and disgrace,
this chancre, this gumboil, this cyst!

These lines I ascribed to the lips of coins of a man sprung from Stint's loins:

Despair, hungry suitors with slavering eyes,
who seek to disgrace me.
No lips but my master's can press my cool cheeks;
why harry me, chase me?
I am crushed like a bundle of myrrh to his chest;
ah, his both hands embrace me!

I sent the following token of my esteem to the academy head, the absent Rabbi Samuel son of Nissim:

O burning bush that is not consumed,
firstborn of Wisdom, of Right begot—
You dwell in deep darkness, as God in dark cloud;
my hope tuns ash while my heart burns hot.
These I recall: your light and your lore
and the flower of your love. I forget you not.

This I wrote to a deserving soul with fists like a rock—deserving of the title Laughing-stock:

Your palm is closed to outstretched palms,
O virgin true.
Would that your mother had been so tight
and spared us you.

This I wrote of a man whose greed defies analysis, a narcissist whose fist is locked in lifelong paralysis:

Stint's loins The following is the translator's freer rendering of the preceding poem.

I am crushed like a bundle of myrrh to his chest [S. of S. 1: 13].

his both hands embrace me [S. of S. 2: 6].

O burning bush that is not consumed Exod. 3: 1–3.

You dwell in deep darkness, as God in dark cloud 1 Kgs. 8: 12.

lifelong paralysis This and the following two poems are free renderings of one poem with a complex pun.

For his many sins
be his recompense myriad:
To petitioners' Ay-Ay! *he cries*
I-I-I! Period!

Growing warmer, I added these lines to the former:

He spares no coins—
then let my words
be sparse:
A gaping mouth;
a grasping fist;
an arse!

And this last blast:

Like gaunt Ali Babas they kneel at his heart's
black cave, all shaking in need.
Open! *they cry.* Open sesame! *and—*
he throws each a sesame seed.

This I wrote over the wedding of a stripling with a maid of more than threescore, rich with no end to the store.

What? Take to husband your very own child
nor wait till the fellow is grown?
Shun every mirror, avoid your own face,
lest in terror you turn to stone.
Your beauty is spare as your husband's years
and your wealth as untold as your own.

This I wrote of Stint's chief heir, a greybeard whose alms cupboard is always bare:

By refusing me help
he adheres to our Laws
(may his front teeth all rot!).
By God's writ was he told
to deny me his gold—
I had simply forgot:

rich, with no end to the store Nah. 2: 10.

The wicked man's sceptre
shall never alight
on the righteous man's lot.

This I wrote of a patron with a gushing mouth, but a hand drier than drouth:

O foremost of our silvered hands—
your praise be sung!
Brighter by far than your raving boast
is your waving tongue.
Despair not: God may yet raise you up
from your hillock of dung.

This I wrote of a man who flung open his mouth's hold, but not that of his silver and gold:

In the race for bright name your opponents are lame,
Wit's bowl and blown Rhetoric's platter:
Let others plod forward on nags of good deeds,
speed thou on the stallion of chatter.

I wrote this turn of wit for a noted hypocrite:

Look at that whoremonger raising a din,
wrapped in his prayer shawl, nose and chin;
Fair as a dovecote in noonday sun—
pure white without, pure black within.

This I wrote of a man whose open hands proved drier than Sahara sands:

I blunder sir,
I wait in vain:
You thunder, sir,
but give no rain.

The wicked man's sceptre shall never alight on the righteous man's lot Ps. 125: 3.

drouth This and the following poem expand upon a single Hebrew poem in the original.

God may yet raise you up from your hillock of dung [Ps. 113: 7].

*T*his I wrote of a Calnite whom I praised, but who then took flight to Haran, where he hid from my sight:

A font of corruption, a pillar of filth,
a trashbin, a turd, a slop-pail;
I polished his name in two tongues, till his fame
turned an anthem o'er hill and o'er dale.
Thereafter I came for my fee, but was told
that the ship of my hope had set sail.
But flee he as far as the depths of the sea
my pen holds his name in Shame's gaol;
Though my prey fled his cat, the latter was quick:
the rat gained his hole less a tail.

I wrote this concerning a living farce, a donkey rhymester and a monkey's arse, Villainy's tongue and throat, a curst fool by the name of Blessing/Berakhot:

Wide fling the windows the moment this scribbler
makes trespass upon the room:
He passes wind, calls it a song,
then wafts it like perfume.
His father fathered a host of sins,
his mother was Evil's womb.
Dead both, they leave the world their son—
a pox, a scab, a rheum.
Beware! He is passing lines again!
No—worse! Arggh—fetch the broom!

*T*his I wrote of that same Curses/Kelalot, who graced me with the curst child of his pen and on the morrow took it back again:

So swift he reclaims his foul gift
you would think him a comet,
This vice-ridden, lice-ridden cur
dashing back to his vomit.

But flee he as far as the depths of the sea [Amos 9:3].

I wrote this . . . Blessing/Berakhot The poem appears in precisely the same words in Gate 18.

cur dashing back to his vomit Prov. 26:11.

This I wrote of a field of promises turned barren, a very Ruse of Sharon:

Behold my love, exceeding keen,
a thorn among the roses:
Last in the ranks of turned-out purses,
first in turned-up noses.

I tendered this to a noted miser who subsequently turned none the wiser:

You cannot conceal your stingy soul,
your flesh belies all your lies:
Greed is a sign, sir, upon your hand
and a frontlet between your eyes.

This I wrote of the delectation of wine's fermentation:

Steep it and keep it
as long as you can:
The greater the pleasure
for God and for man.

More on wine:

The son of the vine plays the traitor, my friends,
my downfall is cunningly sped:
Deftly he slips past the gates of my lips,
then steals to my throat with soft tread;
Before I can rally he binds up my heart,
then rises to conquer my head.

This I wrote to the Daughter of the Vine, whose love I now resign:

O traitor girl who stole my heart
in starts and fits,

Ruse of Sharon [S. of S. 2: 1].
a thorn among the roses [S. of S. 2: 1].
sign, sir, upon your hand and a frontlet between your eyes Exod. 13: 16.
The greater the pleasure for God and for man Judg. 9: 13.
now resign The following poem is a variant translation of the preceding poem.

Too high the cost for the love I lost
on your fulsome teats:
I bade you remove my grief far off,
but you took my wits.

This I wrote of a young gazelle who plucked my heart and kept it well:

This Joseph hath my ribcage cleft,
lifted my heart and swiftly left.
I grovel, the tail of a Q: he towers—
a serif of capital J. Bereft
And fired, I leap to his lips, wrest fruit,
yes, pluck and suck till no juice be left;
But the sun of his cheek has revealed me—alas,
I am sold, lacking means to make good the theft.

This I wrote of the eyes of a gentle deer that filled me with fear:

The bowstrings of his eyes are taut:
my flesh is a-tremble, as well my thought.
My love for a youth has laid down a net
wherein the bird, my soul, is caught
And is forced to sing loud for his new lord's delight,
Great are the things our Lord hath wrought.

More on desire:

A lover, roaming the river's banks
to moan and pine,
Sees a maiden washing her lover's cloak
(Ah! would it were mine!).
He groans as the cloth is raised to her lips—
oh, kiss divine!
Even thus will the drunkard drink straight to the lees,
so honouring the wine.

the sun of his cheek has revealed me—alas, I am sold, lacking means to make good the theft Exod. 22: 2.

filled me with fear The following poem recalls the plight of the patient in Gate 48.

a net wherein the bird, my soul, is caught Prov. 6: 5.

Great are the things our Lord hath wrought [Ps. 111: 2].

This I wrote of tears sprung from the fire of Desire:

Deep, deep in my heart I sequester Desire
but tears show my lust like a wind-filled sail:
By Naḥal Amanah *my heart tents—Faith's Stream;*
but my eye by the Font of the Spy, Ein-Rogel.

This I wrote to tell how tears betray one's griefs and fears:

My secret, long locked within my heart,
is untimely bared; my honour is rent:
My telltale tears have rushed to my eyes
to show me naked within my tent.

This I wrote to deplore a Greek woman who could read the Torah—but was an arrant whore:

Most keen and cunning, of Lilith taught,
hers is a path obscene.
Tehorah *is her name, meaning Pure, on which*
see Ezekiel 24, verse 13.

I composed this rhyme for a foremost writer of our time, who penned a work sublime:

Beacon, we summon you: rise and rule;
command, for none shall resist.
Kiss our hot brow with your love and your truth,
you by God's Presence kissed.
Tower of Honour, be you our king,
a prince of the Lord in our midst.

This I wrote about a tight-fisted prince much put out over the effects of a drought:

by *Naḥal Amanah* my heart tents—Faith's Stream 2 Kgs. 5: 12.
the Font of the Spy, *Ein-Rogel* Josh. 15: 7.
to show me naked within my tent Gen. 9: 21.
arrant whore This and the following poem represent two poems on the same woman in the Hebrew.
***Tehorah* is her name . . . verse 13** [Ezek. 24: 13] 'For your vile impurity—because I sought to cleanse you (*tihartikh*) of your impurity, but you would not be cleansed (*tahart*)—you shall never be clean (*tithari*) again until I have satisfied my fury upon you.'
a prince of the Lord in our midst Gen. 23: 6.

My prince, nasi*: when clouds,* nesi'im,
hold waters from your land,
Be not surprised: your name they bear—
their conduct is taught of your hand.

More on this venality, this failed liberality:

Sir, are your coin clouds constipate—
or have we sinned?
We groan, we moan—you pass
us naught but wind.

This I wrote of the wise Rabbi Joseph, our Western Light, when I journeyed to Zova from the Land of Delight:

Above the flood's waters rise peaks of hope;
the downpour of tears has ceased:
In your banquet heart sings our Holy Tongue,
and Arabic joins the feast.
O scholar and leader, prince of the West,
and prophet in the East—
Aram Zova this day is the shrine of our God
where you serve as our loved High Priest.

This prayer I wrote of a community who denied all petitioners with impunity:

Cleanse Calneh of her hoarded gold
strip every pocket.
Empty every bulging chest
of coin and locket.
Call Ruin; build his palace there,
beam by socket.

This I wrote of Adinah—a glory in her prime, but now a pit of slime:

failed liberality This poem is the translator's expansion on the previous poem.
Above the flood's waters rise peaks of hope; the downpour of tears has ceased [Gen. 8: 1–5].

Lower than low are Adinah's swarm—
the bug, the slug, the worm, the roach.
All mine the right to expose their blight:
let none contend, let none encroach.
Giving is Sinai in all of their eyes;
to wit, not one of them dare approach.
Once holy jewel, now wholly stool;
now Stint's dull shield, who were Giving's brooch.
A curse on their coffers that offer us naught—
no help, no profit, but shame and reproach!

This I wrote to describe a man tight-fisted to ferocity, who held himself a prince of Generosity:

None nobler in his own bright eyes
but in eyes of others, sadder.
He shall soar, like an angel, to fame's white height
when a donkey can climb a ladder.

This I wrote of men of little sense who were so dense that when I praised them they took offence:

I set down lines that nothing lacked
for men who lacked all wit,
Men fit for the insult that they read
but for praise in no way fit.
Anoint them with oil, they shrivel and die,
but thrive when anointed with——.

This I wrote for a noble foe of thrift who gifted me richly and on the next day doubled the gift:

His fingers, outstretched to supplicants,
are lush vines on a golden trellis.

Sinai in all of their eyes; to wit, not one of them dare approach [Exod. 19: 11–23].
brooch Lance, spear, or bodkin.
no help, no profit, but shame and reproach Isa. 30: 5.
like an angel, to fame's white height when a donkey can climb a ladder Gen. 28: 12.
Anoint them with oil 2 Sam. 1: 21.

His right hand spills coin; his left hand sees,
and surpasses it, being jealous.

I wrote these verses for Hiya, king of Spain's streaming purses:

Countrymen, come, seize lyres and strum,
sound the drum for bright Hiya, and fife.
Hungry for justice, he dowries the poor,
while taking fair Wisdom to wife.
If one should approach him entreating his soul
he would willingly offer his life.

*T*his I wrote of an adept of Love's martial arts, whose smiles were swords and whose eyes were darts:

Revenge! The sleek deer who had fled from my heart
is now singed in the fire of my bowels and my breast.
Except he had slain me with waylayers' eyes,
except he had robbed me of health and of rest
I had planted him deep by my rivers of tears,
whereat he had flourished and prospered, blest;
But for locking me out, he is locked in my ribs
and consumed of the fire devouring my chest.

*T*his I wrote concerning a man who had a maid upon whom he and his father coarsely played:

Men of feeling, weep for shame;
angels, burn with righteous flame.
A man and his father go in to the maid
to desecrate My Holy Name.

*T*his I wrote, almost at a loss, seeing a man with a turban two hundred cubits across:

What has he set on his pink, swollen head?
A cloud? An asteroid?

by my rivers of tears, whereat he had flourished and prospered Ps. 1: 3–4.
A man and his father go in to the maid to desecrate My Holy Name Amos 2: 7.
This I wrote, almost at a loss, seeing a man with a turban two hundred cubits across This poem relates to the precentor of Gate 24.

The wider to hide the little beneath:
lo, a world floats over the void.

I wrote these lines concerning a man whose bride was succulent, amorous, and flushed—but one of whose testicles was crushed:

Have at her breasts in the field of Love
and never call a truce:
Sport with your love in Love's bower, friend,
till the grass runs wet with juice.
But alas—one joy will the revels lack
for a bouncy, a merry, a jolly-day:
Your egg, I forgot, cannot be used,
having been born on a holiday!

*T*his I wrote of the leprous spread of silver over my ageing head:

Pale shrouds of white linen
white Death's last night;
So my hair, mourning youth,
dons a mantle of white.

*A*fter this fashion, I wrote with passion:

The jet-black birds
that used to light
upon my head
Have flown to nest
within my heart
instead

*T*his I wrote of my hair in my younger years, then a shield and buckler for my eyes and ears:

Decriers of my jungle vines—
pick and quibble; yes, carp and shout.
Fools! Had Elisha been blessed like me
he had never heard children cry, Baldy, out!

a world floats over the void Job 26: 7.
Your egg, I forgot, cannot be used, having been born on a holiday BT *BB* 45*a*.
Had Elisha been blessed like me he had never heard children cry, ***Baldy, out!*** 2 Kgs. 2: 23.

I took great pains to translate *The Guide of the Perplexed* for a prince of Spain, a lover of learning, Joseph by name. I sent him the work with these lines:

Peace, Wisdom's knight! In your passioned fight
for knowledge, never your spirit tire,
Though 'gainst your hand and bright command
godless and ignorant men conspire.
Here is an arbour of Wisdom's lush trees—
walk in this park to your heart's desire.
Or perhaps you would offer your heart up to God;
then here is the wood, sir, and here the fire.

*I*n the city of Calneh I wrote of a man deserving of undying shame, Hezekiah by name:

Wait for gifts from Hezekiah?
Sooner wait for the Messiah!
Vileness had all but run its course
when he revived its vital force.
Change his name from Hezekiah
to Manasseh—the pariah!

*I*n the West I penned these lines to turn a man of high degree toward the path of morality:

Seeker of Virtue, hold up your soul
to the mirror of truth, and this truth disclose:
Would you walk the world handsome? Then handsomely live:
in the garden of Virtue bloom like a rose.
But fear evil's blight: beware, take care
lest Sin enwrap you—eyes, mouth, and nose.
Bend to my wisdom and bend rivals' backs,
yes, send forth your rage and demolish your foes.

then here is the wood, sir, and here the fire Gen. 22: 7.

Hezekiah A prominent king of Judah: 2 Kgs. 18: 2 ff.

Manasseh—the pariah Reprobate king, son of Hezekiah: 2 Kgs. 20: 21, 21 f.; Jer. 15: 4; 2 Chr. 32: 33 ff.

path of morality The following poem is a variant of the second poem of Gate 9.

send forth your rage and demolish your foes Exod. 15: 7; cf. Gate 9, poem 2.

This I wrote in France of Virtue's largest stumbling-block, the Levite Yitsḥak:

Herald, ye righteous, our sires' bequeath—
Faith, the hero's shield and wreath;
Find, soul, no fairer, Heaven beneath:
bind her in love.
Measure your days by Faith's true clock,
Faith, sweetest off'ring to God, our Rock;
And this be your sign: the Levite, Yitsḥak,
has no portion thereof.

This I wrote in Tultitula, when the prince Rabbi Joseph ben Shoshan, his people's sword, went to his reward:

The year Lord Joseph died
the fountain of Virtue dried:
Departed the merciful shepherd,
woe the sheep!
Our souls bowed low, distressed.
God named the year unblest,
a year of shmitah, *full rest*
from joy and sleep.

Now some two months prior to his death, Egypt reeled under Heaven's rod: Moses went up to God. So I wrote:

Woe upon woe! Our heads are bloodied—
ah, misfortune's stones:
Moses—dead; Joseph—dead;
crumbled Israel's thrones.
The latter lies down at the former's side:
Moses takes Joseph's bones.

the Levite, Yitsḥak, has no portion thereof Deut. 12: 12.

A year of *shmitah*, full rest In the seventh year the land was to lie fallow [Deut. 15: 1–2].

Moses went up to God Exod. 19: 3.

Moses takes Joseph's bones Exod. 13: 19.

This I wrote of the world and its lust, doomed to dust:

Soul, make assize of the World's disguise:
open eyes wide and make off, afraid.
Her jet-black hair—what have you there?
That shine, that fair is doomed to fade.
My soul, have done; that false booth shun
whose searing sunlight exceeds its shade.

This for a rich bragger given to swagger:

After David—Saul;
After pride— a fall.

One Sabbath eve I was jolted awake by a flea with the fangs of a snake. Later I sang:

My nose! My eye! My butt! My thigh!
Damn this flea! Shall naught allay him?
Vengeance is mine, I shouted in pain,
no rest be mine till I richly repay him.
Sabbath or no, his blood will flow:
fingers and palms: rise up, waylay him!
Sabbath! friends hissed. How dare you track him,
whack him, thrash him, lash him, splay him?
I dare, I replied, for our sages declare:
Who seeks your blood early, rise early and slay him.

This I wrote in the month of Ramadan when, daily, Muslims fast, rising before dawn to their repast:

All who are hungry, eat, says God;
He fats the just with wine and grain.

that false booth shun whose searing sunlight exceeds its shade The festival booth of Sukkot must provide more shade than sunlight (Mishnah *Sukkah* 1: 1).

Vengeance is mine [Deut. 32: 35].

Who seeks your blood early, rise early and slay him BT *Ber.* 58*a*, *Sanh.* 72*a*. This poem recalls the description of the flea in Gate 4.

He fats the just with wine and grain [Deut. 32: 14; Ps. 63: 6].

One day a year, but one, a man
is asked to suffer hunger's pain.
Thus shall He give His beloved friends sleep:
you who rise early, you rise in vain.

These lines I set down for the great prince, Rabbi Sheshet, foremost of our altruists and philanthropists:

Time loud attests: behold Rav Sheshet,
bright keystone of Jewry, her spilling treasure:
Although his hair greys, his largesse ages not
but renews—a ripe Sarah!—in youth's sweet pleasure.

Lovers, lovely and pleasant, I tender you this present:

Two foes can fill up Aragon,
Castile and Granada, too;
Yet for a thousand lovers
a thimble's space will do.

These lines laud the folk of Lunel, whose praise I can scarcely tell:

Whose mind is an archer, can sight
on the praise of these savants? Whose mouth the bow?
Who would brighten their name one mite
would tinsel the sun with the moon's pale glow,
Gift the sea with five flagons of water;
with five fig-clusters, Jericho.

I was asked by the blest late priest, Rabbi Jonathan of Lunel, to copy well a mishnaic tractate and send it to a great shepherd of Jewry's flock, Rabbi Moses, blest be his root and stock. I did so, adding these lines:

One day a year, but one, a man is asked to suffer hunger's pain An aspect of the traditional interpretation of Lev. 16: 31, 23: 27, 32.

Thus shall He give His beloved friends sleep: you who rise early, you rise in vain Ps. 127: 2.

keystone Ps. 118: 22.

but renews—a ripe Sarah!—in youth's sweet pleasure Gen. 18: 12.

Lovers, lovely and pleasant 2 Sam. 1: 23.

with five fig-clusters, Jericho 2 Chr. 28: 15.

God show His face and shining grace
to the princes of Learning and Goodly Deeds.
Here Torah camps and lights her lamps;
here Piety pastures and Wisdom feeds.
Bear praise from this least of your serving men:
feast, God's own priest, on the tractate Seeds.

This I wrote of Rabbi Joseph of Egypt, Salvation's sun and the late revered Prince Obadiah's son:

You are sprung of Honour and Courage, prince;
of Grace and of Wisdom, too.
When God set wings on the Joys of Time,
who hither and thither flew,
He commanded: Hasten to Joseph, go,
and all that he tells you, do.

These lines I wrote when younger, racked with Desire's hunger:

Your cheeks shine sapphires, fairest of youths,
your glance a breeze my hot brow soothes.
Lips of honey softly stir,
teeth of pearls and tongue of myrrh,
Beauty's garden, Passion's prize—
ah, the feast that is giv'n my eyes!
But oh, my heart in my hot blood's swell:
eyes in Eden, heart in Hell!

This I wrote in Calneh of a certain Berakhot/Blessings by name, a bastion of sin and shame:

Princes of evil, father and son,
Morality's own castrati;
He is called Berakhot or Blessings—as soon
call the blind Illuminati.

Joseph, go, and all that he tells you, do Gen. 41: 55.
shine sapphires S. of S. 5: 14.
This I wrote in Calneh of a certain Berakhot/Blessings by name, a bastion of sin and shame Once again Alḥarizi hits a favoured target of Gates 18 and 50.

These lines I did indite concerning a pedigreed Adinite, an obscene libertine:

Bestial Adinah, where men mount men
in Lust's lists, to battle.
Why, even their oxen are twisted:
like owners, like cattle.

These lines I wrote to a nobleman wondrously harried; else, why had the wheels of his letters' chariots tarried?

Peace to the mute and the palsied love
whom this missive comes to teach:
Palsied, who pens his beloved no scroll;
mute, who denies him his speech.

This I sent from Damascus to Hamath to the physician Rabbi Moses bar Zedakah:

Forget not true friends: in the waste of your absence
they long for your waters, your sweet perfume.
O, winged cherub, wing homeward once more;
and set in Ḥadrakh ḥadrakh/*your room.*

This I wrote of the grieving soul who would be whole:

She who was nurtured 'neath Heaven's high throne
is become clay's ward.
Sped from the heights she is wed to the worm,
and the worm to Time's sword.
She pines for the day she can shuck fleshly bonds
and claim her reward,
Then shine in Light's robes, bound wondrously round
with ethereal cord.
Praise God, then, who made her for Heaven's domain:
all souls praise the Lord!

Adinite Babylonian.
why had the wheels of his letters' chariots tarried Judg. 5: 28.
O, winged cherub Ezek. 28: 14.
This I wrote of the grieving soul who would be whole This poem relates at once to the Introduction and Gate 13.
all souls praise the Lord Ps. 150: 6.

This I wrote praying God confirm the end of Exile's term:

God of our fathers, forsake us no more;
Lion of Heaven, rise and roar.
Your children, sunken in Exile's pit,
Your mercy plead, Your might implore.
Like a blind man fronting a mute, they ask,
When comes the End foretold of yore?
Forgiveness they seek these long thousand years:
love them anew and their foes abhor.
Oh, Israel restore to the Mount of Harel;
choose Jacob and set him in Salem once more.

This I wrote of synagogue visitation, to offer supplication:

To sing Thy praises morn and eve
I enter the court of Thy Holy Shrine:
Then enter the crannies and nooks of my heart,
for knowledge of that which is hid is Thine.
My heart and my hope abide in Thee:
falsehood and treachery flee the Divine.
Cast sand in the eyes of my foes that they see
not my shame; oh, trample them down like swine.
Lord, set our feet in Jerusalem's gates;
set firm Thy right hand on Thy favoured vine.

This I penned for men whose tongues gushed blessings like an ocean wave, yet whose hearts were malice, their throats an open grave:

I pray for the day when their evil holds sway
o'er their fortunes—when foulness has fenced them.

This I wrote praying God confirm the end of Exile's term This poem relates at once to Gates 22 and 28.

When comes the End foretold of yore? Dan. 5: 19 and elsewhere.

the Mount of Harel Ezek. 43: 15.

choose Jacob [Ps. 135: 4].

and set him in Salem Gen. 14: 18; Ps. 76: 3.

for knowledge of that which is hid is Thine [Deut. 29: 28].

Lord, set our feet in Jerusalem's gates [Ps. 122: 2].

set firm Thy right hand on Thy favoured vine Ps. 80: 15.

whose hearts were malice, their throats an open grave Ps. 5: 10.

How futile their arts to hide their foul hearts:
lo, their faces bear witness against them.

This on Separation, who never spared me, but ever snared me:

How long shall I roam the world like Cain,
drunk, not on wine, but the wine of pain?
Thirsting for rescue, I lift my eyes
to find black clouds and then black rain;
And Time is the wind that sears my flesh
as Wandering hawks his dry refrain.

This I wrote of pompous men whose puffed-out sails are never furled, the worst travellers of this world:

They poison the earth, then foul the sky
with a black aurora;
They preen, who would seem a garden dream,
but are rotted flora;
All vermin and weeds, they surpass the deeds
of Sodom and Gomorrah.

These lines I penned of moneyed men with flapping jaws but fingers curled, obedient to Greed's laws:

Oh, my eyes: behold men in the depths of Stint,
true brothers of Cain.
*Known as lords/*nesi'im, *they are clouds/*nesi'im
with much wind but no rain.

I wrote this of a man whom I held a brother but who, when tested, proved something other:

I thought your love a mighty knot
that bungling Time could sever not

their faces bear witness against them Isa. 3: 9.
How long shall I roam the world like Cain Gen. 4: 12.
drunk, not on wine 1 Sam. 1: 15.
I lift my eyes to find black clouds and then black rain [1 Kgs. 18: 43–5].
they surpass the deeds of Sodom and Gomorrah [Gen. 18: 20].
clouds/*nesi'im* with much wind but no rain Prov. 25: 14.

Or godly manna. Manna it proved:
it melted when the sun grew hot.

This I wrote of an addlepate who bought books by the hundredweight:

Alack his sacroiliac,
this plodding bibliomaniac,
this mule with booksacks on his back.

Herein I praised one of the elect, who showed my art proper respect:

I am crowned by a prince I have crowned with speech
that gives sight to the blind and that speeds the lame.
He sweetens my lot for words sweeter than gold,
lo: honey sprung rich from a lion's frame.

This I wrote of Rabbi Zedakah the judge, the Damascene, once ruler of Good's demesne, whose deeds his name demean:

A man set a tree in his garden,
by night and by day he watered it.
I ate of an apple that tree brought forth
and happy my mouth that savoured it.
Now passing-fair is unfairly past:
Judge, why have you your garden quit?
Yesterday's temple of Truth and Law
is turned a hillock where jackals sit.
Justice I sought, tsedakah*; but found*
tse'akah, *a cry. Alas God's Writ!*
Know that the Lord has set me a sword
of vengeance; 'ware, when my wrath is lit!
My tongue is a pitchfork, bright and honed:
giants it skewers and flings to the pit.

godly manna. Manna it proved: it melted when the sun grew hot Exod. 16: 21.

lo: honey sprung rich from a lion's frame Judg. 14: 8.

Yesterday's temple of Truth and Law is turned a hillock where jackals sit [Lam. 5: 18].

Justice I sought, *tsedakah*; but found *tse'akah*, a cry Isa. 5: 7.

a sword of vengeance [Lev. 26: 25].

I hold back for the nonce; but know: when I thunder
the triple-plate helmet of Time must split.
Whose name shall endure who attacks my name?
Whom, whom shall my ravening pen acquit?

This I wrote in Egypt for the blest late judge, Rabbi Menaḥem, concerning one whose care had sometime veiled me but whose tongue failed me:

Alas that I made me an idol
as my pagan spirit urged.
I took me base silver alloy
thinking it might be purged;
I cast it straightway to the fire
and this dumb calf emerged.

I wrote these stichs concerning passion's pricks:

The gazelle entrapped me in Beauty's arms
and fired my breast to his most cruel pleasure;
But I gave back his apple and forced him to eat;
yes, I repaid him, measure for measure:
I held up my eyes, I mirrored his flame,
and roast him now at my own sweet leisure.

This air was inspired by a singular pair:

This mother and son are naked fools,
conceit their sole regalia,
He like Aháziah, vile as lead,
she as foul as Atháliah.
Lord, send them soon to the final feast,
that earthy bacchanalia
With worms for attendants, for table, stones,
and all pertinent paraphernalia.

Alas that I made me an idol . . . and this dumb calf emerged Exod. 32: 2–4, 21–4.

he like Ahaziah, vile as lead, she as foul as Athaliah 2 Kgs. 8: 25–11: 20.

This I wrote when I heard the clamour of a caged bird:

What succour the broad, beating wing
to the eagle penned?
Even so all the wealth of this world
when man comes to his end.

This I wrote concerning a polished sword:

The sword unsheathed is a tongue of fire:
it speaks, the foeman dies.
To what may we liken it? friends enquire.
I answer, The tongue of the wise.

This I wrote urging men to live up to their station and reputation:

Rank gives no honour. Honour your rank,
then shall your pedigree joy you.
Your fathers will tell you: reap as you plant,
serve Wisdom, beg she employ you.
Do good and that good will uplift you, my child;
do evil and it shall destroy you.

This I sent to a miser who grew never the wiser:

Though the miser seek Heaven on stairways of gold,
misfortune shall cast him down felly.
He swallows his riches to vomit them up:
the Lord casts them out of his belly.

This I wrote concerning the worst of men who ploughed the fields of rapine time and again:

Beaming and fat, he grinds the weak,
he dips his loaf in the poor man's blood—
Himself to be ground in judgement's teeth,
being but an ox that chews the cud.

a polished sword Ezek. 21: 16. This poem relates to the debate between Sword and Pen in Gate 4.

Your fathers will tell you Deut. 32: 7.

He swallows his riches to vomit them up: the Lord casts them out of his belly Job 20: 15.

an ox that chews the cud Deut. 14: 6.

I wrote this in celebration of an expert at expectoration:

Take to the benches, sirs, cover your robes,
send out for rags or the cuspidor:
Behold, he returns, this fellow who reckons
God's chambers his kitchen or bathroom floor.

*T*hese lines I wrote honouring one who tendered breastplate and crowns without flaw for the Scroll of the Law:

These golden crowns are given at the hands
of the man in whom the King delights.
Their note rings out from the Holy Place
like Aaron's bells in Temple rites.
Such be the gifts of Joseph the Prince,
he who has mounted Munificence' heights:
They sing his praise to latter days,
a memorial unto the Israelites.

*T*his on sating on wine; this on mating with the daughter of the vine:

Friends, feast your gaze on my blushing mistress,
see how her lashes wetly blink.
Mature, she shines with youth's delights:
I plunge to her brimming pool and sink.
A thousand years are a day in God's sight,
an epoch—a fortnight; a day—a wink.
Oh, for a cup for a godly year,
then would I drink. And drink. And drink!

*T*his I wrote lust-laden for a nubile maiden:

At midnight, to the house of Love
my dove enticed me, in Fate's despite

the man in whom the King delights [Esther 6: 6, 9, 11].
from the Holy Place like Aaron's bells in Temple rites Exod. 28: 33–5.
a memorial unto the Israelites Exod. 30: 16.
Mature, she shines with youth's delights [Gen. 18: 12].
A thousand years are a day in God's sight Ps. 90: 4.

And loosed her veil. Oh, Abigail!
Oh, moist and full-lipped Shunamite!
She beamed: the mountains skipped like rams,
back turned the Jordan, livid in fright.
Ah me, *I moaned,* the hid is bared!
whereat her hand, a bird in flight,
Skimmed her dark tresses about my head
and brightest day turned darkest night.

On Maimonides' *Sefer hamada*/Book of Wisdom:

A tree by Wisdom's waters blooms—
no further seek for shade or fruit.
Many the books our sages wrote,
but they be branches; this is the root.

This I wrote of a notorious Jerusalemite:

Alas Mount Zion's infamy—
a leprous scourge, a spreading sore:
He spreads himself to each passer-by
and is therefore given the name, Mount Hor.

This I wrote of a man who left his wife abed and lay with his servant girl instead—Jacob his name:

You sons of Jacob, gather and hear
of a Jacob whose deeds your name defame.
His lust run wild, he has got a child
of a serving-maid who supplants his dame.

Abigail 1 Sam. 25: 3 ff.
Shunamite [1 Kgs. 1: 3–15].
the mountains skipped like rams, back turned the Jordan, livid in fright Ps. 114: 3–6.
On Maimonides' *Sefer hamada*/Book of Wisdom The initial book of Maimonides' *Mishneh torah*, wherein he discusses God and His attributes, the angels, the structure of the universe, prophets and prophecy, ethics, penitence, free will, divine providence, and the world to come (*EJ* xi. 769).
A tree by Wisdom's waters blooms Ps. 1: 3.
a leprous scourge, a spreading sore Lev. 13: 7 ff.
Mount Hor Num. 20: 25, 27.
Jacob his name Gen. 32: 28.
You sons of Jacob, gather and hear Gen. 49: 2.

The girl has borne him a female heir
with his same raw face, and foul heart the same.
Jacob, how wretched your tent: not a man
shall delight in your daughter; shame, sir, shame!

I wrote this for a daw with a head of straw:

This poem is vocalized, friend, throughout,
lest for I dunned *you read* I dined—
The better to wean it to your ways,
the better to wed it to your mind.
I have laid down its highways, set banners up,
the surer to guide your young feet, dear hind,
Remembering God's dictate: Put not a block,
no, nor stone nor stick 'fore the feet of the blind.

I wrote this of a man short on sense but otherwise immense:

Slimmer than blade in speech and thought
but in flesh a hemisphere,
A mosquito for wit, but in Fat's vast realm
the true, the sole emir.
Were he plumped in the River of Egypt—why,
the Delta would disappear;
Were he light on his feet as he is in his head,
he would overtake the deer.

*A*n Adinite jackass of singular sensibility penned the following imbecility:

Had Moses seen my neighbour's cheeks
none other can surpass
He had writ not in his Torah
Do not covet thy neighbour's ass.

*I*n a rage, I seized this miscreant's pen and assembled ten men;

Jacob, how wretched your tent [Num. 24: 5].
shall delight in your daughter Gen. 34: 19.
I have . . . banners up [Isa. 62: 10].
Adinite Baghdadian.
Put not a block, no, nor stone nor stick 'fore the feet of the blind Lev. 19: 14.
Do not covet thy neighbour's ass [Exod. 20: 17]. See Analysis.

whereon, adopting his metre and rhyme, we berated him and excommunicated him, time after time. I began, saying:

Samson for all his bravery
cannot this fool surpass
Who rushes upon the Torah
with the jawbone of an ass.

The second declared:

Lord, this firstborn of an ass
is far beyond redeeming:
Send us an angel to break his neck
and spare us his blaspheming.

The third declared:

In kindness to dumb animals
he stands above the mass,
Refusing to let a friend pass by
unless he pet his ass.

The fourth declared:

'Tis told, that of late, at public trial,
this pervert was badly shaken:
A hundred men shouted Mine! *when he asked,*
Whose ass have I ever taken?

The fifth declared:

One son of Jacob this man contemns,
finding him somewhat crass.
We refer of course to Issachar,
who was a bony ass.

Samson for all his bravery . . . with the jawbone of an ass [Judg. 15: 15].
this firstborn of an ass is far beyond redeeming: Send us an angel to break his neck [Exod. 34: 20].
Whose ass have I ever taken? [1 Sam. 12: 3].
Issachar, who was a bony ass [Gen. 49: 14].

The sixth declared:

Hola, young Jews! Know when to refuse
a proffered assignation.
Beware the disgrace of a foul embrace
that may end in as-phyxiation.

The seventh declared:

Lord spare us infection, our flesh is not iron,
nor is our forehead brass.
Remove from our midst dissension and blight,
this plague of a mule and an ass.

The eighth declared:

His hero, no doubt, is the Shunamite,
who cried o'er her son, Alas!
And then, for the saving of life and limb,
hastened and rode an ass.

The ninth declared:

Behold an ardent student of law,
which nobody, sir, denies:
Catch him attentive at every trial,
weighing each assize.

The tenth declared:

Lord, tender this fool his due reward:
a magical looking-glass
Which will shatter in fright at his loathsome sight
and thrust itself up —— ——!

These lines I wrote on turning back from Evil's rack:

our flesh is not iron, nor is our forehead brass [Isa. 48: 4].
plague of a mule and an ass [Zech. 14: 15].
the Shunamite . . . hastened and rode an ass [2 Kgs. 4: 20–4].
These lines I wrote on turning back from Evil's rack This is a variant of the first poem of Gate 9.

How long, O my soul, will you burn for the world
and her tinsel trulls that snigger?
Abandon Lust's ship, that sinking board,
and cling to the Rock with rigour.
Speed like a deer from Earth's rank pit,
that grave, with Time for digger.
Keep faith, my soul, for they who put faith
in the Lord shall renew their vigour.

This I wrote to jolt the resigned and to open the eyes of the blind:

Sleeper, how long will your eyes stay shut,
though brightly Salvation's rays have beamed?
While pagans have streamed to the truth of our God
it is you have reviled Him, defiled Him, blasphemed.
Drowsy-eyed, blowsy-eyed lie-a-bed,
deaf to your days, though long they screamed—
Your friends rise at midnight, hungry for God,
while your eyes stay shuttered. O unredeemed,
Asleep on the breast of the harlot World—
what is this dream that you have dreamed?

This I wrote on asceticism, the soul's best athleticism:

Lengthen your days in the service of God;
in the garden of Virtue, shine like the rose.
Happy that man armed with water and bread:
Appetite's armies he overthrows.
Raise the mind's altar, offer your heart,
weep till the River of Penitence flows.
Remember, your flesh and the world are chaff:
the both shall scatter when Death's wind blows.

Speed like a deer [Mishnah, *Avot* 5: 20].

they who put faith in the Lord shall renew their vigour Isa. 40: 31.

This I wrote to jolt the resigned and to open the eyes of the blind [Isa. 42: 7]. This poem is a variant of the fifth poem of Gate 9.

what is this dream that you have dreamed? Gen. 37: 10.

This I wrote on asceticism, the soul's best athleticism This poem's close is that of the second poem of Gate 9.

Lengthen your days [Exod. 20: 12 and elsewhere].

Unfold, then, the arms of Charity,
widow and orphan and stranger enclose.
Compose you your soul against the long day
when your bones and your flesh shall decompose.
Do this, and every contender down;
rise up in triumph and shatter your foes.

This I offered up in thanks to my God who spared me Wrath's rod:

How great are Your mercies, O Lord of the world;
and oh, what an ingrate and rebel I be.
My cup overflows with Your pity, the while
Sin's goblet is filled to capacity.
Never Your mercies winged out of my sight
though my virtues were dry, and my sin a sea.
When trial lay in ambush and leapt on my soul,
and bore me off whole to captivity,
You opened the coffers of Kindness and Grace;
You ransomed me, Lord, You set me free.
When I wandered a wasteland, weary and weak,
my flesh a hot incandescency,
My parched tongue fixed to the roof of my mouth,
no haven, no refuge, no canopy,
You saved me; and oft as I lauded Your gifts
the more often You favoured and gifted me.
For all of these things my soul renders thanks,
my thoughts bow their head and bend low the knee.
Remember Your pity, O Lord of lords,
forgive this low slave his obstinacy.

widow and orphan [Deut. 24: 19 and elsewhere].
rise up in triumph and shatter your foes Exod. 15: 7.
My cup overflows [Ps. 23: 5].
and bore me off whole to captivity [2 Kgs. 24: 16].
You ransomed me, Lord [Ps. 71: 23].
My parched tongue fixed to the roof of my mouth Ps. 137: 6.
bow their head and bend low the knee [*Aleinu* prayer, all three daily services].
Remember Your pity [Ps. 25: 6].
O Lord of lords Deut. 10: 17; Ps. 136: 3.

Weave the warp of my pleas with Your Kindness's woof
to make of my life a gold tapestry.
Now, water, my eyes, the slim saplings of Hope
till I eat of the Tree of God's clemency.

This I wrote of that angel shape, the daughter of the grape:

Praise the vine's daughter, all wine-soaked tongues,
best balm for pain and dole.
Through her blood shall my blood win rest and repose:
blood alone atones for the soul.

This I wrote for Rabbi Shmuel, son of the great Rabbi Nissim of Spain, and his son, God attend them and defend them:

My heart, reviewing all men of renown,
two alone to head Praise's banquet chose:
Shmuel and his son, Good's standard; all praise!
Begin with the one; with the other, close.

These further lines I penned on his son, God be his sun:

Dawn and darkness bind his brow,
a hail-and-lightning composition,
Mazhir *is his name and so is his mind:*
he gives light *to the blind with his erudition;*
God grant him the rule that his forebears owned:
be this fruit of their loins their sweet fruition.

This I wrote on the subject of desire:

God rip aside her shrouding veil—
I will not reconcile me.
Enough the fire of my Desire—
must even a veil revile me?

On Maimonides, of blessed memory:

The world's chief sages ascended the heights
and on towering summits trod;

eat of the Tree [Gen. 3: 3 ff]. **blood alone atones for the soul** Lev. 17: 11.

They conquered those peaks of wisdom—
but Moses went up to God.

This I wrote of largesse, that lifts man from distress:

Man, sow the seed of righteous deed
and reap tomorrow one-hundredfold.
Let Time shut fast the gates of good:
God holds the key to good and gold.

This I wrote of the world:

Would you sing Time's praise,
laud her twisted ways?
Spare your breath.
Man's life is a vineyard,
the reaper—Time;
the harvest—Death.

Of that which clasps all men, which grasps all men:

Mortal man:
you must drain Time's can
to the hops.
Your wealth, an oil-cruse,
will shatter like you;
the oil stops.

This I wrote for the walls of the synagogue of Ezra our lord:

God of our fathers, Your blessings pour
on Ezra, Splendour's sea and shore,
Renowned in Heaven, revered on earth,
Justice and Righteousness' guarantor.
Israel, this place is the camp of God
where Heaven throws wide its golden door.

but Moses went up to God Exod. 19: 3.
reap tomorrow one-hundredfold Gen. 26: 12.
the oil stops 2 Kgs. 4: 6.
This I wrote for the walls of the synagogue of Ezra our lord This poem relates to Gate 35.
this place is the camp of God Gen. 32: 3.

May his soul be bound in the throne of the Lord,
his dry bones quicken, his spirit soar.
At time's end may God wake him gently from sleep;
that after his death he might live once more.
May his merit defend us, his needy folk,
and silence the Ocean of Troubles' roar;
And may Judah bar Solomon merit His grace
Who yields us delights of His hand evermore.

This I wrote of a man of high estate flanked by rogue and reprobate:

Bend low the knee and sound the horn
for him whose deeds the heavens adorn.
Modest, he lives among arrogant fools
and men who, for spending of silver, mourn.
I am stunned at his dwelling, until I recall
that the Lord spoke to Moses from out of the thorn.

I wrote this further praise to laud his noble ways:

Isaac, God's chosen, has purchased my heart
with love's silver and gold, his since minority.
God's Temple he, his heart, the ark;
his angel tongue, the Law's authority.
Honoured of all, he holds himself light;
but reject a lone voice when it fronts the majority.

This commends the society of friends:

Friendship's days are honey-sweet;
dry and bitter Wandering's night.
Like souls that chafe at the bonds of flesh
my joys awake, shake wings, take flight.
Heavy my woes on the night of farewell;
the joys of the night of friendship, slight.

his dry bones quicken [Ezek. 37: 3–14].
Judah bar Solomon Judah, son of Solomon.
Who yields us delights of His hand evermore Ps. 16: 11.
that the Lord spoke to Moses from out of the thorn Exod. 3: 2.
but reject a lone voice when it fronts the majority BT *Ber.* 9*a*.

This on Desire:

Like a servant maid my soul is sold
to a sleek and heartless hart.
Would God your wrath would cease and the plague
of your wandering far depart.
Why will you torture me with your eyes,
set fires within my heart?
Fulfil the Law's mandate, pay me my hurt—
'twas you the fire did start!

In these lines I abjure a notorious noble of Ashur:

This jeering song I send a prince
unworthy of the name of Jew.
Rich were the promises he trilled;
no blessed note of them, none, rang true.
Never has such a liar been found
from Samarkand to Timbuctoo.
When asked by friends, Shall flowing hands
turn desert sands? Where is your dew?
He said: My hands clutch air, dear friends,
my purse is a sieve the wind blows through.
Daily my coins are sorely taxed;
my needs are vast, my means are few.
A youth is mine whose will is mine,
our bowered couch is ever new.
I am deep in debt to fill his cup
with food and raiment and—'hem—his due.

Done with all this toil, we made our way from Egypt's sands to holy soil. In haste we crossed a sun-seared waste, which place I called Taverah/Hot Lust, for there the barefaced sons of days debased

Fulfil the Law's mandate, pay me my hurt—'twas you the fire did start Exod. 22: 5.
Ashur Mosul, Iraq.
our bowered couch S. of S. 1: 16.
food and raiment and—'hem—his due Exod. 21: 10.
Taverah/Hot Lust Num. 11: 3.

themselves by offering up strange flame—shame, shame! Evil beset them! Curse the day that I met them!

Then on we trekked beneath the desert sun through a land of snake and seraph and scorpion—but water none; yet with tears and sweat we turned it wet: it was river-laced when we were done.

Finally, surviving Travel's straits we came to Gaza's gates: hearts in hand, we sang, we danced our praise to God who brought us cross the burning sand from heathendom to the Holy Land. On we urged, surged through Night's cold and dark on camel ark, and with dawn cried out in happy chorus, for Heaven's gates stood open, Jerusalem lay before us! Low we bowed in God's most Holy City, thanking Him for His bounteous pity; and there we stayed for thirty days, basking in Salvation's rays. Heavens, sound timbrel and fife: those days were stolen from the Tree of Life! Yet daily we would walk over tombs and stones, pitying Zion with our moans, groaning over her children's scattered bones.

After a few days, Desire bade us seek the Mount of Olives and we gained its peak; and there we prayed, yes, offered accolade to Him who Earth and Heaven made; even as, with weeping eye and muffled sigh, we looked upon the Temple court, turned the resort of pagan sport, of heathen sacrifice. We hid our eyes, we could not look upon the site where priest and folk in olden time repented, that field of glory where the Holy Presence tented, where angels hovered, now darkness-covered: nothing remained to take the proud past's part but ashes and rocks to bruise the heart.

Now after all this was past, again we bid our feet rove: we crossed the desert to Damascus which we labelled Esek/Striving, for there we strove. But oh, it joyed our eyes, that wanderer's paradise and treasure-trove, Beauty's cove, green-arboured, turquoise-flowered,

offering up strange flame Lev. 10: 1.

In haste . . . met them The reference is unknown.

a land of snake and seraph and scorpion—but water none Deut. 8: 15.

with dawn cried out in happy chorus, for Heaven's gates stood open, Jerusalem lay before us These lines and those that follow evoke Gate 28.

the Tree of Life Gen. 2: 9, 3: 22.

to Him who Earth and Heaven made [Ps. 146: 6 and elsewhere].

we labelled Esek/Striving, for there we strove Gen. 26: 20. What the text alludes to is entirely unclear.

Beauty's cove See the description of Damascus' beauty in Gate 47.

gold-turreted, and silver-towered. We bade travail cease, for here were ways of pleasantness and paths of peace—kisses of roses beyond count, and many a crystal fount flashing and leaping, laughing and weeping; meadows decked with arbours sweet and fine, and lush with orange, peach, and vine, and waves of bright shrubbery like the waters covering the sea. Eyes, look to the hills where Beauty trips, where sinuous rills twine round Damascus' hips: ho, you who are thirsty, seek these mountains' lips, whence sweetest honey drips. And the city's canals, each a proud sentry giving water entry; and ah, the fair maidens who draw Damascus' waters, Beauty's own daughters; and the white of the mountains, in summer and winter decked with snow's bright fountains.

Now this city holds a mighty congregation of our exiled nation, among them the great doctor Rabbi Moses son of Zedakah, pleasing to God, Right's lifted rod. He alone of all that city made short shrift of foolish thrift: he praised me, raised me, dowered me, and showered me with choicest gift. He alone wears the mantle of praise without reproach: while others dared not draw near to Charity, Moses alone approached.

But then, alas, I learned what travail meant; and would have found no balm for my soul's mortal ailment but that I discovered a man of Adinah named Ezra, come up from Babylon, who raised his rod over Wandering's sea and lo, Pain's waves were gone. Yes, with his sweet fraternation he dried the bitter waters of Separation. But briefly, once more, we knew tribulation: we had to leave that prince and his habitation. On we journeyed to the mine of Sweetness' lode, Virtue's gentlest abode; to wit, Aram Zova, Greatness' sphere—and in its centre, the prince without peer, model of moral fitness, the age's

ways of pleasantness and paths of peace Prov. 3: 17.

like the waters covering the sea Isa. 11: 9. The description of Damascus echoes that in Gate 47.

ho, you who are thirsty [Isa. 55: 1].

these mountains' lips, whence sweetest honey drips [Amos 9: 13].

among them the great doctor Rabbi Moses son of Zedakah The ensuing lines bear overall resemblance to the travelogue of Gate 46.

lifted rod [Exod. 14: 27].

dowered me, and showered me with choicest gift Gen. 30: 20.

while others dared not draw near to Charity, Moses alone approached Exod. 24: 2.

raised his rod over Wandering's sea and lo, Pain's waves were gone [Exod. 14: 27].

witness and sign, its guard against iniquity, righter of obliquity, and keeper of the teachings of antiquity, guide and rock, shepherd of God's flock—Joseph, governor of the land, provisioner of all the people of the land.

Then I raised my voice in song:

Fame and honour and praise vouchsafe
unto Splendour's heir, the fair Yosef.
Justice and giving, savaged by Time,
rush to his pinions and there are safe.

And so, Fate sent Judah before him unto Joseph, come eastward from the West to rise to mighty station: there he became a great and populous nation. Like the sands of the sea he gathers up corn: in Learning's wastes he sounds Torah's horn and lo, his famished people are reborn. He raises Torah's towers, her turrets he emplaces; he bathes in pure water and Sin's grief erases; he cures the poor, heals Time by his shining graces; yea, he wipes away tears from all faces; father and child he has reconciled: therefore our jewelled song his neck embraces.

Then I raised my voice in song:

Praise him whose mouth is our tongue of gold,
whose mantle of praise is wide renowned.
Happy the couch that saw him born:
happy the linen that wrapped him round.
He plundered the gems of Learning; he stole
our hearts and our souls, yet we be the more sound.
We sought him, we caught him, we searched his tent
and there both mantle and tongue were found.

Joseph, governor of the land, provisioner of all the people of the land Gen. 42: 6.

sent Judah before him unto Joseph Gen. 46: 28.

he became a great and populous nation Deut. 26: 5.

he gathers up corn Gen. 41: 48.

he bathes in pure water Lev. 14: 8 and elsewhere.

he wipes away tears from all faces Isa. 25: 8.

jewelled song his neck embraces S. of S. 1: 10.

whose mantle Josh. 7: 21.

we searched his tent Gen. 31: 33–5.

there both mantle and tongue were found Josh. 7: 24.

Then blest be God who has heard our suit and blest be the parents who have borne this fruit. Like father, like son, he is our moon, our peerless sun. Behold him chosen of the Lord, Sinai, the presence of the Lord, our splendour on earth; God alone knows his worth.

Then I raised my voice in song:

There lived in the West a hidden well
unknown to all men in an age of drought;
Then the hands of Honour made search, and sent
and called Joseph and hastily drew him out.

He is Virtue's suzerain, ruling Torah's broad domain, as well an astute physician and acute diagnostician. In the realm of measure his is limitless treasure; he raises the walls of Architecture's halls; in his watch over numbers he neither sleeps nor slumbers; proclaims the laws of Astronomy as Moses God's in Deuteronomy; trills the laws of grammar while rivals stammer; in the Sea of Mishnah's realm, he holds the helm; in the Gemara's domain he is suzerain.

Lo, here is he who has looked upon the King, who is his Maker's seal and signet-ring. None brighter, none more able, his fixed meal is given him daily at the King's table. God-lent, the candelabrum of his intellect stands in the Tent of Meeting in our spirits' sight, upright and bright, our blest and our eternal light.

Behold him chosen of the Lord 1 Sam. 10: 24.
Sinai, the presence of the Lord Ps. 68: 9.
God alone knows his worth [Job 28: 13, 23].
and sent and called Joseph and hastily drew him out Gen. 37: 28 [; 41: 14]. A few more poems are to be found in *ST* 435–46, under the rubric 'Additional Poems from Various Manuscripts of Gate 50 of Taḥkemoni'. Others have been described since. See S–F, *History*, n. 172 and n. 103.
he neither sleeps nor slumbers [Ps. 121: 4].
his fixed meal is given him daily at the King's table 2 Kgs. 25: 30.
the candelabrum of . . . the Tent of Meeting Exod. 40: 24.
eternal light Exod. 27: 20; Lev. 24: 2.

ANALYSES

Analysis of Introduction

In His Name who Teaches Man Wisdom

ALḤARIZI'S INTRODUCTION offers two markedly different explanations of the genesis of *Sefer Taḥkemoni*—the first a quasi-divine charge conveyed in allegorical language, and the second an essentially factual presentation of the enterprise as an answer to the challenge tendered by the *Maqāmāt* of al-Ḥariri of Basra (*c.*1054–1112)[1]—both accounts expressing ire at the neglect and ill-treatment of the Hebrew language. The author's double history, allegorical-fanciful and factual, is preceded by a seemingly unrelated section of praise and petition to God, replete with Neoplatonic imagery focusing on the soul's origin and duties, and its necessary subservience to the intellect. Thematic continuities between these three sections of the introduction make for a rich and somewhat paradoxical overall statement—to be rendered even more complex by a bizarre encounter depicted in Gate 1.

Let us examine in some detail the quasi-allegorical account,[2] which follows the description of the soul's creation and task,[3] a prayer for a composition free of sin and error,[4] and self-advertisement of the author in rhymed prose and metrical verse.[5] Alḥarizi's motivation is externalized: the author's reason, in language drawn from divine charges to the prophets, commands him to be zealous for the Hebrew language, the language of prophecy, a tongue abused and unrealized. Consecrated like Moses, Isaiah, and Jeremiah, the poet describes his fulfilment of this charge through the allegorical reworking of the biblical tale of Abraham's servant Eliezer seeking and finding, at the well of Haran, a bride for his master's son: here Alḥarizi seeks, finds, woos, and weds (for himself) the Hebrew language, engendering a hero—either Hever the Kenite or *Sefer Taḥkemoni* itself—whose potent language puts all rivals to shamed flight.[6]

[1] Tr. Preston, *Makamat*; Chenery (vol. i) and Steingass (vol. ii), *Assemblies*.

[2] *ST* 8. 9–11. 17. [3] *ST* 4. 1–7. 18. [4] *ST* 7. 11–18. [5] *ST* 7. 19–8. 8.

[6] Here Alḥarizi was doubtless influenced by Solomon ibn Gabirol, who prefaced a 400-stich didactic poem on the rules of the Hebrew language, 'Maḥberet ha'anak', with a description of a divine injunction—a *bat kol*—to compose the work, an injunction rich in praise of Hebrew's virtues and in admonition to the Jewish people for not learning and preserving it properly (sts. 18–57: *Secular Poetry* (Heb.), ed. Jarden, i. 377–81; and *Secular Poems*, ed. Brody and Schirmann, 169–70).

In this none too modest presentation Alḥarizi echoes a large medieval philosophical literature, both Arabic and Hebrew, that views the prophet as the highest level of human perfection.[7] Through his projection of an inner compulsion into a richly figured quasi-allegory linking him with prophecy, Alḥarizi accords himself high stature; and this self-advertisement recalls the genre of boast in the metrical Hebrew verse of Spain—and especially the high claims for wisdom of two men: Samuel Hanagid, warrior-statesman of the Berber kingdom of Granada, and Solomon ibn Gabirol, poet and philosopher.[8] As generous as Alḥarizi's self-appraisal is in this first explication of *Sefer Taḥkemoni*'s genesis, it is all the more so when seen against the backdrop of the preceding section, a selective amalgam of Jewish Neoplatonic thought—a philosophical school positing the flow of all existence from God, or the first principle, in hierarchical descent, starting with intellect (or will, then intellect), and emanating from each sphere into the next, concluding with the realm of matter, at the furthest remove from the divine.[9]

[7] See Judah Halevi, *The Kuzari*, trans. Hirschfeld, i. 73, par. 103; and iv. 207–12, par. 3. See also *EJ* xiii. 1177–8, 1181; Lewy, Altmann, and Heinemann, *Three Jewish Philosophers*, index, 'prophecy'; Kreisel, 'Theories of Prophecy', esp. 11–22, 77–84, 218–411; Pagis, 'The Poet as Prophet'; Heschel, 'On the Holy Spirit in the Middle Ages'.

[8] On *shirei hitpa'arut*, the poetry of boast, see Levin, *The Embroidered Coat* (Heb.), 150–208. For additional remarks on Gabirol's self-praise see Or, 'Wisdom and its Quest' (Heb.), 29–36.

[9] Blending philosophical speculation with an essentially religious quest for salvation, Neoplatonism held much that was antithetic to monotheism:

> an impersonal first principle, rejection of creation and revelation, the conception of man as essentially soul, and the . . . submergence of the individual soul in the universal soul. Nevertheless, for monotheistic philosophers the contradictions were not insurmountable. In fact, the method of figurative interpretation cultivated by ancient Neoplatonists . . . was employed by monotheistic philosophers in order to read their Neoplatonic doctrines into the text of Scripture. The ladder of Jacob's dream was thus interpreted as a symbol of the soul's ascent. . . . Creation became a metaphor for eternal procession. Revelation and prophecy were discussed in terms reminiscent of the *unio mystica*. . . . the Arabo-Hebrew milieu was saturated by numerous currents [of Neoplatonism]. (*EJ* xii. 958 ff.)

For a helpful summary of the history and rationale for the theory of emanationism, see Hyman, 'From What is One and Simple'. For additional overviews of the Jewish medieval school of Neoplatonism, see Guttmann, *Philosophies of Judaism*, 84–133, and index; and Husik, *A History of Mediaeval Jewish Philosophy*, 59–196, and index.

A major source of Alḥarizi's Neoplatonism is Solomon ibn Gabirol (b. 1020, d. 1050 or 1058–70, according to differing calculations)—that of his *magnum opus*, a metaphysical dialogue titled 'The Fountain of Life'; and his philosophical-liturgical work, *Keter malkhut* ('The Kingly Crown'), recited to this day on the Day of Atonement in the Sephardi synagogue rite—concerning which see *Selected Religious Poems of Solomon ibn Gabirol*, ed. Davidson, tr. Zangwill, 82–123, 175–86, 228–45 (cited in preference to *The Kingly Crown*, tr. Lewis, as giving Hebrew originals and English translations in facing texts). For a discussion of Alḥarizi's

The hero of Alḥarizi's 'introduction to the introduction' is the cosmic intellect, the very first emanation of divinity, and the agency through which the very world is created and ordered. This same intellect, realized in the individual human being, is the soul's wise and caring mentor, lover, and very salvation: he weds the soul, elevates her from bodily bondage (if she be pure), and restores her to her home with God.

By preceding the description of his call to redeem Hebrew with this dramatization of Neoplatonic theory, Alḥarizi creates an analogy: he is to the Hebrew language as the intellect is to the soul; and his use of Hebrew, in composing *Sefer Taḥkemoni*, is parallel to the holy task of intellect in bringing the soul to her proper station. The correspondence is worked out in some detail: the intellect seeks out, woos, and weds the soul (if she be pure), consummates the marriage, and raises her up; Alḥarizi seeks out, woos, and weds the Hebrew language (once pure, now sullied), consummates the marriage, and raises her up. More: both soul and Hebrew are brought to their pristine state—the soul to God's throne, her origin before her debasing linkage with the body;[10] and Hebrew to its lofty situation in antiquity, the language of revelation, perfect in every way until its abandonment by the Jews and their debased adoption of Arabic.

Furthermore, Alḥarizi blurs the boundaries between the cosmic intellect *per se* and his own intellect with its command: 'then did my intellect call to rouse me'. Stated otherwise, what the persona of the author perceives as profoundly reasonable and a personal imperative is at one and the same time a near-divine charge.[11]

particular debts to this work, see Mirsky, 'On Alḥarizi's Introduction to *Taḥkemoni*' (Heb.).

Other Neoplatonic writers who preceded and influenced Alḥarizi include Isaac Israeli (*c.*850–950), Baḥya ibn Paquda (*c.*1080); the unknown author of *Kitāb maʿānī al-nafs* ('On the Essence of the Soul'; mid-11th–mid-12th cc.), sometimes called Pseudo-Baḥya; Abraham bar Ḥiyya of Barcelona (beginning of the 12th c.); Joseph ibn Zaddik (d. 1149), author of *Olam katan* ('Microcosm'); and Abraham ben Me'ir ibn Ezra (*c.*1092–1167). Judah Halevi (1085–1140) must be mentioned as well: if not a member of any philosophical school, he is variously linked with the Neoplatonic tradition. The reader is directed to the list of specific borrowings at the end of this Analysis.

[10] Our author penned an 11-stich poem in Arabic—one of a cycle of ten philosophic poems—with a number of locutions recalling the description of the soul in this gate, including 'As long as it exercises the intellect, its station is high—but it falls down when it does not . . . and it takes up its abode in a body created by the Will; but when the predestined end comes near, it doffs the bodily cloth in order to put on the most perfectly fashioned robes of glory . . . but his (man's) yearning is for ever for his first dwelling place.' See Stern, 'Some Unpublished Poems by Al-Harizi', 348–9 with English translation, 351–2.

[11] On the phenomenon of medieval Hebrew poets, as well as philosophers, claiming the status of prophet, or hinting at such, see Sirat, *Les Théories des visions surnaturelles*. See also Komem, 'Between Poetry and Prophecy' (Heb.).

The motif of the fountain further links Alḥarizi's enterprise with divine wisdom. The soul's origin is the fount of wisdom; thereafter, in bodily existence, that soul whose eyes are opened by God drinks of the waters of the intellect—and thus gains ascent to the upper realms whence she came. In parallel fashion, Alḥarizi, at the outset of his allegorical encounter, states his determination to draw waters from the holy fountain of the Hebrew tongue; he descends to the spring in order (literally)[12] to 'sate [myself] on the love [or 'breasts', reading *dadei* instead of *dodei*] of wisdom that are better than wine' (S. of S. 1: 2); and finally calls upon his benighted people to drink of his own flowing Hebrew fountain.

Other authors before Alḥarizi had taken world Jewry to task for abandoning Hebrew. He echoes the plaint, and even the phraseology, of Sa'adiah Gaon (882–942), the distinguished leader of Babylonian Jewry, and a luminary of the geonic period:

After the ruin of the holy city, three years before the Greeks had their first king, we began to forsake the holy tongue and to converse in the languages of the alien peoples of the land. When Nehemiah saw us speaking Ashdodite he was grieved;[13] he scolded and quarrelled with the people. We were subsequently scattered through the world, no nation existing which our exiles did not enter. There again we raised our children, studied their languages, so that their gibberish obscured the beauty of our speech.[14]

Alḥarizi voiced these same sentiments in his introduction to his translation of Maimonides' commentary on the Mishnah:

I have rendered this great commentary from Arabic into Hebrew, transferring its lights from west to east. . . . For I am filled with zeal for the commentaries which the Torah has engendered and they have precedence, yet they were born upon the knees of Hagar, maid of Sarah, and Sarah was barren. In amazement I said to myself: 'How can the holy and the profane be joined . . .'[15]

[12] When, in the Analyses, the original Hebrew text is translated literally, not cited from the free English rendering, the fact will be indicated by 'Lit.'.

[13] Neh. 13: 23–7.

[14] Cited in Halkin, 'The Medieval Jewish Attitude', 35–6 and n. 14, citing the repetition of this charge by Sa'adiah Gaon (Zucker, 'From Sa'adya Gaon's Commentary on the Torah', 339).

[15] Maimonides, 53*a*—as cited in Halkin, 'The Medieval Jewish Attitude', 240. For a larger excerpt of this statement of Alḥarizi, see Drory's translation in 'Literary Contacts and Where to Find Them', 296—citing Maimonides, 'Hakdamot leperush hamishnah', 4, in the Appendix. Other works of Maimonides translated by Alḥarizi include *Guide of the Perplexed* and *Ma'amar teḥiyat hametim*. Additional comments on Jewish counterattacks to Arab claims of the superiority of Arabia, the Arab nation, Muhammad, the Koran, Arabic, and Arabic poetry are to be found in Alloni, 'Reflections of the Revolt' (Heb.); id., 'Zion and Jerusalem' (Heb.). See also Brann, *The Compunctious Poet*, index s.v. Arabiyya, and, on the role of Hebrew in the

Other zealots for Hebrew preceding and following Alḥarizi, grammarians and poets, rose to defend the language and lament its misuse and abuse by their fellow Jews.[16]

This impassioned championing of Hebrew, then, couched in an allegorical history (fused with more general Neoplatonic allegory), comprises the first explanation of the origins of *Sefer Taḥkemoni*. Essentially the same rationale is advanced in the second and more realistic exposition of the book's origins, a portrayal of the work as a response to al-Ḥariri's *Maqāmāt*. The exposition, however, is most convoluted: close reading reveals a deliberate effort on the author's part to downplay the part played by his translation of al-Ḥariri's *Maqāmāt* in the genesis of *Sefer Taḥkemoni*.

Having noted al-Ḥariri's wondrous composition,[17] he expresses anger at the Arab's plagiarism of Hebrew sources,[18] and chagrin that the Jews of his own era, ignorantly disdainful of Hebrew's potential, have not produced anything so brilliant. To rectify this situation, says Alḥarizi, he produced 'this

Spanish Jewish culture of Muslim Spain, id., 'Andalusian Hebrew Poetry and the Hebrew Bible'.

[16] See Judah Halevi's statement, in his *Book of the Kuzari*, that 'the divine language which God created and taught to Adam and placed on his tongue and in his heart is undoubtedly the most perfect of languages . . . the angels employ it more than any other tongue' (*Kuzari* 4: 25, as translated by Jospe, 'The Superiority of Oral over Written Communication', 129). For overviews of medieval Jewish praise of Hebrew and criticism of Jewry's abandonment thereof, see Sarna, 'Hebrew and Bible Studies in Medieval Spain', 328–9 and nn. 30, 31; and Halkin, 'The Medieval Jewish Attitude toward Hebrew', 233–48.

Not all Jewish writers were proud spokesmen for Hebrew. In lashing out at those who faulted Hebrew's limitations. Alḥarizi most likely has in mind the translator Judah ibn Tibbon (1120–*c*. 1190), who offered the following justification for Jewish writers' having preferred Arabic: '. . . They did it because it is the language people understood, and also because it is an adequate and rich language for every subject and for every need, for every speaker and every author; its expression is direct, lucid, and capable of saying just what is wanted much better than can be done in Hebrew, of which we possess only what has been preserved in Scripture and [which] is insufficient for the needs of a speaker. It is simply impossible to express the thoughts of our hearts succinctly and eloquently in Hebrew as we can in Arabic, which is adequate, elegant, and available to those who know it' (translator's introduction to Baḥya ibn Paquda, *Duties of the Heart*, ed. Zifroni, 2; see also ibn Tibbon's introduction to Jonah ibn Janaḥ, *Sefer harikmah*, 5: 'and these things [translation] are hard to accomplish because of the inadequacy of the [Hebrew] language [*kotser halashon*]'). For further discussion of the defence of Hebrew and conflicting positions of Hebrew translators from the Arabic—particularly the ibn Tibbons and Alḥarizi—see Drory, 'Literary Contacts', 277–302. Drory points out that it was precisely the shift of Jewish literary creativity to northern Spain that, in general, led to the adoption of Hebrew for many purposes previously reserved for Arabic; and, in the instance of Alḥarizi, to the creation of a work modelled on Arabic literature.

[17] *ST* 11. 18–24.

[18] *ST* 11. 25–8.

work', i.e. *Sefer Taḥkemoni*,[19] and goes on at great length to limn its scope and benefits as fecund composition, moral instruction, and an example both of Hebrew well used and of original writing.[20] He caps this lengthy précis with an insistence that his composition is wholly original, owing nothing to the Arabs—a grotesque claim, inasmuch as whole gates have been lifted and variously adopted from a spate of Arab writers, and first and foremost al-Ḥariri![21]

Only at this point does our author revert to the chronological record, to the topic which he has all but put out of mind—the translation of al-Ḥariri's *Maqāmāt* into *Maḥberot Iti'el* (which he nevers mentions by title!). Other poets who tried to translate al-Ḥariri failed miserably, he observes, but only he succeeded;[22] and following this ultra-terse account he sets down the simple fact that the translation had been commissioned by unspecified Jewish grandees.[23] Then, expressing his shame at having cultivated others' gardens (as a translator), our author leaps back to his preferred and major theme—that he has penned an original work 'to invigorate dry bones' (Ezek. 37), a work whose every chapter 'speaks the tongue of prophecies'.[24] Once again, the overall effect of this tortuous history is to conceal from the reader the true extent of al-Ḥariri's influence on Alḥarizi's enterprise.

[19] *ST* 11. 28–12. 18.

[20] *ST* 12. 19–14. 22.

[21] The fullest summary of our author's indebtednesses, building on earlier lists of Schirmann, 'On the Sources of Judah Alḥarizi's *Sefer Taḥkemoni*' (Heb.), Ratzaby, 'On the Sources of *Sefer Taḥkemoni*' (Heb.), and others, is Maree, 'The Influence of al-Ḥariri's *Maqāmāt* on Taḥkemoni's *Maḥberot*' (Heb.), 279–80. Maree lists ten gates of al-Hamadhani influencing nine of Alḥarizi (Alḥarizi's set in parentheses, following): 11 and 26 (2), 1 (3), 24 (17), 15 (18), 12 (21), 17 (29), 6 (31), 22 (34), and 23 (38); and eighteen of al-Ḥariri influencing fourteen of Alḥarizi (again— Alḥarizi's gates set in parentheses, following): 1, 11, 21, 41 (2), 8 (4), 30 (6), 17 (8), 26 (11), 12 (15), 23 (18), 26 (23), 31 (28), 13 (29), 23 (32), 39 (38), 40 (41), 8 and 19 (48)—as well as other sources. In this very disavowal, Alḥarizi imitates al-Ḥariri in the Arab's own preface, where, speaking ambiguously, he seems to disclaim having borrowed from al-Hamadhani—after having appropriated at least eight tales from his predecessor: see *Assemblies*, tr. Chenery, i. 106. In Maree's thesis, several of Alḥarizi's borrowings and adaptations of entire gates of al-Ḥariri are subjected to detailed scrutiny (including, on pp. 20–8, the introductions of Alḥarizi and al-Ḥariri); and various isolated statements and images from al-Ḥariri are listed in 'Motifs and Themes', 222–42—yet by no means exhausting al-Ḥariri's and others' contributions to *Sefer Taḥkemoni*! Unless otherwise indicated, comparisons made in this book between *Sefer Taḥkemoni* and Arabic sources are my own.

[22] Here, too, our author's language is redolent with overtones of prophecy and suprahuman powers evoking the very opening of his introduction: he calls upon Intellect's heights and brings down rain; speaks to the rock of song—like Moses to the rock in the desert (Num. 20: 8)—and waters gush forth.

[23] *ST* 15. 8–11. The composition of *Maḥberot Iti'el* took place between 1205 and 1215, according to Schirmann, *Hebrew Poetry in Spain and in Provence* (Heb.); or between 1213 and 1216, according to Habermann, 'The *Sefer Taḥkemoni* of Rabbi Judah Alḥarizi' (Heb.), 113.

[24] *ST* 15. 11–22.

In his exuberant self-advertisement, our author is quite frank, even brash, in conveying the largely secular nature of *Sefer Taḥkemoni*. The work contains, he declares, among other things, delightful descriptions of gardens, erotic encounters, as well as riddles, history, drunkenness (!), wars, travels, chicanery, curses (!), and rhetorical exploits—all these categories being interwoven with (far fewer) loftier themes such as prayers, polemics on religious topics, and wise saws.[25] Such the holy issue of Alḥarizi's prior 'coupling' with Hebrew, a fusion mirroring the conjoining of intellect and soul! Further explicating the rationale for producing so bold, and primarily secular, a cornucopia, the author states that the work is geared to every possible reader and specifically to two categories: those who are God-fearing and those who are not. The former category, our author asserts, will find (literally) 'rebukes and prayers and the fear of God',[26] the latter 'pleasures of this world and its good that they stream to the good of the Lord';[27] i.e. non-sacral and non-didactic matter is essentially the means whereby to attract readers to intellectual and moral edification. Herein he closely parallels al-Ḥariri's prefatory statement that matter susceptible of criticism falls within the category of didactic fables designed to guide readers to the right path.[28] Alḥarizi then expands upon his prized theme of the redemption of Hebrew, claiming that this work will not only redound to the honour of the language, but be a source of inspiration and imitation for the writers of the scattered Jewish nation.

What explains this tapestried, multi-level explanation of the book's creation? One may well suspect that Alḥarizi has anticipated criticism of the overriding secular nature, indeed the frequent audacity, of *Sefer Taḥkemoni*. The project, cries the author, is inspired by God and the intellect; in addition, it furthers the holy task of defending Hebrew's honour and restoring her lost vigour. Beyond that, it is a didactic exercise designed to elevate its readers, frivolous and bawdy appearance to the contrary. All this having been said, one cannot and should not reduce completely the author's claims or method to cynical self-serving. As further gates and their analyses will

[25] In openly advocating, and then providing, maximum variety in his works, Alḥarizi echoes Arab philosophy and practice in the literature of *adab* (enlightenment and entertainment; see Analysis 36) with its frequent digressions and shifts from one subject to another. See Scheindlin, 'Rabbi Moshe ibn Ezra on the Legitimacy of Poetry', 105.

[26] *ST* 13. 21–2. Here the author must have in mind the sermon against worldly pleasures (Gate 2); the prayers of Gates 14 and 15; and possibly the history of the Rabbanite–Karaite debate (Gate 17) and the (ostensible) justification of the ways of God to man (Gate 25), on which see the analyses there.

[27] *ST* 13. 22–3; Jer. 31: 12.

[28] Tr. Preston, *Makamat*, 20–2; tr. Chenery, *Assemblies*, i. 103–7.

show, on several occasions the text does indeed demonstrate deep religiosity and convey a keen moral lesson. Moreover, the work as a whole, and many an individual gate, oscillates between the two poles of the sacred and the profane, between roguery and piety.

One further note on the double mask of poet and prophet is in order. Alḥarizi was well aware of a deep-seated disdain on the part of philosophers and others for what they perceived as the essential falsity of poets. This scorn has deep historical roots, going back to Plato's *Republic* (10. 596 ff.), where poetry is described as but a reflection of the reflection of ideal reality —a coarse imitation, morally indefensible.[29] Alḥarizi's revered model, Moses Maimonides, so many of whose works he translated, had some harsh words for poetic (metaphorical) language.[30] Moses ibn Ezra, in his book on Hebrew poetic theory,[31] notes a popular conception that because, logically speaking, metaphorical language is by definition false, the best poetry is the most false, even if its content need not be so. Ibn Ezra's discussion itself seems to echo harsh condemnations of poetry on the part of Andalusian Muslim theologians and thinkers and their predecessors.[32] Later Hebrew poets and philosophers lent their voices to the chorus denigrating poetry on the grounds of falsehood.[33] Shem Tov ben Joseph ibn Falaquera (1224–90), in his *Sefer hamevakesh* ('The Book of the Seeker'), offers this critique:

> These men maintain lies bred by the imagination . . . . 'The happiest of men is he who has, from his youth onward, devoted himself to the science of logic rather than to the vanities of poets.' . . . Their words are of the fifth syllogism, inferior and dark . . . the art of poetry is far removed from the truth . . . Those who practice it use only figurative and metaphorical terms, which are far from the truth, since they refrain from enlightening us in those conventional terms which sincerely wise men employ.[34]

It may well be that here, too, in his apotheosis of his poetic calling, Alḥarizi leaps to his own defence before being attacked.

[29] For other sources, see Pagis, *Secular Poetry*, 43 n. 22.

[30] *Milot hahigayon*, ch. 8. See Twersky, *Introduction*, 250 n. 29.

[31] *Kitāb al-muḥādara wa'l-mudhākara*, ed. Halkin, 119, ll. 4–5.

[32] See Scheindlin, 'Rabbi Moshe Ibn Ezra on the Legitimacy of Poetry'; cf. Bonnebaker, 'Religious Prejudice against Poetry in Early Islam'.

[33] See D. Pagis, *Secular Poetry*, 42, 46–51, 155.

[34] Tr. Levine, ii. 81. See ibid. 113 nn. 96–7 for ibn Falaquera's sources, including Maimonides. For an examination of poets' exploring and exploiting the theme of their falsity, see Brann, *The Compunctious Poet*.

SPECIFIC BORROWINGS FROM JEWISH PHILOSOPHERS

In His name who teaches man wisdom (Ps. 94: 10): Following Arabic example, many medieval Hebrew writers opened their work with praise of God, often singling out divine traits or endowments (such as wisdom or the soul) to be emphasized in the work. Abraham bar Ḥiyya (*c.* 1070–*c.* 1136) declares at the beginning of *The Meditation of the Sad Soul*:

> The meditation commences with the praise of God. Rabbi Abraham bar Ḥiyya of Spain said: 'Blessed is the Lord, God of Israel, Lord of every creature, great in counsel and powerful in deeds, who teaches man wisdom . . .'.[35]

Alḥarizi's immediate model is al-Ḥariri's preface, beginning with the traditional Arabic introduction, 'In the name of God the Merciful, Most Merciful'.[36]

Praise God, the Ever Near but unknown dweller of Heaven's highest sphere: The definition of God by paradox, and particularly in terms of immanence and transcendence, is a hallmark of medieval Jewish and non-Jewish philosophical systems, with roots as well in the Bible. Thus, in Solomon ibn Gabirol's *Kingly Crown* (*Keter malkhut*), sections 2–7 lay out the following divine attributes: unity, being, living, greatness, might, and luminosity.[37]

Come not nigh . . . my land: In Neoplatonic theory, the first essence, transcending all, cannot be perceived by the intellect. See *EJ* xii. 960 and sources cited there.

Now the souls of the righteous aspire to wing home to that glory . . . they strip off their bodies all, to be given . . . royal garments worn of the King: Cf. Alḥarizi's dramatization of the origin, descent, and labour of the soul with the doctrine of Baḥya ibn Paquda, the author of *On the Essence of the Soul*, as summarized by I. Husik:

> In the matter of returning to their own world after separation from the body, souls are graded according to the measure of their knowledge and the value of their conduct. These two conditions, ethical and spiritual or intellectual, are requisite of

[35] Tr. Wigoder, 62. See also Sa'adiah Gaon, *The Book of Beliefs and Opinions*, ed. Rosenblatt, 3; Solomon ibn Gabirol, *Improvements of the Moral Qualities*, 29; Baḥya ibn Paquda, *Duties of the Heart*, ed. Hyamson, 15. See also Altmann in Lewy *et al.*, *Three Jewish Philosophers*, 25 n. 5. Similar dedications in later rhymed prose literature are to be found in Isaac ben Solomon ibn Sahula, *Meshal hakadmoni*, 9, ll. 1–24; Berechiah Hanakdan, *Mishlei shu'alim*, 3; and Immanuel of Rome, *Maḥberot imanuel haromi*, ed. Jarden, i. 3, l. 2.

[36] Tr. Chenery, *Assemblies*, i. 103–4.

[37] *Selected Religious Poems*, tr. Zangwill, 83–6.

fulfilment before the soul can regain its original home. The soul on leaving this world is like a clean, white garment soaked in water. If the water is clean, it is easy to dry the garment, and it becomes even cleaner than it was before. But if the water is dirty, no amount of drying will make the garment clean.[38]

from primal rock in the pit of obscurity: Lit. 'gouged out of the pit of the nethermost [pit] and hewn from the rock of the Rock'. The origins of the soul are in the divine essence. The phrase is taken from section 29 of ibn Gabirol's *Kingly Crown*.[39]

Yes, by the soul's fire man rose from nothing, as Holy Writ proclaims: The Lord descended thereon in flames (Exod. 19: 8): Lit. 'through the heat of the soul man emerged from nothingness to being . . .'. Here Alḥarizi exploits the account of the theophany at Sinai. In utilizing biblical narrative to refer to universal truths or processes in the spiritual plane, Alḥarizi is especially influenced by ibn Gabirol's practice in the *Kingly Crown*.[40] During the later controversy over Maimonides' writings, members of the pro-Maimonidean camp were faulted for excess in this direction.[41]

vegetative soul . . . animal soul . . . upper soul . . . intellect: Alḥarizi's source here is most likely Abraham bar Ḥiyya in *The Meditation of the Sad Soul*:

> To explain this subject, I say that God gave man three faculties (some call them souls). The first is the faculty whereby he grows, as does vegetation. The second enables him to move. These two faculties are shared with all other animals and they are called 'breath of life'. The third faculty is the ability to distinguish between good and evil, between truth and falsehood, between everything and its contrary, and to discern wisdom. This is the soul (Hebrew *neshamah*) by which man is distinguished from other animals. If this soul prevails over the animal soul, man will be distinct from animals and will be perfect and worthy.[42]

The Intellect shall woo her from Lust, raise her from the dust, from the Pit's consummation, to highest station: Lit. 'the Intellect shall teach her the ways of God and lift her from the dust to the station of the elevated and therein

[38] Husik, *A History of Mediaeval Jewish Philosophy*, 113; and see Guttmann, *Philosophies of Judaism*, 111.

[39] *Selected Religious Poems*, tr. Zangwill, 104; cf. Mirsky, 'On Alḥarizi's Introduction', 703–4.

[40] See e.g. *Selected Religious Poems*, tr. Zangwill, 83, ll. 26–7; 86, ll. 68–9; 95, ll. 199–200.

[41] See Sarachek, *Faith and Reason: The Conflict over the Rationalism of Maimonides*, 171–8. See also Silver, *Maimonidean Criticism and the Maimonidean Controversy*, 145 and n. 3, and s.v. 'allegories' in index there.

[42] Tr. Wigoder, 62. See also Guttmann, *Philosophies of Judaism*, 99.

shall she be saved from the descent to the nether world and ascend to the highest station.' Alḥarizi has most likely adapted this description from Joseph ibn Zaddik's conception of the relationship of intellect to soul:

> The rational soul, which is 'like a king' and which is destined to lead man to his eternal bliss, received its 'light' from the intellect, the 'matter' of which is the 'perfect light and clear splendour' which 'emanates from the power of the Creator without any intermediary.' This is a literal quotation from [Isaac] Israeli's metaphysical doctrine, which is itself derived from a pseudo-Aristotelian Neoplatonic treatise describing the coming into being of the intellect.[43]

[43] *EJ* xvi. 912–13.

Analysis of Gate One

Whence this Work Sprung and by Whom it was Sung

THE READER OF GATE I of *Sefer Taḥkemoni* is plunged into a surreal world of paradox. Heman the Ezrahite, who but now has been introduced as the fictitious creation of Alḥarizi, reports the entire chapter as the words of the/his author, spoken by the latter to him! This speech, in turn, records the author's encounter with a quasi-divine youth who charges him with the creation of the very book in which this encounter is recorded; and this youth, who assures the author of his aid and presence, to the extent of meeting him in every chapter, is revealed at the close as Hever the Kenite, whom the author has just presented to the reader in the introduction as the second of his fictional creations. The description of this 'consummate rhetor' is all the more bizarre in its narrative authority: the author describes the youth's behaviour in the tavern (i.e. elsewhere), when this is their first encounter![1]

Nor does impossible circumstance stop at this. Following the youth's impassioned poem of praise for the work's (additional) suggested patron, Josiah, two declarations, ostensibly by the same person, follow: *amar hamagid*, 'said the teller of the tale'; and a few lines thereafter, *amar hameḥaber*, 'said the author'. Now both paragraphs convey essentially the same fact: that the speaker approved the youth's words, and wrote the book![2] Yet while the term 'author' is clear-cut, the 'teller of the tale' could as readily refer to Heman as to Alḥarizi; and indeed in the great majority of instances in the ensuing chapters, it is Heman the Ezrahite that is intended.[3]

Dan Pagis has called attention to the analogy between Alḥarizi and Pirandello, famed for his intricate and dizzying blurring of boundaries

[1] The tavern celebrants, in blending religious and secular wisdom with liberality and rhetorical mastery, are paradigms of Hebrew Spain's new class of courtier-rabbis. See Scheindlin, *Wine, Women, and Death*, 6–7, and introduction to wine poems, 19–33. The laudations here, however, go beyond established norms, inasmuch as the youths are explicitly lauded for including drinking in their behavioural repertoire (ibid. 54–9, poem 5).

[2] There is, of course, a major difference between the two paragraphs: the first focuses on the praiseworthiness and praise of Josiah; the second, on the book itself as a blend of wisdom, rhetoric, and moral preachment.

[3] On Alharizi's adaptation of the origin of *amar hamagid* see Hus, 'The "Magid"' (Heb.); see also Analysis 49 n. 3.

between reality and fiction.[4] What is explicitly stated in Pirandello's *Six Characters in Search of an Author*—the insistent demand of fictitious characters to be made real—is here implicit, when Gate 1 is taken together with the Introduction. The character of Hever the Kenite has assumed, as it were, an independent existence in his creator's mind: his 'life' does not end with the close of the author's work in rendering al-Ḥariri's *Maqāmāt* into Hebrew. He demands continuation.

What has already been stated in the realistic explanation of the book's genesis is recast here: there, abashed at bringing a foreign work into Hebrew rather than writing an original work, the author pens *Sefer Taḥkemoni*; here, the character of the Kenite himself stimulates the author—his creator—to the task. This said, another surreal element of Gate 1 must be mentioned. The character of Hever the Kenite here introduced is neither that met in Alḥarizi's earlier work, *Maḥberot Iti'el*, or in the gates to follow. Hever is usually portrayed as an old man; sometimes his age is not mentioned; but never, elsewhere, is he represented as a youth.[5] Here Alḥarizi makes his clearest differentiation between his own character *in situ* and Hever the Kenite as the twin embodiments of his muse, on the one hand, and his authorial aspirations and shame, on the other.

To speak of Alḥarizi's shame—explicit in the Introduction—is not to overstate the case. So eager is he to downplay his prior work of translation that he engages in yet another blurring of boundaries: he starts by referring to the challenge of translating al-Ḥariri into Hebrew, and through ambiguous phraseology ends up with his composing *Sefer Taḥkemoni*—entirely skipping over the creation of *Maḥberot Iti'el*, in an exercise mirroring a like obfuscation in the Introduction, and sounding similar themes.

Let us look at this process more closely. The youth begins his remarks

[4] See Pagis, 'Variety in Medieval Hebrew Rhymed Narrative', 95–6.

[5] In Gate 6, Hever is complimented for his youthful appearance by a lying matchmaker, whose statement 'the tree of your youth has yielded fruit' (*ST* 75. 21) is best understood to mean that his maturity has borne out the promise of his youth. Also, the context points to the Kenite's being anything but young: in ruminating on the advisability of marriage he says, 'I know not the day of my death'—a citation of Gen. 27: 2, the words of the aged Isaac, setting his house in order in the twilight of his life. In Gate 22 Hever reports that he was in the company of 'Hebrew youths', but gives no hint that he himself was young at the time. Moreover, Heman's prior declaration of his own youth at the outset of that gate is no indication of Hever's tender years: to the contrary, in another gate Heman speaks of himself 'as yet a tender youth' (Gate 18, *ST* 181. 3)—but of Hever as an old man (*ST* 181. 19). Finally, never does Hever speak of himself as a young man or even allude to his youth, as Heman frequently does when speaking of himself; not even in Gate 25, where the Kenite alludes to an incident that had taken place many years before (*ST* 231. 8–9).

with high praise of al-Ḥariri—echoing, and enlarging upon, like praise in the Introduction; then asserts that if al-Ḥariri's work were composed in any other language it would be a disaster, given Arabic's superiority to every tongue. Yet, the author goes on, the language of prophecy can meet this task.

There follows the claim that notwithstanding the loss of so much of the Hebrew language over the centuries, the little remaining will suffice for the production of poems, letters, and varied compositions. At this point the author is not clearly referring to the translation of al-Ḥariri's *Maqāmāt*—though that interpretation could be placed upon his words. He goes on to complain of the lack of patrons; the youth replies (literally): 'if you can compose a book such as this [*sefer kazeh*] . . .'[6]—an ambiguous phrase, for 'this' may mean either al-Ḥariri's *Maqāmāt* or *Sefer Taḥkemoni*. Indeed, following the lengthy praise, in verse and in rhymed prose, of the sought-after patron Josiah, the narrator-cum-author declares: 'I dedicated this tome [*hasefer hazeh*] . . . I composed this tome'—which can refer only to *Sefer Taḥkemoni*! In sum, notwithstanding his acknowledged indebtedness to al-Ḥariri in the Introduction, Alḥarizi here confusingly skips over his having translated his predecessor's *Maqāmāt*—the first stage of the creation of *Sefer Taḥkemoni*.

But to return to the blurring of boundaries between author and characters. In this dizzying overlap and fusion, the author hints at the outset that Hever and Heman be seen as authorial stand-ins. At the same time, inasmuch as they do interact, he reminds us that they are not exactly identical with himself—or with each other. (This paradox and differentation will be crucial in many a chapter, when immoral conduct is presented, or boasted of, or both.) Indeed, to make any sense at all of the plethora of accounts of the book's genesis, we are compelled to view the contradictory accounts as complementary explanations of a complex process—regardless of how many patrons were solicited and of which text was presented to which sponsor. Hever the Kenite, or *Sefer Taḥkemoni* itself, is at once the offspring of Alḥarizi and the Hebrew language, as stated in the Introduction, and the progenitor of the book, as in Gate 1; a natural progression from the translation of al-Ḥariri's *Maqāmāt*, which our author wrote both on commission and to demonstrate Hebrew's suppleness and scope—and the fruit of his shame at having penned *Maḥberot Iti'el* in the first place; it is the fruit of an internal process—yet externally commanded, by his intelligence (Introduction) and the hypostasized Hever (Gate 1).

[6] This is the passage rendered 'For if you can compose a work of metric verse and rhyming prose insightful, delightful, well-groomed, perfumed . . .'.

However, the juxtaposition of Gate 1 and the Introduction reveals not only variation between major themes, but a marked continuity. As noted heretofore, the wedding of Hever to the Hebrew language in the Introduction was analogous to the fusion of the cosmic intellect with the cosmic soul, and the desired fusion of the individual intellect with the individual soul—both unions leading to the restoration of pristine virtue. Moreover, a transcendent reality was responsible for both unions: godly directive, in the case of intellect and soul; and the author's intellect calling upon him, in language taken straight from biblical divine calls to the prophets. Now in Gate 1, the charge to the author is given by Hever, who is linked in various ways through biblical citation to God. Wisdom's taking refuge beneath Hever's wings evokes Ps. 91: 4, where the suppliant is shielded by God. Moreover, in the first poem of the Gate, Hever is implicitly linked with God in uncovering the path of life (Ps. 16: 11), even as he is linked to wisdom in granting life (Prov. 8: 35 and 4: 23)—and, like personified wisdom in Proverbs, in calling out for men's attention, at the outset of the paragraph following the initial poem (Prov. 8: 4). Indeed the authorial persona states explicitly, citing Ezekiel 37: 10, that 'I prophesied as I was commanded'! Thus Gate 1 further intensifies the linkage of Hever—author—(divine) wisdom so emphatically put forward in the Introduction.

The author's high praise of himself complements his effusive and elaborate praise of Josiah—the exilarch of that name in Syria in the early part of the thirteenth century.[7] The praise of Jewish leaders in Hebrew poetry of Spain, including generous use of biblical passages redolent with divine praise and prophecies of salvation, was a widespread practice.[8] Here Alḥarizi renders a virtuoso performance in this tradition as he blends structural and metrical features of well-known models of secular and sacred verse. The metre employed here, and the rhyme-scheme *aaab cccb dddb*, was the creation, and a favourite vehicle of, Dunash ben Labrat (d. *c.*990), the originator of the quantitative metre in Arabic style of Hebrew Spain, albeit Dunash kept one final rhyme throughout in secular verse.[9] The first, and famous, monorhymed panegyric written in Hebrew Spain was executed in this metre and rhyme-scheme (albeit non-stanzaic), honouring Ḥisdai ibn Shaprut, a Jewish

[7] On Josiah son of Yishai—who apparently lived in Mosul—and his family see Gil, *In the Kingdom of Ishmael*, i. 442–3 and n. 259. See also Schirmann, *New Poems from the Genizah* (Heb.), 130–1, 283–4, and notes there.

[8] See Abraham ibn Daud, *Sefer Ha-Qabbalah*, ed. G. Cohen, 276–89.

[9] On the contribution of Dunash to Hebrew poetry generally, see *EJ* vi. 270–1.

grandee in the court of Abdurrahman III.[10] Furthermore, both Alḥarizi's poem and that of Dunash hark back stylistically to early synagogue poetry of the Land of Israel, in *kedushta'ot*, or poetic expansions of the Amidah prayer: there stanzas of four lines or longer, praising God or a bridegroom, would end with a biblical quotation followed by 'as it is written', then followed by the full quotation.[11]

The overall effect of this sacral, archaic style, then, is to render incomparable praise to an incomparable patron—an especially fitting dedication for a self-styled incomparable masterpiece.[12]

[10] Isaac ibn Kaprun, 'Legibor bite'udah' ('To the Hero of the Torah'), in Schirmann, *Hebrew Poetry*, i. 43–8.

[11] See Fleischer, *Hebrew Liturgical Poetry in the Middle Ages* (Heb.), 154–7.

[12] One wonders what Josiah's reactions would have been had he read the dedication to Samuel ibn Albarkoli at the close of the Introduction (presumably not included in the manuscript tendered him!); or those to the other patrons to whom the book was dedicated: we know of Samuel ben Nissim of Aram Zova, Shmariah ben David of Yemen (in dedications in manuscripts only) and Saʿdid al-Dawlah ʿabd al-Qadir of Aleppo and his son Abu Naṣr. See Habermann, 'Judah Alḥarizi's *Sefer Taḥkemoni* and its Editions' (Heb.), 117–18, citing Schirmann, 'Judah Alḥarizi, Poet and Storyteller' (Heb.), 104. On Samuel ibn Albarkoli and his family, see also Gil, *In the Kingdom of Ishmael*, i. 458–61 and n. 267; 474–6 and n. 273. For expansion on this matter see also S–F, *History*, ii. 186–8, where Fleischer asserts that it is not absolutely certain that all the dedications were attached to *Sefer Taḥkemoni*. At p. 190 n. 185, Fleischer quotes an excerpt from the Arabic introduction emphasizing the book's vital contribution to Eastern Jewry, so ignorant of proper Hebrew. Two manuscripts of *Sefer Taḥkemoni* entirely lack the dedication to Josiah (Yahalom, 'Function', 140 n. 19)—doubtless copied from a manuscript meant for a different patron.

Analysis of Gate Two

Brimstone and Wrath against the Worldly Path

IN THIS EPISODE Alḥarizi strikes sombre chords. The grim, even morbid, diatribe against the pleasures of worldly existence, and the grating call to look to humanity's end, spring from established literary traditions: reflective Hebrew poetry, rooted in turn in Arabic verse, and a long tradition of prose diatribe in Arabic, rhymed and unrhymed, castigating worldly delights and those who succumb to their temptations.[1] To a limited degree, Scripture, too, sounds a like note: not pointing to a world to come as rabbinic Judaism does,[2] it knows the pain of the cessation of human life and physical dissolution, as in the famous close of Ecclesiastes:

So appreciate your vigour in the days of your youth, before those days of sorrow come and those years arrive of which you will say, 'I have no pleasure in them'; before sun and light and moon and stars grow dark, and the clouds come back again after the rain:

When the guards of the house become shaky,
And the men of valour are bent,
And the maids that grind, grown few, are idle,
And the ladies that peer through the windows grow dim . . .
Before the silver cord snaps
And the golden bowl crashes,
The jar is shattered at the spring,
And the jug is smashed at the cistern,
And the dust returns to the ground
As it was,
And the lifebreath returns to God
Who bestowed it.
Utter futility—said Koheleth—
All is futile![3]

---

[1] On the genre of *zuhdiyat*, Arabic sermon-like poems preaching asceticism, and one of its major practitioners, Abu'l-Atahiya, see Scheindlin, *Wine, Women, and Death*, 135–7. On the ascetic thrust of Hebrew reflective poetry see Pagis, *Secular Poetry*, 225–52.

[2] On the subject of the world to come in rabbinic thought see 'Olam Ha-ba' in *EJ* xii. 1355–7; 'Reward and Punishment', *EJ* xiv. 134–9; and literature cited in those articles; also Analysis of Gate 25 below.

[3] Eccles. 12: 1–3, 6–8 (NJPS translation, *Tanakh—The Holy Scriptures*).

Medieval tones, however, are even more sombre: at least the author of Ecclesiastes affirms, on occasion, the enjoyment of one's lot and one's wealth, and the blessings of marriage;[4] and in the book of Psalms, references to the finality or bleakness of the netherworld are often offset by passionate pleas or thanksgiving for continued earthly existence.[5] Hebrew medieval literature of *tokheḥah* ('rebuke'), and specifically the stinging sermon before us, offer wholesale condemnation of all the good that earthly existence has to offer.[6]

Undoubtedly the Kenite's searing diatribe was all the more compelling to those of his readers aware of his major sources: no less than four gates of al-Ḥariri's *Maqāmāt*—1, 11, 21, 41—in every one of which the preacher is unmasked at the close as a hypocrite![7] This irony is wholly absent in the Hebrew: Hever's character here is free of moral taint.[8]

Alḥarizi's reworking of his models is the more pronounced for his choice of the tale's placement. In a sense, Gate 2 is the first of the tales of Taḥkemoni, following the threefold explication of the book's genesis in the Introduction and Gate 1: from here on the authorial persona appears no more, and the stage is held by Heman the narrator and Hever the performer (here) or recounter. We may note especially how Alḥarizi opens his work with a manifest reworking of his predecessor's materials, in particular of al-Ḥariri's Gate 1,[9] most obviously changing its close, with its central motif of eating. In the Arabic gate, the preacher Abu Zayd is unmasked at the finish as a glutton.

---

4 Eccles. 5: 17–18, 8: 15, 9: 7–9, 11: 9.

5 To cite a few examples: Pss. 6: 3–6, 16: 9–10, 18: 1–20, 30: 2–4, 9–11, 49: 16, 86: 13, 89: 47–9, 103: 1–4, 116: 1–6. See also Isa. 38: 17–19; Jonah 2: 4–10; Prov. 23: 14; Job 33: 24.

6 Secular Hebrew literature in Spain is rich in poems denigrating worldly pleasures. Examples, with illuminating analyses, are to be found in the section 'Death' in Scheindlin, *Wine, Women, and Death*, 135–75. On Hebrew literature's debt, on this point, to Arabic literature, see id., *The Gazelle*, 3–12. See also Itzhaki, *Man—the Vine, Death—the Reaper* (Heb.). For related prose writings see Baḥya ibn Paquda, *Duties of the Heart*; Ibn Gabirol, *The Improvement of the Moral Qualities*.

7 For comparisons with Gates 11, 21, and 41 of al-Ḥariri, see Maree, 'The Influence', 134–50. For English translations see Preston, *Makamat*, 154–74 (gate 41), 248–67 (gate 11), and 289–310 (gate 21—Preston took the liberty of revising al-Ḥariri's order). See also *Assemblies*, tr. Chenery, i. 163–8 (gate 11; nn. 364–8), 223–8 (gate 21; nn. 455–69); tr. Steingass, ii. 108–13 (gate 41; nn. 251–5).

8 All that remains of another like work in Hebrew is the Arabic title of a lost *maqāma*, namely: 'The *maqāma* of Alexandria, containing an account of a preacher who rebuked the people with smooth tongue but later was caught in (the execution of) the vilest acts.' See Schirmann, *New Poems from the Genizah*, 408.

9 Of course, Alḥarizi is simultaneously refurbishing his own reworking of al-Ḥariri in *Maḥberot Iti'el*, with its very venal Hever the Kenite; see the Translator's Preface and the Analyses of Introduction and Gate 1. More detailed examinations of Alḥarizi's dual reworking of his Arabic sources, and of his own translations/adaptations in *Maḥberot Iti'el*, remain a desideratum.

The gate begins with the narrator bewailing his poverty and hunger:

I had not a meal; I found not in my sack a mouthful . . . as roams the thirsting bird . . . relieve my thirsting.

Thereafter the preacher weaves in reference to the consumption of dainties, literally and metaphorically:

How long wilt thou persevere in thine error, and eat sweetly of the pasture of thy wrong? . . . The dishes of many meats are more desired of thee than the leaves of doctrines.[10]

The suspicious narrator, seeing him lavishly gifted by the enthralled congregation, trails him to a cave and finds him

sitting opposite an attendant, at some white bread and a roast kid, and over against them was a jar of date wine. And I said to him, 'Sirrah, was that thy story, and is this thy reality?' But he . . . went near to burst with rage . . . But when his fire was allayed and his flame hid itself, he recited:

'I don the black robe to seek my meal, and I fix my hook in the hardest prey:

'And of my preaching I make a noose, and steal with it . . .

'Fortune has forced me to make my way even to the lion of the thicket by the subtlety of my beguiling.

'Yet I do not fear its change, nor does my loin quiver at it:

'Nor does a covetous mind lead me to water at any well that will soil my honour.

'Now if Fortune were just in its decree it would not empower the worthless with authority.'

Then he said to me, 'Come and eat . . .'.[11]

—an invitation which the narrator refuses.

The hypocrisy of the preacher, who has just castigated his hearers for worldliness, disregard of God's commandments, and greed, is rendered the more blatant by his faulting Fortune for setting worthless men in positions of authority: Fortune has done precisely that to the congregation on which he preys! He adds insult to injury by claiming that his greed never leads him to dishonour. Finally, by having Abu Zayd stuff his palate and invite the narrator to do the same, al-Ḥariri rounds out the motif of eating.

Alḥarizi departs markedly from his model on all the above-mentioned points.[12] There is no hint of the mercenary in his Gate 2: even at the close, Hever the Kenite remains the model of probity; and the narrator, whose quest at the start had been religious—the acquisition of moral instruction

[10] *Assemblies*, tr. Chenery, i. 109–10. [11] Ibid. 111–12. [12] *ST* 37. 7–8.

—stays at the hero's side for further edification[13] and spiritual and aesthetic delight.

The motif of food and consumption, so central to the Arabic, is deftly reshaped in the service of sincere instruction. In this 'initial' gate of *Sefer Taḥkemoni* worldlings are admonished to put aside their wine;[14] earth consumes those who dwell therein, even as it tenders a cup of bitters;[15] its cup intoxicates and its honey is mixed with wormwood;[16] on the final day, dainties will be abhorred: the throat will not be able to accommodate them;[17] drunkards are called to awaken;[18] the world's breast drips wormwood;[19] death will consume man's spawn;[20] in the grave, flesh will be wanting for those who had had abundance of it, and moist and ample flesh will be dry;[21] men have erred in tasting of the fruit of the world's gardens;[22] the worm and the grub will feast on the bodies of worldly mortals;[23] men are called upon to prepare spiritual victuals, feast upon them, and then pass on to the next world.[24] Finally, in the next to last line of the gate, the narrator gathers the fruits of Hever the Kenite's poetic speech.

No doubt about it: Alḥarizi here plays the game of reversal, declaring loud and clear that *Sefer Taḥkemoni*'s Hever the Kenite is virtue incarnate, precisely the opposite of Abu Zayd in al-Ḥariri's *Maqāmāt* and Hever the Kenite himself in *Maḥberot Iti'el*—especially in the four gates of those works where the preacher is unmasked as a hypocrite, and above all in their opening gates.[25] In the unlikely event that any readers acquainted with the Arabic sources might have missed his intention, Alḥarizi has his preacher warn emphatically, and at great length, against no other sin than that of hypocrisy,[26] significantly expanding upon the relatively brief admonishment of al-Ḥariri; namely:

> Thou commandest to righteousness, but violatest its sanctuary: thou forbiddest from deceit, but refrainest not thyself: thou turnest men from oppression, and then thou drawest near to it.[27]

Alḥarizi, in the manifesto of the Introduction and Gate 1, has set forward various goals, among them entertainment, redemption of the honour

[13] While the Arabic source has a spiritual component in the narrator's quest this is clearly secondary: seeking food and drink, he comes upon a brilliant preacher and decides on the spot to 'catch his profitable sayings, and gather up of his gems' (*Assemblies*, tr. Chenery, i. 109).

[14] *ST* 31. 19.
[15] *ST* 31. 23–32. 1; 32. 9–10.
[16] *ST* 32. 12, 14–15.
[17] *ST* 33. 4–6.
[18] *ST* 33. 9.
[19] *ST* 33. 14–15.
[20] *ST* 33. 19.
[21] *ST* 33. 26–34. 1.
[22] *ST* 35. 6.
[23] *ST* 35. 15–17.
[24] *ST* 36. 11–13.

[25] The reader of *Sefer Taḥkemoni* will be doubly shocked by the work's continuation, as early as the very next chapter, where the Kenite is a prominent glutton! On the contradictions in the character of Hever, see the discussion in the Afterword.

[26] *ST* 34. 10–24.
[27] *Assemblies*, tr. Chenery, i. 110.

of the Hebrew language, and moral instruction. These three aims are given special resonance in Gate 2 by the use of biblical language: the horrors of death and dissolution, as laid out by Hever, are lent rhetorical emphasis through reapplication of verses and whole episodes from the Bible.

In the book of Exodus, the Israelites are assured by God that they shall not leave Egypt paupers:

And I will dispose the Egyptians favourably toward this people, so that when you go, you will not go empty-handed.[28]

Alḥarizi, wrenching this quotation out of its context, speaks of the worms destined to ravage the future corpses of the audience of the caustic sermon: 'when they (the worms) depart, they shall not go empty-handed'![29] Similarly, he converts a neutral reference to a place called Ḥatserot (literally 'court-yards'), a point of passage in the Israelites' desert journey (Num. 12: 16), to a universal statement on human fate: 'They have readied them tombs in the wilderness; afterward the people removed from Ḥatserot.'[30] In ten further instances in Gate 2, in the Hebrew, texts taken from the story of Egyptian bondage, the Exodus, and the sojourn in the wilderness are made metaphors describing the inexorability of death or the efforts needed to attain to the world to come.[31]

This phenomenon is the more marked in being prefigured by a like clustering in the opening of the frame tale.[32] Heman, in presenting his own backsliding, guilt, and yearning for moral rehabilitation, cites five verses of Exodus and Numbers, three of which convert a biblical event into a metaphorical description of the sinner or his soul: Moses' bringing forth water from a rock[33] stands for the preacher's evoking tears in his listener's eyes;[34] the desert encampment of Kibroth-hattaavah[35] represents enslavement to desire; a desired expulsion of Canaanite foes[36] becomes an urge for moral cleansing.

It is this rhetorical intensity, starkness, and urgency that the translation has sought to recreate in the English.

[28] Exod. 3: 21. [29] *ST* 35. 16–17.

[30] The rendering in this translation: 'Crumbled the castles, fallen the forts, for the people have gone forth from Ḥatserot/courts.'

[31] See D. Segal, 'The Opening', 412–13 and nn. 20–1. Of these references, five are retained in the translation here; and three similar passages, not in the original, but similarly reapplied, are inserted. Thus, in transmuting biblical sacrificial injunctions to a call for internal moral cleansing, the English version substitutes a reworking of Exod. 29: 17–18 for Lev. 3: 3 (*ST* 34. 8–9). On the logic and methods of compensatory allusion see the Translator's Preface.

[32] For a discussion of the phenomenon of scriptural citation clustering see Segal, '"Maḥberet Ne'um Asher ben Yehudah"'. [33] Exod. 17: 6; Num. 20: 11.

[34] *ST* 31. 7. [35] Num. 11: 34–5; 33: 16–17. [36] Num. 22: 6.

Analysis of Gate Three

The Mystery and History of the Hebrew Song of Spain

WELL BEFORE THE MAJOR TOPIC of Gate 3 is openly revealed, Alḥarizi hints at what is to come in veiled fashion.

Heman recalls frolicking in a place of *neradim im kefarim*, 'nard and henna'; of Solomon ibn Gabirol's masterpiece for the Day of Atonement Hever declares, 'all its themes are *neradim im kefarim*'.[1] The rocks of the palace found by Heman, flowing with milk and honey, anticipate the first description of Judah Halevi's poems as sweeter than honey.[2] Heman says of the cups in the Hebrew original, 'and the goblets were cast of light, as it were, and overlaid with gold of desire'—*bizehav haḥeshek meḥushakim*; it is precisely this unusual locution that is predicated of the poet ben al-Mu'alim, of whom Heman says, 'There are none like the poems of ben al-Mu'alim *bizehav haḥeshek meḥushakim*'![3] The Day of Atonement poem of Moses ibn Ezra, with words 'more precious than vessels of gold', recalls the 'gilt vessel' held by every serving lad.[4]

More generally, and yet more subtly, the entire discussion on poetry is prefigured by the repetition of the word *batim*, denoting houses, but alluding to a second meaning—stichs:

> . . . and therein were *batim* filled with all manner of good things . . . The *batim* were covered with patchwork of gold and every *bayit* was crowned with all manner of fillets with coverings of fine woven wear laid thereon, making a coat of many colours; and in the *batim* were tables with all good things readied, lush and vibrant . . .'[5]

Relating to the mention of tables above, Hever says of the poems of Rabbi Barukh that 'their source is blessed and their table set for every comer'.[6] The general characterization of the poetry of Spanish Jewry as being golden, gem-like, and flaming harks back to earlier depictions of the wine.

Alḥarizi's game of foreshadowing augments the humour and shock of the portrayal of the protagonist. Ultimately revealed as a consummate rhetor and authoritative literary critic, Hever first appears as a barbarian and a glutton, and comically so.[7] Alḥarizi wrenches biblical citations out of context,

[1] S. of S. 4: 13; *ST* 38. 7; 44. 9–10. [2] *ST* 38. 19–20; 42. 11. [3] *ST* 39. 7; 42. 8–9.
[4] *ST* 39. 22; 44. 21–2. [5] *ST* 38. 20–39. 3. [6] *ST* 44. 16–17.
[7] The kernel of this idea is to be found in gate 1 of al-Hamadhani, where a young and indigent bystander to a literary discussion renders judgement on stellar figures of Arabic poetry;

often wedding them to highly imaginative personifications—for example, the meat as quailing victim of a voracious predator. But there is more to this humour than meets the eye.

Close attentiveness to motifs, especially in the realm of figurative language, and to such details as recurring words and associated synonyms, reveals that Heman's description of Hever's ravaging of the food foreshadows the poetic prowess of the figures Hever discusses—particularly through the motifs of light, gold, eating, intimidation and fear, combat and warfare, and intellect.

Hever's fervent kissing of the cup anticipates the verses of ben Barukh, kissed by the hearts' mouths.[8] The Hebrew's assertion that the poems of Rabbi Abraham ben Ḥarizi[9] are grasped (*aḥuzim*) in 'the hands of intellect' recalls the grasping arm, hands, and palms of the hungry Hever.[10]

Hever consumes all, leaving nothing for anyone else: 'He left not a thing before us; the land was like a garden of Eden *before* him but *after* him a desolate waste' (Joel 2: 3).[11] Of Solomon ibn Gabirol Hever says, 'The poems of bards who were *before* him are, compared with him, wind and chaos—and *after* him there arose none like him';[12] Halevi 'pulls in' every heart with his liturgical poems,[13] and—so Hever asserts both in rhymed prose and metre—stripped song's treasure bare, then left, barring the door behind him.[14]

Indeed, close examination of the long paean of superlative praise of Halevi uncovers sustained military imagery shared with the Kenite. Hever *attacks* the bread and *prisons* the meat with iron bands; the sheep fear the *sword* of his teeth; his lips are called his *spear* by the contemptuous onlookers, and his tongue, a *pitchfork*.[15] Relatedly, Hever describes Halevi as *yoshev*

and even more so in gate 15 (*The Maqāmāt of Badī' al-Zamān al-Hamādhānī*, 26–30, 70–3). Dishon, 'The Poets of Spain: Gate 3 of *Sefer Taḥkemoni*' (Heb.), details several specific commonalities and differences between our text and gate 15 of al-Hamadhani—including a like ring-structure and shared themes. As well, there is clear influence from gate 22 of al-Ḥariri (himself influenced by al-Hamadhani), where a shabby outsider is spurned, then is silenced by a group discussing two kinds of official writing, then reveals himself as an expert on the subject; but when the group apologizes and courts his friendship, he disdains it and leaves in a huff (*The Assemblies*, ed. Chenery, i. 229–34). A similar dynamic obtains in al-Ḥariri, gate 24 (ibid. 243–53); and, to a lesser degree, in gate 42 (*The Assemblies*, tr. Steingass, ii. 113–19), where an old man mocks the efforts of a group contesting one another in riddle-making.

[8] *ST* 40. 22; 41. 26–7.

[9] The familial relationship of this figure to our author is not known.

[10] *ST* 40. 1–2, 9–15; 45. 2.

[11] *ST* 40. 24–5.

[12] *ST* 44. 2–3.

[13] Conversely, Heman's wandering about the cities of Babylon like a captainless ship prefigures the helplessness of the food before Hever's onslaught.

[14] *ST* 46. 7–9; 47. 3–4.

[15] *ST* 40. 5–6, 15; 41. 1–2. As Dishon observes, this last portrayal, *uleshono kilshono*, 'his tongue is his pitchfork', is a clear evocation of a stich in a famous poem of boast of Solomon

beshevet taḥkemoni, 'dwelling in the encampment of Taḥkemoni'—explicitly linking him with this very work, penned by Alḥarizi! Hever then goes on say, quoting the same verse (2 Sam. 23: 8), that Halevi is Adino the Eznite, wielding his *javelin* against giants.[16] Later, Hever says of Halevi that 'none reach the dust of his *chariot wheel*'; that his tongue is *ḥets barur veshaḥut*, 'a beaten *polished arrow*' (Isa. 49: 2); and, in the metric poem, 'in the war of poesy he sets his encomia as his *arms* to battle, and his utterances are his *spears*'.[17]

Heman's characterization of Hever's utterances as fearsome and thunderous prefigures the Kenite's portrayal of Halevi: 'He yells, he roars aloud.'[18] The warriors of poetry are slain by Halevi; the meat declares, while gripped in Hever's teeth, 'God has given me over into hands from which I cannot rise' (Lam. 1: 14).[19]

By looking closely at the lines following upon the metric poem of praise for Halevi, we can detect further intentional linkage between *Sefer Taḥkemoni*'s protagonist and Spain's master poet. Heman declares that Hever's words 'set all wisdom/*ḥokhmah* mute'; Hever had said of Halevi's poems that they 'struck fear into the hearts of the wise/*haḥakhamim*'; and, at the close of his poem of praise, 'when the wise/*haḥakhamim* waged poetry's war, Judah prevailed'.[20]

A close look at Hever's poem of self-praise reveals that the rhetor himself augments the Hever–Halevi linkage conveyed by Heman. Hever declares that his soul is stationed 'atop the Pleiades (*alei rosh ash*)', that the zodiacal sign of the Ram will 'bow its head (*rosh*)' before his genius; and that 'if figured speech has a head (*rosh*), he is its crown'.[21] Previously, Hever had characterized Halevi's lines as being 'a gracious crown atop (*lerosh*) wisdom' and stated that the reader can find in his rhymed prose 'every beautiful figure of speech (*kol melitsah yafah*)'.[22] Following upon Hever's poem of boast, Heman declares that his friend is 'unique in his generation, with no second' —recalling Hever's emphasis on Halevi's singularity, especially in the poem where Halevi is described as having entered poetry's chambers alone.[23]

These many, purposive links between the two poets are yet further strengthened when we examine subtle foreshadowings of the awe with

ibn Gabirol, who says of an ignorant community contemptuous of him, 'Now I shall tread them like clay, for my tongue is my pitchfork—*ki leshoni kilshoni*' (Schirmann, *Hebrew Poetry*, i. 208, l. 28).

[16] *ST* 46. 3–4. On the significance of the word Taḥkemoni, see the Afterword.

[17] *ST* 46. 9–10, 12. 27–8.

[18] *ST* 42. 21–2; 46. 19–20, citing Isa. 42: 13.

[19] *ST* 46. 5; 40. 17–18.

[20] *ST* 47. 14; 46. 5–6; 47. 11–12.

[21] *ST* 47. 118–24.

[22] *ST* 46. 1–2, 15–16.

[23] *ST* 47. 3–4, 25.

which Hever is ultimately regarded, paralleling his own high regard for, and description of, Halevi.

Heman's observations on the light play of goblets and wine, both in rhymed prose and metrical verse (including the Hebrew words *me'orim* and *orot*, both meaning 'light'), prefigures specifically 'they distinguished his blacknesses [ostensibly Hever's gross behaviour] from his lights (*vehikiru misheḥarav me'orav*)'.[24] The fiery torches proceeding from Hever's mouth, conveying his voracity, prefigure the moment when 'they understood that after his (Hever's) lightnings came clouds (*vehevinu ki aḥarei berakav nesi'im*)', these clouds being filled with the rains of intellect; this same moment was prefigured by the description of wine in goblets as hail and lightning (in the original also as coals).[25] The panic of the fare before Hever prefigures the fear characterizing the group of debating banqueters following the Kenite's rebuke: 'when the people heard the pleasantness of his words they trembled at the thunder of his remarks'.[26]

There can be no doubt: Alḥarizi has provided his readers with a paradoxical message. Judah Halevi is the incomparable master of Hebrew poetry and none shall ever hold a candle to him; but Hever the Kenite, or rather his scriptwriter Alḥarizi, in his brilliance and the high esteem in which he is held, does indeed hold a candle to him!

If that were not confusing enough, our author, in Gate 18, clearly puts the laurel of Hebrew poesy on the head of Solomon ibn Gabirol; the reader is referred to that gate and to its analysis, where this contradiction is discussed.

FURTHER READING: THE HEBREW POETRY OF MUSLIM SPAIN

As (subjective) cultural history, the scope of this gate is large indeed. The identification of all writers mentioned and the explication of Alḥarizi's critiques—involving, *inter alia*, interpretations of his figured speech, both conventional and original, and an in-depth comparison of his evaluations with preceding poets—remain weighty desiderata, necessitating much further research in the field: the unearthing and editing of poems not yet known to us, further aesthetic analyses of major and minor figures, and far more comparative studies of poets and their poems than we now have. All this lies beyond this study.

[24] *ST* 39. 5–18; 42. 22–3.

[25] *ST* 40. 12; 42. 23; 39. 9–10, 18. On the conjoining of opposites see D. Pagis, *Secular Poetry*, 61–2 and nn. 18–129; and Zemaḥ, 'On Conventional Imagery' (Heb.).

[26] *ST* 40. 15–18; 42. 21–2.

Two writers of Hebrew Spain preceded Alḥarizi in surveying, variously, the history of Hebrew poetry and poets there: Abraham ibn Daud, author of *Sefer hakabalah* (ed. G. Cohen) and Moses ibn Ezra, author of the Arabic-language *Kitāb al-muḥādhara wa'l-mudhākara* (ed. and tr. A. S. Halkin). Dishon, 'The Poets of Spain', notes several differences in the three writers' length of comments on a number of poets, and some different emphases and evaluations. A most illuminating discussion of Alḥarizi's Arabic writing, and what that creativity implies about cultural cross-fertilization, is Sadan, 'Rabbi Judah Alḥarizi as a Cultural Crossroads', with its rich bibliography.

For modern overviews of Hebrew poetry in Spain, see Pagis, *Hebrew Poetry of the Middle Ages and the Renaissance*; 'Poetry' in *EJ* xiii. 681–90, 693; 'Piyyut', *EJ* xiii. 573–602, *passim* (see too 'Medieval Hebrew Poetry in Spain' in 'Prosody', ibid. 1211–20, 1239–40); Spiegel, 'On Medieval Hebrew Poetry'; Halkin, 'Judeo-Arabic Literature'; Zinberg, *A History of Jewish Literature*, i: *The Arab-Spanish Period*, which, if dated, contains sensitive renderings of the period's poetry; ibid. xii, analytic index; Waxman, *A History of Jewish Literature*, i; Halkin, 'The Judeo-Islamic Age'; Goitein, *Jews and Arabs: Their Contacts through the Ages*; Rosen-Moked, 'Five Hundred Years of Hebrew Literature in Spain' (Heb.); Scheindlin, 'Hebrew Poetry in Medieval Iberia'; Weiss, 'Court Culture'; and Schirmann, 'The Function of the Hebrew Poet in Medieval Spain'. In Cohen's edition of Abraham ibn Daud's *Sefer hakabalah*, see especially pp. 263–304, 'The Typology of the Rabbinate', showing among other things how ibn Daud's criterion of selection for his very particular history was the poets' penning poems that consoled their people in the exile. See also Drory, '"Words Beautifully Put"', for a discussion of the reasons for the appearance of secular Hebrew verse in Spain.

For collections of several poets mentioned in this gate, see, in the bibliography, entries (here arranged chronologically) under Dunash ben Labrat, Isaac ibn Ghayyat, Samuel Hanagid, Solomon ibn Gabirol, Moses ibn Ezra, Joseph ibn Zaddik, Judah Halevi, and Abraham ibn Ezra. For a study of one poet involving his indebtedness to, and relations with, other poets, see Katz, *Rabbi Isaac ibn Ghayyat: A Monograph* (Heb.).

For a selection of book-length offerings of the poems of several, or individual, major poets of Spain translated into English, see the works by Carmi, Davidson, Goldstein, Millgram, Scheindlin, Weinberger, and the translations of ibn Gabirol (Lewis, Zangwill), Judah Halevi (Salaman), and Moses ibn Ezra (Solis-Cohen) cited in the bibliography. At the time of writing, Isaac Goldberg of Netanya was engaged on a major project of recording—with thousands of entries—translations of Samuel Hanagid, Solomon ibn Gabirol, Moses ibn Ezra, and Judah Halevi into English and several other languages; and studies on these poets and their works.

On Isaac son of Abraham ibn Ezra and his conversion to Islam, see Gil, *In the Kingdom of Ishmael*, i. 468–9 and n. 270. On Samuel, son of Judah ben Abbas, briefly alluded to as a reprobate son, see ibid. 471 and n. 271.

One poem singled out in this gate is discussed at length by Levin, 'The Pen and the Horseman' (Heb.), who points out several Arabic conventions drawn upon by the poet, comparing the poem with the reply-poem of Samuel Hanagid.[27]

For a translation of 'Asher ben Yehuda's Declaration', together with an analysis of the stratum of biblical citations in this work, see Segal, '"Maḥberet Ne'um Asher ben Yehudah"'; see too Scheindlin, 'Fawns of the Palace and Fawns of the Field'.

[27] In an essay entitled 'Strange Cohesion' (Heb.), the author shows how Immanuel, in wedding serious praise to three independent, raucous episodes laced with vulgarity and scatological humour, was influenced by the covert cohesion of Gate 3 of *Sefer Taḥkemoni*.

Analysis of Gate Four

A Descant on the Flea and the Ant

GATE 4 OF *Sefer Taḥkemoni* is the first of several debates or verbal confrontations, whether between Hever and one or more opponents;[1] two other opponents;[2] among Hever's pupils, with Hever serving as judge;[3] with Hever himself taking two sides of an issue;[4] or with various other contending characters.[5]

The debate mode, developed extensively in medieval Persian and Arabic literature, has roots extending back to debates of animals, seasons, and other beings in ancient Sumer and Akkad. Its Hebrew origins lie primarily in early liturgical poetry, linked to holidays and special Sabbaths, and covering a broad spectrum of topics, such as the mountains' vying to receive the Torah and the contention of the body and the soul.[6] The genre was not extensively developed in the *maqāmāt* of Alḥarizi's two major Arab predecessors,

[1] Hever and one opponent: Gates 32 (Hever and a youth, a rhetorical contest), 41 (Hever and a woman in a battle of the sexes), and 42 (Hever and an opponent debate on stinginess and generosity); Hever and multiple opponents: Gates 9 (Hever and thirty challengers) and 19 (Hever and seven laudators of various virtues). Gate 5 is a special category: Hever calls on a group of youths to laud a month each, and is called upon in turn to begin the exercise.

[2] Gates 7 (two warriors) and 24 (two synagogue-goers on the issue of poetic additions to the service).

[3] Gates 16 (pupils of Hever vie as poets) and 44 (Hever's pupils vie in turning out apophthegms).

[4] Gates 26 (on the advisability of travel) and 27 (on drinking wine).

[5] Gates 13 (soul, body, and intellect), 39 (day and night), 40 (sword and pen), 43 (sea and land), and 47 (countries). On this subgroup, debates between concepts or inanimate objects, see the respective analyses as well as the Analysis of Gate 5.

[6] On verbal contests between creatures, substances, or other personifications in Babylonian literature, see Lambert, *Babylonian Wisdom Literature*, 150 and n. 4. For an overview of debate literature in general and Jewish literature in particular, see Turniansky, 'The Jewish Debate Poem' (Heb.), where the author notes and discusses the bibliographic information compiled by Steinschneider, 'Rangstreit-Literatur'; Davidson, in 'Thesaurus of Secular and Sacral Poetry' (Heb.); and Habermann, 'A List of Debate Poems on Superiority in Hebrew' (Heb.). Turniansky also cites Wilensky, 'A Critique of Habermann' (Heb.). The earlier scholarly literature—and as yet unpublished Genizah poems—show that the internal origins of debate poems in Hebrew literature lie in synagogue poems written for special Sabbaths and holidays, where debates take place between such entities as Sinai and other mountains, Hanukkah and Purim, and the months of the year—on which topic, see Gate 5 and Analysis. For more on the broader question of debate literature and its origins, see Analysis of Gate 5, nn. 1, 4–5.

al-Hamadhani and al-Ḥariri. It was the Hebrew author who took it upon himself to develop this mode, heavily influencing later authors of Hebrew rhymed prose.[7]

The combatants here, revealed as Hever and son at the close, seem remarkably well matched: each, with energy and flourish, vaunts his skill, disparages the other, claims awesome powers, and demands of his rival the glorification of a specified insect; and each rises to the challenge in witty description rich in tropes and ingenious citation of biblical texts. An examination of the likenesses and singularities of each performance will do much to clarify a covert dimension of this contest.

Called upon to describe the ant, the young man chooses to focus on the creature's industriousness, a trait lauded in two well-known maxims of Proverbs: 'Go to the ant, thou sluggard; consider her ways, and be wise' (Prov. 6: 6) and 'The ants are a people not strong, yet they prepare their food in the summer' (Prov. 30: 25). The youth alludes to both sayings—at the close of his rhymed-prose exposition, and in the body of his poem, respectively.

In both instances, and throughout his performance, he exploits the fact that the Hebrew word for ant, *nemalah*, is feminine: he makes of the insect a model of female service, a traditional woman *par excellence*. A resolute maidservant, the ant rises early and scurries about in the fulfilment of her duties. A well-organized homemaker, she procures food for her family—and that, months in advance. No instinct-guided automaton, no creature of hive or swarm, no annoying pest to be stepped on, she is a devoted, praiseworthy mother. The ant's caring and kindness are the more tellingly brought home through citation clusters heavily emphasized in the Hebrew text as well as in the rhymed translation: the creature is identified time and again with the selfless Ruth the Moabitess; and with Proverbs' woman of valour, who sees to the needs of her household and wins honour for her husband and herself.[8]

Alḥarizi does still more to crown the ant with virtue. She is not merely industrious, but unusually pious: she obtains matzah (unleavened bread) for the feast of Passover, indeed *matsah shemurah* or 'guarded flour' closely scrutinized at all stages of production, starting with the harvesting of the wheat—and preferred by meticulously observant Jews; and she accepts the talmudic dictum (*Ber.* 56*a*) that exile wipes the slate free of sin. This last stance is the

[7] In the *Maḥberot* of Immanuel of Rome this mode predominates, with the author's persona vying in friendly fashion with his patron, almost always for the sake of debate or show.

[8] For a study of the phenomenon of citation clusters, see Segal, '"Maḥberet Ne'um Asher ben Yehudah"'.

more impressive in that no hint of sin—such as the flea's thievery—attaches to the ant's selfless behaviour; to the contrary, she gathers discarded foods—*leket veshikhehaḥ*, the gleanings, that which is forgotten in the field, food that is the due of the poor.[9]

There is further sophistication in Alḥarizi's use of citation. Not content to identify the ant with scriptural idealizations of female virtue, the youth cites, in witty new contexts, descriptions of slatterns! Thus he utilizes, in closest juxtaposition, two consecutive biblical verses that portray the harlot of Proverbs:

She is loud and stubborn; her feet abide not in her house; now is she without, now in the streets, and lieth in wait at every corner.[10]

Lest any reader miss the author's design here, the Hebrew (and rhymed English) text weds the two citations one with the other, and with a third passage likewise wrenched out of context—the depiction of the people Israel as an unbridled ass in heat, welcoming all fornicators:

Like a wild ass used to the wilderness, snuffing the wind in her eagerness, whose passion none can restrain, none that seek her need grow weary—in her season they shall find her.[11]

Alḥarizi's rewoven product is smooth-seamed, as a look at the literal translation will reveal:

. . . (the ant hurries) about paths on hills and in plains, now without, now in the streets; and all through the days of winter she disappears if she be sought, but in the summer months she may be found by all who seek her—in her month they shall find her; and to seek out her food her feet stay not in her house.

With humour and flair, then, the youthful debater has created a persona from a pastiche of biblical verses, several from the same book or even chapter, sometimes inventively reversing their contexts.

The old man responds to the youth's challenge with a will. He offers no sober-insect-as-pious-and-caring-mother; rather, he limns the flea as a cheery, mocking, and very male, rogue,[12] and that in a plethora of biblical verses even more varied than the young man's selection. A noted Israeli scholar has cited a segment of Alḥarizi's *tour de force* in depicting the flea,

[9] *ST* 51. 16–17, referring to Lev. 19: 9 and Mishnah *Pe'ah* 4: 3; and to Deut. 24: 19 and Mishnah, *Pe'ah* 6: 1. [10] Prov. 7: 11–12. [11] Jer. 2: 24.

[12] In his depiction of the flea, Alḥarizi has expanded upon the rhymed prose and metrical verse of the Arab poet ibn al-Shahid (latter half of the 11th c.). See Ratzaby, 'Arabic Influences' (Heb.), 332–4.

some 220 words, identifying twenty-eight citations taken from thirteen biblical books![13]

If his young rival has drawn heavily from the book of Ruth, and Proverbs' 'woman of valour', the old man counters with brilliant citation clusters of his own, drawn from different scriptural sources, but treating of the same subject. Thus the rascality of the flea is heightened by his frequent identification with—the priest! 'Covering loins to thighs' is an exact quotation of Exodus 28: 42, where a garment of the high priest is described; here, the maiden-flesh roamed over by the flea is denoted. Similarly, 'the breast of the wave offering', 'the heave offering of the shoulder', 'the whole rump and the fat thereof' enjoyed by the marauding insect are all perquisites of the priest! Indeed, in the original he is called 'a priest, sprinkler son of a sprinkler'—an honorific title alluding to the priestly sprinkling of the altar with blood as part of the Day of Atonement ritual.[14]

Both of the above citation clusters can be subsumed under the general rubric of ribald secularization of the sacral, a widespread phenomenon in the metrical poetry of Hebrew Spain, especially in erotic verse.[15] Yet another, and brilliant, example of the same phenomenon in Gate 4 is the identification of the flea with the patriarch Jacob, who, on meeting a camp of angels, named the site Maḥanayim or 'double camp', referring here to the maiden's two breasts!

Further humour attaches to the description of the flea as a criminal (as noted above, in deliberate contrast to the ant) within a context of toraitic legislation—laws of the city of refuge, of the spreading of a cloth to determine virginity, of the fate of a virgin who cries out when attacked, and of blood vengeance.

In sum, if the youth is shown to use biblical sources for a 'pious' effect, citing female exempla of virtue on the one hand and 'converting' allusions to Proverbs' harlot on the other, the old man, in kaleidoscopic inventiveness, stands holy verses on their heads to depict a male thief and quasi-rapist!

The game of point-counterpoint extends farther. The youth cites the ant's blackness at the outset of his rhymed prose exposition and twice in his poem. The old man cites the flea's blackness at the outset of his rhymed prose exposition; in the body of his poem (more often than the youth and with richer metaphor); and, implicitly, at the very close of his poem, where he likens the flea to an inkspot.

The youth speaks of the ant going into exile, as she leaves her quarters

[13] Pagis, *Innovation and Tradition* (Heb.), 74–5. See also Carmi, *The Penguin Book of Hebrew Verse*, 27–8.

[14] JT *Ber.* 7: 4.

[15] See Segal, '"Maḥberet Ne'um Asher"', 24–6.

underneath the soil; the greybeard speaks of the winter hibernation of the flea as going into exile.

The word *leḥem*, 'bread', is emphasized in the metric poem describing the ant, at the meeting of biblical allusion and pun: she goes, like Ruth, to Bethlehem—in Hebrew *Beit-leḥem*, which could mean 'house/source of bread'; contrapuntally, Hever, as he begins his description of the flea, declares that the latter 'eats the bread of wickedness', *leḥem resha yilḥam* (Prov. 4: 17).

It is not surprising that of the two debaters it is Hever who lauds the roguish flea—by roguishly 'dishonouring' sacred biblical verses even as the flea ravages his victims, be they king or maiden. Hever's son, too, of course, is a hoodwinker in the two gates in which he appears—as a youngster both here and in Gate 29; but Hever's rascality is more amply attested in *Sefer Taḥkemoni*.[16] In short, the miscreant flea that Hever describes is all but a stand-in for himself.

The contrast of ant/saint with flea/miscreant makes for lively reading and good drama: small wonder that the judge was prepared to part with coin for the pleasures of this impromptu performance (impromptu to his knowledge; planned, to the readers'—though only at the close).

Yet the contrast goes beyond entertainment.

Seen in overview, Gate 4 presents two radically opposite models of behaviour: resolute and hardworking virtue, as against roguish exploitation and sensuality. These two poles relate to the author's explicit declaration in his Introduction as to what his work contains and to whom it is addressed: it holds both preachment and edification on the one hand, and humorous, entertaining tales on the other—even if the author insists that the latter category is intended to woo readers to 'the good of the Lord'.[17] Teaching or preaching predominate in the anti-worldly sermon of Gate 2, the literary history of Gate 3, the model prayers of Gates 14 and 15, a grim portrayal in Gate 25, and elsewhere; entertainment prevails in the rhetorical fireworks of Gate 8 and other gates of verbal display, and in the above-mentioned gates instancing Hever's rascality; and several gates variously weave these two strains together. Gate 4 seems to strike a balance: the judge, after all, calls the contest a draw. Neither rascality nor virtue can claim the victory.

But in a sense, the laurel is due Hever: not only because his insect is more richly realized than the gleaner-mother ant, being thief, attacker, seducer-rapist, glutton, and judge; but because the upshot of the debate is, after all, the bilking of the hoodwinked judge, a deception that sets both debaters, if not their author as well, in the ranks of roguery—to wit, in the camp of the laughing, winking flea.

[16] See esp. Gates 20, 21, 30, and 38.

[17] *ST* 13. 22–3. On the covert level of Alḥarizi's apologia here, see the Afterword.

Analysis of Gate Five

Twelve Poets Sound the Months' Round

THE SINGULARITY OF THIS GATE in *Sefer Taḥkemoni*, and indeed in all Jewish literature, is the inventive, often audacious, description of the year's months in tripartite fashion: as season, Jewish holiday, and always an occasion for drinking wine![1]

The flippancy of the enterprise is most apparent in the months of Tammuz and Av. The seventeenth day of the former commemorates the breaching of the walls of Jerusalem, hardly an occasion for a bacchanalia. Similarly, an unqualified injunction to down wine in the month of Av, the month of the destruction of both the First and Second Temples, is grotesque. Indeed the especially pious refrain from drinking wine at all from 17 Tammuz to 9 Av.[2]

This hardly exhausts, however, the brazenness of this gate's calendar. Several of the transitions from Jewish sacral time to calls for tippling were written with more than tongue in cheek. Such is the case with Tishrei, where the clean soul worthy to look at the face of God the King is described metaphorically as blossoming like the vine, and enjoying a rich table with cup overflowing with wine; thence the speaker readily proceeds to tout the joys of drinking *actual* wine.

The ninth speaker's light-hearted shift from sacral to secular joy is smoothed, if not blurred, via rhyme linkage. The original reads, 'Therefore is

[1] For a discussion of the Hebrew wine poetry of Spain, upon whose conventions our author drew, see Pagis, *Secular Poetry*, 253–66; for further discussion, and translations and analyses of several wine poems, see Scheindlin, *Wine, Women, and Death*, 19–76; for an earlier discussion of wine poetry see Ratzaby, 'The Wine Poetry of Rabbi Samuel Hanagid' (Heb.). Turniansky, 'Debate Poems', 3 n. 7, notes that unpublished manuscripts from the Cairo Genizah contain debates written for the synagogue service, among them an argument of the twelve months of the year over the redemption, for a prefatory prayer for Passover; and a debate between Nisan and the rest of the months, for recitation on the Sabbath of the New Moon. Whether or not this gate is indebted to either of these two poems remains a subject for further investigation.

[2] The three weeks between 17 Tammuz and 9 Av bear the name of *bein hametsarim*, 'between the straits', and comprise a time of mourning; albeit the prescribed renouncements are observed, in most quarters, only from 1 to 9 Av. These include abstention from entertainment, music, weddings, non-ritual bathing, eating new fruits, cutting hair; and, in particularly observant quarters, abstention from eating meat and drinking wine, except on the Sabbath. See *EJ* xv. 1124; and Zevein, *The Holidays in Jewish Law* (Heb.), ii. 409–11.

it fitting for every thinking man at this time to rejoice, *lismo'aḥ*, and bless God over the fruit of the vine; and bless Noah, *No'aḥ*, who, through wine, invented for us rest, *mano'aḥ*'. The call to bless Noah, the second of three rhyme-words, is, syntactically, an expansion of a simple sentence (centring on God) to a compound sentence with a new and earthly focus. Further wit accrues to our text when the reader recalls what appears in Scripture following the word *mano'aḥ*: 'This one (*zeh*) will comfort us from our work and the toil of our hands' (Gen. 5: 21). In Scripture, *zeh* refers to Noah; Alḥarizi makes the word denote wine; and the quote is doubly brazen in that Noah's downfall was wine: drinking to excess, he fell into a stupor in his tent, where he was disgraced by one of his progeny (Gen. 9: 20–7).

Kislev's speaker is not alone in toying with biblical citation. All the contestants use scriptural verses liberally, and all end with a verse either wrenched out of (usually sacral) context or metaphorized or both.

In the book of Ruth, the embittered Naomi, having lost husband and sons, declares, upon her return to Bethlehem, 'Full I went forth but am brought back empty by the Lord' (YHWH, pronounced *adonai* in Jewish tradition; Ruth 1: 21); the same verse is predicated of the drained cup in Nisan, with the last word written out as *adonai*, literally, 'my lords'. 'Delay me not, seeing that the Lord has prospered my way', declares Abraham's servant Eliezer to his master's kin, as he seeks speedy return to Canaan (Gen. 24: 56); in our text, wine is the speaker demanding to be downed in the month of Iyyar. The remedy for the scorpion-stung Israelites in the wilderness is the bronze serpent held aloft: 'And it shall come to pass, that everyone that is bitten, when he sees it, shall live' (Num. 21: 8); here Tammuz's healing cup is proffered to those bitten by sorrow.

The spokesman for Tishrei crowns his flippancy with a citation from tractate *Avot* of the Mishnah (popularly known as *Pirkei Avot* or 'Ethics of the Fathers'), a quote demanding righteous action in view of life's brevity; here, drinking is insisted upon for the same reason. Rivalling this (mis)-appropriation from classical sources is the quotation closing the description of Tevet, lauding the power of wine to wipe out grief: 'and a fire went forth from before the Lord consuming them [i.e. griefs]' (Lev. 9: 24 and 10: 2): the quote in question describes the violent death of two sons of Aaron, ascribed variously in rabbinic literature to their having approached the altar in a state of intoxication![3]

[3] No less than twelve reasons in all were adduced by the rabbis for the sudden demise of these men: they include having offered up a sacrifice on their own initiative, not having married, not having begotten children, and having approached the altar unwashed or improperly attired. The mention of intoxication is found in *Pesikta derabi kahanah* 95; *Leviticus Rabbah*

Thus far this analysis has focused on rhymed prose exposition; but the metric rhymed triplets closing the description of each month, themselves a distinguishing formal stylistic of this gate, partake of the game of transmuting holy to profane. Thus the tippler is enjoined in Elul, traditional month of penitence, to bow before the branches of the fruit tree and to the tree trunk, this 'admonition' being a citation of a verse castigating—idol worship: '. . . I roasted meat and ate it—should I make the rest an abhorrence? Should I bow to a block of wood?' (Isa. 44: 19). The speaker for Marḥeshvan, the month following the New Year and Day of Atonement, toys further with the theme of sin and forgiveness, as he calls on the celebrant to pardon the transgressions and iniquities of time—through drinking!

Alḥarizi's boldness in this gate is all the more striking when viewed against the backdrop of earlier calendric debate in Hebrew literature. No less than three *piyutim*, or poetic expansions of the synagogue service, contain the altercation of the months over the privilege of serving as the time of Israel's redemption from Egypt: an unpublished manuscript from the Cairo Genizah, for recitation on the Sabbath of the New Moon;[4] another fragment, recently published, most likely intended for the same Sabbath;[5] still another, from the 'Fragment Targum of the Pentateuch', for a prefatory prayer for Passover.[6] A citing of the utterances of selected months from this last source will serve to demonstrate several commonalities, pointing to the likelihood that our author was influenced especially—whether directly or through an intermediary version or versions—by this text: the citing of Jewish history and holy days (in the Targum, the overwhelmingly predominating theme); mention of weather and seasonal change; retention of the order of Nisan to Adar; the inclusion of a pun on the name of a month; and ending the Adar section with the theme of drink (here metaphorical):

Sivan answers and says, 'It is in me that they should be delivered, and I am the one who should receive the royal crown for it was in me that Mount Sinai stood arrayed

12: 1 and 5; and the Targum Jonathan on Leviticus 10: 9. All these sources are cited in Shinan, 'The Sins of Nadav and Avihu', 201–14.

4 Turniansky, 'The Jewish Debate Poem', notes several debates in early synagogue poetry: that of the mountains, for the privilege of the revelation of God to the Israelites; of Sabbath and the New Moon; of winter and summer; of body and soul (on which, see Gate 13); and more (Turniansky 3 and nn. 6 and 7). On the (likely) relation of such debates to the genre of debate poem, or *tenson*, in the ancient and medieval Near East, see Gates 13, 39, 40, 43, and 47.

5 Van Bekkum, 'Observations on the Hebrew Debate in Medieval Europe', 80–2. See too Klein, 'Months Compete for the Passover Honour', 14–18.

6 The Paris manuscript of the Fragment Targum, re-edited by Klein, *Fragment Targums*, i. 72–3 (text), ii. 37–9 (translation); cited by Brock, 'A Dispute of the Months', who offers his own translation at pp. 209–11.

like a bridegroom, and all Israel was eager to hear the commandments of the Law which were (coming) from the mouth of the Living One.' . . . Marḥeshvan answers and says,[7] '. . . in me the winter rains begin to fall and the four gates of the earth sway.' . . . Teveth answers and says, '. . . I am good (*tab*) and in me every good thing is a gift.' . . . Shevat answers and says, '. . . in me all the dormant (lit. silent) trees get up and open their mouths to praise the living God with their leaves when they see me,' . . . Adar answers and says, 'I will not give any reply at the present moment for it is a time of great straits and the decrees of the enemy are spread out on the pillars of the synagogue to finish off and destroy the enemies of Israel;[8] and so I am not now at leisure or peace, until I break the decrees and he mix [the cup of punishment] for himself; the cup which he has mixed he shall drink, and the pit he has dug shall he fill.'[9]

There are other arresting facets of this gate.[10] By far the longest description of any month—the most developed in its metaphors and the most original in its use of citation-cum-metaphor-cum-pun (*barak*/lightning melds with the hero Barak of Judges 5)—is that preceding the contest. As such it focuses only, and richly, on the natural aspect of Nisan. Yet the speaker here is not Hever, but Heman the Ezrahite. Relatedly, it is Heman—more than Hever, explicit originator of the contest—who introduces major recurring motifs: the personification of seasons and the garden, warfare between the seasons/forces of hot and cold, and flora as attire. Of course it is given Hever to set up (1) the basic tripartite structure of this jovial calendar; (2) the pattern of closing the rhymed prose paean with an especially arresting biblical quote; (3) wrapping up the praise of the month with a three-stich poem; and (4) beginning each such poem with a pun on the name of the month.[11]

The gate exhibits an unusual breaking of narrative framework, recalling the Introduction and Gate 1. Here both the time-frame and the frame of the tale are shattered. The gate began as a story of a contest viewed by Heman,

[7] All the months but two (Nisan, who hears the others present their claims and is himself awarded the privilege of containing the redemption, and Adar) begin their brief talk with the statement, 'It is in me that they should be delivered, and I am the one who should receive the royal crown.'

[8] 'The enemies of Israel' denotes, euphemistically, Israel.

[9] Brock, 'A Dispute', 209–11. The reader is referred to Brock's arresting article, which includes *inter alia* an anonymous Syriac debate among the months, wherein the excellences of the seasons blend, or vie frequently with, the relation of the months to the biography of Jesus. There is no evidence that Alḥarizi had access to Syriac literature; and the specific relationship of Alḥarizi's calendrical exercise to this or other debates mentioned or quoted in Brock's essay lies outside this study.

[10] For a concealed rhetorical feature of this gate, see the Afterword.

[11] On the intermingling of the identities of author, Hever, and Heman, see Analyses of the Introduction and Gate 1, and the Afterword.

but ends as a past-tense account of the widespread circulation of the text—not the event—with dramatic and comic repercussions on the behaviour of its readership: 'Now when this *maḥberet* was heard throughout the land, drunkards placed it upon their heads as a crown and upon their hearts for safe-keeping'[12]—this being an audacious parody on the commandment for phylacteries: 'You shall set them (divine teachings) as a sign upon your hand and for frontlets between your eyes' (Exod. 13: 16; Deut. 6: 8, 11: 18). The deliberateness of this parody is hammered home in the very next phrase, 'and when the voice was heard in Damascus, its congregations studied it like the study of the recitation of the Shema'—the Shema being the major source of the sign-and-frontlets injunction.[13]

The gate has closed, then, with an especially adroit twist, worthy of its speaker—who can be none other than Alḥarizi himself: 'Here is the numbering of your months: I have set them out in number for you, not a one missing.' Thus the author ends his calendrical *tour de force* by a double shattering of framework: Heman's description of an event suddenly becomes a history of the impact of the entire gate, in which Heman is himself a character; and the author, who has been content to represent himself throughout via the characters of Heman and Hever and the other speakers, steps forward at the close in barely veiled fashion for the readers' applause.

[12] This conclusion is adapted from gate 49 of al-Ḥariri: 'When the sons of Sasan heard these beautiful mandates, they prized them above the mandates of Lokman, and learnt them by heart, as the mother of the Koran is learnt, so that they reckon them to this time the best that they can teach their children, and more profitable to them than a gift of gold' (*Assemblies*, tr. Steingass, ii. 175).

[13] The Shema is the central section of the morning and evening service, known as 'Shema and its blessings'. Discussion of the rules governing the time of the recitation of the Shema in the morning and evening are to be found in Mishnah *Ber.* 1: 1–5. The reciting of the Shema upon the bed is a reference to the recitation of the Shema before sleep. See Hertz, *Authorised Daily Prayer Book*, 'Prayer before Retiring to Rest at Night', 996–1004; and 'Night Prayer', *EJ* xii. 1157–8.

Analysis of Gate Six

Of One Too Swiftly Sped to the Marriage Bed

IN ITS CONTEXT IN *Sefer Taḥkemoni*, Gate 6 surprises the reader in presenting—until the close—the protagonist in a reversed situation, that of victim; and a highly comical situation at that.[1]

A dupe by his own account, Hever seems a far cry from the cunning deceiver of Gate 4: he himself is taken in by a crafty old woman who is far more adroit with words than he. Fiercely aroused by her depiction of quintessential beauty, he walks in a daze through a contraction of marriage with a swindler, and proceeds to a wedding night wherein his bride is revealed as quintessential foulness.

In several instances, the reversals of Hever's expectations and fortunes are quite specific. Described by the old crone as a snarer of women through his beauty, Hever is trapped by the thought of a nubile beauty, and then snared by a woman who is ugliness incarnate. Praised as a man all of whose 'debts have been paid by beauty', Hever is wed to a mate whose mock dowry ensures him penury.

Hever's helpmate, he is promised, will calm his restless nights; wedding her brings him the most horrific night of his life. The promised bride's hair is described as jet-black, 'bringing on the night', but turns out to be white. Her cheeks are called a candelabrum by the enthusiastic matchmaker; her mouth, a source of perfume; her eyes, a doe's. Hever, in his rage, describes these same bodily features as monstrosities.[2]

There are other aspects of the maid's description by the crone that are ironically contrasted in the tale's continuation. Hever is told, in the original text, 'you will walk by the splendour of her countenance'; ultimately he flees in deep darkness (literal and metaphorical) from that very countenance. He is assured that the appearance of the girl's body will split the heart of any onlooker, stir up a fire in his midst, even drive him mad. All of this proves

[1] The comedy of the text is neither unmixed nor devoid of problematic, especially the brutal denouement. This will be dealt with later in the analysis.

[2] For Arabic sources for angry depictions of a foul woman, see Ratzaby, 'Arabic Influences', 329–32. One source is gate 40 of al-Ḥariri, where an irate husband tells his wife, 'I found thee uglier than a monkey, drier than a strip of hide, tougher than a palm fibre, more offensive than carrion, and more troublesome than the cholera and dirtier than a menstrual cloth . . .' (*Assemblies*, tr. Steingass, ii. 103).

literally true, as Hever is driven berserk by what he encounters, a misfeatured woman prefigured (often in detail) by the deformities of the old crone herself.[3] Similarly, the bowled-over Hever is told of his dream bride, *raḥok mipeninim mikhrah* (Prov. 31: 10), rendered by NJPS as 'her worth is far beyond that of rubies'—but translatable in context as 'her worth is far from (i.e. below) that of rubies'.

And the ironies spill on. The lot of him who 'bows, falls down, and lies between her feet' is paradisiacal, the crone declares as she perverts a biblical verse that is itself ironic, Judg. 5: 27: 'At her feet he sank, lay outstretched, at her feet he sank, lay still', where the prophetess Deborah boasts of the downfall of the enemy general Sisera at the hands of a woman whom he (implicitly) lusted after.[4]

Hever's language of anticipation—he speaks of 'a night of vigil', *leil shimurim* (Exod. 12: 42)—bears overtones of revelation, the night wherein God revealed himself as Israel's rescuer in Egypt (Exod. 12: 42); but the revelation awaiting Hever is that of a woman hell-sent.[5]

As ever, Alḥarizi plays the game of thematic prefiguration, overt and covert. Heman's sporting with loved friends, and actively questing for joy and delight, prefigures the partly similar goal of Hever. Looking closely at Heman's language, we read that he sat with *ḥaverim ahuvim mibenei hanedivim*, 'loved friends, sons of generous/princely men'; and the crone's first description of the intended bride is *mibenot hanedivim*, 'of the daughters of generous/princely men'.

The choice of locale, Thebez,[6] is most subtly prefigurative. Thebez was the site of a crushing defeat of a warrior brought about by a wise woman who dropped a stone on his head (Judg. 9: 50–6)![7]

[3] Double wit is provided by the use of Deut. 28: 34, 'Thou shouldst go mad at the sight of thine eyes that thou shouldst see.' The crone guarantees the protagonist ecstasy as she wrenches from its context the assured curse of exile for the Israelites should they abandon Mosaic law. But ecstasy is far from Hever's lot! Nonetheless Hever's encounter with his bride restores the verse to its original meaning, inasmuch as flight is a kind of exile. This citation is used in a similar erotic context in Gate 34.

[4] On the subtleties of his locution, see Alter, *On Biblical Poetry*, 43–9. Further to appreciate Alḥarizi's language here, let the reader recall that the lusted-after woman spoken of in Scripture was the wife of Hever the Kenite!

[5] See the discussion on citations of negative revelation in D. Segal, '"Maḥberet Ne'um Asher", §C-5, p. 26. A specific borrowing from that text is the use of 'I found no vision from the Lord' (Lam. 2: 9).

[6] As well, Thebes in Greece may be intended; see S–F, *History*, ii. 166 n. 83.

[7] The text provides here a yet subtler prefiguration. *Lehitaden min hata'anugim bemarbets* means, literally, 'to delight in the pleasures of lying down'. The non-specified pleasures, be they of lolling about or hints of sexual play, are particularly strange in that the word *marbets*

The question of reader response to this tale is one that cannot be avoided. The reader encounters, at the close, the picture of Heman the Ezrahite rolling on the ground with laughter, having been told of a verbal castigation of an ugly woman unparalleled (in Hebrew literature) in its viciousness[8]—capped by a murder, or at least a brutal beating (the Hebrew is ambiguous).

The question of what is so funny, is a serious one. Clearly one possibility is that Heman is splitting his sides to hear of a deceiver getting his just deserts. Generally an adroit charlatan, this ultimate egotist who seeks not only the perfect sexual object but a source of lucre as well, is saddled, through cunning, with an impoverished monstrosity. Equally as probable, the Ezrahite is guffawing at a tale he knew, or at least suspected, to be fictitious from the start. His early question as to what happened is preceded by the statement that he laughed. Seen in this way, more than half the fun (of Hever's auditor and the reader both) is the savouring of an account whose teller is deliberately laying out his own cupidity, naïveté, and comeuppance for entertainment's sake. The Kenite's early portrayal of the old woman as evil and false, before he cites her words to him, would support this interpretation. And in the light of this reading, Heman would laugh, *inter alia*, at the unmitigated gall of Hever's praising God for his rescue, after having perpetrated a civil and moral crime; and is perhaps laughing at Hever's nerve in having tried to pass off a fantasy as history.[9]

All this, however, will not solve for every modern reader the dilemma of laughter following on the account of the grisly fate of the ugly bride.

If self-ridicule were the goal of Hever, and/or ridicule of Hever on the part of Alḥarizi, our author had a clear model: the very text he borrowed from so selectively. In *Minḥat yehudah sone nashim* ('The Tale of Judah the Misogynist'),[10] we have two ludicrous figures: first, the aged Taḥkemoni, to whom it is 'revealed' in a night vision rife with illogic and scriptural perversion (with highly selective use of rabbinic exegesis), that all mankind's woes are due to women;[11] and second, his son Zerah, who sets out in holy zeal to

is predicated only of animals in the Bible (see BDB 918, *r-b-ṣ*); and a lustful Hever, who did indeed look forward to the delights of lying down (on the marital couch), proceeds to describe his bride as a monstrous animal and ends by acting like a beast!

[8] For the literary roots of Hever's diatribe, see the discussion on the genre of vituperative poetry (modelled on Arabic example) in Levin, *The Embroidered Coat*, 309–14.

[9] On this point see Brann, 'Power in the Portrayal', 9.

[10] For the relevant, and other, excerpts from this tale, see Schirmann, *Hebrew Poetry*, ii. 70–86; for a brief discussion of the work, which was revised by the author in his own lifetime, see ibid. 67–70, and S–F, *History*, ii. 129–36. See also Dishon, 'On the Sources' (Heb.); ead., 'Was Joseph ibn Zabara the Misogynist a Misogynist?' (Heb.).

[11] It may be the case that Alḥarizi's very naming of his work *Taḥkemoni* was intended to

preach to all men of women's evils. The author so orchestrates his characters that the crusader is lured into disregarding his vows by a cunning and extraordinarily beautiful woman, who converts into a shrew following the wedding ceremony. The dupe and the victim is Zerah; the victimizer is his bride, who, in context, arouses no little sympathy in trapping such an arrant misogynist. There is no identification of a woman's foul appearance with moral foulness in *Minḥat yehudah*; there is no verbal or physical brutalization of women; and no one laughing at such things.

One cannot but suspect that the author has revealed a personal bias and a sense of humour that not all his readers will share.[12] This is said with full appreciation of the dangers of facile identification of a writer with his characters, a danger especially great in a work where the author frequently, often transparently, identifies with his creations.[13]

The fact remains, however, that apart from the personified Hebrew language of the Introduction and the (servile) ant of Gate 4, the entire book can be scoured without turning up a praiseworthy woman, excluding a handful mentioned in minuscule anecdotes in Gate 44. Indeed the battle-of-the-sexes debate in Gate 41 could have afforded the author a prime opportunity to right the imbalance, but such is not the case.[14] Furthermore in the poetical

hint subtly at his sympathy towards the misogyny of Zerah's father. If such echoing is deliberate, it can be added to the echoing of 'Hakmoni'—or 'Wisdom'—employed 250 years earlier by the Italian sage Shabbetai Donnolo (913–*c.*982) as the title of a learned commentary on the mystical corpus *Sefer yetsirah* (S–F, *History*, ii. 185 n. 4).

[12] For a consideration of anti-female animus in medieval Hebrew *belles-lettres*, as well as related sentiments in European and Arabic literature, see Rosen, 'On Tongues Being Bound and Let Loose', esp. 75–6. In discussing the excoriation of garrulous and shrewish wives and the praise of silence in women, related to their domestic seclusion, Rosen holds that, in general, courtly poetry and *maqāma* literature served to sanction prevalent thought patterns and the existing social order. For a brief survey of attitudes towards women in Jewish literature from the Bible to the medieval period—including some non-Jewish attitudes—citing important secondary sources and studies, see Dishon, 'Images of Women in Medieval Hebrew Literature'. For a study of the theme of the cunning woman in particular, see Roth, 'The "Wiles of Women" Motif'. See also the discussion on the depiction of the world as an ugly and evil woman—found e.g. in Gate 2 above (*ST* 31–3)—in Levin, 'Time and the World' (Heb.), 68–79; and Dishon, *The Book of Delight of Joseph son of Meir ibn Zabara* (Heb.), index s.vv. *genut nashim* ('disparagement of women'), and *sinat nashim* ('misogyny').

[13] On the blurring of boundaries between the author, on the one hand, and the protagonist and narrator on the other, see Analyses of the Introduction and Gate 1, and the Afterword. On the dangers of assigning an anti-feminist bias to an author whose work contains anti-feminist characters or statements, see Pagis, 'Variety in Medieval Rhymed Narratives', section titled 'Sources, Context, Argument', 91–5.

[14] See Analysis 41 for a close comparison of the strengths and weaknesses of the debaters there.

catch-all of Gate 50 the only woman cited as learned is shamefully promiscuous.[15]

One might well see in this gate a quintessential example of literary coarseness towards women as women, call it chauvinism or what you will. One might have good reason. The definition of womanhood here is that of subservient wife and sexual partner.[16] She must be beautiful. She must have means. She may be beaten.

Some may laugh; others will not.

[15] *ST* 397. 1–12. In another poem in this section—390. 17–22—an unsuspecting father is chagrined to learn that his supposedly virgin daughter is pregnant.

[16] See, in this regard, Dishon, 'The Depiction of the Ideal Woman' (Heb.).

Analysis of Gate Seven

Of Battle Lords and Dripping Swords

AMONG THE MORE SOBER GATES OF *Sefer Taḥkemoni*, the seventh is unique. If later we are to encounter violence and death,[1] Gate 7 alone presents vivid, even horrific, battlefield carnage.

The central episode, that of the confrontation of two mighty camps, is peculiarly constructed: Hever the Kenite briefly portrays, in rhymed prose, the opposing parties (1); lays out, in metrical verse, their ferocity in action (2); reverts, chronologically, to the opposing champions' initial poems of boast (3 and 4); then presents, once more in rhymed prose, the armed slaughter that takes place (5), a description that contradicts the preceding heroic account, all the warriors being shown as devastated victims. Alḥarizi hammers home this inversion, shattering the expectation he has created, and subverting established literary conventions in Hebrew and Arabic martial poetry.

First, let us examine how the expectation of bravery is built up. Among the several motifs that convey fierceness in Hever's initial account, at least four are shared by one or both of the champions' poems: the association or identification of the warriors with savage beasts; enthusiastic, at times erotic, pursuit of injury and death; weapons, personified, as ominous or bloody; and the potency of battlefield shouts. These motifs are summarized below.

1. *The association or identification of the warriors with beasts.* Hever likens the warriors, as a whole, and the two poets specifically, to lions, particularly in terms of their loud cries. The second poet speaks of battle cries as a roar.[2]

2. *Enthusiasm for injury or death.* In Hever's account, the warriors' spear points are honed for death and long for death, having been forged, as it were, in death's crucible. They run to embrace each other like lovers; and view disaster as spice, spear wounds as sweet, and sword cuts as ornaments.

The first speaker holds death his sire, and so ardently seeks death on the field that life is as poison to his taste: death would be sweet to his lips. The second holds himself the very twin of death, who suckled with him at one breast.

---

[1] See Gate 25.

[2] Inasmuch as the translation faithfully mirrors all the cited motifs and figures of speech in their specificity, the Hebrew sources, by page and line, have not been cited.

3. *Weapons, as ominous or bloody, and often personified.* Hever likens the contenders' flashing spears to stars; and their swords to fire, lightning, and blood-red roses.

The first poet claims that his spear and shield witness his prowess, that he sates his thirsty sword with blood, and prefers bow and sword to wealth. His rival boasts that his sword refuses its sheath till it be blood-caked, is the site of terrors, frightens foes in their sleep, and piles up skulls like reapers pile up sheaves of wheat.

4. *Roaring.* In Hever's first account, mountains shudder before the foemen's cries, giants turn into grasshoppers, lion-hearts into wax.

Both poets are presented as roaring fiercely in mutual rebuke; the first poet, specifically, asserts that his battle cry blasts the heavens.

In the face of these various emphases on martial valour, the reader, of course, anticipates a continuation of heroic encounter, with one camp proving to be the more heroic. This anticipation is doubled in that the aggregate of descriptions, literal and figurative, derive from poetry where this is precisely what happens: namely, the Hebrew poetry of Samuel Hanagid, eleventh-century vizier and commander of the armed forces of the kingdom of Granada;[3] and Arabic battle odes, both pre- and post-Islamic.

A few examples of the four above-mentioned motifs in Samuel Hanagid's and Arabic poetry, drawn almost wholly from the most helpful article by Israel Levin on Samuel Hanagid's indebtedness to earlier Arabic example, follow:[4]

1. Association, or identification, of warriors with beasts

Samuel Hanagid

And with us—men like lions . . .

('Hali ta'as', st. 30)[5]

[3] Grammarian, exegete, rabbi, polemicist, talmudist, and commander of the armies of the Berber kingdom of Granada, Samuel ben Joseph ibn Naghrella, or Samuel Hanagid, left a legacy of over forty martial, or war-related poems, running from three to 149 stichs, variously depicting his battles, often in great detail and at times in conjunction with other problems and concerns—ageing, sin, Zion's plight, and more. For an overview of the life and times of Samuel Hanagid see S–F, *History*, i. 183–256; *EJ* xiv. 816–18 and the bibliography there; and especially Levin, *Samuel Hanagid: His Life and Poetry* (Heb.); and Schirmann, 'Samuel Hanagid: The Man, the Soldier, the Politician'. On the genre of martial poetry see Segal, 'Observations on Three War Poems of Samuel Hanagid'.

[4] Levin, 'Martial Poetry' (Heb.). Further examples of several motifs and conventions cited by Levin are to be found in Schippers, *Arabic Tradition and Hebrew Innovation*, 257–89.

[5] *Divan shmuel hanagid*, ed. Jarden, i: *Ben tehilim*, 18.

Lions (warriors) look upon a fresh wound
upon their head as though it were a crown.
('Elohah oz', st. 67)[6]

And every one who roared on the day of ruin like lions—
lions roar over them today. ('Belibi ḥom', st. 58)[7]

Arabic Poetry

Is he ignorant of the wind of the lion until he tastes it?
And the wild beasts know well the wind of lions.
(al-Mutanabbi, ode to Saif al-Daula, st. 34)[8]

Lions of the fray—but for the smiting of our swords
they would never have worn chains or dwelt in prison.
(Ibn ʿUnain, ode on the capture of Damietta, st. 16)[9]

Whenever the squadrons of lions are gored by such under
the dust cloud of battle, they depart before him, but he
does not depart.
(al-Mutanabbi, ode on his prowess, st. 24)[10]

2. Enthusiastic, at times erotic, attraction to injury and death

Samuel Hanagid

Chieftains on the day of rage, wrath,
and zeal choose Death's first-born.
('Eloha oz', st. 53)[11]

Lions (warriors) look upon a fresh wound
upon their head as though it were a crown.
('Eloha oz', st. 67)[12]

They (enemy troops) rush to destroy their flesh,
abhorring the life of flesh.
('Belibi ḥom', st. 41)[13]

(With us were) every swift swordsman and every man running
to slaughter goodheartedly and with joy.
('Hali ta'as', st. 33)[14]

[6] Ibid. 8. [7] Ibid. 84.

[8] Arberry, *Arabic Poetry*, 88: 'The wild beasts take cover when they catch the scent of a lion. The domesticus [foe in this poem] is more stupid, in that he ignored the scent (fame) of the lion he was facing, i.e. Saif al-Daula' (ibid. 89 n.). [9] Ibid. 124.

[10] Arberry, *Poems of al-Mutanabbī*, 52, poem 7. [11] *Ben tehilim*, ed. Jarden, 8.

[12] Ibid. [13] Ibid. 83. [14] Ibid. 18.

Arabic Poetry
Death is sweeter than honey to us,
us sons of Dabah, camel masters.
(Abu Tammam, *Dīwān al-Ḥamāsa*)[15]

Meeting in the straits, they embraced—
their meeting spear-laden, their embrace the swords' blow.
(al- ʿAqqad)[16]

3. Weapons as ominous or bloody, and often personified

Samuel Hanagid
Recall how He (God) sated your sword with blood
like water drawn from the wells of joy.
('Shmuel kademah', st. 36)[17]

With links of mail inlaid like waves
and shields red as [red-skinned] scrolls . . .
You see only the flash of spears . . .
('Hali ta'as', sts. 34, 37)[18]

Arabic Poetry
How many a suckling child they weaned with the edge of
the sword before the time of weaning!
(Ibn al-Rumi, ode on storming of Basra, st. 22)[19]

Our souls leave, flow forth on the points of polished swords.
(Abu Tammam, *Dīwān al-Ḥamāsa*)[20]

My footmen and horsemen storm over them and I impose
my javelins upon them, that will not miss the mark. Flee—
and they will strike your backs; advance—and they will
strike your chests; and if you descend to the plain to the
horsemen, they will descend upon you with sword blows
like the downpour of urine of pregnant milch-cows.
(Shawqi Dayf)[21]

. . . sharp the teeth of their spears and swords.
(Abu Tammam, *Dīwān al-Ḥamāsa*)[22]

[15] Levin, 'Martial Poems' (Heb.), 346 n. 21.
[16] Ibid. 356 n. 61.
[17] *Ben tehilim*, ed. Jarden, 59.
[18] Ibid. 18.
[19] Arberry, *Arabic Poetry*, 64.
[20] Cited in Levin, 'Martial Poems', 347 n. 26.
[21] Cited ibid. 354 n. 51.
[22] Ibid. 355 n. 57.

4. Roaring

Samuel Hanagid

The shout of the multitude was like the shout of the
Almighty, like the shout of the sea and its breakers
when it storms mightily. ('Eloha oz', st. 58)[23]

You see only the flash of the shields,
You hear only the clamour of the exultant.
('Hali ta'as', st. 37)[24]

Arabic Poetry

Had he not led a massive troop on the day of battle,
he would have been accompanied by a clamorous troop
consisting of himself, alone. (Abu Tammam)[25]

. . . glory resides only in the sword . . . and your leaving
behind in the world a great roar as if a man's ten fingers
took turns to stop up his ears.
(al-Mutanabbi, panegyric to ʿAli ibn Aḥmad, sts. 6, 8)[26]

Now these same literary motifs typifying the first four sections of Gate 7's central episode are present in the butchery of the second rhymed prose description but in a context of reversal, overall and specific. The warriors—all of them, not merely those of the vanquished side—become victims.

Real lions, and various beasts, eat the 'leonine' warriors, now powerless: they are described as dying, or as agonized women giving birth. The weapons that served the fighting men become agents in themselves, acting against their wielders. The earlier boasts of bloodthirstiness take on an ironic dimension: hissing arrows pour down, sword and spear rain blood upon a drinking earth and themselves drink at battle's close, swallowing and licking blood. The flash of sword and spear blinds all, not simply the weaker side's combatants.

The same warriors described at first as frightening mountains become a frightened mass. The previous shouts of warriors and champions are paralleled by the din of the serpentine arrows' barrage, the groaning of victims, and the tongueless cries of death and battle. Earlier, the champions' rebukes had kindled flames of fire; now death, identified with the giant Goliath, vents his voiceless cry and blackens the sun. The preceding rebukes of the champions —who are never mentioned after their speeches are concluded!—are paralleled, finally, by the sword's rebuke to the deaf.

[23] *Ben tehilim*, ed. Jarden, 8. [24] Ibid. 18.
[25] Arberry, *Arabic Poetry*, 56, poem 9, st. 40.
[26] Arberry, *Poems of al-Mutanabbī*, 38, poem 5.

Only the barest mention of human victory comes at the close of the Hebrew original, and it is indirect: 'We distanced ourselves from the pursued (to draw near) the pursuing and turned aside from the smitten to the smiters'.[27] Precisely who the conqueror is, or who the vanquished, we do not know at the close, as we did not at the beginning. It is irrelevant. The true victors of war, suggests Alḥarizi, are sword and spear, battle, carnage, and death. The conventions of Hebrew and Arabic martial poetry have been stood on their heads.

In his above-cited article, Israel Levin summarizes the following typical images of ancient Arabic war poetry that he has cited, images that he cites as well from the poetry of Samuel Hanagid. The great majority closely resemble, or are identical with, those that appear in the various sections of Gate 7 of *Sefer Taḥkemoni*; but the reader must recall that in prior Arabic and Hebrew verse, all appear in the context of vaunted/demonstrated superiority of one camp/combatant over the other(s):

> The poetry segments cited deal with war and its horrors. They present its cry in proud first person—plural and singular. War is described as a devastating fire and a watery deluge. Its blackness is emphasized, especially in daylight, with the dust clouds spiralling upward. The dark armies are described, riding angry-faced horses that surge forward in streams, like night and clouds, swift as sudden disaster. The weapons, slashing like lightning, are described in detail—javelin, spear, bow and arrow, sword, armour, and shield. The sword at night resembles a torch; the flashing armour, water ruffled by wind. Violent words and cruel images praise the murderous weaponry that cuts off limbs, splits heads, opens its mouth to eat the flesh of its victims, is thrust into hearts and chests, and sheds blood like water. We are given the provocative or threatening speeches that precede the battle . . . . We hear the shouts of the combatants, their exultant battle cries, their pride in their head wounds; they resemble roaring lions protecting their cubs. Butchery is emphasized in the depiction of corpses fallen under trampling hooves, abandoned to birds of prey and ravening beasts; the crushing of the enemy and the weeping of his widows, as death laughs open-mouthed; and in the end, the inebriation of the victors as they return home.[28]

Again, of utmost importance is the appearance of all these motifs in a context of a clear-cut victory of one army over another. Two examples follow. The first excerpt is taken from a poem of Samuel Hanagid celebrating his victory over rebels against his sovereign, the king of Granada:

> We camped at its foot: in our eyes, his men
> were crickets and worms in the heights of their towers.

[27] *ST* 88. 3–4.

[28] Levin, 'Martial Poems', 357.

My band of warriors struck fast with God's sword;
by the sword was his band struck down and severed
On a day the sky shook from the plunging of stallions,
when earth reeled and quaked at the roar of their stamping
When princes in red-dyed linen were reddened
with arrows, when the high-born were borne off bleeding.
On one hand, the sight of stone hurlers, wall crushers;
shouting, and sounding of horns on the other.
We sprang to the rooftops from ladders of arrows,
we softened their hearts with our spears and our lances.
We paved plunder's highway to every doorstep,
we made of each courtyard an entrance chamber.
We painted the soil a deep red with their blood,
with their corpses we laid on the earth hills and valleys.
Walking, the foot plants a trunk or a skull
and the ear takes the stamp of the cry of the wounded.
On one hand, the rich flow of booty and vengeance;
groans and the lifeblood's gush on the other.[29]

Thus far for a Hebrew example of a clear-cut differentiation between victor and vanquished, and unqualified pride and joy in victory.

In the following excerpt, al-Mutanabbi (915–65), a renowned poet of Muslim Spain, who inherited and developed martial and other conventions of classical Arabic poetry,[30] similarly effuses enthusiasm for the victor of a bloody confrontation. His object of praise is his patron, Saif al-Daula, here celebrated for a raid on Byzantine territory:

The blades have submitted to your blade . . . You ceased not to smite them continuously on the upper parts with a smiting as if the single sword were two, singling out their crania and faces . . . so they flung away what they were flinging with and turned their backs, trampling upon every twanging bow, overwhelmed by the rain of the cloud, distinctly spaced with straight shaft and Indian sword and head. . . . Alas, they were barred from returning by sharp blades whereby many had been slain, and few taken captive . . . Swords side with those whose hearts are sturdy as their hearts, when the two hosts meet. You will find the sword, for all the boldness of its edge, like a coward in the hand of a coward. . . . O, you who slaughter whom you will with your sword, I have become one of those slain by your beneficence . . .[31]

[29] 'Levavi bekirbi ḥam [My heart within me is warm]', sts. 18–27, *Ben tehilim*, ed. Jarden, 37–8. The translation is mine: Segal, '"My Heart Burns"'. For a literal translation see Segal, 'Ben Tehillim of Shmuel Hanagid and the Book of Psalms', 197–201.

[30] On the scope and contribution of al-Mutanabbi's work, see Arberry, *Poems of al-Mutanabbī*, Introduction, 1–15.

[31] Arberry, *Poems of al-Mutanabbī*, 82–9, poem 15, sts. 29, 34–7, 40, 44–5, 48.

Here, as in Samuel Hanagid's poem, the speaker boasts of the crushing defeat his forces have wreaked on the foe, sending them to ignominy and death. In Gate 7, however, weapons, battle, and death are the true victors.

Alḥarizi has used the technique of narrative framing to anticipate the overturning of heroic boast. At the tale's outset, prior to any mention of actual warfare, Hever describes his company as that of warrior noblemen, very 'lions'; but almost immediately thereafter shows them as (self-described) fearful prey in the face of the leonine warring camps before them! Indeed these allegedly bold fighters do not even make the decision to stay in one spot: that step is taken by the realistic and pragmatic elders; the 'warriors'' unquestioning acceptance of this dictate punctures Hever's inflated, if brief, description of the group. All this anticipates the final battle description that gives the lie to the clichés and literary conventions of the two poet-combatants and Hever's initial report of the fray. Moreover, the disappearance of the noble warrior princes from the narrative, as the elders take charge, presages the disappearance of the two declaiming poet-champions.

A closing comment on a seemingly innocuous term at the outset is in order. Sixteen words into the text, Hever is described by Heman as one who 'joys hearts with the sweetness of his *ḥidot*'. The various meanings of *ḥidah* include riddle, enigma, allegory, perplexing moral problem, and a lesson taught indirectly.[32] All these meanings, and especially the last listed, bear upon the thrust of Gate 7: they relate specifically to the confusing, and ultimately symbolic, locale and constituency of the war.

Seven of the ten place-names from which the combatants hail are names of sons of Ishmael, a descendant of Shem: Hadad and Temah, Jetur, Naphish and Kedmah, Mishma and Dumah (Gen. 25: 15); two are names of descendants of Ham, Sabtah and Raamah (Gen. 10: 7); and one is identical with the name of a descendant of Japheth, Togarmah (Gen. 10: 3). In sum, all the groupings of the nations descended from Noah are here represented, to emphasize the universal applicability of the message of this grim literary parody.

In addition, the gate's larger aggregate of place-names most likely serves to hint at the defeat and slaughter that await the warriors: only one biblical source puts together Tyre (Heman's starting-point), Persia and Meshekh (Heman and Hever's starting-point and [unclear] destination), and Togarmah and Raamah; namely, Ezekiel 27, a prophecy of utter devastation.

Finally, the site of the battle, Emek Habakhah, or Vale of Tears, proves to have been yet another symbolic feature and prefiguration.

[32] BDB 295.

Riddled or fooled the reader has been indeed. No standard heroic victory, but an unmitigated carnage, has greeted his eyes, this visual presentation itself highlighted by the verbal bracketing of *me'asher ra'u einav/eineinu*, 'of what his/our eyes had seen'.[33]

A very sombre tale has been told here, hardly what one would have expected from Heman's initial characterization of his friend as 'one who joys hearts with the sweetness of his *ḥidot* and joys souls with his fine delights'; and this deception makes of Heman, whose own expectations had been shattered by Hever, a partner with Hever, and with Alḥarizi—here represented by both of his protagonists—in misleading the reader to serious ends. No light divertissement has been afforded here, but a statement that comes as close as any in medieval Hebrew *belles-lettres* to opposition to war *per se*.

[33] *ST* 83. 6, 88. 3.

Analysis of Gate Eight

In Praise of a Letter of Praise Read Two Ways

IN GATE 8 ALḤARIZI takes on al-Ḥariri with a will, if, as ever, failing to credit his predecessor with the model that serves him here. The reference is to gate 17 of his *Maqāmāt*, translated closely (relatively speaking) into Hebrew in Alḥarizi's *Maḥberot Iti'el*.[1] Al-Ḥariri has his wandering poet Abu Zayd compose a letter that is perfectly reversible, word for word, on the subject of virtuous and prudent living. Now this letter, when read backwards, conveys in essence the very same message that it has when read forward, with minor variation, as Thomas Chenery's translation demonstrates:[2]

'Man is the creature of kindness; and the perfecting of a benefit is the deed of the liberal . . . the keeping from baseness spreads reputation; and the vice of boorishness consists not with excellence; and the essence of the noble is the guarding of secrets . . .'

If one move them in this direction, there is no debate, no contention; but if one desire the reversing of their mould, and the turning of them backwards, let him say, 'Secrets are trusted to the noble; and the nature of excellence consists not with boorishness; and foulness of reputation spreads disgrace' and so on . . .

Alḥarizi's effort differs from his predecessor's on a number of counts,[3] but most prominently in its central effect: in *Sefer Taḥkemoni*, the paean's contents and tone both are reversed with backward reading.[4] Al-Ḥariri's general

[1] Ed. Perets, 141–6. An exact comparison of the Arabic text with Alḥarizi's translation in *Maḥberot Iti'el* remains a desideratum.

[2] *Assemblies*, tr. Chenery, i. 202–3. 'Reversible', in respect both of Abu Zayd's letter and of Hever's panegyric, is said with regard to the written form, not necessarily the vocalization.

[3] Maree, 'The Influence', 164–77, sets forth some differences between the two gates; and some commonalities in the spheres of motifs, plot, and figurative language.

[4] The presentation of the English rendering in two columns is the translator's, designed the better to illustrate the reversal technique. While, in the original, reading backwards without changing one word of the sequence will produce the desired calumny, in this English version the unit is the phrase. Thus the last units of the English, in reverse, will be read as '. . . who-strips-us-of our-glory, who-unsheathes our-life-and-blood: our-unparalleled-lord'. The Hebrew reads, in the first version: *gevirenu tsirenu, magdil yekarenu, mesir anḥatenu*, 'Our lord, our emissary, enlarger of our glory, removing our sighing'; and in reversal, . . . *anḥatenu, mesir yekarenu, magdil tsirenu: gevirenu* '. . . (our sighing), removing our glory, enlarging our pain (another meaning of *tsirenu*): our lord'.

statement produces, in both directions, with but slight variations, the ideal nobleman, blessed with a host of intellectual and moral virtues: association with the wise, cheerfulness, patience, bravery, courtliness, loyalty, prudence, sincerity, eloquence, kindness, and, above all, largesse. Alḥarizi, on the other hand, ostensibly lauds a specific (if unnamed) ideal prince, hailing him as protector of his subjects, famous, upright, humble, lover of wisdom and morality, and God-fearing. All these virtues are obliterated, however, when the missive is read in reverse. In addition, Alḥarizi, expanding on his Arabic model, explicitly adds to the composition the element of well-wishing; that, too, read in reverse, becomes a curse. In presenting himself, with gusto, as a source of praise and condemnation, Alḥarizi taps into a well-established tradition in Arabic and Hebrew poetry whereby the keen-tongued bard is at once a potent friend or scourge of patrons, public figures, or society at large —depending, in no small measure, on the bard's treatment at their hands.[5]

A third, and deeper, difference, emerges from a comparison of the Hebrew and Arabic texts. The true message of Abu Zayd, al-Ḥariri's protagonist, emerges from both readings, forwards and backwards; Alḥarizi's, only from the latter. Here Alḥarizi plays (seriously) with the phenomenon of things being the reverse of what they seem. The Kenite's praise is no praise at all, but vilification, a fitting deception for a man who seems praiseworthy but is, in the estimation of Hever (and Alḥarizi), vile.

Extra jibes are afforded by the stratum of biblical citation: on several occasions, backward reading creates a citation—at times a near-exact quotation—of Scripture, and that where there had either been none before, or the existing one was undone. Thus, *yashpil sotno*, 'let Him lay low His foe', becomes *veyashpil ge'ono*, 'let Him lay low his pride'—evoking Isa. 25: 11, *vehishpil ga'avato*, 'He will humble his pride', referring to the evil kingdom of Moab. The original's *umo'es zedonot*, 'despiser of arrogant acts of evil', evoking Isa. 33: 15, *mo'es bevetsa ma'akashot*, 'spurns profit from fraudulent dealings' becomes *umo'es batorot*, 'he despises (God's) teachings', a citing of Isa. 5: 24, *ki ma'asu et torat adonai*, 'they have rejected the instruction of the Lord of Hosts'; and that reconstruction destroys, in turn, the praise missive's

[5] On the poet as friend or foe, and the question of poetic sincerity in praise poetry, see two comprehensive overviews: Pagis, *Innovation and Change*, 23–41, 'Social and Cultural Change'; S–F, *History*, i. 55–79, 'The Poet in the Society of his Time'. See also Dana, *Poetics of Medieval Hebrew Literature* (Heb.), 211–29, 'The Moral and Social Stature of the Poet: A Survey', esp. 213–15, summarizing the comments of Moses ibn Ezra, on poets' praise and vituperation, in his *Kitāb al-muḥādara wa'l-mudhākara*. See also Cohen, *The Book of Tradition*, 'The Typology of the Rabbinate', 263–89. On denigratory poetry see Levin, *The Embroidered Coat*, 268–324. On a singular tension between genre requirements and a reluctance to laud others' sagacity, see Or, 'And the Doors of Wisdom have Swung Open to Me' (Heb.).

uvoḥer batorot, 'and he chooses (godly) instructions'—echoing the conclusion of the blessing before the recitation of the prophetic portion on Sabbaths and holy days, 'Blessed art Thou, O Lord, who hast chosen the Torah (*haboḥer batorah*) . . .'. Finally, *veyagbiha karno*, 'let Him raise high his horn', evoking 1 Sam. 2: 10, *veyarem keren meshiḥo*, 'He will raise the horn of His anointed one', becomes *veyigda karno*, 'let Him cut off his horn', evoking Lam. 2: 3, *gada beḥori af kol keren yisrael*, 'He has cut off in His fierce anger all the horn [might] of Israel'.[6]

In this gate Alḥarizi seems to downgrade an otherwise favourite theme of his, and one highlighted by al-Ḥariri in his gate 17; namely, monetary support. Abu Zayd emphasizes generosity in his paean, this being both a function of his wretched state and a tool to move his listeners to change it; they indeed endow him generously, although he declines (in this gate, atypically) to accept anything from one person at least—the narrator, whom he terms his student. In Hever's paean, moral probity and intellectuality merit far more attention; and the Kenite makes a point (atypical in *Sefer Taḥkemoni*) of proclaiming at the outset that he will not accept any money for his efforts.

This high stance is variously bolstered. Hever is identified with eminent Jewish leaders: he is the prophet Moses, splitting the sea of wisdom with his words; and he wittily aligns himself with Moses Maimonides as well: the latter wrote the *Guide of the Perplexed*, an aid to the puzzled student of Greek philosophy, while Hever guides perplexed students of rhetoric and poetry.

Hever gains additional status in being the clear leader of companions themselves portrayed, through metaphor and biblical citation, as possessed of miraculous talents. Like the Israelites of old, they cross the sea—here, of knowledge—on dry land; they are fountains of knowledge and song; their utterances are prophetic, and their hearts a valley of vision (Isa. 22: 1) for prophetic song; all are pure-hearted, the Hebrew *barei levav* taking the reader directly to the start of Psalm 73, whose author faults himself for having envied the wealthy, evil, flattered rich; and these youths, like the eminent prophet Balaam, are steeped in knowledge of the Most High (Num. 24: 16).

In addition to being linked to prophecy, Hever's words lay claim to supreme moral weight. He begins his instruction by citing Psalm 34: 12: 'Come, children, listen to me: I will teach you the fear of the Lord.'

Finally, in addition to wrapping himself in the cloak of prophecy, moral rectitude, and probity, Hever dons the mantle of godliness, couching his

[6] *ST* 92. 9, 16–17. This stylistic has been imitated in the translation. Thus 'Raise high his horn' becomes 'Raise high his foeman's gate', the last three words evoking Gen. 22: 17, 'your descendants shall seize the gates of their foes'.

none-too-modest preface to his poetic display with God's words to Moses prior to the revelation in the cleft of the rock at Mount Horeb: 'I shall pass all my good before you' (Exod. 33: 19). Hever will shower his listeners with manna, as God the Israelites in the desert. Indeed his altruistic refusal to accept compensation is couched in words ascribed to God by the prophet Malachi (1: 10): 'I will accept no offering from you'—albeit there the refusal is a condemnation of the would-be donors.

Hever's tone and stance, then, seem directly opposed to what we see of Abu Zayd in the parallel gate of al-Ḥariri's *Maqāmāt*: the latter is more than eager to accept money from his listeners (again, excluding his student); indeed, he insists that this is precisely what he requires.

Of course Hever's posturing is markedly tongue in cheek: we have no high moral display here, but the vendetta of a spurned poet, frustrated in his quest for money. The humour of the exercise is all the greater when the contexts of the above-cited quotations are taken into consideration. 'Come, children, listen to me: I will teach you the fear of the Lord', says the Psalmist, warning specifically against slander, deceit, and hostility: 'Who is the man who is eager for life, who desires years of good fortune? Guard your tongue from evil, your lips from deceitful speech. Shun evil and do good, seek amity [or 'integrity'] and pursue it' (Ps. 34: 12–15).

It is precisely hostile, evil speech in which the Kenite will engage, and will teach his zealous, 'pure-hearted' students!

'I shall pass all my good before you,' God says to Moses on Horeb, and proceeds with a declaration of divine attributes taken by tradition to quintessentialize divine charity and forgivingness:

> The Lord, the Lord [or: 'and the Lord proclaimed, The Lord']: a God compassionate and gracious, slow to anger, abounding in kindness and faithfulness, extending kindness to the thousandth generation, forgiving iniquity . . .[7]

Hever, of course, is the reverse of compassion and kindness.

In sum, Hever has ostensibly praised a lord, but covertly maligned him (overtly to his (Hever's) listeners); and, having claimed to wed poetic excellence with moral instruction, does the opposite, fusing rhetoric not with compassion, but with vindictiveness; not with liberality, but with meanness.

[7] Exod. 33: 17–34: 7. See also Num. 14: 17–19, where Moses begs God's forgiveness for the sinning Israelites on the basis of this revelation. Indeed later Judaism made of this revelation a more pronounced statement of godly compassion. In the repetition of the Amidah on the final service of the Day of Atonement, the Ne'ilah service, the passage is repeated several times, always with the deletion of the last segment, with its brief notation that God will visit the sins of the fathers upon the sons. See Birnbaum, *High Holyday Prayer Book*, 987–95.

Finally, this reversal parallels the actual, physical reversal of the letter of praise.

After all this, the reader is left with no little confusion as to what message the author of *Sefer Taḥkemoni*, as distinct from his protagonist, is ultimately advancing. On this issue, the reader is referred to the discussion in the Afterword on the complex relationship between Alḥarizi and his partial personae, Hever the Kenite and Heman the Ezrahite.

Analysis of Gate Nine

Poetic Invention: One and Thirty in Contention

THROUGH MULTI-PARTY CONFRONTATION in Gate 9 Alḥarizi gets double duty out of his verbal inventiveness: he heightens reader interest (what challenge will come next and how will it be met); and he makes of each poem a fresh victory for his persona. In setting Hever the Kenite against a party of thirty, Alḥarizi evokes Judges 14: 11 ff., where, for a stake of thirty suits of clothing, Samson challenges thirty wedding guests to explain his riddle.

The (not-cited) text of the biblical riddle could be relevant: 'Out of the eater came something to eat, out of the strong came something sweet' (honey in the carcass of a slain lion). Possibly Alḥarizi hints obliquely here at Hever's providing sweet fare for ear and soul, the Kenite being a decidedly 'strong' rhetor and, at least twice in *Sefer Taḥkemoni* (Gates 3 and 21), a glutton! Unlike the biblical episode, however, in this gate no gain accrues to Hever for meeting the challenge, an atypical state of affairs in the book.

The author's initial ingenuity here lies in his having culled Scripture successfully for no less than thirty quotations that can be read as though written originally in the new quantitative metre borrowed from the Arabs[1]—twenty-nine being hemistichs and one a full stich,[2] and all said citations exemplify-

[1] Arabic, as well as Greek, quantitative metre is based upon regular alternations of long and short syllables in standardized units (feet). Dunash ben Labrat, who first introduced this system into Hebrew poetry, had to overcome a major obstacle; namely, that Spain's Hebrew grammarians did not distinguish, for purposes of classification, between long and short vowels of biblical vocalization. Dunash took the mobile *sheva*—as well as the *ḥataf* (a *sheva* combined with a vowel) and *shuruk* meaning 'and'—as the Hebrew equivalent of the Arabic short syllable. Dunash's very limited initial imitation was expanded markedly by Isaac ibn Khalfun and then by Samuel Hanagid. On this topic see Mirsky in *The Collected Poems of Rabbi Isaac ibn Khalfun* (Heb.), 15–18. On quantitative Hebrew metric prosody see *EJ* xiii. 1211–8. For discussions in Hebrew see also N. Alloni, *Metric Prosody*; Y. Bacon, *Topics in the Development of Metre in Medieval Poetry*, 9–41; Schirmann, *Hebrew Poetry*, 719–37 (addendum) and 674–5 (bibliography); and, in various places, S–F, *History*, i. 119–43.

[2] Six texts put forward by the challengers are modified minutely by Hever in his poems: in four instances he deletes an initial *vav* appearing in the biblical text (poems 1, 3, 10, and 13); in one instance he deletes the initial *heh* of the definite article, as he adds three words of the cited biblical source at the end of the challenge phrase (12); and in one replaces the Hebrew word *ki* with an initial *shuruk* (20).

ing well-established monorhyme metres employed by Alḥarizi's predecessors!

To illustrate this point, let us examine the request that leads into poem five and the poem itself.

The challenger demands a poem concluding with Jacob's rebuke to his son Joseph, 'What is this dream that you have dreamed (Are we to come, I and your mother and your brothers, and bow low to you to the ground)?'[3] Again, the very presentation of the challenge to the rhetor registers on the hearer's/reader's ear as an achievement: scriptural narrative has been made to yield up a sentence fragment that can be parsed as the *shalem* metre (*kāmil* in Arabic), long-long-short-long/ long-long-short-long/ long-long-long:

mah ha-ḥa-lom / ha-zeh a-sher / ḥa-lam-ta.[4]

It now devolves upon the respondent to provide the first hemistich of this 'keystone' verse fragment, and working further backwards, compose a preceding, lead-in stich, in this exact metre.[5]

That is precisely what Hever/Alḥarizi does:

Ben ish le-ma-tai ein-nei-kha a-tsam-ta
Oy ki ve-ḥek ha-ta-a-vah nir-dam-ta
Ḥav-lei ḥa-lo-me-kha le-vav-akh lib-be-vu[6]
Mah ha-ḥa-lom ha-zeh a-sher ḥa-lam-ta.[7]

Literally:

Son of man, how long do you shut your eyes?
Alas, you have fallen asleep in the bosom of desire.
The nothingness of your dreams has enticed your heart.
What is this dream that you have dreamed?

[3] *ST* 97. 5–7.

[4] For an example of this metre see Schirmann, *Hebrew Poetry*, ii. 722; for an example of the Arabic metre *kāmil* (acatalectic), see Arberry, *Poems of al-Mutanabbī*, 129–34. In actuality, Hebrew medieval prosodists described this and all metres in a different fashion. Inasmuch as a *sheva* or *ḥataf* was not perceived as an independent syllable, but always linked to the syllable following, prosodists called this compound syllable *yated* and every other simple syllable *tenuah*. Thus the above line, in the *shalem* metre, would have been scanned *tenuah-tenuah-yated/ tenuah-tenuah-yated/ tenuah-tenuah-tenuah*, as follows:

mah ha- ḥalom/ ha- zeh asher/ ḥa- lam- ta.

[5] In two instances in this gate Hever provides two preceding stichs, rather than one, for a total of three stichs: poems 9 and 16.

[6] Here Alḥarizi employs an acceptable variant on the basic metre. Conversely, the opening hemistich could be seen as a variant on the basic metre.

[7] *ST* 97. 9–12.

In my translation:

O nodding soul—your bed of lust,
 this world for which you toiled and schemed
Is but a plot of writhing worms.
 What is this dream that you have dreamed?

In essence Alḥarizi employs here a technique familiar to the liturgical poets of Hebrew Spain, most of whom composed *reshuyot*, or introductory poems, designed to lead into specific blessings or 'liturgical stations' in the service. These generally brief poems, often four or five stichs in length and usually bearing the acrostical signature of the poet's first name, were most often attached to the following prayer by containing, in the last stich, the key word of the text. Thus a brief poem preceding the blessing, 'Blessed are You, O Lord, *yotser hameorot*, creator of the lights', would contain in its last stich the word *maor*, 'luminary' or 'light', or a variant thereof.[8] The probability is very high—to put it mildly!—that the concluding stich, which often contained a modified or exact quotation, was written first, thus dictating the rhyme, metre, and much of the content of the entire poem. Alḥarizi employed this technique extensively in *Sefer Taḥkemoni*, especially when wrenching his citations out of context.

However, the producing of a two-stich poem with predetermined metre, rhyme, and close is but the start of Alḥarizi's achievement here. Hever the Kenite, going beyond the challenge flung down to him, has converted the literal scriptural statement into a metaphor: pursuit of lust is the equivalent of sleep and dreaming.

Fully nine other poems of Gate 9's thirty are built on metaphorizations of biblical verses. These include the fifteenth, where worship of the golden calf symbolizes materialism; the twenty-first, where the mountain (of revelation) that the Israelites dare not ascend becomes the symbol of pride forbidden every man; the twenty-third, where the stew brought to Isaac (Gen. 27: 10) becomes the gift of every son's wise, moral act; and more.[9] Indeed

[8] For further discussion of the mechanics of this style of composition, and of the opportunity given the poet to relate current personal or national concerns to the prayerbook, see Spiegel, 'On Medieval Hebrew Poetry'.

[9] The remaining poems of metaphorization are 7, 8, 12, 14, 18, 19, 23, and 27. All but three of the metaphorized poems make of biblical history or biblical law, statements of ethical obligation or calls for penitence. The three exceptions are poems 14 and 18, where the sheaf of wheat in Joseph's dream, and Moses' rod, respectively, become symbols of the poet's prowess; and 19, exhibiting a similar identification. In the translation—consonant with the method employed throughout—every citation substituted for another has been placed in square brackets. In boldly metaphorizing biblical statement—here and elsewhere (and especially Gate 2, to

only ten keystone quotations retain their literal meaning in a near identical context, those of poems 1, 4, 6, 13, 16, 25, 26, 28, 29, and 30.[10]

The remaining keystone quotations inhabit a middle ground, where the statements remain intact but the referents change: from God to man (2) and vice versa (9); from the people of Israel (Judah) to the individual poet (Judah Alḥarizi; 10); from Moses to every moral man (11); from God versus sinners to the poet versus intellectuals (17); from the Egyptians to a male object of desire (20); from execution by burning, to burning in the world to come (24).

While the overriding theme of Gate 9 is the need for godliness and the avoidance of lust, evil, and evil men, the author has allowed himself minor digressions: poems 20 and 22 comprise erotic verse; and 14 and 17–19 are poems of boast, specifically of the speaker's wisdom and poetic facility. As such they recall many self-congratulatory poems of Hever at the close of various gates, as well as self-encomia from this genre, especially by two proud declaimers, Samuel Hanagid and Solomon ibn Gabirol.[11]

On the whole, this generic interweave makes for a dissonant effect. The eroticism of poems 20 and 22 grate against the gate's overall moral-didactic thrust; they are especially incompatible with poem 5, which faults man for lying asleep in the bosom of desire; and poem 24, which posits that violence is a necessary concomitant of lust.

Similarly, four poems of poetic self-advertisement—14 and 17–19—do not sit well with the overall tone of penitence, contrition, and admonition; and, specifically, with poem 21's adjuration not to climb the mountain of pride!

One can only guess as to Alḥarizi's motives. Certainly, strict confinement to the theme of right living will prove no impediment to the author in

serious ends)—Alḥarizi has copious precedent, too massive to cite extensively. See, in this regard, arresting citations out of context by Solomon ibn Gabirol in *Selected Religious Poems*, e.g. 83, ll. 26–7; 84, ll. 37–8; 86, ll. 62–3; 87, ll. 88–9.

[10] A special instance is that of poem 22, built upon a citation from the Song of Songs. While the citing of this book in its literal meaning was well established in the genre of erotic poetry, in this context it draws attention to itself in a special way. The general context of the gate is that of ethical admonishment and instruction; and traditionally, the Song of Songs has yielded precisely that kind of message in its allegorical interpretation as, primarily, a love song between God and Israel. Thus, in Gate 9, where the literal becomes, generally, allegorical, the allegorical Song has become literal!

[11] For an overall discussion of the genre of poems of boast, with attention to Arabic poetry, see Levin, *The Embroidered Coat*, 150–208. For an example of a unit of boast in a compound war poem, see D. Goldstein, *Hebrew Poems from Spain* (New York, 1966), 54, ll. 5 ff. For poems of boast of Solomon ibn Gabirol, see *Secular Poetry*, ed. Jarden, i. 177–227. For instances of Samuel Hanagid's self-congratulation as poet at the close of multi-sectioned poems, see *Ben tehilim*, ed. Jarden, 26, sts. 137–44, 149; and 70, sts. 40–50.

Gate 33, where an entirely consistent exhortation in rhymed prose homonyms is to be followed by twenty two-stich poems of admonition—again, entirely consistent—progressing in alphabetical acrostic, each containing two pairs of homonyms at the start, and close, of each stich![12] One could maintain that the digressions in this gate lend desired variety beyond that of variance of person.[13] One could maintain, even more readily, that the recurrent tension in *Sefer Taḥkemoni* between didacticism and rascality has led, here, to the intrusion—seemingly superfluous—of the latter.

Gate 9 exhibits a noteworthy rounding out of theme, as well as a sense of climax. Following his excurses into eros and boast, the poet returns to moral concerns—filial piety (23), the ill effects of desire (24), divine punishment (24 and 25), fear and remorse (26 and 27); and a new theme at the close—the plight of God's people Israel and a plea for divine aid (28 and 29). The last gate of the original text can be read in either of two ways: as a summary statement of the poet's situation; or as a cry of Israel in the first person singular—a frequent device in synagogue poetry.[14]

NOTE ON TRANSLATION

In fourteen instances in this unusual gate I have not retained the citation given Hever as a challenge, owing to constraints of rhyme or metre, or both. I have changed the (usually metaphoric) content of every conditional clause in the thirty challenges to Hever, owing to exigencies of rhyme. In every instance I have conveyed the ever-repeating root sentiment, 'If you wish to display your wisdom and/or poetic prowess (compose a poem ending with the following verse)'.

In choosing my 'keystone' citations, more than ever I sought sentiments as close to the original's as possible. Relatedly, I followed Alḥarizi in converting literal statement to metaphor. Thus, in the first poem, I close with 'the young men shall utterly fall' (Isa. 40: 31), a different section of the verse partially cited by the author, 'they who hope in the Lord shall renew their strength'—which, in my rendering, is cited, but not as the challenge verse. In

[12] That Alḥarizi's digression from his central theme was deliberate, rather than an indication of any difficulties he might have had, is made doubly clear by his execution here of a covert and complex rhetorical exercise, regressive or chiastic inclusion—on which see the Afterword.

[13] At times the poet proclaims third-person *sententiae*; and at times addresses himself, man in general, or God.

[14] On the poet adopting the voice of Israel see Hazzan, *The Poetics of the Sephardi* Piyut (Heb.), 268–314, esp. 296–303. See also Fleischer, *Hebrew Liturgical Poetry*, 108, and ibid. 154–5, ll. 1–16, where just such a shift on the speaker's part is cited.

the second poem I end with 'through the might of Your arm they are still as stone' (Exod. 15: 16), where the Hebrew adduces a different verse fragment from the same chapter, 'In Your great triumph You shatter Your opponents' (v. 7). In poem 7 I close with 'Heal me, O Lord, and I shall be healed' (Jer. 17: 14); the Hebrew adduces '. . . have applied it to the rash and it recovered' (Isa. 38: 21). Poem 13 closes, in the original, with 'the Lord will ward off from you all sickness' (Deut. 7: 15); my version, with a similar statement from the Hagiographa, reads, 'He sent forth His word and He healed them' (Ps. 107: 20). In the seventeenth poem I substitute 'the sword, the sword is drawn' (Ezek. 21: 33) for 'I will devour them there like a lion' (Hos. 13: 8): both citations characterize godly punishment in the Bible, but in Alḥarizi's reworking and in my translation represent the poetic potency of the speaker.

I have taken my greatest liberty with my rendering of poem 30:

> Faint is my heart upon enemy soil:
> terror within, and without—the sword.
> Make haste, O God, to deliver me;
> make haste to help me, O Lord.

The original verse is Psalm 36: 11: 'Bestow your faithful care on those devoted to You and Your beneficence on upright men'.[15] The final stich in the original blends personal and collective statement, with emphasis slightly more on the personal:

> Behold, O Almighty, I am brought low
> and forgotten as a dead man out of mind.
> Bestow your faithful care on those devoted to You
> and your beneficence on upright men.[16]

I have chosen to give greater weight to the voice of collective Israel for purposes of a stronger climax to (1) the national, and last, three-stanza section on the trials of the people; and (2) to the poem as a whole.

The original also conveys an additional climax by having the challenger present an entire biblical verse that can be parsed according to the Arabic-style metre as one full stich of a poem. I retain this effect with my substitution.

[15] *ST* 105. 12–13. [16] *ST* 10–13.

Analysis of Gate Ten

Of Rustic Propriety and Winged Piety

THE HERO—and anti-hero—of Gate 10 holds a candle, for vivacity, to Chaucer's Chanticleer; and, for hypocrisy, to his Pardoner, of whom the host declares that the latter would take his own breeches and present them as the relic of a saint, though they were soiled with excrement.[1]

Large is the mantle of sanctity in which the volatile rooster wraps himself to save his skin. He presents his instinct to crow at night as the fulfilment of religious duty—waking the villagers to pray; and their recompense, an attempt to serve him on a platter, as a mockery of any prayer on their part. Indeed he cites prophetic censure of the Israelites of old, whose importunings God rejected precisely because of bloodshed and immorality on their part:

> Moreover, on your garments is found the lifeblood of the innocent poor . . . Bring no more vain oblations . . . it is iniquity . . . . your hands are full of blood . . . Come not to Bethel . . .[2]

The cock buttresses his status as rebuker-in-the-gate by identifying himself with two major religious leaders of the past, Moses and Samuel, also prophets:

> Ye have been rebellious against the Lord from the day that I knew ye . . . behold, while I am yet alive with you this day, ye have been rebellious against the Lord; and how much more after my death? . . . Witness against me before the Lord (: whom have I defrauded) . . .[3]

Having said all this, he castigates his listeners for inattention to their duties as parents: by killing him they would besmirch their names and so leave a tarnished legacy to their children.

Now all this flows from the mouth of a father who offers, in his place, his children; and has the gall to clinch his rhymed-prose argument with a perversion of the Deuteronomic injunction to drive the mother bird away (for

[1] 'The Pardoner's Tale', VI (C) 947–50, in *The Riverside Chaucer*, ed. Larry D. Benson (New York, 1987; Oxford, 1988), 202.

[2] Jer. 2: 34; Isa. 1: 13, 15; Amos 5: 5. Here, as in the entire tale, added humour is lent by having a rooster and (other) non-Jewish characters cite Scripture!

[3] Deut. 9: 24 and 31: 27; 1 Sam. 12: 3.

kindness' sake) when taking her chicks: here the *parent* eagerly invites the predator to take his progeny! To cap his cant, the rooster ends his metric verse recapitulation, in which he once more offers his children, by lambasting the villagers for daring to leave his wife a widow—and separate him from his chicks!

As humorous as this tale is, and as telling a critique of hypocrisy, it is the richer in being circled progressively by narrative elements presenting a bevy of misrepresentations and two-facedness, and prefigurations and echoings of the rooster's grotesque behaviour.

The chief peasant of the village, described by the Hebrew text as *hagadol beineihem*, 'the greatest of their number', at first seems the paragon of hospitality, attending immediately to his guests and their mounts. In his enthusiastic poem of welcome, comic in *mal à propos* similes, he boasts of village hospitality as compared with city dwellers', slaughters a tasty animal for his guests, and rushes to prepare a dairy dish—all evoking the well-known example of Abraham's hospitality to the three angels.[4] On the next day, however, the farmer's boasts turn hollow when, following a substantial morning expedition, he tenders a meal of greens! As the aggrieved Hever puts it, 'All flesh is grass'—a witty inversion of a scriptural comparison of human mortality with the eternity of God's promise to Israel (Isa. 40: 6).

Indeed, a close look at the text reveals that the farmer presages the rooster's offer of his own children by telling his guests that if they had wanted his own son's flesh he would not have denied it them! Moreover, the farmer's own domicile shows him as living like a chicken, as he sloughs through straw and dung. This depiction unmasks as a liar the head of the aristocratic band: it is he who had assured his fellows of an exemplary reception at a village lacking in nothing, inasmuch as all of its inhabitants were beholden to him.

The ring of falsity compasses the Kenite himself, as storyteller: he has promised a wondrous and, by implication, true tale of what had happened to him on the night preceding—an account that turns out (to his listener's delight) to be a fiction. Here the enigmatic self-description of the stranger is unriddled: snaring a fox or ram is a pseudonym for trapping either the astute or the stupid listener; and the specificity of the stranger's self-praise prefigures the Kenite's ultimate snaring (in the fictitious tale) of a rooster to eat.

One more level of deception remains, that of Hever and author together. Heman the Ezrahite commends his friend for having composed a clearly original tale, at which the teller guffaws and departs. The laughter is most likely perceived by Heman as a sign of agreement, of satisfaction with a com-

[4] Gen. 18: 1–8.

pliment; but its true meaning is very much the contrary. Hever is laughing at Heman, and, most likely, Alḥarizi at the reader, for the tale has been lifted directly from an Arab author, one Abu Ḥafiẓ ʿUmar ibn al-Shahid, as set down in a condensed version by Ibn Bassam![5]

Thus the gate ends with a triple deception: of the villagers by the rooster; of Heman by Hever; and, more than likely, of the reader, by Alḥarizi. The hoodwinking of Heman and reader leads us back to the story's close, and meshes with another, if secondary, theme of the gate: gullibility and obtuseness.

The none-too-perceptive villagers buy the rooster's grotesque logic with a will, terming him their leader and mentor who wakes them to God's service. Moreover, their solution to the impasse before them, providing proper hospitality while revering the rooster's life, shows just what dullards they are. Instead of generalizing on the evil of killing a bird who wakens them to prayer they suggest that the farmer serve—another rooster!

[5] See S. M. Stern, 'The Arabic Source' (Heb.), where the Arabic tale, rendered in Hebrew, is presented side by side with the text of *Sefer Taḥkemoni*, revealing Alḥarizi's condensations, expansions, and revisings of his model. Stern's judgement that Alḥarizi's changes detracted from the original's humour has been challenged: 'This claim is hard to accept. Comparison reveals that Alḥarizi replaced certain humorous elements with others, at times bettering the original's wit and sting' (Pagis, *Innovation and Tradition*, 358).

Analysis of Gate Eleven

Of Verbal Show: Using and Refusing the Letter O

THE POETIC OUTPUT of Hebrew Spain was not monolingual: Aramaic poems were penned by Samuel Hanagid, Judah Halevi, and other poets—for all of whom facility in that language was doubtless fed by intimate acquaintance with the Talmud, and the weekly reading in synagogue of the Aramaic translation of the pentateuchal portions.[1] Alḥarizi himself penned a gem of a monorhyme bilingual poem—eighteen stiches in Arabic and Hebrew, praising God.[2] As well, several stanzaic 'girdle poems' (*shirei ezor*) in Hebrew Spain, modelled on the precedent of Arabic *muwashshaḥāt*, displayed lovelorn speakers, who, at the close and climax of the poem, burst into an impassioned one-line statement—in Arabic or Romance.[3] Beyond that, a recently uncovered document by an Arabic literary historian shows the high regard in which Alḥarizi was held among Muslim and Jewish readers of Arabic in the East for his Arabic poems.[4]

This gate, nonetheless, goes well beyond all preceding multilingual poetic achievement in Hebrew,[5] including the author's, falling at the end of

[1] For summary lists of (earlier) Hebrew authors' poems in Hebrew and/or Aramaic; and a discussion of later poems in Hebrew, Aramaic, and Arabic in Yemen—including the presentation of one such by Shabazi; and bibliographic information on other (and later) macaronic verse that included Hebrew—see Tubi, 'Hebrew, Aramaic, and Arabic' (Heb.), *Pe'amim*, 30 (1987), 3–22. See also Ratzaby, 'Arabic Poetry Written by Andalusian Jews' (Heb.); S–F, *History*, ii. 172–4, citing Alḥarizi's accomplishments as a writer of Arabic poems of praise, disparagement, and religious thought—and also a rhymed philosophical summary of the book of Esther, of which only the introduction is extant in manuscript.

[2] See S. M. Stern, 'Some Unpublished Poems by Al-Harizi', *Jewish Quarterly Review* (1960), 349–50; and the English translation, 352–3. The linguistic structure of every two stichs is *abba* (Hebrew–Arabic, Arabic–Hebrew) and the poem shows a quadruple verbal bracketing: *im* and *(ve)higdilu* (though . . . they enlarge) in Hebrew, and *'anta 'l-jalīlu* (You are majestic) in the Arabic. This poem, to be mentioned again in the Analysis of Gate 14, is deserving of a close reading in its own right,

[3] In Arabic girdle poems only Romance endings were accepted. A book-length study of the girdle poem in Hebrew, with bibliographic riches at the close, is Rosen-Moked, *The Hebrew Girdle Poem in the Middle Ages* (Heb.).

[4] Sadan, 'Rabbi Judah Alḥarizi as a Literary Crossroads', esp. 46–63, containing arresting poetic excerpts from Alḥarizi—in Arabic—preceded by Sadan's translations into Hebrew.

[5] Sa'adiah ibn Dana'an, a 15th-c. grammarian and poet, asserts that Samuel Hanagid composed a seven-stich poem honouring his ruler Habbas, each stich in a different language—no mean achievement, if less complex than Alḥarizi's. Nothing of this poem has been recovered. See Dinur, *Israel in Exile* (Heb.), i. 151.

the spectrum of *Sefer Taḥkemoni*'s verbal pyrotechnics. Narrative is minimal, humour or satire absent; here we seem to have rhetoric for rhetoric's sake—that in addition to the overshadowing of al-Ḥariri, who has nothing to match, or approximate, a poem in three languages.[6] In addition, as will often prove the case in *Sefer Taḥkemoni*, Hever supplies his audience with more than is asked for; and gifts them and the reader with yet more artifice than meets the eye.

Of immediate note is the markedly spiritual theme of the trilingual poem offered here (in Hebrew, Arabic, and Aramaic), and that though no topic had been set. In the rhymed prose section, the company *does* dictate a topic, praise of a grandee, within the confines of every word lacking, then containing, the letter *resh*. Hever goes beyond the assigned task, capping each rhymed prose section's encomium with like fireworks in metric verse, as he meticulously holds to the limitation of having every word show, then be void of, the specified letter.[7] In executing his verbal acrobatic, the poet gives pride of place to a favourite theme, largesse, thus laying the groundwork for maximal generosity on the part of his auditors.

So astonishing is Alḥarizi's display in this gate that the reader can readily lose sight of his usual art of framing, prefiguration, echoing, and other modes of cohesion.

Heman, at the outset, travels from Spain (held the farthestmost west) to the land of Israel (the east); Hever proclaims, at the close, that his poems travel to the east and to the west.[8] The narrator speaks at the start of being moved (literally, 'lifted') by his thoughts to depart Spain for the Holy Land;

[6] The reader interested in multilingual composition (macaronic verse) in medieval poetry generally is referred to Diehl, *The Medieval European Religious Lyric*, index. The following titbit is presented on p. 110: 'To my knowledge, the record for the number of languages used in a coherent fashion (or any fashion) in a religious poem goes without question to Bruder Hans von Cleve's Marienlieder of *c.*1400. In his prologue of 180 verses (15 times 12), Hans constructed a gloss on the Ave Maria (the favorite text for the late medieval gloss poem) in which each twelve-line stanza adheres to the following scheme: vv. 1, 5, and 10 are in German; vv. 2, 6, and 12 in French; vv. 3, 7, and 11 in Middle English; vv. 4, 8, and 9 in Latin. Since the rhyme scheme is *aabcddbcceec*, the rhyming sounds each involve different languages: *a* German and French, *b* English and French, *c* Latin (thrice) and French (once), *d* German and French, and *e* German and English. And the author manages to bring off this bravura display with fine effect.'

[7] The idea of the verbal display around the use and disuse of the letter *resh* derives from four gates of al-Ḥariri, as is summarized by Chenery in *Assemblies*, i. 75: 'In the sixth is given an address, the words of which are alternately with and without pointed letters. In the twenty-sixth the artifice is varied, and each alternate letter is pointed, the others being unpointed. In the twenty-eighth and twenty-ninth the orthographical feat is again changed, for they contain compositions in which every letter is destitute of points.'

[8] *ST* 115. 4–5; 122. 1–2, 5.

Hever, at the close, is lifted aloft on the hands of his astounded auditors.[9] Heman, at the outset, travels in fast, deer-like pursuit of sweet figures of speech on (Israel's) mountain slopes;[10] at the close, the Kenite boasts that he is surrounded by poets who race (vainly) to attain his poesy's heights.[11]

The motif of heights, coupled with mention of 'the fair land' (Zion) in Heman's initial remarks, prefigures the praise of God, described as residing in heaven's heights and destined to rebuild His temple on Mount Zion; and Hever echoes the theme of elevation with his above-mentioned, closing self-praise.

Indeed, Alḥarizi most deliberately weds his spokesman, Hever, with divinity, which linkage becomes clearer in the light of the overall thematic structure of the trilingual poem. To clarify this point, I provide here a literal rendering of the ending of the Hebrew original (which is reduced to one tripartite stich in the poetic translation above):[12]

And there we will offer up song
  to the great recompenser,
    yes, awesome in praise.
And among those songs shall mine be sung:
  my praise shall be rung
    in all tongues.
Enviers will moan hearing it;
  it will strike awe
    into the hearts of the wise.
It will whistle at foes
  and bring special honour
    to the Jews of Spain
With words dripping honey
  and with sweet-smelling scent
    ascending to Heaven.
Lo, it is a rare song,
  a crown worthy to be set
    above all nations.

[9] *ST*, 115. 4; 121. 20–1.

[10] *ST* 115. 5–6. Relatedly, Hever declares before his speech (118. 5) that none can come close to his accomplishment in the east or west.

[11] *ST* 122. 15–16. The root *r-w-ts* is a leitmotif in the original. The throng at the outset runs (*ST* 115. 9–10) and is joined in their race by Heman (ll. 13–14); racing lightning, says the Kenite, cannot keep pace with his tropes (ll. 19–20); the poet calls on his muse to race chariots of song in honour of the grandee (118. 15–16), whose heroes race like lightning (119. 1); the grandee's parents taught him to race in right's path (119. 12) and he does just that (119. 13–14); and he races after his Creator (119. 26).

[12] This omission derives from my request to the translator of this poem.

It is a drawn sword
over all the world's heroes,
all the mighty men.
Commanding all hearts,
its fame shall shine
to the end of days.

The eternity of God's praise at the poem's outset is paralleled by the undying repute of this poem itself; the poem's dominance, a drawn sword over heroes, echoes God's mastery and power. God is Most High; Hever's song ascends Heaven's heights. God's love is a river, saturating the earth; Hever is a font of wisdom. God's tabernacle will sit atop the mountains; Hever's song is a crown upon the heads of the people. God's light brightens the night; Hever's fame will shine to the end of days.

Furthering this identification of poet with God the master, Hever proclaims at the gate's close that the three languages kneel before him; and he lends his poetry, metaphorically, superhuman powers: it wanders freely throughout the world, splitting eternal mountains.

The gate's parts cohere even more, with one or both princes being lauded for these very attributes—praise and veneration, dominance, height, (watery) abundance, and crowning light.[13]

While the entirety of the encomia to the princes may be considered praise and veneration, the first grandee is offered hymned praise by splendour itself,[14] and time declares the lauds and exploits of the second.[15] The first prince rules over the lords of his age; the second governs and commands.[16] As regards height: the first Maecenas is the scion of lofty princes, and the poet asks that the second be raised aloft.[17] The might of the first Maecenas is a river; the second's heart is a fountain of wisdom.[18] The first prince is 'the splendour of the chiefs of society' and deserves that God 'lift his crown high'; the second is crowned with glory.[19] As for the theme of light: the poet calls on himself to light the candelabrum of praise for the first leader, illumining the heights of splendour; and says of this prince that he causes Jewry's light to shine—for which reason God is asked to cause the prince's light to shine.[20] Hever calls the second prince a light, splendour, and star, one whose face is a sun unclouded.[21]

In addition to this triple linkage, some virtues are shared by only two of

[13] All these particulars have been retained, in aggregate, in the translation here, though not necessarily in the original order or to the same degree; all are easily identifiable in the Hebrew text.
[14] *ST* 119. 7.
[15] *ST* 121. 5–6.
[16] *ST* 118. 21; 120. 2, 23–4.
[17] *ST* 118. 24–5; 120. 3.
[18] *ST* 118. 27; 121. 12.
[19] *ST* 118. 22; 119. 16–17; 120. 1.
[20] *ST* 118. 19–21; 119. 3, 17.
[21] *ST* 120. 11, 14–15.

the three parties—poet and God, poet and (one or both) princes, God and (one or both) princes. To cite but a few: the ideas of the first prince are a polished sword; Hever's tropes, polished arrows.[22] God will raise up His Temple; the first grandee repairs ruin and the second is a repairer and restorer.[23] God will reveal His salvation; the first prince shepherds his flock, and heals and frees the bound; the second is a saviour and ingatherer of his people, who drink of the water of his salvation.[24]

Through this intricate linkage game of poet, God and (hypothetical) princes, Alḥarizi adds layers of compliment to the various figures. Hever swells his own chest as he likens himself to divinity; increases the tribute to the princes in binding their virtues to God's; and suggests that he is much like the idealized patrons or leaders of the people in many of their excellencies. As well, Alḥarizi pays an implicit compliment to Samuel Hanagid, who introduced and developed this scheme in a number of poems of praise to Jewish scholars.[25]

ADDENDUM

Here follows the literal translation of the Latin and French rendering by Dr Leofranc Holford-Strevens. As ever, the reader interested in a literal rendering of the original Hebrew is referred to V. E. Reichert's translation.

My song shall praise His name
whose workmanship is
of supreme beauty.
The word of God is strong:
to praise the Almighty
is the beginning of speech.
His name is praised in awe:
to the Most High Creator belongs
the mastery of the world.
With all-resplendent sheen
His righteousness lights up
the darkness of the nights.

---

[22] *ST* 118. 27–119. 1; 122. 3.
[23] *ST* 117. 9–10; 119. 2; 120. 24.
[24] *ST* 117. 3; 119. 3–5; 120. 16–18; 121. 3–4.
[25] This linkage of poet, laudee, and God is explicated and exemplified in D. Segal, ' "Truly, to God Who is Beyond Praise" ' (Heb.); id., 'A Poem within a Poem' (Heb.); see Analysis 3. Samuel Hanagid himself imitated the stylistic of the author of Psalm 19, as demonstrated in the first of the two above-cited articles. For further discussion of the genre of boast, see Analysis 16.

Knowledge to man is barred
of Him who views
every mystery.
To the parched earth His love,
which nothing ever hampers,
sends a river.
His kingdom evermore
shall be protected against the fate
of mortal kings.
He shall exalt the meek,
and the tyrannical pride
of the mighty shall He crush.
The horn shall sound that day,
putting an end to the sleep
of those who wait in earth.
His counsel hid no more,
He shall revive the dead,
the champion of the living.
And He shall once more set
His tabernacle on the summit
of the high mountains.
And my song shall not cease
to be the offering of
those who fear God.

Analysis of Gate Twelve

Of the Ferocity of the Wars of Stint and Generosity

STINT IN GENERAL, and Jewish stint in particular, are pet themes of Judah Alḥarizi, who was dependent, like so many Jewish poets of the Middle Ages, on the largesse of patrons.[1]

Here, through witty pseudo-allegory, our author lampoons his people in singular fashion: he makes of stint a hero-king whom dispersed Jewry in their myriads are prepared to defend to the death![2] Many are the ploys Alḥarizi employs to ennoble, as it were, the very figure Hever and friends first described as the epitome of vileness. Biblical citation overlays King Stint with a patina of regality and sanctity. The language of the text evokes Joseph, dreamer of future greatness: like that pitiable youth, the protagonist is cruelly waylaid and flung into the equivalent of a pit to die. This identification with a biblical hero is part of a larger dream-prophecy motif: at the start of Hever's second, and substantial, history of the ascendancy of Stint, he has his protagonist proclaim a symbolic dream, interpreted by his companions as predictive of his future reign over Israel;[3] in the early marketplace scene a savant prophesies this sovereignty; and Stint dreams, in prison, the enigmatic verse of Ps. 68: 14–15, a statement whose meaning and fulfilment (the monarch's rescue) unfolds with the narrative.

Allusions to the book of Esther play their part, too, in shifting reader sympathy away from generosity to its opposite (or in evoking guffaws, depending on the identity or sensibility of the reader). At the start, Stint is linked, through biblical citation, with the honoured Mordecai, robed gloriously at the king's command; while Generosity, forced to lead his rival through the streets and then slink home abashed, evokes the contemptible Haman! Later in this mock saga, the imprisoned monarch's plea to his people is that of Esther to Ahasuerus: 'I am sold to be destroyed, to be slain, to perish.' The

---

[1] See Analyses of Introduction and Gate 1.

[2] No student of Jewish communal organization, with its plethora of institutions and instruments for maintenance of the sick and the poor—see, for example, 'Charity' in *EJ* v. 338–54—will be taken in for a moment by the spokesman for a disgruntled itinerant bard!

[3] Stint's fellows accurately interpret his dream: the fall of the mighty tower and its staunch pillars (the Torah and the leader of Israel) indicate the subservience of world Jewry. A further, and satiric, meaning nowhere stated, but conveyed throughout, is this: that greed is destined to be the ruin of the people and their way of life (the Torah).

news of the capture and imprisonment of Stint is met with the same response as Persia's Jews gave to the evil decree for their imminent extermination—the wearing of sackcloth and ashes and the making of loud lament; and, at the close, the Jews' establishing an annual celebration of Generosity's downfall and the re-enthronement of Stint recalls the like decree of Esther and Mordecai commemorating through the generations Jewry's victory over its evil foe.

More than scriptural verses and verse fragments crown Greed with laurel wreaths or evoke reader sympathy: from his prison cell, the tormented monarch berates his followers for sloth and unfaithfulness—a cry taken up by his courtiers when they spread word of the king's plight throughout the diaspora. Moreover, the king's devotees are presented as observant Jews, adhering strictly to the Torah's dictum of negotiating peace before attacking a city; and the mocking response of Generosity's knights show the latter as coarse, if not villainous!

To the degree that any unwitting reader is snared with sympathy for the harassed 'monarch', Alḥarizi's satire hits doubly home. Any pity for Stint's plight, any joy in his rescue, sets one precisely within the camp excoriated by the author; namely, the perverse Jewish people as a whole (as here portrayed) —a nation overwhelmingly prepared to establish avarice as the organizing, regnant force in their lives. Indeed the poetic credos of the ranked battalions, cumulatively boring in their effect—and doubtless intended as such!—drum home the message: the Jewries of the world are a staunch brotherhood of misers, ready to die the death for their beloved King Greed.[4] The satire is the more stinging here in Alḥarizi's lampoon of the Arabic convention of battle boast, a convention parodied for more sombre ends in Gate 7, where Death emerges as the ultimate warrior of might.

The twelve armies of Stint, drawn from twelve major Jewish centres,[5]

[4] Another satirical touch is found in the description of the king's correspondence: he finds 'a scrap of parchment', further described in the Hebrew as 'about one-fourth of a *zeret*', a *zeret* being the distance between the little finger and the thumb when extended. By having Stint squeeze four lines onto a 5 cm. scrap of paper, the author delivers yet another thrust at niggardliness.

[5] The twelve sites/communities, presented in the order of the poetic declamations of each (*ST* 130. 22–135. 19) are as follows: (1) Adinah = Baghdad (in Isa. 47: 8 Babylon personified, 'the voluptuous one'; and see BDB, 726); (2) Ashur = Mosul, in northern Iraq (*EJ* iii. 783–4); (3) Arbel = Irbil, *c.*100 km. east of Mosul: a site of Jewish settlement continuously from the time of the Second Temple until the 1950s, Irbil was, by the end of the 12th c., a thriving metropolis with a Jewish community noted for its intellectuals (see *EJ* viii. 1462–3); (4) Haran = Harran in Turkey, *c.*100 km. north of Calneh/al-Raqqa (Haran is cited in Gen. 11: 31–2; 12: 45; and see BDB, 357); (5) Aram Naharaim = Mesopotamia, or northern Iraq (Gen. 24: 10, Deut. 23: 5, Judg. 3: 8; BDB, 74); (6) Calneh, the name from Gen. 10: 10 (also Amos 6: 2, Isa.

are suggestive of the twelve tribes of Israel, the more so in being called 'the sons of Judah and Ephraim', respectively the southern and northern Jewish kingdoms in antiquity. Stint's hosts, then, are presented as the totality of world Jewry, implying that the pitifully few defenders of Generosity are beyond the Jewish pale. Indeed, towards the tale's end, the leaders of Stint's army of rescue must remind their troops that the scant fighters for Generosity are, after all, brother Jews as well.

It is only at the last moment (and, in context, almost surprisingly so) that Alḥarizi moves the tale back to where it began, with the narrator's open dismay over greed. Heman—possibly Hever is intended in the ambiguous 'said the teller of the tale'—prays for the re-establishment of Generosity, 'in whose day Judah shall be saved'; i.e. the Jewish people, generally—and Judah Alḥarizi, wandering and despondent poet, in particular!

10: 9) given to al-Raqqa, a city on the Euphrates in northern Syria (*EJ* v. 65, xiii. 1557–8); (7) Pisgah (the reference here being unclear), a mountain in Moab, on the north-eastern shore of the Dead Sea (Josh. 12: 3); (8) Hamath = Hamah, a city north of Damascus (2 Sam. 8: 9; BDB, 333); (9) Damascus (1 Kgs. 15: 18, Ezek. 47: 16–17; BDB, 199–200); (10) the Beautiful Land (of Israel; Ezek. 20: 6); (11) Mitsrayim = Fustat in Lower Egypt, today part of Cairo (Jer. 44: 1; Ezek. 29: 10, 30: 6; BDB, 595, *mitsrayim*, 1a); (12) No-Amon (Nah. 3: 8, where it means Egyptian Thebes) = Alexandria.

Almost all these twelve locales figure prominently in the author's reports of his trip through the East, accounts laced with vitriol at tight-fisted communities and individuals—this despite the support of those Maecenates to whom his work was variously dedicated. (See Gates 46 and 50 and their analyses.)

For recently discovered additions to our knowledge of the Jewish communities of these cities, such as livelihoods and interactions with sages and academies in other centres, see Gil, *In the Kingdom of Ishmael*, esp. i. 507–10, 510 n. 293 (Ashur/Mosul), 510–11, 511 n. 294 (Arbel/Irbil), 512 and 514 n. 295 (Calneh/al-Raqqa), 514 and n. 295 (Haran); index entries at iv. 903 (Alexandria), 905 (Ashur; Baghdad), 914 (No-Amon), and 916 (Adinah).

Analysis of Gate Thirteen

Wherein Shall a Man be Whole? A Debate of Body, Mind, and Soul

HARD ON THE HEELS of Gate 12's rollicking satire we come upon a distinctly spiritual cluster, Gates 13 to 15, wholly devoid of levity or chicanery, but focusing on acts and speech leading to God and the godly life.

The question that sparks the debate and the gate's drama is rooted in a famous rabbinic tale envisioning divine retribution of body and soul—that of the blind man and the lame man. Assigned to guard a fig grove, the two join forces to do what neither could effect singly: the blind man carries the lame man to the appropriate site, under the latter's direction, enabling both to pick and eat the desired fruit. When the king returns, each casts the blame on the other, without whose services the theft could not have occurred. The king then sets the lame man on the blind man's shoulders, as when they sinned, and judges both together.[1]

This parable found its way into *piyut*, or synagogue poetry, in its pre-classical period,[2] specifically within the framework of the *Tokheḥah*, 'Admonition', a sub-genre wherein the poet speaks not as a representative of the nation but as a human being *per se*. Describing his nullity and the vanity of his delights, he asks of the Creator not to judge him harshly:

> . . . His [the poet's] true purpose is to stir the listener to thoughts of repentance and asceticism, and remind him of the day of his death whereon he will have to render accounting for his deeds before [God] . . .[3]

Our midrash is echoed not only in the pre-classical *piyut*, but was reworked as well by four synagogue poets of Spain preceding Alḥarizi: Joseph ibn Avitur, Isaac ibn Mar Shaul, Solomon ibn Gabirol, and Baḥya ibn Paquda.[4]

[1] BT, *Sanh.* 91*b* and *Leviticus Rabbah* 4: 54. One variant reading of the text, as pointed out by Margoliouth, closely resembles Alḥarizi's version: 'Lo I am cast forth like a stone flung upon the earth' (cited in Itzhaki, *Man—the Vine, Death—the Reaper*, 9–10 n. 4).

[2] The precise parameters of the periods of early *piyut* have not been established. The dividing line, if we may speak of such, between the pre-classical and classical periods, falls somewhere in the mid-6th c. BCE (Fleischer, *Hebrew Liturgical Poetry*, 117–19).

[3] Fleischer, *Hebrew Liturgical Poetry*, 95.

[4] Fleischer, 'The Poetic Output of Joseph ibn Avitur' (Heb.), i. 203, cited in Itzhaki, *Man—the Vine, Death—the Reaper*, 10 n. 5. The interested reader will find several direct borrowings

Interestingly, Alḥarizi quickly moves away from the midrashic tale and its reworkings, in that the Kenite never does give Heman the clear answer provided; namely, that God will put body and soul together and judge them jointly. This tack might relate to Alḥarizi's deep Neoplatonism, wherein the body and its delights are seen as very distinct entities, with the former intrinsically inferior, if not sinful, by definition.[5]

Indeed, Gate 13 comprises, more than a recapitulation of the rabbinic parable, an expansion upon the Neoplatonic opening of *Sefer Taḥkemoni*, with its presentation of the origins, travails, and destiny of the soul—descended, painfully, from her pristine home in heaven and set within the body; and desirous of reascending to her Maker—but requiring the intellect's guidance to overcome the temptations of the flesh.[6] Here the drama of that personification is intensified through presenting the body as a potent advocate, one whose tirade is so strong that virtue's battle is all but lost: after but two back-and-forth verbal forays, the soul is so confused that only the swift intervention of the intellect saves the day.

It is at this point in the narrative that the interweave of rabbinic and philosophic sources is enriched, as the Kenite identifies the body with the evil desire, a stereotypic and prominent concept in classical rabbinic literature.[7] Alḥarizi/Hever has the intellect enter the scene, launching upon a lengthy

of Alḥarizi from all four poems, in addition to his use of the talmudic/midrashic tale. A major indebtedness to all four poets is the back-and-forth argumentation between body and soul—most developed in the earliest poem, that of ibn Avitur, with four speeches on the part of the body and three on the part of the soul. The reader is also directed to Rubin, 'From Monism to Dualism' (Heb.) and Yahalom, 'In the Circuit' (Heb.).

The soul–body controversy has ancient and non-Jewish roots as well. In a Syriac dispute of approximately the 6th c., the body says to the soul, 'How greatly did you beguile me with words, drowning me in a sea of sins: you removed me from the love of our Lord and threw me down into the pit of darkness' (Drijvers, 'Body and Soul', 123 n. 11); and the genre goes as far back as Akkad and Sumer, as documented by S. Brock in 'The Dispute between Soul and Body'. An overall intercultural study of this debate tradition remains a desideratum. Finally, the interested reader is directed to two insightful survey-analyses: Bossy, 'Medieval Debates of Body and Soul', and Ackerman, 'The Debate of the Body and the Soul'.

[5] Of course, ibn Gabirol is no less a Neoplatonist and does not digress from the rabbinic model. Significantly, however, in the penultimate line of his poem he asks divine mercy that 'your servant *yinafesh*, revive'—literally, 'be souled' (see Itzhaki, *Man—the Vine*, 14); relatedly: 'The Jewishness of the author, as well as the Neoplatonist in him, may be found in his qualifying of the final repose/stations of the soul as that of seeing the light of his Creator, not the Deity Itself. The One remains beyond all knowing, the first emanation, that of the intellect/light, the most one can hope to attain' (Professor Alfred L. Ivry, of New York University, in private correspondence).

[6] The reader is referred to the start of the Introduction, with its notes, and to the Analysis there.

[7] On the rabbinic concept of the evil desire see *EJ* viii. 1318–19.

exhortation destined to buttress the soul's resolve and avoid the temptations of the flesh. (Here our author hints, perhaps, that the major sinner is, indeed, the flesh.) As a result the soul is convinced that her spiritual mission is possible and that repentance will win kindly forgiveness and ample reward from God. Herein Alḥarizi's dramatization shows further indebtedness to preceding poets' reworking of the rabbinic parable—for in all of them, emphasis is laid on divine forgiveness, whether beseeched or assured.

While being far from comedy, Gate 13 has a touch of humour in that Desire/Body comes forward with the kind of admonitions which, in a different context, would sound as having issued from a preacher's mouth—that the soul shall be nothing after death, that yesterday cannot return, that the soul is destroying itself, that attention must be paid God's largesse, that the soul must leave its dark surroundings and shine.

The audacity of Desire's counsel, of course, lies in its bizarre context—the enjoyment of earthly delights before the final dissolution of the grave; and specifically, the darkness to be abandoned is the intellect's counsel to cleave to God! Desire goes so far as to cite Jeremiah's comforting message to mother Rachel, lamenting from her grave: 'Refrain thy voice from weeping' (Jer. 31: 15). In the Bible the rationale for prophetic comfort is the foreseen return of the Israelites to their land by God's grace; here, comfort is to be had via hedonism![8]

In its heavy sermonizing and counter-sermonizing on the attractions/follies of worldly life, our gate comprises a clear evocation of Gate 2, similarly a serious presentation illustrating the author's announced resolve to educate and elevate his readers. There, too, it will be recalled, the frame begins with the narrator's concern over his sinfulness and his need for repentance. As well, Gate 2's pronounced allegorization of national history—the travail and deliverance from Egypt, and ensuing wanderings in the desert—finds frequent echoing here. The selling of a slave in perpetuity here becomes a charge of soul against body; the intellect cites places of Israel's wayfaring, in order to instruct the soul: she must depart Marah/Bitters for Mitkah/Sweet (Num. 33: 8, 9, 28, 29); the accounting of the Israelites before their taskmasters in Egypt (Exod. 5: 6–19) becomes the soul's accounting before God; the forced labours of the Israelites in erecting storehouse cities for Pharaoh

[8] A. Ivry, in the above-quoted private correspondence, offers a different reading: 'I rather doubt there is a "touch of humour" in the section which has the body advance its thesis of the nothingness which awaits man after his death. The question of the immortality of the soul was a sensitive issue in the middle ages, and the negative thesis is here given a powerful voice. Could the orthodox position which follows, which strikes me as less impassioned, not be simply politically correct, the author being inclined to the more pessimistic view?'

represents the misguided soul's enslavement to delights (Exod. 1: 11–14); and the soul presents herself as the wife (unjustly) accused of adultery and forced to drink potentially lethal waters (Num. 5: 18–27).[9]

As in Gate 2, and as is his general wont, Alḥarizi has used the frame tale for foreshadowing—and this beyond the explicit introduction of the topic of penitence and reward and punishment. Thus the Kenite's declaration of his need to return home, coupled with the citing of Elijah's offer to grant a boon to his disciple Elisha prior to being taken from him, bear heavy overtones of departure from this world; and Heman's thanks in advance, 'God grant you full reward' (Ruth 2: 12), prefigure the divine grace awaiting the soul for right behaviour. Indeed the author has forged a citation bracket for the gate, by using in the soul's final prose statement the very next verse from the book of Ruth, where Ruth's grateful reply to Boaz for having comforted her is repeated by the soul to the intellect.[10]

Finally, Alḥarizi uses the close of his frame further to enrich his theme. In his self-praise, Hever the Kenite in essence models himself on the educative intellect—revealing penitence's gates, and enlightening body and soul that the individual might merit reunion with the Divine Presence; and with this, the reader cannot but be reminded of the implicit identification in the Introduction of Hever, redeemer of the Hebrew language, with the intellect, redeemer of the soul.

[9] There are, as well, several additional allegorizations of Scripture, including citations from Genesis, Judges, 2 Kings, Isaiah, Ezekiel, Hosea, Song of Songs, Lamentations, and Ezra.

[10] This usage is at once a bracketing and a split citation. Another split citation is that of Jer. 31: 16–17, God's comfort to the matriarch Rachel. Alḥarizi uses the first verse for the counsel of (the evil) desire; the second, as part of the intellect's reply.

Analysis of Gate Fourteen

Of a Prayer Beyond Price Hewn from the Mountain of Spice

In composing optional prayers for the individual, Alḥarizi joins a distinguished, if select, list of predecessors—primarily Sa'adiah Gaon, Solomon ibn Gabirol, and Baḥya ibn Paquda; and it is to the first two that he is most indebted.

Sa'adiah Gaon wrote two long private prayers, or *bakashot*, which appear early in his *sidur tefilah*, or book of prayer.[1] Sa'adiah explains his motivation for penning these prayers, for recitation by the individual—especially when he arrives at the synagogue and finds the congregation praying the (obligatory) Amidah, which he has finished—as follows:

> Inasmuch as I have seen a paucity of understanding and feared that he who prays, instead of drawing near to his Master, distances himself from Him through error, I composed a petitionary prayer (*bakashah*) in two versions, containing praise and acclaim to the Lord; and submission on the part of the human being, and confession of sins, and supplication for forgiveness and prosperity in matters of the world, and comfort for the people of Israel and promise of His salvation. One I made forceful and more potent than the other, such that the lighter one would serve for Sabbaths and holidays and days of joy; and the forceful one for fast days and the like. I present first the simpler and easier of them.[2]

Alḥarizi, therefore, is derivative from Sa'adiah Gaon not only in composing a *bakashah*, but in penning two of them, one following upon the other; and in clearly differentiating between them on stylistic grounds. Of the first he (Hever) states that it was 'the crown of praise and tiara of greatness, such that one who recites it with proper intent will be heard of His Creator';[3] of the second: 'Here is the other fair prayer, none second to it in the world. Praise falls silent before it, for the force of its subject and strength of its construction'.[4]

---

1 *Sidur r. sa'adiah gaon*, ed. Davidson, Assaf, and Joel (hereafter *SSG*), 46–81.

2 *SSG* 45–6.

3 *ST* 149. 17–18.

4 *ST* 153. 22–3. Alḥarizi uses precisely the same two words employed by Sa'adiah to characterize his second prayer. He says *leḥozek inyanah uletokef binyanah*, 'for the strength of its matter and the force of its construction'; and the Gaon spoke of his second prayer thus: 'One of them I made *ḥazakah utekifah*, strong and forceful beyond its companion.'

The first,[5] although rife with Neoplatonic concepts, is readily understandable.[6] Not so the second. Its density of figured speech, including metaphorization of biblical citations; its use of rare words; its frequently involuted syntax; its heavy use of balanced, parallelistic statements and intricately constructed word plays—all demand slower and concentrated reading, and indicate a more sophisticated readership.[7]

Sa'adiah was not as consistent as Alḥarizi in the use of rhyme, at times employing it, and at times not.[8] As well, the Gaon liberally employed balanced parallel statement, often with very close rhythmic balance, following the model of the pre-classical liturgists such as Yose ben Yose.[9] Preceding the Spanish Hebrew school and its rootedness in rhyme requirements of Arabic prosody, Sa'adiah's rhymes were less rich than Alḥarizi's.[10]

I have indicated some specific borrowings from Sa'adiah in the notes to the text. Alḥarizi says in both prayers *yehi ratson veraḥamim milfaneikha*[11] or

[5] For explanations of Neoplatonism and its vocabulary, see the Analysis of the Introduction.

[6] For a brief poem of Alḥarizi's recalling this prayer, see Analysis 11 n. 2.

[7] Indeed in the Arabic introduction to his work (S–F, *History*, ii. 190 n. 185) Alḥarizi declares his intention to provide a glossary of difficult terms; and in his list of contents of the various *maqāmāt* he notes, 'The fourteenth is the *maqāma* of two prayers . . . one of which has difficult and opaque locutions . . . The sixteenth is the *maqāma* of difficult locutions. It is a composition that will rarely be understood by anyone dealing with it, unless its matter be explained to him.' A similar dichotomy of style is to be found in the work of the classical liturgist Eleazar Kallir (*c.*6th c. CE), many of whose compositions are yet recited in Sephardi and Ashkenazi rites to this day, on the New Year and the Day of Atonement. A sample of his simple style—but rich statement—is *Atah hu eloheinu*, 'Thou art our God', in the Musaf, the additional service of the Day of Atonement (Birnbaum, *High Holyday Prayer Book*, 633). Yet this same poet was capable of composing prayers in highly obscure language, faulted vehemently by later literati, foremost among whom was Abraham ibn Ezra in his lengthy excursus on Eccles. 5: 1: 'Keep your mouth from being rash, and let not your throat be quick to bring forth speech before God, for God is in heaven and you are on earth; that is why your words should be few.' The Spanish Hebrew critic lambasted the earlier poet for wordiness, opaque speech, licence in the use of biblical vocabulary—and more. See Yahalom, *Poetic Language in the Early* Piyut (Heb.), 11–19. For a lengthier discussion of the opaque, and especially ornate, style of Alḥarizi, and of the translator's method of coping with the same, the reader is directed to the Analysis of Gate 16, where our author employs a similar, yet even denser, rhetoric in a secular context. Here the translator has opted for a more transparent English style and vocabulary, taking more liberties than usual in transposing, deleting, and adding discreet locutions.

[8] Albeit on occasion our author chooses not to rhyme, for emphatic effect. On this point see the Translator's Preface.

[9] On the differing characteristics of early *piyut* and the poetry of Spain, secular as well as sacral, see 'Poetry' in *EJ* xiii. 670–93; and 'Prosody', ibid. 1195–220.

[10] Generally, minimal rhyming morphemes in Spanish Hebrew poetry comprised a consonant plus vowel, or consonant-vowel-consonant—as in *shelakh, kulakh, ulakh* ('yours, all of you, your yoke'); whereas Sa'adiah will rhyme *lakh, itakh, imakh* ('to You, with You, with You')—as in *SSG* 47. 7–8.

[11] 'May it be Your merciful will': *ST* 152. 2; 155. 9.

simply *yehi ratson milfaneikha*;[12] Sa'adiah says frequently, *yehi ratson milfaneikha adonai eloheinu*, 'May it be Your will, O Lord, our God'[13]—an oft-used expression in rabbinic prayer.[14] As well, Alḥarizi ends his first prayer with Ps. 19: 5, the line that closes the Amidah—*yiheyu leratson imrei fi vehegyon libi lefaneikha adonai tsuri vego'ali*, 'May the words of my mouth and the meditation of my heart be acceptable before You, O Lord, my rock and my redeemer'.[15] This is precisely the ending of Sa'adiah's first prayer.[16]

Another clear borrowing from Sa'adiah in Alḥarizi's first prayer—pointed out in the notes to my translation—is the expatiation on the nature of divinity as sole, regnant, eternal, wise, vast, all-powerful, illuminator, creator, and sustainer.

A discreet, and audacious, borrowing is to be found in Hever's proud characterization of his second prayer, *velah tehilah dumiyah*,[17] citing Ps. 65: 2: *lekha dumiyah tehilah adonai betsiyon*, translatable as 'Silence is Your praise, Lord, in Zion'. Alḥarizi, then, says of his prayer that it is beyond praise; whereas Sa'adiah applies this same biblical citation to its original object, God,[18] *ulekha dumiyah tehilah veya'atah berakhah*—'Praise befits You and blessing accords You'.[19]

There are, of course significant differences between Sa'adiah's and Alḥarizi's *bakashot*. Both the latter's are personal. Sa'adiah's first prayer is national, with an emphasis on the history of God's might and salvation of the people and Israel's desire for redemption. Only the second prayer is personal, replete with individual confession, remorse, and supplication for forgiveness.

Another difference: the second of Alḥarizi's poems overlaps generically with the genre of *tokheḥah* or rebuke, a poem where the author rebukes either the anonymous listener and/or his own soul.[20]

Alḥarizi's next indebtedness is clearly to Solomon ibn Gabirol, from whom he borrowed generously in the Introduction to *Sefer Taḥkemoni*, as I

[12] 'May it be Your will': *ST* 153. 6. [13] *SSG* 61. 2, 12; 62. 9.

[14] On this and preceding patterns, see Heinemann, *Prayer in the Talmud: Forms and Patterns*, 320, s. vv. '*yehi ratson milfaneikha*' and '*yehi ratson veraḥamim milfaneikha*'.

[15] *ST* 153. 20–1. [16] *SSG* 63. 12–14. [17] *ST* 153. 20–1. [18] *SSG* 60. 7.

[19] Sa'adiah's understanding of the verse underlies the NJPS translation, 'Praise befits You in Zion, O God'. The discrepancy is ancient: the Septuagint, followed by the most familiar Latin translation (the 'Gallican Psalter') takes it as Sa'adiah does; Jerome's translation 'according to the Hebrews' has 'praise is silent for Thee'.

[20] On the genre of *tokheḥah* see the Analysis of Gate 13; and references there to Fleischer, *Hebrew Liturgical Poetry* and Itzhaki, *Man—the Vine*. For two *tokheḥot* of Alḥarizi himself, see Schirmann, *New Poems from the Genizah*, 286–91. As well, the reader is directed to Hever's call for penitence in the homonym rhymed prose composition of Gate 33, where many of the statements are like, and some identical with, locutions in this gate.

have noted in the discussion there. Like his predecessor Sa'adiah, ibn Gabirol varies his use of rhymed prose, at times employing it and at times eschewing it. He, too, ends his *bakashah* with the same quotation, 'May the words of my mouth . . .'.

More significantly, Alḥarizi's first poem bears a strong overall resemblance to the *Kingly Crown* in its structure, excluding the lengthy second section. Ibn Gabirol, at the very beginning of his poem, in the very first subsection of the first section, lays out God's attributes: greatness, rule, might, mystery, sustainment of the world, omniscience, lovingkindness, reward and punishment, eternal life, supreme rule, emanation of all life. Thereafter, he devotes each of subsections 2–9 to discrete divine attributes: oneness, existence, life, greatness, might (expressed especially in divine forbearance and forgiveness), light, supreme rule, wisdom—this last trait overlapping with the process of creation described as emanation, like light from the eye.

Alḥarizi's first poem, too, is especially rich in Neoplatonic imagery at the outset. Much as in the *Kingly Crown*, our author lists God's attributes, these being almost identical with those set forth by ibn Gabirol. The latter, after a lengthy second section outlining the measure and scope of the entire created world, physical and spiritual, and ending with the creation of the individual soul and body (subsections 10–32), presents in his third section a lengthy and very personal confession and supplication, limning his inadequacies, and the contrast of his baseness with godly perfection and kindness. He castigates himself for the foul counsel and deeds of his evil inclination, pleading to God to bring him back in repentance and to exercise His great mercies in judgement, despite his inadequacies. In like fashion, at the close of his first poem, Alḥarizi begs God to guide him aright and strengthen his resolve to repent; and thanks God for His many kindnesses from his creation onward, even as he confesses the foulness of his sins.

Analysis of Gate Fifteen

A Prayer Sent where Grace Reposes: A Prayer to Godly Moses

GATE 15 STRONGLY REFLECTS the extraordinary stature granted Moses in rabbinic legend. Among the numerous, relevant topics pursued generously in rabbinic compendia are Moses' face as a source of radiant light; Moses as the greatest of the prophets, bringer of God's law, and its expositor; Moses as intercessor on Israel's behalf and intermediary between his people and God. As well he is explicitly mentioned as Israel's leader in the world to come. His ascension to heaven as recipient of the Torah was given special and loving attention in Jewish legend.[1]

What this gate does not reflect in Jewish tradition is the setting up of Moses as an addressee of prayer. Boldly, Alḥarizi expropriates the title of Psalm 90, *Tefilah lemosheh ish ha'elohim*, 'a prayer of Moses, man of God'—using it to denote 'a prayer *to* Moses'. The daring is more than exegetical: Jewish liturgy does not exhibit prayer to any human being. The one substantial reference to Moses in the service, in the Amidah of the Sabbath morning service, if unusual itself in Jewish tradition (being neither a petition or praise of God), is far from a prayer, or even direct address, to Moses:

Moses rejoiced at the lot assigned to him, for thou didst call him a faithful servant. A crown of glory didst thou place upon his head, when he stood before thee on

[1] The easiest starting point for the reader interested in perusing this material is Ginzberg, *Legends of the Jews*, tr. Szold, ii–iii, where the editor weaves into one fluid narrative (at times reconciling contradictory legends) the various midrashic traditions concerning Moses and provides the sources in his copious notes. As well, the reader may turn to vol. vii, Index, under 'Moses'. Any one of the following numerous, and at times overlapping, topics may be explored: (p. 322) Moses surpassed the entire creation;—teacher and judge of Israel;—the radiance of;—modesty of;—wisdom of;—parents of;—birth of; (p. 323)—divided the Red Sea;—received the Torah;—the ascension of;—subsisted on the glory of the Shekhinah;—only abode in the vicinity of heaven;—Law of, the Torah called;—distinction of;—expounded the Torah in 70 languages; (p. 324)—interpreter of the sacred laws;—the halakhah revealed to, on Sinai;—prophetic faculty of;—and the other prophets;—described as the greatest prophet;—the heavenly secrets revealed to;—revealer of mystic doctrines;—gates of wisdom open to; (p. 325)—prayer of, in behalf of various individuals;—intervenes in behalf of Israel;—the intermediator between God and Israel;—prayers of, in behalf of Israel; (p. 327)—compared to the angels;—compared to a burning candle;—compared to the sun;—the leader of Israel in the world to come; (p. 329)—Divine honours paid to;—as best man;—the miracles performed by;—merits of;—Israel protected because of; (p. 330)—merits of;—the world saved on account of;—and Aaron.

Mount Sinai; and in his hand he brought down the two tables of stone, on which was written the observance of the Sabbath, and thus it says in thy Torah.[2]

Moreover, the father of the prophets was not deified. Scripture emphasizes that his burial place—a likely spot for future reverence—is unknown;[3] and for all the abundant rabbinic legends of his accomplishments, miracles, and singular status—particularly his being the one human being to whom God spoke directly—normative Judaism took care not to elevate him to divine status, most likely (at least in part) in reaction to Christian attitudes towards Jesus.[4] One reflection of this discretion is the complete absence of his name from the Passover Haggadah's history of the enslavement in Egypt and the redemption therefrom.

Whether or not Alḥarizi intended his prayer as an optional *bakashah*, 'petition', like the prayers in Gate 14, the question remains as to what lay behind so unusual a composition.

The answer is to be sought in the context of response to the adulation of Muhammad in Islam and the addressing of prayer to the prophet.

One of the tasks that Alḥarizi took upon himself in *Sefer Taḥkemoni* was the combating of *'arabiyya*, or 'Arabism'. This school of thought asserted not only that Islam was superior to all other faiths, the Koran the most sacred of all books and the most elegant, and Muhammad the holiest of men and the choicest of all the prophets, but also, among other things, that Arabic was the fairest language, Arabia the land most conducive to poetic speech, and the Arabs the purest stock of humanity.[5] These points, openly or semi-covertly, Alḥarizi took on variously in *Sefer Taḥkemoni*.[6] It would appear that this impetus is operative here, with Moses being proclaimed the greatest of men and prophets, with Muhammad in mind.

Through the ages Muhammad has been presented as possessed of divine light.[7] His ascent to heaven is central to Islam,[8] and commemorated to

[2] Hertz, *Authorised Daily Prayer Book*, 457. Indeed, the inclusion of so unusual a passage, a relatively late addition to the prayerbook, did not escape opposition. See Wieder, 'The Controversy about the Liturgical Composition "Yismaḥ Moshe"' (Heb.).

[3] Deut. 34: 4 and BT *Sotah* 14*a*. Possibly Alḥarizi's reiteration of this fact was intended to contrast with contending Islamic traditions that ascribe no less than nine sites to Moses' tomb—Jerusalem, Damascus, and elsewhere. See Sadan, 'A Legal Opinion', 235–40.

[4] *EJ* xii. 393.

[5] See Alloni, 'Reflections of the Revolt' (Heb.), esp. 85–98; and id., 'Zion and Jerusalem', 252–8. See also 'Arabiyya' in index of Brann, *The Compunctious Poet*. Brann takes exception to some of Alloni's conclusions on the attitudes of Moses ibn Ezra and Judah Halevi.

[6] See, in this regard, the Introduction and Gate 1 with their Analyses.

[7] See 'The Light of Muhammad and the Mystical Tradition' in Schimmel, *And Muhammad is His Messenger*, 123–43.

[8] See the tradition cited by H. Lazarus-Yafeh, 'The Sanctity of Jerusalem in Islam', 218—

this day in the veneration of the (ultimately accepted) site of this ascent on the Temple Mount in Jerusalem. The peculiar reference to Moses as having been descended 'of choicest loins' could well refer to Muhammad's birth.[9] The very turning to Moses to act as spokesman for the petitioner could well relate to Muhammad's popular role of intercessor, or *shafī'* (if often frowned upon by official Muslim doctrine):

> . . . intercession in its fullness is the prerogative of the Prophet of Islam alone . . . on the whole the belief in his intercession became pivotal in Muslim religious life. This belief reflects the conviction that Divine mercy manifests itself in and through the Prophet; his intercession is in a certain way a result of his position as 'Mercy for the worlds'. . . . There is scarcely any author, be he poet or scholar . . . who has not entreated the Prophet's intercession and, to use Jami's poetical term, did not 'sow the seed of blessing for the Prophet in the soil of asking for forgiveness'.[10]

Finally, the very lavishness of praise tendered Moses in Gate 15 could be intended as a counterweight to the honouring of Muhammad in prose and poetry; and the very medium of rhymed prose, together with several specific locutions, seem to mirror specific *laudes* of Muhammad in Islam:

> the multifaceted and elaborate description of his qualities and virtues was developed during the first centuries in prose rather than in poetry. . . . This sonorous rhyming prose, in which the beauty and strength of the Arabic language reveals itself most expressively and which almost defies translation due to its density, contains numerous works about the . . . signs pointing to the prophet's unique qualities and attributes. At the turn of the first millennium AD Tha'alibi was able to collect a long line of rhyming designations of the Prophet that one should use when mentioning him, for instance, in the introductory sentences of learned works or belles lettres. In his collections one finds statement like these:
>
> 'He brought his community from darkness to light, and afforded shadow for them when the sun was burning bright; Muhammad, God's messenger and closest friend,

and note the similarity to our text: '. . . He ascended this ladder and guided by Gabriel was brought into the upper skies. Here he met many angels and various prophets of Islam . . . and then came before the Divine throne. A thousand fiery veils were removed and he was granted basic precepts of Islam . . .'.

[9] See Tor, *Mohammad: The Man and his Faith*, 33–5, who cites the prediction: 'A soothsayer . . . declared that from among his [Muhammad's father's] descendants a man would arise who would become a world ruler and a prophet of humanity.' Alḥarizi's point is probably that Moses' father, the descendant of Levi, was of a higher class than Muhammad's father, a lesser merchant.

[10] Schimmel, *And Muhammad is His Messenger*, 84–5, 87 ff. It bears emphasizing that Alḥarizi's text often stresses the mercies of Moses: *ST* 159. 4 'the modest and merciful'; 161. 9–10 'commander of salvation and mercy, and pity and consolation'; 1. 15— 'I seize the hem of your glory until you have mercy upon me.'

his prime choice among his creatures, the best one ever created by God and His proof on His earth; he . . . whose birth was blessed and whose arrival was fortunate; radiant is his morning light and glowing his lamp at night . . .[11]

In sum, it would seem that there are enough commonalities between Gate 15's prayer to Moses and Muslim traditions to suggest that Alḥarizi's venture here was motivated, at least in part, by an impulse to compete with similar prayers and texts of Islam.

Finally, one need not search farther afield for proof of this thesis than al-Ḥariri's *Maqāmāt*. Several statements in that work's introduction find clear echoes in the characterization of Moses as intercessor, best of men, greatest of the prophets, lifted up to the highest heavens, Divine envoy, standing in the presence of God and His throne, supreme guide, possessed of authority—as witnessed by the following quotation:

And we call down thy abundant grace and thy bounty . . . also approaching thee through the merits of Mohammed, Lord of men, the Intercessor whose intercession shall be received at the congregation of judgment. By whom thou hast set the seal to the prophets, and whose degree thou hast exalted to the highest heaven;—Whom thou hast described in thy clear-speaking Book and hast said (and thou art the most truthful of sayers): 'It is the word of a noble envoy, of him who is mighty in the presence of the Lord of the throne, having authority, obeyed, yea, faithful'.—O God, send thy blessing on him and his House who guide aright, and his companions who built up the faith; and make us followers of his guidance and theirs, and profit us all by the loving of him and them: for thou art Almighty, and one meet to answer prayer.[12]

[11] Schimmel, *And Muhammad is His Messenger*, 180–1.

[12] Chenery, *The Assemblies*, i. 104. A. Maree, in 'The Influence of al-Ḥariri's *Maqāmāt*' (Heb.), 193–5, points out several affinities of this gate with al-Ḥariri's twelfth: there the protagonist provides travellers with a prayer designed to guard them from harm and increase their wealth, a prayer wherein Muhammad is referred to as seal of the prophets and conveyor of God's messages; in addition, those who heard the prayer learned it thoroughly (Chenery, *The Assemblies*, i. 171, ll. 11–12, 29; 172, ll. 24–6).

Analysis of Gate Sixteen

Airs of Song's Seven Heirs

GATE 16 PROVIDES both translator and reader of *Sefer Taḥkemoni* with an unusual challenge. On the whole, Alḥarizi's vocabulary and style are translucent; however, more than in the case of Gate 14's second prayer the Hebrew author seeks to demonstrate that he can rival al-Ḥariri in the use of archaisms and arcane vocabulary. Generally speaking, the language of the Arabic master's *Maqāmāt* was more demanding than either Alḥarizi's *Maḥberot Iti'el* or his *Sefer Taḥkemoni*; and in some gates he employed recondite terms to tax all but advanced scholars, and even them.[1] Taking a leaf from Alḥarizi, who at the close of gate 19 of *Maḥberot Iti'el* explains opaque locutions (modelling himself on gate 32 of al-Ḥariri, which elucidates recondite riddle),[2] I have explained particularly enigmatic words appearing in my translation. More than rare words, however, characterize our text. Here rhetoric is employed with unusual zeal as the author spins out large sequences of rhyming clauses with convoluted metaphor, both embedded in intricate parallelistic structures syntactical and metrical, and with internal rhyme as well. For an example, let us look at the very opening statement:

[1] On the difficulties of al-Ḥariri's lexicon and style, including his deliberate use of obscure and archaic vocabulary, and especially words from the Koran whose meanings were contested: see Chenery, *Assemblies*, i. 27, 63–6, 70, 74–85. See also the sophisticated use of rare idioms in gate 32 (tr. Steingass, ii. 37–57), where seemingly absurd answers to difficult questions on religious and civil law become comprehensible when a leading word is taken in a more recondite sense.

[2] *Maḥberot Iti'el*, 163. 22–164. 10; cf. al-Ḥariri, *Assemblies*, tr. Steingass, ii. 81–2. It is reported that the author, in addition to writing his own commentaries on difficult gates, taught their correct interpretation to his sons and pupils (Chenery, *Assemblies*, i. 27 and 38). Of his deliberate use of abstruse language, Alḥarizi declares in his Arabic-language Introduction to *Sefer Taḥkemoni*: 'I have collected in it many words that are obscure and difficult to understand so that if the reader is able to understand those opaque expressions, he will have acquired a good deal of knowledge about the Hebrew language, understood many of its meanings, and erected a massive column of its structures. If he persists in reading these *maqāmāt*, Hebrew will run smoothly off the tip of his tongue, and the bridle of his eloquence and clear expression will be slackened. And with God's will we shall explain every phrase that seems difficult or opaque in this collection' (Drory, 'Literary Contacts', 290, based on her edition of the original, 'The Hidden Context: On Literary Products of Tricultural Contacts in the Middle Ages' (Heb.), *Pe'amim: Studies in Oriental Jewry*, 46–7 (1991), 18–20); see too Analysis 14 n. 7. The careful examination of all extant manuscripts for any remains of Alḥarizi's glossary project—if such there be—remains a desideratum.

beterem rigvei hanedodim beḥevrat hayedidim dubaku
ve'afrot haḥevrah lemutsak haperidah hutsaku,

which translates literally as: 'ere the clods of wandering with the company of friends were made to adhere together, and the soils of association into the mould of parting were poured . . .'.

The effect of these two clauses is rendered even denser in that they begin a six-clause rhyming sequence—with a relatively difficult rhyming component at that (*-aku*)—all making essentially the same declaration. Indeed the extraordinarily long introductory section in rhymed prose—ninety-five lines in the Toporovsky text—contains, at root, a very brief kernel of meaning; namely, 'After I had enjoyed good fortune, foul luck allotted me penury, wandering, and grief, until once again good fortune was mine. Then I discovered a band of exquisite poets who contested with one another'.[3]

Part of the effect of the gate's verbal pyrotechnics, then, is variation on a theme: in this instance, tried and true lament over Time's or Fortune's abuses, characteristic of previous metric poetry of complaint. Two major exponents of this genre were Solomon ibn Gabirol and Moses ibn Ezra, the latter in particular: forced to leave the luxuries, friends, and status of Andalusia for the inimical milieu of Christian Spain, he penned several moving complaint poems.[4]

In his rhymed prose display-piece, Heman plays with conventions of the complaint genre where, time and again, the poet excoriates vicious Fate for wresting him from friends and loved ones, bringing pain to his breast and tears to his eyes, or reducing him to penury.[5] I have mirrored the density of Alḥarizi's verbal acrobatics in the translation, where more liberties than usual have been taken. The following will serve as one example:

till an ill	dispensation	gripped me	and savaged me,
a chill	visitation	whipped me	and ravaged me

[3] See, in this regard, Dan Pagis's discussion of characteristic, and like, clothing of a concept in varied and sometimes contradictory metaphors, one line after another, in the (antecedent) secular poetry of Moses ibn Ezra: Pagis, *Secular Poetry*, ch. 4, 'Figures of Speech in Relation to the Rhetorical Structure', 87–100.

[4] On typical themes and figures in poetry of *telunah*, complaint, see Pagis, *Secular Poetry*, ch. 11, 'Poems of Complaint and Elements of Rebuke, Disparagement, and Boast', 281–309. See also I. Levin, 'Poems of Wandering and Suffering of Moses ibn Ezra', and id., *The Embroidered Coat*, ch. 5, 'Poems of Complaint', 209–67.

[5] For a few examples of time/wandering/parting wresting one from friends in the poetry of Samuel Hanagid, see 'Hakhol hayom nesiah vaḥaniyah' ('Shall Wandering and Camping Be My Daily Fate?'; Jarden, *Ben tehilim*, 155–7); and 'Kevodi mide'agah ḥal' ('My Soul Spins'; ibid. 71–3), sts. 1–18. Jarden counts ten poems of *perud* or separation to Solomon ibn Gabirol. See Jarden, *The Secular Poetry of Rabbi Solomon ibn Gabirol* (Heb.), i. 6 (alphabetic pagination).

translating the Hebrew's

ad heniuni *hatenuot* *hameniyot*
vehele'uni *hatela'ot* *hamele'ot*[6]

literally 'until contrary happenings that cancel [one's joys] rendered me as naught, and full torments wearied me'.

At times I have also chosen archaic syntactical forms, such as the absence of the relative pronoun:

Their eyes spoke swords [that] broke Dark's thraw shields;
their lips spilled ploughs [that] tilled Wit's broad fields.

As in the rhymed prose section, one basic pronouncement is repeated in the seven poets' competition; namely, that the speaker is the best singer born. This claim is advanced in variations of near-identical metaphoric statements: that the bard frights/crushes rivals, exhibits miraculous powers; pens lines that shame sun and stars; erects song's tabernacle or altars; creates verse that is wondrous-woven or -grown.[7] In addition several speakers boldly identify with God's might by way of biblical citations. These claims are poetic clichés, drawn from poems of boast, a genre indulged in by all the major poetic figures of Hebrew Spain. Often they described their creations as exquisite artifice or garments; as holy constructs, such as the Temple or Tabernacle. They used military terminology to limn the destruction of rivals; and drew on biblical descriptions of divine wrath or victory to laurel their own prowess.[8] Of course, self-advertisement is a hallmark of *Sefer Taḥkemoni* throughout, in rhymed prose and metric verse, as the protagonist—and sometimes others—vaunt their talents; indeed, both the author's poems of self-praise in the Introduction (where he speaks for himself) anticipate many of the themes and specific locutions of the seven poets here, all of whom, in effect, sound

[6] *ST* 163. 8–9.

[7] My renderings of the stanzas, if at times close enough to the original to encompass specific biblical citations, are generally free adaptations that adhere to the overall sentiments of the poetry, rather than reflecting discrete images or statements.

[8] For an overview of this genre, see 'Songs of Boast' (Heb.) in Levin, *The Embroidered Coat*, 150–208. The vehicle of self-praise may be a poem in its own right, or a segment of a multi-partite poem of praise, complaint, or (in the one case of Samuel Hanagid) of war. For a poem of boast of Samuel Hanagid see Jarden, *Ben tehilim*, 280–3; for the relationship between self-praise and praise of God and friends in his poetry, see Segal, 'Observations on Three War Poems'; id., '"Truly, to God Who is beyond Praise"'; id. 'A Poem within a Poem'. For poems of boast of Solomon ibn Gabirol, see Jarden, *The Secular Poems*, i. 6; and, in the table of contents, 'Shirei hitpa'arut'—albeit many other poems contain segments of boast. For a discussion of poems by Moses ibn Ezra ending in boast, see Pagis, *Secular Poetry*, 194–6.

his praises;[9] and often, as a metric signature, Hever unveils himself at the close with a couplet or more, lauding his singular powers.

Now logically the advancement of such claims as the seven bards put forward skirts grotesquery, on the one hand, and tediousness, on the other; yet Alḥarizi falls into neither pitfall. Here is no satire through parody, as was the case in Gate 12, where twelve communities, symbolic of world Jewry, each rise to declaim, *ad nauseam*, in strict rhyme and metre, their readiness to fight to the death—for greed! Here, contrastingly, Alḥarizi pulls out the stops to demonstrate the suppleness and richness of the Hebrew language (and his own genius), as he had promised to do in the Introduction. Also echoing the Introduction, the author binds tightly together the roles of poet, sage, and prophet—a claim that would hardly have been seconded by Alḥarizi's hero Maimonides, and other philosophers who bore the traditional animus towards poetry as the quintessential perverter of truth.[10]

Structurally, Alḥarizi continues to indulge a favourite and specific game, that of inclusion or exact verbal bracketing. At the outset, Heman the Ezrahite says:

Ere . . . the soils of friendship were cast into separation's mould (*lemutsak haperidah hutsaku*) . . . and hope's daughters had not yet been poured from vessel to vessel (*umikli el kli lo huraku*),

and at the close, speaking of the poets:

After they had emptied their vessels (*heriku keleihem*) and had cast (*hitsiku*) their words . . .

Furthermore, the penultimate word of the gate, *venifradeti*, 'I separated (from them)', closes a circle with the aforementioned *haperidah*, 'separation', in the second line of the text.[11]

A larger, and yet more significant, bracketing is afforded as well. At the close, Hever, in rhymed prose paean, showers his students with accolades rich in metaphorized biblical citations—this as he uses one (unusual) rhyming morpheme, *-lom*, seven times; and for this display he is met with Heman's profound admiration. The reader, on the other hand, cannot but recall the like display of Heman, preceding the poets' tourney; and recall, too, that it was Heman's presentation that was the denser, lengthier, rhyme-richer, and more precious in all respects. In this instance, contrary to surface statement, it is the Ezrahite who must be accorded the laurel.

[9] See *ST* 8. 1–8, 28. 20–29. 16.

[10] See end of Analysis to Introduction, and nn. 28–33.

[11] The translation echoes this stylistic feature in the bracketing of the text with the word 'peace': 'ere the pods of Peace were pounded by Separation's pestle' and 'the seventh (poet) is given Song's covenant of peace'.

Analysis of Gate Seventeen

Rabbanite versus Karaite

THUS FAR, the reader of *Sefer Taḥkemoni* has witnessed ample instances of roguery, wit, and verbal gymnastics for their own sake; Gate 17 (as well as Gates 2 and 13–15) is a reminder that our author can openly and soberly address issues of moral and religious import.

Alḥarizi makes short shrift of the Samaritans, traditionally seen as descendants of populations introduced into ancient Israel by the Assyrians (approximately in the seventh century BCE),[1] who adopted worship of the God of Israel, as well as the Pentateuch[2]—far less of Jewish tradition than our author's chosen target, the Karaites.

Karaism, from its eighth- and ninth-century roots in messianism, anti-rabbinism, and renewed attention to Hebrew language and law, rose to become a movement that variously threatened rabbinic hegemony over the interpretation of Jewish law in all its aspects.[3]

The root meaning of the word 'Karaite' is 'biblicist' or 'adherent of the Bible', deriving from the Hebrew *mikra*, Bible. The precursor of the movement was Anan (8th c.): his dictate that the individual 'search diligently in the Torah' to determine the true meaning of Mosaic command ultimately led to a plethora of interpretation and a splintering of his followers.[4]

While the sect of the Ananites persisted for some centuries, even as other anti-Rabbanite groups arose and vanished, the thrust for reform, or replacement of traditional Judaism took a different direction with the emergence of Benjamin of Nahawendi (*c.*830–60), first to use the term *kara'im*, or *benei mikra*, 'sons of the Bible' or 'biblicists'. Unlike both Anan and the Rabbanites, he based Jewish law on fresh interpretation of the Bible as a whole, not

[1] See 2 Kings 17.

[2] Some recent historians give partial credence to Samaritan traditions and see this community as a subgroup of northern Israel. See 'Samaritans', *EJ* xiv. 726–58. The movement survives to this day in Israel.

[3] *EJ* x. 761–85, especially the bibliography; and i (Index), under 'Karaites'. See also Nemoy, *Karaite Anthology*. A valuable additional resource is Cohen, *Sefer Ha-Qabbalah*, esp. pp. xliii–lxii, 'Sefer Ha-Qabbalah and its Historical Background'.

[4] Karaite historians—al-Kirkisani and others—put their origins back to the time of the split of the northern kingdom of Israel from Judah: claiming that Zadok, leader of the Sadducees, had uncovered a portion of the truth, they held that it was the exilarch Anan who discovered the whole truth (*EJ* ii. 919–22, x. 763–5).

merely the Pentateuch, at the same time making selective borrowings from Rabbanite teaching.[5]

Alḥarizi's critique of the Karaites, blended with an essential feeling of consanguinity, was doubtless influenced by his admired mentor Maimonides, whose works he translated. The latter stated that Karaites 'should be treated with respect, honour, kindness, and humility. . . . They may be associated with, and one may enter their homes, circumcise their children, bury their dead, and comfort their mourners'—all this on the assumption that the Karaites in question do not vilify the Rabbanites.[6]

On the other hand, Alḥarizi's use of the word *minim*, 'heretics' or 'schismatics', links the Karaites with the detested Sadducees.[7] The word *minim* appears in the twelfth blessing of the central prayer of the daily Jewish liturgy, the Amidah. This blessing, in the Sephardi ritual, begins, 'And for slanderers let there be no hope, and let all *minim* perish as in a moment, and let all enemies of your people be cut off swiftly . . .'. The Hertz commentary explains that, historically, this twelfth benediction

> is against slanderers, informers, and traitors. This petition is an addition to the 'eighteen benedictions', which by it became nineteen. It is directed against Jewish sectaries (*minim*) in the generation after the destruction of the Second Temple. They wrought division and havoc in the religious camp of Israel.[8]

Alḥarizi presents the Karaites as utterly opposed to rabbinic exegesis. While one cannot be certain which Karaitic community, or communities, he was most familiar with, it is unlikely that as learned and well-travelled a man as he was totally ignorant of such Karaitic borrowings from rabbinic legal exegesis as Benjamin of Nahawendi's. The extremist position of Daniel ben Moses al-Kumisi, at the end of the ninth century, an opponent of Benjamin of Nahawendi who demanded the strictest adherence to the literal sense of

5 *EJ* x. 766–8.

6 *The Responsa of Maimonides* (Heb.), ed. Blau, no. 449, pp. 729–32—as rendered in *EJ* x. 781. See Blidstein, 'The Approach to the Karaites' (Heb.), who elucidates Maimonides' view that born Karaites (as opposed to converts from Rabbanism) are to be placed in the category of Jewish children abducted by gentiles, and as those whose sin is further mitigated by holding to erroneous practices or beliefs of their parents. See also, on these and related issues, including the sophistication of Maimonides' anti-Karaite polemic, Lasker, 'The Influence of Karaism on Maimonides' (Heb.), 145–61.

7 See Revel, *The Karaite Halakhah*. Alḥarizi was doubtless influenced as well by Sa'adiah Gaon, who earlier had proscribed the movement and its followers. See Poznanski, *Karaite Literary Opponents*; and Malter, *Saadia Gaon*, 58–9, 260–7. On Maimonides' use or non-use of the term *min* to apply to Karaites, depending on their status as converts or children of Karaites, and social-political contexts, see Blidstein, 'The Approach to the Karaites', 505–7.

8 Hertz, *Authorised Daily Prayer Book*, 143–4.

Scripture, was by no means the only, or even dominant, trend within Karaism in Alḥarizi's time. The mid-twelfth-century Karaite authority Judah Hadassi presented in his halakhic compendium *Eshkol hakofer* eighty hermeneutic rules of exegesis, including those applied by the Talmud![9] It seems all but certain that Alḥarizi, in Gate 17 of *Sefer Taḥkemoni*, has deliberately presented a skewed and simplified portrait of Karaite practice and theology, the better to assure his favoured side with unqualified victory.

One can detect a clear influence of Judah Halevi's *Book of the Kuzari*,[10] a fictionalized account of the process of the conversion of the king of the Khazars to Judaism, being mostly a purported record of questions directed by the monarch to a sage representing rabbinic Judaism. This seems particularly true of the allegations of the Karaite spokesman in this gate that the rabbis arbitrarily abrogated or expanded upon the laws of the Torah. Part 3 of *The Kuzari*, paragraphs 22 to the close (74), treats of the challenges of Karaite theology, and their refutation.[11] Thus, in paragraphs 39 to 42 the sage satisfies the Khazar king that post-Mosaic dictates by kings David and Solomon, Ezra the Scribe, and others, do not contravene the Deuteronomic injunction not to expand or diminish toraitic law; but rather that the intent of Scripture is to forbid individual licence. As well, a number of contested doctrines highlighted in Gate 17 are mentioned in this discussion: the laws of the sukkah, and Sabbath practices—the injunction not to leave one's place on the Sabbath, the limits of the Sabbath walk, and the laws pertaining to shared courtyards (*eruv*). Sabbath practices were a major bone of contention between Karaites and Rabbanites. The kindling of Sabbath lights, for example, is treated in Hadassi's *Eshkol hakofer*.[12]

To what degree Alḥarizi's presentation of Karaitic capitulation to the Rabbanites reflects realities in Spain, if it does indeed do that, lies beyond the scope of this study.[13] We do know of efforts by a favourite of Alfonso VI

[9] *EJ* x. 777–8. [10] *EJ* x. 363–6.

[11] H. Hirschfeld, *Book of the Kuzari by Judah Hallevi* (New York, 1946), 142–74.

[12] On this subject see Lewin, 'On the History of the Sabbath Candles' (Heb.), 55–68—cited, with other sources, in Cohen, *Sefer Ha-Qabbalah*, 107, nn. to ll. 19–21 of the Prologue. See also Ehrlich, 'Laws of the Sabbath in Yehudah Hadassi's *Eshkol hakofer*', cited in Lasker, 'The Influence of Karaism on Maimonides', 155 n. 53. Lasker, 'Karaism and the Jewish-Christian Debate', 332 n. 41, notes that the essentials of the Karaite anti-Rabbanite polemic are laid out in Poznanski, *Karaite Literary Opponents*, 131–234.

[13] The reader is referred to the section 'Spain' in J. Rosenthal, 'Karaites and Karaism in Western Europe' (Heb.), *Meḥkarim umekorot*, 8 (1967), 238–44, treating of rabbinic polemical works against Karaites, recorded social tensions, expulsions of Karaites from certain Spanish cities under Rabbanite pressure, and Christian use of Karaite arguments in Jewish–Christian polemic.

One suspects that the Polyanna ending of Gate 17 is as unreliable as Abraham ibn Daud's

of León and Castile that led to the expulsion of the movement's followers from all the Castilian towns after the wife of a deceased leader of the sect took over the reins of the movement, even attempting to win over Rabbanite converts. But at the same time Karaism succeeded in gaining a firm hold in Byzantium.[14]

In using rhymed prose for serious polemic, Alharizi evokes ancient precedent—that of rabbinic Judaism's champion against Karaism, Sa'adiah Gaon, whose rhymed quatrains against one Hiwi al-Balkhi, an eighth-century freethinker, are extant in part.[15] Sa'adiah himself was a virulent opponent of Karaism who won the movement's undying animus.[16]

As is so often the case, Alḥarizi employs subtle prefiguration. Hever the Kenite, identity unknown, is one of the invited guests, *keru'im*—which, with little modification, yields *kara'im*, the very camp that is to be soundly defeated in debate.[17]

assertion in his polemical *Sefer hakabalah* that by his (the author's) lifetime (1110–80) the Karaites had been reduced to an insignificant sect. See Cohen, *Sefer Ha-Qabbalah*, 91–101, commenting on ibn Daud's animus towards the Karaites and his distortions of social-historical realities. For further evidence of the continued existence of the Karaite movement and friction between Karaites and Rabbanites, see 'Attempts at Reconciliation between Karaism and Rabbanism', *EJ* x. 781, which cites a critical tract on the mutual accusations of the two camps by one Sa'd ibn Kammuna (some time before 1284); and a call by an Italian Rabbanite scholar, Shemariah ben Elijah, some fifty years later, that both camps come together 'so that all Israel might once more become one union of brethren'—i.e. the very state of amity proclaimed (over a century earlier) at the close of this gate!

[14] See *EJ* x. 770–2; Cohen, *Sefer Ha-Qabbalah*, xlvi, 94–5, 164–5; and Nemoy, *The Karaite Anthology*, xxi, 124. The authoritative study on this period—albeit not for Spain—is Ankori, *Karaites in Byzantium*. Further information on Spanish Karaism may be found in Lasker, 'Jehudah Halevi and Karaism'; id., 'Karaism in Twelfth Century Spain'.

[15] See I. Davidson, *Saadia's Polemic*, and entries in 'Hiwi al-Balkhi', *EJ* viii. 792–3.

[16] See n. 7 above.

[17] It would be of more than passing interest to determine whether or not Alḥarizi intends a hidden compliment to the movement. This might be the case were it to emerge that Karaitic exegetic scholarship underlay the usage of recondite, or even familiar, biblical words and idioms, in the prose and poetry of *Sefer Taḥkemoni*. On the other hand, that question is complicated by the issue of the degree of identification one ought to posit between Hever, Heman, the author as *persona*, and the actual author—on which topic see the Afterword.

Analysis of Gate Eighteen

The Rise and Reign of Monarchs of Song in Hebrew Spain

COMPLEMENTING THE HISTORICAL survey of Gate 3, Gate 18 renders an account that extends beyond Spain and one which provides further explication of the author's favourable and unfavourable assessments.[1] Before establishing his hierarchy of Spain's poets, Alḥarizi explains their

[1] More than was the case with Gate 3, the scope of this gate is immense, covering not only prior generations of Spain's Hebrew poets but Hebrew poets contemporaneous with the author as well, both in Spain and beyond its borders. Here, too, the amount of surviving materials of the poets mentioned (many unknown but from this history) together with the difficulties of understanding the precise meanings of Alḥarizi's assessments (especially the positive ones) necessitates deferring an 'evaluation of his evaluation' to some future time. On the Arabic source of several of Alḥarizi's strictures for the aspiring poet, see Tubi, 'The Sources'. See also Maree, 'The Influence of al-Ḥariri's *Maqāmāt*', 196 n. 12. The favourably mentioned Greek poet, Michael son of Caleb of Thebez, is perhaps identical with the author of a liturgical poem showing the acrostic 'Michael'; see Weinberg, 'New Poems from the Byzantine Period' (Heb.), 52–3. On Moses ben Sheshet, see Schirmann, 'Moses ben Sheshet, a Spanish Hebrew Poet in Babylon' (Heb.); on 'Toviyah ben Zidkiyah's Declaration' see Yahalom, '"Sayeth Toviyah ben Tsidkiyah"' (Heb.). The Damascene poet, originally from Egypt, excoriated by Alḥarizi is possibly the Karaite poet Moses Dar'i: see S–F, *History*, ii. 159 n. 52. One product of the roundly vilified poet Berakhot ben Yeshuah (*ST* 194 ff.), a poem for a circumcision, has been found and published by Fleischer, 'Remarks on Medieval Hebrew Poetry' (Heb.), with the comment: 'It is of a decidedly inferior standard'. On the other hand, Alḥarizi's blanket condemnation of all Hebrew poets of Baghdad is patently unjustified, as evidenced by the respectable poems of several poets there, and particularly Eleazar ben Ya'akov Habavli, whose *divan* is extant (S–F, *History*, ii. 164 and n. 74).

The need for a scholarly edition of *Sefer Taḥkemoni* is especially evident when one examines this particular gate in differing manuscripts—where additional materials are to be found and other sections are missing. Indeed in some manuscripts the list of poets covered in Gate 18 includes, if only briefly mentioned, the first Hebrew poets in Christian Spain (S–F, *History*, ii. 204).

Moreover, there are several gates with different versions extant—not necessarily scribal corruptions. It is more than likely that the author, in delivering his work to the four or five different patrons to whom it was dedicated, shortened, lengthened, or changed his materials. As has been pointed out (S–F, *History*, ii. 186–7 n. 168), some of these differences have been noted—in Gates 7, 18, and others—in a pamphlet by Stern entitled 'A Brief Announcement on a Scholarly Edition of the Book of Maqamas (Tahkemoni) of Rabbi Judah Alharizi' (Jerusalem, 1937); the pamphlet was intended to have preceded a scholarly edition by S. M. Stern never realized. On versions and editions of the *Sefer Taḥkemoni* see Habermann, 'Judah Alḥarizi's *Sefer Taḥkemoni* and its Editions' (Heb.).

pre-eminence, citing the science of his day, which believed in the significance of locale, especially through the zodiac, in determining human accomplishment and fate. Thus Spain and Babylon were favoured sites of Jewish learning. Furthermore, our author cites the tradition that Spanish Jewry was descended from the tribe of Judah and hence comprised the élite of the Jewish people.[2]

Briefly our author alludes to the acknowledged primacy of Arabic poetry, a theme he grappled with in the Introduction and Gate 1. Here, however, he puts a different twist to the fact of diasporic Jewry's having assimilated foreign ways and models. In the Introduction this was a derogatory statement: streaming to the use of Arabic, the Jews lost command of their own excellent tongue. Here, the fact is praiseworthy: the Jews adapted the best of Arab culture, enriching Hebrew poetry, which had no true (i.e. metric) poetry but only the parallelisms of Job, Proverbs, and Psalms.[3] Not so much as contradicting himself, our author expresses via these two views the same complex and ambivalent attitude towards Arabic poetry as did his predecessor Moses ibn Ezra.[4]

What immediately strikes the reader's eye in Gate 18's account is a shift in preference. In Gate 3 it was clearly Halevi who was ceded the laurel. Here, too, he merits high praise, being rendered the unique compliment of best wedding of all three components of good poetry—lucidity and musicality, deep matter, and excellent figurative speech. Nonetheless, pride of place is clearly given Solomon ibn Gabirol. In the four-figured triad cited in the context of the vile plagiarist, he is king, Halevi being commander of the army (and Abraham ibn Ezra the prince of song, and Moses ibn Ezra the prophet thereof).

As well, in this gate's history of Spain's Hebrew poets Halevi is allotted only four words—*tor hatorah va'adi hate'udah*, 'nightingale of Torah and ornament of godly knowledge'; and this follows upon sixty(!) words given ibn Gabirol, including the following:

> none arose who wafted the perfumes of song like him before or after, none after attained the dust of his feet for his powerful verse.

The central role of ibn Gabirol is prefigured in the gate as well. Heman declares that he set out on his journey while yet a gentle youth—*na'ar rakh*;[5]

[2] Moses ibn Ezra, *Kitāb al-muḥādara wa'l-mudhākara* 54–5, ll. 84 f.

[3] Here Alḥarizi echoes the assessment of Moses ibn Ezra: ibid. 46–7, ll. 16–17.

[4] Scheindlin, 'Rabbi Moshe Ibn Ezra on the Legitimacy of Poetry'. One very significant difference between Moses ibn Ezra and Alḥarizi was the later poet's inclusion of dolts as a category of readers to be pleased—a notion that 'no poet in Andalusia would have entertained' (S–F, *History*, ii. 205 and n. 237).

[5] *ST* 181. 3.

of ibn Gabirol Hever declares that he was 'plucked up while the moistness of youth, *na'arut*, was yet in him'.[6] Heman describes his route as follows:

from the land of Hadrakh to the holy city where the candle of kingship/*ner hamelukhah* was set up and the light of the Presence shone.

Of ibn Gabirol Hever declares, 'at the age of 29 his candle/*nero* was extinguished';[7] and later, in describing the four luminaries of Hebrew poetry of Spain, kingship is given Solomon—'Solomon sitting on his throne'—even if the root *m-l-kh* (king) is not employed there.[8]

Finally, our author most significantly ends the poem of self-praise closing the gate with a boast lifted from ibn Gabirol—'my tongue is a pitchfork';[9] and the high praise Heman then affords his friend subtly bolsters the Hever–ibn Gabirol link: 'When I heard his wondrous utterances/*peliot imrotav* . . .' says Heman; and of ibn Gabirol Hever had said, 'had he lived a long life he would have composed, in song's mysteries, mighty wonders/*pela'im atsumim*'.[10] Indeed Hever's boast before laying out his history, that 'no man but I knows its [your question's] mystery/*sodah*' could relate to this same utterance, for 'in song's mysteries' is, in the original, *besodot hashir*.[11]

The perplexing aspect of Hever's assessments of Halevi and ibn Gabirol in *Sefer Taḥkemoni* arise when the two clusters of superlatives in Gates 3 and 18 are put side by side. Both men are presented as outshadowing (in retrospect) all other Hebrew poets. Specifically, of Halevi Hever had said, in Gate 3, that 'all who went out in his footsteps to learn the artifice of his poems did not attain to the dust of his chariot wheels'; of ibn Gabirol, that 'all the poets who came after him sought to learn from his poems but did not attain to the dust of his feet'.[12] Such an impossible predication of the same primacy to two different poets can hardly be considered a slip of the pen on our author's part. It appears to be the case that he required two different histories in *Sefer Taḥkemoni*—placing them far enough apart to allow for this discrepancy—precisely because he was unwilling unequivocally to grant the

[6] *ST* 185. 17–18.

[7] Here Alḥarizi follows Moses ibn Ezra. Other assessments include ages 35–8 and 50. See *EJ* vii. 236.

[8] At the same time, high praise, if lesser, is accorded Isaac ibn Khalfun. He 'was anointed king' over all the bards of his age—but this is stated after explicit mention of his peers' poor achievements: *ST* 185. 2–10.

[9] 'Niḥar bekori geroni' ('My Throat is Raw from Crying Out'), st. 28: *Secular Poems*, ed. Jarden, i. 230.

[10] *ST* 196. 16; 185. 16–17.

[11] *ST* 182. 3; 185. 16–17.

[12] *ST* 46. 9–10; 185. 15.

highest laurel to either one of the two.[13] At the same time, his covert linkage of his own talents with both bards' excellencies—more pronounced in the case of Halevi—suggests that his insistence that no poet since can rival either is not as ingenuous as superficial reading suggests.

[13] This use of contradiction or paradox to encompass a complex situation recalls the author's contradictory, but complementary, explanations, in the Introduction and Gate 1, for the genesis of *Sefer Taḥkemoni*.

Analysis of Gate Nineteen

Of a Dispute of Poets Seven: Which Virtue is Dearest in the Eyes of Heaven

THE FIRST SEGMENT of Gate 19, the debate between the seven spokesmen of seven virtues, while relating broadly to Arab-style *adab* or moralistic writing,[1] is a clear echo of the mishnaic tractate *Ethics of the Fathers* (*Avot*) 2: 13, where Rabbi Yoḥanan ben Zakkai, a pillar of rabbinic Judaism at the time of the downfall of the Second Temple, challenges his outstanding students:

> He said to them, 'Go and seek out the best path for a man to cleave to.' Rabbi Eliezer said, 'A good eye.' Rabbi Joshua said, 'A good friend.' Rabbi Yose said, 'A good neighbour.' Rabbi Simeon said, 'Foresight.' Rabbi Elazar said, 'A good heart.' He said to them, 'I choose the words of Elazar son of Arakh over your words, for your words are contained essentially in his.'

In and of itself, the literary allusion ostensibly lends a tone of high moral purpose to the text; all the more so in that the announced contest between seven combatants concludes with the good heart, the very trait prized most by Yoḥanan ben Zakkai. As well, Alḥarizi's choice, and his ordering of values, hint that last is best: the first three virtues, humility, industry, and valour, are essentially personality traits, part of one's emotional makeup; the next two, faith and wisdom, are suggestive of commitment to a more refined and spiritual way of life; the sixth virtue, morality, seems *prima facie* to merit higher ranking than all preceding, in that its scope is synonymous with virtue. The seventh virtue, the good heart, especially through the evocation of the rabbis' debate, can be perceived as yet of a higher rank than morality. In classical Hebrew literature, the heart is the seat of both feeling and mental functioning.[2] Hence the good heart is at once a personality trait (cheerfulness and kindness) and a talent (wisdom), a blessing that could well incorporate the six preceding virtues.

The text seems to reiterate that pride of place goes to the good heart through a complex fourfold repetition of one biblical source, culminating in

---

[1] Discussion of *adab* literature has been deferred to the Analysis of Gate 36, a clear exemplum of the genre. See also Gates 44 and 45 with their Analyses.

[2] See the root *l-v-v* in BDB 523–5.

the praise of this faculty. The question posed at the debate's outset was, which virtue is best and is loved above all others, *uve'einei elohim ve'adam ḥashuvah*, 'and is [most] important [or: valued] in the sight of God and man' (Prov. 3: 4). The spokesman for industry, quoting more of the source, declares: *veyimtsa ḥen be'einei elohim va'anashim*, 'he will find favour in the sight of God and men'. The next, and yet longer, citation occurs in the claims of the spokesman for faith: *veyimtsa ḥen vesekhel tov be'einei elohim ve'adam*, 'so shall he find favour and good understanding in the sight of God and man'—which, but for the change of one letter in the Hebrew to indicate the third person rather than the second, is an exact and complete rendering of the biblical clause in its entirety.

The verse is last cited, in this gate, in the closing words of the metric poem that crowns the case for the good heart and concludes, as well, the entire first segment, with its seven speakers. However, in this citation all reference to human approbation is deleted. This is by no means a mere accommodation to the exigencies of a given quantitative metre; rather, speaker and author both seem to suggest a distinctive, elevated, godly status for the good heart:

ki vo yehi ahuv letsuro gam
yimtsa be'einav ḥen vesekhel tov

Literally:

He shall be beloved of his Rock thereby
and also find favour in his eyes and good understanding.

Such a reading of the climax ties in well with earlier argumentation for virtuous living: humility brings one into contact with modest folk; faith is to prophecy as form is to matter (in the English version, as soul is to body), prophecy being the highest status to which a Jew can attain;[3] wisdom distinguishes man from the beast; and the good heart, the climax of the seven-layered debate, is lauded even by the angels.

All of the above, however, is a blatantly partial reading of the first section, one that puts on blinkers against a highly utilitarian message.

The real question in this debate is, which virtue assures its practitioner the most advantage. The major inducements for virtuous living presented here are accretion of social approbation, honour, friends, wealth, power, and reward in the world to come. The motivation for right conduct put forward here is not covenant fulfilment, or *imitatio Dei*, or succouring the oppressed —themes frequently and centrally put forward in pentateuchal and prophetic literature. Certainly no one here urges righteousness for its own sake.

[3] See Analysis of Introduction, n. 7.

The overall tone comes closest to that of Proverbs, where virtue is closely linked with practical wisdom, or prudence: shun evil men and harlots—for they will lead you to ruin (Prov. 1: 10–19, 7: 6–27); disregard of moral instruction ensures grief (5: 12–14); sloth breeds poverty (6: 6–11); avoid contemptuous speech because it is prudent (11: 12); generosity leads to increased wealth (11: 24–6); humility precedes honour (15: 33).[4]

Even in the rhymed prose argument of the proponent of the good heart, the overriding motivation is that of self-seeking—the good-hearted man wins the love of mankind, social elevation, honour, and the praise of friends and foes alike.

It is not utilitarianism alone that uncloaks the debaters as less than moral paragons. Their acerbity reveals them as hostile, rival rhetors rather than dispassionate exponents of ethical or religious truths. With the exception of the first speaker, humility (appropriately), every debater begins his remarks by vilifying his predecessor's!

It is, however, in the second section of Gate 19 that cynicism openly takes sway—and that in the remarks of an unknown and unannounced stranger, appearing inexplicably on the scene. At the gate's outset Heman had cited the number of speakers—seven, a very traditional and significant number in Jewish tradition;[5] and, as has just been explained, the thematic progressions and overall structure of the seven-layered confrontation lend a feeling of finality to the debate up to this point. Yet precisely at this point a new speaker emerges.

At the outset of his remarks, the old man imitates, and goes beyond, the crassness of his predecessors: he insults not one, but all of them, for their ignorance—and that in four rhyming units, whereas every other debater had only used two.

Hever also differs from the preceding seven spokesmen in that he does not proclaim, at once, the virtue which he espouses: his auditors' suspense grows, together with the reader's.

[4] 'Both prophecy and law demand of man in the name of God that he behave properly. Their ethical outlook is . . . not practical utilitarianism, even though they teach the doctrine of reward and punishment. This ethical attitude is given added depth in Psalms, where it becomes a matter of religious feeling that throbs in the heart of the righteous man who seeks closeness with his God . . . the attitude of Proverbs is different. Most of the Proverbs aim at proving to man that it is worthwhile for him to follow the good path from the consideration of simple worldly wisdom' (*EJ* vi. 936; see also 942, bibliography).

[5] Alḥarizi employs the number seven elsewhere in *Sefer Taḥkemoni* as well as in Gate 16, where seven poets vie. There, it is true, Hever is the eighth figure: but his presence is noted from the start. See too Gate 20, with its seven mysterious maidens. On the frequent significance and use of the number seven in the Bible see *EJ* xii. 1257.

Yet slender indeed is the likelihood that a student of ethics will take seriously the Kenite's *laudes* for liberality. Hever makes but the slightest bow in the direction of morality: early on in his defence of giving he says, in the Hebrew, that the practitioner of generosity shall 'thereby be counted among the pious inasmuch as he performs righteous and kindly deeds'.[6] The rest of of his argument is selfishness with a vengeance.

Only two of his predecessors had touched on negative traits of their ideal persona: the advocate of morality had asserted that its practitioner had all his sins removed (in the Hebrew, 'covered'); and the spokesman for the good heart mentioned that such a man would be praised even by his foes.

In Hever's paean to liberality, however, the whitewashing of sin, no matter how foul, and the winning over (read: bribery) of critics and enemies is the very heart of the issue. Going beyond general statement on this point, Hever dispatches, specifically, four rival virtues: he asserts that men of faith, wisdom, humility, and industry will be held up as precisely the opposite, if they lack charity; and that the rankest of sinners who dispense coin with largesse will be held the acme of virtue!

In his rhymed prose exposition, Hever alludes in overall fashion to the well-known and oft-cited role of the poet in medieval Hebrew (and Arabic) society, that of the 'hired pen' (for praise); and that of the dangerous castigator when spurned or mistreated.[7] Without having intimate knowledge of the identity of his patrons, one must wonder to what degree Hever has turned bronze (or tin) to gold when he near-deifies his Maecenas at the close of the Introduction, and of Gates 1 and 50; and what is the measure of truth in his slander of niggardly givers and praise of benefactors in his survey of Jewish communities (Gate 46) and in his potpourri of free-standing metric poems (Gate 50).

What is implicit in Gate 19's rhymed prose becomes explicit in metric verse. Hever closes his poem by baldly stating that he garbs friends with praise and foes with fear; to wit, the very general observations on what happens to tight-fisted men who are otherwise virtuous, and liberal braggarts or dolts or reprobates is a threat on Hever's part. (One fantasizes Alḥarizi recommending to potential patrons that they begin reading his manuscript at this gate . . .).

Hever furthers his sarcasm through mimicking the recurrence and variance of one biblical citation in his opponents' remarks. The first section, it will be recalled, cited on four occasions, in varying lengths, Proverbs 3: 4: 'and he shall find favour and good repute in the eyes of God and man'; with

[6] *ST* 200. 11–12.

[7] See Pagis, *Innovation and Tradition*, 16–42, and 359–62 (notes).

the first appearance of this citation at the start of the debate; and the last, in the metric stichs that close it.

Hever similarly brackets his argument with quotations of varying length from Proverbs 31: 29, the paean to the 'woman of valour': 'Many women have done well, but you excel them all' (or, in the Authorized Version, 'Many daughters have done virtuously, but thou excellest them all'). Close to the start of his remarks, the Kenite delivers, with slight modification, four words from this biblical text—*vehi altah al kulanah*, 'she excels them all'; and at the conclusion of his rhymed prose exposition quotes the entire verse verbatim. He lends the verse further emphasis by quoting it partially in the poem that ends his argument.[8]

Now the scriptural statement under discussion, together with the other verses comprising Proverbs 31, constitutes heartfelt praise for the quintessential representation of altruism—the loving, self-sacrificing wife and mother by whose tireless efforts her husband and children lack for nothing. Here, of course, the quotation is turned on its head: the practitioner of liberality has no one's good in mind but his own; and far from excelling others in virtue, makes up for the vilest of faults through showering friends and foes with gold!

Indeed the context of the quote brings forward, with no little humour, a nuance present in the original text: 'Many women', says the Hebrew text, *asu ḥayil*, 'have done well/virtuously'; but *ḥayil* means, as well, 'wealth': thus, the verse may be said to convey the message that many women have been virtuous and assiduous, thereby increasing (their husbands') wealth! Thus Hever says, at the close of a purported debate on virtues, that generosity tops all other virtues, precisely by making its practitioner even wealthier!

Now even as the reader of *Sefer Taḥkemoni* is all but dizzied by the different and conflicting values that Hever preaches or embodies in its varied gates, even so he must be puzzled, if not astonished, at Heman's attitude, here, towards what the Kenite has said. Unlike Gate 6, where the Ezrahite laughs at Hever's immoral statements or behaviour, considering them a patent and humorous fiction, here he waxes most enthusiastic at the gate's close, at no fewer than three points: reporting his reaction to the reader; complimenting Hever while asking who the latter is; and, following Hever's poem of self-identification, further describing Hever in superlatives, speaking of him as *me'alfenu umorenu ḥever hakeni ḥaverenu*, 'our mentor and teacher, our friend Hever the Kenite'. Teacher indeed! Heman's positive attitude towards Hever is lent further emphasis through the word play of *ḥever . . . ḥaverenu*,

[8] *ST* 200. 8–9; 201. 3, 6.

'Hever our friend'.[9] The reader must decide whether to consider Heman exceedingly dull at this point—blinded, by rhetorical flourishes and display of wit, to a statement defending moral near-anarchy; or as comprising a player in a sarcastic exercise.

Whatever interpretation he opts for, he can perhaps detect a subtle signal as to the author's own assessment of, and distance from, the characters he has created. The opening lines of this *maqāma*, providing the locale for the debate—'I was in the land of Petor, city of Balaam son of Beor'—may veil an ironic statement. The renowned Moabite prophet was summoned by Balak, king of Midian, to curse the Israelites, but concluded by blessing them.[10] Hever the Kenite, not summoned by anyone, steps forward to 'bless' liberality—yet besmirches it; and that by declaring, among other things, that the sin-steeped Maecenas converts (like Balaam) curses to blessings! Indeed, a literal translation of the passage in question reads, 'Those who curse him shall bless him . . .'. Such a reading would put the author at a significant remove from the venality of Hever; and the moral blindness, or complicity, of Heman the Ezrahite.

[9] For a fuller discussion of Heman's varying attitudes towards what Hever says or does, and on punning on the names of the book's protagonists, see the Afterword.

[10] Num. 24: 10: '"I called you," Balak said to Balaam, "to damn my enemies, and instead you have blessed them these three times."'

Analysis of Gate Twenty

Of Seven Maidens and their Mendacity

THIS TALE DIFFERS in more ways than one from most others in *Sefer Taḥkemoni*. Firstly, it is not Hever, wandering rogue-rhetor, who takes centre stage, but Heman. The usual teller of a tale, one told or acted by Hever the Kenite, is himself the actor here, and a very active one indeed: only at the gate's close has Hever qua Hever, anything at all to say and it is brief. Only in one preceding gate is Heman afforded so central a role—Gate 16, where, despite Heman's closing admiration for Hever and his pupils, it is the Ezrahite who merits the laurel for the density and intricacy of his rhymed prose.[1]

Also atypical here is the fact that it is Heman, not Hever, who plays the braggart both in poetry and prose, limning his lineage, his heroic travels, his excellence in study, and his achievements as a lover. As well, his comeuppance bears a resemblance to the downfall of Hever in Gate 6's wedding fiasco.

What explains these role reversals in general, and specifically here?

The answer is not far to seek: both Heman and Hever are reflections, variously, of the author himself, Alḥarizi. Both resemble the author as described and self-advertised in the book's initial poem, Introduction, and first gate: both travel extensively, both are questers, both are admirers and practitioners of elegant language.[2] Here, as in a few places in *Sefer Taḥkemoni*, our author utilizes this identity to render a complex literary statement.

Alḥarizi's immediate source for this narrative is apparent—'The Declaration of Asher son of Judah', by Solomon ibn Zakbel.[3] There a boastful youth inclined to the delights of the flesh becomes involved in a now-you-have-her-now-you-haven't harem imbroglio. Not until the hero is thoroughly enervated does he win to the side of his beloved, where he, too, unmasks a man—a disguised, roguish friend. In both tales the object of desire is portrayed in stereotypic conventions drawn from both Hebrew and Arabic love

---

[1] To a lesser degree, the Ezrahite shows rhetorical skill at the outset of Gate 5, in his description of the month of Nisan. See too Gate 49 and Analysis.

[2] For a complementary discussion of the blurring of boundaries between Alḥarizi, Hever, and Heman, see the Analysis of Gate 49; and see the overall discussion of this topic in the Afterword.

[3] For a literal translation and analysis of this text, see D. Segal, '"Maḥberet Ne'um Asher ben Yehudah"'. See also the translation and comments of Scheindlin, 'Asher in the Harem'.

poetry, where the beloved can be at once a roe and a lioness, ravaging the heart and liver of her suitor, and sporting his blood; she is beauty's acme, possessed of raven black locks and shining white cheeks that put the luminaries to shame; indeed her beauty is godlike and invites worship.[4] In both tales the hero lauds himself to excess but faints away when confronted with a hostile male at the close.

J. Dishon has closely compared these two texts[5] to the detriment of Alḥarizi, holding up ibn Zakbel's creation as far more uproarious and richer in character delineation; it would seem, however, that she has missed Alḥarizi's intent. Of a surety, our author is fully capable of building a hilarious, farcical situation. That is precisely what he does, for example, in Gate 6: there, after a tantalizing build-up, the much-lusted-after young woman turns out to be a monstrosity; and the 'history' of Jewry's enthronement and rescue of King Stint is a *tour de force* of comic social satire. Here, while Alḥarizi has retained the essential farcical plot of ibn Zakbel, he has chosen to render a very different sort of reality.

It is the bizarre conclusion of our tale that gives the clue to what Alḥarizi is about. Hever the Kenite and his mysterious maidens are more than mortal: at the close Hever abruptly disappears, while his maidens, too, vanish instantly:

> Then he hastened to bid me farewell and left me, and the maidens disappeared from my sight—a godly wind carried them off; and I was left alone in my pain.[6]

Here Alḥarizi alludes to the wondrous powers of Elijah:

> They said to him [Elisha], 'Your servants have fifty able men with them. Let them go and look for your master [Elijah]; perhaps the spirit of the Lord has carried him off and cast him upon some mountain or into some valley.'[7]

The maidens accompanying a more-than-human Hever here have the air of the muses about them, albeit very mischievous ones. They are far more than simply voluptuous and enticing; their supra-human nature is hinted at variously. The very word describing their vanishing at the close, *ne'elmu*, 'they disappeared', forms a verbal bracket with their description at their first appearance, when they are surrounded by a 'hidden light', *or ne'elam*.

Indeed the tale's beginning points manifestly to the more than mortal status of the maidens. The very fact that they are seven, a potent number in Jewish tradition, and often linked with the mysterious or sublime, is signifi-

[4] See Segal, '"Maḥberet Ne'um Asher ben Yehudah"', 24–6.
[5] Dishon, 'The Declaration of Asher son of Judah'.
[6] *ST* 207. 21–4. [7] 2 Kgs. 2: 16.

cant.[8] In addition, the women are seen as heavenly bodies casting an extraordinary glow on earth, and are presented as from the stock of Eden. Clearly they are *benot hashir*, 'the daughters of song' of whom Hever boasts intimacy in Gate 8: 'All the daughters of song are possessed (sexually) of me, though they are virgins to all others beside me.'[9]

We have no indication that Alḥarizi was acquainted with the theory and accounts of the muses in classical Greek and Latin literature. In effect, however, he advances his own theory here—and earlier, where Hever himself is presented as the author's muse in the complex, trifaceted explanation of the book's genesis comprising the Introduction and Gate 1, at once the hero and catalyst of each and every gate to follow.

With this key to unlocking Gate 20, Alḥarizi gives us to understand that he has utilized the conventions of erotic poetry not merely for comic effect, but to serious ends: standard hyperbolic praise for feminine beauty hints at the author's genuine passion for that which Hever and his maidens here represent—poetry and poetic inspiration.[10] Heman's initial description of the maidens' beauty and then the splendour of one exceptional maiden (Hever); his ensuing plea to the latter, laced with further praise of her powers and charms; yet another maiden's further praise of their quintessential beauty—all are coded references to the potency and splendour of poetic creativity; and, in this instance, to the specific creativity of the author, Judah Alḥarizi himself.[11]

[8] The reader will recall the seven poets of Gate 17 and the seven speakers for virtues in Gate 19. See 'Seven', *EJ* xii. 1257. The number seven is given further emphasis in the Hebrew title of the tale, lit. 'Of seven virgins (*betulot*) and their tricks (*taḥbuloteihen*)' (the stylistic device mirrored in the translation). Only this gate and Gate 46 have unrhymed titles—which titles are not the author's: in all the manuscripts, rhyming titles are in Arabic (Habermann, 'The Dedications to *Sefer Taḥkemoni*' (Heb.), 138. Habermann suggests that a few words of the original rhyming titles have been lost.)

[9] *ST* 94. 10–11, citing Eccles. 12: 4, 'all the daughters of music (*benot hashir*) shall be brought low' (AV; NJPS translates 'all the strains of music dying down').

[10] In a partially similar and earlier achievement in a riddle poem, Samuel Hanagid prefaces a complaint against a powerful figure with a seemingly convention-laced love poem—which, on close reading, is revealed as an involved metaphoric pre-statement of the very charges that are to be made in the poem's second section. See Segal, 'A Comment on the Love Poetry of R. Samuel Hanagid' (Heb.); and for a dissenting opinion thereon, Y. Ratzaby, 'The Interpretation of "The Comely Gazelle"'.

[11] Sadan, 'Rabbi Judah Alḥarizi as a Cultural Crossroads', sheds further light on this gate, affording appreciation of a fine point of humour. The maiden after whom Heman lusts, and who turns out to be Hever, is noted as being unusually tall: 'Now one of them, from her shoulders and upwards, was the tallest of them' (*ST* 202. 22); this description has been lifted from ibn Zakbel's tale: 'and behold a bevy of delicate women, the choicest of women, and among them a maiden taller than them all from her shoulder upwards' (Schirmann, *Hebrew*

Thus it is not simply a bogus *femme fatale*, but rather Alḥarizi's muse (Hever) who is the acme of beauty, singular, a ruler of nations, eager to display her beauty to all and sundry, flowing with milk and honey, offering beauty available even to the blind and the mute, ringed with honour and majesty, and singular on earth. The threats of the maiden who notes the perils of approaching the fairest of their group hint at the dangers of rashly engaging in the poetic enterprise. The humour and absurdity of the speaker describing a face that is, as we learn from the tale's close, veiled, could additionally relate to the undertaking of the author (represented by Heman) in reaching for a beauty (poetry) that is at once inaccessible and yet vividly present to his imagination.

Hever's constant conversation with his maidens hints at the author's muse seeking yet further and higher inspiration. Moreover, the overall mocking of Heman/the author by his own muse could relate to a profound tension in the book between rascality/roguery, on the one hand, and, on the other, high purpose—moral instruction and the defence of the Hebrew language.

Relatedly: Heman's setting out from Judah's Bethlehem (storehouse) with donkeyloads of desire gives more than veiled prefiguration of the erotic encounter that is to take place; rather, it hints at the passion of the author for literary creation.[12] Indeed the anger of Heman at the close could, on a deeper level, express the occasional frustration of the author seized by the muse in ways unanticipated and at times forced to serve a power outside himself, as it were.

In sum, far from being a slip of the pen, Gate 20 of *Sefer Taḥkemoni*, when read on two levels, reveals Alḥarizi deftly blending humour with an oblique and complex expression of the linkage of his eros with poetic creativity.

Poetry, i. 564, ll. 172–3). The Arabic biographer of Alḥarizi, whose account was based, *inter alia*, on a personal interview with his subject, notes that our author was unusually tall (Sadan, pp. 31, 47; and the Arabic original p. 53, l. 2)!

[12] Again, the Hebrew *beit-leḥem yehudah* means, literally, 'the house/store of bread of Judah', pointing to the intellectual/spiritual 'store' of Judah Alḥarizi. See, in the Introduction and its Analysis, Hever's wooing and wedding of the Hebrew language, and the similar wedding of the intellect and the soul, yet another indication of the intertwining of eros with literary creation in the psyche of the author.

Analysis of Gate Twenty-One

Of a Sumptuous Feast and a Bumpkin Fleeced

IN GATE 21 ALḤARIZI'S debt to al-Hamadhani is large indeed: his product is a wholesale borrowing from the latter's near-identical tale at *Maqāmāt*, gate 12, albeit with significant modifications.[1] Among these are the addition of a frame tale, with heightening of suspense and delivery of a negative moral judgement; and the adding of verve and wit to the description of the hero's hunger and the assuaging thereof. Generally the rogue-rhetor is fouler in the Hebrew: he is more ostensibly empathetic with the peasant, who is presented as more wretched, more naïve, and poorer than in the Arabic tale; and his brazen boast and justification of betraying all and sundry, and especially the wise, is far stronger than the Arabic close.[2]

As ever, Alḥarizi delights in veiled prefigurations, often ironic. Heman's description of wandering round the streets at the outset derives from the Song of Songs (3: 2): 'I must rise and roam the town, through the streets and through the squares . . .'. This is in turn echoed by Hever describing his own wandering, but for literal, not spiritual, victuals; and the latter's joyous discovery of his hapless victims is announced in language echoing the continuation of the borrowed verse: 'Scarcely had I passed them when I found the one I love' (S. of S. 3: 4).

In describing the succulent meat hanging in the market-place, Hever notes that it splits the viewer's heart and, literally, that it 'sends a fire into his ribs'. At the close the peasant declares, in literal translation, 'That rogue who kindled a fire within my heart—oh, would that he could become my sword's dish!'[3]

Heman's declaration at the start that he seeks to cull portions from the fruit of the tongues of wise men (*nevonim*) is a double prefiguration, pointing to the major motif of tasty edibles and to a very different fruit—a technique for gulling the naïve! Hever's concluding boast in metric verse that he makes fools of the wise (*hanevonim*) produces, with *nevonim* of the start, an inclusion, or verbal bracketing of the gate.

[1] al-Hamadhani, *Maqāmāt*, tr. Prendergast, 61–4.

[2] Dishon, 'On the Source of the Twenty-First Gate of *Sefer Taḥkemoni*' (Heb.). Dishon also cites select instances of allusive ironies and prefigurations; I add to these in my analysis here.

[3] *ST* 211. 23–4.

Analysis of Gate Twenty-Two

Of Fate's Rack and the Zodiac

FROM TALMUDIC TIMES down to the Middle Ages, most Jewish sages and philosophers believed in the vital influence of the stars on human destiny.[1] They differed primarily on the degree to which Jews and the Jewish nation were subsumed under this general rule. *Ein mazal le yisrael*, declared Rabbi Yoḥanan, 'Israel has no governing constellation'—a position diametrically opposed by Rabbi Ḥanina bar Dosa.[2]

Several Jewish astrologers made names for themselves in Islamic lands; and post-talmudic Jewish leaders who reckoned astrology a genuine science included Sa'adiah Gaon, Samuel Hanagid, Solomon ibn Gabirol, and many more. Few indeed were outright opponents of star-readers' claims, foremost among them Maimonides, who held the theory and practice of astrology foolishness or fraud. On one point the vast majority of Jewish thinkers agreed: that few humans, if any, could accurately read the future (although the Talmud cites several instances of astrologers whose prediction of coming events came true). It is against this background that the present *maqāma* emerges.

From his first appearance in Gate 22, the stargazer's credentials seem highly dubious. He is presented as a smooth-tongued trickster, a popular fortune-teller rather than a respected court astrologer engaged in legitimate research; indeed, his exaggerated boasts and eagerness to fleece his listeners are much akin to Hever the Kenite's performance as an unscrupulous bogus physician in Gate 30. The initial reaction of Hever and his friends echoes the acerbity of Joseph's scoffing brothers before they tossed their father's favourite into a pit: 'Let us . . . see what shall become of his dreams' (Gen. 37: 20). The savant's claim to know the stars and future, and even control the very constellations, spurs the sceptical Jews to put their impossible question

[1] Islam and Judaism both show significant popular belief in the truth of astrology; and in both, leading figures were sharply divided on the prudence, or very legitimacy, of the enterprise. For a brief and helpful overview on astrology in Jewish civilization, see *EJ* iii. 788–95. See also the discussion on this topic, and the succinct summary of the castigation of astrology by Maimonides, whose thought Alḥarizi championed (in *ST*, in Gates 46 and 50), in Brann, 'Power in the Portrayal', esp. 18–19 n. 37. See too Scheindlin, 'Al-Harizi's Astrologer', especially his discussion of Maimonides' 'Epistle to Yemen', invalidating astrology entirely and specifically warning against the dangers of provoking the Muslims through messianic calculation and giving credence to pretenders. Scheindlin suggests, convincingly, that our text is a clear echo of Maimonides' warning there.

[2] BT *Shab.* 156*a*.

to him; and then demand that he read their minds—exhibiting a telepathic capability to which he never laid claim!

Yet the wizard's reply demonstrates, surprisingly, genuine powers: if far from the superhuman seer he proclaims himself to be, he is no simple confidence man. While never predicting the Messiah's arrival, he identifies his questioners as Jews and does read their minds;[3] indeed, he gives them back their unasked question with a vengeance. They had closed their internal discussion with a circumlocution: 'When shall this fallen one [Israel] be restored?' With dense metaphoric speech drawing richly on biblical (!) sources, the Arab expands upon this query, spelling out, from his perspective, its chief implication—world domination. Labelling his interlocutors as traitors to the crown, he sets the mob upon them and they are all but killed.[4]

In effect, this confrontation, together with the Jews' ultimate rescue, credited to divine intervention, comprises an exemplification of the very dilemma raised by Hever and his friends, and expanded upon by the stargazer: what is to be the fate of diasporic Jewry in hostile lands? The same Jews who had asked when 'this fallen one' would be raised up, themselves fall—being flung to earth and then dragged through the streets; and in his fleshing out of their question, the seer asks, specifically, whether an exiled sheep, walking among wild beasts, can saved from lions' teeth, prefiguring the citation ending the tale, 'Blessed be the Lord, who has not given us as prey to their teeth'.

Relatedly, a citation at the tale's outset hints at the near-allegory to follow. Hever, describing his companions to Heman, uses a singular biblical phrase that is most strange for a Jew to use: he states that he was with 'friends *miyaldei ha'ivrim*/of the Hebrews' children', these being words spoken by Pharaoh's daughter upon seeing the infant Moses (Exod. 2: 6), i.e. by a non-Jew identifying a member of an oppressed minority—which is precisely what Hever and friends prove to be in this tale!

Beyond the description of the stargazer and his boasts, Alḥarizi threads his tale purposively with reference to the stars. In describing how he led his

[3] On this critical point, I differ from Brann and Scheindlin, each of whom has explored this text richly, in the above-cited articles, in the context of Muslim–Jewish relations in Spain, and in the Middle Ages. I construe the stargazer's question, 'Perhaps you are Jews?' as rhetorical and sarcastic in context. It is preceded by his characterization of the men before him as neither Christians nor Muslims, but members of a despised and lowly nation; and is followed by an extraordinary exposition that does demonstrate clear telepathic powers.

[4] Scheindlin, in 'Al-Harizi's Astrologer', 168–9, points out the influence of gate 49 of al-Hamadhani ('The *Maqāma* of Wine'), where a group of mocking young men narrowly escape lynching at the hands of a congregation egged on by a leader of prayer expressing outrage at their irreligiosity (*Maqāmāt*, tr. Prendergast, 178–82).

fellows to test the Muslim sage, Hever declares, 'Now I, ill-fated and star-led' (literally, 'by my wretched luck and ill-fated grief'). Even the seemingly unrelated introductory remarks of Heman weave into the astral theme: 'When dawn *zaraḥ*/shone bright . . . when the stars veered right and left at my command' (literally, 'when I was in my prime and when the stars of my dawn shone and the zodiac circled according to my command').[5] Alḥarizi prefaces a sombre tale of a group of Jews heavily bound by a prototypical Jewish fate with an exaggerated statement of individual control over fate—a claim typical of poetry of boast or self-praise, where the laudandus is touted as fate's master.[6] By the tale's end, Heman in his initial egocentricity—atypical in *Sefer Taḥkemoni* but for Gate 20—is contrasted (implicitly) with Hever and his oppressed fellow Jews, symbolic of suffering Israel.

[5] The astral theme is rendered the more prominent in that *zaraḥ*/shone bright constitutes a pun with Heman *ha'ezraḥi*/the Ezrahite—a pun that serves to emphasize Heman's boastful good spirits.

[6] For discussion of the genre of boast, or self-praise, see Analysis 16.

Analysis of Gate Twenty-Three

Of Hever the Kenite's Wretched Hour and Sudden Rise to Wealth and Power

IF THE MAJOR FOCUS of the preceding *maqāma* was the fate of the Jewish people, Gate 23 explores the theme of fate as it relates to the individual.

In medieval Hebrew metric poetry, fate's machinations and rule play a prominent role.[1] Echoing pre-Islamic, as well as later, Arabic poetry, the genre of Hebrew reflective poetry generally presents man as helpless before the arbitrary power of fate, who hurls down the lofty, turns the rich destitute, and in the end kills all. As Moses ibn Ezra puts it at the close of one such poem,

> What hope is there for mortal man that he should aspire,[2]
> his eyes lifted daily to the pit?
> As though Time were a herdsman, death
> like a knife, and all who live, like sheep.[3]

Generally speaking, time (i.e. fate) and the world are linked in reflective poetry as hostile, at times overlapping, powers—murderous, callous, unstoppable. In a related genre, poetry of complaint, the outlook is the same, with the slight difference that the griefs brought by both, instead of being general, are aimed particularly at the complaining poet: 'And from place to place my fate [literally 'time'] hurls me like a javelin, dart, or lance';[4] 'My time, what makes you plough my back? Hear me and give my heart ease';[5] 'What have I to do with time, who pains one (already) pained (myself), who repeatedly sets a wandering bird wandering?'[6]

Conversely, in poetry of praise (of friends or patrons), or self-praise, as well as in wedding poems, these powers are often portrayed as being subject

[1] For an overview of fate in Hebrew medieval poetry, with discussion of Arabic precedent and example, see Levin, 'Time and the World' (Heb.), and Pagis, *Secular Poetry*, 122–4.

[2] Or: 'What hope is there for man, who awaits death.'

[3] *Secular Poems*, ed. Brody, i. 90, poem 90, sts. 5–6.

[4] Samuel Hanagid, 'Hakhol hayom', st. 3: *Ben tehilim*, ed. Jarden, 156.

[5] Solomon ibn Gabirol, 'Zemani mah lekha taḥarosh begabi', st. 1 (*Secular Poetry*, ed. Jarden, 84).

[6] Moses ibn Ezra, 'Mah li uzeman', st. 1 (Schirmann, *Hebrew Poetry*, i. 380).

to the rule of the person(s) being lauded or celebrated: 'If yesterday I was at the head of them that fear him (Time), Time has risen early today in fear of me; I have overcome the daughters of days as if Israel's nobles were over my army';[7] 'Time falls ill for fear of you, until he thanks you for smiting him on his head; he traps lions in his net but is afraid when he looks upon your snares. Thus are his sons come into the bond of the covenant [Ezek. 20: 37], that they be of your legions.'[8]

There is a decided tension between the concept of this potent entity, fate or time, and the Jewish principle of divine omnipotence: such clashes are mirrored in some war poems of Samuel Hanagid.[9] Relatedly one and the same author can, in different poems of reflective verse, alternately present God, or time, as the regnant power of the universe. Thus Moses ibn Ezra can speak in one of his poems of man being ruled by fate: 'True it is that man's lusts are deep waters—but their (men's) desires are dependent upon the hands of the Pleiades'; and, in another, of God's supremacy: 'God's face alone shall I seek . . . What does one man's hand avail another? Despise the world . . . .'[10]

It is against this background that the *maqāma* under consideration was written. In effect it brings to the fore the inherent contradictions in the treatment of time or fate in Hebrew and Arabic poetry.[11]

[7] Solomon ibn Gabirol, 'Kevar no'ash levavi', sts. 6–7 (*Secular Poetry*, ed. Jarden, 43).

[8] Moses ibn Ezra, 'Tagbir bekhol rega', sts. 7–9 (*Secular Poems*, ed. Brody, i. 46). On the determining influence of genre upon these, and other, recurring motifs, see Pagis, *Secular Poetry*, 116–25, 134–6; esp. 122–4 for further examples of the treatment of the motif of time.

[9] Thus in 'Zeman la'anashim yashk et kos vekuba'at' ('Time Tenders Man a Large Goblet [Filled with Poison]'; *Ben tehilim*, ed. Jarden, 143–5), Time is 'malicious, traitorous, and all-powerful' until st. 19, where it is presented as subservient to God, in all that relates to Samuel Hanagid. In 'Mah lekha el tsevi' ('What Have You to Do with the Gazelle?'; ibid. 100–3), Time gives all men grief, emptiness, and death in the poem's first, pessimistic section, which generically belongs to reflective poetry; whereas, at the poem's close, the poet boasts of divine aid for himself (st. 31) and for his sick son (sts. 36–8). For a discussion of integrative mechanisms in such poems, see Segal, 'Observations on Three War Poems', 165–203. Feldman, *Polarity and Parallel*, discusses typical patterns of cohesion employed by Moses ibn Ezra in multi-genre poems of friendship—specifically poems of praise prefaced by (a) unit(s) of eros and/or wine and/or nature description. Many an element in these prefatory units is prefigurative of (an) aspect(s) of the praised patron, such as his generosity, wisdom, or protection; and at times repeating words or motifs are presented in such a way as to indicate the superiority of the patron to a person (such as an attractive youth) or an inanimate object (such as the sun or moon).

[10] 'Emet ta'avot enosh' and 'Penei ha'el levad' (Schirmann, *Hebrew Poetry*, i. poems 4 and 5, p. 402).

[11] For a lucid review of this topic, see Elizur, 'And Days (Fate) are Commanded of God' (Heb.). Elizur concludes that among the poets of Hebrew Spain, only Judah Halevi reached a philosophically consistent and theologically acceptable synthesis between Jewish tradition and Arab fatalism, as expressed in detail in his poem 'If You Trust in Your God Alone'.

A proper understanding of Alḥarizi's sophisticated game can begin with an examination of the cloak of religiosity Hever dons. Hever's letter to the prince is couched in religious tones and bears a double message: the prince must accept that which he has been accorded by the all-powerful God; and secondly, this same God has ultimately been kind, making good the loss of a daughter with the more valuable gift of a son. Relatedly, Hever credits God with his own change of fortune, when Heman angrily accuses his friend of ingratitude. Finally, the gate closes on the theme of divine power and human trust in the Lord: Heman blesses God, who rewards his servants faithfully.

Yet the overall message of the gate is by no means so simplistic or traditional.

Hever's behaviour contradicts his pious mouthings, as well as his stated philosophy on fate. In his own hour of need, the Kenite relies not on God but his own enterprise; and does not pray, but utilizes his wits and his impressive rhetorical skills to reverse his ill fortune.

Hever's very initiative shows him as anything but gratefully content with divine largesse. Through Heman's hospitality, the Kenite's fortunes *had*, in effect, been reversed: he had been given shelter and food and wine in abundance, by a true friend, one moved to tears by his plight. But this was not enough for a worldling like Hever: he sought greater gain. More than that, he dissembled in his first declamation in a prince's courtyard, making no reference to his friend's considerable help. Indeed it is clear, from the conclusion of the story, that Hever had changed *back* into his filthy rags after Heman had succumbed to the wine, for he rounds out his tale by explicitly noting his new patron's stripping him of foul clothing.[12]

So much for Hever as pietist!

As for the role explicitly assigned fate here, the gate presents contradictory messages, evoking the differing stances of the genres of metric poetry. The lesser prince that Hever first meets is so enthusiastic about the Kenite's poem that he promises not only ample fiscal reward for the required letter but declares that he will render Hever immune from sorrow and the control

There, building on prior conventions, the poet makes of time a mighty force, yet subservient to God, which is given command over the lot of worldlings—but not over those who cleave to God and His ways (ibid. 40–3).

[12] *ST* 272. 17–18. That Hever cites Zech. 3: 4 at this point is pointedly ironic. In a dream vision, an angel declares of Joshua the high priest, 'Take the filthy garments off him', continuing, 'See, I have removed your guilt from you, and you shall be clothed in [priestly] robes'. God goes on to proclaim to the prophet a programme of national salvation, involving Joshua himself. Contrastingly, Hever wrests money from a patron by mouthing alleged truths he himself disbelieves, and gulls a patron out of a magnificent suit of clothes having already had his ragged garb changed!

of fate—a most unrealistic promise under any circumstances (even if modelled on previous poetry), and all the more so here: Hever had reported to Heman his near-death at the hand of brigands, and no gift of any prince could guarantee immunity against such mishap!

It is highly unlikely that Hever would believe such an assurance, especially when he in turn produces an equally glib assurance in his requisitioned letter that the bereaved father, through his newborn son, will rule over time. It is true that this assurance is set in a framework of special divine care, recalling Samuel Hanagid's assertions that God overrules time's (general) ill effect on men, or conventions of praise poetry generally; nevertheless, in this gate's frame of Hever's duplicity and the raw and unavoidable pain of mischance, the promise rings hollow.

Further to enrich the play on the theme of fate, Alḥarizi engages in his usual game of prefiguration and narrative linkage. In overall fashion, the briefly mentioned travails of Heman prefigure Hever's mishap.[13] More specifically, the forced wandering of Heman prefigures, as well, Hever's declared necessity to leave Heman. On this point, Alḥarizi's jibe at convention is scarcely veiled: neither man was compelled. The one word *hishi'ani*, 'he tempted me', predicated by Heman of time, reveals that some thoughts of gain put him to the road; and the necessity cited by Hever in leaving Heman's home (a necessity never clarified to Heman) turns out to be the felt necessity to win more lucre![14]

Now while the attentive reader is aware of the contradictions in Hever's varied utterances, and the contradictions between what he says and what he does, Heman is certainly not. Here he shows decided lack of acumen, to the point of (1) forgetting his (justified) irritation over Hever's ingratitude and mercenary mien; and (2) praising God for not withholding His mercies from His servants, a rank to which Hever hardly qualifies here!

Alḥarizi's repetition of the Hebrew root *s-v-v* has Heman's wandering prefigure Hever's seeking out a patron[15] and bolsters the impression that there is a mercenary side to Heman's peregrination. Heman's comforting of Hever—the root *n-ḥ-m* is used—prefigures the comfort assayed, unsuccessfully, by the lesser prince; and prefigures the comfort that Hever will provide

[13] There is another, and subtle, prefiguration as well: Heman's being bound in the bonds of wandering's friendship prefigures the warm reception to be tendered Hever by Heman.

[14] For a discussion of a related parody on the conventions of erotic, martial, and reflective poetry—and specifically on the motif of time and wandering—see Segal, 'The Tales of Jacob ben Elazar' (Heb.).

[15] *ST* 218. 3–5: *hanedod . . . vehishi'ani . . . leshotet medinot ulesovev me'onot*, 'Wandering . . . tempted me . . . to traverse lands and wander round habitations'; *ST* 219. 23: *sovavti bekhol ha'ir*, 'I wandered round the entire city'.

the greater prince, in his letter.[16] The tendering of wine to make Hever forget his grief prefigures, in overall fashion, the eradication of the prince's grievous loss (of his daughter) by his gain (the birth of a son).

On this last-mentioned, and central, point one can suspect the sincerity of Hever. Is he (or Alḥarizi) speaking with conviction, so readily dismissing the agony of the loss of a daughter? Or is Hever blatantly mouthing what he knows his auditor will welcome? The latter option is the more plausible.[17]

The Kenite walks away from his benefactor lavishly rewarded for declaiming of God and fate what his own words and behaviour belie. Here, as so often, the Kenite's cunning has stood him in good stead to best ill fortune. But Alḥarizi points out between the lines that this success, like that guaranteed the greater prince, is by no means as assured as Hever the Kenite boasts or as Heman the Ezrahite believes.

With this ambiguous message Alḥarizi closes a cluster of gates revolving about the theme of (primarily) the protagonist's chicanery: Gates 19 and 20, where, respectively, Hever the Kenite has come on as a moral nihilist and a mocking deceiver; Gate 22, where he receives his comeuppance in a turning of tables; and this gate, where he has reverted to form, stooping to varied deceits to line his pockets with gold.

[16] *ST* 218. 17–18; 220. 26; 221. 10; 222. 4.

[17] There remains, of course, the possibility that this is but one further evidence of a deeply rooted antipathy on the author's part towards women. On this point see Analyses 6 and 41.

Analysis of Gate Twenty-Four

Of a Jolly Cantor and Folly Instanter

TRADITION DEMANDED much of the precentor. The Mishnah, describing the procedures for prayer on a fast day, stipulates that the prayer leader must be an elder and well-accustomed to the service.[1] The Gemara expands these requirements: he must be humble; desired of the people; sweet-voiced; a seasoned reader of the Pentateuch, Prophets, and Writings; and capable of teaching Midrash, whether haggadic or halakhic; and well versed in all the blessings.[2] These high standards were doubtless a function of the vital role the precentor had to play: excepting congregations of highly learned men, the people, not having prayerbooks, depended upon their cantor's precision in the accurate rendering of the set prayers[3]—and, over the centuries, for any new, poetic accretions to the service.

Perhaps these impossibly high demands, and inevitably conflicting realities, led to harsh condemnations, in halakhic literature, of cantors lacking knowledge or integrity or more. Jewish satirists in Spain, and thereafter, had a field day with the subject, depicting precentors as venal or ignoramuses, or both.[4]

This *maqāma* must be considered the jewel in the crown of this tradition.

Alḥarizi demolishes the cantor of Gate 24 in various ways. First, he presents the man's ignorance of tradition, a failing all the more ludicrous in light of the sextons' extravagant praise of his learning and piety—itself a parody of the above-cited criteria put forward by Rabbi Judah in the Talmud. As significant, to lead Sabbath eve services wearing phylacteries—designated for use during morning, weekday worship—is to show oneself very much less than a sage.[5] To make matters worse, the cantor drags his prayer shawl on

[1] As well, he should be the father of children depending upon him for their livelihood; yet, at the same time, lacking in livelihood—this, that his petition be the more sincere (*Ta'anit* 2: 2).

[2] BT *Ta'anit* 16*a*.

[3] On the obligation of the precentor to fulfil the obligation of the congregant who does not understand the prayer, see BT *RH* 33*b*–34*b*; Maimonides, *Mishneh torah: Hilkhot tefilah/Laws of Prayer*, ch. 8, par. 9, ed. Touger (New York, 1989), 56 f.; *Shulḥan arukh, Oraḥ ḥayim* 124: 1.

[4] See Dishon, 'The Precentor' (Heb.), for an overview of humorous treatment of the cantor in Hebrew *maqāma* literature in Spain, with attention to this gate of Alḥarizi's. See also ead., *The Book of Delight*, 173–82; and entries in the index under *ḥazan* and *sheliaḥ tsibur*.

[5] If the Talmud registers debate on the appropriate and permissible times for putting on phylacteries (*Eruv.* 96*a*–*b*), by Alḥarizi's time the wearing of phylacteries on the Sabbath was clearly forbidden. See *Shulḥan arukh, Oraḥ ḥayim* 31*a*, interpreting *Men.* 36 and *Eruv.* 96.

the ground—hardly a recommendation of refined religious sensibility;[6] and, during the Sabbath morning service, makes ostentatious and exaggerated motions that greatly exceed the permissible.[7] Finally, and most significantly, his misreadings of the prayer text, beginning with those in the 'hundred blessings', are outrageous.[8]

These gross errors, the acme of the gate's satire, are comical enough singly; in aggregate, they are hilarious. Two basic patterns are evidenced, with some overlap: disrespect for God, attaining to blasphemy; and fixation on food.[9] For purposes of closer analysis, the literal translation of the Hebrew text—with which I have taken considerable liberties—is here provided:

Instead of 'Blessed art Thou, O Lord . . . who created man with wisdom/*beḥokhmah*' he said '. . . a beast/*behemah*',[10] and instead of, 'Protect, as well, Thy servant from sinners (or: deliberate sins)', *gam mizedim ḥasokh avdekha*, he said, 'Educate, as well, Thy servant though olives', *gam mizeitim ḥanokh avdekha*; and instead of, 'May he sate you with the fat of wheat', *ḥelev ḥitim yasbi'ekh* (Ps. 147: 14), he said, 'May he sate you with sharp swords', *ḥerev ḥadim yasbi'ekh*; and instead of, 'Who covers the heavens with clouds', *hamekhaseh shamayim be'avim* (Ps. 147: 8), he said, 'Who covers the skies with clothes', *hamekhaseh shamayim begadim*; and instead of, 'Let Israel rejoice in his Maker', *yismaḥ yisra'el be'osav* (Ps. 149: 2), he said, 'Let Ishmael (Araby) rejoice with Esau (Christendom)', *yismaḥ yishma'el be'esav*; and instead of, 'Praise him with lyre and psaltery', *haleluhu beminim ve'ugav* (Ps. 150: 4), he said, 'Praise him, cheeses and cake', *haleluhu gevinim ve'ugah*; and instead of, 'It is in Your power to make all (creatures) great and strong', *beyadekha legadel uleḥazek lakol* (1 Chr. 29: 12), he said, 'It is in Your power to execrate and harm all', *beyadekha legadef ulehazik lakol*.[11]

[6] Note the (much later) remarks in *Beit yosef* (1555), Joseph Karo's noted commentary on Jacob ben Asher's halakhic compendium *Arba'ah turim*—on ch. 21, section four, in the division *Oraḥ ḥayim*: '[The author of the book of] Agur (a compendium of medieval Jewish practice) (section 6) declared in the name of the Hagahot Mordechai: "Anyone who drags his fringes, of him Scripture states (Isa. 14: 23): 'I will sweep him with a broom of extermination'"'.

[7] See discussion below and n. 13.

[8] Jewish law calls for the recitation of one hundred blessings daily (*Shulḥan arukh*, *Oraḥ ḥayim* 46: 2, following *Men.* 43*b*). The term 'one hundred blessings' also designates—as here—a section of the morning service, *birkhot hashaḥar* or 'blessings of the morning'. See Wieder, 'The Hundred Blessings' (Heb.); id., 'The Liturgical Term' (Heb.). Actually most of the errors cited by Hever (in the Hebrew) derive from the second section of the morning service, *pesukei dezimrah*, rather than from *birkhot hashaḥar*.

[9] On food fixation see Dishon, 'The Precentor', 249 and n. 49.

[10] In having the cantor recite 'Blessed art Thou . . . who createdst man a beast/*behemah*', Alḥarizi refers to a blessing in the Italian prayer ritual, *shelo asani behemah*, 'Who didst not make me a beast'. See Wieder, 'On the Blessings' (Heb.).

[11] For the original blessings in their context see Hertz, *Authorised Daily Prayer Book*, 64, 92, 94, 96, 98.

Through these distortions the corpulent cantor stands revealed not only as quasi-illiterate, but also as supremely egotistical, projecting his own behaviour and desires onto the text. Thus, when he speaks of God as 'covering the skies with clothing/*begadim*' rather than 'with clouds/*be'avim*', he recalls his own massive turban! To add insult to injury, a second meaning of *begadim* is 'acts of betrayal', as at Isa. 24: 16 and Jer. 12: 1; and through his blunders, it is the cantor himself who overlays the heavens with traitorous statements!

The original attains to still a further level of humour: so ignorant is the cantor that he even distorts the one text that he should surely understand and render correctly: *ḥelev ḥitim yasbi'ekh*, 'He shall sate you (the pious) with the fat of wheat'. This becomes *ḥerev ḥadim yasbi'ekh*, 'He shall sate you with sharp swords', a statement that is theologically perverse, transmuting the promise of divine protection to assurance of divine murder!

A singular felicity of Alḥarizi's is the cantor's first morning gaffe, the corruption of one of the earliest apostrophes of God in the service: 'Blessed art Thou O Lord our God, King of the Universe, who has created man *beḥokhmah*/with wisdom'—rendered by the cantor as *behemah*, 'beast' (this in the Hebrew text). This error gives the lie to the precentor's claim to erudition (as supported by the sextons), even as it defames God. Moreover, in this 'Freudian slip' the cantor unwittingly refers to himself, identified with beasts by both Hever and, later, the opponent of *piyut*. Finally, this error, together with the sextons' likening their loved leader to a fatted ram, prefigures the other animal characterizations scattered throughout the gate—of the members of the cantor's congregation, and of like ignoramuses scattered throughout the world.[12]

Alḥarizi heightens comic effect in his description of the precentor's exaggerated bodily motion, which, in the original, reads: 'He covered his face, but not in modesty, and stood proudly, making many motions: he moved his shoulders, lifted his right leg and lowered the other, then moved back slightly'.[13]

It would appear that the narrator is faulting the cantor on two scores: for ostentation and exaggeration in customary prayer movements; and for wholly bizarre movements. The covering of the face is apparently a reference to cloaking the head with the prayer shawl when reciting the Amidah silently, a custom observed to this day.[14] The moving backward, beginning with the right leg, could refer to the first two of three steps backward at the conclusion of the silent Amidah.[15] The many motions, and especially of the shoul-

[12] See Dishon, 'The Precentor', 249 and n. 48.

[13] *ST* 225. 2–5.

[14] See *Shulḥan arukh, Oraḥ ḥayim* 91: 6 and Maimonides, *Mishneh torah: Laws of Prayer*, ch. 5.

[15] See *Shulḥan arukh, Oraḥ ḥayim* 123: 1 (and *Oraḥ ḥayim* 95: 1 for steps preceding the Amidah).

ders, might well refer to impassioned swaying (called *shokeling* in Ashkenazi tradition), a practice met with a broad spectrum of rabbinic reaction through the ages, from demanding it to repudiating it—although it would seem that, in general, Sephardi sources opted for a more subdued practice.[16]

Our author weds farce to serious religious critique in this gate, as he lends his voice to a centuries-long attack against the excesses of embellishing the service with *piyut*, synagogue poetry interwoven with the fixed text and leading into key blessings or declarations. Alḥarizi doubtless refers to the end result of a historical process that saw an ancient and respected practice run amok: what originally comprised a limited number of lines in tightly controlled and well-knit, organic poetic compositions, in the course of time spun out of control in Eastern lands, especially throughout the ninth and eleventh centuries: more and more precentors, themselves not the scholar-poets their predecessors had been, and unaware of the original structure and logic of the texts that came down to them, poured on ever growing verses and stanzas. Genizah manuscripts evidence, at times, an amalgam of creations of scores of poets in one kind of composition—the *kedushta*, itself an embellishment of the first three blessings of the Amidah for the Sabbath![17]

A partial summary of the history of the debate over *piyut* has been afforded by A. Z. Idelsohn:

The insertion of poetry into the prayers was by no means met with favour. Many outstanding authorities opposed the piyyut on the grounds that it brought about an interruption in the continuity of the service. Among the opponents were Nahshon Gaon, Judah of Barcelona, and Maimonides. Rabbi Naḥshon said that no piyyut should be inserted and that a *hazzan* who recites piyyut should not be permitted to officiate. A synagogue in which piyyut is recited, he held, the members of that congregation testify concerning themselves that they are not *students*.

Judah of Barcelona opposes all insertions . . . and calls the piyyut 'compositions full of ignorance and exaggerations'. Maimonides rejects the piyyut because it causes a break in the service, because it sometimes expresses obscure and even dangerous ideas, and because we are not allowed to add prayers to those composed by the Great Assembly.

On the other hand, there were men like Gershom 'the Light of the Exile', Rashi, and his grandson, Rabbi Jacob Tam, who were in favor of piyyut. Gershom con-

---

[16] For selected reading on this phenomenon see Sachs, 'On Moving To and Fro'; Berliner, *Selected Writings* (Heb.), ii. 130–1; Millgram, *Jewish Worship*, 359–60; *JE* i. 211, 'Adoration', and ii. 607, 'Swaying the Body'; Ashkenazi, *Each Generation and its Customs* (Heb.), 180–96; Zimmer, 'Laws' (Heb.), esp. 116–27; and Eisenstein, *Thesaurus of Laws and Customs* (Heb.), 269–70.

[17] See Fleischer, *Hebrew Liturgical Poetry* (Heb.), §4, 'Late Eastern *Piyut*', 277–330 (esp. 292–7); also 336, 339–41, 377.

siders the piyyut as divinely inspired. . . . Natronai decided in favor of piyyut even in the Amidah. Mahzor Vitry 325–6 gives a long discussion with regard to the piyyut, and quoting several authorities like Natronai, Rashi, Jacob Tam, Joseph Tov-Elem, he comes to the conclusion that it is not only permissible but even meritorious to insert piyyut into the first three benedictions of the Amidah. In the name of Rashi several decisions are retained which speak in favor of piyyut. A man like Meir of Rothenburg himself composed several piyyutim . . . piyyut became the integral part of the service in Germany, so that Maharil (Jacob Mollin) considered its recitation of great importance and ordered his disciples not to miss the piyyut (Maharil, chapter on tefillah).[18]

Alḥarizi, it is evident, shares Maimonides' animus against *piyutim*: the latter was opposed to their inclusion in the service and to any changes in the obligatory blessings.[19] Objections additional to those cited above include singing, rather than cantorial recitation, of prayer; and the inflation of the service to such a degree that obligatory prayers will not be recited—both practices satirized in this gate.[20]

If Gate 24 reaches its apex of humour early, in the grotesquery of the cantor's misreadings, its apex of acerbity comes at the close, following steadily mounting vituperation against the practice of *piyut*.

Alḥarizi takes pains to have *piyut*'s spokesman mirror, in his argumentation, the very boorishness of Ashur's cantor and congregation: he accuses the scholar of weak argument, asserting that *piyutim* are recited worldwide despite the presence of multitudes of bovine ignoramuses (!); hence, there is nothing wrong with their recitation in the synagogue in question. (At what far remove does this dimwit debater stand from the eminent proponents of *piyut* through the ages!)

Hever's report of a so-called *ḥaver*, or scholar,[21] in Arbel is laced with

[18] Idelsohn, *Jewish Liturgy*, 45–6; and 358, for nn. 35–40, which have not been indicated here. For a recent overview of the Amidah—thematic, structural, and historical-developmental—see Kimelman, 'The Daily Amidah and the Rhetoric of Redemption'.

[19] See Blidstein, *Prayer in the Maimonidean Halakhah* (Heb.), index, p. 340, '*piyut, piyutim, payetanim*', and 'The Sanctity of the Fixed Text and the Problematic of *Piyut*', 123–50, where this topic is examined in detail, with attention to some exceptions to Maimonides' overall objection.

[20] 'Sung melodies are preferable to (recited) supplications' (*ST* 226. 2); and 'Shall it be pleasing in the sight of the Lord to expand the service with idle prayer and leave without the Amidah?' (*ST* 225. 20–2). See Blidstein, *Prayer in the Maimonidean Halakhah*, 134–5; 272–3 nn. 52, 62.

[21] Originally, the title *heḥaver* designated a member of a group meticulous in the observance of the laws of tithing and regulations of purity and impurity. In the geonic period the term denoted high-ranking scholars in the Babylonian academies, then scholars outside the academies. Ultimately, in Muslim lands, it became a synonym for a man of learning. See *EJ* vii. 1489–92.

growing causticness: he likens the man to the speaking ass of Balaam. This Binyamin Heḥaver asserts that the biblical description of God passing before Moses' face and proclaiming His attributes ('The Lord! the Lord!—a God compassionate and gracious ...'—Exod. 34: 6) alludes to a well-known penitential prayer—when, of course, the reverse is true by any stretch of logic![22]

The gate closes with a long excoriation in metric verse, rich in insult, summarizing all the main preceding points. By not ending the gate in the usual fashion, with a continuation of the opening frame, the author leaves the argument precisely where it closes. He does not risk dilution by further narration—certainly not by reverting to, or expanding upon, the avidity of Hever, aligned with the anti-*piyut* camp.

One likely target for Alḥarizi's barbs, especially in the attack on the as-yet-to-be-identified Binyamin Heḥaver, could well be Karaitic tradition: the Karaites were adamant critics of rabbinic expansion of Mosaic law and biblical legislation—even if their opposition softened with time.[23]

Gate 24 exhibits the usual enrichment afforded by the presence of introductory narrative matter.

To a certain extent, the cantor's sullying of sacra is prefigured by Hever's assay: the latter has gone to the synagogue not for spiritual purposes, but to see what material gain might be his.[24]

Another prefiguration is afforded by adroit use of biblical citation. Ashur's Jews do not act as their faith and tradition dictate: they reverse the behaviour of Abraham, founder of the Jewish people, who would not accept from a would-be benefactor anything from 'a thread to a shoe latchet' (Gen.

[22] It is at this point in the debate that the slowest reader must grow suspect of the use of tone: all too simplistically Alḥarizi/Hever tars with heresy's brush what is perhaps the strongest point in the mocked argumentation; namely, that the recitation of the Amidah was not a pentateuchal command, but deduced in a weak and strained fashion by the talmudic sages, who interpreted 'You shall serve the Lord your God' (Exod. 23: 25) as referring to the Shema and the Amidah (BT, *BK* 92*b*). In context, the verse of Exodus certainly does not hint at the Amidah, but rather demands the Israelites' total acceptance of the true God, rather than Canaanite deities, and forbids the erection of pagan pillars: 'You shall not bow down to their gods in worship or follow their practices, but shall tear them down and smash their pillars to bits. You shall serve the Lord your God, and He will bless your bread and your water. And I will remove sickness from your midst' (Exod. 23: 24–5).

[23] See Gate 17's debate between Karaite and Rabbanite, and the Analysis there.

[24] The similitude between the two figures is heightened by a *double entendre* in the Hebrew: *elekha eleiha lidrosh bah* (*ST* 223. 16), meaning 'I will go there [to the synagogue] to seek [my fortune] therein'; or, 'I will go there to preach therein'. Shortly thereafter the sextons extol the cantor as a *ḥazan darshan*, 'a precentor-preacher' (*ST* 223. 24).

14: 23); perversely, they will not give any supplicant the same! This stingy, 'non-Jewish' behaviour in the social realm anticipates inappropriate, 'non-Jewish' behaviour in the religious realm.

Yet another, and subtler, foreshadowing, is afforded in a witty *shibuts shoneh hora'ah*, an exact citation of Scripture with changed denotation.[25] In Numbers 13: 28, the men sent by Moses to spy out Canaan return with pomegranates, figs, and a huge cluster of grapes, and report, 'It is a land flowing with milk and honey and this is its fruit. However (*efes ki*) the people who inhabit the country are powerful . . .'. Here the text, as expanded by Alḥarizi, means, '. . . and this is its fruit: nothing (*efes*), because (*ki*) the people who inhabit the country are fierce (in holding on to their money) . . .'.

Closely related to prefiguration is the arousal of false expectation. The adulation of the sextons for their cantor is contrasted starkly by his exposure as a buffoon. Indeed Hever's very first-quoted sentence in this gate begins the pattern of misleading and enthusiastic description: his announced 'wondrous tale' turns out, in the end, to be a tale of wondrous boorishness!

Finally, Alḥarizi has created a deft contrast and comparison between Hever, consummate rhetor, and the precentor, a consummate fool. Both men twist Holy Writ: Hever, the Bible; the cantor, the prayerbook (including biblical citation therein). But whereas the cantor's mistakes are unintended and demonstrate his lack of control, Hever's wrenching texts out of context is fully intended, and demonstrates exquisite control. While the cantor entertains the reader by baring himself as a clown and an ignoramus, Hever entertains the reader by exposure of others—cantor, congregants, and advocates of *piyut*.

[25] Examples of this usage in medieval Hebrew poetry are provided in D. Yellin, *Spanish Hebrew Prosody* (Heb.), 135–7.

Analysis of Gate Twenty-Five

Of a Hid Place and a Champion of the Chase

GATE 25, perhaps the most chilling in all of *Sefer Taḥkemoni*, is a stark reminder that the medium of rhymed prose, with all the rhyme-rhythmic emphases it can afford, serves grave purposes as readily as comic ends.

Here Alḥarizi uses a technique he does not employ elsewhere in his work, one common to the modern novel and film—the halting of one scene to shift to another, then the bringing of the characters of both scenes together: he shows the fierceness of the hunter, horse, falcon, and hounds; shifts to the idyllic portrayal of the deer cove; then combines all characters in a scene of grisly slaughter. More than creating suspense by this technique, the author builds a sense of horror, inasmuch as the nature of the tale's outcome can hardly be in doubt.

The cruelty of the slayers almost seems paralleled by that of the narrative itself, which seems to revel in the zeal of the hunter and his accomplices, and the strength and efficacy of all weaponry, man-made and natural (teeth, beak, and claws), all these heightened through arresting simile, metaphor, and hyperbole.[1]

The characterization of the vicious hunter as *gibor*, or 'hero', tinges the tale with bitter irony. That term, coupled with narrative emphasis on the hunter's ardour and prowess (and that of his helpers), builds up strong reader expectation of an encounter that will test the skills and strengths so lauded—perhaps with a lion; indeed the text states explicitly that *lions* would be undone by the hero's cry and the sight of his terrifying hounds![2] But no heroic encounter is afforded the reader. The *gibor* in this transparent allegory is personified might; indeed the reader is forcibly reminded that the meaning of *gibor* here is 'strong' or 'mighty', not 'heroic' or 'valorous'.[3]

The harshness of the tale, so deliberately enlarged, serves the deep purpose of Alḥarizi: raising starkly the issue of the suffering of innocents. This purpose is further served by the author's setting in Hever the Kenite's mouth a clearly weak defence of traditional religious thought.

God is enthusiastically and abruptly praised immediately following

[1] See Dishon, 'On the Singularity' (Heb.), 221–32, esp. 225–8, showing how the attributes of speed, shining, strength, and loudness are shared, almost all of them, by the hunter and his animal retinue of hawk, horse, and hounds.

[2] *ST* 231. 11–12; 232. 7.

[3] BDB 150; Ibn Shoshan, *The New Dictionary* (Heb.) i. 154, col. ii.

upon a pronouncement on the innocence of the cruelly slaughtered fawns. And praised for what? For so creating the world that many creatures provide, of their flesh, nurture for others; that the death of one group means life for another. The original reads:

Praise God, Master of the universe, and Him who guides all His creatures justly, and hides from the sons of man His secrets and the reasons for His actions; who gives some of His creatures as prey to others, who prepares the death of some as a reason for the good of others and for their sustenance. He created mighty creatures to the loss of the young, and sent the strong to harass the wretched poor. One He has given to the other for sustaining food; but in their end each will die like the other and all in the netherworld will rot equally and lie down in the dust together.[4]

But Hever's analogy is thoroughly inadequate. The hunter is not described as accompanied by retainers, who might take back the deer meat for human consumption; and even if that were the case, human beings are not carnivores of necessity. No, most of the meat goes to the ravening dogs, who can hardly depend upon such a diet for their survival. The theological justification for the carnage would be suited (perhaps!) to a description of a lion pack at work. But such has not been offered.

Moreover, the assertion that in the end all share the same death, that all go down to the pit, there to rot alike, is hardly a consolation to the victims of savage execution. Indeed this kind of statement characterizes the despairing or cynical attitude of Ecclesiastes:

I mused: 'God will doom both righteous and wicked . . . they [men] are beasts. For in respect of the fate of man and the fate of beast, they have one and the same fate: *as the one dies so dies the other*, and both have the same lifebreath; man has no superiority over beast, since both amount to nothing. Both go to the same place; both came from dust and both return to dust. Who knows if a man's lifebreath does rise upward and if a beast's breath does sink down into the earth?'[5]

The second citation in this 'justification of God's ways' derives from the embittered challenge of Job to God's justice:

Why do the wicked live on, prosper, and grow wealthy? . . . One man dies in robust health, all tranquil and untroubled; his pails are full of milk; the marrow of his bones is juicy. Another dies embittered, never having tasted happiness. They both lie in the dust and are covered with worms.[6]

[4] *ST* 234. 1–8.

[5] Eccles. 3: 17–21.

[6] Job 21: 23–6. Cf. the following observation: 'I am continually unsettled by the frank, and I think cogent, explanation Professor Ginsberg gave in class of why, when God addresses Job out of the whirlwind, God doesn't answer Job's questions about why the righteous suffer but changes the agenda, talking past Job. God, said Ginsberg, does not answer because the author is trying to tell us that actually God does not have any answer' (Greenstein, 'In Memory of H. L. Ginsberg'). See too Kauffman, *Faith of a Heretic*, 153.

So much for the defence of Providence!

It is not as though Alḥarizi lacked for options. He chose to deal with the immense problem of undeserved suffering[7] through the parable of the deer hunt; chose to cite, at the close, unsettling verses from Ecclesiastes and Job, undercutting his justification of God; chose not to content the reader with the well-known dictum, far less offensive than his flawed whitewash, of 'It is not given us to explain the tranquillity of the wicked nor the torments of the righteous' (Mishnah *Avot* 4: 15); and, finally, chose not to include any of myriad rabbinic sources that speak of the rewarding of the just and the punishing of the wicked in the world to come, in the varied understandings of that state.[8]

The author, then, here at *Sefer Taḥkemoni*'s centre, raises the deepest ethical conundrum of religion, and deliberately leaves it unresolved, glaringly so in the light of Hever's superficial preachment;[9] and he further conveys this sense of non-resolution through purposive echoings, in the completion of the gate's frame, of the tale's key words and motifs. Thus Heman's description of Hever echoes the physical prowess of the hunter:

> When I heard his elegant speech and the might (*ḥozek*) of his parables . . . he ran towards me.[10]

The seemingly neutral 'he ran towards me', *rats likrati*, is a deliberate verbal echo: twice the hunter—never the hunted!—is described as running/*rats*; the

[7] Dishon, 'On the Singularity', 232 and n. 24, suggests that the text could constitute an allegory on the suffering of the Jewish people: she points out biblical sources denoting Israel, like the ravaged deer, scattered—and specifically on the mountain tops (Jer. 50: 11, Joel 4: 2, 1 Kgs. 22: 17); and two other citations describing the deer, that in the Bible represent the weary Israelites in the desert and Jerusalem's slaughtered Jewry (Ps. 107: 5, Jer. 4: 30). My preference is for the universal message, as in Gate 7.

[8] On (1) the principle of reward and punishment, and (2) differing rabbinic concepts of the world to come—either as the immediate realm of the deceased following death; or as the soul's final domicile in heaven or hell, according to the judgement following bodily resurrection; or as some intermediate state—see Schechter, *Studies in Judaism*, 'The Doctrine of Divine Retribution in Rabbinical Literature', 105–22. See also Urbach, *The Sages: Their Concepts and Beliefs*, 436–44 ('Reward and Punishment'), 444–8 ('The Reasons for Suffering'), 511–23 ('Interpretation of Theodicy'); Montefiore and Loewe, *A Rabbinic Anthology*, 202–32 ('Reward, Merit and Atonement'), 541–55 ('On Sufferings)', 580–608 (The Life to Come: Resurrection and Judgment). See too '*Olam Ha-ba*', *EJ* xii. 1355–7; and 'Reward and Punishment', *EJ* xiv. 134–9, with the literature cited ad locc.

[9] Another possible reading is to see Hever as speaking with intended irony; i.e. sarcastically, that tone escaping Heman. Yet a third possibility is Heman's capturing the intended sarcasm and hinting, through purposive repetitions of Hever's words and themes, as analysed above, his own unease with Providence.

[10] *ST* 234. 22–5. Note too 232. 8: *beḥamat koḥo*, 'in his (the hunter's) raging strength'.

same root is used to describe both horse and falcon no less than five times;[11] and many synonymous words and phrases are used to convey the speed and pursuit of the hounds and the hunting party.

The two friends' joy, as conveyed by Heman, evokes that of the gambolling deer: 'We delighted ourselves/*hitalasnu* all the days that we were joined together'.[12] Moreover, as Hever had observed: 'the mother was crouching over them and delighting/*mitaleset* in them'.[13] The parting of the two friends as described by Heman—'we were separated from the bosom of companionship and wandered to every side',[14] harks back to the fate of the fawns:

> . . . lying in the bosom of their mother . . . and they, now sleeping in her bosom . . . and now dancing in joy before her, their souls pouring out into their mothers' bosoms . . . the dogs compassing them on every side . . . the foe separating them . . . the dogs compassing them round about on every side.[15]

Given Alḥarizi's deliberate use of verbal repetitions, particularly at the start and close of tales, even one such echoing would have been significant; all the more so this large grouping.

I have, in my translation, sought to preserve these meaningful echoes. I italicize here, for purposes of demonstration, those of my words that convey the above emphases, further indicating with an asterisk words or roots that I have chosen to repeat in my English translation.

> Astounded by what his tale had taught, dumbfounded by this parable's onslaught, I knew the speaker for Hever the Kenite; and he read my thought. *Feet strong and fleeting, he rushed upon me* in warm greeting. I *rejoiced** with him my soul loved best until we were wrested from friendship's *breast*, sent wandering *to every side**—birds *scattered* from their nest.*

Finally, a close rereading of the tale's opening discloses a subtle, and ironic, prefiguration. The valley of Ayalon, Heman's declared destination, was the site of a famous biblical miracle: that of the sun standing still, that God might give the protected Israelites, under Joshua's leadership, maximal time—to slay their foe (Josh. 10: 12–15); here time aplenty is given savage executioners for the butchery of innocents!

[11] *ST* 231. 15, 20; 232. 8, 27; 233. 3. [12] *ST* 234. 25–6. [13] *ST* 232. 19.
[14] *ST* 234. 26–7. [15] *ST* 232. 18, 20–2; 233. 9–10, 13, 22–3.

Analysis of Gate Twenty-Six

Travels: Kudos and Cavils

IN GATE 26 the Kenite once again displays the double gift of rhetoric and chicanery. From the start, his diatribe against wandering rings less than true: his goal is to mulct coin from his hearers—a goal achievable, for all his complaint, only by dint of his having wandered!

Moreover, his initial stance is that of the high-sounding sermonizer.[1] He calls on his listeners to despise transient wealth and set their sights on the world to come. From this pronouncement he specifies the means of ensuring passage to the world to come—giving charity; to himself, of course!

That his hearers are less than convinced of this moralizer's sincerity is evidenced by their response—not the unleashing of gold for his plight, or for their souls' good, as he demanded, but by asking for a reversal of his position in a further display of rhetoric, in both rhymed prose and metric verse.[2] Significantly, in his reply, Hever limits himself almost entirely to the worldly rewards of travel—fame, wealth, and power. He could well have expanded upon the spiritual or intellectual benefits attending upon the itinerant seeker of knowledge. Here, the Kenite evokes but a scant three words in the original in the penultimate line of his poem—the traveller will win understanding and knowledge.

Ironically, it is Heman the Ezrahite, in the opening section, a merchant openly seeking gain through travel, who manifestly relates to the theme of pursuing wisdom. Indeed his reference to his business pursuit is all but an aside; his enthusiasm for the rich, sweet words of the wise young speakers is far more pronounced.[3]

And rich speech is what he gets in Hever's remarks. In addition to the usual blend of varied rhyme and rhythm, biblical citation and figurative language, Hever engages in a technique taken from poems of correspondence

---

[1] Herein Hever adopts—initially—the same tone as that employed in Gate 2.

[2] Alḥarizi's model here is the third gate of al-Ḥariri, wherein Abu Zayd, having provided a poem of praise honouring the dinar, is challenged to offer a poem denigrating the coin—and does so (*Assemblies*, tr. Chenery, 117–21; *Makamat*, tr. Preston, 118–29).

[3] In five other gates Heman's central motivation is the pursuit of wisdom, instruction, or flowery speech: Gates 2, 9, 11, 17, and 21. See Segal, 'The Opening' (Heb.), 408–9. Here Hever doles out an account of the general woes of travel, through which he, personally, has suffered; Heman, seeker of illumination and graceful speech, gains!

or argumentation.[4] In response to an encomium by one Joseph ibn Ḥisdai,[5] Samuel Hanagid sent a poem of praise in return imitating not only the tone of the original poem and themes in sequence, but the same metre and nearly the same rhyme.[6] He exchanged poetic missives in like manner with Isaac ibn Khalfun.[7] Moses ibn Ezra and Judah Halevi wrote to each other in poems of identical rhyme and metre; and other poets did likewise.[8] Here, vying with himself, as it were, the Kenite pens his second poem in exactly the same metre and rhyme as the first. Indeed the words that close the opening stichs of both poems are identical, as are those that close his last[9]—that, as the argument is reversed.

The game of point-counterpoint compasses, as well, particulars of the rhymed prose exposition. In anti- and pro-wandering statements, Hever produces bogus, punning, apophthegms of ancient bards against, and for, wandering.

Of course Alḥarizi does have precedent for both of Hever's stances; and even has precedent in Hebrew medieval *belles-lettres* in having one speaker both denigrate and laud wandering. Samuel Hanagid in his corpus *Ben mishlei* has several scattered apophthegms celebrating travel's benefits, even hailing it as a vital component of the good life; and, contrariwise, has many scattered maxims promoting the stay-at-home life.[10]

[4] See *The Collected Poems of Rabbi Isaac ibn Khalfun* (Heb.), ed. Mirsky, 158, in an asterisked remark. In another rhetor's trick, Hever adopts biblical parlance, in a claim designed to lend added weight to his exhortation: 'Therefore have the bards indited'; but the assertion is bogus: the sayings are the Kenite's own.

[5] 'Halitsevi ḥen': Schirmann, *Hebrew Poetry*, i. 172–5; *Ben tehilim*, ed. Jarden, 161–4. See I. Levine, 'The Pen and the Cavalier'.

[6] 'Hatazkir el yefat mareh': *Ben tehilim*, ed. Jarden, 164–9. The rhyme of Samuel Hanagid's poem is the syllable *nah*; of ibn Ḥisdai's *mah*.

[7] See *Ben tehilim*, ed. Jarden, 179–84, 189–94. For a trenchant reconstruction of the relationship between the two men, and a chronological ordering of their poems of correspondence, based on a close reading, see S. Katz, 'More About the Life of Isaac ibn Khalfun' (Heb.).

[8] See Pagis, *Secular Poetry*, 103, 286–8 with nn. 15–18.

[9] The original shows identical rhymes at the close of each hemistich of the first line (in the rhyme pattern of *abab*) and at the close of the last stich. The translation closely mirrors this pattern of repetition. See, in this regard, Hever's rhetorical display in Gate 27, where he similarly argues both sides of the coin, in lauding and then denigrating wine; there, too, he caps rhymed prose arguments, pro and con, with poems penned in the same metre and rhyme, with several identical rhyming words, and with both poems ending with the very same word.

[10] See *Rabi shmuel hanagid: Ben mishlei*, ed. Abramson, 25 ff., where the editor cites apophthegms of Samuel Hanagid lauding the necessity and benefits of travel; and a cluster of maxims advocating the reverse. In addition, Abramson cites similar contradictions within earlier works of moralistic Hebrew *belles-lettres*—Baḥya ibn Paquda's *Ḥovot halevavot* and the anonymous *Ben hamelekh vehanazir* ('The Prince and the Monk') and medieval biblical exegesis. The poetry of Moses ibn Ezra contains many negative references to wandering. See

Hever's poem of vaunt and self-revelation bares his insincerity. His stance, as a poet, towards others is based not on truth, but on their relation to him, that of friend or foe. If friend, his tongue stands ready to help; if not, to harm.[11]

The boast has two more strata. No longer vying with himself, the Kenite competes with his generous hearers: they have raised him from pauperdom; but he can do better—through diatribe destroy the highborn and haughty (slaying them metaphorically); or through praise, raise the repute (and, by implication, the status and wealth) of the despised. At a third level, the Kenite likens himself, implicitly, to wandering itself, the great destroyer or benefactor. Thus the self-proclaimed victim of wandering becomes a rival of that vast power.

Yet the ironies of the gate do not conclude herewith. On the one hand, in Gate 26 Hever is clearly a stand-in for Alḥarizi, both as a suffering traveller and one who reaps patrons and rewards through journeying. On the other hand, the voices of author and protagonist do not wholly overlap, as is often the case in *Sefer Taḥkemoni*: Alḥarizi's message is broader than Hever's. Travail and ill-fortune may be reversed by industry and rhetorical skill; but simplest logic proclaims that the dangers of the road, and life's journey, are never-ending. Moreover, the attentive reader has not forgotten the near-death of Heman in a sea-storm in Gate 15; the beating of Jews by a mob in Gate 22; and the brigandage of Gate 23 (hinted at here in the noting of the dangers of attack and brigandage during travel). In all these gates, losses were recouped; but there, too, the memory and reality of mortal danger hovered at the close.

Above all, the reader has just been subjected to perhaps the soberest gate of all of *Sefer Taḥkemoni*, that of the deer hunt in the gate preceding, with its reminder of the brute fact of the inexplicable and unjust deaths of the blameless.

In context, then, Gate 26's happy and boastful ending yet reverberates with danger and grief, not only of Hever's foes, but of Hever, and everyman.

the discussion by H. Brody under the lengthy compound entry *perud*, *peridah*, *nedod*, *gerut* ('separation, wandering, and alienation') in 'Index to Commentary' in Moshe ibn Ezra, *Secular Poems*, ed. Pagis, iii. 346–9.

[11] On the capacity of the poet to bring friend or foe into fame or disrepute, see Pagis, *Innovation and Tradition*, 26–36. This theme is central to the latter part of Gate 19.

Analysis of Gate Twenty-Seven[1]

Of the Cup's Joys and Other Alloys

FOLLOWING A RHETOR'S about-face in Gate 26, we have here a like display—a yet more multifaceted rhetorical and ideological confrontation. First, Hever the Kenite, his identity unknown till the close, disputes, then competes with, a handful of wine-praisers, whose laudations he holds pallid. That accomplished, at the challenge of his listeners he contends with himself, as pro-, then anti-, bibbler; and the laurels go to Hever the prohibitionist: his castigation of wine is so powerful as to overwhelm the very audience that asked him, as a rhetorical exercise, to fault wine: many of them take a vow of lifelong abstinence!

The first competition in the gate, that of Hever with the youths, though never judged explicitly, is implicitly won by the former, as witnessed by the sustained interest, and enthusiastic response, of the Kenite's listeners; and by the quality of his reply—the verve and pithiness of his challenge, as he rapidly lists the sensual delights of wine; and the ensuing complexity and variety of his figured speech, enriched by biblical citation and configurations of rhyme and rhythm.

Following the praise and invitation of the literate revellers comes Hever's rhymed prose encomium, presenting wine as a potent, masculine persona. Here, drawing heavily on the conventions of wine poetry, Hever interweaves two central themes, wine's appearance and its banishment of grief. Both traits are highlighted through feigned paradox: wine shows red—but white as well (in the goblet); is little—but downs giants (its drinkers).[2]

Capping his praise with a metric poem, Hever adds variety to his verbal pyrotechnics by depicting wine as a feminine persona—the daughter of the vine, whom he lauds primarily for 'her' visual and sensual appeal.

In his ensuing anti-wine declamation, Hever targets only one of the two

[1] The translator's earlier rendering of this gate appeared in *Mediaevalia: A Journal of Mediaeval Studies*, 10 (1988), 127–32.

[2] For typical motifs in Hebrew wine poetry, derived from Arabic example, see Y. Ratzaby, 'The Wine Poetry of Rabbi Samuel Hanagid' (Heb.). For discussions of wine poetry see literature cited in Analysis 5 n. 1; see too Pagis, 'And Drink Your Wine Good-Heartedly' (Heb.), arguing that a poem of Samuel Hanagid that seemingly crosses the line from irreverence to negation of faith and morality, can be so read as to reconcile (literary) hedonism with religiosity.

earlier foci of his praise; namely, the effects of drinking. His one earlier, indirect allusion to wine's negative potency, that it can down giants, becomes the centre of his attack. Wine and the immoral atmosphere of the tavern lead to drunkenness, base companionship, licentiousness, and economic ruin. While the masculine word *yayin*, 'wine', is employed for the most part in this section, the commanding personification is that of *bat hagefen*, 'daughter of the vine', identified through biblical citation with the harlot of Proverbs 7 and the cunning and powerful Jael, in the book of Judges, who drives a tent peg into the head of Sisera, her unsuspecting victim.

Alḥarizi's close of the rhymed prose diatribe is noteworthy for wit *in loco* and for its function in the gate's overall structure of point-counterpoint. Hever ends his prose speech with a five-word biblical quotation wrenched out of context and, as ever, further emphasized through rhyme: (*veyitbatel min ha'amanut asher ito*) *ki vo shavat mikol melakhto*, '(he ceases working in the craft that he owns) for thereby [through drinking wine] he ceases from all his labour'. Of course, in this biblical verse taken from the account of creation (Gen. 2: 3) *ki vo*, referring to the seventh day, means 'for thereon (God rested from all His labours)'.

Alḥarizi's readers, well versed in the Bible, were quite familiar with this famous citation, not only from its appearance in the yearly cycle of the reading of the Pentateuch, but also from three loci in the prayerbook: the Amidah, or central prayer, of the Friday evening service; a repeating of the citation shortly thereafter; and the Sabbath evening sanctification over wine recited at home.[3] Now by dint of the rhyme scheme employed by Alḥarizi, *ito/melakhto*, readers are doubly cued as to the expected conclusion of the sentence (and section of the gate). Here, as is often the case in *Sefer Taḥkemoni*, the reader (or hearer) becomes, perforce, an active participant in the tale, lips moving with the text in full-knowledged anticipation—and, unless he/she be exceeding sober, smiling the while.

In so ending his rhymed prose attack, Hever further competes with himself, for he rounded off his preceding rhymed prose laudation in just this fashion—with a biblical citation appearing in the liturgy—praise of God as He who sights the blind. *Poke'aḥ ivrim*, 'opens the eyes of the blind' (Ps. 146: 8) is found twice in the daily service—in the *birkhot hashaḥar*, 'morning blessings' ('Blessed art Thou O Lord our God, King of the universe, who opens [the eyes of] the blind') and in *pesukei dezimrah*, the psalm section of the daily morning service, where Psalm 146 appears in its entirety.[4] In the citing of *poke'aḥ ivrim*, as in the later citing of *ki vo shavat mikol melakhto*, we have a

[3] Hertz, *Authorised Daily Prayer Book*, 380, 408.

[4] Ibid. 20, 90.

change of subject with no modification of the quote—if not nearly as arresting or droll as that of Genesis's God (ceasing all holy work) to man (sinking to ruin).

Hever's stylistic competition with himself extends to his metric poems: as was the case in the preceding gate, his poetic rebuttal is identical in rhyme and metre with his poetic paean to wine; he even includes four of the same rhyming words.[5]

Alḥarizi's frame tale makes of this gate something more than a verbal *tour de force*. The tale begins with Heman's religious repudiation of wine—specifically by taking on the abstentions of a Nazirite.[6] The year's vow finished, Heman cancels this repudiation as he rushes to—the tavern! The gate closes with several of the tavern's revellers being so (absurdly) overwhelmed by Hever's rhetoric, that they repudiate wine—not for one year, but forever. The reader, of course, may well suspect that so volatile a group of imbibers, well 'under the influence' at the time of their vow, might hold to their resolve even less than the full year that Heman endured!

Of course, Hever's true assessment of wine and drinking is readily gauged by his enthusiastic tippling in the very tavern where he declaims.[7] The gate, then, in addition to being an exercise in wit and rhetoric, and an (at least partial) attack on swizzling, packs an added satiric punch—mockery of the all-too-swayable masses. Likewise, covert ridicule can be found in Gate 10, where a rooster who would sacrifice his children to save his own life, purveys himself (successfully!) as a quasi-saint to the local peasantry. Of particular note in Gate 27 is that the deceived crowd is well educated: they number poets who can extemporize in rhymed, figured, biblically allusive speech; then invite a more talented display; then ask for a yet more difficult oratorical sleight of hand. The nature of this last request makes Hever's achievement and the audience's reaction all the more impressive.

The narrative frame of the chapter is rendered the more prominent in the original through use of the same root at or near the tale's start and close: both Heman and the revellers commit themselves to a *neder*, a defined religious vow.[8]

[5] The English translation mirrors this phenomenon. *Dameiha*, 'her blood'; *memeiha*, 'her waters'; *yameiha*, 'her days'; and *shameiha*, 'her skies': *ST* 242. 10, 11, 21, 23, 25; 244. 1, 5, 7, 13.

[6] On the institution of the Nazarite, including the examples of the Rechabites and Samson, see 'Nazirite', *EJ* xii. 907–10.

[7] The Kenite's zest and skill as drinker echoes his early depiction at the hands of the author in Gate 1: 'Now he sucks the blood of the goblet, now vents wondrous utterances when he opens his mouth; if he be in the tavern, you will see in him all that is delightful to behold . . .' (*ST* 20. 6–8).

[8] This verbal framing is paralleled in the rhymed translation by the use of 'sworn' and 'swore'.

In his familiar technique of echoing, Alḥarizi closes Gate 27 with Heman's evoking two of its major motifs, wine as fire and wine as oppressor: *ve'azav belibi esh kidodo venafshi ashukah veyado*, 'he left his firebrand in my heart and my soul oppressed at his hand'.

Moreover, even as Heman echoes two major motifs in the body of the gate, he frames the tale with the theme of his craving. At the start, he hungers for asceticism, and then for the pleasures of wine; and at the last, for Hever. The bracketing is the more sophisticated since Hever is associated with the very wine that he himself loves, lauds, and condemns. Wine is linked with fire in both sections of the gate, and in both is a destroyer—of grief in the first and of the drinker in the second.

The reader is left, quite typically in *Sefer Taḥkemoni*, with unresolved tensions between preachment and the celebration of worldly joys. Hever, besting himself in debate, closes with witty and telling castigation of bibbling; but that while his initial behaviour, and Heman's words at the close, tie the Kenite inseparably to all wine's potencies and pleasures.

Analysis of Gate Twenty-Eight

Praise and Pity for David's City

JEWISH VENERATION of Jerusalem is ancient and profound. Since Davidic times the (sometimes) temporal and spiritual centre of the Jewish people, biblical Jerusalem plays prominently in prophetic condemnation and end of days vision, and in pilgrim and other psalms; and the city's demise is mourned in the book of Lamentations, still recited in the liturgy of the Ninth of Av, the commemoration of the destruction of the Temple.[1] Rabbinic exegesis and legend greatly expanded the city's sanctity, making it a mirror of the heavenly Jerusalem and site of the resurrection of the dead.[2] Early synagogue poetry of Palestine retold and further expanded this legacy; and the liturgical poetry of Hebrew Spain is rich in allusion to the city and to the messianic expectations linked thereto.[3] Non-sacral lyric poetry of Spain is rich as well in evoking the past splendour of the Davidic capital and Jewish longing for restoration.[4] Samuel Hanagid, for example, warrior-prince of the petty kingdom of Granada, expresses the hope in a martial ode that he and his son, Levites, will live to see the gathering of the exiles, and sing, in the courts of the Lord, the Nagid's own songs of praise.[5] Especially famous are the Zionides of Judah Halevi.[6] It is against this background, and the

[1] See *EJ* ix. 1549–53 (s.v. 'Jerusalem'): 'In Judaism: In the Bible'.

[2] Ibid. 1556–60: 'In Judaism: In the Aggadah'.

[3] Ibid. 1560–3: 'In Judaism: In the Liturgy'. See also Dana, 'On Appellations of Jerusalem' (Heb.).

[4] See Spicehandler, 'The Attitude towards the Land of Israel', which translates stiches from several such poems.

[5] See Segal, '"My Heart Burns"', and a later, freer version, '"My Heart Seethes"', in Hammer (ed.), *The Jerusalem Anthology*, 194–5; also Segal, 'Observations on Three War Poems of Samuel Hanagid'. Arabic literature, too, is rich in compositions of praise (*faḍā'il*, 'excellences') to Jerusalem; see Livneh-Kafri, 'On the Antiquity' (Heb.), and literature there cited. Alloni cites several poems relating to Jerusalem in 'Zion and Jerusalem'.

[6] See *Poems of Jehudah Halevi*, ed. Brody, tr. Salaman, 2–43, where the Hebrew text is coupled to a facing prose translation; ibid. 151–8, for two poetic renderings. See also D. Segal's translations of two poems of Halevi, '"Earth's Beauty"' and '"The Poet Replies to One who Would Dissuade him from Removing to the Land of Israel"', in Hammer (ed.), *The Jerusalem Anthology*, 198–201; see also *On the Sea: Poems by Yehuda Halevi*, tr. G. Levin. For a very helpful book-length discussion of Jerusalem's (and Israel's) centrality in Jewish sources, see B. Segal, *Returning: The Land of Israel as Focus in Jewish History*.

reality of continuing individual Jewish pilgrimage to the Holy City, that this gate is written.[7]

Especially evident is Alḥarizi's debt, in his metric poem, to Judah Halevi's[8] *Tsiyon halo tishali*, 'Zion, Will You Not Enquire of Your Children's Welfare?', as the following comparison, based on my literal rendering of the Hebrew text (Halevi's poems are indented), demonstrates:[9]

Great joy was hers on the day she (my soul) saw the mountain of God.[10]
    Happy he who waits and merits seeing your light dawn . . . and rejoice in your happiness.[11]
At the ends of the west[12] she was considered dead until she revived/*ḥayetah* in Zion, the Lord's city.[13]
    The air of your land is the souls' life/*ḥayei neshamot*.[14]
Zion: how many lands are glorious; but the human eye has seen no glory like unto hers. [15]
    Shinar and Patros[16]—shall they compare to you in their greatness and shall their vanity resemble your *urim* and *tumim?*[17]
The city wherein the Presence dwelt.[18]
    There the Presence dwelt in you.[19]
She is beauteous: though left stripped of glory and without jewels, the charming gazelle is beauteous.[20]
    Zion, beauty's crown—of old you have decked yourself with love and charm.[21]

[7] On pilgrimages to Jerusalem, see Gate 46, where Alḥarizi mentions his having met several French scholars who came to live in Zion (*ST* 349. 23 ff.); on this group see Kanarfogel, 'The Aliyah of "Three Hundred Rabbis" in 1211'. On routes and rites of Jewish pilgrims in Jerusalem, see Reiner, 'In the Footsteps' (Heb.), esp. 209–15, 'Entering Jerusalem and the Rite of Mourning'. For literature on the significance and praise of Jerusalem in Islamic tradition, see the bibliographic riches in n. 1 of Sadan, 'A Legal Opinion'; and Analysis 47 n. 1. For translated sources from Jewish literature through the ages on Jerusalem, as well as an overview of the city's status in Jewish life and letters, the reader is directed to the fine selections in Hammer (ed.), *Jerusalem Anthology* and to the 'Selected Jerusalem Bibliography' there, 545–7. For a brief discussion of the visits of luminaries of Hebrew Spain to the Land of Israel, generally, and Jerusalem in particular, see Rafa'el, 'My Soul Was Exiled from Zion to Spain'.

[8] On the high esteem of our author for Halevi, see Gates 3 and 18, especially the former, with their respective Analyses.

[9] Often Alḥarizi's debt is doubled, as Halevi frequently cites verses dealing with Jerusalem from Psalms and other scriptural books, as is shown below.

[10] *ST* 245. 17.

[11] 'Zion, Will You Not Enquire', in *Selected Poems of Jehudah Halevi* (hereafter: 'Zion'), 7, hss. (hemistichs) 65–6.

[12] See too the first stich of Halevi's poem *Yefeh nof*: 'Beauteous site, joy of the world, city of the great king—for you my soul yearns from the ends of the west': *Selected Poems*, 19; poetic rendering, 157.

[13] *ST* 245. 24–5.

[14] 'Zion', 5, hs. 31.

[15] *ST* 246. 1–2.

[16] Babylon and Egypt.

[17] 'Zion', 6, hss. 57–8. The *urim* and *tumim* were divining instruments worn by the high priest (Exod. 28: 30; Lev. 8: 8; Deut. 33: 8).

[18] *ST* 246. 5.

[19] 'Zion', 3, hs. 11.

[20] *ST* 246. 11–12.

[21] 'Zion', 6, hss. 47–8.

The rhymed prose lines preceding and following the poem also show indebtedness to Halevi's poem:

And I kissed her ruins and took pity on her dust.[22]
I will fall upon my face to your earth and much desire your stones and pity your dust.[23]
I arose from bended knee to wander about the city.[24]
Would that I could wander about the sites wherein God was revealed to your seers and messengers.[25]
The fire of sighs enflamed my ribs and the blaze of grief burned my ribs and my eyes poured tears.[26]
They [your companions] joy in your tranquillity and ache over your desolation and weep over your ruins.[27]

As significant, there are overall similarities structurally and thematically. Both poems begin with the mention of Zion; both end with a positive picture of the future, in which a pitying God will restore the city and its people. Both emphasize the longing of the speaker for the city.

Though Heman's poem is strongly derivative, in part, from Halevi's 'Zion, Will You Not Enquire', Gate 28, overall, is a horse of a different colour: a fusion of praise of the ideal Jerusalem with excoriation of the Jewish community of the actual Jerusalem.

The poem itself gives no hint of the conversation to follow, and no hint that God's longed-for grace has in any way been actualized; rather, the beauty and glory of Jerusalem are all rooted in the past. In Heman's ode, God is petitioned to return; world Jewry is shown as cast forth from the city, and is still kept afar because of incessant sinning; the Jews look in pained envy at strangers (Christians or Muslims) ascending God's holy mountain. At the close of his poem Heman voices his faith, or fervent wish, that God in His graciousness will renew His love with Israel and redeem them—then walks through the city, tears streaming.

[22] *ST* 245. 10–11. Furthermore, in having Heman declare 'Now I can die, having seen your face'—citing Jacob's words on being reunited with Joseph (Gen. 46: 30)—perhaps Alḥarizi evokes the fate of Judah Halevi, who did indeed die in the Land of Israel following his trip there from Egypt—kneeling at the Western Wall and at the hand of an Arab rider, according to popular legend. For overviews on Halevi's life and his last days in Egypt and the Holy Land, see Schirmann, *Studies in the History of Hebrew Poetry and Drama* (Heb.), i. 319–41, esp. 338–41, and the bottom of p. 41, where Schirmann lists the many relevant articles of S. Goitein on Halevi's life. Goitein's own summary of his findings on the biography of Halevi are to be found in *A Mediterranean Society*, v. 448 ff.; cf. Fleischer, 'Rabbi Judah Halevi' (Heb.), 242 n. 4.

[23] 'Zion', 4, hss. 23–4. Here both Halevi and Alḥarizi draw on Ps. 102: 14.

[24] *ST* 247. 15. [25] 'Zion', 4, hss. 19–20. [26] *ST* 247. 15–17. [27] 'Zion', 6, hss. 49–50.

In this context, the narrator's sudden question to an unidentified resident, 'When did the Jews return here?' is startling: it is predicated on a reality that the reader, up to that point, has not heard of at all. Now, nothing prevented Alḥarizi's placing in Heman's mouth, within his poem, a jubilant note on Saladin's conquest of Jerusalem (1187) and the freedom given Jews to return[28] —or at least some acknowledgement of the same. Instead, the information is conveyed rather matter-of-factly by Hever, who very quickly shifts into a sombre account of the corruption and internecine strife characterizing the Jewish community of Jerusalem.[29] Our author has chosen to split the past from the present (with its new opportunities), even as he maximizes the differing perspectives and emotional states of narrator and protagonist. To render this contrast the starker, he repeats several motifs.

Heman tells of a fire of sighs in his breast, as he laments Jerusalem's radiant past and painful present; Hever speaks of the cursed fire of contention, of fathers kindling these fires, and of others further stoking the flames.

Heman speaks of the purity of Jewish children of old, who prophesied spontaneously; Hever, of fathers and sons locked in mutual hatred, or joined in evildoing; of none doing anything for heaven's sake.

Heman, on arriving in the city, cites the words of the heathen prophet Balaam as he looked over the Israelite encampment in the wilderness, 'How goodly are your tents, O Jacob, your dwelling places, O Israel' (Num. 24: 5); Hever speaks of the rapine and evil in the city's midst.

This extreme polarization ties in with Hever's puzzling behaviour at the gate's close: after his summarizing poem, he laughs at Heman's pain! This laughter seems reminiscent of that of Rabbi Akiba in the face of his colleagues' weeping at the sight of a fox darting from the ruins of the Temple. Pressed for an explanation, Akiba declared that as surely as the prophecies of Zion's ruin had been fulfilled, even so would the prophecies of her restoration.[30] However, it is next to impossible that Hever could be laughing at Zion's situation, which he deems fraught with danger; and the text states implicitly, 'he laughed at my (Heman's) anguish'.[31]

Only one explanation for this oddity seems plausible; namely, that the Kenite holds his friend's sorrow grossly, indeed ludicrously, misplaced. It is

[28] See *EJ* ix. 1417.

[29] To what extent Alḥarizi's account of internecine strife is accurate lies without the confines of this study. For one scholar's view of the Jerusalem Jewry of that era, see Kedar, 'The Jews of Jerusalem, 1187–1267' (Heb.); see too the literature cited there.

[30] *Sifrei on Deuteronomy*, par. 43 (ed. Finkelstein), 95; and BT *Makkot* 24*a*.

[31] *ST* 249. 18.

not over Jerusalem's inaccessibility that tears are called for, Hever suggests implicitly; rather, with tangible evidence of divine favour glimmering, if not dawning; with the real opportunity given Jews to return—it were better (as Hever is doing) to decry the stupidity and callousness of the new and contemporaneous Jewish community of Jerusalem, who give every prospect of bringing about renewed exile. Here the protagonist hints at the dullness of soul, if not the hypocrisy, of lachrymose world Jewry for not performing what was permitted them by the decree of Saladin:

Speak unto the heart of Jerusalem, that all who wish of the seed of Ephraim come thither, those astray in Assyria and Egypt, and those expelled in the ends of the heavens.[32]

This decree, as presented here, is couched in clear prophetic language of redemption—that very redemption whose absence was bewailed by Heman. The citations employed are italicized in the scriptural verses cited below:

Comfort ye, comfort ye, my people, says your God, *speak unto Jerusalem's heart* and declare to her that her term of service is over, that her iniquity is expiated.[33]

And in that day a great ram's horn shall be sounded; *and the strayed who are in the land of Assyria and the expelled who are in the land of Egypt* shall come and worship the Lord on the holy mount, in Jerusalem.[34]

Even if your outcasts are *at the end of the sky*, from there the Lord your God will gather you, from there He will fetch you.[35]

The redemption is here, at hand, now, Alḥarizi all but shouts between the lines at his readership—and at himself, who did not choose to settle in

---

[32] *ST* 248. 14–16. [33] Isa. 40: 1–2. [34] Isa. 27: 12–13.

[35] Deut. 30: 4. Our author might be buttressing his message even more subtly. The date of Saladin's conquest of Jerusalem is given here (*ST* 248. 10–11) as 4950 by the Jewish calendar; the corresponding figure in the Julian calendar is 1190. Now the actual date of Saladin's conquest is 1187 (see *EJ* ix. 1417). Could Alḥarizi have taken the liberty of choosing a date that could yield, by *gematriyah*—hermeneutics through substitution of the numerical equivalents of Hebrew letters—*nidrashta*, 'you were sought out [of God]'? Rearranging *nidrashta* yields *dalet* (= 4[000]), *tav* (= 400), *shin* (= 300), *resh* (= 200), and *nun* (= 50), for a total of 4,950. One may recall, in this regard, 'I responded (*nidrashti*) to those who did not ask' (Isa. 65: 1); and poem 28 of Gate 9, which runs literally: 'Lord who respond (*nidrash*) to Your petitioner, extricate Your people from the churning sea of affliction' (*ST* 104. 18–19). Somewhat similar liberties were taken by the historiographer Abraham ibn Daud, who built upon earlier talmudic tradition. See Cohen, 'The Story of the Four Captives', 103 n. 1; id., *Sefer Ha-Qabbalah*, Analysis, ch. 3, 'The Symmetry of History', 189–92; and esp. 193 n. 19; 194 n. 22; and 201 n. 59. For a general discussion of *gematriyah* and its place in Jewish exegesis see *EJ* vii. 369–74.

the Holy Land despite the miraculously changed circumstance, despite the effectuation of the very prophecies of promised redemption alluded to in the lachrymose performance of Heman the Ezrahite![36]

[36] This reading is buttressed by subtleties of biblical citation at the gate's outset. Jerusalem is designated as *yefei nof*, 'beautiful vista' (Ps. 48: 3), in contrast with Nof (Egypt)—of essentially negative connotations in Scripture. 'The contrast between the cities intensifies in the opening's continuation: "I will bring you up from the wretchedness of Egypt (Exod. 3: 17) . . . to see the good of Jerusalem (Ps. 128: 5)": the author's personal ascent parallels the national redemption of the people of Israel from Egypt' (T. Davidovitz, 'Biblical Substrata' (Heb.), 257).

Analysis of Gate Twenty-Nine

Beggars' Arts versus Frozen Hearts

FOR THE SECOND AND LAST TIME in *Sefer Taḥkemoni*, Hever and son work in tandem, and it is the latter who saves the day. Hever does not succeed as he disparages his auditors' seeming protection against the cold; limns his and his son's former rich, vain state, then sudden plunge to misery; and appeals to his listeners' noble nature and alms, bracketing his plea with a warning that a like fate could be theirs.

That the crowd responds not at all at this juncture suggests that neither the speaker's flattery nor his argument struck their target; or, possibly, that his auditors are far from paragons of charity. The son's speech, while echoing all the major themes of the father's, is a horse of a different colour. His words are primarily a harangue. He begins by admitting to a sense of impotence in the face of callousness[1]—which becomes his major theme. Righteous indignation is followed by a plea to God for rescue—not from the cold, but the inhumanity of the auditors! This in turn is followed by an open accusation of obtuseness and non-repentance, and again obtuseness. Finally, the boy closes with one last call to repentance and a plea to his auditors to picture not themselves in misery but their sons, cold and wretched, and facing as obdurate and stingy a gathering. The son's more stinging supplement to the father's plea turns the trick.

As is often the case, the tale is laced with irony. The son's accusation of obtuseness has doubly hit the mark, for the crowd in the end is blind to the sham that has been practised upon it. The author uses biblical citation as well to augment the irony. In claiming that his father's words could have brought water from a rock, the famous miracle of Moses in the wilderness is evoked: hence the first swindler is linked with Israel's primary prophet.

Indeed it is through Bible-rootedness that the Hebrew *maqāma* differs from its clear source, the seventeenth gate of al-Hamadhani's *Maqāmāt*, which source he has rather closely translated.[2] The major differences be-

[1] The translator has taken the liberty of making the child selectively stutter, a facet absent in the original.

[2] *Maqāmāt*, tr. Prendergast, 74–8. Maree, 'The Influence', 150–63, posits likely borrowings on Alḥarizi's part from gate 13 of al-Ḥariri (*Assemblies*, tr. Chenery, i. 176–81, 380–91). To these one may add a number from gate 14 of al-Ḥariri, where a father and son plead respectively for a mount and for food, and are amply gifted by the company (tr. Chenery, i. 181–5,

tween the two texts are few: the Hebrew author expands slightly on the description of the cold and upon the speeches of both father and son; in the Arabic, the poem of gratitude for the crowd's largesse is longer; and, in al-Hamadhani, the identification of the father occurs in private after the narrator has tracked him down. More significant is the greater emphasis in the Hebrew text on the moral and religious stratum. If the youth's thank-you in the Arabic focuses on the first gift itself—a ring—and its giver, the Hebrew text centres upon God, crediting Him for the crowd's change of heart; but it is primarily through biblical citation that the religious and ethical themes are given greater, and ironic, prominence.

The theme of prophetic chastisement is variously advanced. Fate's indignities and worse, visited upon the ostensibly once rich and smug father and son, are linked with divine punishments for wrongdoing, spoken of by the prophets. Thus the well-fed steeds on which the two rode recall the metaphoric description of the adulterers of Jerusalem:

They were well-fed, lusty stallions, each neighing at another's wife. Shall I not punish such deeds? (Jer. 5: 8–9).

The weapons brought out by time against the two recall the weapons of wrath employed by God in punishment of the Chaldaeans (Jer. 50: 25); the pair's drinking of lees derives from the Psalms:

There is a cup in the Lord's hand with foaming wine fully mixed; from this he pours; all the wicked of the earth drink, draining it to the very dregs. (Ps. 75: 9).

The appallingly sunken eyes of the two men recall the description of sinful Jerusalem:

Her uncleanness clings to her skirts. She gave no thought to her future; she has sunk appallingly . . . (Lam. 1: 9).

The 'reeling cup' of which the two have drunk and of which the father begs his listeners to imagine themselves drinking is a citation from Isaiah, referring to sinful Jerusalem:

Rouse, rouse yourself, O Jerusalem, you who from the Lord's hand have drunk the cup of His wrath, you who have drained to the dregs the bowl, the cup of reeling (Isa. 51: 17, 22).

391–8). In a presentation at the First International Conference on *Maqāma* Literature at Ben-Gurion University (June 1998), Maree, in addition to singling out commonalities between this gate and those of al-Hamadhani and al-Ḥariri, examined another likely source of Alḥarizi here—gate 5 of Abu 'l-Ṭahir Ibn Yusuf al-Saraqusṭi, *Al-maqāmāt al-'azūmiyya*, ed. Daif, 49–64.

The implication of these several citations is clear: we suffered, declare the two beggars, not simply because of fate's turns, but because we sinned.[3] If you have sinned—as indeed you will by denying us charity—you can expect a like fate! This message is buttressed by at least two citations that explicitly link the listeners to sinners in Scripture. The disregard of the lad's plea as irrelevant is based on Malachi 2: 1:

> And now, O priests, this charge is for you: Unless you obey and unless you lay it to heart and do honour to My name—said the Lord of Hosts—I will send a curse and turn your blessings into curses.

The near final plea of the youth, relating to mending the practice of heart and hand, derives from the Deuteronomic injunction:

> If, however, there is a needy person among you, one of your kinsmen in any of your settlements in the land that the Lord your God is giving you, do not harden your heart and shut your hand against your needy kinsman . . . (lest) he will cry out to the Lord against you and you will incur guilt (Deut. 15: 7–9).

Even Heman's description of the crowd's largesse, each man giving according to his means, is an evocation of Deuteronomic instruction to bring gifts to the priests on the pilgrimage to the cultic centre:

> They shall not appear before the Lord empty-handed, but each with his own gift, according to the blessing that the Lord your God has bestowed upon you (Deut. 16: 16–17).

Finally, the poetic outpouring of the happy father, recalling the at first hard hearts of his listeners, cites the prophet Zechariah's condemnation of the leaders of Judah:

> They hardened their hearts like adamant against heeding the instruction and admonition that the Lord of Hosts sent to them by His spirit though the earlier prophets; and a terrible wrath issued from the Lord of Hosts (Zech. 7: 12).

Now of course the humour in all this prophetic citation lies in the hypocrisy of the sermonizers: they it is who are the malfeasants, in their false show and lying preachment; the tightfistedness of the listeners, quite likely rooted in their proper scepticism, pales by comparison.

In this regard, possibly the deftest use of citation is that found at the

[3] Ironically, the description of the father's pause, as though his tongue clove to his jaws, cites the self-imposed curse of another kind of sinner—one who would dare forget Jerusalem: 'If I forget you, O Jerusalem, may my right hand wither; let my tongue stick to my palate if I cease to think of you . . .' (Ps. 137: 5–6).

gate's start. Heman betakes himself to Nineveh, 'a mighty city before the Lord' (Jonah 3: 3), a clear evocation of the divine call to Jonah to speed to a corrupt kingdom and, through his chastisement, bring its inhabitants back to repentance. Here, ironically, the traveller to Nineveh is motivated by no higher motive than profit; and he is witness to a prophet-like, and decidedly effective, rebuke of a populace for its sins—when it is the rebukers themselves who are the sinners!

Analysis of Gate Thirty[1]

Of a Quack and his Bogus Pack

ALḤARIZI WAS NOT ALONE in raising a laugh at the expense of physicians: earlier and later figures in Jewish literature, indeed in all European and Arabic medieval literature, made uncharitable remarks about doctors, especially as they claimed or pretended impossible expertise—clearly the case here.[2] As far as back as the Mishnah we find the dictum, 'The best of doctors—to Gehenna!'[3] Towards the close of *The Book of Delight of Joseph ibn Zabara*, the narrator (ibn Zabara himself) exposes his host, the devil Enan, as a fraudulent and ignorant physician, then launches into a scathing critique of all deceptive doctors.[4] Later the famous Immanuel of Rome, a pronounced imitator of Alḥarizi and contemporary of Dante, will pen (partially in imitation, partially in competition) a spoof of a physician who recommends a diuretic. When the physic does not prove effective, the witty 'doctor' thus characterizes the sick man's poetic composition, penned on the evening when the remedy was to have worked: 'The bodily waste was indeed eliminated, only through another orifice . . .'.[5]

Here, as in other gates, we have the phenomenon of covert prefiguration, encompassing even the seemingly innocuous choice of locale: Baal-Gad means 'possessor of fortune'—recalling the explanation of that name in the book of Genesis, where Leah says, on the birth of her handmaiden's son, *ba gad*, 'Luck has arrived—therefore did she call his name Gad.' The name prefigures the exceptional good luck that the cunning Hever the Kenite will enjoy, mulcting the crowd.

[1] For the Arabic source of this episode, freely reworked by Alḥarizi, see gate 4 of al-Hamadhani's *Maqāmāt* (tr. Prendergast, 35–8).

[2] This is even more so in the English translation, which is freer here than in other sections of *Sefer Taḥkemoni*. The overall effect is of course the same.

[3] *Kid.* 4: 14.

[4] *The Book of Delight*, tr. Hadas, 137–42.

[5] *Maḥberot imanuel haromi*, tr. Jarden, ii. 416, l. 48. For an analysis of this comical gate, and its partial imitation of Gate 3 of *Sefer Taḥkemoni*, see Segal, 'Strange Cohesion'. See too the scathing rhymed prose critique of the physician in the *Even boḥan* of Kalonymos ben Kalonymos, a contemporary of Immanuel (Schirmann, *Hebrew Poetry*, ii. 510–14). For a well-footnoted survey of critical/satirical treatment of physicians in Hebrew and in other languages, see 'physicians' in ch. 5, 'Social Satire' (Heb.) in Dishon, *The Book of Delight*, index, under *rofe'im ramayim* 'lying physicians'; ead., 'The Physician as Mirrored Satirically' (Heb.), *Apirion*, 26–7 (1993), 26–33.

Both the introductory narrative of Heman the Ezrahite and the opening exhortation and boast of the Kenite hint at the evildoing to follow. In describing the physician's instruments as being sharp as a two-edged sword, Heman recalls the well-versed reader to the one source of this exact locution, Proverbs 5: 4, which describes the deceitful woman (harlot) who will lead her victims to ruin: 'For the lips of a forbidden woman drip honey; her mouth is smoother than oil; but in the end she is as bitter as wormwood, sharp as a two-edged sword.' There is an element of irony here: in his depiction of the travelling physician, Heman has evoked the figure of a deceiver whose evil plans and sure ruin are concealed from victims!

An odd instrument noted by Heman, the three-pronged fork, is mentioned but once in the Bible—in Samuel 1 (2: 13), in a description of young men robbing pilgrims to the Shiloh sanctuary of sacrificial meat!

The commencement of the Kenite's speech is a minor *tour de force* of subtle foreshadowing. 'Hear me O peoples' opens the book of Micah, where the prophet announces divine punishment for sin and transgression; 'Attend O ye [mass of] nations' is a quotation of Isaiah 49: 1, whose continuation reads: 'He (God) made my mouth like a sharpened blade, He hid me in the shadow of His hand and He made me like a polished arrow; He concealed me in His quiver.' The treble motif of speech, weaponry, and concealment blend dexterously with the prior locution/citation of Heman the Ezrahite that the medical instruments were sharp as a two-edged sword.

Put otherwise: Hever, in his remarks to the crowd, prefigures in veiled fashion the hoodwinking that is to take place; and Heman, in his narrative introduction to the reader, anticipates this very deception as he imitates Hever's stylistic of foreshadowing through biblical allusion.

To add insult to injury, Heman's concealed prefiguration is laced with a double irony. In declaring that Hever called out to those who were in attendance upon him (*kore lekhol hanitsavim alav*), the book's narrator unequivocally evokes Joseph's impassioned outcry in Egypt:

> Joseph could no longer control himself before all his attendants, and he cried out, 'Have everyone withdraw from me!' So there was no one else about when Joseph made himself known to his brothers.[6]

The irony, of course, lies in the contrast: in the biblical context, Joseph bares his identity to his brothers: here the charlatan veils his identity and intent with every word that he says.

Now clearly Alḥarizi is doing more than poking fun at mercenary and dishonest physicians: he is having a large laugh at the expense of the gullible

[6] Gen. 45: 1.

masses. One more example of ironic prefiguration is relevant here. In declaring his escape from seething (or, proud) waters—fortune's travails, in this context—the Kenite evokes Psalm 124: 5, where an innocent speaker gratefully proclaims his having been rescued from the inundation of proud and overbearing men. Here, however, it is the locals who are about to be inundated, and certainly not saved, by the seething waters of the proud and cunning Kenite.

The reader will recall that this is not the only instance of an overcredulous crowd being put upon in *Sefer Taḥkemoni*: in three previous tales we have met the same constellation. In Gate 9, dimwit villagers wholly accept the protestations of a religious hypocrite, a preaching rooster out to save his own skin through that of his chicks; in Gate 27, tipplers in a tavern—poets, no less—are so overawed by a (solicited!) castigation of wine that they foreswear drinking; and in Gate 29, a bogus tale of woe of father and son parts synagogue-goers from their coin.

The castigation of fate at the end of the gate adds yet another layer in the author's spoof. To foist upon the workings of an indifferent, cruel force the responsibility for the grossly immoral behaviour of the protagonist is unmitigated gall.[7] We have before us a pathetically gullible mob and a thoroughly inadequate critic (Heman), both bilked and outmanoeuvred by an adroit word-huckster.

Having said the above, one must not forget that Alḥarizi's narrator shares, after the fact, in the cunning of the protagonist. Whether or not Heman was indeed nonplussed—we have his report alone to go upon—we have seen that his very purposive narrative introduction is profoundly imitative of the Kenite's: even as Hever has his private laugh at the crowd, covertly alluding to the chicanery that is to come—so Heman, it would appear, has his laugh at the reader, covertly alluding to Hever's chicanery as he prefigures Hever's behaviour and (prefigurative!) style.

To what degree should the reader view the creator of Heman and Hever as sharing in these men's laughter as they toy with crowd and reader respectively? To what degree see the author as an exposer and critic of guile and sham? The question remains open.

[7] Elizur, 'And Days are Commanded of God', 31–2 n. 11, points out that the moral nihilism exhibited here by Hever goes one large step beyond the tensions within metric, reflective Hebrew poetry between the traditional view of God as the moral and sole ruling force in the universe, and a view deriving from Arabic poetry that an omnipotent, cruel, and immoral fate determines all that happens to a human being.

Analysis of Gate Thirty-One

Of a Mocking Knight and a Wormwood Cup of Fright

SURPRISE AND TURNABOUT is the name of the game in the narration before us, somewhat recalling Gate 20 ('The Muses'), where the maiden lusted after by Heman turns out to be a man, his mocking friend, Hever the Kenite. In this gate, the first surprise is the charging horseman's revelation as a woman. The second and greater shock is that maiden's turning out to be very much a man, and a murderer to boot. The third large surprise and reversal is Hever's slipping a knife out of his shoe to slay the warrior.

The denouement is prefigured earlier in the text, as is so often the case in *Sefer Taḥkemoni*: by 'her' report, the 'persecuted maiden' had killed her tormentor and then severed his head; and this is precisely what Hever the Kenite does to the brigand. Relatedly, Hever's closing poem, crediting God for the band's rescue and lauding His mercy, is ironically and variously prefigured. The maiden proclaims her faith in a merciful deity, citing Lamentations 3: 22, 'The kindness of the Lord has not ended'; and blesses God for having allowed her to wreak revenge on her captor. (Indeed Hever and friends echo both statements in thanking God for having rescued them from death.)[1]

In this gate, too, Alḥarizi has utilized the start of the frame tale for purposes of foreshadowing. Heman declares his wish to bare all secrets and ferret out wonders; and, in a tale of serial and astonishing disclosures, finds wonders aplenty.

Gate 31 of *Sefer Taḥkemoni* contains perhaps the most compelling character sketch of psychological perversion in medieval Hebrew literature, a mesh of sadism, transvestism, and a persecution complex. Alḥarizi achieves this through a very deliberate transformation of his Arabic source, gate 6 of al-Hamadhani, where the brigand is male throughout and the theme of homosexual desire is manifest.[2] In the Arabic, even greater emphasis is

[1] The irony is enriched through scriptural citation. Several times in this section, the 'maiden' evokes Lamentations, a dirge over national disaster; and it is a group disaster, to be sure, that looms for Hever and his companions.

[2] For an English rendering of this gate, see *Maqāmāt*, tr. Prendergast, 40–6. For a different comparison of these tales, with a detailing of Alḥarizi's several modifications of his models, see Dishon, 'The Robber: An Analysis of Gate Thirty-One of *Sefer Taḥkemoni* of Judah Alharizi' (Heb.).

given the stranger's description, with his arms and entire body, not only his face, praised. If in both stories the company is impressed with the stranger's beauty, in the Arabic the new arrival removes his outer garment when they reach the oasis, disclosing a transparent, thin undergarment that leaves his onlookers convinced that he is a rival of angels and a fugitive from heaven. When he has the company in his power he compels the narrator to strip naked, following which he slaps every man in the company and removes his own clothing, a clear indication that sexual attack was his design.

All this Alḥarizi alters. Hever, speaking for himself and his friends, is much taken with the stranger's traditionally feminine allure—sparkling teeth; rolling, jet-black hair; and thick, bushy eyebrows. The brigand, in the Hebrew, further arouses their sexual appetites by a tale of abduction by a rapist, one who 'set me up as a target for his arrow' (Lam. 3: 12). Precisely this deft use of biblically laced language suggests the fusion, in the brigand's mind, of eros with brutality, a pairing demonstrated in his own ensuing behaviour: following his 'feminine' display of serving his 'rescuers' by attending to their needs and those of their mounts, he employs his skill with bow and arrows to awe and overpower them; then, having them at last in his power, he tongue-lashes them for their lascivious thoughts—which seem primarily his own projections![3]

The mocking and bitter denunciation poured forth by the desert thief is, dramatically, a continuation of the bitterness of the persona he has created. In his taunting claim that Hever and the travelling band found his breasts, lips, and thighs inviting and doubtless imagined taking all manner of liberties in fondling, kissing, and possessing 'her', the brigand renders a dramatic continuation of the character of the maiden sexually abused by the lascivious lord!

In sum, to the degree that Hever and friends might have been aroused, this was the result in no small measure of the thief's contrived erotic report, by his cultivated feminine look, and by his avowed readiness to serve the company as they pleased—'do with me what you will.'[4] Following his varie-

[3] Alḥarizi's text hardly notes any sexual arousal on the part of Hever and his friends except in their rather restrained—and stereotypic—favourable notice of the maiden's cheek, brow, hair, and lips (*ST* 258. 24–259. 4). Now it is true that the brigand, as maid, tells the group that they may do with 'her' as they will—but they choose the path of compassion and protection. The clearest indication of sexual arousal on their part is to be found (in the Hebrew text) in Heman's assertion, following the brigand's unveiling as a male attacker, that 'love converted to hate and desire turned to war and weapons' (*ST* 261. 20–1); but even there, the reader is not given to understand that any actual designs on the 'maiden' were contemplated.

[4] Indeed the associations of the biblical language are designed for arousal. Of the two closest locutions in the Bible, the first is Gen. 19: 8, where Lot invites the men of Sodom to enjoy his

gated incitement, the brigand kills one of the hosting band (needlessly!); accuses the survivors of brutal sexual designs; and seems about to perpetrate an undefined violence upon them, beyond the presumed theft that will take place.

One critic has posited a deep-seated, general disdain on our author's part against homosexuality[5]—which could perhaps explain his modification of al-Hamadhani's narrative; but only partially so: the Hebrew brigand is, if anything, at a far greater remove from stable and normative behaviour than the warrior of the original tale!

daughters; and the second is Judg. 19: 24, where an Ephraimite host offers depraved townspeople full freedom of his daughters and his guest's concubine, the latter ultimately being raped to death.

[5] Lavi, in the pre-final, and unpublished, version of his doctoral dissertation, 'A Comparative Study of Al-Hariri's Maqamat and their Hebrew Translation by Al-Harizi' (University of Michigan, 1977), 41–114 *passim*. While not agreeing with Lavi on every point, my reading corroborates Lavi's essential position (which he later abandoned)—that Alḥarizi's choice of word and phrase in rendering a specific Arabic text referring to homosexual amours indeed suggests his own disdain, esoterically, through negative overtones of biblical passages chosen (not of necessity). In this regard, it is instructive to consider a cluster of poems in Gate 50 of *Sefer Taḥkemoni* satirizing an apologist for, and practitioner of, sodomy.

Analysis of Gate Thirty-Two

Needlepoint: Point-Counterpoint

As is often the case in *Sefer Taḥkemoni*, assemblage and reader both are afforded more than they are promised in this mêlée of rhetorical vying.[1]

Hever is called upon to engage in verse competition alone, constructing a poetic line that will rhyme with, and complement, in similitude, one that his rival produces—yet the youth and he vie at once in rhymed prose as well.

In most instances here Hever bases his response squarely upon the youth's stich, either by complementing his rival's statement or expanding upon it, usually with arresting simile or metaphor.[2] This dynamic can be seen, in rhymed prose, in the two men's descriptions of mail, horse, myrrh-packet, wolf, lightning, and citron; and in poetry, in their treatments of the sword, myrrh-packet, wolf, stream, nut, harp, and citron.[3] At times, however, the old man goes beyond general relationship in his rhymed prose description to echo one or more specific motifs or locutions that the youth has just advanced, such as the pen's golden colour and capacity to harm; the horse's speed, and association with fire and heights; and the stream as a drawn sword.[4]

Similarly, the youth at times echoes, in his metric stich, a specific element put forward by his rival in the preceding rhymed prose description. Thus, the old man speaks of the letter as proclaiming God's praise; the youth, of the letter being reared in faith.[5]

Thematic echoing is varied by having one character repeat, in his stich, a theme or phrase that he included in his earlier rhymed prose description,

---

[1] Other gates where Hever contends with one or more poets/debaters: 4, 5, 16, 19, and 42.

[2] Several instances of of Alḥarizi's indebtedness to gate 23 of al-Ḥariri are set forth in Maree, 'The Influence', 100–14, among these being that both gates are the longest in each collection, and in both two equals compete, one completing the other's poem.

[3] This same echoing dynamic holds in the Hebrew original for the two men's rhymed prose descriptions of sunlight, and metric verse descriptions of the moon; in these two instances I have been freer in my English rendering. Unless otherwise indicated, references to the text indicate the style and content of both the Hebrew text and my translation. For a close comparison of the Hebrew text, translated literally, with my rhymed rendering, see the addendum to this analysis.

[4] Relatedly, the old man can defer to his metric display an element appearing in the young man's rhymed prose, as in the likening of the horse to an eagle.

[5] *ST* 264. 12–13, 16.

but one that was skipped over by his rival. An instance of such is Hever speaking of the letter as a fair maiden, in rhymed prose and then in metre;[6] and likening the pomegranate, in rhymed prose and then in metre, to a pearl-filled chest.[7]

The gate exhibits a pattern of threefold repetition as well—the old man echoing a locution of the youth and the latter re-echoing the same. Such is the case with the wolf, thrice described as a killer.[8]

In one instance, the description of the myrrh-packet, we have a complex, *fourfold* repetition of a theme—the exposure of that which is hidden. The youth declares, in rhymed prose and in metre, that the sweet scent of the myrrh-packet discloses what the latter was made to conceal—the statement itself constituting a quasi-paradox; Hever illustrates this notion with two similes: he speaks, in rhymed prose, of a lover who would hide his desire but whose eyes tell all; and, in metric verse, of a gossip with tongue cut off, who communicates through his eyes.[9]

In one instance, we have, in the Hebrew, a chiastic, or bracketing, structure (*abba*)—the likening of the horse to an eagle—in the youth's rhymed prose and in Hever's stich; and to lightning—in Hever's rhymed prose and the youth's stich.[10]

While Hever often adopts the tone of his opponent and closely imitates him, reversal is sometimes the case, an example of such being the limning of lightning as a tireless hero in the youth's stich, but a dozing night watchman in Hever's. A literal translation would be:

> The youth sang, saying,
> The lightning plays against (the background of) the clouds
> like a hero racing [Ps. 19: 6], neither wearying nor tiring [Isa. 40: 31];
> And the old man answered, saying:
> Like a night watchman who falls asleep, then opens his eye
> a bit, which in an instant closes.[11]

[6] Further instances in the original: Hever comparing the construction of mail to a camel's body (a burning fire, and having a torch between his eyes) and of the citron as lusting.

[7] *ST* 269. 24; 270. 5–6.

[8] Also, the Hebrew presents three permutations of the root *n-'-m* (pleasant) in three consecutive descriptions of the citron.

[9] In the Hebrew, 'winking his eye', alluding to Prov. 10: [12,] 13: '[A scoundrel, an evil man lives by crooked speech,] winking his eyes, shuffling his feet, pointing his finger.' A further example of fourfold repetition in the Hebrew is the likening of the river to jewellery or craftsmanship, in both men's rhymed prose and metric depictions.

[10] The English translation reorders these elements in *abab* pattern. See, above, the analysis of the description of the pomegranate.

[11] *ST* 269. 1–6.

The above cornucopia of variations on theme repetition itself overlays an extended exercise on repeating and varying traditional images taken from Arabic or Hebrew poetry. Four examples are the description of the pen as an object of desire;[12] of the pen as beneficent and harmful, simultaneously;[13] of wine as having the taste or scent of myrrh;[14] and of the sword-blade, or other weaponry, flashing like lightning.[15]

In this gate's much-varied contests one overall effect, more pronounced in the original, is that of Hever's overshadowing his opponent. While several contests seem evenly matched, with like or contrasting similes and metaphors being put forward, in a significant number of instances Hever's depictions are the more colourful or developed, as in the case of lightning and the stream. In addition, Alḥarizi has the young man fail in one self-imposed mission—to use only one rhyme to describe each entity he chooses: twice, in describing wine and falcon, he uses two.[16]

On the other hand—again, it would seem, for variety's sake and to prevent complete predictability—on at least one occasion the more dramatic imagery is the youth's: in his rhymed prose description of wine he offers a lively and developed personification, whereas Hever's ensuing list is shorter, comprising four unrelated similes.[17]

[12] See Joseph ibn Ḥisdai, 'Halitsevi ḥen' (Analysis 26 n. 5), st. 29, in Samuel Hanagid, *Ben tehilim*, ed. Jarden, 162). See also the discussion of the antecedent traditions of pen description in Arabic poetry and rhymed prose, in the Analysis of Gate 40.

[13] Similarly, in Samuel Hanagid's reply to ibn Ḥisdai, 'Hatazkir el yefat mareh' (Analysis 26 n. 6), 'And this [pen] has a speechless tongue to heat up contention or to quiet dissension' (*Ben tehilim*, ed. Jarden, 168, st. 50).

[14] Similarly ibid., poem 130, p. 279, st. 6; poem 135, p. 285, st. 4; poem 138, p. 287, st. 3.

[15] Arberry, *Poems of al-Mutanabbī*, 52, poem 7, st. 25: 'My flashing blade will cause the lands to forget the lightnings of the sky, and they will be satisfied with the flowing blood, not craving for the rains'; and Samuel Hanagid, 'Eloha oz', st. 61 (*Ben tehilim*, 8): '. . . as if the flung spears were lightning bolts filling the air with light'. See also above, in Analysis 7, the theme of 'Weapons as ominous or bloody, and often personified' in Gate 7, in the poetry of Samuel Hanagid and in Arabic poetry.

[16] Also, in the original, Alḥarizi makes a point of adding a touch of dullness to the youth's presentations. In no less than ten instances, Hever's rival introduces the contest's themes with slight variations on one basic statement—*mah neḥmad, mah na'amah/na'amu*, 'How lovely/pleasant is/are . . . '; and in thirteen instances with 'Behold' (*re'u*—eleven times, *habet*—twice). Aware that often I have rendered the youth's openings with more originality, and more arrestingly, than they appear in the Hebrew, I chose to let the 'improvement' stand, given Hever's overall supremacy in the English version.

[17] Nevertheless Hever overshadows the youth by presenting a fourfold parallelism in meaning, syntax, rhyme, and—almost—syllable count. The original (*ST* 267. 7–13) reads: 'Then the youth spoke of the wine, saying, "Behold the son of the vine, piping (in summons) to joy as he grinds his teeth against sighs; his pleasantness is the life of souls; joy has fallen upon his shoulder; he shoots straight at grief, takes out against him the weapons of his wrath." 'And

Alḥarizi adds yet another flourish to the gate by his ordering of topics. For the most part, he has the younger speaker come forward with pairs of related topics, consecutively. This can be seen in the following summary list, where intrinsically related themes are italicized:

pen and letter
sword and mail
horse and torch
myrrh and wine
falcon and wolf
lightning and stream
pomegranate and nut
harp and water-channel
citron and candle
sunlight and the moon

Even where the paired items are not closely related, they do share at least one intrinsic trait: energy (horse and torch), travel (lightning and stream), flow (harp and conduit), and shine (citron[18] and candle). More significantly, Alḥarizi links these pairs thematically or rhetorically. Thus horse and torch are made to share the motifs of burning and luminescence. Of the horse we read in the original, 'he who walks in darkness shall *beam* in his [the horse's] light' (youth's rhymed prose); 'he *shines* like lightning' (Hever's rhymed prose); and 'the horse runs *like lightning*' (youth's stich).[19] Of the torch, whose light-giving qualities are self-evident, we read in the original, 'How lovely is the burning torch, flashing arrows from its sparks and casting spears' (youth's rhymed prose); 'regard the waxen torch burning and distributing its glow to the eye of loved friends' (youth's stich); and 'resembling a branch of Ophir's gold over whose head an emerald blossoms' (old man's stich).[20]

the old man answered, saying, "He is like the sun in his heat, like the moon in his fullness, like the honeycomb in his taste, and like myrrh in his perfume." '

The Hebrew—here, with syllables indicated—for the last section reads:

Hu kha-she-mesh be-ḥu-mo
ve-kha-sa-har be-tu-mo
ve-kha-no-fet be-ta'-mo
ve-kha-mor be-vos-mo

[18] Tradition assigns the identity of citron (Hebrew *etrog*) to the fruit Scripture mentions—*ets hadar* (Lev. 23: 40). Together with the branches of the palm, willow, and myrtle it is lifted and waved ritually on the Feast of Tabernacles (Sukkot), to which allusion is made in Gate 33. See the commentary of Rashi on Lev. 23: 40, citing BT *Suk.* 35*a*: Rosenbaum–Silbermann, *Pentateuch*, iii. 109, 191–2 nn. 1–3.

[19] *ST* 265. 22, 25; 266. 2.

[20] *ST* 266. 7–8, 14–15, 17–18. The translation preserves the deliberate thematic linkage of horse and torch. Both entities are a source of light or brightness; and the translation intro-

Predictably, paired similar items are often similarly described: falcon and wolf as fierce beasts of prey, both associated with lightning; pomegranate and nut as charming; moon and sun as located in the heavens, while working their effects upon the earth.

In a few instances, Alḥarizi, through figured speech, links consecutive subjects that do not constitute a logical pair: thus letter (preceded, and co-ordinated with, pen) and sword (followed by, and co-ordinated with, mail) are described in linking terms of attire/ornament, and share the related motifs of strength and combat.[21] Similarly, the intrinsically unrelated, yet consecutively appearing torch and myrrh-packet are both likened to lustful lovers.

A further exercise in wit characterizing the gate is the occasional description of one entity in terms of another. Thus lightning, a topic in itself, appears in the descriptions of sword, horse, falcon, wolf, and river![22] Other instances of this phenomenon are the appearance of mail in the description of the stream; pen and letter (implicitly) in the description of the lightning; the sword, in the description of the river and the moon; and the moon, in the description of the wine.

Still another feature of the rivals' descriptive competition in Gate 32 is fictitious paradox, a frequent device in preceding Hebrew poetry, and one given special emphasis by Moses ibn Ezra:[23] the letter speaks, though mute;[24]

duces a trait of the horse, soaring, into the depiction of the torch flame—a red dove soaring over darkness' waters. As well, the translation introduces a commonality of fierceness between horse and torch: 'He [the horse] lunges, flies; fire, his eyes, his breath—shot steam . . .' (youth's stich); 'The torch is a red-horned ox can gore through darkness' stable, wall and door' (youth's rhymed prose). Finally, the translation introduces, faintly, the linkage of gladdening: the horse 'joys eye and mind' (Hever's rhymed prose) and 'the wizard torch transmutes the gloom' (youth's stich).

There are other deliberate linkages in the original between paired entities not closely related intrinsically. Thus the river, whose description follows lightning's, is portrayed, among other things, as being like the lightning of a drawn sword; harp and water conduit each contain a contrast of weeping and crying (a contrast preserved in the translation); and candle and citron are both likened to lusting lovers.

[21] The related themes of strength and combat encompass, as well, the pen, the item preceding and paired with the letter.

[22] Moreover, in the Hebrew, these figures of speech always alternate between the two men, creating the impression of yet another stratum in the competition, as if each poet were saying, 'And now I will (yet) add to the (growing) stock of similitudes using lightning.' The English retains this pattern with the exception of Hever's rhymed prose description of the horse, which lacks the figure of the lightning (the addition of which would work against other significant components of the description).

[23] See Pagis, *Secular Poetry*, 64–86.

[24] See Moses ibn Ezra, 'Emet al hazeman', *Secular Poems*, ed. Brody, i. 13, poem 9, st. 42, with commentary ii. 21, citing eight further instances of this specific feigned paradox.

and the sword flies without wing.[25] Paradoxicality is specially highlighted —as noted above—in the fourfold repetition of the theme 'hidden yet revealed': the myrrh is hidden (visually)—but revealed (by its scent), a phenomenon Hever likens to an exercised lover whose face betrays his inner passion; then to a winking, tongueless gossip. Now all the above rhetorical flourishes and exercises of wit come in addition to 'standard' structural features of *Sefer Taḥkemoni* that advance or emphasize the gate's thematic content—such features as inclusion, prefiguration, echoing, and biblical citation; all of which intermesh richly and variously.[26]

Inclusions—enwrapping of the gate with the very same word or permutations of the same root—include in the Hebrew, *(ha)melitsot* (figured speech); *hayofi/hayafot* (beauty); *sekhel* and *ḥakhamim/ḥokhmot* (wisdom); and *piv, piha, befiv* (mouth).[27] By encasing his gate with these specific words, Alḥarizi lends further emphasis to the theme of his speakers' (his own) rhetorical skill.

As is often the case, the author prefigures several of the gate's significant themes in his introductory section. Song as attire prefigures the description of mail; the linkage of the young rhetor's skill with pearls prefigures Hever's later description of the pomegranate; and Hever's boast that he can illumine dark matters anticipates not only the topics of torch, lightning, candle, sunlight, and moon, but of other light-related images scattered through the gate.

Echoing, at the close, includes the metaphorical description of Hever's rhetoric as sensual (recalling myrrh) and a substance to be ingested;[28] and of Hever as one who removes grief (recalling wine).

An especially adroit structural echoing occurs in the rhyming configurations. In the Hebrew's next to last exchange between the young poet and Hever, the latter once again echoes the youth's closing rhyme, in this instance greatly expanding the proportion of rhyming units (seven, to the youth's three);[29] even as he overshadows the former, as he has often done already, in

[25] See, in an encomium by Moses ibn Ezra, praise of a certain scholarly work that 'travels, yet without thigh or foot; and flies, yet without wing or pinion', ibid. i. 33, poem 30, st. 3, with commentary ii. 67.

[26] For a discussion of yet another, veiled, rhetorical display in this gate, see the discussion on hidden rhetoric in the Afterword.

[27] This phenomenon is paralleled in the translation in the use of the following words: pearl(s), minds/mind's, wisdom's, song's, and tongue('s).

[28] Hebrew original: 'I smelt the scent of his perfume (*ST* 274. 14–15) . . . he left his remembrance in my mouth like a phial of manna' (l. 18); translation: '. . . quell all my cares at wisdom's well. But few were the days I drank his tongue's rich mel . . .'.

[29] *-eikha*, the suffix meaning 'your', in the Hebrew (*ST* 273. 22–274. 3); *-ine* in the translation, where the number of rhyming units is the same as in the Hebrew.

A comparison of literal and rhymed translations with the original (*ST* 267. 7–19)

Transliteration	Literal translation	Rhymed translation
	Youth: Rhymed Prose	
		Blest not of the Nazirite (NUM. 6: 1-4)
Re'u ben sorek	Behold the vine's son	the Vineson
lismaḥot shorek	piping (summoning) joy	Joy's fine son
vela'anaḥot shino ḥorek	gnashing his teeth against sighs	is blest with might (JOB 16: 9 and elsewhere)
ḥayei nefashim no'omo	his sweet is the life of souls	he puts sinner Grief to flight (PROV. 14: 30)
vehasimḥah naflah beshikhmo	joy falls upon his shoulder	to the heart's delight (ISA. 9: 5)
yoreh hayagon betumo	he shoots grief in its full measure	as he shepherds Joy's pilgrims to the goblet's holy site
veyotsi elav kelei za'amo (JER. 50: 25)	he takes out his weapons of wrath against him	
	Old Man: Rhymed Prose	
		Blest sprite—though blest not of the Rechabite (JER. 35: 2–18)
Hu kashemesh beḥumo	He is like the sun at its hottest	he is sun's bright
vekhasahar betumo	and like the moon in its perfection	moon's light
vekhanofet beta'mo	and like flowing honey in its taste	myrrh's bite
vekhamor bivosmo	and like myrrh in its scent	Joy's rite and the sufferer's right
	Youth: Metric Stich	
Yedei mashkeh yerikun yein adamdam	The server's hands spill reddish wine	The server's hands shed
yeḥayu lev enosh et yishpekhu dam	reviving man's heart as they spill blood	blood-red wine, whose fire grief chills
	Old Man: Metric Stich	
ne'im ta'mo kemo rok pi tseviyah (EZEK. 37: 1–13)	Its pleasing taste is like the saliva of the mouth of a gazelle	Our hearts revive, our dry bones draw breath
umareihu keleḥyah hame'odam	and its appearance is like her reddish cheek	as the red blood spills

the richness of his figurative language. Rounding out this game, Heman, in his closing paragraph, produces ten rhyming units, the first seven of which (in the Hebrew) are one rhyme.[30] In having Heman produce this paragraph —which is laced, as well, with inclusions, verbal echoing of themes and imagery, and rich metaphorical description—Alḥarizi hints to the close reader of the overlap in identity of Heman and Hever; and of their both being embodiments of their poet-creator, Judah Alḥarizi.[31]

In general in this chapter, and specifically in this instance, the literary translation closely approximates the style and content of the Hebrew. In two significant instances I take a freer tack—firstly, in the introduction of Nazirites and Rechabites, two groups who abjure wine.[32] This expansion of the rhymed prose component parallels the overall echoing stylistic of this chapter, even as it adds the vital flavour of biblical citation, otherwise lost here in the English. As well, my rendering of the old man's stich substitutes one frequent tactic of the gate (the old man minting an image unrelated to the youth's effort) for another (the old man's reworking and expansion of his young rival's imagery). Here, the addition of the citation from Ezekiel's vision of dry bones lends a climactic element to the mini-poem even as it creates a paradox (a frequent device in the gate)—the tendering and drinking of wine involves murder (shedding blood) and resuscitation. In my rendering of the preceding stich I augment the paradoxicality of the text by having wine heat (the drinker) and chill (grief) at the same time—again a common antithesis in wine poetry of Hebrew Spain.

In sum, here, as throughout the chapter, I aim for a far greater fidelity to the text than word-for-word equivalency. I seek to produce an English version informed by Alḥarizi's style and those modalities he employs—as well as authentic conventions of Hebrew medieval poetry—to create a lively, witty, contest.

[30] *ST* 274. 14–18. In the English I take the liberty of using one rhyme, *el*, ten times.

[31] On the relation of the author to his protagonists, see the Afterword; and in particular Analyses of the Introduction and Gates 1, 20, 48, and 49.

[32] The Nazirites were forbidden the drinking of wine (Num. 6: 1–21). The Rechabites, too, drank no wine: for this they were singled out by the prophet Jeremiah as exemplars of men who kept faith with their ancestors (Jer. 35: 6).

Analysis of Gate Thirty-Three

Homily, Hymn, and Homonym

ONCE AGAIN the reader is reminded, if he requires it at this relatively late point in the narrative, that the persona of Hever is not consistent throughout the book. Given so pronounced a focus on morality, piety, repentance, and prayer in both the rhymed prose and metrical verse segments of the gate, one might have expected the protagonist to exhibit, as in other gates, a contrast between lofty theme and high preachment on the one hand, and venality or grossness on the other.[1] No such contrast, however, is afforded here. Heman has sought wise and fragrant teachings which will bring him to a happy and pleasant life; Hever has provided him with this wisdom, artfully couched.[2]

Alḥarizi was not the first Hebrew poet to value the use of homonym and homonym rhyme so highly. All major Hebrew medieval poets, like their Arabic predecessors and contemporaries, made liberal use of verbal pun, whether within their stichs or, on occasion, as rhyming words, where the phenomenon of the perfect homonym was exhibited—the same word appearing in completely different meanings.[3] Examples of such rhymes are to be found in the poetic output of all the major figures of Hebrew Spanish poetry —as Samuel Hanagid, Solomon ibn Gabirol, Judah Halevi, and Moses ibn Ezra. Indeed the latter produced an entire corpus of homonym poems, *Sefer ha'anak* (*Book of the Necklace*) or *Tarshish* (*Jasper*[?]—Exod. 28: 20), divided into ten gates or chapters devoted to discrete, if at times overlapping, themes, such as descriptions of natural phenomena, wine and wine-fest, fate, and more.[4] Most of ibn Ezra's poems were two stichs in length, although more than a few were of three stichs, and some even four.

Following in ibn Ezra's footsteps, Alḥarizi produced his own homonym compendium, also called *Sefer ha'anak*.[5] Alḥarizi's high regard for Moses ibn

[1] See, in this regard, Gates 19 and 27 and their Analyses.

[2] On the varied and contradictory behaviours of Hever, see the Afterword.

[3] The categories of homonyms in medieval Hebrew poetry are laid out in ch. 11 of the pioneer modern study of medieval Hebrew poetics, Yellin, *Spanish Hebrew Prosody*, 216–42.

[4] *Secular Poems*, i. 297–404; iii, ed. D. Pagis (Jerusalem, 1977), 37–153.

[5] Two extant versions are available: the scholarly presentation of Brody, 'Hidden Treasures', and that of Avronim, *Rabi yehudah alḥarizi: Sefer ha'anak*. For a brief discussion of ibn Ezra's *Sefer ha'anak*, and Alḥarizi's, and later such compilations, see Schirmann, *History*, i. 387–91.

Ezra is particularly evident in Gate 18's history and evaluation of Hebrew Spanish poetry, where he refers to the bard as Moses, prophet of Hebrew song;[6] and characterizes his predecessor's poetry as of particular appeal to other poets, because of its figured speech and *no'am ta'am melakhto*, 'pleasant, tasty craftsmanship'.[7] Here, Alḥarizi is clearly intent on rivalling and surpassing ibn Ezra. The creation of a lengthy rhymed prose excursus on the evils of this world and the need to repent, comprised wholly of homonym rhyme, is impressive enough;[8] but in his metric section he tops ibn Ezra's achievement even further as he constructs a yet more complex homonym rhyme, offering an *abab* pattern for a two-stich poem, the *a* being the word beginning each stich and *b* the word ending it (occasionally the same word is broken in two —a phenomenon found as well in Moses ibn Ezra's *Sefer ha'anak*). On top of all this, Alḥarizi gives himself the arduous task of arranging said poems in doubled alphabetic acrostic—the same letter providing the first and last word(s) of each stich.[9] And he succeeds stunningly in this enterprise.[10]

---

[6] *ST* 186. 24–5.

[7] The most careful, and very illuminating, discussion of ibn Ezra's elaborate and characteristic figures and tropes is to be found in Pagis, *Secular Poetry*, 64–86.

[8] I provide here a literal translation of the first few lines: 'Praise (*tehilah*) be to God whose praise (*tehilato*) is vast and whose splendour (*tehilato*) fills the world (Hab. 3: 3). Light and glory are His columns and capitals (*gulato*); they who thirst for His goodness (see Amos 8: 11) shall be sated at the fountain of His spring (*gulato*). Who gives every sinner the medicament of his penitence (*teshuvato*) that his spirit might ascend on high, high heaven being his point of return (*teshuvato*) (1 Sam. 7: 17) that he might hide from God's wrath and rage (*veḥamato*) and wash his steps in His butter (*baḥamato*) (Job 29: 6) . . . In the battles of travail his righteousness shall be his shield (*tsinato*) (Ps. 91: 1–4) that he might be concealed in its cover against His wrath and His cold (*tsinato*).'

[9] In rendering the art of Alḥarizi into English, the translator has taken great liberty: I have never followed any one poem literally or even attempted to capture its specific content. Rather, following the thrust and conventions of this genre of *tokheḥah* or chastisement/preachment (often to one's self)—I have created, in overall fashion, parallel rhymed admonishment and preachment (see Analyses 2, 13 and 14)—and that within the strict confinements of the gate's verbal display. A literal rendering of the eleventh stanza (*ST* 279. 9–12) follows: 'The fiery spark (*kidod*) of Hell's flame is readied for you; therefore awake, and for the service of your God yearn (*kesof*); for friend (*ki dod*) and brother will not help you at the time of your death, and the start of your life shall return to its close (*kesof*).'

[10] As if all this were not enough, our author has created an intricate and hidden chiastic scheme harking back to the model of the first chapter of Lamentations—on which the reader is referred to the Afterword, where this achievement is summarized and discussed, along with the presentation of like structures in other gates.

Analysis of Gate Thirty-Four[1]

Of a Host Bombastic and a Feast Fantastic

GATE 34 OF *Sefer Taḥkemoni* is a prooftext of the rich potential of the medium of rhymed prose—and Alḥarizi's stylistic—for rich literary statement. Herein the author presents his readers with a multifaceted attack on the garishness of the *nouveaux riches*. In indiscriminate brag, the host spews forth all that he is and has, from his pedigree to his wife's scullery and coital skills; and then to his pool water, gate sockets, and the personal (very!) services of his valet. All this show is punctuated with telltale admonitions to look at (*re'eh*) and pay attention (*sim libekha*) to everything. Compounding ultra-conspicuous display with literary pretension,[2] the merchant comes out with two absurd conflations of figured speech, when he lauds his wall engravings, and then—water in a basin!

The host is rendered the more comical by Alḥarizi's exploitation of the *maqāma*'s stylistic hallmark, rhymed prose.[3] The linking function of rhyme is very much in evidence in Gate 34, where the host lists fact after fact and item after item. The inventorial aspect of the text is highlighted through the rhyming of relatively short phrases, often end-stopped—with further emphasis lent, at times, through parallelism:

Now when I had grown	*vekha'asher gadalti*
and had learnt the way of wisdom	*vederekh tevunah lamadeti*
and grew wiser than all my teachers	*umikol melamdai hiskalti*
until I frustrated the wise	*ad ki ḥakhamim sikalti*

As the statement builds to a climax of arrogance, the host's excess is aug-

[1] This analysis is slightly revised from Segal, 'Of a Host Bombastic and a Feast Fantastic'.

[2] It is this latter point that most separates Alḥarizi's tale from his source, gate 22 of al-Hamadhani (*Maqāmāt*, tr. Prendergast, 88–97). In the Arabic tale, which Alḥarizi follows quite closely, the merchant does not put on literary airs. Indeed, at one point he bites the leg of a table to show how solid it is (ibid. 96, l. 1)! For a presentation of the Arabic text in Hebrew translation, with observations on Alḥarizi's adaptation, see Dana, 'On the Source' (Heb.). For a superb reading of this gate see Monroe, *The Art of Badi az-Zaman al-Hamadhani*, 145–60. Many discrete points in Monroe's analysis resemble my own, which was written independently before I had encountered Monroe's book.

[3] For suggestions on the significance of rhymed elements—morphemically, onomatopoeically, and other—in Hebrew metric verse in Spain, see A. Mirsky, 'On the Significance of Rhyme in the (Hebrew) Poetry of Spain' (Heb.), *Leshonenu*, 33 (1969), 150–95; and Dana, 'The Relation of Rhyme to Content' (Heb.).

mented syntactically by the superfluity of everything past *gadalti*: the main clause of the sentence starts after *sikalti*, with the merchant's father choosing a bride for his son: *gadalti*, then, and each of the next two rhyme-words, could have ended a dependent clause; instead, the sentence spills on and on.

This effect of verbal padding is further buttressed by rhyme: the common denominator of all the rhyme-words is the suffix *ti*—first person, past tense; yet the third unit of the cluster rhymes more fully with the first—*alti*: *gadalti, lamadeti, hiskalti*: and the fourth unit's close lengthens the rhyme component still further (*his*<u>*kalti*</u>—*si*<u>*kalti*</u>). A rhythmic technique evident in Gate 34 is the shortening of rhyming units to two words or even one. Such shortening mirrors, in this context, faster or more intensive activity, even as the use of identical rhyming elements emphasizes the likeness of the activities engaged in or the objects described:

Sir, pay attention	*sim libekha adoni*
to this hall—how fine it is;	*lezeh ha'ulam mah tuvo*
and regard the windows that are in it;	*ure'eh haḥalonim asher bo*
and set your eyes on the beauty	*vesim eineikha al yefi*
of the walls	*hakirot*
and the beams	*vehakorot*
and the rooms	*vehabirot*
and the towers	*vehatirot*
and the turrets	*vehasekhiyot*
and the upper chambers	*veha'aliyot*
and the carven figures.	*ufituḥei hamaskiyot.*[4]

A frequent device in Alḥarizi and in Hebrew rhymed prose generally, often noted in this analysis, is used in Gate 34 to comic advantage; namely, the citing of Scripture out of context. Such quoting is especially apt here: the host misappropriates, if not misunderstands, his sources, and so bares his ignorance. This technique is often, and typically, coupled with rhyme for further emphasis and for climactic effect, as in the case of a rhyme cluster (especially one closing a unit or sub-unit of the narrative) ending with a biblical verse or verse fragment. In just this fashion the host caps off his encomia to his most-domestic wife:

happy the man she sits beside	*ashrei ish asher hi yoshevet etslo*
and happy the people in such a case	*ve'ashrei ha'am shekakha lo*

This is from Psalm 144: 15, which continues: 'happy the people whose God is

[4] Reichert (ii. 199) renders, 'the engravings of the mosaics'. Dishon, 'Medieval Panorama', shows that several details of the realia described in the merchant's home, including the engraved figures, accord with evidence from the Cairo Genizah.

the Lord'; present here are absurd overtones of sanctity and the suggestion that the wife's sooty face and clean pots are the cause of neighbourhood rapture!

An even droller malapropism is the climax of the merchant's exhibitionistic recital of his bedroom revels. He assures his guest that could he be but present on the scene,

your thoughts would be astounded	*tamhu ra'ayonekha*
by this pleasant coition	*lezeh haḥibur hana'eh*
'until you are driven mad	*vehayita meshuga lemareh*
by what your eyes behold'	*eineikha asher tireh*
(Deut. 28: 34)[5]	

Parody is another important comic strategy. The guest-narrator's laughable plight is underscored by open reactions: wry comment and terse asides (such as 'After all this torment he summoned his servant to bring in the table') and his expression of disgust to the host at the close, when the latter invites him to the privy.

It is in Hever's mental parodying of the merchant that the tale reaches the heights of farce. Carrying to absurdity the host's windy and irrelevant digressions—as on water in a jar and wall art—the guest envisages a near-treatise on the bread (like water, a common feature of a meal) and its most distantly related phases of preparation. The hungry guest goes on to mimic stylistically the garrulous host, who earlier had rushed from one item to the next.

Anticipating the merchant's expatiation on his condiments and kitchenware, the guest conveys his frustration first through a list in mocking singsong rhythm and then in a spewing of like items one after another; his catalogue is given further emphasis by shortening the rhyme units; near-rhyming the consecutive units; and, at the close, by expanding rhyme components, the last two rhyme-words—*vehatsapaḥat vehatsalaḥat*—being four-syllable near-homonyms (five, if one holds initial *sheva* to be a syllable).

Attentiveness to the stylistic phenomenon of root repetition in *Sefer Taḥkemoni* leads to an appreciation of two more facets of this complex tale. The first of these is the function of the frame. In Gate 34 there is general and open prefiguration in Hever's exasperation and Heman's questioning him thereon; and there is the very specific prefiguration of the significant recurring root *re'eh* (*adoni*), 'See, (my lord)' in the stranger's imprecation, 'Cursed be lust that makes its owner a laughing-stock, *ra'avah* (literally, "display")'.[6]

[5] In Scripture, the assurance of going insane is presented as a crushing divine punishment, which overtones carry into the host's speech, much contrary to his intention.

[6] I prefer Schirmann's reading of *ra'avah*, 'display' (*Hebrew Poetry*, ii. 180. 5) as in Ezek. 28: 17, to Toporovsky's *da'avah*, 'misery', (*ST* 282. 8) precisely on the grounds of the significance

Similarly the close of this *maqāma* is linked verbally with the main tale. Hever had said of the merchant, 'He seized and drew me (*umeshakhani*) and brought me to the privy.' Heman uses precisely that word and in just that form to describe a desired coercion: 'He drew me (*umeshakhani*) with the sweetness of his speech.'[7] Finally, of the neighbours of the merchant in pursuit, Hever had said, 'They gathered about me and struck me (*vehikuni*)'; and of fate (wandering) Heman says at the close, 'He struck me (*vehikani*) with the rod of his wrath.'

The blurring of boundaries between fiction and reality is another central feature of the text. Hever's proud unveiling in metrical verse at the gate's close—a frequent characteristic of *Sefer Taḥkemoni*'s *maqāmāt*—insistently calls for comparison, in this context, with the verbal behaviour of the host.[8] In stating (literally), 'I compose *maqāmāt* of delightful (*ḥamudot*) veiled tales, sweeter than the honeycomb to the hearer's palate', Hever recalls the tantalization—and frustration—of the guest's (Hever's!) taste-buds by the host. In the final line of his brief poem Hever picks up on a significant repeat word, *no'am*, as he boasts of his poetic prowess: 'From my pleasant fire (*esh no'omi*) I kindle flames and from the rock of my speech I draw swords.' Twice in this tale the host underscores the pleasantness of his possessions by the repetition of this root. He gloats over his servant's 'pleasing stature', *no'am komato*; and describes tasty food to come as 'the pleasant dishes', *hamatamim hane'imim*.[9] This root is also picked up by Hever even before the tale's end in his ruminations on 'the bread and its pleasantness', *une'imuto*, and 'the spices and their pleasantness', *veno'omam*.[10]

The final poem's echoing of a significant theme and a significant root encompasses the realm of biblical citation. In declaring, 'From my pleasant speech I kindle flames (*aḥtsov lehavot*) and from the rock of my speech I draw swords', Hever hints at his quasi-divine stature ('The voice of the Lord kindles flames of fire', *ḥotsev lahavot esh* (Ps. 29: 7)—relating to the host's description of his house in terms evoking the Tabernacle or the Temple).[11] In short, in this typical self-advertisement of Hever at the *maqāma*'s close, Alḥarizi has his hero continue to experience himself as the character he

of prefiguration and recurring roots in *Sefer Taḥkemoni* (and indeed in medieval and much prior Hebrew *belles-lettres* generally). The root *r-'-h* occurs in the following lines: *ST* 282. 5, 20; 283. 3, 7, 8, 12, 17, 20, 23, 27; 284. 1, 3, 7; 285. 4, 18, 19, 20.

[7] Added humour derives from contrastive allusion to the romantic-idyllic declaration of S. of S. 1: 4, 'Draw me (*moshkheni*), we will run after thee; the king hath brought me (*heviani*) into his chambers . . .'.

[8] This feature is lacking in al-Hamadhani.

[9] *ST* 284. 17, 26.

[10] *ST* 285. 5, 9–10.

[11] *ST* 283. 4–7; 284. 3–4.

played in his own tale, and so vent his spleen on the obnoxious host—his own invention![12]

The circle of identity-blur and braggadocio extends even further. In this instance (as in many others), Hever is the spokesman of Alḥarizi, who makes similar claims in the introduction to *Sefer Taḥkemoni*: Alḥarizi's verbal powers are described as a rock, and his words as fiery and sword-like.[13]

TRANSLATION METHODOLOGY: A CASE STUDY

As a translator, I have striven to parallel the comic technique of the original, especially rhyme and rhythm, for emphasis and variation and, as much as possible, root repetition. Frequent repetitions in the original meant frequent repetitions in English: 'Look for' for *re'eh*, 'mark you' for *sim libekha*, 'good' for *tov*, and 'lovely' for *yafeh*. Even words repeating infrequently in the original have not been slighted in the English: Alḥarizi has his host clearly link his wife's lust with her animation in cleaning rooms—the identical phrase, *vehi lo mitapeket* ('and she not restraining herself') is used. Relatedly, he has Hever say concerning his hasty exit from the merchant's home, *velo hitapakti*.[14] I use the phrase '*sans* restraint' in all three instances.

In trying to retain the humorous juxtapositions of the original, I have tried to keep the same groupings of rhyme elements; however, rather than strain unduly for a string of four or five rhyme-words, at times I subdivide a longer cluster, as in the following instance (where I italicize rhyme-words for emphasis):[15]

Literal Rendering		*Rhymed Version*
(The vessel is) large and spacious	(*yadayim*)	It is opulent and *wide*:
containing (much) water—	(*hamayim*)	two men could bathe *inside*.
about 20 cubic yards.	(*se'atayim*)	
Mark you, my lord, this water	(*hamayim*)	And mark thou, sir, these waters,
for it is a delight to the eye	(*einayim*)	the dream of a lusting *eye*—
as though they were tears poured	(*yetsukim*)	as though from the *sigh*-filled *tears*
from the eyes of lovers	(*ḥoshekim*)	of lovers they had quite *congealed*...

[12] The reader is reminded of a somewhat similar blurring of boundaries, albeit entirely within the main tale, in Gate 31, where the brigand's rage at 'her' sexual abuse by the company of travellers carries forward 'her' rage at the (fictitious!) sexual abuse committed by the lascivious lord.

[13] Poetic speech as fire: *ST* 3. 3–4; 8. 24; 11. 10–11; 19. 21–4; 20. 26–7; 28. 26–7. As (a) rock: *ST* 9. 17–18; 29. 12. As a sword/weapon: *ST* 11. 10–11; 14. 24–5; 19. 21; 20. 25–6. For a related discussion see Pagis, 'Variety', 95–8 ('Fact and Fiction'). On the blurring of identities between author and characters see the Afterword and the Analyses of the Introduction and of Gates 1, 21, 28, 48, and 49.

[14] *ST* 282. 21; 283. 25–6; 285. 24.

[15] *ST* 284. 8–10.

Stilted English has been avoided (except where the host strains to make an impression on his guest). To this end I have allowed myself the use of off-rhyme.[16]

In partial compensation for the host's frequent and laughable quoting of Scriptures I have him toss off some French phrases. Similarly, I have him stumble in English: 'Lift your eyes aloof' (rather than 'aloft')—an error bringing out his snobbishness as well as his ignorance. Finally I have emphasized the host's bombast and rabid materialism with more than usual selective capitalization. This same device serves to emphasize, especially, Hever's sarcastic imitation of the merchant.

I have tried to ensure that divergences from the original were compatible not only with the style, content, and dynamic of the original but of the English version as well. Thus where a literal rendering of the host's remark about his wife would have read, 'And the maiden is fair of face and even more so in her activities' I have him declare, 'Fair she is of form and face (more I would say in another place)', creating a *double entendre*—suggesting that the merchant is referring to other bodily assets of his wife; and that he is reticent to discuss, in this circumstance, so intimate a matter. Both meanings relate to what follows, when the host indeed says more, in another room, about the virtues of his wife as a bedmate! When I have the host say of his home, 'Mine is the fairest of them all', I introduce overtones of 'Snow White', thus associating the merchant with the wicked stepmother, an archetype of egocentricity.

One section in particular demanded free reworking: the climactic bathroom confrontation, where the wit and burlesque of the Hebrew are richly realized. The host's penultimate *laudes* boast a more than triple entendre: 'It cannot be that you should leave before seeing the privy, for therein *yishlam hama'aseh*.' These last two words can be construed to mean at least: (1) your need for a privy shall be met here; (2) this undertaking (the display of all I own) will end there; (3) therein the art (of my home) attains its zenith; and

[16] Near-equivalents of off-rhyme are to be found in *Sefer Taḥkemoni*. Throughout, Alḥarizi has adopted as his minimal requirement for rhyme the rhyme known as *ra'uy* or 'worthy' in medieval Hebrew prosody, comprising an initial consonant followed by a vowel (designated CV), e.g. *une'imato* [its pleasantness] . . . *utevuato* [and its harvesting] (*ST* 285. 5) or an initial consonant followed by a vowel and a consonant (designated CVC), e.g. *vehasipot* [and the pots] . . . *vehakapot* [and the spoons] (*ST* 285. 11); indeed, most of his rhymes are fuller than that. In using *ra'uy* as the minimal rhyming component, Alḥarizi follows the practice of all preceding poets who composed in metric rhyme. Very rarely does he use the rhyme called *over*, or 'passing'—merely a terminal vowel sound, or that followed by a consonant (designated VC), e.g. *tal* [dew] . . . *yizal* [drips](*ST* 284. 13–14); in context, the effect in the Hebrew approximates that of off-rhyme in English. See 'Rhyme in Medieval Poetry' in 'Prosody', *EJ* xiii. 1218–20.

(4) therein the tale attains its consummation (here Alḥarizi's voice comes through). Examining and reworking my version I allowed for the changes that at once contributed to the climactic aspect of this section of the story; and harked back to the tale's prominent motifs and key words, mirroring the dynamic of the Hebrew. I render the aura of climax in the English with the host's 'this breathtaking sight, the very Acme of Delight'. The capitalized word 'Delight' relates as a motif to all that the host has displayed and is a significant repeating word in the English as also in the Hebrew (*neḥmad*): the host says that as a child he was a delight (*neḥmad*) to the eye ; he speaks of his courtyard's 'walls and their delightful faces' and calls water in the pool 'God and man's delight'.[17]

The English version tries to convey a sense of climax, creating the host's perhaps most grandiose literary posturing: 'Look sir, alone on Naked Beauty Bare'—this being a distortion of Edna St. Vincent Millay's 'Euclid alone has looked on Beauty bare.' The host's misquotation and its redundancy show him to be anything but the savant he has claimed to be; and his 'Naked Beauty Bare' ties in with his lumping together, throughout, of erotic delights and the pleasures of conspicuous display. In addition, the (mis)quoted poem is a paean to abstract and intellectual beauty—at a far remove from the merchant's vulgar materialism.

'Look, sir, alone' is apt in still two more ways: it recalls the merchant's wishing that his visitor could see him alone in bed (with his wife alongside him); and highlights another aspect of the vexed guest's predicament: he is in no way alone but ever attended by his galling host!

[17] Lit. 'God and man's joy'; the root *ḥ-m-d*, 'delightful', has been used in the Hebrew only a few words before: *gulot hamayim haḥamudim*, 'the conduits of the delightful waters'.

Analysis of Gate Thirty-Five

Of the Grave of Ezra the Blest and Poems Celeste

HEVER—and, it would seem, the author—go to great lengths to press for the authenticity of the miraculous nature of the phenomena reported at the site of the grave of Ezra the Scribe. The first reaction of the protagonist to the tales of the wondrous site contain a strong measure of scepticism: he is convinced that the legendary accounts of the discovery of Ezra's grave, its removal to its permanent site, and the attendant flames had to be lies, plain and simple; but shortly thereafter, in our narrative, Hever insists that his eyewitness experiences corroborated the miracle. Anticipating, perhaps, reader reaction, Alḥarizi has his hero give voice to further scepticism, a suspicion that neighbouring peoples lit bonfires for the purposes of deception and mockery; but Hever rules out such an interpretation, noting that the light was by no means red—hence of earthly origin—but pure and clear. Then the Kenite passionately repudiates the assertion that a naturalistic interpretation is available, as he presents details inconsistent with such an explanation.

What is one to make of so stubborn a claim for an impossible display, and that on the part of a narrator/performer distinguished for fraud and chicanery throughout this book?

The answer lies perhaps in an account by a previous Jewish traveller of the medieval period and of the responses of his contemporaries and later Jewish authorities. Eldad the Danite, a ninth-century traveller of mysterious origins, claimed to have discovered, and lived with, the lost tribes of Naphtali, Gad, and Asher in their strong and independent kingdom in Africa. He also spoke of 'the sons of Moses' living beyond a miraculous river of rolling stones, the Sambatyon, quiescent and passable only on the Sabbath.[1] Eldad's account may have been rooted in legends based in their turn on actual Jewish peoples and rulers: namely,

> the sixth-century Arabian king Joseph Dhu Nuwas of Himyar who, along with his subjects, converted to Judaism; the Falashas in Ethiopia, who were possibly independent in the early Middle Ages; and the Khazar state, whose rulers, along with many of their subjects, converted to Judaism. His aim was probably to raise the spirits of

[1] *EJ* vi. 576–8. For a sampling of Eldad's account, see Leviant, *Masterpieces of Hebrew Literature*, 146–57.

the Jews by giving them news of tribes of Israel who lived in freedom and by creating an attractive Jewish utopia. The report of the existence of such Jewish kingdoms undoubtedly encouraged and comforted Eldad's hearers by contradicting the Christian contention that Jewish independence had ceased after the destruction of the Second Temple. For the Jews his stories obviously had far-reaching messianic implications.[2]

Whether reluctant to prick a pin in this utopian and comforting vision, or whether themselves accepting the Danite's claim wholly or in part, several Jewish leaders were sympathetic to Eldad: Meir ben Baruch of Rothenburg and Abraham ibn Ezra regarded Eldad as an impostor, but his *halakhot* concerning ritual slaughter, even if mostly not accepted, were quoted by many of the outstanding scholars of the Middle Ages (Rashi, Asher ben Jehiel, the tosafists, and others). Neither was he rejected by his contemporary Zemaḥ Gaon, who stated that the possibility of different traditions existed.[3]

The text of Gate 35 clearly supports the interpretation that Alḥarizi was indeed bent on bolstering his readers' faith in continued divine love, by providing physical evidence of it. Prior to his poem at the grave of Ezra, Hever thanks God for having preserved a redeemer and remnant for the Jewish people. In the poem proper, in language redolent of human encounter with the divine and prophetic messages of comfort, Hever points to the phenomena surrounding Ezra's grave as convincing evidence to the heathen that God's glory yet resides among the Jews.[4]

A similar message of comfort is evident in the poem of praise and petition over the grave of Ezekiel. That prophet's vision of the end of days is given the traditional interpretation of God's assurance of ultimate individual resurrection. This section of the gate, too, is miracle-laden. Attended by angels, the prophet's resting-place exudes fragrance. More significantly, Hever claims that, astonishingly, the body of the prophet has known no dissolution, echoing Muslim folk belief that 'deceased' buried prophets actually live in their graves.[5] Finally, even pagans flock to the site in acknowledgement of the mystery and potency of the prophet. This last point echoes the awe and reverence accorded the grave of Ezra, earlier emphasized.[6]

[2] EJ vi. 577. [3] Ibid.

[4] For the latest and fullest discussion of Ezra's grave and the phenomenon treated of by Alḥarizi, see Gil, *In the Kingdom of Ishmael*, i. 494–6 and n. 286; see also *EJ* vi. 1107—which records Muslim reverence for the site—and bibliography.

[5] E. Shinar, private conversation.

[6] Alḥarizi's was by no means the only written account of the grave of the prophet Ezekiel. First mentioned in the epistle of Sherira Gaon (*c*.986), the tomb was described in detail *c*.1170 by Benjamin of Tudela, who speaks at length on the veneration of this site. See *The Book of the Journey of Rabbi Benjamin* (Heb.), ed. Adler, 43 ff. See also *The Journey of Rabbi Petaḥyah*

The close of the gate is unusual for *Sefer Taḥkemoni*. Nothing follows upon the poem to Ezekiel, which is the longest single poem in the book: we encounter no reaction of Heman the Ezrahite, no further interchange between the two, no description of parting—nothing that might take away from the immediacy of the reverence of Hever (and, in this instance, the author).[7] The reader should note as well a phenomenon singular in *Sefer Taḥkemoni*, but by no means singular in Hebrew medieval poetry: for special emphasis, the final hemistich of the poem is exactly the same as the first.[8] Finally, our author has perhaps hinted at the gravity of his topic in the gate's introduction: Heman all but openly reveals himself as Alḥarizi, declaring, 'at that time Judah [i.e. Alḥarizi] departed his brothers'[9]—this preceded by a description that is a slightly rearranged citation of a line from a poem by Judah Halevi describing his journey to Zion.[10]

of Regensburg (Heb.), ed. Grinhut, 14 ff.; and Goitein, 'On the Journey to Prostration' (Heb.). The last three sources are cited in S–F, *History*, ii. 166 n. 79. It was later described by others, Jews and non-Jews alike. For further description of the tomb, still a revered site, see *EJ* vi. 1096–7. On the custom of Jews in Muslim lands of making pilgrimage to the tombs of Ezra and Ezekiel, see Goitein, *A Mediterranean Society*, v. 18 ff. E. Shinar, in private conversation, emphasized that the Jewish practice of reverence for holy men's tombs was clearly derivative from Muslim practice.

[7] Like endings occur in Gates 17 (the Karaite–Rabbanite debate) and 24 (the boorish cantor and the excesses of *piyut*), where, similarly, the polemical thrust of the text is heightened by the absence of a closing frame.

[8] For an earlier example, see Judah Halevi, 'Elohai negdekha kol ta'avati' ('My God, all my desire is before you'), analysed in Tsur, *Studies in Medieval Hebrew Poetry*, 83–99 and further mentioned at pp. 40, 50, 57, 173–4. Biblical precedent is to be found in Ps. 103: 'Bless the Lord, O my soul . . . Bless the Lord, O my soul' and Ps. 104: 'Bless the Lord, O my soul . . . Bless the Lord, O my soul. Halleluyah.'

[9] Citing Gen. 38: 1. On this tactic, and the author's identification variously with Heman and Hever, see the Afterword.

[10] This citation of Halevi is noted in S–F, *History*, ii. 154 n. 39.

Analysis of Gate Thirty-Six

Challenge and Reply: Sweet Words Fly

GATE 36 EXEMPLIFIES a wide-ranging genre, or thrust, of Arabic literature called *adab*. This term covers an extensive spectrum. Originally denoting (praiseworthy) customs, one pronounced signification was superior upbringing and moral stature, as well as urbanity and courtesy; and, in the course of time, the ethical literature that inculcated these same virtues, including anecdotes, dialogues, and poetry. The word's broadest import was humanity or culture.

More narrowly defined, *adab* refers to epigrammatic wisdom emphasizing moral living—anecdotes, riddles, and the like. In earlier Arab collections, from the ninth century CE, these sayings were scattered randomly; later they would appear in categories—such as faith, patience, and friendship—with some compendia presenting the advantages of a given trait followed by its disadvantages. Aiming at universal truths, such collections set the wisdom of the Greeks and the Persians alongside that of Arabs.[1]

Hebrew translations of Arabic *adab* literature include *Mivḥar hapeninim* ('A Choice of Pearls'), which some have attributed to Solomon ibn Gabirol;[2] *Musarei hapilosofim* ('The Moral Teachings of the Philosophers'), compiled in the ninth century by the Syrian Ḥunayn ibn Isḥaq; and *Kalīla wa-Dimna*.[3] Metric verse creations in Hebrew that show a heavy influence of *adab* literature are Moses ibn Ezra's homonym-rhyme compendium *Sefer ha'anak* or *Tarshish* and a similar work of the same name by Alḥarizi;[4] and Samuel Hanagid's *Ben mishlei* and *Ben kohelet*.[5]

In one sense the precursors of Gate 36 go all the way back to the book of

[1] For a fuller discussion of *adab* in Arabic and medieval Hebrew literature, see Ratzaby, '*Adab* Maxims in Medieval Literature' (Heb.). Ratzaby cites influences evident as early as in the writing of Ḥai Gaon (939–1038). For a representative anthology of anecdotes and epigrams in Hebrew translation, see Ratzaby, *Arabic Wisdom* (Heb.).

[2] *Mivḥar hapeninim*, ed. Habermann; for further discussion on editions and theories of authorship, see ibid. 68 ff.; and *EJ* xii. 163–4.

[3] Ratzaby, '*Adab*', 114–18. *Musarei hapilosofim* was translated by Alḥarizi himself in unrhymed prose at the request of the sages of Lunel. See S–F, *History*, ii. 175–7.

[4] See Analysis 33 above, esp. nn. 3–5.

[5] *Divan shmuel hanagid*, ed. Jarden, ii (*Ben mishlei*) and iii (*Ben kohelet*). A related work is the compendium of the Jewish sage and convert to Catholicism Petrus Alfonsi, the *Disciplina Clericalis*.

Proverbs, which is, in its major part, a compendium of saws and adages on disparate themes, all designed to bring home to the student the lesson that moral living is the prudent course to follow. In this, Gate 44 can be grouped with Gate 19; and close reading reveals that here, too, if in less pronounced fashion, satire and cynicism are not very far beneath the surface of the text.

The particular literary genre encountered in Gate 36 is that of question and answer. Encompassing a wide spectrum, the tester throws out one question after another, not necessarily related; and the respondent must answer adroitly and, in this framework, in rhyme.

The earliest example in narrative Hebrew rhymed prose of the modality of question and answer is to be found in Joseph ibn Zabara's *Sefer sha'ashuim* ('The Book of Delight'). The enigmatic figure of Anan, to be revealed in the end as a very devil, challenges the narrator, Joseph, to reply to a series of questions on a variety of scientific topics, which Joseph does. Immediately Joseph turns the tables, whereat the seemingly sophisticated Anan proves a very inept respondent.[6]

What recommends Alḥarizi's reworking of the tradition he has inherited is, above all, the frame that he creates for this contest and the ironic contrasts forged. Hever's responses may be divided into two categories: counsels of prudence, essentially; and dictates that carry a moral imperative or overtones of preachment. The former and utilitarian category is slender, with wisdom its major theme. Stupidity is denigrated, as well as insincere service of one's king; wisdom is proclaimed as the road to success, even for society's rejects; and wisdom's (or cunning's) success is the more assured when the surrounding society is ignorant.

The rest of Hever's replies all bear in some way on the moral life. The Kenite's dicta, however, do not accord with his conduct; indeed, Hever often preaches precisely the opposite of his practice. His praise of silence and the virtues of a good name are far removed from his behaviour here, and generally; and his dunning of appetite, levity, folly, and brazenness stand in stark contrast to his antics amidst the tipplers of Seva'im, between cup and fetching youth.[7] Finally, his promotion of humility is ludicrous, given his arrant boasting.

[6] *Sefer sha'ashuim*, ed. Davidson, 101–23 (chs. 9–10); *The Book of Delight*, tr. Hadas, 126–42. See Segal, 'Certain Delights of the Book of Delights', esp. 198. See too Dishon's book-length study, *The Book of Delight*, esp. 147 ff. The most recent overview is to be found in S–F, *History*, ii. 106–28. Yet an earlier example of question and response—though the respondent quotes, or alludes to, the challenge of the questioner—is to be found in a polemical debate: the responses of Sa'adiah Gaon to the heretical challenges of Hiwi al-Balkhi—on which, see Rosenthal, *Hiwi al-Balkhi: A Comparative Study*—cited among other sources in *EJ* viii. 792–3.

[7] The youth who is the object of desire is referred to in the Hebrew as 'a gazelle'. On the use of such terms see Scheindlin, *Wine, Women*, index; and Roth, '"Deal Gently with the Young Man"'.

Alḥarizi has set up a dramatic situation that blends irony with disdain for the swayable mass. On the one hand, both questioner and admiring crowd cannot know that several of Hever's high-sounding replies are belied by his degraded lifestyle. At certain points, however, tester and assemblage should have seen through the hypocrisy and pretension of their guest orator: he certainly exhibited no love of silence or humility; and his initial inflated self-advertisement presented him as an impossible paragon of learning.[8]

In addition, his pronouncements on piety should have given his listeners pause. In an unusually lengthy reply to one question, Hever stresses that tearful and contrite prayer guarantees divine help. He submits, as well, that true might is the fear of God—and advances that same virtue over all others at the close. Relatedly, Hever had told Heman, in the narrative preceding his rhetorical display, that he praised God warmly for effecting his escape. However, it is industry and initiative that really save the day for the protagonist, the very virtues he lauds in his closing poem to Heman; and these laudations ring much truer than all that has gone before.

Now if the none-too-perceptive crowd has been gulled by Hever, Heman's enthusiasm at the close, including his bowing to the Kenite, presents him, as well, as lacking in perspicuity; or high moral standards; or both.[9] Hever has supplied his friend with enough ammunition for a barrage against hypocrisy—an attack that could have complemented Heman's first outburst—the more so given Hever's open venality at the finish, as he gloats (implicitly) over the locals' filling his purse with coin. Indeed this brag is a sterling illustration of a prior assertion by Hever that the more ignorant one's society, the more effective wisdom—i.e. cunning. Finally, Hever has advanced a tale so improbable that Heman should respond with more than a little scepticism. How likely is it that a besieging army would so liberally allow the appearance of a stranger in their midst; and would welcome, or be impressed by, references to Jewish texts? And how could Hever think of exposing himself as a Jew under such circumstances?[10]

The Ezrahite emerges as either a bamboozled admirer of moralistic rhetoric or, whether consciously or no, an admirer of successful self-seeking. The latter reading is bolstered by a re-examination of Heman's opening

[8] For like listings, praising, respectively, a precentor and a patron, see Gates 24, at the start, and 50, at the close. A partially similar boast is to be found in Gate 30, as Hever as a quack-salver takes in a crowd of locals.

[9] On this point see Analyses 19 and 44; and, in the Afterword, the discussion of the relationship between Hever and Heman.

[10] The reader may recall Gate 22, where a Muslim savant unmasks Hever and his companions as Jews, and nearly has them killed.

statement, which is, in effect, a proclamation of hedonism, lacking only the element of erotic fulfilment; and even that could be hinted at in the Hebrew's *ulehitales*, 'to delight', harking back to the harlot of Proverbs: 'Let us delight (*nitalsah*) in amorous embrace' (Prov. 7: 18).

The Ezrahite's initial condemnation of Hever's libertinism, therefore, could be more a projection of self-censure than unequivocal moral judgement of a friend; and this interpretation, in turn, could explain Heman's willingness instantly to trade his condemnation for curiosity and then praise.[11]

[11] On the larger question of Alḥarizi's attitude towards the venality and trickery of Hever, and of Heman's admiration thereof, if not complicity therewith, see the discussion in the Afterword.

Analysis of Gate Thirty-Seven

In the Clasp of a Deadly Asp

THOUGH HEVER's venality is not absent from this gate (he demands payment, in advance, for the cure he renders) and though he laughs, while the company trembles, the overall effect of the *maqāma* is serious. As such, it falls between the category of self-seeking adventurism and such serious gates as original prayers (14 and 15) and the allegory of the slaughter of the innocents (25) witnessed by the narrator and his companions.

Alḥarizi would have had no difficulty in framing his tale in a different fashion, such that Heman would have heard of, rather than witnessed, this supernatural display; and then could have at least challenged the account's credibility; or laughed at the same—as he laughed at the far more credible tale of Hever's marriage with an ugly bride. But no such thing transpires. Heman is witness to a genuine, yet impossible, rescue.[1]

Gate 30 at once comes to mind—the boisterous Hever as physician, mulcting a gullible crowd after making preposterous claims as a healer. Conversely, here, Hever's claim as healer is terse in the extreme; it is the cure itself and all involved therein that is decidedly fantastical—yet actual. A comparison with Gate 22 is in order too: there a vainglorious stargazer who claims little less than absolute power over fate is suspected of charlatanism, but shows himself possessed of mind-reading capabilities and almost life-and-death power over the band of mocking Jewish questioners, but for the kindness of a righteous judge. In Gate 37, a declared capability that is not, on the surface, supernatural, is, when performed, thoroughly miraculous.

Yet the text provides foreshadowing of the miracle. Through the stratum of biblical citation, both Hever's claim and his saving acts are enlarged, through identification with divine powers. Even the seemingly modest assertion that he will heal the victim, *ani erpa maḥalato umaḥats makato*, 'I will heal his sickness and the injury he has suffered', is a conflation of two statements by God in Scripture: '. . . There is no God beside Me. I deal death and give life; I wounded and I will heal . . .' (Deut. 32: 39) and '. . . when the Lord binds up His people's wounds and heals the injuries it has suffered . . .' (Isa. 30: 26). Hever's claim that every eye shall witness the cure is a citation of God's promise: '. . . for every eye shall behold the Lord's return to Zion' (Isa. 52: 8).

[1] Here I differ with Dishon, who sets this gate together with 30 and 48, holding all three to be 'full-fledged parodies of bogus cures' (*The Book of Delight*, 191 n. 4).

The metaphoric 'drawn sword' whereby Hever adjures the summoned vipers is, in Scripture, always associated with a threatening angel.[2] The threatened blight of 'wrath, indignation, and angels of evil' (Ps. 78: 49) is the biblical description of the havoc wreaked upon the Egyptians by God. As well, the eclipse of the sun evokes depiction of divine powers: 'And in that day—says the Lord God—I will make the sun set at noon' (Amos 8: 9). The company's fear of being eaten alive evokes a like fear in Scripture, where God is credited for the rescue: 'they would have swallowed us alive. . . . Blessed is the Lord, who did not let us be ripped apart by their teeth' (Ps. 124: 3–6). The admonition to 'stand and witness' is a citation of Moses' command to the Israelites to 'stand and witness the deliverance which the Lord will work for you today' (Exod. 14: 13).

Now all this linkage of Hever with divine might contrasts with the impotence of the band of travellers, described at the outset—ironically, in retrospect—as *metei zeroa im gevurah*, 'men whose arms were endowed with might', evoking Ps. 89: 14, *lekha zeroa im gevurah*, 'Yours is an arm endowed with might', predicated of God. The company, far from being endowed with divine might, is reduced to impotence and tears when one of their number is bitten by a deadly snake.

No, the true divine power is possessed by Hever the Kenite, who is further linked with God at the end of the tale, via a near-citation of the traditional blessing recited on seeing one possessed of exceptional wisdom in the Torah: 'Blessed are You, O Lord our God, King of the universe, who has apportioned His wisdom to them that revere Him.'[3]

Herein, however, lies a final irony: though Hever has performed a genuinely benevolent deed, that of saving a human life (if for pay), yet he has transgressed a specific prohibition of the Torah:

> When you enter the land that the Lord your God is giving you, you shall not learn to imitate the abhorrent practices of those nations. Let no one be found among you who . . . is an augur, a soothsayer, a diviner, a sorcerer, one who casts spells (*ḥover ḥovarim*), or one who consults ghosts . . . For anyone who does such things is abhorrent to the Lord.[4]

It is precisely the appellation of *ḥover ḥovarim* that Hever uses in his closing poem of self-presentation. Of course, one must bear in mind that in Scripture itself there is one exception to the rule that only rational and non-magical

[2] Num. 22: 23, 31; Josh. 5: 13; 1 Chr. 21: 16.

[3] Hertz, *Authorised Daily Prayer Book*, 992.

[4] Deut. 18: 9–12. On the prohibition of magic in Jewish healing see *EJ* xi. 703–15 ('Magic'); and 'Medicine', 1179–80 and bibliography, 1204–5.

cures are permitted or described; namely, the case of the Israelites *bitten by snakes*.[5]

Whatever conclusion the reader draws as to the religiosity or no of Hever's behaviour, our author continues insistently to offer a very varied representation of both his protagonist and reality.

[5] Num. 21: 9.

Analysis of Gate Thirty-Eight

Of Men and Ship in the Storm's Grip

TOGETHER WITH Gates 35 and 47, Gate 38 advances the theme of breaking the natural order of things, whether through unsolicited divine miracle (at the graves of Ezra and Ezekiel), wonder-cure (of snakebite), or effecting escape from danger through amulets. As opposed to the earlier two gates, Hever reverts to his more usual pattern of sham, winning ill-got coin for his chicanery. The clearest indication of his fraudulence is the unambiguous assessment of Heman the Ezrahite at the close, and the fact that (only) in this instance, Hever whispers his closing poem of boast rather than flaunting it aloud.

In a study rich in discussion of realia and Hebrew poetry mirrored in this gate (Halevi's poems, the dangers of sea voyage, and amulets and conflicting attitudes thereto in Judaism), J. Dishon points out several purposive changes introduced by our author as he adapted his two sources, gate 23 of al-Hamadhani and gate 29 of al-Ḥariri, especially in the use of biblical citations linking the bogus potency of Hever and his cameos with divine power.[1]

Further buttressing Dishon's analysis, one can see a creative adaptation of al-Ḥariri's protagonist's frequent tauting of his religiosity: Abu Zayd cites the Koran, as he credits God with directing the ship; cites traditions concerning Allah and learning; cites the Koranic account of Noah; declares that he takes refuge with Allah; invokes God's blessing, citing the Koran; calls on Allah to be his witness; and in a second segment of the tale prostrates himself, praises Allah, and asks His forgiveness, prior to preparing a charm to aid in a difficult birth. In addition, the narrator says of the protagonist that 'he sighed with the sigh . . . of the fervent servants of Allah, the revered ones'.[2] Similarly, Heman declares his trust in God. Hever, through biblical citation, often alludes to God's power and promise; explicitly declares that his secret is beloved of the Creator; and closes, in his poem, by praising God—implicitly, for having granted him with enough intelligence to bilk the seafarers! Furthermore, the passengers, who had concluded that God has given of His intelligence to Hever, close with prayers to God.

Relatedly, Hever deftly swears not by God, but by the life of the secret

[1] Dishon, 'Travel by Sea'.

[2] *Assemblies*, tr. Steingass, ii. 95. 14–17, 25–32; 96. 9–22; 99. 10–13; and notes, pp. 234–8.

that he possesses. Now Hever possibly impresses his audience with his belief in the potency of his charms, and by avoiding taking an oath on God's name, in violation of the third commandment. At the same time, he avoids the danger (to himself) of taking such a false oath.

As ever, prefiguration and echoing figure in Alḥarizi's artistry. Wandering bears Heman upon its pinions; thereafter, the wind lifts and flings down the vessel he has boarded. Heman, crushed by wandering, is still and silent at the start; later an assured Hever is still and silent while his shipmates wail and scream in the face of the storm.[3]

[3] There is even the possibility that a framing theme in the Hebrew echoes a major episode in al-Ḥariri that Alḥarizi did not choose to incorporate. The Arabic author brings the vessel to an island where a pregnant woman is having a dangerous and difficult labour. The protagonist, asserting that he can deliver the baby through a potent charm, writes a poem (seen only by the narrator) calling on the infant to stay safe in the womb rather than enter a false world—and is credited with the ensuing successful delivery! And the gate closes with the narrator wishing that babe and mother had died, inasmuch as his well-rewarded friend decided to stay on the island (without him).

In the Hebrew, Alḥarizi introduces an early image of the (laden) ship as a woman crouching to give birth, not in al-Hamadhani or al-Ḥariri; and in the closing poem has Hever describe himself as suckling at wit's breast, again not in either Arabic source. Relatedly, at one point the anguish of the seafarers is conveyed in the phrase 'the people cried out with their hands on their loins'—being a clear citation of only one biblical text, Jer. 30: 6: 'Ask and see: Surely males do not bear young. Why then do I see every man with his hands on his loins like a woman in labour?'

Analysis of Gate Thirty-Nine

The Debate of Day and Night: Whose the Greater Might and Delight

THUS FAR THE READER of *Sefer Taḥkemoni* has encountered several debates and near debates: the boasting confrontations of the warrior poets (Gate 7); the argument of body and soul on whose is the responsibility for sin (13); the disputation of Karaite and Rabbanite (17) and pro- and anti-*piyut* spokesmen (24); and the disputation over which virtue should be regarded as supreme (19). As well one can recall the praise and dunning of wine by Hever in Gate 27; and, of course, the near debate of the descriptions of months (5). With Gate 39 begins a five-gate debate cluster: day–night (39), sword–pen (40), man–woman (41), generosity–stinginess (42), and sea–land (43). Four of these—day–night, sword–pen, man–woman, and sea–land—together with Gate 13 (body–soul) provide the clearest examples of the Arabic literary debate, a genre going back to the debate poem—known also as the disputation, precedence poem, *altercatio*, or *tenson*—of the ancient Near East.[1] The characteristic elements of the Arabic literary debate have been summarized as follows:

> . . . a text in prose, often rhymed or in poetry, in which two or more contestants, often objects or concepts, are represented as speaking in turn and proclaiming their own superiority and the inferiority of the other by means of praise and blame. Rhetorical persuasion may alternate or combine with logical argumentation, and quiet reasoning with violent vituperation. Additional optional elements include an introduction in which the situational context or the occasion for the dispute is given, and a conclusion in which a judgment is pronounced by an arbiter, who may be the author of the text or its dedicatee. The conflict may end either undecided, or with a clear victory of one of the contestants, or with a reconciliation.[2]

[1] The broadest overview of this topic is to be found in Reinink and Vanstiphout, *Dispute Poems*; see especially the introduction, 1–6, and the rich selective bibliography, which includes the classic pioneer study by Steinschneider, *Rangstreit-Literatur*. One school of thought, holding that the debate literature of the Arabs was an autochthonous creation, is that represented by Wagner, 'Die arabische Rangstreitdichtung'. A much more convincing view, asserting cultural continuities and circumstantial evidence when the lines of transmission to the Arabs are not always clear, is that laid out by van Gelder, 'The Conceit of Pen and Sword', 334–6; at p. 336 n. 25 earlier supporters of this position are listed.

[2] Van Gelder, 'The Conceit', 330.

But for the absence of an arbiter or judge, the confrontation of Gate 39 fits the above description perfectly. As well, it relates to another characteristic of at least some Arabic literary debates: the combatants are at once both antithetic and complementary—as belly and back, and winter and summer.[3] This trait goes back to Sumerian literature.[4]

A strong blend of argument and vituperation characterizes Alḥarizi's display here, along with a peculiar blurring of boundaries at the outset: Day's first claim to dominance is élitist: his whiteness, and his rival's blackness, indicate divine ordering of rank. In other words, a luminary cites, in justification of his claim, the given social order on earth, as perceived by Alḥarizi and the medieval world—when, in terms of the narrative, no such society had yet developed! This order is rooted in the biblical tale of the shaming of Noah by his grandson Canaan, son of Ham, progenitor of the black races.[5] Bizarrely enough, Day terms Night a descendant of Ham and himself a descendant of Shem, when, of course, both day and night were created before the heavenly bodies, let alone human beings!

The major ground of argument in this altercation is utilitarian: which combatant best pleases, or meets the needs, of humanity;[6] albeit the argument, already laced with insult, shifts wholly towards *ad hominem* attacks at the close.

Night cites the difficulties humanity has in working by day, and the relief and regeneration that night affords. Then, reverting to the issue of the inherent superiority of whiteness, he shows an example of black's superiority to white—the eye's pupil being superior to the white of the eye. Day adroitly seizes the last image advanced by his rival to turn the argument back to utilitarianism: the eye blackens (cannot see properly) at night, but shines by day, allowing men to do what they need to in order to advance their gains. Day then cites Night's inutility: it is appropriate for clandestine, and hence immoral, activity—thievery and whoring.

[3] Van Gelder, 'The Conceit', 333.

[4] H. Vanstiphout, 'Lore, Learning, and Levity in the Sumerian Disputations', in Reinink and Vanstiphout, *Dispute Poems and Dialogues*, 26–7; Yahalom, 'In the Circuit' (Heb.), 121–2.

[5] Gen. 9: 18–27. At this episode's conclusion Noah curses the descendants of Canaan son of Ham, proclaiming them the slaves of the descendants of Shem. On the genealogies of the sons of Noah—Japheth, Ham, and Shem—and the prominence accorded the Shemites, see Sarna (ed.), *The JPS Torah Commentary: Genesis*, 67–80, esp. 69.

[6] This trait, too, has ancient roots in the genre, as in the Sumerian debates of hoe and plough, and ewe and wheat: '. . . the pleasure and comfort people derive from hoe, their lowly but constant companion, is also an important subtheme . . . the overall general point of the debates is perhaps less the question which of the contenders is of more *use* to mankind than the question which of them is more *pleasing* or *comforting*' (Vanstiphout, 'Lore, Learning, and Levity', 31 n. 32).

In the ongoing play of turn and turnabout, Night points to a laudable community who require dark's cover, lovers: these deserving folk specifically are discomfited by Day's brightness. Day, eschewing comment on his rival's example, counters with a greater show of his own utility, the sun's vital powers that create food and vegetation.

It is at this point that Night, with no telling rebuttal to offer Day's last salient point, shifts ground, and the text moves full sail into the vituperation that has already played a significant role in the confrontation. A review of this facet of the gate is in order here.

From the outset, Day has proved the more aggressive, indeed insulting, of the disputants: contumely is not shared equally here—as it was, say, in Gate 4 (the flea–ant debate) and the first half of Gate 19 (the proponents of seven virtues). Initially described by Hever as overweening, Day promptly calls the Night his slave.[7] With the exception of Night's next mention of Day as an irredeemable slave (literally, 'he has been sold without redemption'), it is Day who spews *ad hominems*. Night's presumption, Day growls, reverses the very order of nature, making the lowly high and the reverse. Citing Job, Day curses Night: 'Barren be that night!' Following Night's (understandable) assertion that Day is the foe of clandestine lovers, Day (again citing Job) curses the day(!) he was born, in that worthless youngsters mock him and that insects attack the stars. Herein insult blends with irony: the stars are a component of the night sky!

As previously noted, it is at this point—following Day's vaunting the benefits of sunshine for agriculture—that utilitarian argument gives way wholly to personal insult. While the Hebrew word *shemesh* can be either masculine or feminine in the Bible, it is generally feminine—and so construed by Night: he identifies the paling and setting of the sun with the shamed and fearful withdrawal of a woman to her chambers, as the moon, a male monarch, ascends amid a glorious retinue of stars.[8] As we have seen already, Alḥarizi chooses *yare'aḥ* (masculine) rather than *levanah* (feminine) to denote the moon.

Day's final counterattack is variously climactic. He begins with the strongest invective thus far: Night is (literally) a 'shepherd of wind' and a 'steaming pot'.[9] Then, balancing Night's portrayal of the female sun in shamed and fearful flight, Day depicts the moon, at dawn, as a shamed—and, by implication, fearful—thief; and herein Day returns to his earlier claim that Night

[7] At the close, Night presents himself as vice-suzerain of Day, certainly no slave. To the degree that Day accedes, a compromise of sorts has been effected.

[8] The reader is recalled to the misogynistic tone of Gate 6.

[9] *ST* 310. 18, echoing Jer. 1: 13 and Hos. 12: 2.

is the time of thievery, but ups the ante: here the lord of the night is himself the thief. Moreover, by using the adjective *levanah*, 'white', to describe the pallor of the moon (*yare'aḥ*), Day adds injury to insult, inasmuch as another meaning of *levanah* is—as noted above—'moon'! All this complements the scientific argument advanced by Day, that the moon's light is no rival at all, being but the reflection of the sun.

Finally, the closing words of Day's attack, likening the embarrassment of the moon to that of a thief when caught, suggest that the persona of Night has been caught out in argument and has been ultimately shamed. In addition, the narrator's assertion, in the next paragraph, that Night's eye was opened echoes Day's earlier argument that men see better by day!

As is typical of *Sefer Taḥkemoni*, in this gate, too, the introductory section hints at what is to come. The contentiousness of the nobles of Rimon Perets prefigures the argumentation of Day and Night. The constituency of the gathering, 'lords of communities and sockets of praise',[10] prefigures the regal status of the debaters and their self-adulation. As well, Night's demise and Day's victory and combativeness are prefigured in the description of spring, the season when nights shrink and days increase, even as the two grow more presumptuous and prepare for battle.

Finally, the text evidences a subtler prefiguration in the realm of biblical citation: in his first speech, Night cites the book of Job three times; and twice in the course of his exchanges with Night, Day heatedly cites the book of Job to convey an attitude of holier-than-thou. In the introduction, Hever cites Job as he adopts a stance of the wiser-than-thou one who is a repository of ancient and privileged knowledge which 'wise men bore from their fathers and have not withheld' (Prov. 15: 18);[11] therein the Kenite (1) hints at his own preference for the argumentation of Day and (2) prefigures Day's supremacy in the debate.

[10] *ST* 308. 4–5. [11] *ST* 308. 7–8.

Analysis of Gate Forty

The Battle of Sword and Pen for Mastery of Men

BASED ON A LONG TRADITION of conflict between pen and sword in Arabic literature,[1] Gate 40's debate is skewed from the start to the side of the pen. The very opening, where Hever rebukes Heman for his impatience and for his display of temper (violence) against the pen, sets the moral of the tale in a nutshell: in the confrontation between pen and sword, the former must be favoured. As well, at the tale's close Alḥarizi sets in Heman's mouth the inscribing of Hever's words upon the heart with iron pen, that they might never part. Endurance and ultimate worth accrue not to violence but to the fruits of the spirit.

Several peculiarities characterize this narrative. The gate's drama begins as a somewhat puzzling quasi-allegory: all civilization is represented by the history of one kingdom, when logic would necessitate the mention of others, inasmuch as the monarch is confronted often by enemies. Beyond this, the opening claims of the two camps representing counsel/spirit versus valour/might are narrowly utilitarian: both the king's counsellors and the king's generals seek self-justification in the service of political power.

The gate is afforded no little irony and dramatic flair in the second, and more purely allegoric section, where pen and sword confront each other: each is described, partially, in terms appropriate to the other.[2] The very fact that the sword speaks at all sets him in one category with the pen, the very instrument of articulation. Conversely, the meeting of the two combatants, like bedouin warriors in an ancient battle ode—recalling the combat of Gate 7—sets both as practitioners of violence. As well, the pen, even while vaunting his attachment to spiritual values, even as he prides himself as a source of counsel and a mainstay of law, does not hesitate to use the metaphoric language of violent conflict, even to sword-wielding.[3]

[1] The excellent article of van Gelder, 'The Conceit of Pen and Sword', traces the motif of pen and sword, as representatives of civilization and brute force, in Arabic literature; and summarizes and examines in some detail a text penned by Aḥmad ibn Burd the Younger (d. 1053–4), with themes, structures, and characterizations closely resembling several in our gate. A detailed comparison of this text, and earlier ones, with Alḥarizi's remains a desideratum.

[2] This tactic recalls the complex thematic weavings of Gate 32.

[3] The linked potencies of sword and pen recall, as well, the Introduction, where the progeny of the fusion of the author and the Hebrew language—i.e. Hever the Kenite or *Sefer Taḥ-*

Throughout, the argument of the pen is by far the more varied and impressive. Against the monotonous boast of might and terror on the sword's part, and his denigration of his rival's puniness,[4] the pen lays claim to prophecy, wisdom, moral probity, and the creation of open and hidden communication. This last talent is of special significance, for that which the pen represents, literary creativity, is by implication the power that has given rise to this very conflict in this very tale. Finally, in emphasizing the relationship between literacy and righteous laws as the mortar of the realm, the pen contravenes the sword's claim that fear and raw might are the foundations of civilization.

As ever, our author has carefully stacked his deck. The sword could well have represented heroic defence against the invader, like Horatio at the gate. Relevant biblical episodes, of course, are not lacking, one such being that of Gideon and his small band, with their cry of 'The Lord's sword—and Gideon's!'[5] The pen, conversely, could have represented unjust laws, cunning, and slander. But this does not happen.

At most, our author gives the faintest hints at the less-than-moral side of the pen. Thus the pen at the close of his first statement says, literally, 'but for the scribe's pen . . . all allegories (*ḥidot*) and wise devisings (*mezimot*) would be lacking', another meaning of *mezimah* being 'evil devices'.[6] Relatedly, the scribes claim at the outset that the pen 'makes the simple wise'. In context, this refers to the civilizing effects of literacy and education; but it could hint at the practice of court poets who praised not-always-brilliant patrons as founts of wisdom.[7]

At the close the author lends more authority to the pen by ceding it the right to close the debate with metric verse, ever the crowning touch in argumentation throughout this work. Characteristically, Alḥarizi has constructed a frame tale that enriches his theme. Heman's behaviour towards the pen prefigures the verbal behaviour—threats and insults—of the sword. Another foreshadowing is provided by the narrator's 'My ear is pierced at your word's door', evoking the forceful boring through of a servant's ear as a sign of permanent slavery: thus, even as Alḥarizi sets out to show the superiority of the

kemoni as a whole—'rose up to lay siege to the fortresses of high counsels and conquer the keeps of wisdom with thoughts hewn of flames, sword-sharp; and utterances of polished lances, javelin wielders, etc.' (*ST* 11. 6–17).

[4] In variously presenting the pen as puny but powerful, Alḥarizi builds upon Arabic-Jewish tradition. See Levin, 'The Pen and the Cavalier' (Heb.), 143–73; and ibn Burd, as translated in van Gelder, 'The Conceit of Pen and Sword', 77: 'ugly face, sickly body, cut nib'.

[5] Judg. 7: 20.

[6] BDB 273.

[7] See Pagis, *Innovation and Tradition*, 26–41. Indeed, Alḥarizi himself in this work gushes praises for both hypothetical and specific leaders, in the Introduction and Gates 1, 8, and 50.

pen he metaphorizes a biblical citation drawn from the semantic field of the sword.

Finally, what wandering does to Hever at the start[8] and to Heman at the close is almost synonymous with the violence brought about by the sword. The narrator declares at the end, 'I dwelt many days with him to spend my days well, my years in pleasantness, until Time shot me with his shafts of parting and weaned me from the breasts of his friendship.'[9]

The intermixture of metaphors during this debate—articulate swords and cutting pens—seems to be more than a mere play of wit on Alḥarizi's part. The reader of *Sefer Taḥkemoni* knows full well that Hever, the figure most aligned with the brilliance of the pen as creator of literary triumphs, is by no means consistently aligned with law, order, rationality, ethics, and godliness. It would seem that the presentation of pen as conqueror-slayer and sword as metaphorizer, rhymer, rhetor, and debater reveal on a deeper level the ever-conflicting camps of roguery and morality, reason and anarchy, warring within the breast of Hever the Kenite—and, perhaps, his creator, Judah Alḥarizi.

[8] An as yet unnoticed influence in this particular episode is that of the fifth gate of the *Maqāmāt* of al-Hamadhani (tr. Prendergast, 38–40). In our tale, Hever, arriving at night unannounced, replies when asked, 'Who calls in the gloom, in the dark of night?', 'One strayed from the track and trembling mightily from want' (*ST* 312. 6–8); al-Iskandari, arriving in the same circumstance, describes himself (at greater length) as 'the defeated and hunted of hunger . . . in the leash of misfortune . . . who asks aid against hunger . . . an exile . . .' (tr. Prendergast, 39. 2–13). Like Hever, al-Iskandari is welcomed hospitably, although al-Hamadhani's hero announces at once that his declaration was false.

[9] *ST* 316. 25–6.

Analysis of Gate Forty-One

Badinage: Man and Woman Rage

IT WOULD SEEM that Gate 41 comes to counterweigh, albeit slightly, Gate 6, where a mercenary and lusting male figure, Hever the Kenite, hoodwinked into a marriage with an impoverished and foul-looking woman, damns his wife in his thoughts and to her face; and ends by beating her, probably to death. Here, in the cluster of debate gates, we have a back-and-forth tirade on which is the superior sex: each speaker heaps contumely on the opposing camp and no winner is declared.

If anything, the narrator seems to tilt the scales towards the woman, as he explicitly labels Hever the Kenite, at the close, as a consummate liar, and all his argumentation worthless. This conclusion is patently true of the man's contention that women were not obligated to fulfil divine commands because of their being's quintessential sensuality. The sages freed women of carrying out all time-linked commandments, such as prayer and ritual, because they saw women's home duties as child-rearers and caretakers being incompatible with such an obligation.[1] Moreover, some commandments do devolve upon women, among such being the lighting of the Sabbath candles before sunset, setting aside a portion of dough used in food preparation, and, of course, many procedures and restrictions relating to conjugal relations.[2] Beyond these distortions, and even prior to Heman's assessment, the male debater is seen as undercutting his own position; a self-professed member of the chosen gender charged with God to keep His commandments, and source of prophets and saints, he fouls his mouth with invective.

Nonetheless, closer reading reveals a different balance. The opening argument is the man's, setting the tone and focus of the debate; and his is the last word in more ways than one: he produces a rejoinder to one of the woman's best arguments (that women prophesied, too), and to this rejoinder the woman is silent. As well, he alone produces a closing poem, ever an indication in this book of rhetorical potency; and, more often than not, comprising the identifying signature of Hever the Kenite.[3] Hence Alḥarizi has struc-

[1] With a few specific exceptions, women are freed of carrying out any time-fixed religious obligations, including prayer and synagogue ritual. See, in *EJ* x. 1566, the discussion of Mishnah, *Kid.* 1: 7 and BT *Kid.* 34*a*–36*a*.

[2] Ibid.

[3] A further and subtle strengthening of Hever's last statement lies in his citing a biblical verse following directly upon that cited by the woman earlier—what may be called a 'split citation'.

tured the work to afford the male figure a very important element of that supremacy which he has claimed all along. More importantly, Hever comes across as the stronger debater: he offers more rejoinders to the woman than she to him, and that more promptly. Two of his claims are contested by the woman: that woman is inferior, being created of man's rib; and that only men prophesied. Other claims she simply ignores—such as that man, specifically, was given command over all earth's creatures. Now, she could have readily punctured that claim by citing Genesis 1: 28: 'God blessed them and God said to them [i.e. man and woman both!], "Be fertile and increase, fill the earth and master it; and rule the fish of the sea, the birds of the sky, and all the living things that creep on earth."' But she does not.

Again, she never counters Hever's false claim that (1) women are obligated by no commandments whatever (2) because they are gross and lustful. Tradition is quite clear that women are freed from almost all time-indicated commandments (especially prayer)—not for any flaw in women's nature, but because these were viewed as incompatible with women's perceived roles as homekeepers, child-bearers, and child-raisers.

When the man taunts her that female prophecy arose when Israel was rife with sin—a debater's invention!—the woman could have asked wherein male prophecy differed a whit on that account. When the man boasts that women were formed of man's flesh, the better to let her know that she was designed to serve him, how easily she could have replied that this servitude was the result of the apple-eating episode in Eden and no part of the original divine plan. To the contrary, biblical narrative draws quite a different moral from the progeniture of woman: 'Hence a man leaves his father and his mother and clings to his wife, so that they become one flesh' (Gen. 2: 24). Contrary to Hever's disgust with desire, Scripture elevates it!

The woman is to be faulted for yet other debater's omissions. She does not cite the famous biblical paean, Proverbs' 'Woman of Valour',[4] and never mentions that the very first divine commandment in Scripture is procreation—and that in the context of mutual rule over all living creatures: 'God blessed them and said to them, "Be fertile and increase, fill the earth and master it; and rule the fish of the sea, the birds of the sky, and all the living things that creep upon the earth"' (Gen. 1: 28).

In the Hebrew, the woman declares, 'May He who is terrible in deed (Ps. 66: 5) cut off a pretentious tongue'; Hever, in his closing poem, speaks of the prophets 'who turned the sea to dry land', citing Ps. 66: 6.

[4] Prov. 31: 10–31. That Alḥarizi was very conscious of the potency of this poem is evident from his deft usages thereof in Gates 4 (in describing the altruistic and hard-working ant) and 19 (in linking this portraiture with the virtue of largesse).

Beyond these failings, the woman mirrors and even outdoes the man in splenetic outbursts and foul language; and that in clear contrast with this debate's closest model in al-Ḥariri's gate 40, where the man's viciousness and vulgarity exceed the woman's by far.[5]

The discerning reader, then, can see that Alḥarizi has given Hever the upper hand here by miscitation and misrepresentation—and by his opponent's inferior debating skills (her best retort is her accurate, but unsubstantiated, assertion that her rival is a liar); and can guess that this skewed imbalance, rife with denigration of female sexuality and man's attraction to woman, is the product of the author's anti-female bias.[6]

[5] A detailed comparison of this gate with the Arabic model is to be found in Maree, 'The Influence', 114–32, with a diagrammatic comparison of the structure of both gates on pp. 126–7.

[6] On an anti-female animus in medieval literature, generally, and medieval Hebrew literature and *Sefer Taḥkemoni*, in particular, see the Analysis of Gate 6, above, and especially n. 12.

Analysis of Gate Forty-Two

Generosity or Greed—Which the Better Creed or Deed?

ONE WOULD THINK that Alḥarizi would have thus far plumbed adequately his beloved theme of generosity versus niggardliness. Five gates have dealt with this topic centrally. Gate 8, with its reversible letter of praise, focuses heavily on the virtue of largesse. In Gate 11, where the Kenite is challenged first to make a statement where every word exhibits a given letter, then a second statement where every word lacks that letter, he focuses heavily on liberality, producing cliché-ridden praises of prince-patrons. Gate 12 limns the history of Stint's usurpation of rule over the Jewish people. In Gate 19 Hever taunts generosity for its ability to convert the foulest miscreant into an honoured leader of the community. In Gate 29, father and son strive to open the hard hearts and closed fists of a fur-wrapped audience on a bitter, wintry day.

In several other gates Alḥarizi has at least touched upon the virtues of liberality and vileness of greed. In Gate 3, the old glutton at the feast's start, later to be revealed as Hever the Kenite, is faulted by the shocked guests for the greedy eater he has shown himself to be. In Gate 4, where the virtues of ant and flea are compared, the ant is the giving altruist and the flea the quintessence of greediness. In Gate 6, outraged over the meagreness of his bride's dowry, Hever cruelly abuses her. In Gate 10, part of the rooster's claim to gratitude and honour is his announced liberality in offering his children's flesh to all and sundry(!). In Gate 23, Hever rises to fame and fortune by penning a special poem and letter to a bereaved prince, thereby gaining the prince's liberality. In Gate 24 the Kenite makes his way to the synagogue in hopes of mulcting profit from those in attendance.

And there are yet more gates to come wherein this theme will be dealt with. In Gate 46, recording Hever's (Alḥarizi's) travels, special animus is reserved for those individuals and communities who proved tight-fisted before the author's need, and the reverse. Finally, some of the juiciest titbits of verse in the potpourri that is Gate 50 revolve about stint.

Nonetheless, our author has worked in yet another variant on his favourite theme, boldly putting his matchless rhetor's talents to use in order to malign—liberality! This gate also differs in having the Kenite bested, the only such episode in the book, with the exception of his losses in Gates 6 (the marriage) and 22 (the stargazer); albeit the author 'gets off the hook' by having the Kenite assert that he well could have put the youth down as an exercise in debating but deliberately did not do so, out of veneration for the virtue the latter was defending! Finally, the Kenite has neither sought out nor attained reward for his verbal pyrotechnics, a rare tactic in *Sefer Taḥkemoni*.

In some of these special emphases and techniques our author owed a patent debt to his Arab predecessors, whom he imitates and vies with. In gate 41 of al-Hamadhani's compendium al-Iskandari preaches, upon request, against both generosity and greed.[1] In al-Ḥariri's gate 43, Abu Zayd reports being bested and confounded by a young rhetor/sage offering him contradictory advice on the benefits of marriage versus celibacy.[2]

There is a great deal of tit-for-tat, of close polemic, and of echoing argumentation in this gate. The game of point-counterpoint even extends to the realm of biblical citation: both speakers quote Proverbs and Job. Both progress from the materialistic benefits or losses of liberality to the more internal/spiritual benefits and gains. Both use the motifs of warfare and suppression.

Both men speak of generosity as a woman: the youth, as a mistress and protector, and as the fairest woman of the world; Hever, as the personification of destruction, bringing men low.[3] Both present generosity as a powerful entity: the youth portrays her as armed with might; Hever, as one who brings low the high and noble, and empties hands.

In terms of structure this gate evidences an unusual foreshadowing. First, there is Heman's characterization of the group he has joined as both wise and generous: this point he develops metaphorically as they lavish their wisdom and rhetoric on one another. Then an unannounced guest outdoes them all in his wisdom, poetry, and magnanimity: he showers them with his knowledge and rhetorical ability, treats his audience to a lavish meal and precious gifts,[4] and then departs. This very shared experience sparks the major confrontation of the gate. The group's reaction to the liberality of the stranger prefigures their reception of the message of the youth, and their judging him the victor in the debate.

A mystery remains at the close: who was the giving stranger? The author might have intended him as nothing more than a slightly sketched character to fulfil the role of poet-Maecenas. Yet who, might we ask, could be worthy of such praise as is tendered by Heman here, who hails the visitor for unparalleled wisdom and rhetoric; and in this regard, it will be recalled that

[1] This is the 'Maqāma of Advice', *Maqāmāt*, tr. Prendergast, 153–5.

[2] Steingass, *The Assemblies*, ii. 119–32.

[3] *ST* 326. 22–5; 327. 8–10.

[4] Alternatively, the repast could be interpreted metaphorically, and would thus refer to the verbal gifts.

neither the old man nor the youth is credited with having surpassed him. It is quite plausible that here, as in several other gates, the author has allowed himself the sport of intruding into a story of his own making—a cameo role *à la* Alfred Hitchcock, if you will.

If this be the case, we have been presented with yet another irony in this work: for once Alḥarizi, so markedly the complainer (openly or through the persona of Hever) at not having got enough support hither and yon, is the endower of an exemplary company. As well, he here hints at the greater largesse that is his to give: the cornucopia of *Sefer Taḥkemoni* itself.

Analysis of Gate Forty-Three

The Sea Roars its Worth against Proud Earth

THIS CHAPTER can be categorized variously. Seen in the context of a smaller grouping, it belongs with the gates of debate-confrontation, those chapters wherein we witness not only opposition in debate, as in Gate 27 (where the selfsame character opposes the virtues and errors of drinking) or in Gate 42 (where two characters debate the merits of generosity and stinginess), but where the subjects of the debate are themselves the debaters. These gates are 39 (day and night), 40 (pen and sword), 41 (man and woman), and 43 (sea and land)—all, as noted heretofore, standing in the long tradition of the precedence poem, or *tenson*, going back to Sumer.[1]

No two confrontations run precisely the same course. This is especially true of the debates' outcomes. In Gate 39, night accedes to day. While no conclusion is reached explicitly in Gate 40, the frame of the tale, where Hever admonishes Heman to respect the pen for its many virtues, makes it clear—together with other indications—whose the supremacy is. In Gate 41, the debate between man and woman, though the former's argument is riddled with duplicity, the author goes out of his way to give him the edge. Here, in the debate between sea and land, a standoff is reached.

In two gates—here and in 40 (pen and sword)—we have a conflation of two elements: confrontation on the grounds of raw strength and claims of superiority in the moral sphere. Here the sea is presented at the outset as overbearing and contemptuous, and its bullying personality, much like the sword's, remains constant throughout the tale. The sea threatens to smash the earth to smithereens and flood it; earth makes no similar counter-threat. Perhaps it is at this point that the author hints at his disdain for violence: from the lips of the land we hear that it is precisely butchery and violence that characterize the sea.

Time boundaries are blurred in this tale. The story begins at the moment of creation. In short order, however, we find ourselves in another time-frame—the revelation at Sinai; and the redemption of the Israelites is past history, as the sea claims credit for having rescued the Jews of the Exodus![2] More-

[1] See the outset of the Analysis of Gate 39, especially nn. 1–6.

[2] Even prior thereto, the earth speaks of kings raising fortresses and banners upon its plains and mountains.

over, prior and following claims concerning the terrors and deaths inflicted by the ocean upon seafarers presuppose the rise of civilization.[3]

To complicate matters further, by the tale's end the elders of both camps make peace between the feuding parties—making the two figures tribal leaders at a *ṣulḥ*, or bedouin ceremony of reconciliation!

In the sphere of morality, the edge in argumentation is clearly the earth's. While both speakers seem vexed and prideful, the land seems by far to be more justified therein. Repeatedly earth accuses the sea of cruelty and havoc, a charge that the sea, for the larger part of the gate, takes no pains to rebut. To the contrary, the sea is proud of its might and threatens repeatedly to use the same to efface its rival earth—even as it boasts of its power to wreck vessels and, by implication, their passengers. Towards the end of the disputation, the sea briefly defends his name on moral grounds, emphasizing the role of the Red Sea waters in rescuing the Israelites, and the sea's role, generally, in bringing sinners to penitence through fear; but this is too little and too late to put down the earth's attack.

So while the outcome of this controversy is ostensibly a draw, reader sympathy has been steadily drawn from the violent persona of the sea to his rival, earth. With all this said, one cannot but notice that, in a subtle prefiguration, Hever the Kenite is linked by Heman with the more violent of the contenders: 'his words were a hammer, *shattering rock*' (Jer. 23: 29)!

[3] This blurring of boundaries relates to the larger question of blurred boundaries (between reality and fiction) in *Sefer Taḥkemoni*. See the Analyses of the Introduction and Gate 1, and the Afterword.

Analysis of Gate Forty-Four

Life's Laws: Proverbs and Saws

THE READER will recall Gate 36, an exemplum of *adab*—moralistic, often epigrammatic writing—and question-and-answer-play, where Hever the Kenite fields a bevy of queries on varied topics. There, while propounding dicta of a traditional nature—including the validation of silence, noble reputation, and humility—the protagonist's actual practice is, on several points, the opposite of what he preaches. Here, although it is Hever's students who speak, the dynamic is markedly similar.

In this gate, Alḥarizi has drawn liberally from Arabic *adab*: thus far thirteen of the fifty sayings have been linked with specific sources.[1] Stylistically, Gate 44, like all other gates of *Sefer Taḥkemoni*, shows the characteristic hallmark of root inclusion. The wise students surrounding the flashing-eyed teacher are *ḥamudim*, 'delightful'; at the close, Heman declares that Hever is 'the crown of learning, who gathers together all delights—*haḥamudot*'. Relatedly, Hever asks each of his students to come forward with an adage that is *neḥmad*, 'delightful'.[2]

The gate evidences, in its frame, a thematic contrast: Heman the Ezrahite takes pains to emphasize the piety and modesty of the old preacher/teacher at the start; indeed, the metaphor of the old man's wearing a veil of piety evokes the veil that Moses wore to contain the brilliant radiance of his face from the encounter with divinity (Exod. 34: 33–5). This initial characterization is turned on its head at the close, when one of the preacher's students is asked by the narrator to disclose the elderly teacher's identity: the preacher himself intrudes to boast of his accomplishments in stichs designed to make a mockery of Heman's initial description.

The very fact of intrusion shows how eager Hever is to boast: he well could have let his student make reply; and in stating that were he to keep silent, his deeds would attest to splendour's having called him by name—he speaks very much with tongue in cheek, inasmuch as in speaking he chooses *not* to keep silent; and that, when he earlier praised that very virtue and condemned loquaciousness.

That we have here a very purposive framing on the author's part cannot

---

[1] Ratzaby, 'On the Sources of *Sefer Taḥkemoni*'.

[2] The translation uses the word 'sweet' at these junctures, or close by, to capture the inclusion.

be in doubt: at the close of many gates in *Sefer Taḥkemoni* the Kenite presents himself and his mission quite variously. There is nothing to have prevented him from emphasizing his role as a mentor, especially since the wisdom presented in this gate is that of his students; only indirectly, if at all, can he be credited.

Furthermore, the Kenite's boast stands in sharp contradiction to more than one utterance of his pupils, especially that lauding restraint: 'He who practises restraint knocks at the gates of salvation'![3] Indeed in one sense the Kenite's intemperate brag provides a negative illustration of the very first maxim offered: 'A man gains prestige or is denigrated in the hour of trial and test':[4] having just given unqualified praise to his students, the teacher will not allow one of them to reveal their master's name, but must himself butt in, adding what was not asked for—self-praise!

In this light, the enthusiasm of Heman the Ezrahite, and his specific utterance, hardly do him credit. The praise of the Kenite as master of every area of learning is exaggerated on the basis of what has just happened: the students have come forward with arresting saws, not the teacher; and the Kenite is hardly *osef kol haḥamudot*, 'the amalgam of all that is delightful',[5] when such an amalgam should include the very modesty that he lauded at the outset!

The unwary reader is in danger of being hoodwinked. As the book approaches its finish, Alḥarizi once more has the main protagonist present himself as a spokesman for virtue and wisdom, in general; and here, specifically, for modesty, restraint, and spare speech. For his display he wins praise, even as his behaviour puts him at a clear remove from the very virtues he espouses.

[3] *ST* 335. 23.

[4] *ST* 334. 16.

[5] *ST* 337. 25—alternatively, 'the gatherer'.

Analysis of Gate Forty-Five

Hid Learning: Saws of Men of Discerning

ALḤARIZI'S DEBT to Arabic moralistic writing is large, and even more evident here than in the case of the preceding gate. Of the twenty-six anecdotes, fourteen have been linked to specific sources.[1] As in that corpus of writing, here one finds a free and easy relationship between rhymed and unrhymed matter.

If the frame tale in this gate is rather spare, it yet has a modest role to play: almost every one of the twenty-six episodes is prefigured thematically, at times by a specific root that will repeat.

The overriding theme, appearing in nearly half the anecdotes, is that of recompense—whether of God toward the righteous and miscreants, or of rulers to incautious subjects; at the start, Hever proclaims his obligation to recompense his friend for his hospitality.[2]

Similarly, the theme of debt/obligation prefigures several episodes. Hever's determination to be giving prefigures magnanimous behaviour asked of God, or given by Him; or shown by a monarch.[3] God, cited as the Creator in the introduction to the gate, figures in several episodes, and is called the Creator in the eighth. The banqueting of Hever and Heman prefigure four anecdotes: the anger of the prisoner to be flayed ('Do you invite me to a banquet?'); obliquely, the anecdote of moderate drinking; mention of the old man who falls asleep after his meals; and the gluttony of the miser in the next to the last episode.

[1] Ratzaby, 'On the Sources of *Sefer Taḥkemoni*'. For a collection of anecdotes similar in tone and scope—including some brief questions and answers like those in the gate preceding—see the parables of the elderly host in *The Book of Delight by Joseph ben Meir Zabara*, tr. M. Hadas (New York, 1932), 101–10. Another similar corpus, with 216 adages and tales, many including metric verse, was apparently penned by Alḥarizi: *Peninei hamelitsot* ('Adage Gems'), ed. H. Y. Gurland in *Ginzei yisra'el besaint petersburg*, iv (St Petersburg, 1865). I. Reifmann, in his introduction to this edition, and an addendum (pp. 35 ff.), shows that forty-six of the two hundred anecdotes and tales are identical with items in Gates 45 and 50 of *Sefer Taḥkemoni* (S–F, *History*, ii. 170–1 and n. 96).

[2] There is yet another subtle prefiguration in the original: Heman's board is *arukh*, 'set'; and the account in the world to come is *arukh*, 'set'.

[3] The linkage is pronounced between the introduction to the gate and anecdote 12. Hever declares, *ki ḥasdekha gadol alai*, 'because your kindliness toward me is great'; and a sage tells a grieving king, *vehamavet higdil aleinu ḥasdo*, 'and death has acted with great kindness towards us' (*ST* 338. 10–11; 341. 8–9).

This last-noted linkage is pronounced for two reasons. By dint of biblical allusion the reader can sense that Hever is being gluttonous (recalling Gate 3)—a behaviour at odds with the moralistic bent of his twenty-six apophthegms; and by its placement, the castigation of the miser almost forms a motif envelope of the gate—to add to the verbal inclusion of 'thoughts' and Heman's holding fast to Hever.

Nor does this wholly describe the bracketing phenomenon operative here. A look at the ending shows that the central figures in the last four episodes are deficient, comical, or evil: the old man ever hungry, dozing, with his sexual functioning gone awry except when he is asleep (anecdote 23); the dunned, womanizing, gluttonous miserly prince (24); another tight-fisted, rapacious miser (25); and a coward and braggart (26). Now Hever, at the start, is seen as an inordinate eater; moreover, his voracity is conveyed, in the Hebrew, in language lifted from Deuteronomy, the description of a dissolute Jewish nation: 'When I bring them into the land flowing with milk and honey that I promised on oath to their fathers, and they eat their fill and grow fat and turn to other gods and serve them, spurning Me . . .' (Deut. 31: 20–1).

Finally, in anecdote 3 a pious man rejects others' praise; in anecdote 26, two braggarts vie in self-praise. Another contrary kind of bracketing—overall, rather than within the body of the twenty-six apophthegms—is the presentation of Heman at the outset as the ideal and generous host, as opposed to the skinflints lambasted in anecdotes 24 and 25.

Analysis of Gate Forty-Six

Of This and That Community Sung with Impunity

ALḤARIZI'S DESCRIPTION of Spain at this gate's outset is of special interest both for what it does, and does not, incorporate. In his enthusiastic outpourings over the physical beauty of his country, its pure air, sunshine, fragrance, star-like gardens, and its incomparable splendour, he echoes a significant native Arabic tradition of praise of al-Andalus as well as specific cities therein. This is also evident in his reference to Spain as 'the rose of Sharon, the lily of the valley', an exact citing of the description of the beloved in the Song of Songs (2: 1); and by citing desire as his motivation for seeing the land, he parallels sentiments such as those of the Castilian poet ibn Daraji: 'Bow your head and prostrate yourself before Cordova for me, even as I would press her to my body and my chest.'[1] In this instance, Hever—whose birthplace, of course, is Elon Zaananim—surely speaks for the author, recalling the prefatory poem, where Spain is presented as Alḥarizi's birthplace; and again, if in veiled fashion, in Gate 20, where Heman the Ezrahite points to Spain as his native land. This 'patriotic cluster' stands against Gate 28, where the true home of the Jews has been presented as Jerusalem—and it is in that gate that two other major themes that figure in Andalusian poems of cities are found: longing for home from exile and lament over the city's destruction.[2] This deeper 'patriotism' will figure in Gate 50 as well.

Alḥarizi was one of a number of medieval Jewish writers to have rendered accounts of their travels. First, and perhaps most famous, is Benjamin of Tudela (second half of the twelfth century), whose journeying led to his *Sefer hamasa'ot* ('The Book of Travels'):

> There is no general account of the Mediterranean world or of the Middle East in this period which approaches that of Benjamin of Tudela in importance, whether for Jewish or for general history. . . . He tells who stood at the head of Jewish communities, and who were the most notable scholars. He gives the number of Jews he found in each place . . . He notes economic conditions . . . He was deeply interested in Jewish scholarship, and his account of intellectual life in Provence and Baghdad

[1] Al-Maqqari, *Nafḥ aṭ-ṭīb*, ed. Aḥsan 'Abbas, i. 139, cited in Doron, 'Cities in the Hebrew Poetry of Spain' (Heb.).

[2] Doron, 'Cities in the Hebrew Poetry of Spain', 69–78.

is of singular importance, as is his characterization of the organization of synagogal life in Egypt . . . The importance of the work can be gauged from the fact that it has been translated into almost every language of Europe, and is used as a primary source-book by all medieval historians.[3]

Alḥarizi's travelogue, while doubtless of significance to students of history, is far less factually reliable.[4] The tone and thrust of the account is set by Heman's questions—which communities were distinguished on grounds of morality and piety, and which not. Hever here fills the dual role of laudator-castigator, a talent of which he boasts elsewhere and which, in general, had been vaunted by his predecessors—court poets and others who were lavish in praise of patrons or scholars, or conversely showered abuse on any who slighted them, especially by denying support.[5]

Here Alḥarizi has six main foci. In praise, he centres on largesse, scholarship, and moral probity—the first and third being inextricably bound in his mind, especially where his needs were concerned. In denigration, he centres on tightfistedness and immorality (again, often twinned), the latter at times extending to homosexuality as well as irreligious cultic practice; and on stupidity—especially that of dimwit poetasters. Indeed Alḥarizi seems at his most enthusiastic and sincere, with no question as to authorial intent, when lacing into hypocrites, tightwads, and dullards—although in the absence of external evidence one cannot know how truly lacking in talent, integrity, or even generosity, were the objects of his scorn.

The translator refrains from analytic comment on the body of this gate, letting the stinging attacks of the author speak for themselves. The elucidation of historical data touched upon in this travel account will be left to historians.[6] The reader is also referred to the translation into Hebrew of the greater portion of Alḥarizi's Arabic-language *maqāma* written later and reporting this very same journey, his only Arabic *maqāma* that we possess;

[3] *EJ* iv. 537. Other literary travellers include Pethahiah of Regensburg and Jacob ben Netanel, who focused mainly on holy places and tombs. See the discussion of Gate 35, and *EJ* xv. 1351 ff. For observations on these and other medieval travellers to Jewish communities of the east, see Gil, *In the Kingdom of Ishmael*, 'Index of Persons, Peoples, Factions, and Cults', iv. 821 ff.

[4] What the determining factor in Alḥarizi's travels was we may never know. Certainly his quest for patrons bore fruit; and we do know that peregrination in search of learning and experience is well attested in Arabic and medieval Jewish civilization, both as an ideal and a reality. In this regard the reader is directed to Gate 26, with its discussion of the advantages of travel, and the Analysis.

[5] On the poet as laudator or castigator, see Analysis 8, esp. n. 5.

[6] See, in this regard, 'The Trip to the East: *Sefer Taḥkemoni* as a Biographical Source' and 'Stations on the Great Journey' (Heb.) in S–F, *History*, ii. 153–68, 171 n. 101. Among other topics discussed is the very difficult question as to which cities cited in *Sefer Taḥkemoni* were the scenes of actual events recorded in the book.

therein the author, if still focusing largely on benefactors and niggards, and lavishing even more metric verse on the former than here, provides an essentially realistic discussion that touches upon political and social realia.[7] In general fashion the reader is referred to the *Encyclopaedia Judaica* for detailed discussions of medieval Jewish communities in the lands and cities cited in this chapter.[8] A few specific entries relating to prominent known persons or locales mentioned by Alḥarizi have been cited in the notes to the text.[9]

[7] Ratzaby, 'An Arabic *Maqāma*' (Heb.), pointing out that the Arabic record is far richer in portraitures of individuals, and that in poems or even single metric stichs; and also touches upon significant events, including a four-year conflict between the Jews and Christians of Fustat and Cairo (p. 10). Ratzaby also posits the order of the actual journey, country by country—Egypt, the Land of Israel, Syria, and Iraq—and city by city (10–11). Notes 2–7 record earlier studies on this Arabic *maqāma*, including Stern, 'A New Description' (Heb.), and id., 'Rabbi Judah Alḥarizi in Praise of Maimonides'. Alḥarizi's praise of Maimonides is substantially larger in his Arabic text, where he cites specific contemporary rabbinic luminaries who praise Maimonides effusively; and he puts Maimonides in the rare category of Ezra the Scribe and Sa'adiah Gaon as singular leaders of world Jewry, near prophets who rescued their brethren from ignorance and folly. On the relation of Alḥarizi to Maimonides, see also Analysis 50. Yet another account of this journey was composed by Alḥarizi in Hebrew, paralleling in large measure that of the Arabic and this gate—presented in Stern, 'An Unpublished Maqama by al-Harizi'.

[8] On the Jewish communities of Baghdad, Mosul, Irbil, Haran, Calneh/al-Raqqa, Hamath, Damascus, Fustat, and No-Amon/Alexandria see Analysis 12 and n. 5 there. On other centres the following may be said: Tavekh or Tokh, meaning literally 'within' or 'middle', refers to Wasit, which lies midway between Baghdad and Basra (see Schirmann, *Hebrew Poetry*, ii. 99; S. Stern, 'A New Description', 147; and Gil, *In the Kingdom of Ishmael*, i. 494–6, incl. n. 286); Serug refers to Sürüç, located south of al-Raqqa and north-west of Haran; the city is mentioned in Gen. 11: 20 (Sarna, *The JPS Torah Commentary: Genesis*, 85; and see Gil, *Kingdom*, i. 515–16 and n. 296).

[9] A little more information on some personages is to be obtained in Gil, *In the Kingdom of Ishmael*: i. 436–7 and n. 255, on the exilarch David, resident in Mosul; 465–6 and n. 275 on Joseph ben Shever, (alleged) miser of Baghdad. For recently discovered and highly credible biographical information on Alḥarizi's date of birth, last years, the record of his death in Aleppo in 1225, and encounters during his journey to the East, see Sadan, 'Rabbi Judah Alḥarizi as a Cultural Crossroads': pointing out the high regard in which our author was held for his Arabic poetry (!), and evidence of growing appreciation and support in Irbil and Aleppo, Sadan raises the possibility that Alḥarizi remained in the East permanently—despite his 'patriotic fervour' for Spain at the outset of this gate.

Analysis of Gate Forty-Seven

Nation Contends with Nation for Rank and Station

In the present gate Alḥarizi has adapted a popular genre in Arabic literature, that of boasting debate between cities or lands.[1] Here the basis of comparison is varied, albeit the dominant motifs are clear: rule, splendour, godly presence, might, and fame; they are summarized in the table at the end of this analysis.

There are other claims to fame as well: Zova and Baghdad vaunt their wise men, and three sites attach holy history to themselves: Egypt, locus of the miraculous redemption of the Israelites; Acre, where Elijah contended with the prophets of Baal; and Jerusalem, home of prophecy (overlapping with the capital's being home to the divine presence). Neither Spain nor any of its cities is mentioned. While this hardly accords with the high praise given Spain in the preceding gate, it is perhaps understandable in light of the overall pull in *Sefer Taḥkemoni* between Spain and Jerusalem as homelands of the author.[2]

What is more than curious is the lack of a designated, even clear-cut, winner in this seven-sided competition—even if several are praised in all major categories.[3] Nonetheless, the text does seem to point to the worthy victor—Jerusalem, variously depicted as the most singular contestant.

If other sites boast rule, it is unique Davidic rule that is alluded to in the

[1] On the Arabic genre of praise of locales, and debates over which deserves pre-eminence (*faḍā'il*), see *EI* ii. 728–9; and Livneh-Kafri, 'On the Antiquity'. See also Sivan, 'The Beginnings', and Hasson, 'The Literature of Praise of Jerusalem in Islam' (Heb.)—both cited in Sadan, 'A Legal Opinion', 232 n. 1. Specific locales mentioned in this gate were subjects of praise compilations in Arabic literature, one such being Damascus (n. 4, Livneh-Kafri). Maree, 'The Influence', 200 n. 20, mentions a long discussion on this subject in al-Makri, *Nafḥ aṭ-ṭīb*, 125–228. An in-depth comparison of this gate with Arabic literature of praise of cities, including the cities boasting and vying between themselves, remains a desideratum. Schirmann posits that a satiric thrust might underly this gate, citing the mixed assessments of the Jewish communities of cities in Gate 46 and one poem in the addenda to Gate 50, in which the Jewries of these same cities are excoriated for ignorance, grossness, and stinginess (S–F, *History*, ii. 162–3 and n. 62).

[2] See Analyses 28 and 46.

[3] See the Table of Places and Properties at the close of this analysis. In two other gates we find seven contenders: Gate 19, where seven proponents of different virtues vie but are overshadowed by Hever, cynical spokesman for largesse; and Gate 16, where Hever awards the laurel to all seven of his poet-pupils. The number seven figures also in Gate 21, with its seven muses.

case of Jerusalem. Israel's holy capital makes no attempt to contend seriously with the others—particularly Damascus—on the grounds of beauty; rather, she vaunts the presence of God and angels.

Other contestants implicitly acknowledge the special status of the Jewish city: Acre, by boasting a facet of Jerusalem's advantage, prophetic history—that of Elijah's confrontation with the prophets of Baal; Egypt, by making her first claim to fame 'beauty like Jerusalem's'.

There are further signs of the gate's pro-Jerusalem bias. In the last line of the Hebrew text, Heman says to Hever, 'May God spread over you His canopy of peace'—a clear echo of the close of the Sabbath evening prayer *Hashkivenu*, coming shortly before the Amidah: 'and spread over us Your canopy of peace. Blessed are You, O Lord, who spreads a canopy of peace over us and over all His people Israel, and over Jerusalem'. In addition, we must note the very opening words of this gate, citing Song of Songs 2: 12, 'the voice of the turtledove is heard in our land', an indirect allusion to the land of Israel.

There is yet another hint of the overriding importance of Jerusalem, conveyed through subtle prefiguration. The awakening of Hever is described thusly in the Hebrew text: *veka'asher karavti elav venitsavti alav hekits vehu ḥared mitenumato*, 'now when I drew near him and stood over him, he awoke from his sleep very frightened'[4]—an evocation of the divine revelation afforded Jacob at Bethel: 'And behold the Lord was standing over him (*nitsav alav*—or, standing atop *it*, i.e. the ladder) . . . and Jacob awoke (*vayikats*) from his sleep . . . and he was afraid' (Gen. 28: 13, 16, 18).

The site of this revelation, Luz/Bethel in Scripture, was identified with Jerusalem in rabbinic exegesis and, thereafter, in the commentary of Rashi (1040–1105).[5] The revelation motif in Gate 47 is augmented by the immediate response of Heman, *Shalom lekha al tira*, 'Peace be unto you, fear not'[6]—a citing of yet another divine revelation, that of the angel to Gideon on the threshing-floor (Judg. 6: 23). Of course, the fact of biblical citation does not gainsay a light touch here: it is no divine revelation that awaits Hever, but the discovery of his friend Heman.

Now all this having been said, one cannot but notice in our text a subtle and opposite bias, one favouring Baghdad.

At the start of his declamation, Hever says that the 'fair lands/*hamedinot ha'adinot* contended'; Adinah is a Hebrew name for Babylon, which here denotes Baghdad. That land begins her boast by using Adinah as a rhyming word: *ani adinah pe'er kol medinah*, 'I am fair/*adinah*, glory of every nation';

[4] *ST* 367. 11–12. [5] Tr. Rosenbaum and Silbermann, i. 131–4. [6] *ST* 367. 13.

Table of places and properties

Site	Rule	Splendour	God's presence	Might	Fame	Other
No-Amon	•	•	•	•	•	Sea
Fustat		•		•		Jewish history/ miracles
Jerusalem	•(David)	•	•	•		Jewish history/ prophecy
Acre		•		•(holy)		Prophet Elijah
Damascus	•	•	•	•	•	Gardens
Aleppo	•	•	•	•		Wise men
Ashur	•	•	•	•	•	Envied
Baghdad	•	•		•	•	Wise men

and this same rhyme and statement opens Baghdad's poem: 'I am the crown of time, the land of Adinah and my soil is the glory of every nation/*medinah*.' Moreover, the third and closing stich of this poem ends with the rhyme-word *shekhinah*, a key word in Jerusalem's boast.[7]

Also noteworthy is the fact that Baghdad is afforded the last word, closing the list of contestants. Finally, Baghdad says of the exiled Jews, 'I hid them in my shade', a benevolence prefigured by the earlier description of Heman's escape from the punishing heat of the sun.[8]

[7] Babylon's poem reads, literally, as follows: 'I am time's crown, land of Adinah, and my earth is the glory of every nation. Truly all lands are as stones in a catapult, whereas I am a jewel. And God's sages dwelt/*shakhenu* in me, but in their hearts the Presence/*shekhinah* dwelt/*shakhenah*' (*ST* 372. 6–11).

[8] Alḥarizi might well have given voice here to an ambivalent position on which centre merited the higher praise; and that internal division could reflect a historic tug of war—political and religious—between Palestine and Babylon, the latter steadily gaining in prestige and influence in the talmudic period and thereafter. See Malter, *Saadia Gaon*, 69–88; Margaliot, *The Controversies* (Heb.), ch. 1, 'Relations between Babylonia and the Land of Israel from the Close of the Talmudic Period until the Close of the Geonic Period', 1–23; and L. Ginzberg, *A Commentary on the Palestinian Talmud* (Heb.), i. pp. xli–l, repr. in id., *On Jewish Law and Lore*, 29–37.

Analysis of Gate Forty-Eight

The Heart's Grief and Relief

As *Sefer Taḥkemoni* approaches its close, Alḥarizi brings the art of point–counterpoint to a new high, and that in an unusual display of riddle-cum-metaphor and sophisticated narrative framing.

The Hebrew text of Gate 48, aptly called by Schirmann 'Lovesickness and its Cure',[1] leaves open the possibility of multiple and even contradictory readings; and I have striven to preserve this ambiguity in the English version.

The central episode is open to two very different interpretations. According to the first, and the more plausible, the self-proclaimed patient is no true victim of rejection, but a witty rhetor. It is highly unlikely that a man so deeply agitated by lack of love would have the patience and presence of mind to deliver so sophisticated a presentation as the one we are afforded, and a bipartite one at that. According to this reading, the doctor guffaws at his challenger's wit and gives back payment in coin: for two metaphoric extravaganzas, a double *tour de force*.

The first riddling presentation of the 'patient' is doubly paradoxical: he claims to have been mortally wounded in battle, then asserts that only his slayer can cure him! Following the doctor's angry response, the patient pledges plain speech—and plunges into a 'decipherment' that is heavily metaphoric, laced with, and based upon, the conventions of metric erotic poetry of the Hebrew Spanish school: lover as gazelle, eyes/glances as wounding weapons piercing liver and heart, and love as an illness calling for a doctor and cure.[2]

The doctor's emotional and verbal response strongly suggests that he considers the description that he has received as a challenge not to his healing acumen but to his oratorical and rhetorical skills. Laughing heartily at the brilliance of his opponent, he responds to a doubly limned dilemma with a double cure, condensable to four words: 'Make love—or suffer!' Each cure, however, is stretched out in loving and ingenious detail, and at greater length than the patient's; and more originally, as well, in terms of the literary traditions of Hebrew Spain. To enrich the element of contest and jest, the doctor

[1] Schirmann, *Hebrew Poetry*, ii. 190.

[2] For a sampling of love poetry of Hebrew Spain, exhibiting these and other conventions, see Scheindlin, *Wine, Women, and Death*, sect. 2, 'Women', 77–134.

includes in each apothecarial concoction specific ingredients that pick up on specific locutions of the patient—such bodily features as eyes and hearts; words expressive of cure—*te'alah* (cure), *mazor* (medication), and *tsori* (balm) *lirefuatah* (for its healing)—echoing *tsori* (balm), *refuah* (healing), *mazor* (medication), and *te'alah* (cure);[3] and words relating to suffering: *ha'anaḥot* (groans) and *begaḥalei lehavim min ha'ahavim* (flaming coals of love)—echoing *bemilḥemet ḥeshek ve'ahavah* (in the war of lust and love), *lehavot min ha'ahavot* (flames of love), and *vesame'aḥ le'anḥati* (and rejoicing in my groan).[4]

The rhetorical achievement of the doctor is manifold. There is, first of all, the very conceit of bodily assets and amorous favours as pharmaceuticals; then there is the aptness of the preparation of the 'potion'—gathering, squeezing, crushing, laying on of unguents, extraction of juice,[5] all suggestive of amours; and the verve of copious pun and alliteration, as in *ve'esev ha'anaḥot* (and the grass of sighs) *ve'otsev haruḥot* (the sadness of winds [sighs]) . . . *peri haperidah* (the fruit of separation) *ve'anfei heḥori vehaḥaradah* (branches of wrath and fear).[6] The translation mirrors these essential virtues of the Hebrew.

The brilliance of this tit-for-tat gives the lie to the doctor's feigned irritation and ignorance at the close of the lamenter's first speech; for anyone capable of concocting so witty a 'prescription' as did the doctor, surely grasped his patient's 'dilemma' before requesting, and receiving, a second presentation.

Finally, the doctor's reply can be seen to hold yet another stratum of wit: the patient, following one strain of Hebrew erotic poetry—again, based on Arabic models—had clearly spoken of a male lover; the doctor, in his prescriptions, calls implicitly for heterosexual involvement/fulfilment.[7]

All the above notwithstanding, there is an alternative reading. The patient, genuinely distressed and a brilliant rhetor, is loath to state baldly in public that he loves a man; so he employs literary convention to mask his dilemma to all but cognoscenti of literary tradition—hopefully people who might be open to the admissibility of such a union—including the doctor. Seen in this light, the doctor's aggravation may not be entirely feigned; and his laughter might be—at least in part—at the plight of a man for whom literary convention has become a reality (or whose proclivities and torment underlie the literary convention).

From this perspective, the healer's answers, partially veiled as were the questions put him, contain a deft rebuke: leave off pursuit of men and turn

[3] *ST* 375. 10–11—echoing 373. 22, 374. 1–2.
[4] *ST* 375. 26, 376. 6—echoing 374. 9, 13, 21.
[5] *ST* 375. 13–18.
[6] *ST* 375. 26–7.
[7] See Roth, '"Deal Gently with the Young Man"'.

to women—hinted at in the citing, specifically, of breasts (*shadayim*, a term predicated of women). Beyond that, the patient is to plunge into sensual gratification—with a woman!—frequently (three times a day), and so forget both his torment and his homosexual inclination. If he cannot effect this change, he must be prepared to suffer, giving vent to his grief daily for years, until his pain subsides. Let time do its work.

The overtones of one biblical citation could indeed be suggestive of genuine repugnance on the doctor's part: the Hebrew reads that the prescription of gratification is to be taken, *lo yom velo yomayim velo ḥodesh velo shanim*, 'not one day and not two days and not one month and not years (but daily . . .)'[8] —this being a clear allusion to the ravenous, grumbling Israelites, told by God through Moses that they would be given meat until they were disgusted with it:

> You shall eat not one day, or two, not even five days or ten or twenty, but a whole month, until it comes out of your nostrils and becomes loathsome to you. For you have rejected the Lord who is among you, by whining before Him and saying, 'Oh, why did we ever leave Egypt?'[9]

In short, the doctor, in disgust at the patient's proclivities and complaint, urges the cure of indulgence in sexual union *ad nauseam*![10]

Now having examined the two major alternative interpretations of the body of the gate, let us examine the frame. Prefiguring the patient's display, Heman speaks in riddling metaphor, even more so than the patient. On the one hand, he presents himself as the victim of a high fever and actual physical discomfort; on the other, the metaphoric site of his suffering—'where the king's prisoners are kept'[11]—is highly enigmatic. The reader might suspect that Heman is the victim of time/fate—i.e. of ageing, although such an interpretation could only be tentative. It is only when the text is read through, and the several and specific similarities between Heman and the love-struck patient are noted, that it becomes clear that both men suffer the same affliction. Both are ill, both are wounded in the heart by sharp weapons, both weep, both writhe on a bed of pain, both require balm/*tsori*.[12]

A careful reading of the close of the gate strengthens this identification.

[8] *ST* 375. 21–2.

[9] Num. 11: 19–20.

[10] Then again, the very use of a biblical citation in markedly different context could itself be part of the game conducted by the two rhetors in jocular interchange.

[11] *ST* 373. 5–6.

[12] The patient's closing poem in the Hebrew contains, as well, the statement 'How is it that I cry "Violence!" when Gilead's balm is here, next to me, you being the doctor?' (*ST* 374. 27–8), recalling that Heman had been referred to the land of Gilead, there to find balm for his pain (*ST* 373. 8–9).

Hever proclaims in song to Heman that he is *ḥever ḥaverakh gam yedidakh*, 'Hever, your friend, your beloved'. 'Whenever you wish to know me,' says Hever, 'turn to your heart and find that I dwell in it', *be'et tirtseh ledati shuv lelibakh vetimtsa ki ani shokhen betokho.*[13] The Hebrew root *yod–dalet–ayin*, translatable as 'to know', connotes in biblical Hebrew intimate knowledge, to the inclusion of sexual congress, as in 'Adam (or: the man) knew his wife Eve and she conceived', *vayeda ha'adam et ḥavah ishto vatahar* (Gen. 4: 1). Here—according to one possible reading—Hever, in more gentle and veiled fashion than the speech addressed to him by the judge, adjures Heman to be content with platonic (non-physical) love. Heman, however, does not pick up the message: his frustration at the disappearance of his beloved friend is expressed in an exact quotation from the Song of Songs, describing the search of a physically and emotionally aroused woman for her beloved: 'I sought him, but I could not find him; I called him, but he gave me no answer' (S. of S. 5: 6).[14]

These words of Heman are themselves an echo of the patient's description of his frustration when denied satisfaction by his beloved: *ekra elav velo ya'aneh ve'etsak velo yifneh*, 'I call to him and he answers not; I cry aloud and he turns not.'[15] Here too, then, the plight of Heman and the patient (Hever) are identified.

An alternative interpretation would take the word *yedidakh* in the first stich of Hever's poem to mean 'dear, true friend'. By this reading the Kenite simply is adjuring his comrade to take hope and sustenance in his absence through recollection and spiritual contact; and Heman, in his great longing, finds that he cannot put this advice into practice at once.

We have far from exhausted the complexity of the gate's thematic interplay and its studied ambiguities. On the (likely) assumption that Hever as patient was by no means afflicted, but was merely engaging in a favourite occupation—challenging a rival to a rhetorical contest—then his bogus pain and frustration contrast with the very real love-longing of Heman at the gate's start and close. If, on the other hand, Hever was genuinely afflicted with love-longing—a less satisfying interpretation, to my mind—two different readings of the close suggest themselves: Hever, doubly vexed, spitefully leaves his friend in like frustration; and/or, ironically, denies himself the fulfilment of having a lover who pines for him. Alternatively, having absorbed the message of the physician to eschew homosexual involvement, Hever conveys essentially the same message to Heman, even as he points to the more refined solution of platonic love.

[13] *ST* 376. 14–17. [14] *ST* 376. 19–20. [15] *ST* 373. 23–4.

Whatever interpretation one puts on the inner tale, or the outer frame, the author must be seen as deliberately and richly exploring the theme of frustrated love and literary convention, and the entanglements of the two.

Finally, we are left with one last riddle, even though it is not presented as such: the identity of the doctor, who, in his verbal gymnastics, bests Hever the Kenite—given the most likely reading of the original Hebrew, that it is the patient who is followed by Heman the Ezrahite at the end.[16] Never before in *Sefer Taḥkemoni* has Hever been so seriously overshadowed. He has had rivals: in his debate with a woman (most likely his wife) over the relative worth of man or woman (Gate 41); and in his vying with a younger man in Gate 32, where he completes his rival's descriptions in rhymed prose and then in metric verse. In both instances, however, Alḥarizi clearly stacks the deck in favour of the Kenite, whose argumentation and/or display put his opponent's into the shadow. Similarly, in Gate 4, in the debate over the ant and the flea, the Kenite's depiction is at once more imaginative and racy than that of his rival (who is also his son). In Gate 17, Heman the Ezrahite executes a *tour de force* of complex rhymed prose exposition in a lengthy introduction to a contest between seven poets, but in that gate Hever is not a presenter/competitor. In Gate 29, the son's presentation is apparently more effective than the father's in winning contributions from auditors, but not clearly superior in its construction or flourish. In Gate 42, where the Kenite defends stinginess in a debate with an unidentified youth, the latter seems to win the day—but the Kenite claims, to his listeners' credence, that he held back telling argument/display so as not to give the laurel to greed.

Astonishingly, in this text we have not only an unidentified rival but one who has the last word and far exceeds Hever in metaphoric conceit and in the richness of the sound stratum of alliteration and pun!

There is but one likely candidate for the mystery doctor: Alḥarizi himself, who in the work's Introduction and first gate speaks of his own talents, and displays them proudly, as he interacts complexly and variously with both Heman and Hever—and returns to do so here.[17]

[16] 'Now, upon my leaving the doctor I hurried after him'—*ST* 376. 10. Even if a manuscript reading were to yield 'upon *his* leaving'—*betseto* rather than *betseti*—this interpretation would still hold.

[17] The reader will recall that the author did subtly intrude into one other prior chapter—Gate 5, where the final boast of presenting twelve months in rich description can only be, in context, that of Alḥarizi; and most likely in Gate 42, in the guise of the generous visiting rhetor.

Analysis of Gate Forty-Nine

In Praise of the Fruits of the Garden Trees

GATE 49 IS THE LAST TRUE GATE of *Sefer Taḥkemoni*, Gate 50 being essentially a catch-all of metric verses. It seems all the more peculiar, then, that precisely here the author breaks the pattern that he has followed throughout, with rare exception; namely, that the narrator, Heman, encounters Hever, and the former observes/hears the latter's rhetorical or other display, frequently voicing admiration for his accomplished friend.[1] Here it is Heman who commands the stage, to the point of *his* receiving the adulation of Hever the Kenite, who appears only briefly, at the close. To compound this conundrum, the introductions to Heman's poems on the garden's components mix first- and third-person statements: *vaya'an hameshorer*, 'the poet declared'; *vayisa meshalo*, 'he took up his theme';[2] *va'esa meshali*, 'I took up my theme'; and *vaya'an vayomer*, 'he spoke, saying'.[3]

A convenient path to take in unriddling this conundrum is to follow the argument of M. Itzhaki, who has called attention to yet two more puzzling features of the text: the fruits and flowers cited could not possibly appear simultaneously, as they blossom at different times; and the site's design differs from described practice in Jewish and Muslim Spain, where gardens were centred on a palace, fountain, or drinking site.[4] Focusing on the number (seven) and the nature of the specific fruit trees chosen by our author, on Jewish literary sources (the Bible, Midrash, and exegetic literature) as well as the Koran, and prior analyses of the Muslim garden as a representation of

[1] Gates wherein Heman shows a positive reaction comprise 2–4, 5, 7, 8, 10, 14, 15, 17, 18, 25, 27, 28, 32–4, 36, 37, 39, 40, 42–5, and 47; a negative reaction—19, 20, 29, 38, and 41. In Gates 23 and 30 Heman's reaction is mixed. See Segal, 'The Opening', 408–9. The only gates without the usual Heman–Hever encounter pattern are the Introduction and Gate 1; and Gate 20, where the central figure is Heman as hopeful, then frustrated, suitor.

[2] This particular rendering taken from the NJPS translation of the tale of Balak and Balaam (Num. 23: 7, 18; 24: 3, 15, 20, 21, 23). I have translated *vayisa meshalo* as 'He lifted his voice in song.'

[3] Before this, on seven occasions in this work, *amar hamagid* 'the narrator said', has been predicated of Hever rather than Heman: Gates 6 (*ST* 37. 14), 10 (*ST* 109. 11), 12 (*ST* 135. 20), 30 (*ST* 217. 9), 31 (*ST* 261. 18), and 34 (*ST* 285. 3)—as pointed out by Yahalom, 'Function', 140 n. 19. This phenomenon is, however, less problematic than it seems. In all these instances, Hever is indeed a narrator, relating a tale to Heman; hence, he can legitimately be called a narrator. In Gate 49, however, the unfolding episode has already been presented as the tale of Heman the Ezrahite. See also Hus, 'The "Magid"' (Heb.).

[4] '"In Praise of Garden Fruits"' (Heb.).

paradise on earth, Itzhaki concludes that the text leans in the direction of allegory; that what we are given here is 'an imaginative, poetic realization of the heavenly Garden of Eden'.[5] She goes on to suggest a specifically Jewish allegoric interpretation: citing further and varied midrashic sources, she holds that the specific fruits variously recall the Jewish people or the Torah or divine power. She tempers this reading by stating, at the close, that the text 'is by no means constructed as a perfect allegory' but blends, in inconsistent fashion, realia of the courtier wine fests, a 'transcendental stratum of Paradise, and [differing] traditions of the perception thereof; and the allegoric stratum . . .'.[6]

While Itzhaki's careful attention to the non-realistic aspects of Gate 47 is most helpful, her conclusions are questionable. The cited midrashic interpretations of various fruits are not compatible with our text in its specificity. Thus the nut is spoken of in the Midrash as a symbol of three different kinds of Jews, the last being the kind that must be coerced into giving charity but, like a smashed nut, is worthless open. However, our text clearly speaks of the need to crack open *every* nut. Similarly, forced interpretation would be required to see the apple, blood-red in appearance and delicious for human consumption,[7] as Israel; or the *rimon*/pomegranate, running with juice and blushing blood-red, as emblematic of the high priest's gown.[8]

As for the garden of Eden interpretation: frequent and open similitude is not enough for allegory, the more so when Itzhaki takes pains to show that Alḥarizi's garden is not laid out like the actual court gardens said to symbolize the Muslim paradise. The several allusions to Eden here, as well as related repetition of the root *ayin–dalet–nun*, come to emphasize the supreme delight and more than earthly nature of the site—which, withal, is not in heaven.

Itzhaki is on far safer ground in her pointing out the book's overall circular composition—i.e. the significant linkage of our gate with the book's beginning. In the Introduction to his work Alḥarizi declares:

> And whoever wishes to see the pleasantness of its themes and to delight in the gardens of its utterances and draw [waters] from its flowing fountains, will find therein gardens and groves, and garden beds and myrtle trees, and cups of sweet juices . . . hewn from the rocks of my ribs and cut from the trees of my counsel.[9]

Moreover, Alḥarizi has already spoken of the holy tongue as 'rivers of Eden' or 'the source of Eden'.[10]

[5] Ibid. 313. [6] Ibid. 317–18. [7] *ST* 378. 22–4; Itzhaki, '"In Praise"', 316.
[8] *ST* 379. 1–12; Itzhaki, '"In Praise"', 316. The explicit likening of the pomegranate/*rimon* to the *rimonim*/bell-shaped ornaments on the high priest's gown does not justify an allegoric interpretation. [9] *ST* 12. 20–7. [10] *ST* 12. 13, 15.

At the close of Gate 49, in the description of the handsome youths, he again alludes to the same theme:

The source of the intellect was in their utterances and the fountain of song in their ideas.[11]

This finale moves away from the sensual ambience of the gate as a whole, lending the text a more abstract meaning, possibly allegorical. If we take into account the fact that the Gate 50 is not a usual one, but a compendium of metric poems lacking the typical narrative framework, it well might be that our gate concludes, essentially, the entire collection of *maqāmas*. We have, then, the effect of rounding out—a poetic realization, if you will—of the promise given in the Introduction, 'that this book might be like a *garden* containing all manner of delights and pleasant plantings'.[12]

Itzhaki buttresses her position by noting that one meaning of the *pardesim*/groves promised in the Introduction is, according to the medieval Jewish commentator David Kimḥi, 'a garden of fruit trees'[13]—hence the presentation of the fruit trees at the close fulfils the promise at the start. Indeed, a look back at the author's promise further strengthens Itzhaki's thesis, revealing, in the Introduction, an abundance of detail and specific locutions that are to recur in Gate 49: a garden of sweet delights in its utterances, with bounteous waters—one filled with groves, gardens within gardens, and garden beds; beauteous structures; and 'a singing maiden, a maid firing love'—all these formed of the author's 'rocks of his ribs and of the trees of his counsel'.[14] The book, the author repeats, is intended to be

like a garden containing all manner of delights and pleasant plantings wherein every seeker can find what he seeks and acquire all that he desires but lacks . . . and he who pays no mind to God's word will find therein the delights of and good things of the world and [then] flow to the good of the Lord . . . let anyone who hungers enter and eat.[15]

Rounding out the garden theme, Alḥarizi declares, referring to his guilt at having translated al-Ḥariri's *Maqāmāt* before composing his original work, 'My own vineyard I did not guard'.[16]

A close comparison of our text with that of Gate 1 will leave little doubt that the reader is being recalled to the setting in which, according to Heman's report, the author encountered a group of incomparable youths, handsome and brilliant, led by Hever the Kenite.[17]

[11] *ST* 382. 18. [12] *ST* 13. 17–18; Itzhaki, '"In Praise"', 315–16. [13] Ibid. 316 and n. 21.
[14] *ST* 12. 20–7. [15] *ST* 13. 17–23; 14. 9–10. [16] *ST* 15. 17—a citation of S. of S. 1: 6.
[17] The reader is referred, at this point, to the table at the close of this analysis, detailing this identity.

Table of echoes: Gates 1 and 49

Gate 49	Gate 1
baḥurei ḥemed	*yeladim ein bahem kol mum vekhol dofi mele'im ḥokhmah*[†] *ukhelil yofi*
handsome youths (*ST* 382. 16)	youths free of taint and stain, beauty's perfection (*ST* 19. 17–18)
maḥmadei einayim	*tireh bo kol maḥmad ayin*
the eyes' delight (*ST* 382. 16)	in him [Hever] you might see every delight of the eye (*ST* 20. 8)
*maḥpirim beyofyam** *kokhevei shamayim*	*be'oram kokhevei shaḥak ya'alimu ufenei shaḥar yakhlimu*
shaming with their beauty heaven's stars (*ST* 382. 16–17)	hiding with their light heaven's stars and shaming dawn's face (*ST* 19. 8–9);
	vehayofi al panav yaḥaneh
	beauty camps on his [Hever's] face (*ST* 20. 4)
vehem mishtashe'im beshirei neginot	*imratam tserufah umelitsatam retsufah*
they delighting in melodious song (*ST* 382. 17)	their speech was refined and their poetic utterance inlaid (*ST* 19. 21)
mekor hasekhel behegyoneihem	*alu besulam sikhlam ad ḥug erets . . . amud esh hasekhel ya'ir le'eineihem*
the source of intellect was in their utterances (*ST* 382. 19)	with their intellect they ascended to the heavens . . . the pillar of the intellect's fire lit their eyes (*ST* 19. 9, 12–13);
	vehasekhel al pihem yisa veyaḥaneh
	the intellect would journey and camp at their command (*ST* 19. 19–20)
umotsa habedolaḥ bein shineihem	*mileihem sapirim*
the source of bdellium was between their teeth	their words were sapphires (*ST* 19. 6)
umizraḥ hashemesh al peneihem	*ufeneihem meorim*
sunrise lay upon their faces (*ST* 382. 19)	their faces were luminaries (*ST* 19. 6–7)

Gate 49	Gate 1
vehineh rubam ḥevel nevi'im	*reḥibarti hasefer hazeh ka'asher min hashamayim hor'eti vehinabeti ka'asher tsuveti*
lo, most of them were a band of prophets (*ST* 382. 24)	so I composed this book as I was instructed by Heaven and I prophesied as I was commanded (*ST* 28. 13–14)
vayipol al tsavari vayishakeni	*nashak bein einai*
he fell upon my neck and kissed me (*ST* 382. 26)	he kissed me between my eyes (*ST* 29. 21–2)

* The printed text reads *beyofyah*, 'in *her* beauty'.
† Dan. 1: 4.

In addition to the many and manifest links between Hever and his band in Gates 1 and 49, cited in the table above, we have the further commonality of imbibing wine:

ulefaneiha gevi'im me'odamim bidemei bat hakeramim	*pa'am demei hakos yimtseh*
And before her were goblets reddened with the blood of the daughter of the vineyards (*ST* 382. 9)	at times he sucked the blood of the cup (*ST* 20. 6)

Finally, the section on the lute-playing maiden[18] is paralleled with the citing of Hever as one who, 'if he played, delivered up grief into the hands of joy'.[19]

At the start and close, then, of *Sefer Taḥkemoni*, wisdom, beauty, wine-drinking, music, and rhetoric are all linked in a lofty enterprise—paralleling the overall play, throughout the work, of enlightenment and entertainment, the sacred and the profane.

The book has indeed come round full circle: in Gate 1, amidst a band of rhetor-prophets, Hever the Kenite kisses the author as a sign of affection and gratitude, designating him the supreme poet, destined to redeem the Hebrew language. In Gate 49 Hever, 'father of awesome songs', kisses Heman the Ezrahite, announcing to *ḥaverav*/his companions, the band of rhetor-prophets, that only now, following Heman's lengthy poetic display, have they arrived at

[18] *ST* 381. 20–382. 8.

[19] *ST* 20 8–9.

their true heritage.[20] Herein is the conundrum of the mixed first and third person introductions to Heman's poems—'he/I took up his/my theme', etc.—solved: these are no slips of the pen of author or copyists, but a mirroring of the deliberate overlapping of identities of the author with Hever and Heman—in the Introduction and at various junctures throughout the work. Whether or not we agree with Hever's laudation of his friend's achievement (Alḥarizi's boast of his own), the author has given us to understand that he has indeed accomplished what he set out to do in Gate 1—redeem the Hebrew language and demonstrate its equality with, if not superiority to, the *Maqāmāt* of al-Ḥariri.

There is one last linkage to be considered: 'Spain, I answered, is the land of my birth,' declares Heman, 'and I have set my feet toward the fairest land on earth.' The narrator all but quotes, here, the concluding section of *Sefer Taḥkemoni*'s prefatory poem, sung by the author, Judah Alḥarizi:

> He abandoned his land and his dwelling
> to run, trembling, to Zion's domain.
> He is Judah, wise Solomon's offspring;[21]
> his birthplace and country is Spain.[22]

Sefer Taḥkemoni, then, opens and closes with Alḥarizi's self-praise, and that in the context of his profound attachment to the land of Israel.

[20] *ST* 382. 26–383. 2.

[21] Lit.: 'He left the habitations of the land of his domicile and ran trembling to the land of the Lord; his name is known as Judah son of Solomon and the name of his land and his birthplace is Spain.'

[22] *ST* 3. 23–6.

Analysis of Gate Fifty[1]

Varia and Nefaria

IN THIS POETIC POTPOURRI Alḥarizi almost takes leave of the restrictions of the *maqāma* genre, as he casts off metric verse, one poem after another, on topics varied and sundry, many—as has been indicated in the notes—harking back to characters and episodes in the book. Several poems witness the special regard of our author for Maimonides, whose works he translated and whose honour he here defends.[2] Finally, Alḥarizi attacks with gusto his favourite dual theme of largesse/benefaction and stint/skinflints.

Thematically and stylistically, special emphasis is given one outspoken and crass homosexual, whether he be a genuine historical figure or reflection thereof, or a figment of the author's imagination.[3] With his ten-poem barrage, Alḥarizi reminds his reader of a number of prior characters and episodes: the violent transvestite of Gate 31; the repugnant, if highly comical, merchant of Gate 34, spare (relatively) in his description of his wife's beauty but lavish in his praise of his serving lad, presented all but openly as the object of his lust; Heman's ire at his friend, found embracing simultaneously cup and youth in a tavern (Gate 36); Berakhot, dissolute of Ashur (Gate 46), never to be trusted with money, maid, or young man; and, possibly, the covert animus of the physician towards the homosexual infatuation of his 'patient' (Gate 48). It would appear that our author, despite obeisance to convention in scattered poems of desire for the fair (male) youth—here and in Gate 9—harbours a deep-seated animus against sexual deviants, or at least persons flaunting any such proclivity.[4]

---

[1] As in the Analysis of Gate 46, in most instances the translator does not address questions of identification and background that are the province of historians.

[2] See Analysis 46 n. 7.

[3] The Hebrew text of the first poem of this ten-poem set (*ST* 418. 15–421. 15) concludes *ve'et zakhar*, a shortened version of Lev. 18: 22: 'Do not lie *with a male* as one lies with a woman: it is an abhorrence'. The ensuing ten poems in the Hebrew all involve rhymes or word-plays with *zakhar*.

[4] On the figure of the 'gazelle', or desired young man, in Hebrew Spanish poetry, see Schirmann, 'The Ephebe'; and Alloni, 'The Gazelle and the Camel' (Heb.). See also on the topic of homosexuality Roth, '"Deal Gently with the Young Man"'. Zemaḥ has provided three especially astute readings of homoerotic poems by Samuel Hanagid: two, of *Yeshureni*, 'He Looks upon Me', and *Sima yeminakh*, 'Set Your Right Hand' in Zemaḥ and Rosen-Moked, *A Sophisticated Work* (Heb.), 128–34, and the third in '"Should My Heart Leave My Body"'.

Despite the uniqueness of this catch-all gate, it does enter the rounding-out dynamic that has been evidenced in Gates 48 and 49. If only slightly, the gathering of brilliant youths at the outset, in the rhymed prose section, recalls the sterling group at the opening of Gate 1;[5] and here, as there, the champion of the assemblage is Hever. Beyond this, the introductory poem of *Sefer Taḥkemoni* set forth the fact of the author's wanderings; this theme (which lay at the heart of Gate 46) reappears here at the close, and—as at the start—with emphasis on the author's travails (if the circumstances of the journey and the identity of his travelling companions remain a mystery). As well, prominence is given the ascent to Jerusalem in Gate 50, as is done at the close of the introductory poem.[6] The dedication to highly praised patrons is a prominent component of the Introduction and Gate 1; here, it closes the work.[7]

In addition, the wording of the last stich of the gate's initial poem could hardly have been coincidental:

> With water of my tears wipe out my transgression (*pishi*)
> and let not the sin of Judah be written.[8]

This prayer recalls the author's explicit plea at the book's start, citing the very same biblical text, that the reader may overlook his deficiencies: 'I entreat every reader of it, upon finding any sin or element worthy of censure, that he judge me charitably, for love covers all transgressions (*pesha'im*);[9] and let not the sin of Judah be writ on his heart.'[10]

There is even an internal closure of sorts operative in Gate 50, involving the word 'Judah': following on the first of three poems in a section of fulsome conclusory praise, Alḥarizi cites the account of the patriarch Jacob, in

[5] The parallel between the two groups is much more extensive and detailed in Gate 49; see the Analysis, with table.

[6] The longing for holy sites—Jerusalem (Gate 28) and the graves of Ezra and Ezekiel (Gate 35)—is pronounced in *Sefer Taḥkemoni*. Of special interest are the different attitudes of Hever: in Gate 28 he mocks the grieving Heman; here, he reports on his own sincere grief. This seems but one more instance of Alḥarizi's ability, even penchant, to have Heman and Hever represent different facets of himself—on which subject, see the Afterword. Further evidence of the author's zeal for Jerusalem is afforded in the following lines of one of his dedications for *Igeret leshon hazahav* ('The Tongue of Gold Missive'): 'Spain is my home . . . whence God took me, that I rode the sea in a vessel, making my longed-for goal Jerusalem . . . eager I hasted to the Land of Israel, journeying through lands of the heathen, coming from the far islands to walk before the Lord in the land of the living' (Habermann, 'The Dedications to *Sefer Taḥkemoni*', 140.) Here, too, we have another bracketing of the book with the ascent to Jerusalem.

[7] As well, the text's inflated praise recalls Heman's self-advertisement in Gate 21 and the sextons' extravagant laudation of the precentor in Gate 24.

[8] *ST* 385. 10–11; Jer. 17: 1.

[9] Prov. 10: 12.

[10] *ST* 15. 25–7; Jer. 17: 1.

reference to one Joseph, Maecenas of Aram Zova, saying, 'He sent Judah ahead of him to Joseph'[11]—which, in context, is to be construed as Time's having directed Judah Alḥarizi to this generous benefactor.

Yet another element of the gate adds to the rounding out of the work as a whole—the fulsome praise of Joseph of Aram Zova, recalling the extravagant praise of the Maecenates of *Sefer Taḥkemoni*'s dedications.

Finally, the last words but eight in the gate are a citation of the final verse of the historical section of First Prophets—the books of Joshua, Judges, First and Second Samuel, and First and Second Kings: 'A regular allotment of food was given him.'[12] In Scripture, this refers to the auspicious fortune of King Jehoiachin; here, to the unending portion of wisdom allotted the grandee (and, indirectly, to the ongoing and regular help sought by Alḥarizi). By closing his work on this positive note, which finalizes a major portion of biblical history, Alḥarizi further adds to the finality of his closure, which has been marred by the appearance of so large a poetic catch-all.

[11] *ST* 432. 8; Gen. 46: 28.

[12] *ST* 433. 19; 2 Kgs. 25: 30.

Afterword

ONE CAN HARDLY DENY that a full reading of *Sefer Taḥkemoni* substantiates the author's initial claim that he has created a cornucopia thematically and generically, one that can attract, variously, seekers of preachment and instruction—or light entertainment. The work has unrolled serious polemic and mock debate, cutting satire, fantastical narrative, firework rhetorical displays, sombre and rollicking parody, literary history and literary criticism, travel accounts—most with frequent overlap thematically and generically and all within a dynamic of interaction between a wandering, boastful, oft-disguised rhetor and his (usually) admiring friend and recorder. A deeper understanding of this varied and often subtle interrelationship requires a closer look at the genesis and significance of the names of these two men—a topic that has commanded too little attention thus far. A logical starting point for such an enquiry must be Alḥarizi's previous work, *Maḥberot Iti'el*. In rendering into Hebrew al-Ḥariri's *Maqāmāt*, Alḥarizi chose to give Abu Ḥarith ibn Hammam, the narrator, the name of Iti'el. The narrator's name in Arabic has overtones of sanctity, comprising two (of four) names allegedly recommended by Muhammad as appropriate names for sons—al-Ḥarith (the ploughman) and al-Hammam (the fearful).[1] Aptly, then, the Hebrew name means 'God is with me.' Relatedly, Iti'el, in his one appearance in Scripture, is a purveyor of worthy wisdom.[2]

The appellation of the narrator in Hebrew as *magid* is also apt. One of its meanings is a messenger, one who bears official news: 'Runner dashes to meet runner, messenger (*magid*) to meet messenger (*magid*), to report to the king of Babylon that his city is captured.'[3] The term employed in the Arabic, *rāwī*, implies authority and accuracy; it denoted earlier a conveyor of traditions concerning the prophet Muhammad.[4]

[1] This on the testimony of al-Sharishi, a primary commentator on al-Ḥariri's *Maqāmāt*, and al-Ḥariri's biographer Ibn Khallikan—cited in Lavi, 'Why and How' (Heb.), 173.

[2] Note Abraham ibn Ezra's commentary on Prov. 30: 1, 'The words of Agur son of Jakeh . . . to Ithiel, to Ithiel and Ucal': '"The words of Agur": In the days of Solomon he was a man of integrity, learned and honoured in his generation; therefore King Solomon collected his wise sayings in his book. . . . Iti'el and Ucal were friends of Agur or his students.'

[3] Jer. 51: 31. See also 2 Sam. 15: 13 and 18: 11.

[4] Relatedly, the name Iti'el appears in the phrase *ne'um hagever le'iti'el* (Prov. 30: 1); and *ne'um*, or 'declaration/word', has a weighty connotation of highly authoritative pronouncement, frequently preceding the word 'Lord'. The first maqamist to employ it was Solomon ibn Zakbel, who preceded Alḥarizi (Lavi, 'How and Why', 175–6; for an English article paralleling the Hebrew, see Lavi, 'The Rationale').

Alḥarizi chose to name the cunning Abu Zayd al-Saruji (i.e. from the town of Serug) Hever the Kenite. This choice seems appropriate for a number of reasons pointed out by Lavi. Like Iti'el, the name is biblical; and the use of biblical lexicon, syntax, and morphology in Hebrew literary composition was a central feature of the medieval Jewish response in Muslim lands to *arabiyya*, that theory and movement within Arab civilization vaunting the superiority of Arabic along with the incomparability of the Koran.[5] Secondly, the Kenites were nomadic; and this could relate to the protagonist's constant state of wandering.[6] Thirdly, this overtone is augmented by the appellation *mitsa'ananim*, 'of the locale Zaananim', inasmuch as the root meaning of *tsadi-ayin-nun* is 'to wander', as in Isaiah 33: 20—and was so used by Alḥarizi in translating the very same root from the Arabic in al-Ḥariri's fourth gate, with the meaning of 'journeyed'. In this regard, al-Ḥariri has his wandering protagonist Abu Zayd of Serug declare in Gate 5, 'I am from Serug (*sarūj*) and was raised on saddles (*surūj*)'—making for yet another correspondence, with Hever's home locale attesting, in punning fashion, to his wanderer's avocation, even as the title al-Saruji pointed to Abu Zayd's proclivity for wandering.[7]

Fourthly, according to some biblical commentators, the Kenites were identical with the Rechabites, a group of Jews who had forsworn drinking wine (1 Chr. 2: 55; Jer. 35: 2–7); and inasmuch as Abu Zayd transgressed the Islamic prohibition on drinking of wine in a number of gates of al-Ḥariri's *Maqāmāt*, often flagrantly, the choice of a Kenite, or Rechabite, as the Hebrew protagonist was especially felicitous (albeit drinking *per se* is not forbidden in Jewish tradition).[8]

To the above-cited reasons of Lavi three more can yet be added. Scripture's Hever the Kenite is of a group related to the Jews historically: the Kenites are described in the Bible as descendants of Moses' father-in-law Hovav and living in close proximity to them.[9] This consanguinity relates to Alḥarizi's very translation enterprise—bringing into Jewish culture a work from a closely related group; for the Jews and Arabs of Spain not only lived in close proximity but had rich cultural interchange.

Next, one understanding of the Kenites is Ishmaelites, or Arabs.[10] In

[5] This movement and the Jewish response thereto was noted in the Analyses of the Introduction and Gate 15.

[6] See Gen. 15: 19; Judg. 1: 16; 1 Sam. 15: 16.

[7] Lavi, 'How and Why', 177–9. Indeed, twice more in *Maḥberot Iti'el*, in gates 21 and 25, this verb, *tsa'anti*, is used in precisely the same form and with precisely the same meaning (*MI* 173. 10, 219. 6). In addition, *vayitsan*, 'he journeyed', appears in gate 2 (*MI* 12. 7).

[8] Lavi, 'How and Why', 179.

[9] Num. 10: 29; Judg. 4: 11.

[10] *Pirkei rabi eliezer*, 69*a* (ch. 30) and *Nistarot shel rabi shimeon bar yoḥai*, cited by R. Brann, 'Power in the Portrayal', 25–6 n. 67.

this light, the ethnic and religious identity of the Abu Zayd of al-Ḥariri's *Maqāmāt* carries over directly into Hever of *Maḥberot Iti'el*.

Finally, the name Hever provided a special opportunity, in rendering several gates of al-Ḥariri's *Maqāmāt*, to provide an emphasis not present in the Arabic; namely, through pun and root repetition, highlighting the salient themes of friend (*ḥaver* in Hebrew), and group or society (*ḥevrah* or *ḥavurah*).

The most prominent instance of this is an appellation used three times in *Maḥberot Iti'el*[11]—*ḥaverenu ḥever hakeni*, 'our friend Hever the Kenite', so rendering the Arabic *shaykhunā* (our sheikh, or leader) *'abū zayd al-saruji*; when a closer equivalent for *shaykhunā* would have been *morenu* or *me'alfenu*, 'our teacher', or other synonyms denoting or connoting leadership.[12]

Two examples of the use of this phrase, together with word pun and root repetition, will demonstrate Alḥarizi's lending added emphasis in his translation to a major theme in the Arabic original. Close to the start of gate 15, the narrator declares, in the Hebrew text, 'I longed and yearned . . . that God would provide me with a wise friend (*ḥaver*)'. Shortly thereafter the narrator, who has ushered in a guest on a rainy night, declares, 'I brought the candle and looked at him with a scrutinizing eye and behold: *ḥaverenu ḥever hakeni* in truth!' Close to the gate's conclusion the Kenite declares, 'I thank the days of separation that brought me to your sweet companionship (*ḥevratekha*) and I said to him, "How pleasant is your friendship (*ḥevratekha*) to my heart."'[13] None of this added emphasis through root repetition and bracketing is present in the Arabic.

A like technique obtains in the Hebrew gate 20. There the narrator begins by stating: 'I journeyed to the land of Zidon with friends (*ḥaverim*) . . . I was with them as one who has not visited his own family and society (*veḥevrato*)'. Later in the tale, uncovering the identity of the protagonist (who has deceived the group), Iti'el says, 'And lo it was *ḥaverenu ḥever hakeni*.' At the tale's close he says, 'I returned to my friends (*ḥaverai*) and told them what I had seen'.[14]

Indeed there is scarcely a gate in *Maḥberot Iti'el* devoid of any permuta-

[11] Gates 2 (*MI* 16. 5), 15 (*MI* 125. 10), and 16 (*MI* 139. 10). A related phrase occurs at the close of gate 24 (*MI* 206. 15): 'Then I knew he was Hever the Kenite, lamp of friends (*ner haḥaverim*).' In the Arabic original, which lacks punning at this juncture, the phrase is 'the light of Seruj' (Chenery, i. 248).

[12] Scheindlin, in a response to an oral presentation on this topic, held that *ḥaverenu* is indeed an apt rendering of *shaykhunā*, inasmuch as one significant meaning of the term *ḥaver* in the post-talmudic period is 'scholar'. See *EJ* vii. 1491–2. One difficulty with this interpretation lies in the fact that the use of *ḥaver* in this meaning with a possessive suffix is not otherwise attested.

[13] *MI* 125. 8; 126. 8; 132. 7–8.

[14] *MI* gate 20, 167. 2; 169. 17; 170. 5–6.

tion of the root *ḥ-b-r*, and in some the root is used lavishly. In gate 3, called *Maḥberet haḥevrah*, 'The Gate of Society'—the Hebrew title itself employing pun for emphasis—friendship is the central theme. The narrator, travelling with a band of friends, overhears a father and son discussing the theme of proper behaviour towards others. The youth declares that one must revere friends and injure neither foe nor friend. The father rebukes the boy, insisting that measure for measure is the norm to follow. After the two are gifted generously by Iti'el and friends, father and son leave abruptly—and that on false pretence, giving the lie to both their arguments. Here are a few citations from the text:

We were journeying in a pleasant company (*beḥevrah*) . . . now when the company (*haḥavurah*) had sat down . . . I heard a man saying to his fellow (*ḥavero*), 'Tell me: how would you comport yourself with your friends (*ḥavereikha*) and neighbours . . .?' 'I would elevate my friend (*ḥaveri*) . . .' 'Know that I would not join (*etḥaber*) with any other than a friend (*leḥaver*) . . . I would not reward . . . him who despises my friendship (*ḥevrati*) . . . Let none oppress his friend (*ḥavero*) . . . What sort of friendship (*ḥevrah*) shall be pleasant? . . . I shall pay the debt of friends (*haḥaverim*) . . . Always despise anyone who despises his friends (*ḥaverav*). . .'

I saw (it was) Hever (*ḥever*) the Kenite and his son speaking . . . and I praised their wisdom to the members of the group (*haḥavurah*) . . . and the members of the group (*haḥavurah*) joined (*hitḥaberu*) them . . . the group (*haḥavurah*) awaited them . . . I said to my friends (*ḥaverai*) . . .[15]

The closing poem of this gate, described as written 'in the handwriting of Hever the Kenite', provides strong evidence of the use of puns by design to emphasize—here, ironically—the character of the protagonist: 'O soulmate, and choicest (*umivḥar*) of all my friends . . .' The pun on *Ḥever*—*umivḥar* would have been doubly emphatic for medieval readers, inasmuch as our author has here used, at the outset of his metric self-disclosure, the opening stich of a poem by Isaac ibn Khalfun, identical but for the replaced word *umivḥar*: 'O soulmate, and the soul (*venefesh*) of all my friends'.[16]

Alḥarizi was, of course, limited in his freedom to pun on his protagonist's name, inasmuch as *Maḥberot Iti'el* was a translation. The potential of punning on Hever is more richly exploited in *Sefer Taḥkemoni*—and consequently suggests an additional, and powerful, motive for the retention of the essentially *inappropriate* name of Hever the Kenite, a non-Jew in Scripture,

15 *MI* 27. 9, 20–2; 28. 6, 14–15, 21; 29. 12, 16–17; 30. 9–11, 21, 30; 31. 1, 3, 14, 19.

16 Schirmann, *Hebrew Poetry*, i. 70, poem 17; Isaac ibn Khalfun, *Collected Poems*, ed. Mirshy, 84. 1. In *Sefer Taḥkemoni*, at the close of Gate 30 (*ST* 257. 4–5) Alḥarizi employs the same pun: '*ha'atah ḥever hakeni* . . . *anokhi mivḥar yedideikha*/"Are you Hever the Kenite?" . . . "I am the choicest of your friends" . . .'.

in a work abounding with Jewish referents: in this very Jewish compendium, Hever composes prayers for his coreligionists; defends the honour of the Hebrew language; debates synagogue practice; polemicizes against Karaism; mocks a mourner of Jerusalem's ruin, but later himself bemoans the destruction of Jerusalem; twice surveys the history of Spanish Jewish poetry; and more.[17]

This punning is varied. After curing a victim of snakebite (Gate 37), Hever declares, '*Ani ḥever veḥaver laḥaverim*/I am Hever and a friend to friends, *velineḥashim ani ḥover ḥovarim*/but for snakes I cast spells.'[18] At the close of Gate 48, with its emphasis on lust, love, and infatuation, Hever declares, '*Ani ḥever ḥaverakh gam yedidakh*/I am Hever your friend, yes, your dear friend'.[19] It is, however, the permutations of *ḥ-b-r* denoting 'linking' and 'composition' that Alḥarizi uses most in pun formation; and in so doing, further emphasizes the protagonist's representation of the author.

One specific meaning of the word *ḥibur* in medieval Jewish literature is 'metric verse', that which is (tightly) linked, as opposed to *nifrad*, that which is separated (rhymed prose); hence one who links, or versifies metrically, is a *meḥaber*. At the close of his verbal acrobatics in Gate 32, where he fleshes out the rhymed prose, then metrical, challenges of a young opponent, Hever declares, '*Hakhi kare'u shemi ḥever lema'an aḥaber kol pezurei haḥamudot*/Truly they named me Hever because I link together all scattered delights.'[20] In another instance, the moral and intellectual aspect of Hever's (Alḥarizi's) creativity is stressed: at the close of Gate 42's debate on the pros and cons of largesse, the rhetor boasts, '*Ani ḥever vekhishmi ma'asai ki aḥaber nifzerei musar beshiri*/I am Hever and my deeds are as my name for I link together scattered wisdom in my song.'[21] Indeed the declaration '*Ani ḥever meḥaber*/I am Hever who composes (or authors or links)' appears more than any other signature in the compendium's fifty gates:

Ani ḥever meḥaber shir . . . aḥbir leshon ever vekedar ve'aram/I am Hever composer of song . . . I bind together the Hebrew, Aramaic, and Arabic tongues.[22]

Ani ḥever meḥaber shir yedidot . . . ve'aḥbir milevavi niv hitulim/I am Hever, composer of loving song . . . I compose from my heart comic utterance.[23]

---

[17] On the retention of the name of Hever as a reflection of the character's being hypostasized in the author's mind, see the Analyses of the Introduction and Gate 1.

[18] *ST* 305. 4–5.

[19] *ST* 376. 14–15. Similarly, the protagonist opens his poems of boast and self-disclosure at the end of Gates 18 and 39 (*ST* 196. 19; 311. 7), 'I am a friend/*ḥaver* of whoever seeks me out'—in this instance *ḥaver* implying Hever, the two words being nearly identical. Relatedly, at the close of Gate 28 (*ST* 249. 18–19) Hever announces himself in rhymed prose as '*ḥaverkha ḥever hakeni*/your friend Hever the Kenite'. See also Hus, 'The "Magid"'.

[20] *ST* 274. 12–13.

[21] *ST* 328. 7–8.

[22] Gate 8, *ST* 121. 16–17; 122. 7–8.

[23] Gate 10, *ST* 114. 6–9.

Amnam ani ḥever meḥaber shir . . . aḥbir leshon ever vekedar va'aram/Indeed I am Hever, composer of song . . . I link the languages of Ever, Kedar, and Aram.[24]

Ani ḥever meḥaber hatehilot/I am Hever, composer of hymns . . . *aḥaber lasekhalim mahatala'ot ve'e'erokh laḥasidim niv tefilot*/I compose folly for fools but set forth for the pious polished prayers.[25]

Ani ḥever meḥaber shir ḥamudot/I am Hever, composer of delightful song.[26]

Ani ḥever meḥaber hapeninim/I am Hever, stringer of pearls.[27]

Ani ḥever melabev halevavot . . . aḥaber maḥberot ḥidot ḥamudot/I am Hever, who stirs hearts . . . I compose *maqāmāt* of sweet riddles.[28]

The last of the above-cited examples is an especially strong self-advertisement, inasmuch as the Hebrew word *maḥberet* is the chosen term to represent *maqāma*.[29] The author in effect is having his protagonist say, 'I am Hever (i.e. Alḥarizi), the composer of *maqāmāt*.'[30]

The emphasis and punning on the name Hever as an indication of author-protagonist identification is not confined to the closing poems of the book's gates. In some instances in those very gates the same or like use of the root *ḥ-b-r* appears at the outset, in effect framing the tale. Thus, at the start of Gate 14, which closes with Hever's claim to be composer/*meḥaber*, of prayers, we find, 'let him compose (*yeḥaber*) a work for us from the jewels of his thought'.[31] Even when the concluding poem lacks a pun on *ḥ-b-r*, a gate can still show inclusion, or root bracketing. Thus, at the outset of Gate 4, one of a group of poets declares, 'I am the Lord's: He called me from the womb to compose (*uleḥaber*) figures of speech (*hamelitsot*).' At the end of this tale, in a threefold root-motif repetition, we read of the judge's compliments to Hever and his 'rival': 'even as God apportioned/*heḥbir* figures of speech/*hamelitsot* between you, join in friendship/*hitḥaberu* both of you'; and in the closing poem Hever declares, 'I am Hever and this is my fruit; but he and I are the lions of figured speech/*melitsot*'; and thereafter: 'When I heard his poem I knew that he was *ḥaverenu ḥever hakeni* . . .'.[32]

[24] i.e. Israel, Araby, and Christendom: Gate 11, *ST* 121. 25; 122. 7.

[25] Gate 14, *ST* 157. 21–4. [26] Gate 19, *ST* 201. 14. [27] Gate 26, *ST* 239. 5–6.

[28] Gate 34, *ST* 286. 11–14.

[29] On the discussion of *maḥberet* as the translation of *maqāma* see Klar, 'Four Titles of Compilations', 247–8.

[30] In the Introduction the author uses the root *ḥ-b-r*, 'to compose', in metric verse referring to himself: '*aḥaber ḥamudot meshalim veḥidot*/I compose delightful utterances, parables, and allegories' (*ST* 8. 1); and refers to himself as *meḥaber*/author in prose: 'Said the author/*hameḥaber* upon seeing this book of wondrous worth' (*ST* 16. 10). Relatedly Heman declares at the outset of Gate 1: 'Indeed the author/*meḥaber* of this work told me' (*ST* 19. 3); and reports later in that gate, 'The author/*hameḥaber* declared, "When I heard his words . . ."' (*ST* 28. 11).

[31] *ST* 149. 9–10. [32] *ST* 49. 12; 58. 6–7, 11–12, 15.

The linkage of author and Hever through pun and root repetition is of a piece with another tactic used by Alḥarizi—Hever's speaking of himself as the author, citing for this purpose biblical verses describing the biblical Judah.

In Gate 9, in answering a challenge to compose a poem ending, 'The Lord will take Judah unto Himself' (Zech. 2: 16), Hever so constructs the poem as to make it clear that the Judah referred to is Judah Alḥarizi—yet not without some tongue in cheek: the poem expresses the speaker's (Hever's) loyalty to God's word, and his disdain of gain and the mercenary!

In Gate 35, Hever says of his departure from Spain, citing Gen. 38: 1, 'Judah left his brothers at that time.'[33] Towards the close of that gate, Hever declares 'May his (Ezekiel's) merit stand him for an intercessor to quiet the tumult of the sea of upheavals; and may He in whose hand is strength and in His right hand pleasantness (Ps. 16: 11) deal kindly with Judah son of Solomon'—recalling the author's introducing himself by that name in the final stich of the poem that opens the work.

In Gate 46, towards the close of a scathing attack on an untalented plagiarist, Hever declares, alluding to the biblical episode of Tamar and Judah: 'now when Judah saw her [his ruined poem], he held her a whore, such that he cried out against her . . . "Away with her—let her be burnt!" '[34]

In the first of the catch-all of poems that comprise Gate 50, Hever concludes his confessional by citing Jer. 17: 1: 'Let the sin of Judah be writ no more'; and towards the gate's conclusion he says, in praise of a specific patron's support of him (i.e. Alḥarizi, of course), 'And so, he (fate) sent Judah before him unto Joseph'—citing Gen. 46: 28, describing an action of the patriarch Jacob.[35]

To sum up: Hever is bound to the author openly by similar boast-like description of talents, and journeying; the linkage of *ḥever—meḥaber*, Hever—author; and through citation of biblical verses referring to Judah son of Jacob.

All this having been said, let us return to the name and character of Heman the Ezrahite to explore his relationship and linkage with Judah Alḥarizi.

Let us recall that at least in one gate the character of Heman is all but openly identified with that of the author—Gate 21, concerning the mysteri-

[33] *ST* 287. 18.

[34] *ST* 353. 24–6—citing Gen. 38: 15 and 24.

[35] Alḥarizi uses such a biblical citation in speaking of himself as a persona. Thus in the Introduction, the author closes a poem of self-praise by declaring, 'Scattered tropes I return grouped together | and from them Judah gathers the dispersed' (Isa. 11: 12)—this being a witty *shibuts shoneh hora'ah*, or citing of Scripture in such a fashion as to change the meaning: the original reads, 'He will . . . assemble the banished of Israel and gather the dispersed of Judah from the four corners of the earth.'

ous seven maidens: there Heman boasts of the poetic prowess that Alḥarizi cited in the Introduction and Gate 1; and points to the peregrination of which Alḥarizi spoke in the prefatory poem. Relatedly in Gate 49, as has been shown, Heman reverses roles with Hever as extemporizing poet *par excellence* and as the object of Hever's praise at the close.

What might have motivated the choice of this name? In Scripture Heman the Ezrahite is author of one psalm, Ps. 88; hence the name carries over roughly the status of religious overtones of Iti'el, the surrogate name for Abu Ḥarith ibn Hammam of al-Ḥariri's *Maqāmāt*, while being a more decisively Jewish personage. As well, the name carries overtones of discernment: the full rubric of Ps. 88 is *maskil leheman ha'ezraḥi*, the word *maskil* (from the root *s-k-l*/wisdom) suggesting a literary artifice distinguished by wisdom or craftsmanship.

Yet there is more here. Heman is also one of five noted wise men in the ancient world. Of Solomon we read, 'He was the wisest of all men: [wiser] than Ethan the Ezrahite, and Heman, Chalkol, and Darda the sons of Mahol' (1 Kgs. 5: 11). This emphasis on wisdom would further bolster the reliability of the narrator.

Looking further into Scripture we find yet another possible signification of this name. First, however, the reader will recall that one reading of the outcome of the author's coupling with the Hebrew language was the birth of Hever. Now one interpretation offered by Abraham ibn Ezra of Ps. 88: 1's 'Heman the Ezrahite' is '. . . and there are those who say that the *alef* [of the word *ha'ezraḥi*] is (an) added (letter) and that he is the son of Zerah, as is his brother Eitan'. According to Num. 26: 20 one of the sons of Judah is Zerah. Hence an additional, if more veiled effect, of the name Heman the Ezrahite is to create a further analogy between Hever and Heman: both are 'progeny' of Judah Alḥarizi.

And now let us return to the matter of the usage of the name Judah, purposively used on a number of occasions to link Hever with the author. Heman, too, is identified with the biblical patriarch. 'Taking desire for provision I journeyed forth from *beit leḥem yehudah*/the house of bread of Judah'—or, the storehouse of Judah (*ST* Gate 20, 202. 7–8).

To complete this list, let us examine the close of Gate 12, where the reader encounters a sudden, passionate plea for the demise of stint and the restoration of the rule of generosity: 'Break the reign of Stint . . . and cause the horn of fair Generosity to flourish; in his days Judah shall be saved'[36]—referring at once to the people of Israel in general, and specifically to Judah Alḥarizi.

[36] *ST* 137. 5–7.

Now this declaration is prefaced by *amar hamagid*, 'Thus spoke the narrator'—usually indicating Heman the Ezrahite. Here, however, it could as readily refer to the narrator of the satiric allegory on the rise of stinginess[37] among Jewry, to wit, Hever the Kenite. Either reading is justifiable; however, it would seem that the author, while confusing some readers, could be hinting to others that *both* his characters are stand-ins for himself.

All this having been said on the identification of the author with both of his characters, yet one more facet of this identification may be put forward. Every letter of the Hebrew alphabet has a numerical equivalent: *alef* equals 1, *bet* 2, *yod* 10, *kof* 100, and exegetes throughout the ages, some more than others, found esoteric hints and teachings in Scripture through the exegesis of calculations, or *gematriyot*. For example:

It is used as supporting evidence and as a mnemonic by R. Nathan. He states that the phrase *eleh hadevarim* ('These are the words') occurring in Exod. 35: 1 hints at the 39 categories of work forbidden on the Sabbath, since the plural *devarim* indicates two, the additional article a third, while the numerical equivalent of *eleh* is 36, making a total of 39 (*Shab.* 70*a*).[38]

Now the numerical value of *heman ha'ezraḥi* is 436,[39] and of *ḥever hakeni*, 385,[40] the two totalling 721. The numerical value of *yehudah alḥarizi ben shelomoh*[41] is 723; but if we take the liberty of using the Arabic *ibn* for son instead of *ben*, and the further liberty of writing the shortened form of *ibn*, namely a *nun* with a slash (as was often done in the medieval period), we emerge with—721! Once again, and this time in veiled fashion, our author signals—this time to a small fragment of—his readership, that he is to be identified not with one of his two figures in this book, but with both. Judah Alḥarizi is at once Heman the Ezrahite and Hever the Kenite: rhetor—and (self-)promoter; poet—and admirer; rogue—and castigator.[42]

[37] The reader is recalled to the summary statement at the outset of Analysis 42, on Alḥarizi's treatment of the theme of niggardliness.

[38] *EJ* vii. 369–70.

[39] *Heh* = 5, *yod* = 10, *mem* = 40, and *nun* = 50, all these totalling 105; *heh* = 5, *alef* = 1, *zayin* = 7, *resh* = 200, *ḥet* = 8, and *yod* = 10, these letters totalling 231. The two words thus total 436.

[40] *Ḥet* = 8, *bet* = 2, *resh* = 200, together comprising 210; *heh* = 5, *kof* = 100, *yod* = 10, *nun* = 50, and *yod* = 10, together comprising 175. The two sums total 385.

[41] Yehudah ben Shelomoh is precisely the name used by the author in the last stich of his prefatory poem to the work: *ST* 3. 25.

[42] Well might it be that the limning of Hever as a frequent conniver and dissembler and opportunist indeed reflects actual penchants of the author: Sadan, 'Rabbi Judah Alḥarizi as a Cultural Crossroad', points out very significant disparagement in the description of our

GIVEN THE POTPOURRI nature of *Sefer Taḥkemoni*, it is not surprising that the work has been seen as a compendium whose parts have been arbitrarily ordered, such that one could shift any gate to any other with no change effected. That this is not the case has been noted more than once in this study, particularly in respect of the book's beginning and close. The opening matter could not be shifted without damage to the whole. The initial poem, the Introduction and Gate 1 lay out the identity of the writer and the complex process of the genesis of the work; Gate 2, essentially the first gate in the book-wide pattern of Heman the Ezrahite encountering Hever the Kenite, presents the latter as a truly moral figure—that after the very serious declarations of the book's purpose (preceding) and in contrast to the clearest Arabic source, where the preacher (in al-Ḥariri's opening gate) is an arrant hypocrite; and Gate 3, laying out the history and evaluation of Hebrew poetry in Spain, delivers an esoteric message that Alḥarizi is the true heir, if not rival, of his illustrious predecessors and, in particular, Judah Halevi.

Indeed a case may be made for the aptness of the shock effect of having the preachment of Hever the Kenite in Gate 2 followed by the display of his grossness in Gate 3—in effect creating a bracketing of incongruous and coarse behaviour with very serious messages. In Gate 3, it will be recalled, the disgusted assemblage is forced to concede, shamefacedly, that their rejection of the crude glutton was shortsighted, and that his coarse exterior belied his true genius.

The logic of the book's ordering at the start is paralled by the effect of closure in the concluding gates, by which time the blending of Alḥarizi with his personae has become patent. Gate 46 picks up a major theme of the work, largesse and its lack—the very theme that figured so prominently in Gate 1—even as it echoes the fact of the author's journeying, highlighted in the introductory poem. Gate 47 with its vying of seven cities relates, again—but now in obverse fashion—to the author's initially emphasized wandering, and recalls the emphasis on Jerusalem in the introductory poem. Gate 48, a virtuoso display of rhetoric and literary structuring as the book approaches its close, brings to its most sophisticated display the interaction of Hever and Heman throughout the work, while recalling the bizarre interactions of author, narrator, and protagonist in the Introduction and (especially) Gate 1.

author by al-Mubarak ibn al-Sha'ar. The latter, while praising him warmly for his poetic talents and citing others who did the same, observed that he was a man not be trusted, always(!) mocking every person that he ever praised (Sadan, pp. 32, 46; and in the Arabic original, 52, ll. 3–5)! Of course, one such statement does not constitute proof of such a proclivity—but the characterization comes tantalizingly close to the behaviour of Hever in many a gate in *Sefer Taḥkemoni*.

Gate 49, shattering the convention of almost all gates preceding that it is Hever who is the rhetor-hero and Heman his awed audience, comes to drive home the dual identification of author with Heman and Hever both. Finally, though Gate 50 is indeed a poetic catch-all, its closing brief mention of the trip through the East, including the grief over viewing the ruins of Jerusalem, links up with the initial poem wherein the author ends on the theme of his wandering, and his journeying to Zion. Moreover, the repeated skewering of tightwads in this gate, as was the case in Gate 46, rounds out the bitter complaint of the author in Gate 1 that poetry and writers are spurned world-wide by a boorish and tight-fisted Jewish people; conversely, the effusive dedications to Samuel ibn Albarkoli at the close of the Introduction and to Prince Josiah at the close of Gate 1 are paralleled by the fulsome praise tendered Joseph of Aleppo at the book's end.

In addition to this designedly bracketing structure, there are some subsections or clusters of consecutive gates—at times including an additional gate one gate removed—comprising variations on a genre or a common theme (while by no means exhausting said theme or genre in the work as a whole). Thus Gates 13, 14, 15, and 17 deal with serious religious subjects: divine retribution (13), original prayers (14 and 15), and the Karaite–Rabbanite controversy (17). Fate's rule and power, a theme appearing frequently in *Sefer Taḥkemoni*, is variously explored in Gates 22, 23, 25, and 26 (and 29 as well). The theme of miraculous rescue is explored in Gates 37 and 38. Literary debate, or *tenson*, though found in several loci in the book, is clustered in Gate 39 (in whose analysis the genre's history is discussed), and Gates 40, 41, and 43. Two gates of maxim and anecdote are 44 and 45.

As well it would seem that the often stark conjoining of disparate gates is no sure indication of arbitrary arrangement: frequently it could be part of the game of shocking the reader while playing authorial hide-and-seek. The sincere preacher of Gate 2 turns glutton in Gate 3; the practitioner of horrific violence in Gate 6 is awed by the horrors of battle carnage in Gate 7; the preacher against corruption in Jerusalem (Gate 28) becomes a hypocrite preacher in Gate 29.

Now putting all these elements together we can see that Alḥarizi's bifurcation is more than a whim or game. This work has often run at cross-purposes. The stated goal of *Sefer Taḥkemoni* has been to give added wisdom to the wise and to lead other readers, through light and secular entertainment, to 'the good of the Lord'. Such a declaration must be seen as far from adequate to account for the many and profound contradictions and tensions within the book. The sophisticated and multi-level splitting of the author into two personae, neither of which is consistently identified with honesty, morality, or religiosity—albeit Heman represents probity more than Hever—hints at the divisions within the actual author himself.

If the shifting stances, even personalities, of Hever the Kenite present a somewhat dizzying display to the reader, and rightly rule out any simplistic 'message' of the work, one aspect of the Kenite—and of his author—prevails in almost every gate: a penchant for concealment. In the overwhelming majority of instances, the identity of Hever is concealed until the end, when the narrator 'discovers' who he is—more often by the calibre of his metric display than by explicit visual recognition! In addition, Heman as well as the reader have been misled more than once as to what will be told, or as to the veracity of the episode.

Beyond all this lies a deeper stratum, a number of complex literary structures not unrelated to the later bracketing of the work as a whole, heretofore discussed—structures that neither the persona of the author or Hever, executor of the same, boasts of or even mentions.

The reader will recall the elaborate rhetorical display of Gate 33, wherein Alḥarizi has his protagonist expound an arresting rhymed prose diatribe, entirely in homonym rhyme, against the follies of this world; and follows this display with twenty-two two-line double homonym poems. Of this achievement Hever the Kenite credits himself expansively, as is his wont in the book, and the audience is duly impressed with his display; but he has accomplished yet more—to understand which will require a brief excursus.

In previous gates the reader's attention has been drawn to a widespread scriptural stylistic, the phenomenon of inclusion, or bracketing of the gate with one or more identical words, or words deriving from the same root. In recent decades, biblical scholarship has given growing attention to this bracketing, at first of psalms and other poetic creations, then of prose compositions or parts thereof. Such bracketing may comprise the very first and last word(s) of the composition (such as the bracketing of each of Pss. 146–50 with *halleluyah*); the bracketing of the poem with an identical verse (Ps. 118: 'Praise the Lord for He is good, for His mercy endures for ever'); or providing an identical word or root in the very first and last verse,[43] or in the initial and closing verses.[44] A very special development of biblical inclusion overlaps with the phenomenon of chiastic parallelism, represented in graphic short-

[43] Ps. 29: 1, 11.

[44] Examples of such would be *lehagid* in Ps. 92: 'To proclaim (*lehagid*) Your steadfast love at daybreak, Your faithfulness each night' (v. 3) and 'in old age they still produce fruit . . . attesting (*lehagid*) that the Lord is upright, my rock, in whom there is no wrong'. An early list of inclusions in Psalms is to be found in S. Liebreich's 'Psalms 34 and 145 in the Light of their Key Words', *Hebrew Union College Annual*, 27 (1956), 183 n. 7.

hand as *abba* (for example: 'They-stirred-him-to-jealousy with-strange-gods, with-abominable-practices they-provoked-him-to-anger'—Deut. 32: 26).[45] In the first chapter of Lamentations, which is written as an alphabetical acrostic, this chiastic bracketing includes the sharing of a common root in the first and last verses, then the second and twenty-first, and so on, right to the middle verses.[46] The sharing of words in the first and last two verses is presented herewith:

1. Alas! Lonely sits the city once great (*rabati*) with people. She that was once great (*rabati*) among nations is become like a widow; the princess among states is become a thrall.

> 22. Let all their wrongdoings come before You, and deal with them as You have dealt with me for all my transgressions. For my sighs are many (*rabot*) and my heart is sick.

2. Bitterly she weeps at night, her cheeks wet with tears. There is none to comfort her of all (*ein lah menaḥem mikol*) her friends. All (*kol*) her allies have betrayed her; they have become (*hayu*) her foes (*le'oyevim*).

> 21. When they heard how I was sighing, there was none to comfort me (*ein menaḥem li*); all my foes (*kol oyevai*) heard of my plight and exulted, for it is Your doing: You have brought on the day that You threatened. Oh, let them become (*veyihyu*) like me!

The entire scheme of this full chiastic bracketing can be represented as follows:

1	*rabati . . . rabati*	22	*rabot*
2	*ein lah menaḥem mikol . . . kol . . . le'oyevim*	21	*ein menaḥem li . . . kol oyevai*
3	*hametsarim*	20	*tsar li*
4	*kohaneiha*	19	*kohanai*
5	*halekhu shevi*	18	*halekhu bashevi*
6	*bat tsiyon*	17	*tsiyon*
7	*hayu*	16	*hayu*
8	*kol*	15	*kol*
9	*lo*	14	*lo*
10	*paras*	13	*paras*
11	*re'eh . . . vehabita*	12	*habitu ure'u*

[45] Cited in the discussion of biblical parallellism in 'Poetry', *EJ* xiii. 673.

[46] This phenomenon is presented in Renkema, 'The Literary Structure of Lamentations', who cites the earlier discovery of this phenomenon in 1932. My list differs slightly, in that I have accepted only root repetitions, whether of verbs, adjectives, prepositions, or adverbs, and have disregarded the parallelisms of synonymous words. Both Condamin and Renkema

A careful reading of the poetic homonym rhymes of Gate 33 reveals this very phenomenon. Here follows a literal rendering of one set of matching poems according to this scheme—*Tet* versus *Nun*, the ninth poems from the start and close.

Tet

You, drowning in the sea of evil: know, pray, that (*ki*) that man is happy who has dipped in the river of truth. Good he is [held] before his God (*elohav*) and as well before every man (*kol adam*); hence he shall never be lacking in good.

Nun

We wait on You, our God (*eloheinu*), for (*hakhi*) Yours is that greatness poured out upon man (*adam*). Yet we cover our utterances with the gilt of vanity; a mask covers every (*kol*) heart.

The entire scheme is represented in Table 1 at the close of this discussion.

Now if this hidden rhetorical achievement were not enough, Alḥarizi has given his (most discerning!) readers yet more of the same. A close reading of the gate's entire homonym display—the rhymed prose preachment of the Kenite together with his acrostically organized metric verse—reveals full bracketing inclusion of both, when they are taken as one unit. Let us look at the meeting point of this phenomenon—the last lines of rhymed prose and the immediately ensuing first three poems, the latter presented here in reverse order, in accordance with the bracketing phenomenon.

Rhymed Prose

. . . an angel of His presence will be his messenger and emissary (*vetsiro*) to bandage his wound and his hurt (*vetsiro*) and if he eschew lust he will rejoice (*yismaḥ*) at the end of his days of being a Nazirite and his mitre will shine upon him (*alav*).

Poetry

Gimel

Gilead's balm (*tsori*) is there none for your injuries (*tsireikha*)
until you exile the troops of your sin;
Eternal joy shall you then find
when Time's sea stirs up filth and muck.

point out a like phenomenon in ch. 2 of Lamentations. In a study now under preparation I consider the possibility that this full bracketing phenomenon includes paronomasia. If this proves to be the case, the findings in Alḥarizi would deserve fresh scrutiny.

Bet
The tester of hearts will search out your heart's secret;
therefore hold fast to probity ever, my son.
Therein find favour and good when time changes your joy for disaster
and your happiness (*vesimḥatakh*) for moaning.

Alef
Faith is the ornament of regents and princes
and is queen: every king is her prisoner.
Raised in her bosom was my soul and therefore (*ve'al ken*)
I shall not remove her from my heart.

The full chart of correspondences of this chiastic bracketing is to be found in Table 2 at the close of this discussion.

In Gate 33, then, Alḥarizi chooses to deliver far more than his hero has boasted that he is capable of—a tactic not new in *Sefer Taḥkemoni*, but far less difficult to discern heretofore.[47]

Now Gate 33's concealed bracketing pattern is not alone in *Sefer Taḥkemoni*. In no less than five other gates of this work our author has produced a like esoteric display, if never quite so intricate.

When one extracts the twelve poems of praise for the months of the lunar year in Gate 5, one discovers that precisely three bracketing roots/words link the first month, Nisan, with the last, Adar; the second, Iyyar, with the next to last, Shevat; and so on until the inclusions meet in the middle with Elul and Tishrei.[48]

In Gate 9, the bracketing pattern here described is to be found by comparing the poems requested of Hever, together with the preceding requests in rhymed prose.[49]

In Gate 32, it appears in the rhetorical contention of the aged Hever and the youth in the description of varied phenomena, with Hever completing, first in rhymed prose and then in metric verse, his rival's description.[50]

In Gate 12, the poems of boast of the twelve Jewries gathered to defend King Stint—in aggregate symbolizing the Jewish people (the twelve tribes of Israel)—the same pattern is evidenced, with two or more roots or words being shared by the poetic declarations of loyalty put forth.[51]

Even in the anecdotes of Gate 45 the same phenomenon is evidenced.[52]

Whom was our author out to impress? Most likely but a handful of readers

[47] See e.g. Gates 8 and 11 and their respective Analyses.
[48] See Table 5 at the close of this discussion. [49] See Table 4 at the close of this discussion.
[50] See Table 6 at the close of this discussion. [51] See Table 7 at the close of this discussion.
[52] See Table 8 at the close of this discussion.

—perhaps the same group of poets-cognoscenti that he posited would most appreciate the very difficult tropes and figures of Moses ibn Ezra, whom he held up as a model of a poet who wrote for poets.[53] That our author had Moses ibn Ezra in mind is certain, for herein he has imitated a stylistic not only of Lamentations, but of this admired predecessor, with whom he here vies—on an esoteric level! A careful perusal of Moses ibn Ezra's *Sefer ha'anak*, a ten-section compendium of homonym rhymes, reveals in the sixth gate, treating of the topic of fate and its treacheries, a full bracketing-receding inclusion. A particularly strong linkage is that of poems 7 and 18:

Poem 7

I am vexed with a friend (*re'a*) who conducted himself duplicitiously (*belev valev*, 'with two hearts'), as he demonstrated (by his actions) and spoke: he alighted upon the oil of my friendship like a fly until he stank and spoilt it.

Poem 18

Every theft is trivial compared with the theft of a friend (*re'a*) I had held as my rib. My heart (*levavi*) had imagined that he would serve him (i.e. my heart) as a rock on the day of danger, but he rejoiced on the day of my misfortune.[54]

In this hidden rhetorical display Alḥarizi, then, is at once heir of both Moses ibn Ezra and the author of Lamentations.[55] Furthermore, he joins a distinguished cadre of medieval Hebrew writers who practised esoteric communication for different reasons: Maimonides, in his *Guide of the Perplexed*, to safeguard for his chosen audience (ostensibly the one recipient of the book) philosophic knowledge beyond the ken of the masses;[56] Abraham ibn Daud, whose elaborate dating-system in his *Sefer hakabalah* has been shown to treat of the tabooed topic of calculating the end of the exile;[57] and Samuel Hanagid, who not only likened himself openly to King David as psalmist, but esoterically linked several poems in his *Divan*, or anthology of secular poetry, with specific hymns in the book of Psalms.[58] Yet even as all these

[53] Gate 18, *ST* 189. 3–190. 2.

[54] For the chart of correspondences, see Table 3 at the close of this discussion.

[55] In actuality, Moses ibn Ezra follows the same pattern in a number of his ten gates, as I mean to show in a future study. Alḥarizi imitated, competed with, and surpassed ibn Ezra's accomplishment in his own *Sefer ha'anak*, where every gate exhibits the phenomenon of full receding inclusion. For a discussion of this issue, with listings and charts, see Segal, 'Imitations'.

[56] The classic study is Strauss, 'The Literary Character'. A succinct and summary discussion may be found in Sirat, *A History of Jewish Philosophy in the Middle Ages*, 162, 175–9, 199, 284.

[57] Cohen, *Sefer Ha-Qabbalah*, esp. ch. 3 of the analysis, 'The Symmetry of History', pp. 189–222.

[58] D. Segal, 'Ben Tehillim of Shmuel Hanagid and the Book of Psalms', 119–322.

writers variously hint at the esoteric component of their writing, so has Alḥarizi in Gate 33, albeit very obliquely. At the start, Heman expresses his desire to attend the *ḥidot* of the *ḥakhamim*, 'wise'.[59] *Ḥidah* is defined variously as 'riddle, enigma, perplexing saying or question', 'dark, obscure utterance', 'something put indirectly and needing interpretation', 'a lesson taught indirectly', and 'riddle, enigma, to be guessed'.[60] None of these definitions quite fit what follows in the text, on the surface. Only when the reader/listener goes beyond the apparent rhetorical display-cum-preachment will he reach this particularly hidden level—and hidden it is.

***Table 1.* Receding inclusion in the homonym poems of Gate 33**

Poem	Shared root/word	Poem	Shared root/word
Alef	*lo*	***Tav***	*velo*
Bet	*levavot . . . ki*	***Shin***	*levavi . . . ki*
Gimel	*hazeman*	***Resh***	*hazeman*
Dalet	*ha'el . . . lev*	***Kof***	*libi . . . ha'el*
Heh	*al*	***Tsadi***	*alai*
Vav	*enosh*	***Peh***	*enosh*
Zayin	*al*	***Ayin***	*alav*
Ḥet	*nafshi*	***Samekh***	*nafsham*
Tet	*ki . . . elohav . . . kol adam*	***Nun***	*eloheinu hakhi . . . adam . . . kol*
Yod	*divrei*	***Mem***	*devar*
Kaf	*lekha*	***Lamed***	*lekha*

[59] *ST* 275. 4. [60] BDB 295.

***Table 2.* Receding inclusion in the rhymed prose and homonym poems of Gate 33 when taken as one unit (page and line references are to *ST*)**

Page	Rhymed prose		Poetry	
	Lines	Word(s)	Word(s)	Letter
275	23–4	*tehilah . . .* *tehilato . . . tehilato*	*tehilah*	***tav***
276	1	*tuvo*	*tov*	***shin***
	1	*kol*	*kulam*	***resh***
	2	*la'alot*	*alav*	***kof***
	2	*lema'alah*	*alai*	***tsadi***
	5	*hasekhel . . . halev*	*levav maskil*	***peh***
	7, 11	*veliheyot . . . hayetser*	*tehi . . . yitsrekha*	***ayin***
	13	*haḥet*	*ḥet*	***samekh***
	14	*el*	*eloheinu*	***nun****
	14	*el*	*ha'el*	***mem***
	15	*veliheyot*	*hayu*	***lamed***
	16	*elohim*	*eloheikha*	***kaf***
	16	*kol . . . yekarah*	*kol yekar*	***yod***
	18	*haresha . . . hatov*	*rasha . . .* *tov . . . tov*	***tet***
	19	*leveito*	*beit*	***ḥet***
	20	*keven*	*ben*	***zayin***
	21	*movao*	*bevo*	***vav***
	23–4	*hayetser*	*yitsrekha*	***heh***
	24	*ha'el*	*ha'el*	***dalet***
	26	*vetsiro . . . vetsiro*	*tsori* *letsireikha*	***gimel***
	27	*yismaḥ*	*vesimḥatakh*	***bet***
	27	*ve'alav*	*ve'al*	***alef***

* This is the only instance of the pairing of word-play rather than a shared or identical root. The *el* of the rhymed prose means 'to' or 'towards'; *eloheinu* = 'our God'.

Table 3. Receding inclusion in Gate 6* of Moses ibn Ezra's *Sefer ha'anak*, or anthology of homonym rhymes

1	*ish*, man	24	*ishim*, men
2	*al*, on	23	*al*, on
3	*el . . . lo*, with . . . not	22	*el . . . lo*, with . . . not
4	*dodim*, friends	21	*yedidut*, friendship
5	*al . . . me'enosh*, over . . . of mankind	20	*ish . . . alai*, man . . . against me
6	*yelekhu*, they walk	19	*yelekh*, he walks
7	*re'a belev valev*, a duplicitous friend	18	*re'a . . . levavi*, a friend . . . my heart
8	*ish*, a man	17	*ish*, a man
9	*veliyedidim yemei*, with friends who, during the days	16	*beyom . . . ledodi*, on that day . . . towards a friend
10	*veyosher*, and probity	15	*veyashar*, the most upright
11	*le'anshei*, to the men	14	*enosh*, man
12	*ahav*, love	13	*ahavai*, my loves

* Gate 6 contains twenty-four poems.

***Table 4.* Receding inclusion in Gate 9**

Root/word	No.	Rhymed prose	Poem	Poem	Rhymed prose	No.
ki, r-ts-h	1	*retsonekha*	*ki*	*hakhi*	*tirtseh*	30
al, h-y-h	2		*tihyeh*	***vehayetah***		
			. . . al	*. . . alai*		29
asher	3		*asher*	*asher*		28
shir,	4	*shirkha . . .*	***shelakh***	***yishlakh***	*beshirkha*	27
sh-l-kh		***shelakh***				
'-v-h	5	*te'aveh*	*hitavah . . .*		*titav*	26
asher,	6		***asher*** *. . .*	***asher***		25
ʿ-s-h			***asot***	***ya'aseh***		
ruaḥ	7		*ruḥi*	*veruḥo*		24
s-kh-l, al	8	*sikhlekha*	*ve'al ken*	*sikhlekha*	*al*	23
lev,	9	*levav . . .*	*libi . . .*	*levav . . .*		22
mayim		***mayim***	*kamayim*	***mayim***		
sekhel,	10	*sikhelekha*	*enosh . . .*	*sekhel*	*sikhlekha*	21
ish/enosh			*ish*	*ve'anshei*		
levav,	11		*bilevavkha*	*levavi*		
ayin			*. . . eino*	*. . . eini*		20
shir, rosh	12	*shirkha*	*lerosh*	*rosh . . .* ***rosh***	*hashir*	19
kol	13	*kol*		*kol*	*mikol*	18
shir,	14	*shirkha . . .*	*uve'et*	*leshiri . . .*	*shir . . .*	17
n-ts-v,		*shir*	*. . . shir*	*shir*		
et		***nitsavah***	***nitsavah***	*nitsevu . . .*		
				be'et hashir		
kol,	15	*kol . . .*		*kol*		16
yehi		*yehi*			*yehi*	

Explanation: Words presented in the challenge citation to Hever and which appear in his closing hemistich are in bold type. In the Root/word column, recurring words that occur in their exact form are given as words; verbs occuring in different forms are given as roots.

Table 5. Receding inclusion in Gate 5: Descriptions of the months of the year

1	Nisan	*beinot . . . yemei . . . kosan*	*bein . . . koskha . . . biyemei*	Adar
2	Iyyar	*ki . . . alei . . . yagon*	*yagon . . . ki . . . alei*	Shevat
3	Sivan	*kosot mekhusot . . . hakos . . . leshon hakos betsuf*	*hakos . . . tsuf . . . uleshonkha . . . mileshon . . . koskha*	Tevet
4	Tammuz	*zeman . . . yehi . . . usemaḥ . . . tehi*	*mizeman . . . tihyeh . . . semaḥ*	Kislev
5	Av	*hakos . . . tirveh . . . yegonot*	*harvan . . . bekhos . . . yegonot*	Ḥeshvan
6	Elul	*tenah hakos . . . ets . . . be'ets*	*tenah . . . hakos . . . ke'ets*	Tishrei

Summary of shared roots and their meaning

1 *bein*, among; *yom*, day, season; *kos*, cup
2 *ki*, because; *al*, on; *yagon*, grief
3 *kos*, cup, *mekhuseh*, covered; *tsuf*, fine honey; *lashon*, tongue
4 *zeman*, time; *h-y-h*, to be; *semaḥ*, rejoice
5 *kos*, cup; *r-v-h*, satiate; *yagon*, grief
6 *tenah*, give; *kos*, cup; *ets*, tree

Table 6. Receding inclusion in Gate 32: Fleshing out of descriptions

Subject	Specific words	Specific words	Subject
Pen	*vene'ehav*, loved	*ahavah*, love	Moon
Missive	*me'orah*, luminary	*leha'ir*, to shine	Sunlight
Sword	*me'or*, light *leshon*, tongue	*or . . . or*, light *leshon*, tongue	Candle
Mail	*ein*, eye	*ayin*, eye	
Steed	*lekhol*, to all *uvanahar*, and in the river	*lekhol*, to all *neharim*, rivers	Water Conduit
Torch	*bokhah vetsoḥeket*, weeps and laughs	*mevakah . . . vetsoḥeket levikhyo*, weeping and laughing at his weeping	Harp
Myrrh	*ne'im*, pleasantness	*na'amu*, pleasant; *ne'imim, na'im*, pleasant	Nut
Wine	*adamdamim . . . hamo'adam*, reddish *ne'im*, pleasantness	*admonim*, reddish *no'am*, pleasantness	Pomegranate
Hawk	*keruaḥ*, like the wind *habarak*, the lightning	*ruaḥ*, wind *barak*, lightning	Streams
Wolf	*kaberakim*, like lightning	*barak, vehabarak*, lightning	Lightning

Table 7. Receding inclusion in Gate 12: Poems

Group	Shared words	Shared words	Group
1 Haran	*al, ad*	*al, nital, ad*	Damascus
2 Aram Naharaim	*keravot oyevav, ad, la'adoneinu, demei, bedamim*	*keravot, hakerav, laoyev, adei, adoneinu, dam*	Hamath
3 Calneh	*naḥnu, benei, na'arokh, na'avor, lo neḥsheh ad ki adoneinu, miyedei*	*naḥnu, benei, na'arokh, avru, lo neḥsheh ad ki adoneinu, miyad*	Pisgah
4 Adinah	*ḥaravot, namut, adoneinu*	*beḥarbeinu, umavet, adoneinu*	No-Amon
5 Ashur	*adoneinu, hakerav, lakerav, lo . . . ad*	*adonai, kerav, hakerav, lo . . . ad*	Mitsrayim
6 Arbel	*yelekhu, lefaneinu, adoneinu, el, elohim, ad ki, ad*	*halekhu, lefaneinu, adoneinu, ha'el, ve'ad ki*	Erets Hatsevi

Glossary (1) *al*, on; *ad*, until; *nital*, we shall ascend. (2) *kerav*, battle; *oyev*, foe; *ad/adei*, until; *adoneinu*, our lord; *demei/dam*, blood. (3) *naḥnu*, we; *benei*, sons of; *arokh*, wage (war); *na'avor/avru*, cross over; *lo neḥsheh ad ki adoneinu . . . miyad/miyedei*, we will not hold silent until we [rescue] our lord from the hand(s). (4) *ḥerev*, sword; *namut*, we shall die, *umavet*, and death; *adoneinu*, our lord. (5) *adonai*, lord; *krav*, battle; *lo . . . ad*, not . . . until. (6) *yelekhu/halekhu*, go; *lefaneinu*, before us; *el/elohim*, God; *(ve')ad ki*, until.

Table 8. Receding inclusion in Gate 45

	Repeating words	Repeating words	
1	*al*, on, *eikh*, how	*al, eikh*	26
2	*meshakrim*, lie	*sheker*, falsehood	25
3	*bevo*, at the coming of	*ba*, came	24
4	*tishe'al*, ask	*sha'al*, he asked	23
5	*kavarta*, you buried	*kever, kever*, grave	22
6	*ishah*, woman, *shetei* (× 3), two	*ishtekha*, your wife, *shenei*, two	21
7	*ishah*, woman, *mibenot*, from the daughters of	*liveno*, for his son, *be'ishah*, upon a woman	20
8	*beḥayim*, alive	*ḥai*, by the life of	19
9	*ḥesed*, grace, *ish eḥad min*, a certain man of	*haḥasidim, heḥasid*, the pious *ish min, eḥad min*	18
10	*ish min haḥakhamim*, a wise man	*ish min*, a man of *veḥokhmah*, and wisdom	17
11	*ve'amar ish*, a man said, *amar*, he said	*sha'alu le'ish*, they asked *amar*, he said	16
12	*ve'amar, ish*	*ve'amar, le'ish*, to a man	15
13	*ish eḥad*, one man *amar lo*, he said to him *amar*, he said, *alav*, over him	*ish*, a man, *le'eḥad*, to one *ameru lo*, they said to him *al*, over	14

Bibliography

ABRAHAM BAR ḤIYYA, *The Meditation of the Sad Soul* [*Hegyon hanefesh ha'atsuvah*], tr. G. Wigoder (London, 1969).

ABRAHAM IBN DAUD, *Sefer Ha-Qabbalah: The Book of Tradition, by Abraham ibn Daud*, ed. G. Cohen (Philadelphia, 1967).

ABRAHAM IBN EZRA, *The Religious Poems of Abraham ibn Ezra* [*Shirei hakodesh shel avraham ibn ezra*], ed. I. Levin (2 vols., Jerusalem, 1975–80).

—— *The Torah Commentaries of Abraham ibn Ezra* [*Ibn ezra: perushei hatorah lerabenu avraham ibn ezra*], ed. A. Weizer: *Genesis* (Jerusalem, 1977).

—— *Ḥai ben mekits* [*He who Lives, Son of Him who Wakens*], ed. I. Levin (Tel Aviv, 1983).

ACKERMAN, R. W., 'The Debate of the Body and the Soul and Parochial Christianity', *Speculum*, 37 (1962), 541–65.

AL-HAMADHANI, *The Maqāmāt of Badí' al-Zamān al-Hamādhānī: Translated from the Arabic with an Introduction and Notes, Historical and Grammatical, by W. J. Prendergast* (London, 1915).

AL-ḤARIRI, *Makamat or Rhetorical Anecdotes of Al Hariri of Basra, translated from the Arabic with Annotations by T. Preston* (London, 1850).

—— *The Assemblies of Al-Hariri*, i, ed. T. Chenery (London, 1867); ii, tr. F. Steingass, prefaced and indexed by F. F. Arbuthnot (London, 1898).

See also under ALḤARIZI

ALḤARIZI, JUDAH, *Machberoth Ithiel*, ed. T. Chenery (London, 1872).

—— *Rabi yehudah alḥarizi: Sefer ha'anak*, ed. A. Avronin (Tel Aviv, 1945).

—— *Al-ḥariri: Maḥberot iti'el betirgum rabi yehudah alḥarizi*, ed. Y. Perets (Tel Aviv, 1951).

—— *Sefer Taḥkemoni*, ed. Y. Toporovsky (Tel Aviv, 1952).

ALLONI, N., *The Scansion of Medieval Hebrew Poetry: Dunash, Judah Halevi and Abraham ibn Ezra* [*Torat hamishkalim shel dunash, yehudah halevi ve'avraham ibn ezra*] (Jerusalem, 1951).

—— 'The Gazelle and the Camel in the (Hebrew) Poetry of Spain' ['Hatsevi vehagamal beshirat sefarad'], *Otsar yehudei sefarad*, 4 (1961), 16–43.

—— 'Reflections of the Revolt against "Arabiyeh" in our Literature in the Middle Ages' ['Hishtakfut hamered ba'arabiyeh besifrutenu biyemei habeinayim'], in C. Rabin (ed.), *M. Wallenstein Jubilee Volume* [*Sefer me'ir valenshtein*] (Jerusalem, 1979), 80–136.

—— 'An Anthology of Twelfth-Century Prose Letters and Works from (Hebrew) Spain' ['Kovets igerot sefardiyot mehame'ah hasheteim-esrei'], *Sefunot*, 16 (1980), 63–82.

ALLONI, N., 'Zion and Jerusalem in the Poetry of (Hebrew) Spain' ['Tsiyon viyerushalayim beshirat sefarad'], in Ben-Ami (ed.), *The Legacy of the Jews of Spain and the East*, 235–59.

ALMAGOR, D., 'On Physicians and the Sick' ['Al rofe'im veḥolim'], *Yediot aḥaronot*, 6 Jan. 1978.

—— 'Social Satire in *Maqāma* Literature' ['Satirah ḥevratit besifrut hamakamot'], *Alei siaḥ*, 7–8 (1979), 132–58.

ALTER, R., *On Biblical Poetry* (New York, 1985).

ALTMANN, A., *Biblical and Other Studies* (Cambridge, 1963).

ANKORI, Z., *Karaites in Byzantium* (New York, 1959).

ARBERRY, A. (ed. and tr.), *Arabic Poetry: A Primer for Students* (Cambridge, 1965).

—— (ed. and tr.), *Poems of al-Mutanabbī* (Cambridge, 1967).

ASHKENAZI, S., *Each Generation and its Customs* [*Dor dor uminhagav*] (Tel Aviv, 1977).

ASHTOR, E. *The Jews of Moslem Spain*, tr. A. Klein and J. Machlowitz (3 vols., Philadelphia, 1983–4).

AVINERI, I., 'The Old Man in the Bible and the Talmud' ['Hazaken bamikra uvatalmud'], *Sinai*, 98 (1986), 218–77.

AVRONIM, A., *Rabi yehudah alḥarizi: Sefer ha'anak* (Tel Aviv, 1945).

—— 'Maḥberot itiel' (reviewing Perets's edition), *Gilyonot*, 25 (1951), 314–15.

BACON, Y., *Topics in the Development of Metre in Hebrew Poetry* [*Perakim behitpatḥut hamishkal shel hashirah ha'ivrit*] (Tel Aviv, 1968).

BAḤYA IBN PAQUDA, *Al-hidāya 'ilā 'l-farāiḍ al-qulūb*, tr. M. Mansoor *et al.*, *The Book of Directions to the Duties of the Heart* (London, 1973); Heb. trans. *Ḥovot halevavot* (*Duties of the Heart*), ed. A. Zifroni (Jerusalem, 1928); ed. M. Hyamson (Jerusalem, 1970).

BARNETT, R. D., *The Sephardi Heritage: Essays on the History and Cultural Contribution of the Jews of Spain and Portugal* (London, 1971).

BEKKUM, W. J. VAN, 'Observations on the Hebrew Debate in Medieval Europe', in Reinink and Vanstiphout, *Dispute Poems*, 77–90.

BEN-AMI, I. (ed.), *The Legacy of the Jews of Spain and the East: Studies* [*Moreshet yehudei sefarad vehamizraḥ: meḥkarim*] (Jerusalem, 1982).

BENJAMIN OF TUDELA, *The Book of the Journey of Rabbi Benjamin of Blessed Memory* [*Sefer masaot shel rabi binyamin zikhrono liverakhah*], ed. M. Adler (London, 1907).

BEREKHIAH HANAKDAN, *The Fox Fables of Rabbi Berekhiah the Grammarian* [*Mishlei shualim lerabi berekhiyah hanakdan*], ed. H. Schwarzbaum (Kiron, 1979).

BERLINER, A., *Selected Writings* [*Ketavim nivḥarim*] (Jerusalem, 1949).

BIRNBAUM, P., *High Holyday Prayer Book* [*Maḥzor hashalem lerosh hashanah veyom kipur*] (New York, 1951).

—— *The Daily Prayer Book* [*Hasidur hashalem*] (New York, 1977).

BLIDSTEIN, G., 'The Approach to the Karaites in Maimonidean Teaching' ['Hagishah lakara'im bemishnat harambam'], *Teḥumin*, 8 (1987), 501–10.

—— *Prayer in the Maimonidean Halakhah* [*Hatefilah bemishnato hahilkhatit shel harambam*] (Jerusalem, 1994).

BONNEBAKER, S. A., 'Religious Prejudice against Poetry in Early Islam', in Clogan (ed.), *Medieval Poetics*, 77–100.

BOSSY, M. A., 'Medieval Debates of Body and Soul', *Comparative Literature*, 20 (1976), 144–63.

BRANN, R., 'The "Dissembling Poet" in Medieval Hebrew Literature: The Dimensions of a Literary Topos', *Journal of the American Oriental Society*, 107 (1987), 39–54.

—— 'Andalusian Hebrew Poetry and the Hebrew Bible: Cultural Nationalism or Cultural Ambiguity?', in D. R. Blumenthal (ed.), *Approaches to Judaism in Medieval Times* (Atlanta, 1988), iii. 101–31.

—— *The Compunctious Poet: Cultural Ambiguity and Hebrew Poetry in Muslim Spain* (Baltimore, 1991).

—— 'Power in the Portrayal: Representations of Muslims and Jews in Judah Alharizi's Tahkemoni', in C. Issawi and B. Lewis (eds.), *Princeton Papers in Near Eastern Studies*, i (Princeton, 1992), 1–22.

BROCK, S., 'A Dispute of the Months and Some Related Syriac Texts', *Journal of Semitic Studies*, 30 (1985), 181–211.

—— 'The Dispute between Soul and Body: An Example of a Long-lived Mesopotamian Literary Genre', *Aram*, 1: 1 (1989), 53–64.

BRODY, H., 'Hidden Treasures: Section Two: The Book of Pearls of Rabbi Judah Alḥarizi' ['Matmunei mistarim: maḥberet bet—sefer ha'anak lerabi yehudah alḥarizi'], in D. B. Gunzburg and I. Markon (eds.), *Harkavy Jubilee Volume* [*Sefer zikaron leharkavi*] (3 vols., St Petersburg 1908; repr. Jerusalem, 1969), iii. 309–50.

BROWN, F., DRIVER, S. R., and BRIGGS, C. A., *A Hebrew and English Lexicon of the Old Testament with an Appendix Containing the Biblical Aramaic, based on the Lexicon of William Gesenius, as translated by Edward Robinson* (corr. repr. Oxford, 1959).

CARMI, T., *The Penguin Book of Hebrew Verse* (New York, 1981).

CASSUTO, U., *A Commentary on the Book of Genesis: Part One—From Adam to Noah*, tr. I. Abrahams (Jerusalem, 1961).

CHOTZNER, J., *Hebrew Satire* (London, 1911).

CLOGAN, P. M. (ed.), *Medieval Poetics = Medievalia et Humanistica: Studies in Medieval and Renaissance Culture*, NS 7 (Cambridge, 1976).

COHEN, G., 'The Story of the Four Captives', *Proceedings of the American Academy for Jewish Research*, 29 (1960–1).

—— *Sefer Ha-Qabbalah: The Book of Tradition by Abraham ibn Daud* (Philadelphia, 1967).

CRANE, HART, *Complete Poems and Selected Letters and Prose*, ed. B. Weber (New York, 1933).

DANA, J., 'The Relation of Rhyme to Content in the Hebrew Poetry of Spain' ['Zikat heḥaruz letokhen hashir bashirah ha'ivrit bisefarad'], *Tarbiẓ*, 48 (1979), 107–16.

—— 'The Moral and Social Stature of the Poet' ['Demuto hamusarit vehaḥevratit shel hameshorer'], in id., *Poetics of Medieval Hebrew Literature According to Moses ibn Ezra* [*Hapoetikah shel hashirah ha'ivrit biyemei habeinayim bisefarad lefi rabi moshe ibn ezra umekoroteiha*] (Jerusalem, 1982), 211–29.

—— 'On Appellations of Jerusalem in the Sacral Poetry of (Hebrew) Spain' ['Al kinuyei yerushalayim beshirat hakodesh hasefaradit'], *Meḥkerei-ḥag*, 4 (1992), 88–97.

DAVIDOVITZ, T., 'Biblical Substrata in the Twenty-Eighth *Maqāma* of Judah Alḥarizi's *Sefer Taḥkemoni*' ['Tashtiyot mikra'iyot bamakamah ha'esrim ushemoneh besefer taḥkemoni liyehudah alḥarizi'], *Talpiyot* (1991–2), 248–61.

DAVIDSON, I., *Saadia's Polemic against Hiwi Al-Balkhi* (New York, 1915).

—— *Thesaurus of Secular and Sacral Poetry from the Time of the Completion of Scripture till the Beginning of the Haskalah Period* [*Otsar hashirah vehapiyut mizman ḥatimat kitvei hakodesh ad reshit tekufat hahaskalah*] (4 vols. and supplement; Jerusalem, 1925–38).

DIEHL, P. S., *The Medieval European Religious Lyric: An Ars Poetica* (Berkeley and Los Angeles, 1985).

DINUR, B. Z., *Israel in Exile* [*Yisra'el bagolah*] (10 vols., Tel Aviv, 1960–73).

DISHON, J., 'On the Sources of the Maḥberet "The Offering of Judah the Misogynist" of Judah ibn Shabbetai and its Influence on the Marriage *Maqāma* of Judah Alḥarizi' ['Limekoroteiha shel hamaḥberet minḥat yehudah liyehudah ibn shabetai vehashpa'atah al makamat hanisuin liyehudah alḥarizi'], *Otsar yehudei sefarad*, 11–12 (1969), 57–73.

—— 'Solomon ibn Zakbel's "The Declaration of Asher son of Judah" and the Twentieth *Maqāma* of Judah Alḥarizi's *Taḥkemoni*' ['Ne'um asher ben yehudah lishelomoh ibn tsakbel vehamakamah ha'esrim betaḥkemoni liyehudah alḥarizi'], *Bikoret ufarshanut*, 6 (1974), 57–65.

—— 'The Precentor in the Hebrew *Maqāma* in Spain' ['Haḥazan bamakamah ha'ivrit bisefarad'], *Sinai*, 74 (1974), 242–51.

—— 'On the Source of the Twenty-First Gate of *Sefer Taḥkemoni*' ['Limekorah shel hamaḥberet ha'esrim ve'aḥat besefer taḥkemoni'], *Bikoret ufarshanut*, 13–14 (1979), 9–26.

—— 'Alḥarizi's *Maqāma* of the Brigand' ['Makamat hashoded le'alḥarizi'], *Bikoret ufarshanut*, 16 (1981), 71–83.

—— 'Narrative in Judah Alḥarizi's *Sefer Taḥkemoni*' ['Hasipur besefer taḥkemoni liyehudah alḥarizi'], *Yeda am*, 21 (1982), 21–7.

——'On the Motif of Disguise in Hebrew *Maqāma* Literature of Spain' ['Lemotiv hahithḥapsut bamakamah ha'ivrit bisefarad'], *Yeda am*, 22: 51–2 (1984), 41–53.

——*The Book of Delight of Joseph son of Meir son of Zabara* [*Sefer hasha'ashuim leyosef ben me'ir ibn zabara*] (Jerusalem, 1985).

——'Was Joseph ibn Zabara the Misogynist a Misogynist?' ['Ha'im hayah yosef ibn zabara sone nashim sone nashim'], *Bitsaron*, 7: 27–8 (1985), 46–52.

——'On the Singularity of the Depiction of the Hunter in Judah Alḥarizi's *Sefer Taḥkemoni*' ['Leyiḥudo shel te'ur hatsayad besefer taḥkemoni liyehudah al-ḥarizi'], in Malakhi (ed.), *Aharon Mirsky Jubilee Volume*, 221–32.

——'The Depiction of the Ideal Woman' ['Te'ur ha'ishah ha'ide'alit'], *Yeda am*, 23: 53–4 (1986), 3–15.

——'Medieval Panorama in Tahkemoni', *Proceedings of the American Academy for Jewish Research*, 56 (1989), 11–27.

——'Travel by Sea: On the Thirty-Eighth *Maqāma* in Judah Alḥarizi's *Sefer taḥkemoni*' ['Hanesiah bayam: sha'ar 38 misefer taḥkemoni liyehudah alḥarizi'], in Dishon and Hazzan (eds.), *Studies in Hebrew Literature*, 377–94.

——'The Physician as Mirrored Satirically in Medieval Hebrew Literature' ['Harofeh bire'i hasatirah basifrut ha'ivrit biyemei habeinayim'], *Apirion*, 26–7 (1993), 26–33.

——'The Poets of Spain: Gate Three of *Sefer Taḥkemoni*' ['Meshorerei sefarad: hamaḥberet hashelishit besefer taḥkemoni'], in Tsur and Rosen (eds.), *Israel Levin Jubilee Volume*, i. 79–94.

——'Images of Women in Medieval Hebrew Literature', in J. R. Baskin (ed.), *Women of the Word* (Detroit, 1994), 35–49.

——and HAZZAN, E. (eds.), *Studies in Hebrew Literature and Yemenite Culture: Jubilee Volume Presented to Yehuda Ratzaby* [*Meḥkarim besifrut am yisra'el uvetarbut teiman: sefer hayovel liyehudah ratsabi*] (Ramat Gan, 1991).

DORON, A., 'Cities in the Hebrew Poetry of Spain' ['Arim bashirah ha'ivrit bisefarad'], in Tsur and Rosen (eds.), *Israel Levin Jubilee Volume*, i. 69–78.

DRIJVERS, H. J. W., 'Body and Soul: A Perennial Problem', in Reinink and Vanstiphout, *Dispute Poems*.

DRORY, R., 'The Hidden Context: On Literary Products of Tricultural Contacts in the Middle Ages' ['Haheksher hasamui min ha'ayin: al totsarim sifruti'im shel mifgash telat-tarbuti biyemei habeinayim'], *Pe'amim: Studies in Oriental Jewry*, 46–7 (1991), 9–28.

——' "Words Beautifully Put": Hebrew Versus Arabic in Tenth-Century Jewish Literature', in J. Blau and S. C. Reif (eds.), *Genizah Research after Ninety Years: The Case of Judaeo-Arabic* (Cambridge, 1992), 53–66.

——'Literary Contacts and Where to Find Them: On Arabic Literary Models in Medieval Jewish Literature', *Poetics Today*, 14: 2 (1993), 277–302.

DUNASH BEN LABRAT, *Poems* [*Shirim*], ed. N. Alloni (Jerusalem, 1947).

EHRLICH, B., 'Laws of the Sabbath in Yehudah Hadassi's *Eshkol hakofer*' (diss., Yeshiva University, 1974).

EISENSTEIN, Y., *Thesaurus of Laws and Customs* [*Otsar hadinim vehaminhagim*] (New York, 1917).

ELBOGEN, I., *Jewish Prayer in its Historical Development* [*Hatefilah beyisra'el behitpatḥutah hahistorit*], tr. and rev. J. Heinemann *et al.* (Tel Aviv, 1972).

ELIZUR, S., 'And Days (Fate) are Commanded of God' ['Vehayamim metsuvim me'eloha'], in Tsur and Rosen (eds.), *Israel Levin Jubilee Volume*, i. 27–43.

FELDMAN, Y., *Polarity and Parallel: Semantic Patterns in the Medieval Hebrew Qaṣīda* [*Bein hakotovim lekav hamashveh: shirat yemei habeinayim—tavniyot semantiyot bashir hamurkav*] (Tel Aviv, 1987).

FINKELSTEIN, L., *The Jews: Their History, Culture and Religion* (2 vols., 4th edn., New York, 1960).

FLEISCHER, E., 'The Poetic Output of Joseph ibn Avitur' (Ph.D. diss., Hebrew University, 1968).

—— (ed.), *Shimon Halkin Jubilee Volume* [*Meḥkarei sifrut mugashim leshimon halkin*] (Jerusalem, 1973).

—— 'Remarks on Medieval Hebrew Poetry' ['Inyenei piyut ushirah'], in id. (ed.), *Shimon Halkin Jubilee Volume*, 183–204.

—— *Hebrew Liturgical Poetry in the Middle Ages* [*Shirat hakodesh ha'ivrit biyemei habeinayim*] (Jerusalem, 1975).

—— 'Rabbi Judah Halevi: Clarifications on his Biography and Work' ['Rabi yehudah halevi: berurim bekorot ḥayav uveyitserato'], in Tsur and Rosen (eds.), *Israel Levin Jubilee Volume*, i. 241–76.

FRANKL, D. (ed.), *Alexander Marx Jubilee Volume* (New York, 1943).

GELDER, G. J. VAN, 'The Conceit of Pen and Sword: On an Arabic Literary Debate', *Journal of Semitic Studies*, 32: 2 (1987), 329–60.

—— *The Bad and the Ugly: Attitudes Towards Invective Poetry (Hiǧāʾ) in Classical Arabic Literature* (Leiden, 1988).

GIL, M., *In the Kingdom of Ishmael* (Publications of the Diaspora Research Institute, ed. M. Rozen, 117; The Haim Rosenberg School of Jewish Studies, Tel Aviv University; 4 vols., Jerusalem, 1997).

GINZBERG, L., *A Commentary on the Palestinian Talmud* [*Perushim veḥidushim liyerushalmi*] (New York, 1941).

—— *On Jewish Law and Lore* (Philadelphia, 1955).

GINZBERG, S., *Legends of the Jews*, tr. H. Szold (7 vols., New York, 1956).

GOITEIN, S., 'The *Maqāma* and the *Maḥberet*: A Chapter in the History of Literature and Society in the East' ['Hamakamah vehamaḥberet: perek betoledot hasifrut vehaḥevrah bamizraḥ'], *Maḥberot lesifrut*, 5 (1951), 26–40.

——*A Mediterranean Society* (5 vols., Berkeley, 1967–88).

——*Jews and Arabs: Their Contacts through the Ages* (3rd edn., New York, 1974).

——'On the Journey to Prostration on the Grave of Ezekiel' ['Baderekh lehishtateḥut al kever yeḥezkel'], in S. Moreh (ed.), *Studies in the History and Culture of Iraqi Jewry* [*Meḥkarim betoledot yehudei irak uvetarbutam*], i (Or Yehuda, 1981), 12 ff.

GOLDSTEIN, D. I., *Hebrew Poets from Spain* (London, 1965); repr. as *The Jewish Poets in Spain, 900–1250* (Harmondsworth, 1983).

GOLDZIHER, I., *Muslim Studies*, ed. S. M. Stern, tr. C. R. Berber and S. M. Stern (London, 1967).

GREENSTEIN, E., 'In Memory of H. L. Ginsberg', *Jewish Studies Network*, 5: 2 (1991), 7–8.

GRUNEBAUM, G. E. VON, *Unity and Variety in Muslim Civilization* (Chicago, 1955).

GUTTMANN, J., *Philosophies of Judaism: The History of Jewish Philosophy from Biblical Times to Franz Rosenzweig*, introd. R. J. Z. Werblowsky, tr. D. W. Silverman (London, 1946).

HABERMANN, A., 'A List of Debate Poems on Virtues in Hebrew' ['Reshimah shel shirei vikuaḥ lama'alot be'ivrit'], in Frankl (ed.), *Alexander Marx Jubilee Volume*, Hebrew section, 59–62.

——'The *Sefer Taḥkemoni* of Rabbi Judah Alḥarizi' ['Sefer taḥkemoni lerabi yehudah alḥarizi'], *Sinai*, 31 (1952), 112–27.

——*Studies in Secular and Synagogue Poetry in the Middle Ages* [*Iyunim bashirah uvapiyut shel yemei habeinayim*] (Jerusalem, 1972).

——'Judah Alḥarizi's *Sefer Taḥkemoni* and its Editions' ['Sefer "taḥkemoni" liyehudah alḥarizi umahadurotav'], in id., *Studies in Secular and Synagogue Poetry*, 115–36.

——'The Dedications to *Sefer Taḥkemoni* and the Table of Contents of its *Maqāmāt*' ['Hahakdashot lesefer taḥkemoni ureshimat tokhen makamotav'], in id., *Studies in Secular and Synagogue Poetry*, 137–53.

HALKIN, A. S., 'The Judeo-Islamic Age', in L. Schwarz, *Great Ages and Ideas of the Jewish People* (New York, 1956), 213–63.

——'Judeo-Arabic Literature', in Finkelstein (ed.), *The Jews*, ii. 121–54.

——'The Medieval Jewish Attitude towards Hebrew', in A. Altmann (ed.), *Biblical and Other Studies* (Philip W. Lown Institute of Advanced Judaic Studies, Brandeis University, Studies and Texts, 1; Cambridge, Mass., 1963), 232–48.

HAMMER, R. (ed.), *The Jerusalem Anthology* (Philadelphia, 1995).

HASSON, I., 'The Literature of Praise of Jerusalem in Islam' ['Sifrut shivḥei yerushalayim be'islam'], in M. Sharon (ed.), *Studies in the History of the Land of Israel under Muslim Rule* [*Sugiyot betoledot erets yisra'el taḥat shilton ha'islam*] (Jerusalem, 1976), 43–68.

HAZZAN, E., *The Poetics of the Sephardi* Piyut *according to the Liturgical Poetry of Judah Halevi* [*Torat hashir befiyut hasefaradi le'or shirat rabi yehudah halevi*] (Jerusalem, 1986).

HEINEMANN, J., *Prayer in the Talmud: Forms and Patterns*, tr. R. Sarason (Berlin, 1977).

HERTZ, J. H., *The Authorised Daily Prayer Book: Revised Edition* (New York, 1952).

HESCHEL, A., 'On the Holy Spirit in the Middle Ages' ['Al ruaḥ hakodesh biyemei habeinayim'], in Frankl (ed.), *Alexander Marx Jubilee Volume*, Hebrew section, 175–208.

HIRSCHFELD, H., *Judah Hallevi's Book of Kuzari* (New York, 1946).

HODGSON, M., *The Venture of Islam* (3 vols., Chicago, 1974).

HUS, M., 'The "Magid" in the Classic Maqama: Towards Term Clarification' ['Hamagid bamakama haklasit: leveiruro shel munaḥ'], *Tarbiẓ*, 65 (1996), 129–79.

HUSIK, I., *A History of Mediaeval Jewish Philosophy* (Philadelphia, 1958).

HYMAN, A., 'From What is One and Simple Only What is One and Simple Can Come to Be', in L. Goodman, *Neoplatonism and Jewish Thought* (Albany, 1992), 111–35.

IBN SHOSHAN, A., *The New Dictionary* [*Hamilon heḥadash*] (3 vols., Jerusalem, 1979).

IDELSOHN, A. Z., *Jewish Liturgy and its Development* (New York, 1932).

IMMANUEL OF ROME, *Maḥberot imanuel haromi*, ed. D. Jarden (2 vols., Jerusalem, 1957).

ISAAC BEN SOLOMON IBN SAHULA, *Meshal hakadmoni* (Tel Aviv, 1953).

ISAAC IBN GHIYYAT, *The Poems of Rabbi Isaac ibn Ghiyyat—A Tentative Edition* [*Shirei rabi yitsḥak ibn giyat: mahadurah tentativit*], ed. Y. David (Jerusalem, 1987).

ISAAC IBN KHALFUN, *The Collected Poems of Isaac ibn Khalfun* [*Kol shirei rabi yitsḥak ibn khalfun*], ed. A. Mirsky (Jerusalem, 1961).

ITZHAKI, M., *Man—the Vine, Death—the Reaper: Studies in the* Tokheḥah *Poetry of Spain* [*Haḥai gefen vehamavet botser: iyunim befiyutei tokheḥah misefarad*] (Lod, 1987).

—— '"In Praise of Garden Fruits": Three Ways of Reading a *Maqāma*' ['"Beshevaḥ peirot ilanei hagan": sheloshah keriyot efshariyot bemakamah'], in Dishon and Hazzan (eds.), *Studies in Hebrew Literature*, 307–18.

JONAH IBN JANAH, *The Book of Rikmah in the Hebrew Translation of Rabbi Judah ibn Tibbon* [*Sefer harikmah betirgumo ha'ivri shel rabi yehudah ibn tibon*], ed. M. Wilensky (2 vols., Berlin, 1928–30; repr. Jerusalem, 1964).

JOSEPH BEN MEIR IBN ZABARA, *Sefer Sha'ashuim: A Book of Medieval Lore*, ed. I. Davidson (New York, 1914).

—— *The Book of Delight*, tr. M. Hadas (New York, 1932).

JOSEPH IBN ZADDIK, *Poems* [*Shirei yosef ibn tsadik*], ed. Y. David (New York, 1982).

JOSPE, R., 'The Superiority of Oral Over Written Communication: Judah Halevi's *Kuzari* and Modern Jewish Thought', in Neusner, Frerichs, and Sarna (eds.), *From Ancient Israel to Modern Judaism*, 127–56.

JUDAH HALEVI, *Selected Poems of Jehudah Halevi*, ed. H. Brody, tr. N. Salaman (Philadelphia, 1924; repr. 1974).

—— *Jehuda Halevi: Kuzari*, ed. J. Heinemann (New York, 1965).

—— *The Kuzari: An Argument for the Faith of Israel*, tr. H. Hirschfeld (10 vols., New York, 1968).

—— *On the Sea: Poems by Yehuda Halevi*, tr. Gabriel Levin (Jerusalem, 1988).

KANARFOGEL, E., 'The *Aliyah* of "Three Hundred Rabbis" in 1211: Tosafist Attitudes toward Settling in the Land of Israel', *Jewish Quarterly Review*, 76: 3 (1986), 191–215.

KATZ, S., 'More on the Life of Isaac ibn Khalfun and his Links with Samuel Hanagid' ['Od al ḥayei yitsḥak ibn khalfun ukesharav im shmuel hanagid'], *Bikoret ufarshanut*, 28 (1991), 31–49.

—— *Openwork, Intaglios, and Filigrees: Studies and Research on Solomon ibn Gabirol's Poetry* [*Pituḥim petuḥim va'aturim: iyunei meḥkar biyetsirat rabi shelomoh ibn gabirol*] (Jerusalem, 1992).

—— *Rabbi Isaac ibn Giat: A Monograph* [*Rabi yitsḥak ibn giyat: Monografiyah*] (Jerusalem, 1994).

KAUFMAN, W., *Faith of a Heretic* (Garden City, 1963).

KEDAR, B. Z., 'The Jews of Jerusalem, 1187–1267' ['Yehudei yerushalayim, 1187–1267'], in id., *Chapters in the History of Jerusalem in the Middle Ages* [*Perakim betoledot yerushalayim beyemei habeinayim*] (Jerusalem, 1989), 122–36.

KIMELMAN, R., 'The Daily Amidah and the Rhetoric of Redemption', *Jewish Quarterly Review*, 79 (1988–9), 165–97.

KLAR, B., 'Four Titles of Compilations' ['Arba'ah shemot sefarim'], *Kiryat sefer*, 16 (1939–40), 241–58.

KLEIN, M. L., *The Fragment Targums of the Pentateuch According to their Extant Sources* (*Analecta Biblica*, 76; 1980).

—— 'Months Compete for the Passover Honour: Targumic Fragments Reveal How Hebrew Months Vied for Pesach', *Moment*, 14 (Apr. 1989), 14–18.

KOMEM, A., 'Between Poetry and Prophecy: An Enquiry into the Poetry of Judah Halevi' ['Bein shirah linevuah: iyunim beshirato shel yehudah halevi'], *Molad*, 11–12 (1969), 676–97.

KREISEL, H., 'Theories of Prophecy in Medieval Jewish Philosophy' (Ph.D. diss., Brandeis University, 1981).

LAMBERT, W. G., *Babylonian Wisdom Literature* (Oxford, 1960).

LASKER, D., 'Jehudah Halevi and Karaism', in Neusner, Frerichs, and Sarna (eds.), *From Ancient Israel to Modern Judaism*, 111–25.

LASKER, D., 'The Influence of Karaism on Maimonides' ['Hashpa'at hakara'ut al harambam'], *Sefunot*, 20, NS 5 (1991), 145–61.

——'Karaism in Twelfth Century Spain', *Journal of Jewish Thought and Philosophy*, 1–2 (1992), 179–95.

——'Karaism and the Jewish-Christian Debate', in H. Walfish (ed.), *The Frank Talmage Memorial Volume* (Haifa, 1993), i. 323–32.

LAVI, A., 'A Comparative Study of Alhariri's Maqamat and their Hebrew Translation by Alharizi' (Ph.D. diss., University of Michigan, 1977).

——'Why and How did Judah Alḥarizi, in *Maḥberot Iti'el*, Judaize the Names of the *Maqāmāt* of al-Ḥariri?' ['Madua ve'eikh yiḥed alḥarizi bemaḥberot iti'el et hashemot shebemakamat alḥariri'], *Bar Ilan Annual*, 20–1 (1983), 172–81.

——'The Rationale of al-Ḥarīzī in Biblicizing the Maqāmāt of al-Ḥarīrī', *Jewish Quarterly Review*, NS 74 (1984), 280–93.

LAZARUS-YAFEH, H., 'The Sanctity of Jerusalem in Islam' in J. M. Oesterreicher and A. Sinai (eds.), *Jerusalem* (New York, 1974), 211–25.

——*Some Religious Aspects of Islam* (Leiden, 1981).

——*Intertwined Worlds: Medieval Islam and Bible Criticism* (Princeton, 1992).

LEVIANT, C., *Masterpieces of Hebrew Literature: A Treasury of Two Thousand Years of Jewish Creativity* (New York, 1969).

LEVIN, I., 'Time and the World in Medieval Secular Hebrew Poetry in Spain' ['Zeman vetevel beshirat haḥol ha'ivrit bisefarad biyemei habeinayim'], *Otsar yehudei sefarad*, 5 (1962), 68–79.

——*Samuel Hanagid: His Life and Poetry* [*Shmuel hanagid: ḥayav veshirato*] (Tel Aviv, 1963).

——'Poems of Wandering and Suffering of Moses ibn Ezra' ['Shirei hanedudim vehasevel shel moshe ibn ezra'], *Otsar yehudei sefarad*, 9 (1966), 66–83.

——'Weeping Over the Ruins of the Encampments and the Wandering Night Figure' ['Habekhi al ḥorvot hame'onot vehademut haleilit hameshotetet'], *Tarbiẓ*, 36 (1967), 278–96.

——'The Martial Poetry of Samuel Hanagid against the Background of Ancient Arabian Heroic Poetry' ['Shirat hamilḥamah shel shmuel hanagid al reka shirat hagiborim ha'aravit ha'atikah'], *Hasifrut*, 1 (1968), 343–67.

——'The Poem of Apology in the Hebrew Secular Poetry of Spain' ['Shir hahitnatslut beshirat haḥol ha'ivrit bisefarad'], *Hasifrut*, 2 (1969), 176–93.

——'The Pen and the Horseman: On the "Singular Poem" of Joseph ibn Ḥisdai and the Qaṣīda [Compound Poem] in the (Hebrew) Secular Poetry of Spain' ['Ha'et vehaparash: al "shirah yetomah" leyosef ibn ḥisdai ve'al hakatsidah beshirat haḥol bisefarad'], in Malakhi (ed.), *A. M. Habermann Jubilee Volume*, 143–73.

——*The Embroidered Coat: The Genres of Hebrew Secular Poetry in Spain* [*Me'il tashbets: hasugim hashonim shel shirat haḥol ha'ivrit bisefarad*] (Tel Aviv, 1980).

LEWIN, B. M., 'On the History of Sabbath Candles' ['Letoledot ner shel shabat'], in I. Davidson (ed.), *Essays and Studies in Memory of Linda R. Miller* (New York, 1938), Hebrew section, 55–68.

LEWIS, B., *The Jews of Islam* (Princeton, 1984).

LEWY, H., ALTMANN, A., and HEINEMANN, J. (eds.), *Three Jewish Philosophers: Philo: Selections*, ed. H. Lewy; *Saadya Gaon: The Book of Doctrines and Beliefs*, ed. A. Altmann; *Jehuda Halevi: Kuzari*, ed. J. Heinemann (New York, 1965).

LIEBREICH, S., 'Psalms 34 and 145 in the Light of their Key Words', *Hebrew Union College Annual*, 27 (1956), 181–92.

LIVNEH-KAFRI, O., 'On the Antiquity of Compositions Dedicated to Jerusalem in Arabic Literature' ['Al kadmutam shel ḥiburim hamukdashim liyerushalayim basifrut ha'aravit'], *Cathedra*, 44 (1987), 21–6.

—— 'The Ancient Tradition on Jerusalem' ['Hashiah hakedumah ve'emdatah kelapei yerushalayim'], *Bitaon lamoreh le'aravit*, 14–15 (1993), 130–6.

—— 'Jerusalem: the Earth's Centre in Islamic Tradition' ['Yerushalayim: tabur ha'arets bimesoret ha'islam'], *Cathedra*, 69 (1994), 105–79.

LOEWE, R., 'Ibn Gabirol's Treatment of Sources in the *Kether Malkhuth*', in S. Stein and R. Loewe (eds.), *Studies in Jewish Religious and Intellectual History Presented to Alexander Altmann on the Occasion of his Seventieth Birthday* (London, 1979), 183–95.

—— *Ibn Gabirol* (London, 1989).

LURIA, B. Z., *Sefer avraham even-shoshan* (Jerusalem, 1985).

MAIMONIDES, *Moreh nevukhim*, tr. Judah Alḥarizi, ed. L. Schlossberg and S. Scheyer (3 vols., London, 1851–79).

—— *The Guide of the Perplexed*, tr. M. Friedlander (New York, 1881).

—— *Milot hahigayon*, ed. Israel Efros, *Maimonides' Treatise of Logic: The Original Arabic with Three Hebrew Translations = Proceedings of the American Academy for Jewish Research*, 8 (1937/8) (with English translation); 'Maimonides' Arabic Treatise on Logic', ibid. 34 (1966), roman pagination 155–60 (introduction), Hebrew pagination 9–42 (text).

—— *Hakdamot leperush hamishnah (Introduction to the Commentary on the Mishnah)*, tr. Judah Alḥarizi, ed. M. D. Rabinovitz (Jerusalem, 1960).

—— *The Responsa of Maimonides (Teshuvot harambam)*, ed. J. Blau (Jerusalem, 1960).

—— *Ma'amar teḥiyat hametim* [*The Treatise on the Revival of the Dead*], ed. A. S. Halkin, *Kovets al yad*, 9 (*Minora Manuscripta Hebraica*) (1989), 129–50.

—— *Maimonides' Mishneh Torah: Hilkhot Tefillah (II) and Birkat Kohanim: The Laws of Prayer and the Priestly Blessing*, tr. E. Touger (New York, 1989).

MALAKHI, Z. (ed.), *A. M. Habermann Jubilee Volume* [*Shai leheiman: meḥkarim basifrut ha'ivrit shel yemei habeinayim mugashim le'a. m. haberman*] (Tel Aviv, 1977).

MALAKHI, Z. (ed.), *Aharon Mirsky Jubilee Volume: Essays on Jewish Culture* [*Be'oraḥ mada: meḥkarim betarbut yisra'el mugashim le'aharon mirski*] (Lod, 1986).

—— 'Hamakamah ha'aravit vehashpa'atah al ha'alegoriyah ha'ivrit' ['The Hebrew *Maqāma* and its Influence on Hebrew Allegory'], *Maḥanayim*, 1 (1991), 176–9.

—— and DAVID, H., *Studies in the Work of Solomon ibn Gabirol* [*Meḥkarim beyitsarat rabi shelomoh ben gevirol*] (Tel Aviv, 1985).

MALTER, H., *Saadia Gaon, his Life and Works* (New York, 1926).

AL-MAQQARI, *Nafḥ aṭ-ṭīb min ghusn al-Andalus ar-raṭīb*, ed. Aḥsan ᶜAbbas (Beirut, 1968).

MAREE, A., 'The Influence of al-Ḥariri's *Maqāmāt* on *Sefer Taḥkemoni*' ['Hashpa'at makamot al-ḥariri al sefer taḥkemoni'] (MA thesis, Bar Ilan University, 1986).

—— 'The Influence of al-Ḥariri's *Maqāmāt* on Taḥkemoni's *Maḥberot*' ['Hashpa'at makamot al-ḥariri al maḥberot taḥkemoni'] (Ph.D. diss., Bar Ilan University, 1996).

MARGALIOT, M. (ed.), *The Controversies between Eastern Jewries and the Residents of the Land of Israel* [*Haḥilukim shebein anshei mizraḥ uvenei erets yisra'el*] (Jerusalem, 1938).

Midrash Rabbah: Exodus, ed. H. Freedman and M. Simon (London, 1939).

Midrash tanḥuma hakadum vehayashan [*The Ancient Text of Midrash Tanhuma*], ed. S. Buber (Lvov, n.d.; repr. Jerusalem, 1964).

MILLGRAM, A., *Jewish Worship* (Philadelphia, 1975).

MIRSKY, A., 'On Alḥarizi's Introduction to Taḥkemoni' ['Limekoroteiha shel hakdamat alḥarizi letaḥkemoni'], *Ha'arets*, 28 Sept. 1952, repr. in id., Piyut: *The Development of Post-Biblical Poetry in Eretz Israel and the Diaspora* [*Hapiyut: hitpatḥuto be'erets yisra'el uvagolah*] (Jerusalem, 1990), 699–704.

MONROE, J., *The Art of Badi' az-Zaman al-Hamadhani as Picaresque Narrative* (Beirut, 1983).

MONTEFIORE, C., AND LOEWE, H., *A Rabbinic Anthology* (London, 1938).

MOSES IBN EZRA, *Secular Poems* [*Shirei haḥol*], vols. i and ii, ed. H. Brody (Berlin, 1935, 1941).

—— *Selected Poems of Moses ibn Ezra*, ed. H. Brody, tr. S. Solis-Cohen (Philadelphia, 1945).

—— *Kitāb al-muḥādara wa'l-mudhākara: Sefer ha'iyunim vehadiyunim al hashirah ha'ivrit* [*The Book of Enquiries and Discussions on Hebrew Poetry*], ed. and tr. A. S. Halkin (Jerusalem, 1975).

—— *Secular Poems* [*Shirei haḥol*], vol. iii, ed. D. Pagis (Jerusalem, 1977).

AL-MUTANABBĪ, *see* ARBERRY

NEMOY, L., *Karaite Anthology* (New Haven, 1952).

NEUSNER, J., FRERICHS, E. S., and SARNA, N. (eds.), *From Ancient Israel to Modern Judaism* (Atlanta, 1989).

NICHOLSON, R., *A Literary History of the Arabs* (Cambridge, 1907).

OR, S., 'Wisdom and its Quest: A Personal Theme in the Secular Poetry of Rabbi Solomon ibn Gabirol' ['Haḥokhmah uvakashatah: nose ishi beshirat haḥol shel rabi shelomoh ben gevirol'] (MA thesis, Bar Ilan University, 1993).

——'"And the Doors of Wisdom have Swung Open to Me, though Closed to All the Sons of my People": On the Limitations of Praise for Wisdom in the "Songs of Affection" (Shirei yedidut) by Solomon ibn Gabirol' ['"Vedaltei hatevunah nifteḥu li vehen al kol benei ami segurot": al tsimtsum shivḥei haḥokhmah beshirei hayedidut lerabi shelomoh ben gevirol'], *Bikoret ufarshanut*, 32 (1997), 7–24.

PAGIS, D., *Secular Poetry and Poetic Theory: Moses ibn Ezra and his Contemporaries* [*Shirat haḥol vetorat hashir lemoshe ibn ezra uvenei doro*] (Jerusalem, 1970).

——'And Drink Your Wine Good-Heartedly' ['Usheteh belev tov yeinekha'], in Fleischer (ed.), *Shimon Halkin Jubilee Volume*, 131–51.

——*Innovation and Change in Hebrew Secular Poetry: Spain and Italy* [*Ḥidush umasoret beshirat haḥol ha'ivrit: sefarad ve'italiyah*] (Jerusalem, 1976).

——'Variety in Medieval Rhymed Narratives', *Scripta Hierosolymitana*, 27, 'Studies in Hebrew Narrative Art Through the Ages' (1978), 79–98.

——'The Poet as Prophet in Medieval Hebrew Literature', in J. L. Kugel, *Poetry and Prophecy: The Beginnings of a Literary Tradition* (Ithaca and London, 1990), 140–50.

——*Hebrew Poetry of the Middle Ages and the Renaissance* (Berkeley, Los Angeles, and Oxford, 1991).

——*Poetry Aptly Explained: Studies and Essays on Medieval Hebrew Poetry* [*Hashir davur al ofanav: meḥkarim umasot beshirah ha'ivrit shel yemei habeinayim*], ed. E. Fleischer (Jerusalem, 1993).

PERCIKOWITSCH, A., *Al-Harizi als Übersetzer der Makamen al-Hariris: Ein Beitrag zur Geschichte der Literatur-Übertragungen* (Munich, 1932).

PETHACHIAH OF REGENSBURG, *The Journey of Rabbi Pethachiah of Regensburg* [*Sibuv harav rabi petaḥyah miregensburg*], ed. A. Grinhut (Jerusalem, 1905).

PETRUS ALFONSI, *The Disciplina Clericalis of Petrus Alfonsi*, translated from Latin to German (*Die Kunst, vernünftig zu leben*) and edited by Eberhard Hermes; translated into English by P. R. Quarrie (The Islamic World Series; London, 1977).

PETUCHOWSKI, J., *Theology and Poetry: Studies in the Medieval Piyyut* (London, 1978).

POZNANSKI, S., *Karaite Literary Opponents of Saadiah Gaon in the Tenth Century* (London, 1908).

RAFEL, Y., 'My Soul Journeyed from Spain to Zion' ['Nafshi letsiyon misefarad galetah'], *Et-mol*, 17: 4 (1992), 3–5.

RATZABY, Y., 'On the Sources of *Taḥkemoni*' ['Limekorotav shel taḥkemoni'], *Tarbiẓ*, 26 (1957), 424–39.

RATZABY, Y., 'Adab Maxims in Medieval Literature' ['Pitgamei adab besifrut yemei habeinayim'], *Otsar yehudei sefarad*, 4 (1961), 114–24.

——*Arabic Wisdom: Classic Tales and Sayings* [*Siḥot arav: misifrut hamofet ha'aravit*] (Tel Aviv, 1966).

——'Arabic Influences in the (Hebrew) Literature of the Spanish Period' ['Hashpaot araviyot besifrut tekufat sefarad'], *Bar Ilan Annual*, 6 (1968), 314–38.

——'The Wine Poetry of Rabbi Samuel Hanagid' ['Shirat hayayin lerabi shmuel hanagid'], *Bar Ilan Annual*, 9 (1971), 423–74.

——'The Interpretation of "The Comely Gazelle" of Rabbi Samuel Hanagid—How (to View It)' ['Perush tsevi na'im lerabi shmuel hanagid—keitsad'], *Tarbiẓ*, 42 (1973), 185–7.

——'The Motif of Old Age in the Spanish Hebrew Poetry of Spain' ['Motiv hazik-nah bashirah hasefaradit ha'ivrit'], *Bar Ilan Annual*, 16–17 (1979), 193–220.

——'An Arabic *Maqāma* Penned by Alharizi' ['Makamah aravit me'eto shel alḥarizi'], *Bikoret ufarshanut*, 14 (1980), 5–51.

——'Arabic Poetry Written by Andalusian Jews' ['Shirah aravit befi yehudim ba'andalusiyah'], in Tsur and Rosen (eds.), *Israel Levin Jubilee Volume*, i. 329–50.

REICHERT, V. E., *The Tahkemoni of Judah Alharizi: An English Translation* (2 vols., Jerusalem, 1965–73).

REINER, E., 'In the Footsteps of Jewish Pilgrims to Jerusalem in the Middle Ages' ['Be'ikvot olei regel yehudiyim liyerushalayim biyemei habeinayim'], *Ariel*, 13, nos. 83–4 (1992), 107–46.

REININK, G., and VANSTIPHOUT, H., *Dispute Poems and Dialogues in the Ancient and Mediaeval Near East* (Leuven, 1991).

RENKEMA, J., 'The Literary Structure of Lamentations', in W. van der Meer and J. C. de Moor (eds.), *The Structural Analysis of Biblical and Canaanite Poetry* (*The Journal for the Study of the Old Testament*, suppl. 74; Sheffield, 1988), 294–396.

REVEL, B., *The Karaite Halakhah and its Relation to Sadducean, Samaritan, and Philonian Halakhah* (Philadelphia, 1913).

ROSEN(-MOKED), T., *The Hebrew Girdle Poem in the Middle Ages* [*Le'ezor shir: al shirat ha'ezor ha'ivrit biyemei habeinayim*] (Haifa, 1985).

——'On Tongues Being Bound and Let Loose: Women in Medieval Hebrew Literature', *Prooftexts*, 8 (1988), 67–87.

——'Five Hundred Years of Hebrew Literature in Spain' ['Ḥamesh meot shenot sifrut ivrit bisefarad'], *Zemanim*, 41 (1992), 54–69.

ROSENBAUM, M., and SILBERMANN, A. (trs.), in collaboration with A. Blashki and L. Joseph, *Pentateuch with Targum Onkelos, Haphtaroth, and Rashi's Commentary* (5 vols, New York, 1930).

ROSENTHAL, J., 'Hiwi al-Balkhi', *Jewish Quarterly Review*, NS 38 (1947–8), 419–30.

——*Hiwi al-Balkhi: A Comparative Study* (Philadelphia, 1949).

——'Karaites and Karaism in Western Europe' ['Kara'im vekara'ut be'eiropah hama'aravit'], *Meḥkarim umekorot*, 8 (1967), 234–52.

ROTH, N., 'The "Wiles of Women" Motif in the Medieval Hebrew Literature of Spain', *Hebrew Annual Review*, 2 (1978), 145–66.

——'Satire and Debate in Two Famous Medieval Poems from al-Andalus: Love of Boys vs. Girls, the Pen, and Other Themes', *Maghreb Review*, 4 (1979), 105–13.

——'"Deal Gently with the Young Man": Love of Boys in Medieval Hebrew Poetry of Spain', *Speculum*, 57 (1982), 20–51.

RUBIN, N., 'From Monism to Dualism: the Relation of Body to Soul in Rabbinic Thought' ['Mimonizm ledualizm: yaḥas guf–nefesh bitefisat haḥakhamim'], *Da'at*, 23 (1989), 33–63.

SA'ADIAH GAON, *The Book of Beliefs and Opinions*, ed. S. Rosenblatt (New Haven, 1948).

——*Sidur r. Sa'adiyah gaon: Kitāb jamīʿ aṣ-ṣalawāt wat-tasābīḥ* [*The Prayerbook of Sa'adiah Gaon: The Book of All the Prayers and Petitions*], ed. I. Davidson, S. Assaf, and B. I. Joel (3rd edn., Jerusalem, 1970).

SACHS, S., 'On Moving To and Fro during Study and Prayer' ['Al devar hitno'a'ut bishe'at halimud uvishe'at hatefilah'], *Hamitspeh*, 4 (1885), 9–12 (folklore section).

SADAN, Y., 'A Legal Opinion of a Muslim Jurist Regarding the Sanctity of Jerusalem', *Israel Oriental Studies*, 13 (1993), 231–45.

——'Rabbi Judah Alḥarizi as a Cultural Crossroads' ['Rabi yehudah alḥarizi ketsomet tarbuti'], *Pe'amim*, 68 (1996), 16–67.

SAMUEL HANAGID, *Rabi shmuel hanagid: Ben mishlei*, ed. A. Abramson (Tel Aviv, 1948).

——*Divan shmuel hanagid* [*The Collected Poetry of Samuel the Prince*], i: *Ben tehilim* [Psalmiad] (rev. edn., Jerusalem, 1985); ii: *Ben mishlei* [*Proverbiad*] (Jerusalem, 1982); iii: *Ben kohelet* [*Ecclesiasticon*], ed. D. Jarden (Jerusalem, 1992).

SARACHEK, J., *Faith and Reason: The Conflict over the Rationalism of Maimonides* (New York, 1970).

AL-SARAQUSṬĪ, ʾABŪ 'L-ṬĀHIR IBN YŪSUF, *Al-maqāmāt al-ʿazūmiyya li'l-saraqusṭī* [*Al-Sarakusti's* Maqāmāt *in Prescribed Rhyme*], ed. B. Daif (Cairo, 1982).

SARNA, N., 'Hebrew and Bible Studies in Medieval Spain', in R. Barnett, *The Sephardi Heritage: Essays on the History and Cultural Contributions of the Jews of Spain and Portugal* (London, 1971).

——(ed.), *The JPS Torah Commentary: Genesis* (Philadelphia, 1989).

SCHECHTER, S., *Studies in Judaism* (Philadelphia, 1958).

SCHEINDLIN, R., 'Rabbi Moshe Ibn Ezra on the Legitimacy of Poetry', in Clogan (ed.), *Medieval Poetics*, 101–16.

——'Fawns of the Palace and Fawns of the Field', *Prooftexts*, 6 (1986), 189–203.

SCHEINDLIN, R., *Wine, Women, and Death: Medieval Hebrew Poems on the Good Life* (Philadelphia, 1986).

——'Asher in the Harem', in D. Stern and M. J. Mirsky (eds.), *Rabbinic Fantasies: Imaginative Narratives from Classical Hebrew Literature* (Philadelphia, 1990), 253–73.

——*The Gazelle: Medieval Hebrew Poems on God, Israel, and the Soul* (Philadelphia, 1991).

——'Hebrew Poetry in Medieval Iberia', in V. B. Mann, T. F. Glick, and J. D. Dodds (eds.), *Convivencia: Jews, Muslims, and Christians in Medieval Spain* (New York, 1992), 38–59.

——'Al-Harizi's Astrologer: A Document of Jewish-Islamic Relations', in R. Nettler (ed.), *Studies in Muslim-Jewish Relations* (Berne, 1993), 165–75.

SCHIMMEL, A., *Mystical Dimensions of Islam* (Chapel Hill, 1975).

——*As Through a Veil: Mystical Poetry in Islam* (New York, 1982).

——*And Muhammad is His Messenger: The Veneration of the Prophet in Islamic Piety* (Chapel Hill, 1985).

SCHIPPERS, A., *Arab Tradition and Hebrew Innovation: Arabic Themes in Hebrew Andalusian Poetry* (Amsterdam, 1988).

SCHIRMANN, J., *Die hebräische Übersetzung der Maqamen des Ḥariri* (Frankfurt am Main, 1930).

——'Judah Alḥarizi, Poet and Storyteller' ['Yehudah alḥarizi hameshorer vehamesaper'], *Moznayim*, 11 (1940), 101–15, repr. in id., *Studies in the History of Hebrew Poetry and Drama*, i. 353–68.

——'Samuel Hanagid: The Man, the Soldier, the Politician', *Jewish Social Studies*, 12 (1951), 99–126.

——'On the Sources of Judah Alharizi's *Sefer Taḥkemoni*' ['Leḥeker mekoratav shel sefer taḥkemoni liyehudah alḥarizi'], *Tarbiẓ*, 23 (1952), 198–202.

——'The Function of the Hebrew Poet in Medieval Spain', *Jewish Social Studies*, 15 (1954), 235–52.

——*Hebrew Poetry in Spain and in Provence* [*Hashirah ha'ivrit bisefarad uviprovans*] (2 vols., Jerusalem, i: 1954, rev. 1961; ii: 1956, rev. 1960).

——'The Ephebe in Medieval Hebrew Poetry', *Sefarad*, 15 (1955), 55–68.

——*New Poems from the Genizah* [*Shirim ḥadashim min hagenizah*] (Jerusalem, 1965).

——'Yehudah alḥarizi', in id., *New Poems from the Genizah*, 282–91.

——'Moses ben Sheshet, a Spanish Hebrew Poet in Babylon' ['Moshe bar-sheshet, meshorer ivri-sefaradi bevavel'], in Malakhi (ed.), *A. M. Habermann Jubilee Volume*, 323–8.

——*Studies in the History of Hebrew Poetry and Drama* [*Letoledot hashirah vehadramah ha'ivrit: meḥkarim umasot*] (2 vols., Jerusalem, 1979).

——*The History of Hebrew Poetry in Muslim Spain* [*Toledot hashirah ha'ivrit bisefarad hamuslemit*], edited, supplemented, and annotated by E. Fleischer (Jerusalem, 1995); cited as S–F, *History*, i.

—— *The History of Hebrew Poetry in Christian Spain and Southern France* [*Toledot hashirah ha'ivrit bisefarad hanotserit uviderom tsarfat*], edited, supplemented, and annotated by E. Fleischer (Jerusalem, 1997); cited as S–F, *History*, ii.

Sefer mivḥar hapeninim [*The Book of Choicest Pearls*], ed. A. M. Habermann (Tel Aviv, 1947); tr. A. Cohen, *Solomon Ibn Gabirol's Choice of Pearls* (Library of Jewish Classics; New York, 1925).

SEGAL, B., *Returning: The Land of Israel as Focus in Jewish History* (Jerusalem, 1987).

SEGAL, D., 'A Comment on The Love Poetry of R. Shmuel Hanagid' ['He'arah lama'amar, "Ha'ahavah beshirat rabi shemuel hanagid"'], *Tarbiẓ*, 41 (1972), 238–40.

—— 'Ben Tehillim of Shmuel Hanagid and the Book of Psalms: A Study in Esoteric Linkage' (Ph.D. thesis, Brandeis University, 1975).

—— 'Certain Delights of the Book of Delights', *Hebrew Annual Review*, 1 (1977), 181–203.

—— '"My Heart Burns" by Shmuel Hanagid: A Studied Translation', *Hebrew Studies*, 19 (1978), 63–7.

—— 'Observations on Three War Poems of Shmuel Hanagid: A Study in Internal Poetic Cohesion', *Association for Jewish Studies Review*, 4 (1979), 165–203.

—— '"Maḥberet Ne'um Asher ben Yehudah" of Solomon ibn Zaqbel: A Study of Scriptural Citation Clusters', *Journal of the American Oriental Society*, 102 (1982), 17–26.

—— 'Of a Host Bombastic and a Feast Fantastic: Rhyme and Reason in the Thirty-Fourth Gate of Alharizi's Tahkemoni', *Prooftexts*, 3 (1983), 51–62.

—— '"Truly, to God, Who is beyond Praise"' of Samuel Hanagid and Psalm 19' ['Emet la'el asher ein lo tehilah lishemuel hanagid umizmor 19 bitehilim'], *Meḥkarei yerushalayim besifrut ivrit*, 4 (1984), 43–58.

—— 'The Tales of Jacob ben Elazar: Understanding Gate Seven' ['Mishlei ya'akov ben elazar: lemahut hamaḥberet hashevi'it'], in Malakhi (ed.), *Aharon Mirsky Jubilee Volume*, 353–63.

—— 'A Poem within a Poem: Intrusion or Organic Unity' ['Shir betokh shir: hadḥasat neta zar o aḥdut shirit'], *Eshel be'er sheva: meḥkarim bemada'ei hayahadut*, 3 (1986), 119–35.

—— 'Gate Twenty-Seven of *Sefer Taḥkemoni* of Judah Alharizi: Of the Cup's Joys and Other Alloys', *Mediaevalia: A Journal of Mediaeval Studies*, 10 (1988), 127–32.

—— 'The Opening, the Conclusion, and the Frame Tale in Judah Alḥarizi's *Sefer Taḥkemoni*' ['Hapetiḥah, hasiyum, vehasipur ha'otef besefer taḥkemoni liyehudah alḥarizi'], in Dishon and Hazzan (eds.), *Studies in Hebrew Literature*, 407–21.

SEGAL, D., 'Strange Cohesion: A Study of Esoteric and Quasi-Esoteric Patterns of Linkage in Gate Twenty-Three of the *Maḥberot* of Immanuel of Rome' ['Sedarim lo she'arum: iyun bemaḥberet 23 shel maḥberot imanuel haromi'], *Pe'amim: Studies in Oriental Jewry*, 81 (1999), 43–55.

——'Imitations of a Singular Chiastic Structure obtaining in Lamentations, in the Hebrew Poetry of Spain' ['Ḥikuyei degem kiasti yiḥudi misefer eikhah betokh hashirah ha'ivrit misefarad'], in B. Bar-Tikva and E. Hazan (eds.), *Mesoret hapiyut*, 3 (forthcoming).

SELLS, M. A. (tr.), *Desert Tracing: Six Classical Arabian Odes* (Middletown, 1989).

S–F, *History, see under* SCHIRMANN

SHEM TOV BEN JOSEPH IBN FALAQUERA, *Studies in Judaica: The Book of the Seeker (Sefer Ha-Mebbaqesh) by Shem Tob ben Joseph ibn Falaquera*, ed. and tr. M. Levine (New York, 1976).

SHINAN, A., 'The Sins of Nadav and Avihu in Rabbinic Legend' ['Ḥata'eihem shel nadav va'avihu ba'agadat ḥazal'], *Tarbiz*, 48 (1979), 201–14.

Sifrei on Deuteronomy, ed. L. Finkelstein (Berlin, 1939).

SILVER, A. H., *History of Messianic Speculation in Israel* (Boston, 1959).

SILVER, D., *Maimonidean Criticism and the Maimonidean Controversy* (Leiden, 1965).

SILVERMAN, M., *High Holiday Prayer Book* (Hartford, Conn., 1960).

SIRAT, C., *Les Théories des visions surnaturelles dans la pensée juive du moyen âge* (Leiden, 1969).

——*A History of Jewish Philosophy in the Middle Ages* (Cambridge, 1985).

SIVAN, E., 'The Beginnings of the *Faḍā'il al-Quds* Literature', *Der Islam*, 48 (1971), 100–10.

SOLOMON IBN GABIROL, *Improvement of the Moral Qualities*, tr. S. S. Wise (New York, 1902).

——*Selected Religious Poems of Rabbi Solomon Ibn Gabirol*, ed. I. Davidson, tr. I. Zangwill (Philadelphia, 1924; repr. 1974).

——*The Fountain of Life of Rabbi Solomon ibn Gabirol* [*Sefer mekor ḥayim lerabi shelomoh ibn gevirol*], tr. J. Bluwstein, ed. A. Zifroni (Jerusalem, 1925–6).

——*The Kingly Crown*, tr. B. Lewis (London, 1961).

——*The Fountain of Life* [*Fons Vitae*] *of Solomon ibn Gabirol*, abr. and tr. H. E. Wedecker (London, 1963).

——*Secular Poetry of Rabbi Solomon ibn Gabirol* [*Shirat haḥol lerabi shelomoh ibn gevirol*], ed. D. Jarden (2 vols., Jerusalem, 1975–6).

——*Secular Poems* [*Shelomoh ibn gevirol: shirei haḥol*], ed. H. Brody and J. Schirmann with the participation of J. Ben-David [Hebrew] (Jerusalem, 1975).

SPICEHANDLER, E., 'The Attitude towards the Land of Israel in Spanish Hebrew Poetry', in M. Sharon, *The Holy Land in History and Thought* (Leiden, 1988), 117–40.

SPIEGEL, S., 'On Medieval Hebrew Poetry', in Finkelstein (ed.), *The Jews*, ii. 82–120.

STEINSCHNEIDER, M., *Rangstreitliteratur: ein Beitrag zur vergleichenden Literatur- und Kulturgeschichte* (Sitzungsberichte der Philosophisch-Historischen Klasse der Kaiserlichen Akademie der Wissenschaften, 155/4; Vienna, 1908).

STERN, S. M., *A Brief Announcement on a Scholarly Edition of the Book of Maqamas (Tahkemoni) of Rabbi Judah Alharizi* (Jerusalem, 1937).

——'The Arabic Source of Alḥarizi's "Rooster *Maqāma*"' ['Mekorah ha'aravi shel "makamat hatarnegol" le'alḥarizi'], *Tarbiẓ*, 17 (1946), 87–100.

——'Some Unpublished Poems by Al-Ḥarizi', *Jewish Quarterly Review*, 50 (1960), 269–76, 346–64.

——'A New Description by Judah Alḥarizi of his Journey to Iraq' ['Te'ur ḥadash mirabi yehudah alḥarizi al nesiato levavel'], *Sefunot*, 8 (1964), 147–56.

——'An Unpublished Maqama by al-Ḥarizi', in *Papers of the Institute of Jewish Studies*, ed. J. G. Weiss (London, 1964), i. 186–201.

——'Rabbi Judah Alḥarizi in Praise of Maimonides' ['Rabi yehudah alḥarizi beshivḥo shel harambam'], in M. Zihari and A. Tertakover (eds.), *Jewish Thought in Europe* [*Hagut ivrit be'eiropah*] (Tel Aviv, 1969), 91–103.

STRAUSS, L., 'The Literary Character of the Guide for the Perplexed', in id., *Persecution and the Art of Writing* (Glencoe, 1976), 38–94.

Tanakh—The Holy Scriptures: The New JPS Translation According to the Traditional Hebrew Text (4th edn., Philadelphia, Pa., 1988).

TOPOROVSKY, Y., *Rabi yehudah alḥarizi: taḥkemoni* (Tel Aviv, 1952).

TOR, A., *Mohammad: The Man and his Faith*, tr. T. Menzel (London, 1936).

TSUR, R., *Studies in Medieval Hebrew Poetry* [*Iyunim bashirah ha'ivrit biyemei habeinayim*] (Tel Aviv, 1969).

——*Medieval Hebrew Poetry in a Double Perspective: The Versatile Reader and Hebrew Poetry in Spain* [*Hashirah ha'ivrit biyemei habeinayim beferspektivah kefulah: hakore haversatili beshirat sefarad*] (Tel Aviv, 1987).

——*Toward a Theory of Cognitive Poetics* (Amsterdam, 1992).

——and ROSEN, T. (eds.), *Israel Levin Jubilee Volume* [*Sefer yisra'el levin*] (2 vols., Tel Aviv, 1994).

TUBI, Y., 'Hebrew, Aramaic, and Arabic in the Poetry of the Jews of Yemen, Particularly in the Poetry of Rabbi Shalom Shabazi' ['Ivrit, aramit, ve'aravit beshirei yehudei teiman, bimeyuḥad beshirat rabi shalom shabazi'], *Pe'amim*, 30 (1987), 3–22.

——'The Sources of Harizi's "tena'e ha-shir" (Conditions of Poetry) in "Amud al-Shi'r" of Arabic Poetry', *Medieval Encounters*, 1–2 (1995), 175–87.

TURNIANSKY, H., 'The Jewish Debate Poem and its Evolution in Franco-German Jewry' ['Shir havikuaḥ hayehudi be'ashkenaz'], *Hasifrut*, 32 (1982), 2–12.

TWERSKY, I., *Introduction to the Code of Maimonides* (New Haven, 1980).

URBACH, E., *The Sages: Their Concepts and Beliefs*, tr. I. Abrahams (Jerusalem, 1975).

VAJDA, G., *L'Amour de Dieu dans la théologie juive du moyen âge* (Paris, 1957).

—— *La Théologie ascétique de Bahya Ibn Paquda* (Paris, 1974).

VANSTIPHOUT, H., 'Lore, Learning, and Levity in the Sumerian Disputations', in Reinink and Vanstiphout, *Dispute Poems*, 23–46.

WAGNER, E., 'Die arabische Rangstreitdichtung und ihre Einordnung in die allgemeine Literaturgeschichte', *Akademie der Wissenschaften und der Literatur in Mainz: Abhandlungen der geistes- und sozialwissenschaftlichen Klasse*, 1962/8, 435–76.

WASSERSTEIN, D., *The Rise and Fall of the Party Kings: Politics and Society in Islamic Spain* (Princeton, 1985).

WATT, W. M., *A History of Islamic Spain* (Edinburgh, 1965).

WAXMAN, I., *A History of Jewish Literature* (3 vols., New York, 1930–6; 2nd edn. 4 vols., 1938–41, 5 vols., 1960).

WEINBERG, J., 'New Poems from the Byzantine Period' ['Shirim ḥadashim mehatekufah habizantinit'], *Hebrew Union College Annual*, 39 (1968), 1–62.

WEINBERGER, L., *Jewish Prince in Moslem Spain: Selected Poems of Samuel ibn Nagrela* (Alabama, 1973).

WEISS, Y., 'Court Culture and Court Poetry: Towards an Understanding of the Hebrew Poetry of Spain' ['Tarbut ḥatsranit veshirah ḥatsranit: berurim lehavanat shirat sefarad ha'ivrit'], in *Proceedings of World Congress of Jewish Studies*, i (Jerusalem, 1952), 396–403.

WIEDER, N., 'The Hundred Blessings = The Morning Blessings' ['Me'ah berakhot = birkhot hashaḥar'], *Sinai*, 44 (1959), 258–60.

—— 'On the Blessings Pertaining to "Heathen", "Slave", "Woman", "Beast", and "Ignoramus"' ['Al haberakhot "goy", "eved", "ishah", "behemah", u"bur"'], *Sinai*, 85 (1979), 97–116.

—— 'The Controversy about the Liturgical Composition "Yismaḥ Moshe"—Opposition and Defence' ['Yismaḥ moshe: hitnagedut vesanegoriyah'], in J. Petuchowski and E. Fleischer (eds.), *Studies in Aggadah, Targum, and Jewish Liturgy in Memory of Joseph Heinemann* [*Meḥkarim be'agadah, targumim utefilot yisra'el*] (Jerusalem, 1981), Hebrew section, 75–99.

—— 'The Liturgical Term "One Hundred Blessings"' ['Hamunaḥ haliturgi "me'ah berakhot"'], *Sinai*, 96 (1985), 36–45.

WILENSKY, M., Critique of Habermann, *Kiryat sefer*, 23 (1946/7), 200–1.

YAHALOM, Y., *Poetic Language in the Early* Piyut [*Sefat hashir shel hapiyut ha'erets yisra'eli hakadum*] (Jerusalem, 1985).

—— 'The Function of the Frame Story in Hebrew Adaptations of the *Maqāmāt*'

['Tafkido shel sipur hamisgeret be'ibud makamot ivriyim'], in Tsur and Rosen (eds.), *Israel Levin Jubilee Volume*, i. 135–54.

——'"Sayeth Tuviyah ben Zidkiyah": The *Maqama* of Joseph ben Simeon in Honour of Maimonides' [' "Ne'um toviyah ben tsidkiyah: hamaḥberet shel yosef ben shimon likhevod harambam'], *Tarbiẓ*, 64 (1997), 543–78.

——'In the Circuit of Debate: The Argument between Body and Soul in Liturgical Poetry ['Bema'agal hahitnatsḥut: havikuaḥ bein guf vanafesh beshirat hakodesh'], *Mabua*, 32 (1998), 114–23.

YELLIN, D., *Spanish Hebrew Prosody* [*Torat hashirah hasefaradit*] (Jerusalem, 1940).

ZEMAḤ, E., *As the Root, So the Tree* [*Keshoresh ets*] (Jerusalem, 1962; 2nd edn. Merhavia and Tel Aviv, 1973).

——'On Conventional Imagery' ['Al hadimui hakonventsiyonali'], in id., *As the Root, So the Tree*, 199–213.

——'"Should My Heart Leave My Body": On Homo-Eroticism in the Poetry of Samuel Hanagid' ['Im ya'azov gufi levavo: al ahavat gevarim etsel shmuel hanagid'], *Moznayim*, 6 (1983), 111–13.

——and ROSEN-MOKED, T., *A Sophisticated Work: An Examination of Poems of Samuel Hanagid* [*Yetsirah meḥukamah: iyun beshirei shmuel hanagid*] (Jerusalem, 1983).

ZEVEIN, S., *The Holidays in Jewish Law* [*Hamo'adim behalakhah*] (2 vols., Jerusalem, 1944).

ZIMMER, Y., 'Laws Pertaining to the (Disposition of the) Body during Prayer' ['Tikunei haguf bishe'at hatefilah'], *Sidra*, 5 (1990), 89–130.

ZINBERG, I., *A History of Jewish Literature*, tr. and ed. B. Martin, i: *The Arab-Spanish Period* (12 vols., Hoboken, NJ, 1972–8).

ZUKER, M., 'Miperusho shel rabi sa'adyah gaon latorah' ['From Rabbi Sa'adiah Gaon's Commentary on the Torah'], *Sura: Sefer shanah yisra'eli-amerikai lemeḥkar ule'iyun beva'ayot yisra'el vehaolam be'avar uvahoveh*, 2 (1954–5), 313–55.

Index of Biblical References

The great majority of biblical references in the Hebrew original have been preserved in the translation, although some have not and others have been replaced with citations of like thrust or tone (see the Translator's Preface). Page numbers in brackets refer to biblical references introduced by the translator.

Jeremiah

Index of Persons and Peoples

Because of the constraints of translation, patronymics sometimes occur in the text in alternative forms, for example 'ben', 'ibn', or 'son of'. Page numbers in square brackets are references to names introduced by the translator. 'Rabbi', often the equivalent of 'Sir' or 'Mr' in the text, is used here only to designate religious functionaries.

Index of Places

Page numbers in brackets refer to names introduced by the translator.

General Index

A

acrostic 475, 577
Alḥarizi, Judah:
  Arabic poems 419 n. 10, 617, 618 n. 9
  Arabic writings 442, 618 n. 7
  misogyny 457, 533 n. 17, 606
  name Judah linked with Heman and Hever 644–5
  Peninei hamelitsot 614 n. 1
  praise of Maimonides 618 n. 7, 633
  revisions of *Sefer Taḥkemoni* 511
  Sefer ha'anak 576, 588
  self-naming in *Sefer Taḥkemoni* 3, 9, 18
  self-praise 417, 418, 423, 431, 505, 632, 643 n. 35
  translations from Arabic: of al-Ḥariri, *Maqāmāt* (*Maḥberot Iti'el*) xvi, 18, 421–2, 425, 429–30, 468, 503, 629, 637, 639–40; of Maimonides 389, 420
  travels 617 n. 4, 618 n. 7
  see also authorial persona *and* Index of Persons and Peoples
allegory 417–21, 488, 493–4, 527, 541, 601–2, 628
Amidah 95 n., 110 n., 148 n., 218, 221–3, 432, 495, 497, 499, 508, 536–8, 539 n. 22, 620
Arabic language:
  arabiyya 500, 638
  preferred by Jewish writers 421 n. 16, 430, 512
Arabic literature 614
  adab 423 n. 25, 515, 588, 612
  debate mode 444–5
  maqāmā, *maqāmāt* xiii; of al-Hamadhani 562 n. 1, 565–6, 578 n. 2; of al-Ḥariri 421, 453, 468–71, 483, 502–3, 632, 638–9, 644
  rhymed prose 501
  translations from, *see under* Alḥarizi; Hebrew literature
Arabic poetry (metric) 175–6, 512, 576
  genres 433; battle odes 460–5, 489; boast 476 n. 11; debate 597, 598, 619; *muwashshaḥāt* 482; praise of locales 619; *zuhdiyat* 433 n. 1
Arabism, attempts to combat xvi, 500
Aramaic language 482
archaisms 432, 503–6
  see also rare words, use of
astrology 526–8; Gate 22
authorial persona in *Sefer Taḥkemoni* 616
  'the author' 19, 23, 30–1, 428, 609, 626
  Judah = Alḥarizi, *see* Index of Persons and Peoples
  Judah = Heman 92, 587, 644–5
  Judah = Hever 279, 413
  overlap with protagonists 428–32, 452–3, 457, 467, 472, 510 n. 17, 520, 521, 523, 547, 575, 581–2, 587, 621, 626, 632, 634 n. 6, 643–8

B

backward reading, *see* reversal
biblical citations, *see* scriptural citations
biblical parlance 56 n. 4
blurring of boundaries:
  between characters 428, 575, 581–2
  between cosmic intellect and Alḥarizi's own 419
  between reality and fiction 428–30, 582
  temporal 598, 610
  see also authorial persona: overlap with protagonists
bracketing 646–7
  chiastic 648–51
  structural 648
  verbal 467, 494, 506, 522, 525, 544, 551, 569, 573, 615, 639, 648; *see also* inclusion, receding

C

calendar, Hebrew 449–53; Gate 5
  debates of months 449–52
cantors, *see* precentors

Q

R

S

T